Leading Issues in Black Political Economy

Leading Issues in Black Political Economy

Thomas D. Boston
editor

Routledge
Taylor & Francis Group
LONDON AND NEW YORK

Originally published as Spring 1998 of *The Review of Black Political Economy*, Vol. 25, No. 4; Summer/Fall/Winter/Spring 1998/1999 of *The Review of Black Political Economy*, Vol. 26, No. 1/2/3/4; and Summer 1999 of *The Review of Black Political Economy*, Vol. 27, No. 1.

Published 2002 by Transaction Publishers

Published 2017 by Routledge
2 Park Square, Milton Park, Abingdon, Oxon OX14 4RN
711 Third Avenue, New York, NY 10017, USA

Routledge is an imprint of the Taylor & Francis Group, an informa business

Library of Congress Catalog Number: 2001041592

Library of Congress Cataloging-in-Publication Data

Leading issues in Black political economy / Thomas D. Boston, editor.
p. cm.
Originally published as Spring 1998 of the Review of Black political economy, Vol. 25, No. 4; Summer/Fall/Winter/Spring 1998/1999 of the Review of Black political economy, Vol. 26, No. 1/2/3/4 and Summer 1999, Vol. 27, No. 1.
Includes bibliographical references.
ISBN 0-7658-0759-9 (pbk. : alk. paper)
1. African Americans—Economic conditions. 2. African Americans—Economic conditions—Forecasting. 3. African American business enterprises. 4. United States—Economic conditions—1945- 5. United States—Race relations—Economic aspects. I. Boston, Thomas D. II. Review of Black political economy.

E185.8 .L38 2001
338.6'42'08996073—dc21

2001041592

ISBN 13: 978-0-7658-0759-5 (pbk)

DEDICATION

To Andrew F. Brimmer

Distinguished economist and public servant, former member of the board of governors of the Federal Reserve System, former vice president of The American Economic Association, and past president of the North American Economic and Finance Association.

To Robert S. Browne

Distinguished economist and public servant, co-founder of the National Economic Association, founder of *The Review of Black Political Economy*, and former U.S. Executive Director of the African Development Bank Group.

Contents

Minority Business Development

Income Inequality

Economic History and Public Policy

Health, Welfare and Development

Discrimination, Affirmative Action and Public Policy

Preface

The essays contained in this book were written in celebration of the twenty-fifth anniversary of *The Review of Black Political Economy*. This is indeed a momentous occasion. To recognize it appropriately, I solicited twenty-eight contributions from the nation's leading authorities on the issue of race and economics. *Leading Issues in Black Political Economy* reflects their views on the economic status of African Americans and African peoples at the dawn of the new millennium. Robert S. Browne, the distinguished founder of *The Review of Black Political Economy*, should be pleased with these essays. They are a continuing reflection of the journal's steadfast commitment to its founding principles. Today's revolutionary advances in information technology and the unparalleled accumulation of wealth are widening the gap between blacks and whites, even as some policymakers proclaim that racism is dead. Under these circumstances, there continues to be a critical need for the sobering analyses presented year after year in the pages of *The Review*. In short, its mission is as timely now as it was twenty-five years ago. That mission is as follows:

> *The Review of Black Political Economy* is a scholarly journal devoted to the examination of issues related to the economic status of black and Third World peoples. Its aim is to encourage and promote the analysis and empirical study of inequality in economic status and opportunity based on race and ethnic origin. It is self-consciously oriented toward an emphasis on the identification and analysis of policy prescriptions designed to reduce racial economic inequality, and to achieve the possibilities for fulfillment of economic opportunity for people of color in the United States and throughout the world.
>
> *The Review of Black Political Economy* is committed to the principle that knowledge and understanding of the roots and dynamic operation of current institutional arrangements that perpetuate racial inequality is the beginning of wisdom required for the eventual elimi-

> nation of such barriers to the full expression of economic opportunity by black people. The journal is conceived in the belief that public and private policies play a critical role, both in the creation of economic inequality and its ultimate eradication. Thus, research on economic trends and developments, and on the institutional environment in which policy is formulated and implemented, will help deepen our understanding of ways to achieve greater economic opportunity.

As editor of *The Review*, I thank each of the contributors to this book, and I wish to especially thank all of the scholars who have written for the journal over the years and served as anonymous referees. I also wish to thank members of the editorial board and the National Economic Association. Without your support, this celebration would not be possible. Finally, I wish give a special thanks to Andrew F. Brimmer. Despite an enormously busy schedule, Andrew continues to publish in *The Review* and participate in the NEA panels at the annual meetings. Indeed, he agreed to write the introductory essay to this book with little advance notice.

Thomas D. Boston

1

INTRODUCTION AND OVERVIEW

Andrew F. Brimmer

The twenty-eight essays in this book cover a wide spectrum of issues and challenges facing African Americans at the beginning of the twenty-first century. These include education, training, and employment. Several of the papers treat macro-economic concerns of business development—with special attention given to long-term trends of black-owned businesses. This work also emphasizes public welfare considerations in an era when anti-welfare attacks are gaining ground. Likewise, it shows the need for affirmative action when support for the latter is weakening in many quarters. Attention is also devoted to the role of race in the continuing disparity in the level and distribution of income in the United States. Finally, two essays explore some problems and opportunities in stimulating economic development in Africa.

Thomas D. Boston, the editor, persuaded an outstanding roster of leading economists to prepare the essays in this volume. For the most part, they were written as part of the celebration of the twenty-fifth anniversary of *The Review of Black Political Economy*. The editor has performed another outstanding service by bringing the essays together in the present volume.

BUSINESS DEVELOPMENT

The two articles which examine the survival and growth of businesses—if read together—provide a number of insights into the development of black-owned enterprises. While they both stress recent changes, the evolution of these firms over time can also be traced.

The essay by Andrew F. Brimmer, entitled "Long-Term Trends and Prospects for Black-Owned Businesses," is a further examination of the theory of black business development that he first advanced in 1966. In that work, Brimmer demonstrated that racial segregation in the United States served as a protective barrier behind which most black enterprises originated and expanded. He also predicted that, as racial segregation declined and opportunities for black entrepreneurs in the broader society increased, black-owned businesses would stagnate and eventually decline—while the black community as a whole would improve its relative position in the nation's economy.

On several occasions in the intervening years, Brimmer has documented the linkage between segregation-and-growth and integration-and-stagnation of black-owned businesses. The analysis presented in the present essay shows that the comparative position of black-owned businesses in the American economy deteriorated from the mid-1980s through the early 1990s. This was due principally to their failure to compete successfully for the rising incomes of the black middle class. Some firms did make measurable progress through the mid-1990s—mainly by diversifying away from retail trade and into computer-linked activities.

The bulk of Brimmer's article consists of a detailed examination of the statistics on black-owned businesses as reported in the Census Bureau's "Survey of Minority-Owned Business Enterprises: Black," for the years 1982, 1987, and 1992. The analysis is mainly at the industry level. The number of firms and business sales of black-owned enterprises are compared with those of all firms in the country. The results are presented primarily in the form of disparity indexes that, among another indicators, show the changing degree and pattern of participation by black firms in the American economy.

Brimmer, in looking ahead to 1995 through the year 2000, had predicted that gains of black firms would be quite uneven. Fairly high growth rates were projected for the fields of engineering, technology, and telecommunications. Traditional fields (which have long served mainly the black consumer market) were expected to grow very slowly. Moreover, those industries (such as public construction and television) which have benefited substantially from affirmative action would lag behind.

In her article entitled "Minority Business Formation and Survival: Evidence on Business Performance and Viability," Jan E. Christopher undertook a large assignment. Essentially, she set out to identify and weigh the factors that influence the formation and survival of black-owned businesses. Some attention is given to business ownership by other minorities and women, but her main interest is the experience of black owners. Christopher relies heavily on statistics and other information contained in two U.S. Census Bureau publications: (1) "Characteristics of Business Owners" (CBO), and (2) "Survey of Minority-Owned Business Enterprises" (SMOBE). Drawing mainly on these sources, she studies a variety of attributes of minority owners and their firms in the context of both socioeconomic and financial theories. Geographic and industrial criteria are stipulated as part of the estimated models and explicative frames of reference. In carrying out the research, the probability of business survival was observed, estimated, and evaluated with reference to the characteristics of the individual business owner as well as of the minority-owned firms.

This study focuses on the years between 1987 and 1991. Over this period, survival rates of minority-owned businesses (including women-owned firms) ranged from fifty-five to eighty-five percent. More specifically, during this period approximately twenty percent of the owners in the CBO survey dissolved their businesses.

The most significant determinant of business survival was found to be the age of the firm. (In passing, the reader must be alert to avoid misinterpreting this statement. Read quickly, it might appear to predict that a firm will survive in the future because it has survived so far. Instead, "age" seems to be a form of shorthand that captures the influence of other variables that are associated with time.) The age determinant is followed by the level of capital investment, formal education, and years of employment experience—in that order. Furthermore, survival rates are observed to increase at a decreasing rate with nominal increases in the levels of capital investment.

The author reports much unevenness in the influence of racial identifiers. She also notes that considerable emphasis is currently being placed on the length of business ownership as an indicator of contemporary business performance and future business survival. However, she cautions that non-economic factors have significant roles in the determination of business success. These include business continuity in a specific geographic area as well as the businesses' contribution to the local and regional economies.

ECONOMIC INEQUALITY

Five of the papers in this volume explore the nature and extent of economic inequality suffered by African Americans. Three of these do so with respect to measures (such as employment, occupations, wages, and other incomes) traditionally used by economists. Two others seek to explain racial differences in income by the introduction of more novel variables—including cognitive skills and political cooperation among groups.

The contribution by Octavian Ngarambé and Stephan J. Goetz is described sufficiently by its title: "Determinants of Regional Income Distribution in the U.S. South, 1980-1990: Roles of Net Migration and Human Capital Accumulation." The authors examine the differential effects of net migration and education on black-to-black, white-to-white, and overall income inequality. Their analyses are based on county-level statistics for the U.S. South for the decade 1980 through 1990. The evidence suggests that net migration produced a decrease in overall income inequality. However, it had a clear, positive effect on black income equality. The improvement in educational attainment also had an equalizing effect on overall inequality. Finally, it was found that the impact of both net migration and education on spatial income disparities varied across southern county-types.

In a similar vein, Lonnie K. Stevans assesses "The Effect of the Occupational Crowding of Immigrants on the Real Wages of African Americans Workers." The investigation is based on a sample of 2,695 blacks drawn from the 1990 National Longitudinal Survey of Youth. Specifically, the study estimates the effect of immigration on the real wages of black workers in both skilled and unskilled occupations. The results include the discovery of relatively strong negative wage effects on indigenous and non-U.S. citizen black workers who were already in this country. This outcome resulted from the occupational crowding of immigrants into unskilled occupations. In contrast, the real wages of skilled black workers were not affected by the entry of a relatively large number of immigrants into their occupations.

Economists frequently ask the question: is racism in the United States permanent or transitory? According to Jeremiah Cotton, the answer depends on both the theoretical orientation and the selection of empirical data analysts bring to the assignment. Cotton takes up the question in the essay "On the Permanence or Impermanence of Black-White Economic Inequality." He asserts that the issue occurs in both orthodox and heterodox economics where it is posed with respect to black-white inequality in wages, earnings, employment, occupation, capital ownership, and wealth.

In Cotton's view, economic orthodoxy predicts that racism will disappear in the long run because economic discrimination cannot survive in the face of competitive forces which are inherent features of capitalist markets. On the other hand, economic heterodox analysis looks at present and past differences in black-white unemployment, family income, wealth, and poverty rates as demonstrating that racism has continued and will continue to divide the United States.

Cotton asserts that the record supports his own belief in the permanence of racism. For example, he notes that black unemployment rates have been twice as high as white rates for nearly fifty years. In 1954, the black teenage unemployment rate was about fifteen percent. Forty-four years later, it had more than doubled to thirty-one percent. Furthermore, there has been an almost constant three-to-one ratio of black to white poverty rates for nearly forty years.

To narrow the black-white economic gap, Cotton argues that an economic rights crusade must follow the civil rights movement that did so much to end racial segregation in the 1960s. Such a movement should certainly demand increased black community economic development, employment opportunity, and equal earnings. But it must demand full employment for the whole economy as well. While benefiting blacks, full employment would also benefit working class whites. It might also help to mitigate white bigotry since much of the latter is fueled by their perception of blacks as competitors for the scarce jobs on which they should have first claim. Resistance to the demand of an economic rights movement will be strong. However, because of the persistence of racism, it should be launched anyway.

A less conventional approach to the study of economic inequality is embodied in the article entitled "Race, Cognitive Skills, Psychological Capital and Wages," by the team of Arthur H. Goldsmith, William Darity, Jr., and Jonathan R. Veum. The authors enter vigorously into the long-running debate over the extent to which blacks suffer from discrimination in the labor market. The conclusion that blacks in the United States earn less than otherwise comparable whites has been a long established tenet of labor economics. It is also generally believed that the gap is due to racial discrimination.

In recent years however this conventional view has been challenged by "conservative" investigators. Some of the latter argue that the apparent linkage between discrimination and wages is the result of faulty scholarship on the part of "liberal" economists rather than a correct description and measurement of wage determination. Some of the most vocal critics argue that the finding tracing wage differentials to discrimination flows from the failure to test for the influence of cognitive ability on wages. For these critics, research that adopts an appropriate specification of the wage equation demonstrates that black employees are paid as much as comparable white workers. For example, they cite studies that purport to account for cognitive ability (which is a productivity-related characteristic) and that they say show that black and white employees earn wages that are essentially identical. Consequently, they assert that black workers in the United States are not victims of systematic race based wage discrimination.

In this article, the Goldsmith-Darity-Veum team presents findings that raise considerable doubts about the validity of the non-discrimination conclusion. Drawing on literature in psychology, they argue that psychological capital is an important determinant of personal productivity, and, hence, of wages. Yet, with few exceptions, the influence of psychological capital on wages has been neglected in empirical models of wage determination. Moreover, they report that—when psychological capital is incorporated in such models—blacks earn significantly less than otherwise comparable white workers. Therefore, the evidence they present appears to be consistent with an important adverse discriminatory effect on the wages of black workers.

In the final essay in this section, "The Shadow of the Future and the Complexity of Cooperation," John W. Handy outlines a framework for enhancing cooperation among different ethnic groups. At the core of this framework is a game-theoretic model of a societal-scale prisoner's dilemma: by groups focusing on short-term gains as a reflection of narrow self-interest, social outcomes are often suboptimal. The conflicts between narrow self-interest and socially optimal outcomes are a very common result of mutual defections from policies and actions where everyone would be better off with mutual cooperation.

Conflicts in American society concerning racial justice, the allocation of resources between central cities and suburbs, and affirmative action often reflect a suboptimal zero-sum mentality based on the assumption that there must always be winners at the expense of losers in a never-ending struggle for primary access to resources and opportunities. Instead, Handy argues that cooperative solutions to the repeated prisoner's dilemma can demonstrate that there are long-term compromises that are more enlightened and which also increase the payoffs to all parties. He applies his model in assessing a range of socioeconomic issues, including employment niches, occupations, income distribution, integrational wealth transfers and affirmative action.

ECONOMICS OF RACE IN HISTORICAL PERSPECTIVE

Four of the essays in this volume examine economic aspects of race in historical perspective. They range from a pioneering evaluation of the changing status of blacks in the United States during the transition from an agrarian to an industrial society, evolution of "Negro" jobs, an assessment of the impact of racial discrimination in the market place, to the case for reparations to compensate present and future generations of blacks for the exploitation suffered by their ancestors in the past.

Lynn C. Burbridge, in "W.E.B. DuBois as Economic Analyst," does a masterful job in tracing the training and intellectual development of DuBois in the field of economics. Although DuBois is best known for his work in history and sociology, his earliest contributions (in both research and teaching) were in economics. In fact, DuBois researched and wrote (in German) a "first" doctoral dissertation on the organization and development of small-scale agriculture in the United States before the Civil War—although, because of a lack of funding, he did not obtain his degree from the University of Berlin. His "second" dissertation, which examined the suppression of the slave trade, was submitted to Harvard University, which did award him a Ph.D. in history. However, the economic aspects of the trade in human beings were highlighted. Subsequently, his research on the status of blacks in Philadelphia and other large cities put most of the emphasis on social and political conditions, but the impact of economic and industrial changes was not overlooked. Moreover, DuBois' classic debate with Booker T. Washington over the best ways for blacks to develop their community was actually as much about economics as about education.

In "No More Servants in the House," Beth T. Bates uses the record of employment of "Pullman Porters" on the railroads to illustrate how the availability of jobs for blacks was influenced substantially by stereotypes held by employers. When blacks were seen as "servile," they were liked by both employers and passengers. When they were organized into unions and became "uppity," this changed perception—along with rising labor costs and increased air travel—contributed to the near extinction of the Pullman Porter.

In the essay "The Economics of Racism," Marcus Alexis demonstrates that the study of racial discrimination is a proper subject for economists. However, until Gary Becker published *The Economics of Discrimination* in 1957, the assessment of racism was considered to be beyond the boundaries of economics as a discipline. Even so, Becker, and most of those who followed him, stressed the economic consequences of market discrimination as narrowly defined in a neo-classical context.

Actually, some economists did go beyond the confines of the traditional competitive market framework to assess the effects of racial discrimination. For example, in 1951, I completed a masters thesis entitled "Some Economic Aspects of Fair Employment." For the study, I formulated a model which enabled me to show how discrimination, as practiced by employers and trade unions separately, influenced the different types of skills possessed by black and white workers—which, in turn, shaped (1) the size and composition of the labor force and employment, (2) the industrial and occupational distribution of workers with jobs, and (3) wage differentials and the distribution of income. Although the thesis was not published at the time, parts of it were used extensively in economics courses taught by professors who knew of its existence.

Some years later (1966), I refined the original model and applied it in making a comprehensive appraisal of the black role in the American economy. This approach "...highlighted the strategic factors influencing the conditions under which [blacks] participate in the economy and share the benefits of national production. This [method], which is basically analytic and statistical, emphasize [blacks'] adaptation to the malfunctioning of the market place. In general, both resource allocation and income shares are determined by the price system in an economy such as that found in the United States. But the existence of racial discrimination and the mosaic of social disorganization associated with segregation have severely restricted [blacks'] opportunities to acquire skills and property and to offer them in exchange for income. Partly because of the resulting limited ability to earn—but also because of additional barriers—[blacks] in turn have a restricted access to the market for consumer goods and services."

In the study included in this volume, Alexis also develops a model that breaks sharply from the neo-classical approach. He also makes a distinction between discrimination and racism. He argues that the Becker-style concentration on market consequences is unnecessarily limited in that it prevents a consideration of the role that racism and discrimination play in a wider social context. Furthermore, if racism is not an end in itself but a way to achieve larger objectives, emphasis on consequences restricts the economist's role as a commentator on broader social issues. In the paper, Alexis demonstrates that economics has much to say with respect to the market and non-market dimensions of racism.

In "Reparations and Public Policy," Richard F. America extends his seminal analysis of the effects of both past and present discrimination on the economic status of blacks. In his view, to correct the continuing inequality which blacks suffer will require substantial investment in their education and skills (human capital) paid for by federal tax revenues.

At the center of Professor America's numerous studies is the concept of reparations. This concept is the key to understanding the public policy dimensions of the race problem and fundamental to resolving them. The driving force underpinning both his analyses and methods of resolution is the Restitution Principle. The latter states that, whenever a social group, a nation, or a race decides that past behavior by those with power was wrong—and has made it illegal—then it is also wrong for those same possessors of power today to receive and retain the benefits produced by those actions.

America draws from extensive historical evidence to support his case. He states that, for 357 years, slavery directly enriched owners and directors in agriculture, mining, transportation, manufacturing, and the development of major publics works, such as roads, bridges, and dams. Slavery also indirectly benefited millions of others who had no first hand role in the slavery regime. It released them from low level occupations and allowed them time to pursue education and training for the betterment of themselves and their descendants. On the other hand, these same 375 years of slavery were the equivalent to theft of black human capital. This banditry deprived African Americans of adequate training and education, and it has left them unable to compete equally in the contemporary economy.

To compensate for this moral injustice, America prescribes reparations. The latter should be in the form of public investment in black education and training, housing, health, and business development. These redistributive investments should be made in ways that enhance recipients' human capital and ability to compete. Moreover, this public policy should not simply subsidize subsistence for the underclass but should help develop discipline, a work ethic, and respect for low and "middle class" ways of looking at life and behaving. Professor America concludes that, if reparations were used to develop responsible adults, then social costs would be greatly reduced to the benefit of the country as a whole.

In passing, it should be noted that America, in this essay, clarifies the concept of reparations as he employs it. From his early writings, many readers got the impression that he wanted the descendents of slave owners and others who benefited from slavery to make payments personally and directly into a community-owned pool similar to a mutual fund on which only blacks could draw to finance their education, training, and business development. In this essay, he makes it clear that he seeks payment for the improvement in black people's human capital from the public treasury.

HEALTH AND WELFARE

Two of the articles in this volume focus principally on the impact on African Americans of Federal Government programs to improve health and welfare in the nation at large. One examines the effects of the divergent ways in which health and housing benefits are provided. The other is concerned more specifically with black infant health.

Wilhelmina A. Leigh, in "21st Century Pollination: Federal Housing and Health Policies," examines some of the issues that might emerge in the future if health and public housing programs continue to be funded separately. She observes that it has long been recognized that housing has considerable impact on health while health requirements influence housing demand. Yet, despite these interrelations, federal health and housing programs have been developed and financed with very little coordination.

The author analyzes some of the features of the Low-Rent Public Housing and discretionarily funded housing assistance programs and considers their implications for the Medicaid health insurance program for the poor and disabled. Features considered include: block granting, cashing out the subsidy, waiting lists, cost sharing and income mixing, and portability. She concludes that, although altering the funding basis for health programs might affect Black Americans and other disproportionately poor populations first, this type of change would have implications for the nature of assistance for all eligible population groups.

Employing an historical perspective, Geoffrey Warner examines "Black Infant Health: Where to in the 21st Century?" The essay is essentially an analysis of the economics of health care with specific reference to black infant health in the United States from slavery through the present. He presents a highly useful chronology of important legislative efforts by the federal government to improve infant health. The body of research on infant health is summarized. Some strategies for infant health improvement that are relevant to the black community are also discussed.

Warner arrays the principal infant health issues confronting the black community as follows: the amount of curative health care to give up in order to increase the amount of preventive health care; the amount of health care to give up in order to increase the efforts towards solving the social and economic problems which have serious adverse health effects; the degree to which the current balance between free and regulated markets should be altered as a tool to increase black infant health; and the degree to which the black community should turn towards itself and away from the white community in regards to solving its infant health problem.

MARGINALIZATION AND ECONOMIC DEVELOPMENT IN AFRICA

Two of the essays focus on problems and opportunities for economic development in Sub-Saharan Africa. One explores the challenges within a regional framework, while the other does so in the context of international assistance.

Professor E. Ike Udogu presents his analysis in "Economic Community of West African States: From an Economic Union to a Peacekeeping Mission?" He argues that the marginalization of most African states within the global economic system has created a hardship for the majority of the population living on the African continent. It took a number of years following the end of colonization for African leaders to appreciate the situation. But once the impact of these changes on political stability in the region was realized, lawmakers hastened to find strategies to reverse the trend.

The approach pursued varied depending on the countries' heritage. In both Francophone and Anglophone countries, efforts were made to establish economic unions. Among these was the Economic Community of West African States (ECOWAS). The organization of 16 countries was formed on May 28, 1975, under the leadership of Nigeria. Among other goals, its principal task was to tackle the intractable economic problems confronting the region. However, despite the group's concerted efforts so far, it has not been able to achieve many tangible results.

One reason for the lack of progress has been the difficulty of achieving a consensus on industrial policy. For two years (1977-79), I served as Economic Adviser to the ECOWAS Development Fund based in Lome, Togo, and I witnessed the struggles being played out on a daily basis. For example, Nigeria was not only the largest country in Sub-Saharan Africa, but it also had a huge lead in industrialization. Nevertheless, Nigeria pressed its plan to industrialize as quickly as possible—even at the expense of other countries in the community. Over time, the effort to promote regional economic integration in West Africa eroded.

Today, under the leadership of Nigeria, ECOWAS is engaged in peace-keeping missions that have the look and feel of civil war. The author of this article contends that economic revitalization and prosperity are imperative for peace and stability. Moreover, he asserts that it is only when ECOWAS pursues vigorously the tenets of its treaty within the framework of economic liberalization and political democracy will the West Africa region be spared conflicts of the types that have devastated Liberia and Sierra Leone.

Kempe Ronald Hope, Sr. contributes a paper entitled "Development Prospects and Policy for Africa: Structural Adjustment and Beyond." He states that economic crises in Africa during the 1980s led to the emergence of policy reform, which was dominated by donor-sponsored structural adjustment programs (SAPs). In his review, Hope finds that most SAPs have had mixed results. Yet, for the most part, they have been successful in restructuring and liberalizing many African economies. Therefore, African leaders can see that a number of economic performance indicators have been showing positive trends since the early 1990s. In the article, Hope demonstrates the positive economic impact of SAPs in Africa and assesses the development prospects and policy in the post-SAPs era—beyond 2000.

Employment, Training and Education

2

THE DECLINING SOCIAL AND ECONOMIC FORTUNES OF AFRICAN AMERICAN MALES: A CRITICAL ASSESSMENT OF FOUR PERSPECTIVES*

James H. Johnson, Jr.
Walter C. Farrell, Jr.
Jennifer A. Stoloff

Considerable research has been devoted to the steadily deteriorating social and economic status of the African American male in urban America over the last quarter century. Their rates of school failure, joblessness, homicide, incarceration, and other antisocial behaviors far exceed those of their white, Hispanic, and Asian male counterparts. In fact, the magnitude of these problems has led some researchers to characterize the African American male as an endangered species.[1]

A range of theories spanning the entire political spectrum has been advanced to explain the declining socioeconomic fortunes of the African American male vis-à-vis other males in American society. In this article, we provide a general overview of four of the competing perspectives on "the African American male problem": *the spatial isolation hypothesis, the cultural capital/employer preference hypothesis, the search and destroy hypothesis,* and *the social capital hypothesis.* Following the discussion of the theoretical underpinnings of each of these schools of thought, we review recent empirical studies that attempt to evaluate the relative weight of the various factors undergirding these competing perspectives which have been culled from the extant literature.[2] To set the context for these analyses, we begin by reviewing selected social and economic indicators of the status of the black male in American society.

---

* The authors gratefully acknowledge the expert technical assistance of Ms. Cathy Mae Nelson of the University of Wisconsin-Milwaukee's School of Education word processing pool.

CRITICAL BACKGROUND AND THEORETICAL FOUNDATION

Declining Economic Fortunes of the African American Male

During the last two decades, the economic fortunes of black males have declined precipitously.[3] In the 1980s, as Figure 1 shows, the jobless rate for twenty-year-old black men (21.6 percent) was almost five times higher than the rate for their white counterparts (4.8 percent). And for twenty-year-old men with less than a high school education, the racial disparity in joblessness was even greater: 10.3 percent for white men and 36.1 percent for black men. During the 1960s, the disparity in the jobless rate for young black and white men, with and without a high school diploma, was not nearly as stark. Moreover, among high school graduates, the average white male jobless rate rose from virtually zero to 2.5 percent between the mid-1960s and the mid-1980s; for comparable blacks, the jobless rate increased from zero to 14.3 percent.[4]

Joblessness is not the only area in which racial divergence has occurred in recent years. Similar disparities were observed in weeks worked and earnings, as shown in Figure 2.[5] Among twenty-year-old white males who worked at all during the year, the number of weeks worked increased slightly, from 40.5 to 44 between the 1960s and the 1980s; for their black male counterparts, the number of weeks worked actually decreased during this period, from 39.9 to 38.6. Among white male high school dropouts who worked at all during the year, the number of reported weeks worked increased from 38.5 to 40.8. For comparable black males, the number of weeks worked decreased noticeably from 39.1 to 33.6. Among black high school graduates, the average number of weeks worked declined from 41.3 to 40.5 compared to an increase among white high school graduates from 41.7 to 45.2 weeks.[6]

In terms of weekly earnings, as Figure 3 illustrates, all white males and white male dropouts registered a decline, while all black males showed a small increase in earnings, and black high school dropouts registered a small decline in earnings. Because of the dramatic rise in joblessness occasioned by recessions, real annual earnings fell between the mid-1960s and the mid-1980s—by 5 percent for white males, from $10,859 to $10,303; however, earnings declined by 19 percent among comparable black males, from $6,857 to $5,589, as noted in Figure 4. Real annual earnings (in 1987 dollars) among white male high school dropouts fell from $10,000 to $7,880, a decline of 17 percent, but earnings for compa-

FIGURE 1
U.S. Joblessness for Twenty-Year-Old Black and White Males

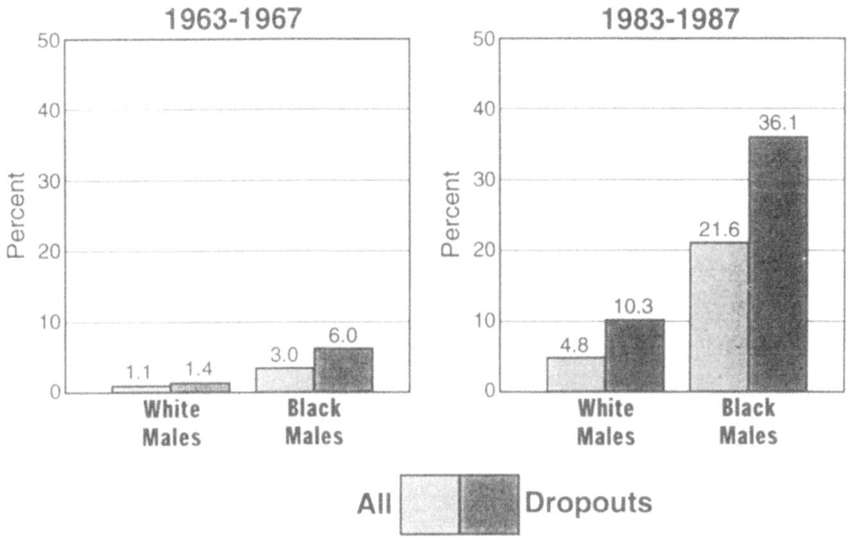

rable black males fell dramatically, from $5,754 to only $3,029. More recent research suggests that these trends have continued during the 1990s.[7]

Explanations of Hypotheses

As we noted earlier, a wide range of views and perspectives has been advanced to explain the racial disparities in joblessness, weeks worked, and earnings depicted in Figures 1 through 4. Here we shall focus on the four schools of thought and/or hypotheses which we believe are representative of the diverse opinions that have been expressed in the literature.

The first, based primarily on the works of Wilson[8] and Massey and Denton,[9] is what we term the *spatial isolation hypothesis.* It posits that the plight of African American males is intricately linked to their increasing social and geographical isolation and economic marginalization from mainstream educational and employment opportunities in U.S. society.[10] In contrast to the urban black communities of the 1950s, today's African American males are constrained, for the most part, to inner-city residential areas, variously referred to as "ghetto poor," "hypersegregated," or "concentrated poverty communities," where the structure of opportu-

FIGURE 2
Weeks Worked for Twenty-Year-Old Black and White Males

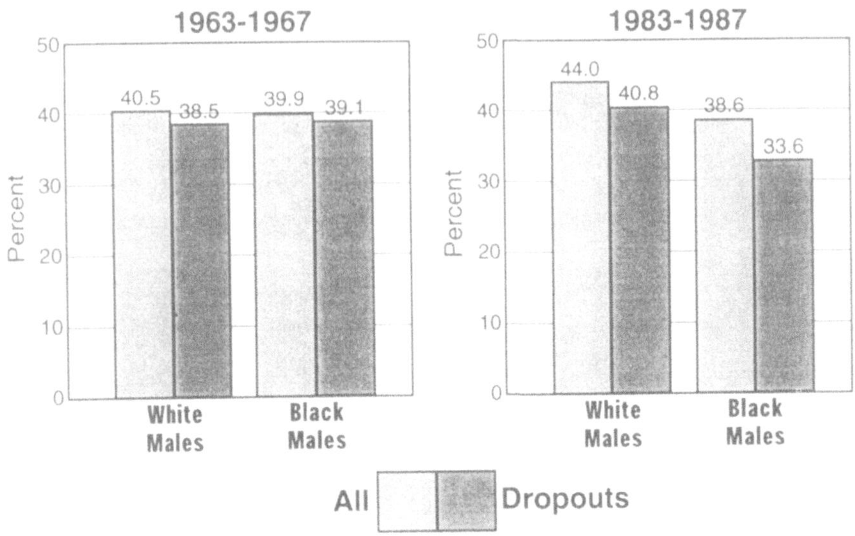

nity, including access to jobs, has been substantially diminished. In the absence of mainstream employment opportunities which organize and structure daily life,[11] and given persistent racial discrimination in the metropolitan housing market[12] which constrains access to housing, education, and employment opportunities in the suburbs and beyond, inner-city communities have become "islands of despair," characterized by high rates of black male joblessness and a wide array of other antisocial behaviors.[13]

These conditions, according to Wilson,[14] Massey and Denton,[15] and others,[16] were created, on the one hand, by the anti-discrimination laws enacted during the 1960s and 1970s, which fostered the "selective" out-migration of the black middle class from inner-city communities and, on the other, by wholesale changes in the U.S. economy, which have left the most disadvantaged African Americans in general, and African American males in particular, trapped or mired in a state of poverty and severe economic distress.

One of the dominant forces contributing to the increasing spatial isolation and economic marginalization of African American males, according to Grant and Johnson,[17] is the U.S. government's efforts during the past twenty-five years to create a deregulated business environment in an

FIGURE 3
Annual Earnings for Twenty-Year-Old Black and White Males

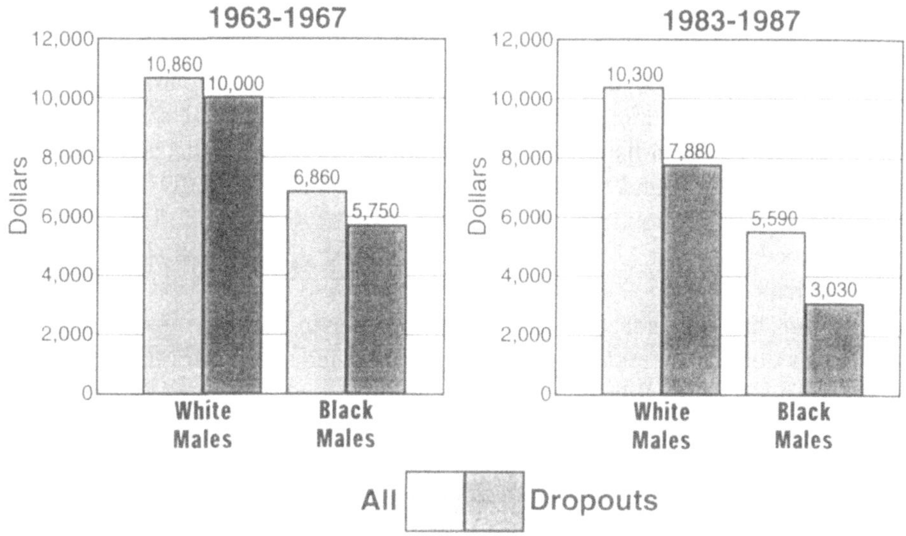

FIGURE 4
Weekly Earnings for Twenty-Year-Old Black and White Males

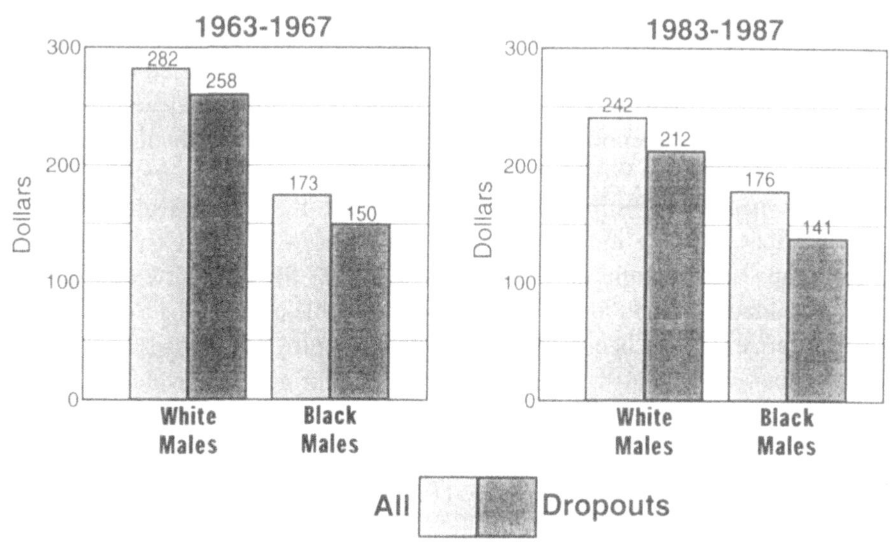

effort to increase the competitiveness of U.S. firms in the global marketplace. It has been noted that changes have been made in antitrust laws, and their enforcement, which have resulted in a growing concentration of large, vertically- and horizontally-integrated firms in key sectors of the economy; that these large conglomerates, due to their economic power and control of markets, have been able to move capital quickly and efficiently to select national and international locations to take advantage of cheap labor;[18] and that the federal government, especially during the Bush Administration, may, in fact, have used taxpayers' dollars to provide incentives for U.S. firms to relocate abroad, especially to Central American countries.[19]

Grant and Johnson also argue that in order to facilitate the competitiveness of firms remaining in the U.S., the federal government, under President Ronald Reagan, relaxed environmental regulations and substantially cut both the budgets and the staffs of governmental agencies charged with the enforcement of laws governing workplace health, safety, and compensation, as well as hiring, retention, and promotion practices.[20] Other authors have drawn similar conclusions.[21]

This shift toward a deregulated business environment, according to several researchers, is partially responsible for the wholesale exodus of high-wage, highly unionized, heavy-manufacturing employment from major metropolitan centers in the industrial Northeast and Midwest, where large numbers of blacks were concentrated, a process referred to as deindustrialization.[22] Further, they assert that it also precipitated the emergence of new industrial spaces in the suburbs, exurbs, and non-metropolitan areas in this country, as well as the movement of manufacturing activities to Third World countries, a process known as *employment deconcentration.* To support the latter assertion, they cite research which shows that the new industrial spaces which have emerged on the U.S. landscape are typically situated in places where there are few blacks in the local labor market and few within a reasonable commuting distance.[23]

Moreover, it has been argued that black employment losses resulting from massive deindustrialization and manufacturing job deconcentration have not been offset by emerging employment opportunities in the growth sectors of the U.S. economy: advanced services, high-technology manufacturing, hospitality services (e.g., hotel, motels, restaurants, etc.), and craft-specialty (e.g., garment, furniture, and jewelry making) industries.[24] This appears to be the case irrespective of whether this job growth occurs in central cities, where many blacks are concentrated, or outside of these communities.[25]

Proponents of the *spatial isolation hypothesis* argue that blacks are substantially disadvantaged in their efforts to secure employment in these growth sectors due to changes in the way in which employers fulfill their labor needs.[26] Employers are shifting to more flexible modes of production, primarily those in the craft-specialty sector of the economy, in an effort to remain competitive in the global marketplace.[27] To improve efficiency and keep labor costs down, Scott notes that work is either farmed out to contractors and subcontractors, or labor demand is met through informal preferential hiring practices.[28] This flexibility in fulfilling labor needs is made possible by the growing presence of women and immigrants in the U.S. labor market over the last three decades.[29]

The second school of thought, gleaned from the extant literature on the African American male problem, is what we term the *cultural capital/ employer preference hypothesis.* According to this view, the decline in the economic fortunes of the African American male is not due to the structural constraints advocated by proponents of the *spatial isolation hypothesis*; rather, the joblessness problem reflects character deficiencies and deviant values of inner-city residents, especially black males.

Advocates of this perspective, to whom we shall collectively refer as the cultural capital theorists,[30] allege that inner-city black males actually choose not to work regularly, and this unwillingness to work is embedded in the nature and culture of the inner city. Negative attitudes toward work, they suggest, are rooted in slavery and the southern sharecropper system, both of which inculcated in blacks "values that are impediments to work, savings, education, and upward mobility."[31] Cultural capital theorists argue further that neither slavery nor the southern sharecropper system fostered personal responsibility; under both systems, they contend, "lack of initiative, evasion of work, half-done work, unpredictable absenteeism, and abuse of tools and equipment were pervasive," especially under slavery.[32] Lemann indicates that the blacks who migrated from the South brought these behavioral traits with them to the urban North, where they were once again reinforced by the liberal social welfare policies of the 1960s.[33]

Shaped by this set of forces, inner-city African American males, in this view, do not have the appropriate set of cultural capital attributes—morals, values, attitudes, and behavioral traits—to compete for jobs in the contemporary American labor market. Rather than suffering from material poverty, as proponents of the *spatial isolation hypothesis* maintain,[34] Bennett et al. conclude that inner-city African American males suffer primarily from moral poverty, which they define as follows:

> By "moral poverty" we mean the poverty of being without loving, capable, responsible adults who teach the young right from wrong. It is the poverty of being without parents, guardians, relatives, friends, teachers, coaches, clergy, and others who habituate . . . children to feel joy at others' joy; pain at others' pain; satisfaction when you do right; remorse when you do wrong. It is the poverty of growing up in the virtual absence of people who teach these lessons by their own everyday example, and who insist that you follow suit and behave accordingly. In the extreme, it is the poverty of growing up surrounded by deviant, delinquent, and criminal adults in a practically perfect criminogenic environment—that is, an environment that seems almost consciously designed to produce vicious, unrepentant predatory street criminals.[35]

Moral poverty, they and others assert, is primarily responsible for the previously described racial disparities in joblessness and earnings, as well as the sharp increase in out-of-wedlock births, family disruption, long-term welfare dependency, and illegal activities revolving around gangs, drug dealing, and other criminal acts in the African American community.[36]

How is the perceived lack of moral health viewed in the labor market? It translates into African American males being perceived as lazy, inarticulate, uneducable, untrainable and, most importantly, dangerous.[37] In an economy where increasing numbers of jobs require direct interface with the public, proponents of this school of thought reason that high rates of joblessness exist among young black males, in large measure, because most do not possess the cultural capital or "soft" skills—values, attitudes, appearance, and behavioral disposition—that are highly valued in the contemporary labor market.[38]

A third school of thought or theme that runs through the extant literature on the African American male problem is what we characterize here as the *search and destroy hypothesis.* It posits that the African American male is being systematically targeted for discriminatory treatment and exploitation in at least three domains: the labor market, education and job training, and the criminal justice system.[39]

With respect to the labor market, Kirschenman and Neckerman, based on their interviews with a sample of Chicago-based employers, show how negative stereotypes of black men—that they are lazy, inarticulate, and dangerous—are often applied categorically in the recruitment and hiring process.[40] Their research demonstrates how, irrespective of their socioeconomic status or their human capital skills, employers will often use the type of school attended or residential address to screen out or reject African American male job applicants. More recent research, involving interviews with employers in other cities, confirm that these screening procedures are widely used.[41]

Johnson and Oliver note that some of the previously mentioned undeserved stereotypical images that employers hold of black men—that they are dishonest, lazy, inarticulate, uneducable, untrainable, and dangerous—are themselves a function of the failure of recent social policy.[42] They conclude that urban black males, in particular, have been negatively impacted by recently implemented policies designed to remedy what is increasingly perceived as a failing urban public educational system.[43] In the process of dissecting and challenging the "crisis" in American public education, they reason that analysts and policy makers have instituted a series of "get tough" education policies, such as tracking by ability group, grade retention, the increasing reliance on standardized tests as the ultimate arbiter of educational success, and extreme disciplinary sanctions, which have educationally disenfranchised large numbers of black (and other minority) youth.[44]

With respect to tracking, data indicate that black youth are underrepresented in the gifted and talented or college-bound tracks and overrepresented in the vocational, general education, and special education or non-college-bound tracks. Moreover, individuals who have little or no training in child development often do this tracking. In addition to the adverse effects of tracking, school officials have tightened requirements for both high school graduation and college admission without paying proper attention to whether qualified teachers and the necessary facilities are available at the primary and secondary public school levels.[45] These developments have been especially problematic for urban blacks from impoverished backgrounds who attend economically and educationally inferior inner-city schools.[46]

In addition, Oliver and Johnson cite the increased reliance on standardized general and subject-specific tests as yet another barrier, owing to well-established biases that characterize such tests in predicting black (and other minority) student academic success in higher education. Finally, they draw attention to research which shows that blacks generally, and black males specifically, are more likely than their white counterparts to be subjected to extreme disciplinary sanctions, including permanent expulsion from school.[47]

A number of studies confirm that these and related "get tough" educational policies are directly responsible for the recent rise in the dropout rate and the decrease in the college-going rate of black youth, especially black males. Because many of those who drop out of high school or fail to qualify for admission to college or a university do not possess the skills to compete for jobs in the rapidly growing high-wage sectors of the U.S. economy, Johnson and Oliver argue that these policies have further exacerbated joblessness among young black males.[48]

Heckman contends that black males have also been disadvantaged in the labor market by federal employment and job training programs.[49] Fitzgerald and McGregor specifically note that:

> The limited effectiveness of the JTPA (Job Training and Partnership Act) training is related to the need to meet federal regulations. Job placement assistance is preferred over training, because it is the shortest, and thus the cheapest, service. Fifty percent of enrollees receive placement assistance only. Evidence suggests that the JTPA program creams off the most employable individuals for the most effective types of training in order to meet placement criteria. *Specifically, white males seem to be channeled into on-the-job training programs, which provide the highest reemployment opportunities, while women, minorities, the long-term unemployed, and public assistance recipients are more likely to receive classroom than on-the-job training*. [emphasis added][50]

They also conclude that black males who successfully complete federal job-training programs "frequently find that there is no demand for their newly acquired skills in the local labor market."[51] However, it is in the area of crime policy that the evidence that black males are being systematically targeted for discriminatory treatment is strongest and most convincing. For nearly three decades, states, with the encouragement and support of the federal government, have pursued a policy of resolving the problems of the inner city through the criminal justice system.[52]

The state of California, once a leader in the rehabilitation of criminals, epitomizes this shift in anticrime policy. In 1977, the California Legislature enacted the Determinant Sentence Law; it encouraged punishment over rehabilitation, mandated specific prison sentences for several crimes that were previously eligible for probation, and dramatically escalated the rate at which probation and parole violators were returned to prison.[53] As a consequence of the passage of this law, the California prison population skyrocketed from 22,000 in 1980 to 106,000 in 1992, an increase of nearly 400 percent.[54]

Following California's lead, a number of other states have enacted determinant sentence laws and also have gone on a prison construction binge to accommodate the resulting increase in their prison population. Freeman notes that, as a consequence of this "lock them up and throw away the key" approach to the crime problem, state spending on criminal justice has far outstripped total spending and spending on education.[55] According to Petersilia, over a five-year period, spending on the criminal justice system increased by 70 percent in California, approximately four times greater than total state spending, while state spending on education increased by only 10 percent.[56]

Several writers have argued that the unprecedented rise in rates of incarceration over the last two decades is not simply a function of rising crime rates. In an empirical study, Arvantes and Asher demonstrated that extralegal factors, including unemployment, economic inequality, and the presence of minorities, influences "the level of crime control independent of the level of crime.[57] Based on these findings, they conclude that crime control bureaucracies are reacting not only to the *incidence* of crime but also to the *threat*—real or perceived—of crime. "Without underestimating the serious crime problem in the U.S.," they further conclude, "it is unfortunate that politicians, the media, and the public seem to be unaware that crime is not the sole cause of the incarceration frenzy in this country."[58]

Miller presents forceful and persuasive evidence that black males have been affected disproportionately by these "get-tough-on-crime" policies. Commenting on his experiences as an official in the Massachusetts correctional system, he provides scenarios to show that African American males are the targets of a "search and destroy" mission by federal, state, and local crime control bureaucracies:

> I learned very early on that when we got a black youth, virtually everything—from arrest summaries, to family history, to rap sheets, to psychiatric exams, to "waiver" hearings as to whether or not he would be tried as an adult, to final sentencing—was skewed. If a middle-class white youth was sent to us as "dangerous," he had to have done something very serious indeed. By contrast, the black teenager was more likely to be dealt with as a stereotype from the moment the handcuffs were first put on—easily and quickly relegated to the "more dangerous" end of the "violent-nonviolent" spectrum, albeit accompanied by an official record meant to validate each of a biased series of decisions.[59]

With respect to his views on the juvenile justice system, Miller states:

> [In] . . . juvenile justice processing . . . black teenagers were more likely to be detained, to be handled formally, to be waived to adult court, and to be adjudicated delinquent. If removed from their homes by the court, they were less likely to be placed in the better-staffed and better-run private-group home facilities and more likely to be sent into state reform schools.[60]

In reference to the "drug war," he concludes that this is where "race falls out of the closet. . . . [It] was a disaster-in-waiting for African Americans from the day of its conception."[61] He goes on to point out that

> [i]n Baltimore, 11,107 of the 12,965 persons arrested for "drug abuse violations" in 1991 were African American. In Columbus, Ohio, where African American males made up less than 11 percent of the population, they comprised over 90 percent of the drug arrests and were being arrested at 18 times the rate of whites. In Jacksonville, Florida, 87 percent of those arrested on drug charges were African American males, even though they comprised only 12 percent of that county's population. In Minneapolis (where a state court held that punishments mandated by the legislature for possession or sale of crack cocaine were racist in their effect), though black men made up only about 7 percent of the population, they were being arrested at a ratio of approximately 20:1 to white males.[62]

After noting that "penalties follow the same trend [as arrests]," Miller observes that

> [i]n 1991, 90 percent of the "crack arrests" nationally were of minorities, whereas three-fourths of the arrest for powder cocaine were of whites. However, sentences for the possession of crack were usually three to four times harsher than those for possession of the same amount of powder cocaine. Blacks were sent to prison in unprecedented numbers and were kept there longer than whites. Ninety-two percent of all drug possession offenders sentenced to prison in New York were either black or Hispanic, and 71 percent in California.[63]

Miller continues by stating the following about drug treatment:

> [I]n [the] drug war . . . African Americans were less likely to be assigned to treatment programs than whites. In California, for example, whereas 70 percent of inmates sentenced for drug offenses were black, two-thirds of the drug-treatment slots went to whites.[64]

Elaborating on this discriminatory treatment, Freeman estimates that

> [i]n 1993, about 7 percent of black men over 18 were incarcerated. One black man was in prison for every eleven black men in the workforce; and approximately one was under the supervision of the criminal justice system for every three to four black men in the workforce. Combine race and age and you find that 12 percent of black men aged 25–34 were incarcerated.[65]

In 1994, blacks constituted 44 percent of the U.S. prison population. What impact did this high rate of incarceration have on the African American community? As Johnson and Oliver note, for the African American male, "incarceration breeds despair, and hopelessness, and in the employment arena, it is the 'Scarlet Letter' of unemployability."[66] Such high rates of incarceration also threaten black family structure and the future economic viability of the African American community; it is, probably, most distressing for the estimated 825,000 black children in the U.S. whose fathers are currently incarcerated.

Finally, the *social capital hypothesis* suggests that social isolation as a function of economic restructuring and racial discrimination in both the labor market and the housing market is a critical determinant of joblessness and wage inequality. It also acknowledges the findings of recent ethnographic studies which indicate that in the increasingly hostile and dangerous neighborhoods of the inner city, a "code of the streets" often emerges, particularly among young African American males, where the demand for respect through periodic violence is a form of human capital, and gang membership is a form of social capital—a social support network and source of protection for young African American males.[67]

But they are also quick to assert that not all residents of inner-city communities who are isolated, socially and economically, from the mainstream are jobless and poor. Likewise, they note that not all youth who grow up in these environments engage in antisocial or dysfunctional behaviors. In these environments, they argue, some adults manage to find jobs, and some youth manage to eschew underclass behaviors despite their residence in a ghetto poor or hypersegregated neighborhood.[68]

The distinguishing factor, according to social capital theorists, is what they term bridging social networks, which are defined as ties that connect individuals to a different world of information, resources, and opportunities. Jarrett has demonstrated how some poor women in the inner city have been able to develop social networks that connect them, and especially their children, with individuals and institutions beyond the boundaries of their neighborhoods. Her research revealed that the children of these women were more likely to engage in "community-bridging" behaviors than the children of their counterparts who were not embedded in bridging social networks.[69] The latter group of youth was more likely to engage in "community-specific" behaviors, that is, antisocial or dysfunctional behaviors consistent with those described in the literature on the urban underclass.[70]

With respect to the previously described racial disparities in joblessness and earnings, social capital theorists contend that one of the major problems is that African American men, especially those who reside in the inner city, are embedded in homogenous networks which disadvantage them in the labor market.[71] If we are to improve the economic fortunes of African American men, social capital theorists reason that the key is figuring out how to embed them in heterogeneous networks, that is, networks in which all members differ on such characteristics as place of residence, race, gender, and class. What African American men need, in network terms, are advantageous weak ties, ties that serve as bridges to the economic mainstream.[72]

Assessing the Utility of the Four Schools of Thought

The debate on the underlying causes of the black male crisis in American society is highly polarized. For the most part, researchers and policymakers alike have embraced one or another of the foregoing schools of thought and have ignored the possible effects of forces highlighted in other schools of thought in their analyses and interpretations of the problem.[73] Only recently have researchers begun to develop analytical models that are designed to provide empirical insights into the relative weight of the various factors undergirding the four schools of thought reviewed above. Below, we highlight some of the most salient findings of these recent empirical studies.

Most of the studies that have attempted to assess the relative effects of these competing hypotheses have utilized data from the Los Angeles Survey of Urban Inequality (LASUI).[74] They indicate that in terms of gaining access to jobs in the Los Angeles labor market, black males are hurt tremendously by their low levels of education and their connection with the criminal justice system.[75] More specifically, according to research, black men with less than a high school education are 92 percent less likely to be working than their counterparts who have 12-plus years of schooling, and those with a criminal record are 76 percent less likely to be gainfully employed than their black male counterparts who have avoided an encounter with the law. To which of the hypotheses do these findings lend support? Given our field research in Los Angeles concerning urban inequality along the lines of gender and race, we lean toward the *search and destroy hypothesis* for the following reasons.

First, it is well documented that both the Los Angeles Police Department (LAPD) and the Los Angeles Sheriff's Department (LASD) have strategically targeted South-central Los Angeles, which is the heart of Los Angeles' black community, and young African American males within this community in their war on gangs and drugs.[76] Second, it has also been confirmed that, in an effort to lure international capital to Los Angeles, city officials have pursued, consciously and aggressively, a strategy of downtown and Westside redevelopment, at the expense of the neighborhoods and communities that make up South-central Los Angeles.[77] Partly as a function of the city's wholesale disinvestment in South-central Los Angeles communities, the area has become host to a disproportionate number of alcohol outlets and other locally unwanted land uses. Commenting on the impact of a high concentration of alcohol outlets in socially isolated and economically marginal communities like South-central Los Angeles, Bennett et al. state:

> In economic terms, . . . high densities of alcohol outlets create negative "externalities" that compete against, cancel out, or overwhelm the positive "externalities" associated with traditional institutions and behaviors like church going. Whether or not they themselves drink to excess, hang out in bars, or engage directly in related behaviors, it is probable that poor, inner city youths who grow up in places where drinking is common and liquor outlets are everywhere are more likely than otherwise comparable youths to have diminished life prospects that include joblessness, substance abuse, and getting into serious trouble with the law.[78]

Moreover, research shows that city officials' neglect of South-central Los Angeles coincided with massive cuts in federal aid to cities.[79] Both of these developments were occurring precisely at the time that the primary institutions in poor communities like South-central Los Angeles—families, schools, churches, and others—were being swamped with huge increases in the juvenile population. As Bennett et al. point out, partly as a function of these cuts in local and federal government assistance, the primary institutions in South-central Los Angeles (and other inner-city communities) started "to crumble at the very moment when they were needed to be towers of strength."[80]

Other studies reveal that in the past, such community-based institutions as the Boys' and Girls' Clubs, the YMCA, and the YWCA were successful mediators in poor inner-city environments; they encouraged disadvantaged youth to pursue mainstream avenues of social and economic mobility and discouraged them from engaging in antisocial or dysfunctional behavior.[81] Today, owing to budget constraints occasioned by federal and local government cuts in financial support, these organizations are not as successful as they were in the past.[82]

Third, at the state level, over this same period, there has been a drastic reallocation of resources from the public education system to the criminal justice system. Research shows that this reallocation process has been a double-edged sword for African American males. Cuts in education have contributed to their school failure, and the increased spending in "lock-them-up-and-throw-away-the-key" crime control policies has been used to brand them with the scarlet letter of unemployability. African American males are the only group in our Los Angeles research for whom having a criminal record exerted a statistically significant negative effect on their likelihood of employment.[83]

Our retrospective analyses of the life courses of more than two dozen young black male violent offenders, now serving life sentences for murder, serve as a powerful illustration of what happens to youth who grow up in communities, like South-central Los Angeles, where the social safety net has been systematically dismantled.[84] Their childhoods were plagued by a common set of problems.

They grew up in families—in most cases two-parent families—in which there was a history of spousal and child abuse, alcohol and drug abuse, and chronic joblessness or, at best, weak attachment to the labor market. Moreover, they often suffered from undiagnosed and/or untreated learning disabilities, other mental problems, and alcohol and drug problems. They also were victimized by the discriminatory tracking and social promotion system in the Los Angeles public school system, which in turn led to school failure and involvement in gangs, drug dealing, and other criminal activities.[85] It is clear from the retrospective data that these black males might be on a different life course trajectory today had they not been residents of South-central Los Angeles, a community that is bereft of the kinds of social, psychological, and institutional supports that characterize working-class, middle-class, and upper-class communities.

Other data in the LASUI also illustrate how widespread the disparate treatment along racial lines is in American society. Research on the labor market experiences of prime working-age males in the Los Angeles labor market indicates that not only race but also skin tone plays a major role in determining who works and who does not in Los Angeles.[86]

Despite federal, state, and local statutes which bar discrimination based on race and skin tone, analyses of the LASUI data reveal that being a dark-skinned African American male reduced the odds of working by 52 percent.[87] In 1994, according to the LASUI, only 8.6 percent of white males were unemployed compared with 23.1 percent of black males in general and 27 percent of dark-skinned black males. Light-skinned African American males were more likely to be working than their dark-skinned counterparts, although their rate of unemployment was still relatively high compared to that of white males (Figure 5).

While education and job training widen employment for black males, race and skin tone still play a significant role. In the Los Angeles survey, only 10.3 percent of light-skinned African American men with 13 or more years of schooling were unemployed, compared with 19.4 percent of their dark-skinned counterparts with similar education. Indeed, the unemployment figure for light-skinned black males compared favorably with the 9.5 percent rate of unemployment for white males with comparable schooling (Figure 5). Among males who have participated in job-training programs, light-skinned black males actually have a lower jobless rate than their white male counterparts—11.1 percent compared to 14.5 percent. Yet dark-skinned African American males who had undergone job training had a jobless rate of 26.8 percent. This is 15 percent higher than their light-skinned counterparts and 12 percent higher than white males (Figure 5).

The Los Angeles data suggest that race and skin tone matter even for those who have not played by the rules governing American society. In Los Angeles, where there are far more job seekers than there are available jobs, a criminal record is the scarlet letter of unemployability—irrespective of race and skin tone. But a criminal record is especially problematic for dark-skinned black males whose 54 percent jobless rate was 13 percent and 29 percent higher, respectively, than the rates for their light-skinned black male counterparts, whose jobless rate was 41.7

FIGURE 5
Percent of Males not Working by Skin Tone

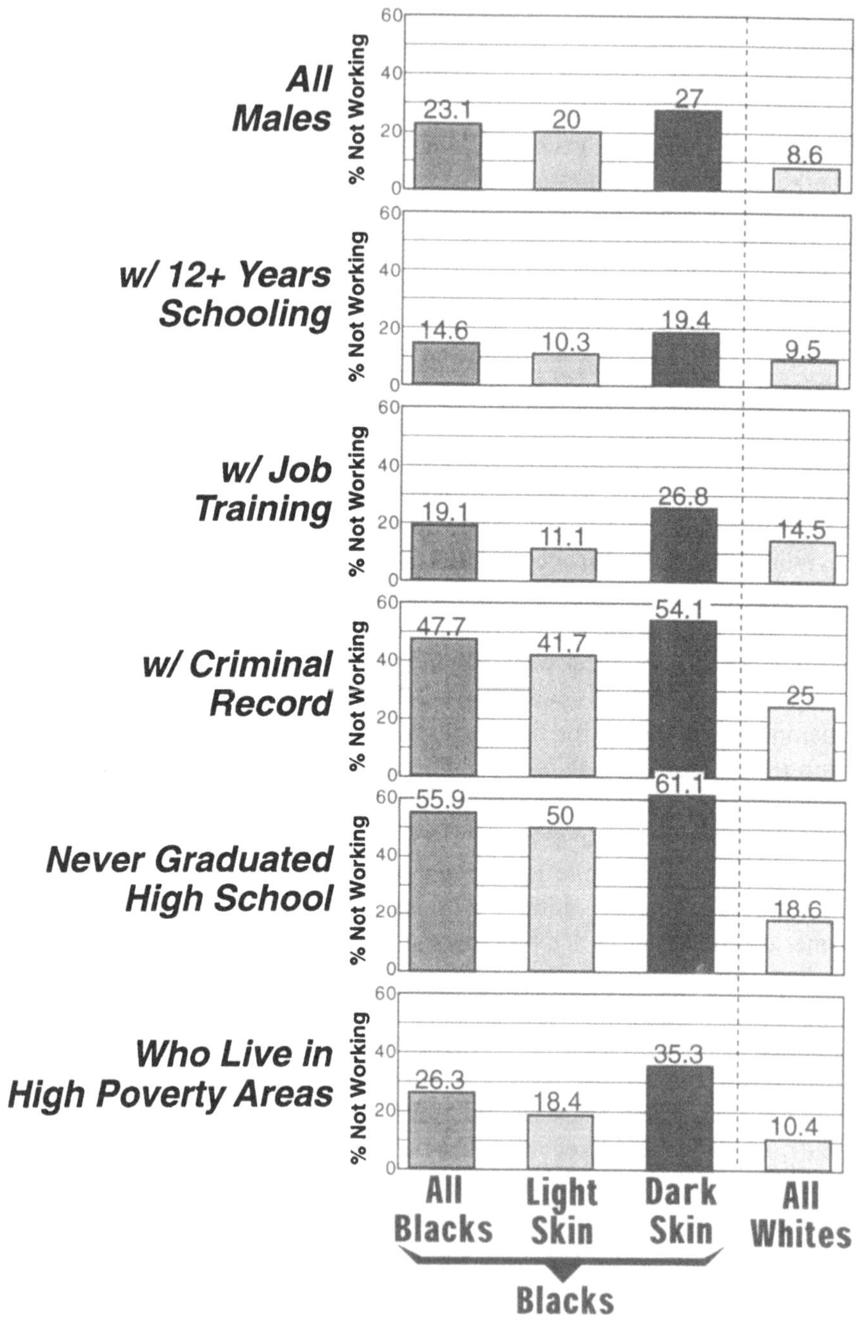

percent, and for their white male counterparts, whose jobless rate was 25 percent (Figure 5).

The same pattern held true for Los Angeles survey respondents who were high school dropouts and for those who lived in poor ghetto neighborhoods (i.e., neighborhoods where the poverty rate exceeds 30 percent). Some 61 percent of dark-skinned African American men with less than twelve years of schooling and 35.9 percent of dark-skinned blacks who lived in poor ghetto neighborhoods, compared with 35.3 percent of light-skinned black men who were high school dropouts and 21.4 percent who lived in ghetto neighborhoods, were unemployed. The comparable figures were 18.6 percent for white men without high school diplomas and 12.7 percent for whites in high-poverty neighborhoods (Figure 5).

These data suggest, in short, that while a lack of basic skills (as measured by years of school completed), engagement in antisocial behavior (e.g., involvement in illegal activities), and geographical isolation from mainstream employment opportunities are major impediments in the U.S. labor market, employers do not respond to these constraints in a race-neutral way. There is an additional disadvantage if you are a black male, and the situation is even worse if you are a dark-skinned black male, especially when confounded with other disadvantaging attributes such as a criminal record.[88]

SUMMARY AND CONCLUSIONS

In this paper, we have attempted to assess the utility of four schools of thought/hypotheses that have been advanced to explain the crisis of the black male in America. One of these schools of thought, *the spatial isolation hypothesis,* views the plight of the African American male as essentially a structural problem, which is primarily rooted in the globalization of the economy and the persistence of racial discrimination in the U.S. housing market. A second school of thought, *the cultural capital/ employer preference hypothesis,* characterizes the problem as "a crisis of values and morals," which are reflected in negative attitudes and behaviors that cause black males to be shunned in the mainstream labor market. The third school of thought, *the search and destroy hypothesis,* views black males as being systematically targeted for discriminatory treatment, especially in the public education system, the labor market, and the criminal justice system. The fourth perspective, *the social capital hypothesis*, views the black male problem as one of a lack of embeddedness in individual and institutional networks that serve as "bridges" to the educational and economic mainstream.

Studies that attempt to assess the relative utility of these four schools of thought, using data from the LASUI, lend empirical support to the *search and destroy hypothesis*. In the criminal justice arena, but also in other critical policy domains, including education and job training and employment, black males appear to be systematically targeted for disparate treatment. Anger, rage, and a sense of despair and hopelessness are among the behavioral manifestations of this discriminatory treatment. In much of the extant literature, such behaviors are often mischaracterized as subcultural norms rooted in slavery, the southern sharecropper system, and most often the social welfare policies of the 1960s.

If the *search and destroy hypothesis* appears to explain the so-called African American male problem, what steps can be taken to ameliorate the situation? Studies suggest that instead of the paternalistic and punitive policies that have been implemented to date, programs designed to build "bridges" to mainstream educational and employment opportunities will go a long way toward solving the "African American male problem."[89]

NOTES

1. B. W. Austin, ed., *Repairing the Breach: Key Ways to Support Family Life, Reclaim Our Streets, and Rebuild Society in America's Communities* (Dillon, CO: Alpine Guild, Inc., 1996); E. Cose, *A Man's World: How Real is Male Privilege—And How High is Its Price?* (New York: Harper Collins, 1995); J. T. Gibbs, *Young, Black, and Male in America: An Endangered Species* (Dover, MA: Auburn House, 1988); N. McCall, *Makes Me Wanna Holler: A Young Black Man in America* (New York: Vintage Books, 1995).
2. J. H. Johnson, Jr., "The Real Issues for Reducing Poverty," in *Reducing Poverty in America,* ed. M. R. Darby (Thousand Oaks, CA: Sage Publications, 1996), pp. 337–363.
3. B. Bluestone, M. Stevenson, and C. Tilly, *An Assessment of the Impact of "Deindustrialization" and Spatial Mismatch in the Labor Market: Outcomes of Young White, Black, and Latino Men and Women Who Have Limited Schooling* (Boston, MA: John McCormick Institute of Public Affairs, 1992).
4. *Ibid.*
5. R. B. Freeman, "Towards an Apartheid Economy?" *Harvard Business Review* (1996), pp. 114–121.
6. Bluestone, Stevenson, and Tilly, *An Assessment of the Impact of "Deindustrialization."* For an earlier discussion of the impact of deindustrialization on American wages, see B. Bluestone and B. Harrison, *The Deindustrialization of America* (New York: Basic Books, 1982).
7. Bluestone, Stevenson, and Tilly, *An Assessment of the Impact of "Deindustrialization"*; R. B. Freeman, "Towards an Apartheid Economy"; L. Mishel, "Rising Tides, Sinking Wages," *The American Prospect* (1995, Fall), pp. 60–64.
8. W. J. Wilson, *The Truly Disadvantaged* (Chicago: University of Chicago Press, 1987); W. J. Wilson, *When Work Disappears* (New York: Alfred A. Knopf, 1996).
9. D. Massey and N. Denton, *American Apartheid: Segregation and the Making of the Underclass* (Cambridge, MA: Harvard University Press, 1993).

10. D. Massey, "The Age of Extremes: Concentrated Affluence and Poverty in the Twenty-First Century," *Demography* 33 (1996), pp. 395–412.

11. Wilson, *When Work Disappears.*

12. L. D. Bobo and C. Zubrinsky, "Attitudes on Residential Integration: Perceived Status Differences, Mere In-Group Preference, or Racial Prejudice," *Social Forces* 74 (1996), pp. 171–186; Massey and Denton, *American Apartheid.*

13. J. T. Bernard, "Angry Aggression Among the 'Truly Disadvantaged,'" *Criminology* 28 (1990), pp. 73–95; J. Hagan, "The Social Imbeddedness of Crime and Unemployment," *Criminology* 31 (1993), pp. 465–491; Wilson, *The Truly Disadvantaged.*

14. Wilson, *When Work Disappears.*

15. Massey and Denton, *American Apartheid.*

16. J. H. Johnson, Jr., and M. L. Oliver, "Structural Changes in the U.S. Economy and Black Male Joblessness: A Reassessment," in *Urban Labor Markets and Job Opportunity*, eds. G. E. Peterson and W. Vroman (Washington, D.C.: The Urban Institute Press, 1992).

17. D. Grant and J. H. Johnson, Jr., "Conservative Policymaking and Growing Urban Inequality in the 1980s," in *Research and Politics and Society,* eds. R. Ratliff, M. Oliver, and T. Shapiro (Greenwich, CT: JAI Press, 1995).

18. Johnson and Oliver, "Structural Change in the U.S. Economy and Black Male Joblessness."

19. M. D. Hinds, "Survey Cited to Assail Bush on Overseas Jobs," *New York Times* (1992, December 23), p. Al.

20. Grant and Johnson, "Conservative Policymaking and Growing Urban Inequality."

21. Mishel, "Rising Tides, Sinking Wages"; J. L. Palmer and I. V. Sawhill, eds., *The Reagan Record* (Washington, D.C.: The Urban Institute Press, 1984).

22. Bluestone and Harrison, *The Deindustrialization of America*; Johnson and Oliver, "Structural Changes in the U.S. Economy and Black Male Joblessness"; Wilson, *The Truly Disadvantaged* and *When Work Disappears.*

23. R. E. Cole and D. R. Deskins, "Racial Factors in Site Location and Employment Patterns of Japanese Auto Firms in America," *California Management Review* 31 (1988), pp. 9–22; D. Foust and M. Mallory, "The Boom Belt: There's No Speed Limit on Growth Along the South's I-85," *Business Week* (1993, September 27), pp. 98–104; K. Labich, "The Geography of an Emerging America," *Fortune* (1994, June 27), pp. 88–94; A. MacCormack, L. Newman, III, and D. B. Rosenfield, "The New Dynamics of Global Manufacturing Site Location," *Sloan Management Review* (1994, Summer), pp. 62–69; R. A. Melcher and K. Kelly, "America's Heartland: The Midwest's New Role in the Global Economy," *Business Week* (1994, July 11), pp. 116–124.

24. A. J. Scott, "Flexible Production Systems and Regional Development: The Rise of New Industrial Spaces in North America and Western Europe," *International Journal of Urban and Regional Research* 12 (1988), pp. 171–186.

25. Johnson and Oliver, "Structural Changes in the U.S. Economy and Black Male Joblessness"; B. Stocking, "Workplaces Welcome Hispanics," *The News and Observer* (1996, September 2), p. Al.

26. R. Waldinger, *Who Makes the Beds? Who Washes the Dishes? Black/Immigrant Competition Reassessed.* Unpublished manuscript, Department of Sociology, University of California at Los Angeles, 1992.

27. S. Head, "The New Ruthless Economy," *The New York Review of Books* (1996, February 26), pp. 47–52.

28. Scott, "Flexible Production Systems and Regional Development."

29. R. H. Hayes, "U.S. Competitiveness: 'Resurgence' Versus Reality," *Challenge* (1996, March/April), pp. 36–44.

30. W. J. Bennett, J. DiIulio, and J. P. Walters, *Body Count: Moral Poverty . . . and How to Win America's War Against Crime and Drugs* (New York: Simon and Shuster, 1996); L. E. Harrison, *Who Prospers? How Cultural Values Shape Economic and Political Success* (New York: Basic Books, 1992); N. Lemann, *The Promised Land* (New York: Alfred Knopf, 1991); L. Mead, *The New Politics of Poverty* (New York: Basic Books, 1992); C. Murray, "Reducing Poverty and Reducing the Underclass: Different Problems, Different Solutions," in *Reducing Poverty in America: Views and Approaches*, ed. M. Darby (Newbury, CA: Sage Publications, 1996), pp. 82–110; T. Sowell, *Ethnic America* (New York: Basic Books, 1981); T. Sowell, *Race and Culture: A World View* (New York: Basic Books, 1994); The Editors, "Foul Shots," *The New Republic* (1997, December 29), p. 11.

31. Harrison, *Who Prospers?*, p. 194.

32. Sowell, *Ethnic America*, p. 200.

33. Lemann, *The Promised Land.*

34. Wilson, *When Work Disappears*; Massey, "The Age of Extremes."

35. Bennett, DiIulio, and Walters, *Body Count*, p. 14.

36. *Ibid.*; Harrison, *Who Prospers?*; Mead, *The New Politics of Poverty*; C. Murray, *Losing Ground* (New York: Basic Books, 1984); Murray, "Reducing Poverty and Reducing the Underclass"; Sowell, *Race and Culture.*

37. J. H. Braddock, II, and J. M. McPartland, "How Minorities Continue to be Excluded from Equal Employment Opportunities: Research on Labor Markets and Institutional Barriers," *Journal of Social Issues* 431 (1987), pp. 5–39; J. Culp and B. H. Dunson, "Brothers of a Different Color: A Preliminary Look at Employer Treatment of White and Black Youth," in *The Youth Employment Crisis*, eds. R. B. Freeman and H. J. Holzer (Chicago: University of Chicago Press, 1996), pp. 223–259; H. Cross, G. Kenny, J. Mell, and W. Zimmerman, *Employer Hiring Practices: Differential Treatment of Hispanic and Anglo Job Seekers* (Washington, D.C.: The Urban Institute Press, Report No. 90–4, 1990); J. Kirschenman and K. Neckermann, "We'd Love to Hire Them, But: The Meaning of Race for Employers," in *The Urban Underclass*, eds. C. Jencks and P. E. Peterson (Washington, D.C.: The Urban Institute Press, 1991), pp. 203–224; K. Neckerman and J. Kirschenmann, "Hiring Strategies, Racial Bias and Inner City Workers," *Social Problems* 38 (1990), pp. 433–447; M. A. Turner, M. Fix, and R. J. Struyk, *Opportunities Denied, Opportunities Diminished: Racial Discrimination in Hiring* (Washington, D.C.: The Urban Institute Press, Urban Institute Report, 1991).

38. H. J. Holzer and K. Ihlanfeld, *Customer Discrimination and Employment Outcomes for Minority Workers,* unpublished manuscript, Michigan State University, 1996; The Editors, "Foul Shot."

39. J. L. Jackson and J. L. Jackson, Jr., *Legal Lynching, Racism, Injustice, and the Death Penalty* (New York: Marlowe and Company, 1996); J. Miller, *Search and Destroy: African American Males and the U.S. Criminal Justice System* (New York: Cambridge University Press, 1996).

40. Kirschenman and Neckerman, "We'd Love to Hire Them, But"; Neckernan and Kirschenman, "Hiring Strategies, Racial Bias and Inner City Workers."

41. Holzer and Ihlanfeld, *Customer Discrimination and Employment Outcomes for Minority Workers.*

42. Johnson and Oliver, "Structural Changes in the U.S. Economy and Black Male Joblessness"; Grant and Johnson, "Conservative Policymaking and Growing Urban Inequality."

43. M. L. Oliver and J. H. Johnson, Jr., "The Challenge of Diversity in Higher Education," *The Urban Review* 20 (1988), pp. 139–145.
44. G. Orfield, "Exclusion of the Majority: Shrinking College Access and Public Policy in Metropolitan Los Angeles," *The Urban Review* 20 (1988), pp. 147–163.
45. Oliver and Johnson, "The Challenge of Diversity in Higher Education."
46. J. Kozol, *Savage Inequalities: Children in America's Schools* (New York: HarperCollins, 1992).
47. Oliver and Johnson, "The Challenge of Diversity in Higher Education."
48. Johnson and Oliver, "Structural Changes in the U.S. Economy and Black Male Joblessness."
49. J. Heckman, "Is Job Training Oversold?" *The Public Interest* (1994, Spring), pp. 91–115.
50. J. Fitzgerald and A. McGregor, "Labor-community Initiatives in Worker Training," *Economic Development Quarterly* 7 (1993), p. 174.
51. *Ibid.*
52. Miller, *Search and Destroy;* M. Mauer, "America Behind Bars," *Criminal Justice* 6 (1992), pp. 12–18, 38.
53. J. Petersilia, "Crime and Punishment in California: Full Cells, Empty Pockets, and Questionable Benefits," in *Urban America: Policy Choices for Los Angeles and the Nation,* eds. J. B. Steinberg, D. W. Lyons, and M. E. Vaiana (Los Angeles: Rand Corporation, 1992), pp. 175–206.
54. Petersilia, "Crime and Punishment in California."
55. R. B. Freeman, "Why So Many Young American Men Commit Crimes and What We Might Do About It," *Journal of Economic Perspectives* 10 (1996), pp. 25–42.
56. Petersilia, "Crime and Punishment in California."
57. T. M. Arvantes and M. Asher, "The Direct and Indirect Effects of Socioeconomic Variables on State Imprisonment Rates," *Criminal Justice—Report* 7 (1995), pp. 27–53.
58. *Ibid.*, p. 47.
59. Miller, *Search and Destroy*, p. 78.
60. *Ibid.*, p. 72.
61. *Ibid.*, p. 82.
62. *Ibid.*, pp. 81–82.
63. *Ibid.*, p. 82.
64. *Ibid.*, p. 83.
65. Freeman, "Towards an Apartheid Economy," p. 26.
66. Johnson and Oliver, "Structural Changes in the U.S. Economy and Black Male Joblessness," p. 144.
67. E. Anderson, *Streetwise: Race, Class and Change in an Urban Community* (Chicago: University of Chicago Press, 1990); E. Anderson, "Code of the Streets," *Atlantic Monthly* (1994, May), pp. 81–94; Massey, "Getting Away with Murder: Segregation and Violent Crime in Urban America," *University of Pennsylvania Law Review* 143 (1995), pp. 1203–1232.
68. R. Jarrett, "Growing Up Poor: The Family Experiences of Socially Mobile Youth in Low Income African American Neighborhoods," *Journal of Adolescent Research* 10 (1995), pp. 111–135; M. Sullivan, *Getting Paid: Youth Crime and Work in the Inner City* (Ithaca, NY: Cornell University Press, 1989).
69. Jarrett, "Growing Up Poor."
70. Wilson, *The Truly Disadvantaged.*
71. Braddock and McPartland, "How Minorities Continue to be Excluded from Equal Employment Opportunities."

72. W. C. Farrell, Jr., J. H. Johnson, Jr., M. Sapp, R. M. Pumphrey, and S. Freeman, "Redirecting the Lives of Urban Black Males: An Assessment of Milwaukee's Midnight Basketball League," *Journal of Community Practice* 2 (1996), pp. 91–107; J. H. Johnson, Jr., E. J. Bienenstock, and W. C. Farrell, Jr., "Bridging Social Networks and Female Labor Force Participation in a Multi-Ethnic Metropolis," in *Fault Lines in the Metropolis: Race and Economic Inequality in Metropolitan Los Angeles,* eds. L. D. Bobo and J. H. Johnson, Jr. (New York: Russell Sage, in press).

73. Johnson, "The Real Issues for Reducing Poverty."

74. J. H. Johnson, Jr., M. L. Oliver, and L. D. Bobo, "Understanding the Contours of Deepening Urban Inequality," *Urban Geography* 15 (1994), pp. 77–89.

75. Johnson, Farrell, and Stoloff, "Bridging Social Networks."

76. M. W. Klein, *The American Street Gang: Its Nature, Prevalence and Control* (New York: Oxford University Press, 1994).

77. Grant and Johnson, "Conservative Policymaking and Growing Urban Inequality"; J. H. Johnson, Jr., and W. C. Farrell, Jr., "The Fire This Time: The Genesis of the Los Angeles Rebellion of 1992," in *Race, Poverty, and American Cities,* eds. J. C. Boger and J. W. Wegner (Chapel Hill, NC: University of North Carolina Press, 1996), pp. 166–185.

78. Bennett, DiIulio, and Walters, *Body Count*, pp. 73–74. Also see M. P. Dawkins, W. C. Farrell, Jr., and J. H. Johnson, Jr., "Spatial Patterns of Alcohol Outlets in the Washington, D.C., Black Community," *Proceedings of the Pennsylvania Academy of Science* 53 (1979), pp. 89–97.

79. P. NiBlack and P. Stan, "Financing Public Services in Los Angeles," in *Urban America: Policy Choices for Los Angeles and the Nation,* eds. J. Steinberg and M. Vaiana (Santa Monica, CA: Rand Corporation, 1992).

80. Bennett, DiIulio, and Walters, *Body Count*, p. 14.

81. M. L. Oliver, "The Urban Black Community as Network: Towards a Social Network Perspective," *Sociological Quarterly* 29 (1988), pp. 623–625.

82. W. C. Farrell, Jr., and J. H. Johnson, Jr., "Access to Local Resources Key to Problems in Inner City," *Wisconsin Review* (1994, October), p. 24; Johnson and Farrell, "The Fire This Time."

83. J. H. Johnson, Jr., E. J. Bienenstock, and J. Stoloff, "An Empirical Test of the Cultural Capital Hypothesis," *The Review of Black Political Economy,* 24 (1995), pp. 7–27; J. H. Johnson, Jr., and W. C. Farrell, Jr., "Race Still Matters," *The Chronicle of Higher Education* (1995, July 7), p. A48.

84. J. H. Johnson, Jr., W. C. Farrell, Jr., and M. Sapp, "African American Males and Capital Murder: A Death Penalty Mitigation Strategy," *Urban Geography* 18 (1997), pp. 403–433; J. H. Johnson, Jr., W. C. Farrell, Jr., and M. Sapp, "The Daniel Green Case: A Death Penalty Mitigation Strategy," *Negro Educational Review* 47 (1996), pp. 94–115.

85. Johnson, Farrell, and Sapp, "African American Males and Capital Murder."

86. Johnson, Bienenstock, and Stoloff, "An Empirical Test of the Cultural Capital Hypothesis"; J. H. Johnson, Jr., and W. C. Farrell, Jr., "Race Still Matters."

87. *Ibid.*

88. *Ibid.*

89. Farrell, Johnson, Sapp, Pumphrey, and Freeman, "Redirecting the Lives of Urban Black Males"; Johnson, Bienenstock, and Farrell, "Bridging Social Networks."

3

ECONOMICS RESEARCH AT HISTORICALLY BLACK COLLEGES AND UNIVERSITIES: RANKINGS AND EFFECTS ON THE SUPPLY OF BLACK ECONOMISTS*

Jacqueline Agesa
Maury Granger
Gregory N. Price

INTRODUCTION

In recent years, a literature has emerged that examines the research productivity of economics departments at non-research universities.[1] With the exception of Hartley and Robinson,[2] who include Morehouse and Spelman colleges in their sample, nothing in the literature provides insight into the research productivity of economics departments at Historically Black Colleges and Universities (HBCUs) exclusively. In this paper we rank forty HBCUs that have faculty roster listings in the 1996 Prentice Hall Guide to Economics Faculty.[3] Our method of ranking HBCUs is based on two measures of research productivity. One measure captures research productivity exclusively in the discipline of economics. The second measure captures research output across a spectrum of disciplines, including economics. The latter measure is especially useful as many economics faculty at HBCUs are housed in multidisciplinary departments.

An analysis and ranking of the research productivity of economics departments at HBCUs is of interest for at least two reasons. First, Bodenhorn argues that at teaching-oriented liberal arts colleges, an increasing emphasis is being placed on scholarly productivity, and these colleges are now making significant contributions to the literature of economics.[4] A ranking of economics departments at HBCUs, the majority of which are teaching oriented, would provide insights into the extent to which their faculty are engaged in scholarly activity and making con-

* We are grateful to Shanta Harris for outstanding research assistance.

tributions to the stock of economics literature. Finally, Hartley and Robinson report a positive correlation between the research productivity of an economics department and the number of its undergraduates that earn Ph.D.s in economics.[5] This suggests that scholarly productivity by economics faculty is one dimension of teaching effectiveness that cultivates an interest in undergraduates to pursue doctoral degrees in economics. In this analysis, we also rank economics departments at HBCUs by the number of their undergraduates that earned Ph.D.s in economics. To the extent that the correlation between HBCU economic research productivity and the number of its undergraduates earning doctorates in economics is positive, an implication is that HBCUs could enhance the pipeline of black Ph.D. economists by committing more resources to faculty research.

The remainder of this paper is organized as follows. The first section below describes the data and methodology. The second section provides rankings of HBCU economics departments on the basis of research productivity and the number of undergraduates that earned a Ph.D. in economics. Forty HBCUs are ranked on the basis of eight variants of two research productivity measures. In the second section we also examine the possibility of a causal relationship between faculty scholarship in economics and the graduate school achievements of students, and compute correlation coefficients between research productivity measures and the number of students that earned doctorates in economics.

DATA AND METHODOLOGY

Ranking HBCU economic departments on the basis of research productivity required the following data: (1) a listing of economics faculty at HBCUs and (2) an account of journal articles, book chapters, and book reviews published by the faculty. Faculty listings were obtained from the *1996 Prentice Hall Guide to Economics Faculty*. Although there are 103 HBCUs in the United States, the *Prentice Hall Guide* included detailed faculty listings for only forty HBCUs.[6] The rankings provided here are therefore more or less representative of research productivity of economics faculty at HBCUs—as there may be some biases in the rankings as a result of omitting those HBCUs for which we did not have faculty listings.

Two measures of research productivity are utilized. The first is based upon the number of articles, notes, comments, book reviews, book chapters, and books each faculty member produced between 1983 and 1997 that were indexed in the EconLit database.[7] This database is available on

CD-ROM and covers all journals catalogued in the *Journal of Economic Literature* (JEL). In this sense, it is a proper measure of research exclusively in economics. While the first measure is traditionally used in determining research productivity in economics, our second measure is not so traditional. The second measure is based upon the number of articles, notes, and comments each faculty member produced that were indexed in the CARL Uncover database for the years 1987–1997.[8] The CARL Uncover database is a searchable index of nearly 17,000 English language periodicals covering essentially all academic disciplines.[9] The second measure is thus a measure of the extent to which economics faculty at HBCUs are engaged in scholarly activity, either within the discipline of economics or not. In addition, since many of the economics departments at HBCUs are housed in multidisciplinary units in which economics is listed as the lead discipline, our second measure allows us to capture the total productivity of the organizational unit in which economics faculty are housed.

Ranking economics departments at HBCUs on the basis of the number of their graduates that earned Ph.D.s in economics required data on doctoral counts for each institution. For the HBCUs in the sample, the number of undergraduates from each school that obtained a Ph.D. in economics over the 1980–1995 period was obtained from the National Science Foundation's Computer-Aided Science Policy Analysis and Research Database.[10]

RANKINGS

Research Output

Table 1 presents a ranking of HBCUs by total research output. Schools are ranked in four categories: (1) total JEL catalogued output (this includes journal articles, book, and book chapters); (2) total JEL output with an adjustment for coauthorship (e.g., a paper with three authors was counted as one third for each co-author); (3) total CARL-indexed periodicals; and (4) total CARL-indexed periodicals with an adjustment for coauthorship. Research output varies dramatically depending on the measure used. Indeed, the total JEL output of HBCUs was 228 journal articles, book reviews, and book chapters, while total CARL-indexed output at HBCUs is 150 articles. The larger JEL output is partially the result of the larger time period covered.[11] However, the remaining discrepancy indicates the need for both measures. Moreover, the JEL measure is larger as a result of the inclusion of book chapters and book reviews, while the CARL measure captures multi-disciplinary work (over 10 percent of which are not JEL indexed). Moreover, each captures a unique aspect of research output and together provides a thorough assessment of scholarly activity at HBCUs.

The total number of publications is highly concentrated among the top-ranked schools. Using total JEL output, the top-ranked school, Howard University, accounts for 36.8 percent of all publications at HBCUs, while the top five schools account for 68.4 percent, and the top ten account for 87.7 percent. Using total CARL output, concentration is almost equally as pronounced. Using this measure, the top-ranked school, North Carolina A&T State University, accounts for 28 percent of the total, the top five account for 64 percent, and the top ten account for 87.7 percent. Additionally, a substantial portion of HBCUs have zero output using either measure (37.5 percent using JEL and 47.5 percent using CARL). These findings suggest that faculty at many HBCUs are not engaged in scholarship.

The adjustment of each index for coauthorship alters the rankings only slightly. However, it appears that the largest change in rankings is a result of the index used. For example, Howard University is ranked number one using the JEL index but falls to number five using the CARL index. This shift is a result of the large number of books and book chapters in Howard's JEL output. At the same time, multidisciplinary departments, such as North Carolina A&T State University and Alabama A&M University, have a substantially larger output using the CARL measure.

A potential argument against the above rankings is that they do not control for department size. As such, they are biased in favor of larger departments. Thus a ranking of research output at HBCUs adjusted for department size is presented in Table 2.

Additionally, the rankings in Tables 1 and 2 are not adjusted for quality—an adjustment that is typically done in studies that rank economics departments in terms of research productivity. In order to provide a quality ranking, we identify the thirteen HBCUs in the sample of forty with faculty that published an article in one of the 130 economics journals rated by Laband and Piette.[12] We utilize the Laband and Piette quality measure based on citations per article. This quality measure rates each of the 130 rated journals relative to the top-rated journal, the *Journal of Economic Literature*. For a given HBCU economics department, total

TABLE 1
Ranking of HBCUs by Research Output

	Ranking Source							
	Author Adjusted JEL		JEL		Author Adjusted CARL		CARL	
School:	Rank	Number	Rank	Number	Rank	Number	Rank	Number
Howard University	1	84	1	51.67	5	10	3	10.00
Alabama State University	2	27	2	19.00	2	22	2	15.50
North Carolina A&T State University	3	21	3	15.50	1	42	1	22.98
South Carolina State University	4	12	4	8.33	3	11	5	7.00
Tennessee State University	4	12	5	8.17	6	9	6	6.83
Cheyney University	6	11	9	6.33	13	2	18	.83
Southern University	6	11	8	6.83	3	11	7	5.50
Florida A&M University	8	8	7	7.00	11	3	11	2.50
University of the District of Columbia	8	8	6	7.50	13	2	12	2.00
Grambling State University	10	6	10	5.50	10	4	12	2.00
Alabama A&M University	11	4	11	3.33	8	8	10	2.66
Clark Atlanta University	12	3	14	1.67	17	1	18	.83
Fayetteville State University	12	3	12	2.33	6	9	4	7.83
Fort Valley State University	12	3	16	1.00	11	3	9	3.00
North Carolina Central University	12	3	13	2.00	9	5	8	4.50
Hampton University	16	2	23	.83	17	1	20	.33
Tuskegee University	16	2	15	1.33	13	2	20	.33
Benedict College	18	1	24	.50	22	0	22	0
Bethune Cookman College	18	1	16	1.00	22	0	22	0
Delaware State University	18	1	16	1.00	17	1	15	1.00
Jackson State University	18	1	16	1.00	22	0	22	0
Morehouse College	18	1	16	1.00	17	1	15	1.00
Prairie View A &M University	18	1	25	.33	22	0	22	0
Texas Southern University	18	1	16	1.00	22	0	22	0
Virginia State University	18	1	16	1.00	13	2	14	1.33

TABLE 1 (continued)

	Ranking Source							
	JEL		Author Adjusted JEL		CARL		Author Adjusted CARL	
School:	Rank	Number	Rank	Number	Rank	Number	Rank	Number
Albany State University	26	0	26	0	22	0	22	0
Alcorn State University	26	0	26	0	22	0	22	0
Central State University	26	0	26	0	22	0	22	0
Dillard University	26	0	26	0	22	0	22	0
Fisk University	26	0	26	0	22	0	22	0
Kentucky State University	26	0	26	0	22	0	22	0
Lincoln University (MO)	26	0	26	0	22	0	22	0
Lincoln University (PA)	26	0	26	0	22	0	22	0
Mississippi Valley State University	26	0	26	0	22	0	22	0
Morgan State University	26	0	26	0	17	1.00	15	1.00
Morris Brown College	26	0	26	0	22	0	22	0
Norfolk State University	26	0	26	0	22	0	22	0
University of Arkansas–Pine Bluff	26	0	26	0	22	0	22	0
West Virginia State University	26	0	26	0	22	0	22	0
Winston Salem State University	26	0	26	0	22	0	22	0

quality adjusted publications is defined as E $w_i^{1/2}$, where w_i is the weight assigned to a given journal according to citations per article relative to an article published in the *Journal of Economic Literature*.[13] Table 3 reports quality adjusted publication rankings for total and coauthored adjusted publications for the period 1987–1997.[14]

The Production of Black Doctorates and Research Output

McCaughey suggests that academic environments with good teaching and "mentoring" encourage students to aspire to professional study of a subject and eventually teach it.[15] Thus, given the intense academic rigor of graduate study in economics, it is conceivable that faculty who are engaged in scholarship are better suited to mentor students in preparation for this rigor. Indeed, recent studies provide compelling evidence of a

TABLE 2
Ranking of HBCUs Adjusted for Department Size

	Ranking Source							
	JEL		Author Adjusted JEL		CARL		Author Adjusted CARL	
School:	Rank	Number	Rank	Number	Rank	Number	Rank	Number
Howard University	1	3.818	2	2.349	12	.455	9	.455
Alabama State University	2	3.375	1	2.375	1	2.750	1	1.938
Cheyney University	3	2.750	3	1.583	10	.500	12	.208
South Carolina State University	4	1.500	5	1.041	4	1.375	5	.875
Florida A&M University	5	1.333	4	1.167	10	.500	10	.417
Tennessee State University	5	1.333	7	.908	6	1.000	6	.759
North Carolina A&T State University	7	1.235	6	.912	2	2.471	3	1.352
Southern University	8	1.222	8	.759	5	1.222	8	.611
University of the District of Columbia	9	.800	9	.750	17	.200	14	.200
Clark Atlanta University	10	.750	12	.418	15	.250	12	.208
Fort Valley State University	10	.750	16	.250	8	.750	7	.750
Fayetteville State University	12	.600	11	.466	3	1.800	2	1.566
Grambling State University	12	.600	10	.550	13	.400	14	.200
North Carolina Central University	12	.600	13	.400	6	1.000	4	.900
Alabama A&M State University	15	.364	15	.303	9	.727	11	.242
Benedict College	16	.333	17	.167	22	0	22	0
Bethune Cookman College	16	.333	14	.333	22	0	22	0
Hampton University	16	.333	21	.138	18	.167	20	.056
Prairie View A&M University	19	.250	25	.083	22	0	22	0
Tuskegee University	20	.222	19	.148	16	.222	21	.037
Texas Southern University	21	.167	17	.167	22	0	22	0
Virginia State University	22	.143	20	.143	14	.286	16	.190
Jackson State University	22	.125	22	.125	22	0	22	0
Morehouse College	22	.125	22	.125	19	.125	17	.125
Delaware State University	25	.091	24	.091	21	.091	19	.091
Albany State University	26	0	26	0	22	0	22	0

TABLE 2 (continued)

	Ranking Source							
	JEL		Author Adjusted JEL		CARL		Author Adjusted CARL	
School:	Rank	Number	Rank	Number	Rank	Number	Rank	Number
Alcorn State University	26	0	26	0	22	0	22	0
Central State University	26	0	26	0	22	0	22	0
Dillard University	26	0	26	0	22	0	22	0
Fisk University	26	0	26	0	22	0	22	0
Kentucky State University	26	0	26	0	22	0	22	0
Lincoln University (MO)	26	0	26	0	22	0	22	0
Lincoln University (PA)	26	0	26	0	22	0	22	0
Mississippi Valley State University	26	0	26	0	22	0	22	0
Morgan State University	26	0	26	0	19	.125	17	.125
Morris Brown College	26	0	26	0	22	0	22	0
Norfolk State University	26	0	26	0	22	0	22	0
University of Arkansas – Pine Bluff	26	0	26	0	22	0	22	0
Winston Salem State University	26	0	26	0	22	0	22	0
West Virginia State University	26	0	26	0	22	0	22	0

direct relationship between faculty research output and the achievements of their students in graduate school.[16] In this light, it is useful to rank HBCUs by the number of doctorates produced and to explore the relationship between research output and doctorates produced.

Table 4 presents a ranking of HBCUs by the number of black doctorates produced in economics from 1980 to 1995. Howard University clearly outperforms all other HBCUs in the production of black doctorates, producing 400 percent of the next HBCU. These findings are not surprising given that Howard University is the only school in the sample with a Ph.D. program in economics. Thus, Howard may be creating a pipeline from its undergraduate to its graduate program.[17]

The Pearson correlations between the various measures of research output and the production of black doctorates are presented in Table 5. The correlation between JEL output and the number of black doctorates produced is large and positive (.8292). The correlation between the coau-

TABLE 3
JEL Quality Adjusted Publications: 1987-1997

School:	Rank	Coauthored Total	Adjusted	Rank
Alabama State University	1	2.69	2.20	1
Howard University	2	2.08	1.82	2
North Carolina A&T State University	2	2.08	1.71	3
Florida A&M University	4	0.93	0.93	4
University of the District of Columbia	5	0.82	0.82	5
Cheyney University	6	0.68	0.38	6
Hampton University	7	0.40	0.13	9
Southern University	8	0.39	0.13	9
Fayetteville State University	9	0.38	0.38	6
South Carolina State University	10	0.22	0.07	12
North Carolina Central University	10	0.22	0.11	11
Tennessee State University	12	0.18	0.18	8
Morehouse College	13	0.17	0.08	13

thored JEL measure and black doctorates produced is almost equally as large (.8054). When the CARL index and author-adjusted CARL measures of research output are used, the correlations are .1926 and .2718, respectively. Although not reported in the table, the correlations remain positive when the quality-adjusted rankings are used.[18] These findings support the notion that scholarly research by economics faculty at HBCUs may cultivate an interest in students to pursue doctorates in economics. An extension of this argument would suggest that increasing research output at HBCUs may be a viable means to increase the number of black doctorates in economics.

CONCLUSION

To our knowledge, no previous research exists that examines the research productivity of economics departments at HBCUs.[19] The rankings provided here are therefore an initial look at the scholarly output of economics departments at HBCUs. As in the case of teaching-oriented liberal arts colleges, the rankings provided here show that economics faculty at HBCUs are also making contributions to the stock of knowl-

TABLE 4
Ranking of HBCUs by Black Doctorates Produced 1980–1995

School	Rank	Number	School	Rank	Number
Howard University	1	24	Kentucky State University	15	1
Alabama A&M University	2	6	Lincoln University (MO)	15	1
Tuskegee University	2	6	Tennessee State University	15	1
Morgan State University	4	5	University Arkansas – Pine Bluff	15	1
Jackson State University	5	3	Winston Salem State University	15	1
North Carolina A&T State University	5	3	Alabama State University	25	0
			Albany State University	25	0
Hampton University	7	2	Benedict College	25	0
Lincoln University (PA)	7	2	Bethune Cookman College	25	0
Morehouse College	7	2	Cheyney University	25	0
North Carolina Central University	7	2	Delaware State University	25	0
Norfolk State University	7	2	Dillard University	25	0
University of the District of Columbia	7	2	Fayetteville State University	25	0
			Fort Valley State University	25	0
Virginia State University	7	2	Grambling State University	25	0
Southern University	7	2	Mississippi Valley State University	25	0
Alcorn State University	15	1	Morris Brown College	25	0
Central State University	15	1	Prairie View A&M University	25	0
Clark Atlanta University	15	1	South Carolina State University	25	0
Fisk University	15	1	Texas Southern University	25	0
Florida A&M University	15	1	West Virginia State University	25	0

edge. Our measures of research productivity are also novel in the sense that we utilize a broader measure of scholarly activity which includes research outside the discipline of economics.

Our findings suggest that a substantial portion of the economics departments at HBCUs are not engaged in scholarly activity in terms of published research. Thirty-five percent have no research output based on our JEL measure, 47 percent using the CARL measure, and 70 percent using the quality-adjusted JEL measure. However, this should not be viewed as a pathological finding, or as a dysfunctional attribute unique to HBCUs. The research inactivity of the HBCUs in our sample is quite compatible with previous findings on faculty research. In a study of liberal arts colleges, McCaughey finds that 38 percent of the faculty never published in a professional journal, 69 percent of the faculty had never published a book, and 49 percent are not engaging in research that will lead to publication.[20]

We also report correlations between various research productivity measures and the number of HBCU graduates that earned doctorates in eco-

TABLE 5
Correlation Coefficients between Number of Black Doctorates Produced and Research Output

	Ranking Source			
	JEL	Author Adjusted JEL	CARL	Author Adjusted CARL
Number of Black Economics Doctorates Produced 1980–1995	.8292	.8054	.1926	.2718

nomics. The correlations are consistently positive, suggesting a link between the research productivity of economics faculty at HBCUs and a certain kind of teaching effectiveness—teaching that encourages black students to pursue graduate studies in economics and eventually become Ph.D. economists themselves.[21] In this context, HBCUs could be a valuable asset in enhancing the pipeline and supply of black economists. The positive correlations suggest that if HBCUs commit more resources to economics faculty research, a substantial pay-off in black Ph.D. economists would result. Of course correlations do not imply causality, and the positive correlations reported here could be spurious. However, to the extent that faculty research productivity and the doctoral achievements of students are causally related, a positive correlation between them is a reasonable expectation. An interesting extension of this research would be to explore in detail the possible causal mechanism between economics faculty research productivity at HBCUs, and the number of black students who earn doctorates in economics.

NOTES

1. See for example: Howard Bodenhorn, "Teachers and Scholars Too: Economic Research at Elite Liberal Arts Colleges," *Journal of Economic Education*, Fall 1997, pp. 323–336; James E. Hartley and Micheal D. Robinson, "Economic Research at National Liberal Arts Colleges: School Rankings," *Journal of Economic Education*, Fall 1997, pp. 337–449, Hirschel Kasper et al., "The Education of Economists: From Undergraduate to Graduate Study," *Journal of Economic Literature*, September 1991, pp. 1008–1109.
2. See Bodenhorn (1997) and Hartley and Robinson (1997).
3. James R. Hasselback, *The 1996 Prentice Hall Guide to Economics Faculty*, Englewood Cliffs, NJ: Prentice Hall, 1996

4. Howard Bodenhorn, "Teachers and Scholars Too: Economic Scholarship at Elite Liberal Arts Colleges."

5. James E. Hartley and Michael D. Robinson, "Economic Research at National Liberal Arts Colleges: School Rankings," *Journal of Economic Education*, Fall 1997, pp. 337–349.

6. The reported value for the number of HBCUs in the United States was obtained from The College Fund/UNCF (formerly the United Negro College Fund) Mission statement. It is available via the Internet at http://www.uncf.org/mission.htm.

7. Each measure of research output counts the published works of faculty members on the roster of these forty HBCUs in 1996. Because faculty members may have been employed at different institutions prior to and after 1996, these measures may capture research produced at other institutions. While this is a shortcoming, it is a standard way of measuring research productivity in the rankings literature. See Bodenhorn (1997).

8. The use of different time periods to gauge research output using the CARL and JEL measures are the consequence of using the largest time window available in each index (a fifteen-year window is available using JEL, and a ten-year window is available using CARL).

9. CARL Uncover is available via the Internet at http://uncweb.carl.org/.

10. This database, also called WEBCASPAR is available via the Internet at http://www.nsf.gov/srs/srsdata.htm. The doctorate records file allows one to identify the baccalaureate institution of those who earned a doctorate in economics in a given year. As in the case of our measures of research output, the temporal window is somewhat arbitrary. Nonetheless, to the extent that the decision of HBCU graduates to purse doctorates in economics is subject to short-run fluctuations, a fifteen-year window allows a more steady-state perspective.

11. Total JEL output for HBCUs over the period 1987–1997 is 183 journal articles, books, book reviews, and book chapters.

12. See David N. Laband and Michael J. Piette, "The Relative Impacts of Economics Journals: 1970–1990," *Journal of Economic Literature,* June 1994, pp. 640–658.

13. The square root of the weight is taken to reduce the wide discrepancies in cardinal rank that exist between the top-rate journal and all of the rest. See Bodenhorn (1997), p. 325. In this weighting scheme, an article published in the *Review of Black Political Economy*, for example, has a weight of .167. A faculty member with one published article in the *Review of Black Political Economy* therefore has published .167 *Journal of Economic Literature* equivalent articles.

14. Nineteen eighty-seven was the earliest year in which we observed a faculty member for the HBCUs in our sample publishing in one of the 130 journals ranked by Laband and Piette (1994).

15. See Hartley and Robinson (1997), p. 344.

16. See Hartley and Robinson (1997).

17. The doctorate records file in the WEBCASPAR database allows one to identify the baccalaureate institution in which a doctorate recipient earned their degree. However, it is not possible to discern the Ph.D. granting institution. Thus, we cannot substantiate this claim using this data source.

18. For the quality adjusted rankings the correlation coefficients are approximately .45 in both cases. Of course the sample size in both cases is much smaller than the initial sample.

19. There is, however, an interesting analysis of HBCU research productivity in sociology. See John L. Huggins, "The Segmentation of Southern Sociology? Social

Research at Historically Black Colleges and Universities," *Social Forces*, March 1994, pp. 885–893.

20. Robert McCaughey, "But Can They Teach? In Praise of College Professors Who Publish," *Teachers College Record*, Winter 1993, pp. 242–257.

21. Interestingly, McCaughey (1993) reports positive correlations between faculty research productivity and teaching evaluations. This suggests that faculty research productivity also enhances teaching quality as perceived and measured by students.

4

WORKER RE-TRAINING AND LABOR MARKET OUTCOMES: A NEW FOCUS FOR LABOR RESEARCH PUBLISHED IN *THE REVIEW OF BLACK POLITICAL ECONOMY**

James B. Stewart

INTRODUCTION

Intensive examination of factors affecting employment patterns and earnings profiles of black workers has been one of the hallmarks of *The Review of Black Political Economy.* This analysis extends the *Review*'s focus on labor market issues through the exploration of the impact of retraining on the earnings and employment of displaced workers. This topic, as well as the broader analysis of training outcomes, has received little attention in the pages of the *Review.*

Evidence is presented here about program participation and the earnings and employment outcomes for a sample of dislocated black, Hispanic, and white male and female workers who participated in training programs funded under Title III of the Job Training Partnership Act of 1982. This act was amended in 1989 by the Economic Dislocation and Worker Adjustment Act of 1988 (EDWAA), which is administered by the Employment and Training Administration of the U.S. Department of Labor.[1] Thus, the assessments are most directly relevant to the pre-EDWAA operation of Title III. The present study summarizes selected findings from a more in-depth investigation.[2]

The organization of the study is as follows. The treatment of vocational training issues in the *Review* and in other organs is discussed in the second section; the third section describes Title III in more detail; the fourth section describes the methodology and data; and the results are

* This paper is based on research conducted under Contract B9A42869 for the National Commission for Employment Policy. As with all such contracts there is no implied official responsibility for the findings or conclusions.

presented in the fifth section, followed by a summary of the findings and suggestions for future research.

STUDIES OF TRAINING AND LABOR MARKET OUTCOMES: AN OVERVIEW

During the early 1970s, structural barriers limiting equitable participation by blacks in U.S. economic institutions came under close scrutiny in the *Review.* At the most global level, these barriers were seen as endemic to the capitalist system, with particular manifestations at the local, national, and international levels. Articles in the inaugural issue by James Boggs, Robert Browne, and Daniel Fusfeld, in particular, focused exclusively on discussions of systemic barriers.[3]

These and other analyses provided an impetus for the use of macroeconomic and economic development models to examine the feasibility of quasi-autonomous economic development strategies.[4] Much of the literature exploring community economic development highlighted the importance of black-owned business enterprises. However, concern about persisting structural barriers limiting the opportunities of black workers was an implicit impetus for this line of research. As an illustration, Frank Davis's advocacy of quasi-separate inner-city economies was driven by the assessment that the interplay of technological displacement and the distribution of jobs relegated most black workers to unskilled occupations compensated at or near the minimum wage.[5] In discussing strategies to ameliorate this situation, however, Davis did not include provisions for training unskilled workers.

Given the early emphasis of the *Review,* it is not surprising that the foundations of a detailed focus on labor market issues, per se, did not begin to emerge until circa 1974. At that time, some researchers began to offer policy proposals to neutralize structural barriers and increase access of black workers to higher-paying jobs. Still, however, the analyses typically failed to consider vocational training issues specifically. As an example, Jack Nelson's examination of the changing position of black urban workers led to proposals for greater access to suburban jobs through affirmative action hiring policies and residential relocation. While taking note of improvements in the relative educational attainment of blacks, he made no mention of the need for expanded vocational training.[6] In a study of the occupational and industrial distribution of black workers, Lloyd Hogan and Harry Harris also recommended aggressive affirmative action enforcement policies along with lawsuits to end discrimination in schools and discriminatory hiring practices. Again, there was no discussion of vocational training.[7] Ranjit Singh and James Heffner's examination of discrimination in selected basic industries also failed to explore training issues even though the industries studied were highly unionized.[8]

Early attention to training issues in the *Review* was limited to three analyses. David Kaun approached this subject matter indirectly in an analysis of racial differences in "quality of work."[9] Kaun drew a careful distinction between formal occupational training and education; however, he relegated training to secondary status in the study by reporting empirical results only for education. Marshall Medoff examined factors contributing to the lack of black apprentices in trade unions.[10] Specifically, Medoff explored whether this pattern reflected personal decisions related to expected rate of return from apprenticeship training or the effect of monopoly power of trade unions. He concluded that the small number of black apprentices was due primarily to exclusionary practices of trade unions but offered no policy recommendations to address this problem. Finally, Bradley Schiller scrutinized the experience of blacks in the Work Incentive Program (WIN) from 1974–75.[11] Schiller reported that while many blacks did benefit from participation in WIN, the average gains were substantially less than for white participants. In fact, the relative status of blacks declined. Schiller did conclude that specific employment services, especially on-the-job training, can benefit participants.

As more focused and refined studies of labor market issues began to appear in the *Review,* the limited attention devoted to training issues persisted. Theoretical and empirical tendencies within labor economics contributed substantially to this pattern. For example, wage studies using human capital models rarely include any specific measure of training as a determinant of earnings. In fact, specific measures of training are generally unavailable. Substantive analysis of the relationship between job training and labor market outcomes has been absent from virtually all types of studies, including those examining labor market discrimination, returns to human capital, occupational crowding, inter-industry comparisons, inter-regional comparisons, worker displacement, and employment impacts of foreign trade.

The absence of systematic attention to training issues has limited the usefulness of many analyses examining labor market implications of major structural shifts in the U.S. economy. Although Barry Bluestone's analysis of deindustrialization in the early 1980s included a number of policy recommendations including plant closing legislation, worker buyouts, a full employment tax and expenditure budget, and a national planning mechanism, worker training and retraining programs were not discussed.[12] Thomas Hyclak and James Stewart documented the fact that black unemployment rates are significantly more responsive to changes in aggregate demand growth and wage flexibility than is the case for whites and Hispanics.[13] However, they provided no suggestions regarding the extent to which targeted training programs can reduce the differences in unemployment rate sensitivity. From the work of Bartholomew Armah we know that international trade has contributed to employment shifts and that new employment opportunities are created in some sectors simultaneously with the loss of jobs in others.[14] We do not know, however, whether retraining programs can assist displaced workers in taking better advantage of new employment opportunities.

There are two exceptions to the general pattern of limited attention to training issues in recent work published in the *Review*. Joan Fitzgerald and Wendy Patton undertook a case study of a job training program targeted at young blacks.[15] Studies that provided a point of departure for their investigation yielded three important conclusions: (a) the operation of the Jobs Training Partnership Act (JTPA) programs seems to perpetuate labor market discrimination; (b) black JTPA participants are less likely to find jobs following completion of training; and (c) race is a better predictor of re-employment success than training.[16] Emily Blank examined the rate of return of on-the-job training using data from the Panel Study of Income Dynamics.[17] Blank did not have explicit measures of on-the-job training; rather, she constructed estimates based on job tenure and information about the time required for a worker to be fully trained. Blank found that the rate of return to an additional month of training was higher for nonwhites than whites.

Given that this study is particularly concerned with displaced workers, it is necessary to identify relevant literature from other sources. Two concerns reflected in most studies of worker dislocation/displacement are (a) the likelihood of re-employment following displacement and (b) the relative magnitude of earnings prior to dislocation and earnings after re-employment and the factors affecting this relationship.

A variety of factors have been shown to influence the magnitude of the earnings losses experienced by re-employed workers (the difference between pre- and post-displacement earnings). Generally, researchers have not found large reductions in earnings following dislocation, although a significant proportion of workers do experience substantial earnings losses. As an example, Swaim and Podgursky found that about 30 percent of re-employed full-time blue collar workers and 25 percent of re-employed white collar and service workers received wages that were more than 25 percent below pre-dislocation levels.[18] One critical factor affecting earnings losses is a worker's pre-displacement industry. Generally workers formerly employed in durable goods manufacturing had higher losses than workers in other industries.[19] A number of studies have found that pre-dislocation tenure is an important determinant of post-displacement earnings, and specifically that longer pre-displacement tenure is associated with higher earnings losses.[20] Finally, there is some evidence that depressed local labor market conditions increase workers' losses and unemployment duration.[21]

The extent to which earnings losses and re-employment probabilities differ across socio-demographic groups is of special interest to this investigation. Jacobson, LaLonde, and Sullivan reported that most of the studies using DWS data find that gender is not a very important determinant of earnings losses.[22] There do appear, however, to be significant differences across racial groups. Kletzer found that both blue- and white-collar nonwhite men and women had lower probabilities of re-employment and lower post-displacement earnings than whites.[23] Swaim and Podgursky found longer unemployment durations for blacks than whites.[24]

Several studies indicate the potential for training programs to play a vital role in assisting the adjustment of dislocated/displaced workers. To illustrate, Seitchik and Zornitsky argue that for many groups, particularly those from the lower half of the wage-age salary distribution, relatively modest investments in remedial education, entry-level job training, and job search assistance can be potentially valuable.[25] Bloom's analysis of four demonstration projects in Texas led to the conclusion that a relatively inexpensive mix of job-search assistance and limited occupational skills training can be a cost-effective means of assisting *some* displaced workers.[26]

An extensive review of pre-EDWAA training programs by Leigh provided a set of particularly useful conclusions: (1) classroom training does not appear to generate additional benefits beyond job search assistance alone; (2) on-the-job training has a larger net impact than classroom training but does not yield consistently positive effects on earnings; (3) the net benefits from training appear to be larger for men than for women; (4) there is little difference in the benefits between blacks and whites; and (5) workers under forty-five years old benefit more from training than older workers.[27]

While the preceding information is of value to the present study, it must be recalled, as noted by the Congressional Budget Office, that in general there is limited information currently available about the effectiveness of JTPA Title III training programs.[28] Efforts to evaluate the effectiveness of training programs is complicated by continuing disagreement among researchers about the appropriate methodologies to be used in estimating training effects. There is a significant literature that debates the issue of the relative merits of experimental versus non-experimental approaches to program evaluation that has been effectively summarized by Bowman.[29]

The data available in the present study do not allow the use of the type of nonexperimental techniques advocated in the preceding studies. First, there is no control group of non-program participants available to allow comparisons with program participants. In addition, the data set does not contain a sufficient amount of pre-program enrollment information to allow the estimation of workers' earnings trajectory if no "shock" to earnings had occurred to precipitate a decision to enroll in a training program. Only four quarters of pre-program entry data are available, making it difficult to quantify accurately the size of the wage dip that occurs at the time of dislocation. An additional complication arises because many participants had long periods of tenure with former employers and were eligible for significant severance payments. These payments are generally spread out over an extended period of time and are reported as earnings. As a consequence, the observed earnings pattern diverges from the traditional image of a dislocated worker as having no income other than possibly unemployment compensation. This phenomenon also has the potential to introduce additional biases if the decision to complete or not complete a training program is highly correlated with the level of pre-program participation earnings.

Given the absence of a control group of non-program participants, an alternative strategy used by Romero involved comparing outcomes for completers and non-completers of a given program.[30] Assuming that the background characteristics of these two subpopulations are comparable, inferences regarding the relative effects of specific training activities can be generated. This is the approach taken in this study.

TITLE III—AN OVERVIEW

The original Title III legislation designated three groups of workers as eligible for assistance: (1) workers who have been terminated or laid off or received notice of impending termination/layoff, with eligibility for unemployment insurance benefits and with little likelihood of returning to their previous industry or occupation; (2) workers who have been terminated or received notice of impending termination due to permanent closure of a plant or facility; or (3) the long-term unemployed with little chance of re-employment in a similar occupation in their current geographical area, including older workers facing employment barriers associated with age.[31]

Most existing studies of the national cohort of dislocated workers are based on analyses of data collected by the Bureau of Labor Statistics in the Displaced Worker Survey (DWS) conducted in January 1984, 1986, 1988, 1990, and 1992 as a supplement to the CPS. In this survey, any civilian twenty years of age or older who loses or leaves a job because of a "plant closing, an employer going out of business, a layoff without recall, or some similar reason" is defined as a dislocated or displaced worker.[32]

The Congressional Budget Office (CBO) raised several questions regarding the measurement conventions associated with this definition.[33] The CBO revised the measurement convention to include only full-time workers who lost jobs and generated a set of annual estimates of job losses. Specifically, the CBO estimated that the number of dislocated/displaced workers fell from 2.7 million in 1982 to 1.5 million in 1988.[34]

The CBO report noted that the characteristics of displaced workers were remarkably stable during the 1980s. This stability occurred despite a wide swing in the business cycle, changes in industrial composition, and changes in a broad array of government policies.[35] Selected trends during the 1980s highlighted in the CBO report included: (1) 20 percent of dislocated/displaced workers were forty-five years old or more; (2) 60 percent were males; and (3) those with schooling beyond high school grew from about 30 percent to 40 percent.[36]

Under the auspices of Title III, dislocated workers were offered a specific but flexible training program designed to help participants find new jobs. The basic categories of training activities available to participants are (1) occupational classroom training, (2) remedial/basic education, (3) on-the-job training, (4) work experience, (5) employment and training services, (6) job search assistance/direct placement, and (7) other. The category of job search assistance/direct placement is sometimes used as a control category for the purpose of assessing the relative effectiveness of various training activities, which are presumably more intense. Most previous investigations have focused only on the first training activity recorded in a participant's record. In this investigation a more detailed examination of the sequence of training activities is undertaken.

One thrust of the present study is the examination of the relationship between program completion/non-completion and subsequent earnings and employment outcomes. EDWAA places greater emphasis on training services for dislocated workers than was previously the case by eliminating basic readjustment services such as job search assistance from allowable training activities.[37] Consistent with the practice found in other investigations, job search assistance is used as a control for the examination of the incremental benefits associated with participation in other training activities in this study.

EDWAA required that states distribute 60 percent of program funds to sub-state areas using a formula that takes into account a variety of factors reflecting the presence or potential presence of a large group of dislocated workers, i.e., insured unemployment, unemployment concentrations, plant closings and mass layoffs, declining industries, farmer-rancher hardship, and long-term unemployment.[38] In the present study an effort is made to examine whether variations in local economic conditions affect post-program earnings and employment outcomes.

In summary, the objective of this study is to examine factors affecting variations in post-program earnings and employment outcomes of JTPA participants, with particular attention to the following issues:

- variation across demographic characteristics,
- the effect of program completion status,
- variation across training activities, and
- effects of local economic conditions.

DATA AND METHODOLOGY

A. Data

The data used in this study were generated as a result of a project undertaken by the National Commission for Employment Policy, begun in 1988, to determine if states' Unemployment Insurance (UI) records could be used in place of telephone surveys to ascertain JTPA program participants' post-program earnings. These data are available for eleven states.[39] This data source provides more complete information about earnings, including severance payments, that may affect participants' job search and program completion decisions than other data sources.

The original sample used in this investigation consisted of 5,436 observations. Incomplete data for some variables reduced the usable num-

TABLE 1
Comparisons of Original and Restricted Sample Sizes

JTPA Title III Sample Whites, Blacks, and Hispanics
by Race and Sex—Ages 25–64

Category	Original Sample Size	Restricted Sample Size	Pct. of Original Sample
White Men	2018	1090	54.0
White Women	1425	674	47.3
Black Men	516	215	41.7
Black Women	594	198	33.3
Hispanic Men	595	451	75.8
Hispanic Women	288	201	69.8
Total—Men	3129	1756	56.1
Total—Women	2307	1073	46.5
Total	5436	2829	52.0

ber of observations to 2,829 (Table 1). A description of ail variables is provided in the Appendix. For whites and blacks, one principal effect of the sample restrictions is to reduce the prevalence of high school drop-outs and increase the likelihood that participants will have undertaken some post-secondary education. The reverse is true for Hispanics. In the case of employment status, there is a substantial increase in the proportions of the sub-samples of blacks that are unemployed. Interestingly, there is an increase in the proportion of whites and blacks not claiming unemployment compensation with little effect on the other indicators of engagement with the unemployment compensation system. For all sub-samples except Hispanic males there is a slight decrease in the relative frequency of individuals unemployed for fifteen of the last twenty-six weeks. The sample restrictions increase the likelihood that whites and Hispanics were employed at the time of termination from the training program. Finally, there is little impact on the proportion completing the training program for any of the sub-samples.

Turning to the issue of the distribution of pre- and post-program par-

TABLE 2
JTPA Title 3 Sample
Relationship Between PREWAG4* and PREWAG1**

Whites, Blacks, and Hispanics
Men and Women—Ages 25–64

Wages 4 Quarters Pre-Enrollment	Wages 1 Quarter Pre-Enrollment	Pattern	N of Cases	Pct. of Cases
PREWAG4 = 0	PREWAG1 = 0	No Change	355	12.55
PREWAG4 > 0	PREWAG1 = 0	Wage Decline	558	19.72
PREWAG4 > 0	PREWAG1 > 0; PREWAG4 > PREWAG1	Wage Decline	742	26.23
PREWAG4 > 0	PREWAG1 > 0; PREWAG4 < PREWAG1	Wage Increase (Reverse Dip)	924	32.66
PREWAG4 = 0	PREWAG1 > 0	Wage Increase (Reverse Dip)	250	8.84
Total			2829	100.00

* PREWAG4 = Wages 4 full quarters prior to enrollment; ** PREWAG1 = Wages 1 quarter prior to enrollment; Includes only cases with Complete Training Activity Information and UI Wage Information for at Least One Quarter.

ticipation earnings, as noted previously a variety of patterns can be observed. Summary data, not disaggregated by race and gender, are provided in Table 2.

The most significant conclusion to be derived from Table 2 is that less than half of the cases exhibit a decline in earnings during the quarters preceding program entry. If data for eight quarters prior to program entry were available, presumably a higher proportion of cases of declining earnings should be observed. The cases exhibiting a "reverse wage dip" reflect the distorting effects of severance payments discussed previously. The wide variation in earnings profiles suggests that the most useful way of analyzing the relationship between pre- and post-program participation earnings is to treat each pattern separately. When the data are disaggregated by race and gender, mean earnings differences are uniformly greater for men within a given race and the general ranking of inter-racial differences is whites>blacks>Hispanics. The only exceptions to this pattern occur in two cases where the earnings change for black women is greater than for white women. There is also substantial variation in the relative representation of racial groups across earnings patterns.[40]

With respect to the types of training received by participants, space does not permit a complete discussion of the descriptive data. To summarize, job search assistance/direct placement is by far the most likely first training activity (42.6%). However, in 15.6 percent of the cases, job search assistance/direct placement was followed by another training activity. As a consequence, if job search assistance/direct placement is used as a control category, then only those cases where there has been no participation in any other training activity should be used for this purpose.

Women were more likely to be assigned initially to occupational classroom training and less likely to be assigned to on-the-job training and work experience. There were also differences in the initial assignment to training activity across racial groups. These patterns may reflect group differences in educational attainment and work experience and must be taken into account in assessing training outcomes. For men, the most significant difference was the extremely high proportion of Hispanics assigned initially to work experience. Black men were more likely than their white and Hispanic counterparts to be assigned to occupational classroom training and less likely to be assigned to on-the-job training. Hispanic women were also disproportionately assigned initially to work experience, producing the same pattern of under-representation in other activities found for Hispanic men. However, Hispanic women were also over-represented in on-the-job training. Black women were the most likely to be assigned to job search assistance/direct placement.

The methods used to model the determinants of workers' training decisions and post-training earnings and employment outcomes are described below.

B. Methodology

Given the pattern of pre-enrollment earnings instability described previously, a preliminary analysis was conducted to identify any factors systematically associated with the reporting of non-zero earnings during specific quarters prior to program enrollment. The model used to make this assessment took the following form:

(1) $$\text{EARN4B}_i = b_0 + b_1\,\text{AGE} + b_2\,\text{HIGHSCHL} + b_3\,\text{POSTHIGH} + b_4\,\text{BLACK} + b_5\,\text{HISP} + b_6\,\text{BLK*HS} + b_7\,\text{BLK*PHS} + b_8\,\text{HISP*HS} + b_9\,\text{HISP*PHS} + b_{10}\,\text{EMPGTH} + b_{11}\,\text{PCINGTH} + b_{12}\,\text{PCTTRGTH} + b_{13}\,\text{WGSALJB} + u$$

In equation 1, $EARN4B_i$ is a dichotomous variable assigned the value 1 if a participant reported positive earnings during the fourth quarter prior to program entry and 0 otherwise. EARN1B is defined analogously for the last quarter prior to entry. The results obtained from estimating the model failed to identify a fixed set of factors that allow prediction of whether participants had earnings during specific quarters prior to program enrollment.

The second step in the preliminary investigation involved regressing the same set of independent variables on each of a set of dichotomous indicators describing the relationship between earnings four quarters prior to program entry and one quarter prior to entry. Few strong associations were found between pre-enrollment earnings receipt patterns and the demographic indicators. There was some evidence that earnings recipiency patterns for Hispanics were more closely associated with demographic characteristics than for whites and blacks. Earnings recipiency patterns exhibited a small degree of responsiveness to changes in local economic aggregates, but the patterns were not consistent.

The findings from the preliminary analyses suggested that few biases would be introduced by regressing the set of independent variables directly on a dichotomous indicator of program completion. The basic model was augmented to allow a determination of the extent to which program completion probabilities vary systematically across different types of training activities, as shown below in equation 2.

$$(2)\quad COMPL_i = b_0 + b_1 AGE + b_2 HIGHSCHL + b_3 POSTHIGH + b_4 BLACK + b_5\, HISP + b_6\, BLK{*}HS + b_7\, BLK{*}PHS + b_8\, HISP{*}HS + b_9\, HISP{*}PHS + b_{10}\, EMPGTH + b_{11}\, PCINGTH + b_{12}\, PCTTRGTH + b_{13}\, WGSALJB + b_{14}\, JBSRCH{*} + b_{15}\, OCCUP + b_{16}\, BASIC + b_{17}\, OJT + b_{18}\, WK\ EXP + b_{19}\, EMP\ SRV + b_{20}\, OTHER + u$$

In equation 2, COMPL is a binary variable assigned the value 1 if participant i completed a training program and 0 otherwise. The variables OCCUP, BASIC, OJT, WK EXP, EMP SRV, and OTHER are dummy variables indicating the first training activity in which a participant was enrolled, and are assigned the value 1 if a participant was enrolled in a given training activity and 0 otherwise. JBSRCH* is defined in a slightly different manner; this variable is assigned the value 1 if the first training activity that a participant was enrolled in was job search assistance/direct placement, and the participant was subsequently enrolled in another training activity. This construction is designed to allow participation in job search assistance/direct placement with no subsequent enrollment in any other training activity to serve as the control. Thus, the coefficients of each of the indicators of first training activity and, in the case of JBSRCH* (job search assistance/direct placement augmented by additional training), capture the incremental effect of more intense training interventions relative to job search assistance alone. As was the case in the preceding analyses, equation 2 was estimated separately for men and women. The samples were again restricted to participants between the ages of 25 and 64 for whom complete information was available.

The next phase of the investigation involved modeling earnings outcomes. A set of independent variables was regressed on two measures of earnings outcomes. One of these measures is highlighted below in equation 3.

(3) $EARN1Y_i = b_0 + b_1\ AGE + b_2\ HIGHSCHL + b_3\ POSTHIGH + b_4\ BLACK + b_5\ HISP + b_6\ BLK{*}HS + b_7\ BLK{*}PHS + b_8\ HISP{*}HS + b_9\ HISP{*}PHS + b_{10}\ EMPGTH + b_{11}\ PCINGTH + b_{12}\ PCTTRGTH + b_{13}\ WGSALJB + b_{14}\ NCOMP + b_{15}\ OCCUP + b_{16}\ BASIC + b_{17}\ OJT + b_{18}\ WK\ EXP + b_{19}\ EMP\ SRV + b_{20}\ OTHER + b_{21}\ DIFF2 + b_{22}\ DIFF3 + b_{23}\ DIFF4 + b_{24}\ DIFF5 + b_{25}\ PREWAG1 + u$

In equation 3, $EARN1Y_i$ is a dichotomous variable assigned the value 1 if a trainee has four consecutive quarters of positive earnings during the first year following termination from the training program and 0 otherwise. A parallel specification, $EARN2Y_i$, is defined for the earnings history of trainees during the second year.

The final phase of the investigation involved modeling of employment outcomes using equation 4 below. The usefulness of this exercise was limited because of the large amount of missing information related to post-training employment outcomes. Only 1285 of 1756 observations for men and 866 of 1073 for women had complete information. In addition, it was not possible to include the program completion status indicator in the model due to multi-collinearity problems.

(4) $EMPL_{13} = b_0 + b_1\ AGE + b_2\ HIGHSCHL + b_3\ POSTHIGH + b_4\ BLACK + b_5\ HISP + b_6\ BLK{*}HS + b_7\ BLK{*}PHS + b_8\ HISP{*}HS + b_9\ HISP{*}PHS + b_{10}\ EMPGTH + b_{11}\ PCINGTH + b_{12}\ PCTTRGTH + b_{13}\ WGSALJB + b_{14}\ JBSRCH{*} + b_{15}\ OCCUP + b_{16}\ BASIC + b_{17}\ OJT + b_{18}\ WK\ EXP + b_{19}\ EMP\ SRV + b_{20}\ OTHER + u$

In equation 4, $EMPL_{13}$ is assigned the value 1 if a participant was employed during the thirteenth week following termination from the program and 0 otherwise. A variant of equation 4 was used to examine factors associated with the number of weeks worked during the last twenty-six weeks prior to the survey. In this case the dependent variable was the actual number of weeks worked, and standard OLS regression techniques were used to estimate the model.

The results obtained from estimating the models are summarized below.

RESULTS

Space does not permit the presentation of the detailed results obtained from the estimations of equations 2–4. The detailed results are available from the author upon request. Brief summaries of the principal results from each estimation are presented below.

A. Program Completion

The likelihood of program completion was largely unrelated to demographic and human capital characteristics of program participants. The only exception occurred for race/ethnicity, where blacks were found to be the most likely race/ethnic group to complete training. Higher rates of economic growth had a small positive effect on the likelihood of program completion. Finally, program completion probabilities varied across first training activities. Men and women for whom work experience was the first training activity were the most likely to have completed the training process. Gender-specific patterns were found for basic/remedial education (men) and on-the-job training (women).

B. Earnings Outcomes

(1) Former trainees not completing a program were more likely than completers to have four consecutive quarters of positive earnings during the first post-program year, but not during the second post-program year.

(2) Initial enrollment in the occupational classroom or work experience training activities was generally associated with a greater likelihood of four consecutive quarters of positive earnings during either the first or second post-program year; initial enrollment in on-the-job training was associated with a reduced likelihood of four consecutive quarters of positive earnings during the first post-program year.

(3) Older, less educated trainees were more likely to have positive earnings during all four quarters of the first post-program year.

(4) Virtually no differences were found among racial/ethnic groups in the likelihood of having positive earnings during all four quarters of either post-program year.

(5) Former trainees with zero earnings during both the fourth and last quarter prior to program enrollment were more likely than those with other pre-enrollment earnings profiles to have four consecutive quarters of positive earnings during either post-program year.

(6) Earnings during the quarter immediately preceding enrollment had no indicated effect on the likelihood of four consecutive quarters of positive earnings during either the first or second post-program year.

(7) Variations in local economic growth rate aggregates had no observable effects on the likelihood of four consecutive quarters of positive earnings during either post-program year.

C. Employment Outcomes

Results obtained from the two variants of equation 4 exhibited a number of discrepancies relative to the findings from the analysis of earnings outcomes. However, as noted previously, these results are suspect due to the large quantity of missing information.

CONCLUSION

The results of this study suggest the need for additional research on a number of topics. Studies that rely exclusively on workers' self-reported earnings to assess program impacts are subject to substantial bias associated with under-reporting of earnings. This is a particularly significant problem in the case of older workers who were eligible for sizable severance payments at the time of dislocation. Workers' decisions regarding length and intensity of participation in training programs can be influenced by the magnitude of assets that can be devoted to job search and consumption.

In contrast to previous studies of other populations, post-program outcomes for workers not completing training programs were superior to those who completed programs. The mechanisms producing this outcome are unclear but appear to be associated, in part, with the phenomenon of severance and/or other lump sum payments discussed above. In addition, however, the sequencing of training activities may affect both completion decisions and post-participation outcomes. Most previous studies have limited the consideration of training activities to the first activity in which a participant is enrolled. The results presented here strongly indicate a need for a more in-depth examination of training activity sequencing. Although basic information about the actual training sequences was available, information about the amount of time spent in each activity was not reliable.

The availability of accurate information about the length of training sequences could enable much more effective training programs to be designed. As an example, an analysis could be undertaken to determine the inflection point, say t*, where the amount of time in a training activity begins to have a statistically significant impact on post-program participation employment and earnings. This inflection point could be used to segment the sample of trainees into three sub-samples: (a) individuals whose time in a particular activity is less than t*; (b) individuals participating in the training activity for a period of time greater than t* but who did not complete the training program; and (c) individuals participating in a particular activity longer than t* and who completed the program. In combination with activity-sequencing information, it would be possible to determine the optimal timing and sequencing combinations to optimize post-program outcomes for participants with various mixes of background characteristics. Such an approach bears similarity to the analysis presented in Blank's study of returns to on-the-job training discussed previously.[41]

The present study was constrained by the limited information about the background characteristics of trainees. Unlike many previous studies, the available information was limited largely to age, education, race/ethnicity, and gender. Previous studies have indicated that the earnings losses experienced by dislocated workers vary by industry of previous employment and job tenure. The absence of this information hampered efforts to develop models to examine several critical relationships including determinants of particular patterns of quarter-to-quarter pre-program enrollment earnings and program completion. The absence of reliable post-program employment information also limited the extent to which consistent implications could be drawn from the results. Better information would allow the incorporation of the focus on the supply side of the market, as reflected in the studies by Armah and Hyclak and Stewart, discussed previously.[42]

The measures of local economic conditions used in this investigation are crude and require refinement. Development of refined indicators could help identify areas where training programs are most likely to lead to improved earnings and employment outcomes.

In summary, the results of this study suggest that a large amount of additional research is needed before definitive conclusions can be reached regarding the effectiveness of Title II-A and EDWAA training programs. Efforts to develop and assessment effective training and retraining programs will, in all likelihood, intensify in the future, particularly if rapid economic transformation continues. Given the distribution of benefits associated with past and present training efforts, without a greater understanding of the factors contributing to positive outcomes, blacks and other similarly situated population groups will continue to be disproportionately ill-served by existing training programs. Such a situation is suggested by the fact that blacks were found to have the greatest likelihood of completing a training program, with no apparent returns resulting from this decision. Evidence of racial "crowding" into specific types of training was also found.

The *Review* clearly has an important stake in becoming a major outlet for the publication of future research in this area. Taking on such a role would surely honor and continue the twenty-five year tradition of scrutinizing those issues most critical to improving the economic status of blacks and similarly-situated groups.

NOTES

1. See National Commission for Employment Policy, *Assisting Dislocated Workers: Alternatives to Layoffs, and the Role of the Employment Service under the Economic Dislocation and Worker Adjustment Assistance Act*, Special Report Number 30, Washington, D.C.: National Commission for Employment Policy (October 1991), p. 44.

2. The current research is extracted from J. Stewart, "An Analysis of Earnings and Employment Outcomes of JTPA Title III Program Participants," Final Report Submitted to the National Commission for Employment Policy, Contract #B9A42869, (November 1995).

3. J. Boggs, "The Myth and Irrationality of Black Capitalism," *The Review of Black Political Economy* 1:1 (1970), pp. 27–35; R. Browne, "Toward an Overall Assessment of Our Alternatives," *The Review of Black Political Economy* 1:1 (1970), pp. 18–26; D. Fusfeld, "The Basic Economics of the Urban and Racial Crisis," *The Review of Black Political Economy* 1:1 (1970), pp. 58–83.

4. W. David, "Black America in Developmental Perspective, Part I," *The Review of Black Political Economy* 3:2 (1973), pp. 89–104; F. Davis, "Problems of Economic Growth in the Black Community—Some Alternative Hypotheses," *The Review of Black Political Economy* 1:4 (1971), pp. 75–107; T. Spratlen, "Ghetto Economics Development—Content and Character of the Literature," *The Review of Black Political Economy* 1:4 (1971), pp. 43–71.

5. F. Davis, op. cit.
6. J. Nelson, "The Changing Economic Position of Black Urban Workers," *The Review of Black Political Economy* 4:2 (1974), pp. 35–48.
7. L. Hogan and H. Harris, "The Occupational-Industrial Structure of Black Employment in the United States," *The Review of Black Political Economy* 6:1 (1975), pp. 8–28.
8. R. Singh and J. Hefner, "Relative Job Discrimination in Basic Industries," *The Review of Black Political Economy* 6:1 (1975), pp. 29–40.
9. D. Kaun, "Black-White Differentials in the Quality of Work," *The Review of Black Political Economy* 6:1 (1975), pp. 41–58.
10. M. Medoff, "Investing in Human Capital: The Lack of Black Apprentices," *The Review of Black Political Economy* 7:2 (1977), pp. 176–182.
11. B. Shiller, "The Pay-Off to Training for Blacks: The WIN Experience," *The Review of Black Political Economy* 8:2 (1978), pp. 211–217.
12. B. Bluestone, "Deindustrialization and Unemployment in America," *The Review of Black Political Economy* 12:3 (1983), pp. 27–42.
13. T. Hyclak and J. Stewart, "Racial Differences in the Unemployment Response to Structural Changes in Local Labor Markets," *The Review of Black Political Economy* 23:4 (1995), pp. 29–42.
14. B. Armah, "The Demographics of Trade-Affected Services and Manufacturing Workers (1987–1990): A Comparative Analysis," *The Review of Black Political Economy* 23:4 (1995), pp. 43–268.
15. J. Fitzgerald and W. Patton, "Race, Job Training, and Economic Development: Barriers to Racial Equity in Program Planning," *The Review of Black Political Economy* 23:2 (1994), pp. 93–112.
16. L. Kletzer, "Job Displacement, 1979–1986: How Blacks Fared Relative to Whites," *Monthly Labor Review* 114 (1991), pp. 7–25; J. Fitzgerald, "The Effect of Education and Training on the Reemployment Success of Displaced Workers in Ohio." Report submitted to the Ohio Bureau of Employment Services and the Ohio Job Training Partnership (1991).
17. E. Blank, "Changes in the Stock of On-the-Job Training, Race, and Wage Growth," *The Review of Black Political Economy* 17:4 (1989), pp. 45–57.
18. P. Swaim and M. Podgursky, "The Distribution of Economic Losses Among Displaced Workers: A Replication," *Journal of Human Resources* 26:4, pp. 742–755.
19. See, for example, L. Jacobson, "Earnings Losses of Workers Displaced from Manufacturing Industries," in W. Dewald, ed., *The Impact of International Trade and Investment on Employment,* Washington, D.C.: U.S. Department of Labor (1978), pp. 87–98; P. Flaim and E. Seghal, "Displaced Workers of 1979–83: How Well Have They Fared?" Bulletin 2240, Washington, D.C.: U.S. Department of Labor, Bureau of Labor Statistics (1985).
20. See, for example, J. Portugal and P. Portugal, "Job Displacement, Relative Wage Changes, and Duration of Unemployment," *Journal of Labor Economics* 7 (1989), pp. 281–302; L. Kletzer, "Earnings after Job Displacement: Job Tenure, Industry, and Occupation," in J. Addison, (ed.), *Job Displacement, Consequences and Implications for Policy,* Detroit: Wayne State University Press (1991), pp. 107–135.
21. See, for example, L. Jacobson, R. LaLonde, and D. Sullivan, *The Costs of Worker Dislocation,* Kalamazoo, MI: W.E. Upjohn Institute for Employment Research (1993); L. Jacobson, "A Tale of Employment Decline in Two Cities: How Bad Was the Worst of Times?" *Industrial and Labor Relations Review* 37 (1984), pp. 557–569, and P. Swaim and M. Podgursky, "Displacement and Unemployment," in J. Addison, op. cit. (1991), pp. 136–161.
22. Jacobson, LaLonde, and Sullivan, op. cit., p. 33.

23. Kletzer, "Earnings After Job Displacement: Job Tenure, Industry, and Occupation," op. cit.
24. Swaim and Podgursky (1991), op. cit.
25. A. Seitchik and J. Zornitsky, *From One Job to the Next: Worker Adjustment in a Changing Labor Market,* Kalamazoo, MI: W.E. Upjohn Institute for Employment Research, (1989), p. 115.
26. Howard S. Bloom, *Back to Work: Testing Reemployment Services for Displaced Workers,* Kalamazoo, MI: W.E. Upjohn Institute for Employment Research, (1990), p. vii.
27. Duane E. Leigh, *Does Training Work for Displaced Workers? A Survey of Existing Evidence,* Kalamazoo, MI: W.E. Upjohn Institute for Employment Research (1990).
28. Congressional Budget Office, *Displaced Workers: Trends in the 1980s and Implications for the Future,* Washington, D.C.: Congressional Budget Office (February 1993), p. 39.
29. William R. Bowman, *Evaluating JTPA Programs for Economically Disadvantaged Adults: A Case Study of Utah and General Findings.* Research Report No. 92–02. Washington, National Commission for Employment Policy (1993).
30. Carol Romero, *JTPA Programs and Adult Women on Welfare: Using Training to Raise AFDC Recipients Above Poverty.* Research Report No. 93–01. Washington, National Commission for Employment Policy (1994).
31. National Commission on Employment Policy, op. cit.
32. Congressional Budget Office, *Displaced Workers: Trends in the 1980s and Implications for the Future,* Washington, D.C.: Congressional Budget Office (February, 1993), p. 5.
33. *Ibid.*
34. *Ibid.*
35. *Ibid.*, p. 9.
36. *Ibid.*, pp. 9–10.
37. National Commission on Employment Policy, op. cit., p. 52.
38. National Commission on Employment Policy, op. cit., p. 52.
39. National Commission on Employment Policy, op. cit., p. 51.
40. When the data are disaggregated by race it appears that, in general, nonwhites have a greater likelihood than whites of having zero earnings during the fourth quarter prior to entry and positive earnings one quarter prior to entry. This pattern is particularly true for Hispanics. Among males, whites are relatively over-represented in the population of participants with zero earnings during both quarters. Blacks are over-represented in cases where earnings decline and are non-zero during both quarters. Hispanics are over-represented in situations where earnings decline and earnings are zero in the quarter immediately preceding program enrollment. Among women, Hispanics are over-represented within the sub-population with zero earnings during both quarters, in addition to those cases where there are zero earnings four quarters prior to enrollment and positive earnings during the period immediately preceding entry into the program. Whites are over-represented among participants whose earnings profiles exhibit a traditional wage dip with non-zero earnings in both quarters, while Hispanics are under-represented in this category. Blacks are slightly over-represented within the categories where earnings are non-zero four quarters prior to enrollment and zero immediately prior to enrollment, and where earnings are non-zero during both quarters and higher during the quarter immediately preceding program entry.
41. Blank, op. cit.
42. Armah, op. cit.; Hyclak and Stewart, op. cit.

APPENDIX
VARIABLE DEFINITIONS

Variable	Definition
EARN4B	Dichotomous variable = 1 if participant had positive earnings 4th quarter prior to entry; else 0
EARN1B	Same as EARN4B measured during last quarter prior to program entry
COMPL	Dichotomous variable = 1 if participant completed training program; else 0
EARN1Y	Dichotomous variable = 1 if participant reported 4 consecutive quarters of positive earnings during first year following termination from program; else 0
EARN2Y	Same as EARN1Y, measured for second year following termination
EMPL13	Dichotomous variable = 1 if participant was employed during 13th week following termination from program;
AGE	Continuous variable indicating the age of the participant
HIGHSCHL	Dichotomous variable = 1 if participant completed high school; else 0
POSTHIGH	Dichotomous variable = 1 if participant had some post-high school education; else 0
DROPOUT	Dichotomous variable = 1 if participant did not complete high school; else 0
BLACK	Dichotomous variable = 1 if participant is black; else 0
HISP	Dichotomous variable = 1 if participant is Hispanic; else 0
BLK*HS	Dichotomous variable = 1 if participant is black and completed high school; else 0
BLK*PHS	Dichotomous variable = 1 if participant is black and has some post high school education; else 0
HISP*HS	Dichotomous variable = 1 if participant is Hispanic and completed high school; else 0
HISP*PHS	Dichotomous variable = 1 if participant is Hispanic and has some post-high school education; else 0
JBSRCHA	Dichotomous variable = 1 if participant's only training was job search assistance; else 0
JBSRCH*	Dichotomous variable = 1 if participant's first training was job search assistance and enrolled in another training activity; else 0
OCCUP	Dichotomous variable = 1 if participant's first training type was occupational training; else 0

Variable	Definition
BASIC	Dichotomous variable = 1 if participant's first training type was basic training; else 0
OJT	Dichotomous variable = 1 if participant's first training type was on-the-job training; else 0
WK EXP	Dichotomous variable = 1 if participant's first training type was work experience; else 0
EMP SRV	Dichotomous variable = 1 if participant's first training type was employment services; else 0
OTHER	Dichotomous variable = 1 if participant's first training type was other; else 0
NCOMP	Dichotomous variable = 1 if participant did not complete a first training program; else 0
DIFF2	Dichotomous variable = 1 if participant's earnings 4 quarters prior to entry were positive and earnings 1 quarter prior to entry were 0; else 0
DIFF3	Dichotomous variable = 1 if participant's earnings 4 quarters prior to entry were positive and earnings 1 quarter prior to entry were 0; else 0
DIFF4	Dichotomous variable = 1 if participant's earnings 4 quarters prior to entry were positive and earnings 1 quarter prior to entry were 0; else 0
DIFF5	Dichotomous variable = 1 if participant's earnings 4 quarters prior to entry were positive and earnings 1 quarter prior to entry were 0; else 0
PREWAG1	Earnings one quarter prior to program enrollment
PREWAG 4	Earnings four quarters prior to program enrollment
EMPGTH	Growth rate in participant's metropolitan area employment between 1986 and 1988
PCINGTH	Growth rate in participant's metropolitan area total income between 1986 and 1988
PCTRGTH	Growth rate in participant's metropolitan area total transfer payments between 1986 and 1988
WAGSALJB	Growth rate in participant's metropolitan area total wage and salary jobs between 1986 and 1988

5

EMPLOYMENT AND TRAINING SOLUTIONS FOR THE ECONOMICALLY DISADVANTAGED: AN ESSAY

Bernard E. Anderson

In the midst of the best economic performance in a generation, it is most appropriate to review what can and should be done to improve the economic status of the urban poor. For more than thirty years, national policy makers have grappled with the problem of urban poverty, but thus, far have not found a fully satisfactory solution. The quest for ways to improve the income of the least fortunate among urban dwellers is a vexing task that will continue to challenge the capacity of social and behavioral scientists as we move toward the millennium.

In searching for remedies to improve the economic status of the urban poor, it is necessary to begin with a clear understanding of the root cause of barriers to their participation in the economy. That search is not made easier by use of the term "urban underclass," and I refuse to use that term. Underclass implies that the reason some people are poor is their attitudes, values, and behavior. Underclass further implies that poverty is imbedded in the folkways and mores of a cultural lifestyle.

Rather than accept that view of the problem, it is important to recognize that urban poverty is grounded in the limited economic opportunities available to the urban, economically disadvantaged population. The attitudes, values, and behavior that might seem endemic to the urban poor reflect the inevitable adaptation to blocked opportunities that characterize the lives of many who live in low-income, urban areas.

As Daniel Patrick Moynihan said some years ago, while serving as the White House domestic policy adviser for President Richard M. Nixon, "the reason people are poor is that they don't have money." Urban poverty has little to do with values, attitudes, and behavior. The urban poor would like to be income maximizers, as described in economic theory, but many factors conspire to block their opportunity to achieve that goal.

THE STRATEGY: LABOR MARKET SOLUTIONS

An important and indispensable requirement for improving the economic status of the urban poor is to increase the quality and quantity of their participation in the labor market. Increased labor market participation will generate increased income and contribute to an improvement in the standard of living of the economically disadvantaged.

Over the past quarter century, many efforts have been made to improve the labor market experience of the economically disadvantaged in urban areas. Most such efforts were initiated and funded by the federal government, but other institutions also played an important role. In particular, credit must be given to private foundations such as the Ford, Rockefeller, and MacArthur foundations, each of which has funded important demonstration projects aimed at finding solutions to the problems of urban poverty. The Carnegie Corporation and the Edna McConnell Clark, Mott, and William Penn foundations also played an important role in providing seed money to test the effectiveness of promising interventions designed to address the problem. Virtually no stone has been left unturned in the search for innovative and creative ways to improve the economic status of the urban poor. But as is evident in most urban areas throughout the nation, progress has been slow, and success has been limited in finding effective ways to improve the income of the economically disadvantaged.

KEY STRATEGIES

In pursuing the employment and training option, the main strategy has been to target resources toward services for specific groups. There are four major program groups:

1. Employability development for youth. This includes the summer youth employment programs and out-of-school youth programs. In-school programs should be classified under education initiatives, rather than employment and training;
2. Adult training programs, aimed at young adults, many of whom have limited work experience;
3. Welfare-to-work programs. These efforts include both workfare and the job training/transition to work initiatives; and
4. Direct job creation.

At various times these categorical program strategies played a major role as weapons in the arsenal of the federal government aimed at increasing the employment and raising the income of the economically disadvantaged. But other employment and training programs, especially the dislocated worker initiatives, while important devices for improving worker labor market experience, were not designed to address the problem of urban poverty.

IMPACT OF EMPLOYMENT AND TRAINING

The central policy question that should be raised concerning employment and training programs and the urban poor is: what impact have these efforts had in helping to expand economic opportunity for the economically disadvantaged? Does the experience with such programs justify continued investment in them? Indeed, should the investment in employment and training be increased, perhaps at the expense of support for other strategies to improve the income of the urban poor?

The answers to these questions can be gleaned from the results of the voluminous social science research on the impact of employment and training programs. Several research summaries on this issue were prepared over the past two decades.

The first was prepared by a labor market research group at the Wharton School, University of Pennsylvania, in the late 1970s.[1] The review assessed the research on the impact of government manpower programs from their initiation during the War on Poverty up to 1974, the year in which federal policy shifted from categorical program funding to the Comprehensive Employment and Training Act (CETA). CETA reduced the role of the U.S. Department of Labor in designing program strategies, and greatly increased the role of state and local government in determining how federal funds would be used.

More recent summaries of the research literature on employment and training programs include the National Research Council study of youth employment programs,[2] and the U.S. Department of Labor study of employment and training economic impacts.[3] Finally, much of what we know about the impact of this strategy in recent years is based on the National JTPA Study conducted jointly by Abt Associates and the Manpower Demonstration Research Corporation (MDRC) under contract to the Department of Labor.[4]

The research summaries cover more than one hundred studies of categorical programs, demonstration projects, and pilot programs funded by the federal, state, and local governments and by private foundations. Collectively, the social science evidence contained in these studies tell us what's working and what's not in producing an economic impact on the income status of the economically disadvantaged population in urban areas. In contrast to the oft-repeated claim that nothing works, the social science evidence tells us a great deal about both the opportunities and the limitations of the employment and training solution to the problem of urban poverty.

LESSONS FROM THE RESEARCH

Four key lessons can be drawn from the social science research:

Lesson 1. Small but important victories are possible from the employment and training strategy. The net impacts for both adult men and women are modestly positive, and employment and training programs pay for themselves in terms of increased earnings for the two adult groups. But the results for out-of-school youth are disappointing. There is little evidence that such youth, most of whom are economically disadvantaged, are better off from participating in the JTPA program than they would be in the absence of such participation. Similar modest or even negative income results were found among youth who participated in MDRC's Supported Work and JOBSTART demonstration studies. None of the training programs designed and implemented thus far show statistically significant, positive results in improving the earnings of disadvantaged youth.

Studies of state work-welfare programs for women on AFDC in the early 1980s found statistically significant, positive impacts in the first two years after entering the program that ranged up to about $1,000 per year. These findings are similar to those observed in the National Supported Work Demonstration project, but the Supported Work costs per participant were much higher.

Lesson 2. The replication of successful intervention models is very difficult, and as a result, replication is rarely achieved. For example, one of the most successful programs identified in the national search for effective models is the Center for Employment and Training in San Jose, California. CET serves a predominantly Hispanic population, many of whom have limited English-speaking proficiency, but CET has shown the capacity to provide skills training in a variety of occupational fields, while improving participants' basic communication and computation skills. The program's job placement rate remains consistently high, and former participants have a high rate of job retention.

Still, it has been very difficult to replicate the successful CET experience in other communities on the West Coast, much less other regions of the country. Is that because the vibrant Silicon Valley labor market is unique? Are there other locational factors that limit the replicability of a successful model? Experience has shown that many successful community based job training programs are *sui generis*; it is not easy to identify the key factors that contribute to their success. For that reason, the knowledge learned in one place seems limited in its application elsewhere.

Lesson 3. Public job creation is indispensable to success, especially for out of school youth. Even successful job training programs rarely live up to all the expectations placed on them. Training programs *alone* cannot lift disadvantaged participants entirely out of poverty. For some groups, direct job creation might be necessary. Support for this conclusion can be found in the experience of minority group youth during the summer of 1978. At that time, the federal government supported a broad range of youth employment programs, including some funded under the Public Service Employment program that was expanded to more than 500,000 jobs in 1977. Through a variety of grants made to state and local governments and to non-profit community-based organizations, nearly 80 percent of all minority group youth who were employed during the summer of 1978 held publicly subsidized jobs. The policy designed to saturate selected low-income communities with public jobs for disadvantaged youth paid off, as reflected by the significant increase in the employment/population ratio for minority youth. But the program was only temporary; when funding was cut at the end of the summer, the minority youth employment rate reverted to its previous low level.

Lesson 4. The market won't solve the problem. A conclusion that logically follows lesson three is that public policy intervention is indispensable to success in addressing the economic problems of the urban poor. No automatic market adjustment to lower operating costs, cheaper labor in inner city communities, or other neoclassical economic nostrums will stir the backwaters of depressed urban areas where large numbers of the economically disadvantaged jobless reside.

Publicly funded economic incentives are vital to the process of community economic development through which locally based, private-sector jobs might be created. The employment requirements of welfare reform, combined with the persistent long-term joblessness of economically disadvantaged youth, have produced a formidable job creation challenge in the cities. In Philadelphia alone, city officials expect a shortfall of 35,000 jobs below what is required to meet the welfare reform job placement goal during the next two years. A variety of public initiatives, including empowerment zones and enterprise communities, are necessary to stimulate job creation aimed at increasing the income of the urban poor. Market forces alone will not do the job.

CONCLUSION

The persistence of urban poverty and the presence of economically disadvantaged families in our cities is a continuing challenge to national aspirations for equal opportunity and economic justice. A continuing bifurcation of society between those who enjoy an increasing share of economic prosperity and others who are stuck on the lowest rung of the economic ladder should be unacceptable. The search must continue for ways to improve the productivity and earning power of those who need assistance in getting a foothold on the escalator to a middle-income standard of living.

Employment and training programs remain one of the options necessary to achieve that goal. While past programs have not been a panacea, they have contributed to a modest improvement in income among many who participated in them. In the choice of weapons required to combat urban poverty, employment and training programs should be part of the arsenal. The experience of the past, while limited, justifies continued investment in the employment and training option, and the continued experimentation with programs to address the needs of specific target groups. Only by testing new and increasingly comprehensive training models will we find the right mix to accelerate the decline in urban poverty. To achieve success in reducing urban poverty, it is important to maintain steady, balanced economic growth, and persist in the experimentation with job training models.

NOTES

1. Charles R. Perry, Bernard E. Anderson, Herbert R. Northrop, and Richard L. Rowan, *The Impact of Government Manpower Programs: In General, and for Minorities and Women,* Philadelphia: University of Pennsylvania Press, 1975.

2. Charles Betsey, Robinson Hollister, and Mary Papageorgius, *An Evaluation of Youth Employment Programs,* Washington, D.C.: National Research Council, 1985.

3. Lawrence Katz and Alan Krueger, *Youth Employment Programs: What Works and What's Not?*, Washington, D.C.: U.S. Department of Labor, 1994.

4. James J. Kemple, Fred Doolittle, and John W. Wallace, *The National JTPA Study,* New York: Manpower Demonstration Research Corporation, 1993.

Minority Business Development

6

LONG-TERM TRENDS AND PROSPECTS FOR BLACK-OWNED BUSINESSES

Andrew F. Brimmer

The relative status of black-owned businesses deteriorated somewhat from the mid-1980s through the early 1990s. Between 1987 and 1992, sales of black firms rose as a fraction of total sales, but the number of black businesses as a percentage of all businesses rose slightly faster. As a result, the Disparity Index for black firms declined noticeably. In those industries where blacks did make significant progress, they did so by diversifying into new areas.

Looking ahead, between 1995 and 2000, gains of black firms will be quite uneven. Fairly high growth rates are projected for technology and engineering, along with selected fields in telecommunications. In contrast, traditional areas (such as retail trade, which has long served mainly the black consumer market) will grow very slowly. Moreover, construction and television (which have benefited substantially from various types of affirmative action) will lag behind.

In the following article an overview of the growth of black-owned businesses is presented, as well as a discussion of trends in market shares and, finally, long-term prospects for black firms are examined.

GROWTH OF BLACK BUSINESSES: OVERVIEW

In 1992 (the last year for which official Census Bureau figures are available), there were 621,000 black-owned firms in the United States, accounting for 3.599 percent of the total of 17.3 million. The black firms had sales and receipts of $32.2 billion in that year, representing 0.969 percent of the $3.3 trillion reported by all firms. In 1987, there were 424,000 black firms with total sales of $19.8 billion. The corresponding figures for all firms in that year were 13.7 million and $2 trillion, respectively. Therefore, blacks represented 3.096 percent of all firms and 0.991 percent of total sales. By these measures, blacks' share of firms decreased slightly while their share of sales edged up. These figures yielded Disparity Indexes of 26.9 in 1992, compared with 32.07 in 1987. Consequently, over the five-year period, the overall position of black-owned businesses deteriorated somewhat.

The official measures of black-owned businesses in 1987 and 1992 presented above understate the size and growth rate of black-owned businesses. In compiling the estimates, the Census Bureau included data from the U.S. Internal Revenue Service for individual proprietorship or self-employed person (IRS Form 1040, Schedule C), partnership (1065), and subchapter S Corporation (11205). Thus, firms filing a regular IRS Form 1120 tax return were not included. The exclusion applied to both black firms and firms in the nation at large.

The effect of this change in survey methodology on the scope of black business activity was substantial. The magnitude of the impact stands out clearly in the figures for 1982 (see Table 1). The estimates for that year were based on the original methodology which incorporated filings of regular corporations, i.e., IRS 1120 forms. The black firms on this larger roster had sales of $12.4 billion, equal to 0.301 percent of the total. The revised method (which excluded IRS 1120 returns) produced $9.6 billion of sales by black-owned firms, equal to 0.233 percent of total sales by all firms.

Historically, most black businesses have been sole proprietorships, and many of them have adopted the subchapter S form of organization in recent years. More importantly, however, they have increasingly relied on the 1120 form as their businesses have grown in size. By excluding the latter from the data, the Census Bureau has failed to capture information on some of the most dynamic black-owned businesses.

To correct for this shortfall, I re-estimated sales of black-owned businesses in 1987 and 1992. Guidelines for the new estimates were derived from the level of sales and comparative growth rates of the firms on the *Black Enterprise* BE100 Lists for the top 100 black-owned industrial and commercial firms and a similar list for the top 100 black-owned automobile dealerships. The results are shown in Table 1. As a result of re-estimation, sales of black companies in 1987 were raised from $19.8 billion to $25.6 billion. For 1992, the level was raised from $32.2 billion to $49.3 billion. The corresponding black business shares were lifted from 0.991 percent in 1987 to 1.282 percent; in 1992, the lift was from 0.969 percent to 1.482 percent.

Nevertheless, despite these adjustments, black-owned businesses are continuing to play a very modest role in the American economy. As

TABLE 1
Comparative Growth of Black-Owned Businesses, 1982–1992
(Amounts in Millions of Dollars)

Category	1982	1987	1992	Average Annual Percentage Change 1982–87	Average Annual Percentage Change 1987–92
Sales: All U.S. Firms					
Census of Business	4,130,150	5,394,437	6,717,585	5.5	4.5
MBE Survey	—	1,994,808	3,324,200	—	10.7
Percentage of CB	—	36.98	49.49	—	—
Sales: All Black-Owned Firms					
MBE Survey					
Original Method	12,444	25,570[1]	49,275[1]	22.0	14.0
Revised Method	9,619	19,763	32,197	9.7	10.3
Black as Percentage of:					
All U.S. Firms					
Original Method	0.301	0.474	0.734	—	—
Revised Method	0.233	0.366	0.479	—	—
All MBE Survey Firms					
Original Method	—	1.282	1,482	—	—
Revised Method	—	0.991	0.969	—	—
Sales: BE 100 Firms					
Reported Sales	2,170	6,095	12,365	23.0	15.2
BE 100 as Percentage of					
All U.S. Firms	0.053	0.113	0.184	—	—
All MBE Survey Firms	—	0.306	0.372	—	—
All MBE Black Firms					
Original Method	17.44	23.84	25.09	—	—
Revised Method	22.26	30.84	38.40	—	—

[1] Estimated by Brimmer & Company, Inc.
Source: Prepared by Brimmer & Company, Inc. Data from U.S. Department of Commerce, Bureau of the Census, *1987 Economic Censuses Survey of Minority-Owned Business Enterprises: Black*, July, 1990, and *1992 Survey of Minority-Owned Business Enterprises: Black-Owned Businesses* (Excerpts), December 11, 1995.

already noted, their share of total business sales climbed from 0.233 percent (revised method) in 1982, to 0.366 percent in 1987, to 0.479 percent in 1992. Measured using the original estimating method, their shares rose from 0.301 percent in 1982, to 0.474 percent in 1987, and to 0.734 percent in 1992.

Likewise, black businesses are sharing only moderately in the growth of income being achieved in the black community. As shown in Table 2, blacks' money income rose from 7.09 percent of the total in 1982, to 7.53 percent in 1987, to 7.56 percent in 1992. In the same years, sales of black firms represented 8.34 percent of blacks' money income (relying on the original method) in 1982; the proportions rose to 11.37 percent in 1987 and to 17.33 percent in 1992. The revised method of estimating black business sales yielded the lower shares indicated.

Several factors help to account for the slight increase in the percentage of the black households' income received by black-owned firms. The latter are diversifying so that they are better able to supply the goods and services demanded by black consumers as their incomes rise. Some black firms are also following their customers to the suburbs as they increasingly abandon core cities. Moreover, an increasing number of black firms are expanding their participation in the economy at large, and those sales helped boost their overall standing.

TRENDS IN MARKET SHARES

Blacks' share of total business activity in the United States, which was already very small in 1987, declined further over the following five years. Measured by the broadest gauge of participation (the Disparity Index-DI), their relative position decreased from 32. 01 in 1987 to 26.92 in 1992.

The Disparity Index is calculated as follows:

$$DI = \frac{S_b}{S_t} \div \frac{N_b}{N_t} \times 100,$$

Where:

S_b = Sales of black firms
S_t = Sales of all firms
N_b = Number of black firms
N_t = Number of all firms.

If the DI is equal to 100.00, blacks' share of total sales matches their share of total firms in an industry. This ratio indicates that blacks' market access is unimpeded. If the DI reading is below 100.00, it implies that blacks are excluded from full participation. To some extent, the latter may be due to discrimination. A DI above 100.00 suggests that blacks enjoy special advantages in the particular industry.

The DIs for blacks in ten broad industry groupings in 1987 and 1992 are presented in Tables 3 and 4, respectively. The underlying figures on

TABLE 2
Business Sales and Black Money Income, 1982, 1987, and 1992

	1982		1987		1992	
Category	Amount	Percentage of Total	Amount	Percentage of Total	Amount	Percentage of Total
Business Sales and Receipts						
All U.S. Firms	4,130,150	100.00	5,394,437	100.00	6,717,585	100.000
Black-Owned Firms						
Original Method	12,444	0.301	25,570[1]	0.474	49,275[1]	0.734
Revised Method	9,619	0.233	19,763	0.366	32,197	0.479
Money Income in the United States						
Total	2,061,691	100.00	2,988,548	100.00	3,822,005	100.00
Black	149,130	7.09	224,893	7.53	284,327	7.56
Black Firms' Sales as Percent of Black Money Income						
Original Method	—	8.34	—	11.37	—	17.33
Revised Method	—	6.45	—	8.79	—	11.32

[1] Estimates by Brimmer & Company, Inc.

Source: Prepared by Brimmer & Company, Inc. Data from U.S. Department of Commerce, Bureau of the Census.

TABLE 3

Number of Firms, Business Sales, and Disparity Indexes, By Industry, 1987
(Numbers in Thousands. Amounts in Millions of Dollars)

	All Firms		Black Firms				
Category	Number	Sales	Number	Percentage of Total	Amount	Percentage of Total	Disparity Index
All Industries	13,695	1,994,808	424	3.096	19,763	0.991	32.01
Agriculture	357	20,585	7	1.961	217	1.054	53.75
Mining	121	15,084	1	0.826	54	0.358	43.34
Construction	1,651	232,372	37	2.241	2,174	0.936	41.77
Manufacturing	433	226,824	8	1.848	1,023	0.451	24.41
Transportation & PU	593	76,355	37	6.239	1,573	2.060	33.02
Wholesale Trade	439	298,264	6	1.367	1,327	0.445	32.55
Retail Trade	2,241	544,768	66	2.945	5,890	1.081	36.71
Fin., Ins., R.E.	1,227	123,710	27	2.200	804	0.650	29.55
Services	5,938	417,105	210	3.537	6,120	1.467	41.48
Other Industries	695	39,741	27	3.885	580	1.459	37.55

Source: Calculations by Brimmer & Company, Inc. Data from U.S. Department of Commerce, Bureau of the Census. *1987 Economic Censuses: Survey of Minority-Owned Business Enterprise: Black*, July, 1990.

TABLE 4

Number of Firms, Business Sales, and Disparity Indexes, By Industry, 1992
(Numbers in Thousands. Amounts in Millions of Dollars)

	All Firms		Black Firms				
Category	Number	Sales	Number	Percentage of Total	Amount	Percentage of Total	Disparity Index
All Industries	17,253	3,324,200	621	3.599	32,197	0.969	26.92
Agriculture	433	29,665	10	2.309	265	0.893	38.67
Mining	150	32,661	1	0.667	66	0.327	49.03
Construction	1,830	307,123	43	2.350	2,651	0.863	36.72
Manufacturing	518	451,719	10	1.931	1,319	0.292	15.12
Transportation & PU	699	130,033	49	7.010	2,498	1.921	27.40
Wholesale Trade	538	641,051	8	1.487	2,944	0.459	30.87
Retail Trade	2,478	722,713	87	3.511	6,968	0.964	27.46
Fin., Ins., R.E.	1,941	322,251	40	2.061	3,777	1.172	56.87
Services	7,784	661,284	333	4.278	11,057	1.672	39.08
Other Industries	882	25,699	39	4.422	652	2.537	57.37

Source: Calculations by Brimmer & Company, Inc. Data from U.S. Department of Commerce, Bureau of the Census.

number of firms and amount of sales are also shown. Changes in DIs are shown in Table 5. Sales figures for a number of more narrowly defined industry groups in 1987 and 1992 are shown in the Appendix Table.

It will be noted that all of the DIs were considerably below par in both years. The highest industry reading in 1987 (53.75) related to agricultural services, forestry, and fishing, and most of the activity was in farming. Mining followed with a DI of 43.34. In this case, oil and gas extraction accounted for the bulk of the sales by black firms.

Next in line were construction (41.77) and services (41.48). Within the construction industry, special trade contractors were responsible for more than half the activity. Much of the latter reflected blacks' participation in government-sponsored projects at Federal, state, and local levels. Blacks' share of services rested substantially on their provision of personal services to black consumers who were frequently excluded from service establishments catering to whites.

Retail trade (36.71) also mirrored the legacy of black merchants selling primarily to black customers during the era of segregation. The DI for wholesale trade (32.55) reflected, to a large degree, blacks' role in the beverage business. In the case of transportation and public utilities, the DI was 33.02. Here, the bulk of black firms' receipts came from the operation of taxis and local trucking enterprises.

The DI for manufacturing (24.41) was the lowest calculated. Within this industry, blacks' factories were engaged primarily in the production of lumber, fabricated metals, apparel and textiles, and printing and publishing. A smaller proportion of sales came from food processing. Between 1987 and 1992, the DIs for six of the ten industry groups decreased. Declines were particularly noticeable in agriculture (–15.08 percentage points), manufacturing (–9.29 percentage points), and retail trade (–9.25 percentage points). The decrease in agriculture reflected the continued exit of blacks from farming. The declines in manufacturing and retail trade—to some extent—probably were partly due to the fact that 1992 was a recession year. But, in both industries, blacks were not well represented in those segments which did achieve above-average growth rates.

Over the time period under review, blacks did make noticeable gains in a number of industries (see Appendix). Among these were subdividers and land developers in the construction industry. These were mainly builders of low-income tract housing, where the average annual growth rate was 22.4 percent (vs. 3.7 percent for all firms). Black food processors increased their sales by an average of 27.4 percent, compared with

TABLE 5
Changes in Disparity Indexes For Black-Owned Businesses, 1987–92

Industry	1987	1992	Change: 1987–92 (Percentage Points)
All Industries	32.01	26.92	–5.09
Agriculture	53.75	38.67	–15.08
Mining	43.34	49.03	5.69
Construction	41.77	36.72	–5.05
Manufacturing	24.41	15.12	–9.29
Transportation & PU	33.02	27.40	–5.62
Wholesale Trade	32.55	30.87	–1.68
Retail Trade	36.71	27.46	–9.25
Fin., Ins., R.E.	29.55	56.87	27.32
Services	41.48	39.08	–2.40
Other Industries	37.55	57.37	19.82

Source: Calculations by Brimmer & Company, Inc. Data from Tables 3 and 4.

14.8 percent for all firms. This gain reflected a few large-scale acquisitions by blacks as well as the growth which some existing enterprises achieved internally.

The receipts of black-owned local and inter-urban transportation firms expanded by 16.2 percent (vs. 10.7 percent for all firms). Again, much of this growth was traceable to the ability of blacks and other newcomers to enter the industry as the latter was deregulated. Blacks in the communications industry saw their sales rise almost twice as fast as those for the industry as a whole. The increase for blacks was 37.5 percent, compared with 19.3 percent for the total. A large proportion of the expansion by black companies reflected purchases of radio and television stations under special tax incentive programs sponsored by the Federal Communications Commission (FCC).

Gains in sales by blacks in wholesale trade (17.3 percent vs. 16.5 percent for all firms) were due primarily to distributors of non-durable goods—particularly food and alcoholic beverages. In retail trade, increases were recorded by apparel and accessories stores (7.8 percent vs. 5 percent) and eating and drinking places (10.5 percent vs. 7.2 percent).

In general, those black-owned businesses which were able to increase their market shares between 1987 and 1992 did so primarily by diversifying into new fields of activity. The latter were most often found in the general market rather than relying heavily on black consumers. Those businesses which remained wedded to the provision of services almost exclusively to blacks experienced slow growth, with some suffering actual declines.

LONG-TERM OUTLOOK FOR BLACK-OWNED BUSINESSES

The prospects for firms owned by blacks can be described as only moderately optimistic over the next five years. Their sales will grow only slightly faster than those of all businesses, and they will continue to attract only a small proportion of the income of the black community.

In Table 6, the trend of black firms' sales from 1987 through 1995 is shown along with a number of macroeconomic variables. Projections through 2000 are also presented.

Several features stand out. Over the coming five years, blacks will constitute a larger fraction of the U.S. population (i.e., 12.84 percent in 2000 vs. 12.57 percent in 1995). They will also see a noticeable rise in their share of total money income to 8.26 percent vs. 8 percent.

Sales of black-owned businesses are estimated to have increased from $49.3 billion in 1992 to $72.5 billion in 1995, lifting their share from 0.734 percent to 0.919 percent of the total. It is estimated that the level of black firms' sales will have risen to $119.8 billion by 2000. If this growth materializes, their share of total sales would climb to 1.202 percent.

Black businesses appear to have been competing somewhat more successfully for black consumers' dollars in recent years. In 1987, their sales represented 11.38 percent of blacks' money income. The percentage then rose as follows (percentage): 1992, 17.34; 1994, 18.61; and 1995, 19.64. A further rise to 24.79 percent is projected for 2000.

In the years ahead, the strongest expansion of black businesses is expected to occur mainly through diversification into new fields rather than in areas where they have traditionally been active. An indication of what these growth areas are likely to be is provided by the data in Table 7. The figures show the industry distribution of sales of the businesses on *Black Enterprises'* list of the largest 100 black-owned automobile dealerships and the largest 100 industrial and commercial firms. The sales are for 1987 and 1994, and they are ranked according to the 1994 levels.

It will be noted that in 1987, automobile dealers accounted for 33.4 percent of combined sales of $6.1 billion. The largest category was food

TABLE 6
Long-Term Economic Growth and the Expansion of Black-Owned Businesses, 1987–2000
(Amounts in Billions of Dollars)

Category	1987	1992	1994	1995	2000
Population	242,289	255,082	260,711	263,434	276,241
Black	29,325	31,635	32,631	33,117	35,469
Percentage	12.10	12.40	12.52	12.57	12.84
Gross Domestic Product	4,539.9	6,020.3	6,738.4	7,077.5	8,939.9
Personal Income	3,802.0	5,144.9	5,701.7	6,051.0	7,669.0
Percentage	83.75	85.46	84.62	85.50	85.78
Money Income	2,988.5	3,761.1	4,350.4	4,614.2	5,849.9
Percentage of:					
GDP	65.83	62.47	64.56	65.20	65.44
PI	78.60	73.10	76.30	76.26	76.28
Black Income	224.9	284.3	339.3	359.1	483.1
Percentage of:					
GDP	4.95	4.72	5.04	5.22	5.40
PI	5.91	5.53	5.95	6.10	6.30
Money Income	7.53	7.56	7.80	8.00	8.26
Business Sales: Total	5,394.4	6,717.6	7,513.3	7,891.4	9,968.0
Percentage of GDP	1.188	1.116	1.115	1.115	1.115
Black-Business Sales	25.6	49.3	63.1	72.5	119.8
Percentage of:					
GDP	0.564	0.891	0.936	1.024	1.340
Black Income	11.38	17.34	18.61	19.64	24.79
Total Business Sales	0.474	0.734	0.840	0.919	1.202

Source: Prepared by Brimmer & Company, Inc. Historical data from U.S. Department of Commerce, Bureau of the Census and Bureau of Economic Analysis.

and beverages (37.5 percent). This level reflected the acquisition by blacks of a very large formerly white-owned company in that year. Following these two categories, there was a sharp falloff in the shares of total *BE*-200 sales accounted for by other industry groups. In percentage terms they were: construction, 6.4; media, 5.5; computers and information, 4.6; and health and beauty aids, 3.5.

By 1994, a significant change had occurred in the industry distribution of total *BE*-200 sales of $11.7 billion. Automobile dealers had raised their proportion to 42.6 percent, while food and beverages had declined to 23.6 percent.

TABLE 7
Industry Distribution of Sales of BE200 Firms, 1987 and 1994
(Amounts in Thousands of Dollars)

Industry	1987 Amount	1987 Percentage	1994 Amount	1994 Percentage	Average Annual Growth Rate, 1987–94 Percentage
Automobile Dealers	2,036,681	33.4	4,983,747	42.6	13.6
Food & Beverages	2,284,032	37.5	2,768,213	23.6	2.7
Engineering and Technology	281,300	4.6	1,050,261	7.0	21.0
Computers and Information	281,300	4.6	—	—	—
Engineering	—	—	167,564	1.5	—
Technology	—	—	882,697	7.5	—
Media	336,210	5.5	920,654	7.9	15.5
Manufacturing	129,315	2.1	682,810	5.8	27.0
Construction	389,221	6.4	393,332	3.4	0.2
Health & Beauty Aids	210,711	3.5	240,900	2.1	2.0
Miscellaneous	428,018	7.0	671,288	5.6	6.6
Entertainment	143,000	2.3	—	—	
Transportation	109,076	1.8	—	—	—
Security—Maintenance	49,662	0.8	—	—	—
Commodities	—	—	—	—	—
Health Care	—	—	—	—	—
Other Misc.	126,289	2.1	—	—	—
Total	6,095,488	100.0	11,711,205	100.0	9.8

Source: Prepared by Brimmer & Company, Inc. Data from *Black Enterprise*, June, 1988, and June, 1995

In marked contrast, the share of engineering and technology had almost doubled, rising from 4.6 percent to 7 percent. Most of the latter share (7.5 percent) was provided by technology. Again, much of the growth in technology sales was directly tied to computers and computer-assisted activities, areas in which blacks have been making considerable headway.

Media firms also achieved some improvement in their relative position. They lifted their share of total sales from 5.5 percent to 7.9 percent. While much of this expansion reflected the internal growth of existing firms, a major share was due to the acquisition by blacks of previously white-owned companies. To a considerable extent, as noted above, those acquisitions were stimulated by the tax incentive program operated by the FCC and designed to promote minority ownership of radio and TV stations.

Blacks also made noticeable gains in manufacturing. This category accounted for 2.1 percent of total *BE*-200 sales in 1987. By 1994, the fraction had risen to 5.8 percent. As late as 1987, much of the industrial activity of black firms consisted of printing and publishing and the production of cosmetics for black consumers. In recent years, however, blacks have "lost" some factory capacity as several previously-owned black firms (especially cosmetics and food producers) have been sold to whites. These transfers have been more than offset by blacks' expansion into other manufacturing fields, particularly electronics, textiles and apparel, and fabricated metals.

The position of black firms in the construction industry lagged noticeably between 1987 and 1994. In the earlier year, receipts of construction contractors represented 6.4 percent of the total sales of *BE*-200 firms. By 1994, the proportion had fallen to 3.4 percent. To a large degree, the lag reflected the slowdown in construction in the nation as a whole during these years. But it also mirrored the diminished role of affirmative action programs under whose auspices blacks had been able to make considerable gains.

Expected growth rates of black-owned businesses over the next five years, by major industry groups are presented in Table 8. Projections of GDP and total business sales are also shown for comparative purposes.

It will be noted that black business receipts are projected to increase faster than total sales between 1995 and 2000—at an average annual rate of 10.6 percent vs. 4.8 percent. However, the rate of increase for blacks is less than that recorded during the earlier period.

The biggest gains are expected to occur in the technology field. Here the growth rate may average 25 percent per year. The driving force will be the spread of computers and computer information systems. The expansion of black firms will exceed that anticipated for all businesses (18 percent). The higher growth rate for black firms will partially reflect the much smaller base from which they start, but genuine growth will also be achieved. The receipts of black engineering firms may expand at an annual rate of 20 percent, compared with 15 percent for all businesses combined.

Black firms in communications will also expand rapidly, at an annual

TABLE 8
Differential Growth Rates: Total and Black-Owned Businesses, 1987–94 and 1995–2000
(Percentage)

	Average Annual Growth Rate (Percentage)		
		1995–2000	
Category	1987–94	Black Firms	Total
Gross Domestic Product	5.8	–	4.8
Business Sales: Total	4.9	–	4.8
Business Sales: Black Firms	13.7	10.6	–
Automobile Dealers	13.6	12.0	6.0
Food & Beverages	2.7	6.0	4.0
Engineering and Technology	21.0	22.0	16.0
Engineering	–	20.0	15.0
Technology	–	25.0	18.0
Media	15.5	12.5	5.5
Manufacturing	27.0	7.0	3.5
Construction	0.2	3.0	4.0
Transportation	–	10.0	7.5
Communications	–	15.0	10.0
Telephones	–	12.0	4.0
Wire lines	–	10.0	5.0
Cellular/PCs	–	30.0	22.0
Radio	–	15.0	8.0
Television	–	5.0	6.0

Source: Prepared by Brimmer & Company, Inc. Data from U.S. Department of Commerce, Bureau of the Census, Bureau of Economic Analysis, and the International Trade Administration. Tables 6 & 7.

rate of 15 percent vs. 10 percent for all businesses. The growth rate in cellular telephones and personal communications systems may be especially strong, 30 percent vs. 22 percent. Black-owned radio stations are expected to do particularly well (expanding at 15 percent vs. 8 percent for all such stations). In contrast, black-owned television stations may lag considerably. They are projected to see an annual increase of only 5 percent, compared with 6 percent for all TV stations combined. The stagnation in black ownership of TV stations reflects the repeal of the

FCC minority ownership program, which has come under both Congressional and judicial attack in recent years.

In a similar vein, sales of black construction firms may rise very slowly, i.e., by only 3 percent per year. Overall, construction will also rise slowly, by 4 percent. To a considerable extent, the expansion by blacks in this industry in the past could be traced to a variety of affirmative action programs adopted by federal, state, and local governments. However, beginning with an adverse Supreme Court decision in 1989, many of those programs have been abandoned or scaled back significantly.

In manufacturing, blacks will most likely see their sales grow twice as fast as those for the industry at large. Many of these firms will be participating in joint ventures with white-owned enterprises.

On balance, blacks in business will make further progress over the next five years. Nevertheless, the fairly high growth rates recorded in the 1980s probably will not be repeated.

APPENDIX

	1987			1992			Average Annual Percentage Change	
		Black Firms			Black Firms			
Industry	All Firms	Amount	Percentage	All Firms	Amount	Percentage	All Firms	Black Firms
All Industries	1,994,808	19,763	0.991	3,324,200	32,197	0.969	10.8	10.3
Agricultural Services	16,875	190	1.126	25,340	244	0.963	8.4	5.1
Mining	15,085	54	0.358	32,661	66	0.202	16.7	4.1
Construction	232,372	2,174	0.936	307,123	2,651	0.863	5.8	4.0
Gen. Building	86,562	636	0.735	118,100	840	0.711	6.4	5.7
Heavy	20,684	156	0.754	33,669	156	0.463	10.2	0.0
Special	105,185	1,314	1.249	126,672	1,466	1,157	3.8	2.2
Subdividers	19,941	69	0.346	28,682	189	0.659	3.7	22.4
Manufacturing	226,824	1,023	0.451	451,719	1,319	0.292	14.8	5.2
Food	27,351	61	0.223	54,512	204	0.374	14.8	27.4
Lumber	19,450	211	1.085	29,244	248	0.848	8.5	3.3
Apparel and Tex.	16,235	65	0.400	29,633	83	0.280	12.8	5.0
Printing and Pub.	24,440	126	0.516	40,420	180	0.445	10.6	7.4
Fab. Metals	20,608	116	0.563	39,034	91	0.233	13.6	–5.0
Transportation and Pub.	76,355	1,573	2.060	130,033	2,498	1.921	11.2	9.7
Local and Interurban	3,369	218	6.471	5,602	462	8.247	10.7	16.2

Trucking and Ware.	40,866	1,010	2.471	58,771	1,347	2.292	7.5	6.0
Transport Services	14,043	223	1.588	15,695	161	1.026	2.3	–6.7
Communications	9,918	82	0.827	23,929	401	1.676	19.3	37.5
Elect., Gas, San.	3,059	20	0.654	18,084	110	0.608	42.7	40.7
Whole Sale Trade	298,264	1,327	0.446	641,051	–2,944	0.459	16.5	17.3
Durable Goods	141,477	629	0.445	303,865	1,107	0.364	16.5	12.0
Nondurable Goods	156,786	699	0.446	337,186	1,837	0.545	16.6	22.4
Retail Trade	544,768	5,890	1.081	722,713	6,968	0.964	5.8	3.4
Building Mat.	33,923	190	0.560	32,571	140	0.430	–0.8	–6.3
Gen. Merchandise	7,757	44	0.567	10,620	47	0.443	6.5	1.3
Food Stores	79,112	1,001	1.265	103,602	980	0.946	5.6	–0.4
Auto Dealers	211,843	2,156	1.018	294,443	2,384	0.810	6.8	2.0
Apparel and Access.	18,327	140	0.764	23,425	204	0.871	5.0	7.8
Furniture	28,858	187	0.648	37,546	181	0.482	5.4	–0.7
Eating and Drinking	73,114	1,084	1.483	103,659	1,786	1.723	7.2	10.5
Misc. Retail	91,835	1,086	1.183	116,848	1,247	1.067	4.9	2.8
Finance, Insurance & R.E.	123,710	804	0.650	322,251	3,777	1.172	21.5	36.3
Real Estate	68,541	506	0.738	212,510	1,553	0.731	25.3	25.2
Other FIRE	55,169	298	0.540	109,741	2,224	2.027	14.7	49.5
Services	417,105	6,120	1.467	661,284	11,057	1.672	9.7	12.6
Hotel & Lodging	26,380	128	0.485	46,546	208	0.447	12.0	10.2
Personal	30,196	960	3.179	40,023	1,469	3.670	5.8	8.9
Business	98,137	1,570	1.600	122,558	2,371	1.935	4.6	8.6
Auto Repair	29,990	427	1.424	41,050	558	1.359	6.5	5.5
Misc. Repair	11,839	154	1.301	16,226	170	1.048	6.5	2.0
Motion Pictures	5,401	62	1.148	21,739	86	0.396	32.2	6.8
Amusement	19,409	503	2.592	31,820	665	2.090	10.4	5.9

APPENDIX (Continued)

	1987			1992			Average Annual Percentage Change	
		Black Firms			Black Firms			
Industry	All Firms	Amount	Percentage	All Firms	Amount	Percentage	All Firms	Black Firms
Health	81,091	1,351	1.666	142,206	2,859	2.010	11.9	16.2
Legal	55,293	336	0.608	77,735	551	0.709	7.1	10.4
Educational	3,305	65	1.967	5,092	71	1.394	9.0	1.8
Social Services	5,469	224	4.096	11,824	582	4.922	16.7	21.2
Engineering & Management	n.a.	n.a.	—	93,695	1,353	1.444	—	—
Services, n.e.c.	40,596	340	0.672	10,769	121	1.124	—	—
Industries not Classified	39,741	580	1.459	25,699	652	2.537	–9.1	2.4

Source: Prepared by Brimmer & Company, Inc. Data from U.S. Department of Commerce, Bureau of the Census, *1987 Economic Censuses Survey of Minority-Owned Business Enterprises: Black,* July, 1990, and *1992 Survey of Minority-Owned Business Enterprises: Black-Owned Businesses* (Excerpts), December 11, 1995.

7

MINORITY BUSINESS FORMATION AND SURVIVAL: EVIDENCE ON BUSINESS PERFORMANCE AND VIABILITY

*Jan E. Christopher**

INTRODUCTION

Empirical analyses of the factors influencing business performance and viability have shown that minority businesses, compared with the non-minority population of small businesses in the United States, experience a lower business formation rate and a higher dissolution rate. Black, Hispanic, and other minority business owners have historically experienced severe economic problems when forming and maintaining business enterprises. Inadequate human and physical capitalization, as well as discrimination, have often restricted the growth in the number and size of minority-owned businesses. African American business owners have experienced particular problems in the formation and viability of their businesses. African American proprietors have cited many obstacles and difficulties, including limited demand for their products and services, racial discrimination, limited vocational or educational opportunities,[1] unpredictable business cycles in the economy, and limited access in securing credit for business ownership. These phenomena, in essence, have excluded many African Americans, as well as other minorities, from successfully participating in business opportunities and obtaining the financial and non-pecuniary (e.g., freedom, independence, profit potential) rewards associated with being self-employed.

---

* Sincere gratitude is expressed to Professors Satish Wadhawan, Charles Betsey, Rodney Green, Michael Bosse, and Cleveland Chandler. Special thanks to Gavin Chen, William Darity, Jr., Donald Snyder, Charles Ou, Richard Boden, Jules Lichtenstein, and Ed Starr for supportive commentary; and Margaret Simms, Stephen Prowse, Greg Duffee, Thomas Simpson, Hank Leddon, Portia Thompson, Janet Reid, Johnetta Davis, Tyrone Boyd, and Catherine Core in bringing this work to print.

There is evidence to suggest that minorities have had major difficulties starting businesses in a number of industries and occupations. Many scholars have cited numerous barriers to business performance and viability. These barriers have included (1) low levels of education in the minority community, (2) low earnings levels among the clientele, (3) unfavorable commercial bank behavior, (4) lack of starting capital (e.g., personal savings or wealth) to form a business entity, (5) competition by non-minority owned businesses, (6) lack of political influence, (7) limited markets, (8) inability to collect debts, and (9) low financial returns on investment. These difficulties have traditionally hampered minority participation in many types of business activities which could facilitate substantial returns on net investment.

Black, Hispanic, and other minority-owned businesses are generally small. All small businesses in the United States, however, have a greater than 50 percent dissolution rate within their first five years of operations.[2] Larger firms, however, experience greater return on shareholders' equity and larger owner/executive compensation than smaller firms. Economies of scale and the rate of experience of larger firms play major roles in contributing to business performance. Empirical evidence also suggests that larger firms that are highly sophisticated in their strategies and planning procedures are even more viable.[3]

This article considers two facets of business performance and viability. First, explanations for business survival may be based on the characteristic of the individual business owner and on geographic location. Second, the ability of a business owner to have a viable business may be based on general economic conditions. In fact, the findings presented here may have major implications for the classification and definition of race and ethnicity in the next millennium, as well as for policy solutions related to the self-employed.

DEVELOPMENT OF HYPOTHESES

The hypotheses developed in this research study have several objectives, including the examination of the attributes of individual business owners, the identification of the business conditions experienced by minority business owners, and exploration of the factors that influence varying degrees of business success.

The research question addresses the hypothesis that businesses are more successful when business owners invest in human and physical capital. A primary objective is to test the importance of owners' human capital in fostering business performance and increasing business viability. The research objectives assert that the success of minority entrepreneurs rises with formal education, through continuing informal and non-formal education, through years of work experience, through length of business ownership, and with significant financial capitalization. The specific hypotheses relating to human capital, and the utilization of investment capital in business formation, were that: (1) minority business survival increased with the number of years of formal education of the owner; (2) minority business survival increased with greater work experience of the owner; (3) minority business survival was higher in the industries where starting capital requirements were low and did not hinder entry into particular lines of business; and (4) minority business survival increased with the utilization of commercial bank financing in business formation, where education served as a proxy for a sole proprietor's ability to obtain bank credit.

A Taxonomy on Minority Business Enterprise

Three important concepts are presented in the literature on minority business enterprise that should be noted here: accessibility to financial capital, business success, and business dissolution.

Accessibility to Financial Capital. Access to, or availability of, financial capital is influenced by the following factors: years since business was established, age of owner, educational attainment of owner, starting capitalization, percentage of borrowed capital, source of borrowed capital, source of equity capital, racial characteristics of owner, wealth holdings of owner, region or location of residence or business, and marital status of owner.[4]

Business Success. A business is successful if it assists in economic activity at the local level and weathers local business conditions. Business performance, survival, and viability are enhanced by how well an establishment contributes to the local economy, maintains positive accounting profits, and provides ample self-employment income for the business owner to remain successful. Another short-term economic indicator of business success includes the employment of local residents.

Business Dissolution. A business dissolution is when a business owner decides to terminate operations. Dissolution includes the voluntary termination of operations because net sales or profits are too low; the retirement of the business owner; or the decision of the owner to seek wage-and-salary employment as an alternative to self-employment. Business failure, on the other hand, can take many forms. Current data on business failures do not fully disclose whether a firm has dissolved or merely reorganized.[5]

OVERVIEW OF THE RESEARCH DESIGN

The data used in this research study are from both primary and secondary sources. The bulk of the primary data are from the U.S. Bureau of the Census, *Characteristics of Business Owners* (CBO) database that is not publicly available.[6] Special tabulations from the CBO database were obtained through the Center for Economic Studies of the U.S. Bureau of the Census.[7] The results in this article were verified by U.S. Census Bureau employees who have direct access to the raw data. The CBO database is comprised of two different information sources: survey response data and administrative records that are attached to each individual survey response.

Secondary data sources providing information on various facets of the characteristics of metropolitan areas were extracted from the 1987 and 1992 *Survey of Minority-Owned Business Enterprises* (SMOBE) and the *State and Metropolitan Area Data Book: 1991.* These publications provided summary information of firms, sales and receipts, legal form of organization, and number of employees.

The characteristics of business owners and their firms were surveyed by the Census Bureau in February 1991, requesting information as of 1987.[8] A follow-up telephone survey was performed if the surveys were not completed and returned to the U.S. Bureau of the Census by June 1991. Listed in Table 1 are the units of analysis defined as owner attributes and firm characteristics that exist in the 1987 and 1992 CBO databases and were given consideration in this study.

The geographic units of Metropolitan Statistical Area (MSA), county, and state were combined to create spatial variables to conform to various model specifications and research designs. This study, as presented in this article, selected the Census Regional Division as its geographic unit of analysis.[9]

Four classifications of ethnicity have been selected—Black (African American), Hispanic (Latino American), Asian/Other (Asian Americans, Pacific Islanders, Native Americans, and Alaska Natives), and White (Non-minority)—on the basis of the availability of comparable data from earlier censuses. This approach also facilitated comparisons with other research studies.

TABLE 1
The Characteristics of Business Owners (CBO): Units of Analysis

Owner Attributes	Firm Characteristecs
Age	Age of Firm
Marital Status	Size of Firm
Immigrant to the U.S.	Industry of Operation
Veteran	Markets for Products or Services
Education	Number of Employees
Work Experience	Legal Form of Organization
Household Income	Size of Payroll
Location of Residence	Physical Location of Firm
Average Hours Managing Business	MSA where firm is located
Months Per Year Managing Business	State/County of Location of Firm
Founder of the Business	Home-Based Business
Prior Business Ownership	Sales Level of Firm
Starting Capital Used to Start Business	Profits (losses) of the Firm
Sources of Debt Capital	Percentage Women Employees
Sources of Equity Capital	Percentage Minority Employees
Assets and Liabilities	Percentage Minority Customers
Received Government Assistance to Start Business	Percentage Exports Outside U.S.
Racial Characteristic of Owner	Franchised Business
Gender of Owner	Government Sub-Contractor

Source: Compiled from the Characteristics of *Business Owners, 1987, CB087-1*, 1992. Washington, D.C., U.S. Department of Commerce, Bureau of the Census.

Firm-specific data on individual business-owner characteristics were classified according to owner ethnicity. For comparisons of general patterns of variability among and between racial or ethnic minorities, major industry categories were used. In an analysis of the determinants of industrial distribution, the two-digit SIC industry was employed as the unit of analysis and 70 industrial classifications were utilized.

CHARACTERISTICS OF MINORITY-OWNED BUSINESSES

The distribution of employment and sales receipts among minority-owned business enterprises compared to all small businesses throughout the United States revealed that approximately 82 percent of all small businesses in the U.S. had no paid employees. The 18.2 percent of the firms having paid employees, however, were the bigger businesses, with 87.5 percent of all sales and receipts. The proportion of African Americans, particularly African American women, who owned businesses with no paid employees was far greater than the national average (92.5 percent vs. 81.8 percent). An analysis of sales receipts data evidenced that firms with no paid employees have lower self-employment incomes.

Survey data indicate that 68.6 percent of all small businesses in the U.S. had 0–4 employees; 92.9 percent of all small businesses had fewer than 20 employees; and 95.3 percent of all minority-owned businesses fall into the 0–19 employee category. Sales and receipts of small businesses in the U.S. that had 0–19 employees comprised only 37.6 percent of all sales receipts in 1992 dollars, yet the very small minority-owned firms earned 54.9 percent of the sales and receipts of minority-owned business enterprises. This phenomenon indicates that there are very few large minority-owned firms. Approximately 1.1 percent of all U.S. small business firms surveyed had more than 100 employees, yet these firms collected only 33.9 percent of all sales and receipts. Among minority firms, only 0.5 percent had more than 100 employees and these larger firms collected 21.2 percent of all minority-owned business sales and receipts.

The major ancestry groups, presented in Table 2, are African American (Black); Hispanic American (Latino); and Asian/Other (Asian Americans, Pacific Islanders, American Indians, and Alaska Natives). Although the distribution of employment is relatively consistent across each minority group, sales and receipts by firm size varied significantly by ancestry group. In 1992, the variation in sales and receipts of the very smallest firms with fewer than 20 employees was 51.5 percent for African American businesses, 55.3 for Hispanic enterprises, and 55.4 percent for Asian/Other business enterprises.

THE REGIONAL DISTRIBUTION OF MINORITY-OWNED BUSINESSES

The relationships among the various minority groups within the regions of the United States are shown in Tables 3 and 4. Minorities, as a group and within their individual ancestries, differ in their regional composition of population, business participation rates, and business performance. A regional perspective provides insight into the differential patterns of minority business ownership in various sections of the United

TABLE 2
Minority Group Employment and Sales Receipts by Firm Size: 1992 (Percent)

Firm Size	All U.S. Firms	All Minority Firms	African American	Hispanic American	Asian/ Other
Employment					
0–19	92.9	95.3	96.2	95.1	95.0
20–49	4.6	3.4	2.6	3.5	3.7
50–99	1.4	0.8	0.7	0.8	0.8
100+	1.1	0.5	0.5	0.6	0.5
Total	100.0	100.0	100.0	100.0	100.0
Sales and Receipts					
0–19	37.6	54.9	51.5	55.3	55.4
20–49	16.2	14.4	13.6	15.6	13.7
50–99	12.3	9.5	9.3	10.4	8.9
100+	33.9	21.2	25.6	18.7	22.0
Total	100.0	100.0	100.0	100.0	100.0

Note: Employment and Sales Receipts of minority-owned business enterprises with paid employees indicates that firms with fewer than 20 employees comprised 96.2 percent of all African American businesses, 95.1 percent of Hispanics American businesses, and 95.0 percent of Asian/Other businesses in 1992. The corresponding sales and receipts were 51.5 percent for African American businesses, 55.3 for Hispanic American businesses, and 55.4 percent for Asian/Other businesses.
Source: *1992 Survey of Minority-Owned Business Enterprises*, vol. 4, *Summary* MB92–4, 1997. Washington, D.C.: U.S. Department of Commerce, Bureau of the Census. Tables 9 & 14.

States (Table 3). The Pacific Census Division, for example, has the most minority-owned businesses, with concentrations of Latino American, Native American, and Asian American businesses. African American-owned businesses are more heavily concentrated in the South Atlantic region.

The regional distribution of the minority populations is provided in Table 4. Like their businesses, the African American population is heavily concentrated in the South Atlantic region. Latinos and Asian Americans are more heavily concentrated in the Pacific division. Native Americans live and work predominantly in the West South Central, Mountain, and Pacific divisions. A comparison of Table 3 with Table 4 indicates that the overall regional distribution of minority-owned businesses is not equivalent to the regional distribution of the minority population.

TABLE 3
Minority-Owned Businesses, by Census Region and Division: 1992
(Percent)

Region	All U.S. Firms	Total Minority	African American	Hispanic American	Asian/ Other
Census Region					
Northeast	19.8	15.2	16.4	11.9	18.3
Midwest	22.9	9.8	16.3	5.2	8.7
South	33.5	38.5	53.3	40.6	20.4
West	23.8	36.5	14.0	42.3	52.6
Total	100.0	100.0	100.0	100.0	100.0
Census Division					
New England	5.9	2.1	2.3	1.8	2.1
Mid-Atlantic	13.9	13.1	14.1	10.1	16.2
East North Central	15.1	7.9	13.3	4.1	6.9
West North Central	7.8	1.9	3.0	1.1	1.8
South Atlantic	17.1	20.6	32.4	18.8	10.7
East South Central	5.4	3.1	7.9	0.5	1.4
West South Central	11.0	14.8	13.0	21.3	8.3
Mountain	6.4	4.8	1.7	8.2	3.8
Pacific	17.4	31.7	12.3	34.1	48.8
Total	100.0	100.0	100.0	100.0	100.0

Note: Minority-Owned Businesses, by Census Region and Division provides the percentages of minority-owned business enterprises that operate in the various Census regions and divisions.
Source: *1992 Survey of Minority-Owned Business Enterprises*, vol. 4, *Summary* MB92–4, 1997, Washington, D.C.: U.S. Department of Commerce, Bureau of the Census, Tables 2 & 11.

CONCENTRATION QUOTIENTS

The relative business ownership of minority groups is examined through the calculation of concentration quotients for minority-owned businesses. Concentration quotients (CQ) are statistical measures used to identify the relative concentration of businesses in a regional economy. The concentration quotients shown in Tables 5 and 6 utilize specific data on the number of minority-owned businesses in a region and compares this statistic with the minority group's population in the region (in a percentage format).

TABLE 4
Minority Population Distribution, by Census Region and Division: 1990 (Percent)

Region	U.S. Population	African American	Hispanic American	Native American	Asian American
Census Region					
Northeast	20.4	18.7	16.8	6.4	18.4
Midwest	24.0	19.1	7.7	17.3	10.6
South	34.4	52.8	30.3	28.7	15.4
West	21.2	9.4	45.2	47.6	55.6
Total	100.0	100.0	100.0	100.0	100.0
Census Division					
New England	5.3	2.1	2.5	1.7	3.2
Mid-Atlantic	15.1	16.6	14.3	4.7	15.2
East North Central	16.9	16.1	6.4	7.7	7.9
West North Central	7.1	3.0	1.3	9.6	2.7
South Atlantic	17.5	29.8	9.6	8.8	8.7
East South Central	6.1	9.9	0.4	2.1	1.1
West South Central	10.8	13.1	20.3	17.8	5.6
Mountain	5.5	1.2	8.9	24.5	3.0
Pacific	15.7	8.2	36.3	23.1	52.6
Total	100.0	100.0	100.0	100.0	100.0

Note: Minority Population Distribution by Region provides the 1990 Decennial Census depiction of minorities in the various Census regions. The Northeast and Midwest have fewer minorities in their population than the overall distribution of the U.S. population among various states and regions. The South consisting of the South Atlantic, East South Central, and West South Central Divisions are the areas where approximately 52.8 percent of the African American population lives. Hispanic Americans predominate in the South and West with 75.5 percent of Hispanic Americans in these regions. The West has 47.6 percent of the Native American population and 55.6 percent of the Asian American population.
Source: *State and Metropolitan Area Data Book: 1991* Washington, D.C.: U.S. Department of Commerce, Bureau of the Census, Table E, pp. 202–210.

$$CQ = \frac{\text{Minority-Owned Firms in Region}_k \div \text{All Small Firms in Region}_k}{\text{Minority Population in Region}_k \div \text{Total Population in Region}_k}$$

A concentration quotient approximates the business formation and performance per unit of regional population. The general rule is that quotients greater than 100 percent indicate that the level of business success of the minority group is greater than the minority group's proportion in the population; those quotients less than 100 percent denote that minority-owned businesses are less successful or economically viable to the regional economy in relation to their population.

Asian Americans, for example, have been extremely successful in establishing business entities, as shown in Table 5 by the fact that their overall concentration quotient is 94.7 percent. This compares with 29.8 percent for African Americans, and 49.8 percent for Hispanics Americans in 1992. Asian-American business ownership is representative of the Asian-American population in the Mid-Atlantic, South Atlantic, and East South Central divisions. The Hispanic American population is economically viable in the South Atlantic division.

The concentration quotients for sales and receipts of minority-owned businesses are much lower than 100 percent. In aggregate, minority-owned business enterprises underperform economically in their respective regional economies when compared to their populations in these regions, as depicted in Table 6.

INDUSTRIAL DISTRIBUTION OF MINORITY-OWNED BUSINESSES

Significant variation in minority business ownership exists across industries (see Table 7). Hispanic-owned businesses are the more successful in Agriculture and Construction. African American-owned businesses tend to be highly represented in Transportation & Public Utilities and the Service industries. Asian Americans are highly represented in the Wholesale and Retail Trade industries, as well as in Finance, Insurance, and Real Estate.

DESCRIPTIVE STATISTICS ON FIRMS WITH PAID EMPLOYEES

The 1987 and 1992 *Survey of Minority-Owned Business Enterprises, Summary* provided the data necessary to analyze the economic conditions facing minority business ownership. Minority-owned businesses, in these surveys, were very small businesses, with over 95 percent of those business enterprises having fewer than 20 employees (Table 2). Moreover, the number of all small businesses in the U.S. was approximately 17.3 million in 1992 (Table 8). Small businesses also accounted for about $3.3 trillion in gross sales and receipts during this period. Minority-owned businesses comprised 11.4 percent of all U.S. small businesses and garnered 6.1 percent of sales and receipts. The number of

TABLE 5
Concentration Quotients for Minority-Owned Firms, by Census Region and Division (Percent)

Region	Minority Firms	African American	Hispanic American	Asian/ Other
All Regions	57.8	29.8	49.8	94.7
Census Region				
Northeast	50.7	27.0	36.4	113.1
Midwest	38.0	26.8	35.4	72.6
South	56.3	30.9	68.5	108.3
West	72.2	39.6	41.4	82.2
Census Division				
New England	44.9	30.1	32.0	63.5
Mid-Atlantic	53.2	27.4	38.3	128.4
East North Central	39.9	27.6	35.7	93.5
West North Central	35.5	27.3	39.2	38.2
South Atlantic	58.6	33.3	100.1	119.0
East South Central	31.8	26.9	69.7	107.3
West South Central	62.5	28.9	50.9	93.7
Mountain	61.7	35.4	39.0	40.4
Pacific	74.6	40.5	42.2	89.9

Note: Concentration Quotients for Minority-Owned Business Enterprises by Region. The degree that minority-owned businesses are represented in the regional economies of the United States are indicated by the concentration quotients. A concentration quotient is calculated as the ratio of the percentage of minority-owned firms in a region to all small businesses in that region divided by the percentage of the ancestry group in the regional populations.
Sources: *State and Metropolitan Area Data Book: 1991* Washington, D.C.: U.S. Department of Commerce, Bureau of the Census, Table E, pp. 202–210. *1992 Survey of Minority-Owned Business Enierprises* vol. 4, *Summary* MB92–4, 1997. Washington, D.C.: U.S. Department of Commerce, Bureau of the Census. Tables 2 & 11.

minority-owned businesses with paid employees in the United States was 311,695 in 1992; these firms earned about $158.8 billion in gross sales and receipts in 1992 dollars.

Minority-owned firms with paid employees were only 15.9 percent of all minority-owned firms, yet earned 78.6 percent of all sales and receipts. African American businesses with paid employees were 10.4 percent of all African American-owned business enterprises and earned 70.2 percent of all sales and receipts of African American-owned businesses. Similar patterns were exhibited by Hispanic and Asian/Other-owned businesses. Hispanic and Asian/Other business enterprises with paid employ-

TABLE 6
Concentration Quotients for Sales and Receipts, by Census Region and Division (Percent)

Region	Minority Firms	African American	Hispanic American	Asian/ Other
All Regions	30.8	8.0	24.4	80.8
Census Region				
Northeast	23.6	5.8	14.7	36.3
Midwest	21.7	8.2	22.2	49.3
South	27.9	7.6	41.6	71.6
West	48.1	17.7	19.4	57.8
Census Division				
New England	21.2	8.1	12.7	48.3
Mid-Atlantic	24.0	5.5	15.1	90.5
East North Central	22.1	8.2	21.9	93.9
West North Central	19.6	8.1	23.4	37.7
South Atlantic	30.9	8.1	77.0	104.0
East South Central	12.4	6.0	50.4	130.0
West South Central	29.6	7.5	23.5	79.9
Mountain	36.8	15.6	20.6	34.2
Pacific	49.0	17.7	18.9	80.3

Note: Concentration Quotients for Sales and Receipts by Region. The extent to which minority-owned businesses are represented in the regional economies of the United States is calculated. A concentration quotient is the ratio of the percenage of sales receipts of minority-owned firms in a region to receipts of all small businesses in the same region; this proportion is then compared to the percentage of the mmority population in the regional population.
Sources: *State and Metropolitan Area Data Book: 1991* Washington, D.C.: U.S. Department of Commerce, Bureau of the Census, Table E, pp. 202–210. *1992 Survey of Minority-Owned Business Enterprises*, vol. 4, *Summary* MB92–4, 1997. Washington, D.C.: U.S. Department of Commerce, Bureau of the Census, Tables 2 and 11.

ees were 14.9 and 22.5 percent of their respective total number of firms. They, moreover, had sales and receipts of 78.5 percent and 81.3 percent, respectively.

WOMEN-OWNED BUSINESSES

The gender of the minority business owner varied by major ancestry group. The number of women-owned businesses was approximately 717,435 in 1992. Women-owned businesses were 36.5 percent of all minority-owned businesses. Additionally, women proprietors owned 44.7

TABLE 7
Minority-Owned Businesses by Industry Division: 1992 (Percent)

Industry	Minority To All U.S.	Total Minority	African American	Hispanic American	Asian/ Other
Minority-Owned Businesses, All Industries	11.4	100.0	31.6	39.3	30.9
Agriculture and Mining	9.9	100.0	17.9	57.0	26.4
Construction	9.1	100.0	26.1	58.6	17.0
Manufacturing	9.1	100.0	22.2	39.1	40.2
Transportation & Public Utilities	17.0	100.0	41.3	40.2	20.5
Wholesale Trade	8.3	100.0	16.8	39.5	44.7
Retail Trade	13.0	100.0	27.0	33.5	41.1
Finance, Insurance & Real Estate	7.8	100.0	26.9	32.4	42.6
Services	12.0	100.0	35.5	37.0	29.2
Industries, n.e.c.	13.4	100.0	33.2	44.6	24.0
Sales and Receipts All Industries	6.1	100.0	15.9	36.0	49.4
Agriculture and Mining	5.4	100.0	9.8	52.6	39.1
Construction	5.1	100.0	16.8	52.0	32.7
Manufacturing	3.5	100.0	8.4	39.2	53.2
Transportation & Public Utilities	6.4	100.0	30.0	44.5	27.0
Wholesale Trade	5.2	100.0	8.8	37.4	54.5
Retail Trade	7.3	100.0	13.3	33.7	54.7
Finance, Insurance & Real Estate	5.4	100.0	21.8	27.9	51.9
Services	8.0	100.0	23.2	31.8	48.5
Industries, n.e.c.	10.9	100.0	15.9	40.7	38.0

Note: Minority-Owned Businesses by Major Industry Division provides the distribution of minority-owned businesses to all small business enterprises using major industry divisions. Table 10 also indicates the distribution of the number of minority-owned businesses that fall into each major industry classification. In this configution, the distributions do not sum to 100 percent because of the multiple classifications of some minorities.

Source: *1992 Survey of Minority-Owned Business Enterprises*, vol. 4, *Summary* MB92–4, 1997. Washington, D.C.: U.S. Department of Commerce, Bureau of the Census, Tables 1 & 10.

TABLE 8
Minority-Owned Firms, by All Industries: 1992

	Number of Firms	Sales & Receipts [$Millions]	Average Receipts Per Firm	% Δ in Avg Receipts 1987–92
U.S. Small Businesses	17,253,143	$3,324,200	$192,672	19.66%
Minority-Owned Firms[a]	1,965,565	$202,011	$102,775	44.96%
Black-Owned	620,912	$ 32,197	$ 51,854	0.67%
Hispanic-Owned	771,708	$ 72,824	$ 94,367	45.78%
Asian./Other-Owned	606,426	$ 99,710	$164,422	64.62%
Firms with Paid Employees	3,134,959	$2,907,132	$927,327	71.14%
Minority Firms w/Paid Employees[a]	311,695	$158,806	$509,493	102.54%
Black-Owned w/Paid Employees	64,478	$ 22,590	$350,347	94.11%
Hispanic-Owned w/Paid Employees	115,364	$ 57,187	$495,709	109.69%
Asian/Other-Owned w/Paid Employees	136,351	$ 81,084	$594,671	106.68%

Note: Minority-Owned Businesses with Paid Employees compares the number of firms, sales and receipts and average receipts per firm for all firms and firms with paid employees. The percentage change of average receipts per firm in real 1992 dollars is illustrated.
[a] Firms and Sales Receipts of minority-owned firms do not sum to total due to multiple classifications of minority groups.
Source: *1992 Survey of Minority-Owned Business Enterprises*, vol. 4, *Summary* MB92–4, 1997. Washington, D.C.: U.S. Department of Commerce, Bureau of the Census. Tables 1 and 11.

percent of all African American-owned businesses, 31.9 percent of all Hispanic-owned businesses, and 34.4 percent of all Asian American-owned businesses. In terms of sales and receipts, however, women business owners earned only 26.4 percent of all African American sales receipts, 23.6 percent of Hispanic sales and receipts, and 24.9 percent of Asian American sales receipts.

Minority women-owned businesses with paid employees comprised 29.1 percent of minority firms with paid workers. African American women-owned businesses were 32.4 percent of all black-owned businesses with paid employees. Hispanic women owned 26.3 percent of Hispanic-owned enterprises with paid employees, whereas Asian American women-owned businesses were 30.2 percent of all Asian American-owned businesses with paid employees.

PRELIMINARY CONCLUSIONS

African American, Hispanic, and other minority-owned businesses are generally small. The economic profiles of these businesses differ for each specific minority classification. The relative business ownership of minorities with respect to their numbers was introduced using concentration quotients that compared minority businesses with the proportion of the minority group in the total regional population. The concentration quotients revealed that Asian Americans have been successful in establishing business enterprises; however, significant variation in minority business ownership existed across industries. The business performance and viability of women-owned businesses tended to mirror the general business success of their intergroup male counterparts.

The four major minority groups presented in this research were African American (Black), Latino American (Hispanic), Native American, and Asian American. Minorities, within their individual cultures, differ in their regional composition of population, business participation rates, and business performance. Like their businesses, the African American population is concentrated in the South Atlantic region. Latinos and Asian Americans are more heavily concentrated in the Pacific region, and Native Americans live and work predominantly in the West South Central, Mountain, and Pacific regions.

EMPIRICAL MODELS OF BUSINESS PERFORMANCE AND VIABILITY

The primary data source used in this study was the *1987 Characteristics of Business Owners* (CBO) Database of the U.S. Bureau of the Census. A random sample of 88,111 observations of small businesses in the United States was selected. Of these observations, approximately 46,000, or 52 percent, were sole proprietorships (and single-owner subchapter S corporations). An extract file was created of 26,514 individual business owners. A "weight" variable that adjusted for owner survey nonresponse based on the results of the 1987 Economic Censuses was available for use with the CBO database. The weight variable allowed CBO sub-samples to simulate the 1987 Economic Censuses, and adjusted the CBO data to reflect the 14 million small businesses in 1987 (see Tables 9 and 10). It

TABLE 9
Survival Model, Weighted and Unweighted Means

Variable		Number of Business Owners	Weighted Mean	Unweighted Mean
Dependent Variable				
S	Survived	21,142	.719 (.041)	.797 (.003)
SBL	Black Firms which Survived	4,432	.020 (.013)	.167 (.002)
SHI	Hispanic Firms which Survived	4,670	.021 (.013)	.176 (.002)
SAS	Asian/Indian Firms which Survived	4,282	.019 (.013)	.161 (.002)
SWH	Noru-ninority Firms which Survived	7,758	.659 (.043)	.293 (.003)
Independent Variables				
COL	College Graduates	10,780	.394 (.044)	.407 (.003)
EXP	Years of Experience	26,514	14.0 (1.14)	13.4 (.075)
FOUN	Founder	19,606	.815 (.035)	.739 (.003)
FRAN	Franchised	1,399	.032 (.016)	.053 (.001)
HOME	Home-Based Business	9,656	.553 (.045)	.361 (.003)
K	Starting Capital	26,514	$27,463 (11538)	$67,455 (1516)
LOC	Firm located within MSA	20,357	.752 (.039)	.768 (.003)
MGMT	Managerial Experience	12,353	.401 (.045)	.466 (.003)
SEX	Women-Owned Businesses	7,969	.289 (.041)	.301 (.003)
Industry				
IND_1	Construction	2,491	.120 (.030)	.094 (.002)
IND_2	Manufacturing	1,766	.027 (.015)	.067 (.002)
IND_3	Transportation	1,409	.034 (.017)	.053 (.001)
IND_4	Wholesale Trade	2,723	.031 (.016)	.103 (.002)
IND_5	Retail Trade	5,530	.167 (.034)	.209 (.003)
IND_6	Finance, Insurance, Real Estate	1,693	.091 (.026)	.064 (.002)
IND_7	Services	6,244	.367 (.044)	.235 (.003)
IND_8	Personal Services	1,304	.090 (.026)	.049 (.001)

was also assumed that these business owners operated in a competitive environment in which there were a large number of identical entrepreneurs (approximately 14 million firms in 1987 and 17 million firms by 1992), and that outcomes were independent across firms.

RESEARCH DESIGN

The "Survival Models" explored the factors that influenced individual motivation to continue business operations (i.e., to stay self-employed) by using a discrete dependent variable, S, defined as business survival between 1987 and 1991. From an empirical perspective, the decision to terminate or stay in business is not always the owner's to make. Many

TABLE 9 (Continued)
Survival Model, Weighted and Unweighted Means

Variable		Number of Business Owners	Weighted Mean	Unweighted Mean
Age of Firm				
FA_1	Firm Age 1–2 Years	7,823	.390 (.0.44)	.295 (.003)
FA_2	Firm Age 3–9 Years	10,459	.354 (.043)	.394 (.003)
FA_3	Firm Age 10 + Years	8,232	.256 (.040)	.310 (.003)
Census Division				
CR_1	New England	1,951	.065 (.022)	.074 (.002)
CR_2	Mid-Atlantic	2,481	.132 (.031)	.094 (002)
CR_3	East North Central	2,684	.161 (.033)	.101 (.002)
CR_4	West North Central	2,278	.094 (.027)	.086 (.002)
CR_5	South Atlantic	4,961	.165 (.034)	.187 (.002)
CR_6	East South Central	1,596	.050 (.020)	.060 (.001)
CR_7	West South Central	2,867	.099 (.027)	.108 (.002)
CR_8	Mountain	2,631	.062 (.022)	.099 (.002)
CR_9	Pacific	5,065	.172 (.034)	.191 (.002)
Ethnicity				
AS	Asian/Other	5,266	.026 (.015)	.199 (.002)
BL	Black	5,700	.028 (.015)	.215 (.003)
HI	Hispanic	5,943	.030 (.016)	.224 (.003)
WH	White	9,605	.916 (.025)	.362 (.003)

Note: Summary Statistics for the Survival Model: Weighted and Unweighted Means provides the number of business owners in the sample who exhibit various characteristics. In the sample, 21,142 business survived between 1987 and 1991, or approximately 80 percent.
N = 26,514; Numbers in parentheses are standard errors.
Source: Characteristics of Businesses Owners Database. Unpublished data.

exogenous influences also play an important role. This decision-making process can be expressed mathematically as a binary choice variable for survival, S=1 or 0. The binary outcome represents whether the business survived or did not survive. The functional form of the Survival Models, therefore, represents the marginal changes in the prospect of succeeding in business, S, associated with each of the independent variables.[10] All coefficients are evaluated using the standard normal density function and the cumulative normal distribution.

In the Survival Models, the dependent variable is a dichotomous variable, and the independent variables have been logically divided into exogenous and endogenous explanatory variables. Exogenous variables are factors that the individual business owner cannot control, e.g., gender.

TABLE 10
Survival Model Augmented by Selected Variables, Weighted and Unweighted Means by Race/Ethnicity

Variable		Number of Business Owners	Weighted Mean	Un-weighted Mean
Dependent Variable				
S	Survived	21,142	.719	.797
SBL	Black Firms which Survived	4,432	.710	.778
SHI	Hispanic Firms which Survived	4,670	.699	.786
SAS	Asian/Indian Firms which Survived	4,282	.731	.813
SWH	White Firms which Survived	7,758	.719	.808
Augmented Variables				
Interaction (Gender and Race/Ethnicity)				
SEX	Women-Owned Businesses	7,969	.289	.301
SEXBL	Black Women-Owned Businesses	1,753	.348	.308
SEXIII	Hispanic Women-Owned Businesses	1,140	.254	.192
SEXAS	Asian Women-Owned Businesses	1,158	.307	.220
SEXWH	White Women-Owned Businesses	3,918	.288	.408
Interaction (College Graduates and Race/EthnicIry)				
COL	College Graduates	10,780	.394	.407
COLBL	Black College Graduates	2,095	.341	.368
COLHI	Hispanic College Graduates	1,737	.243	.292
COLAS	Asian College Graduates	3,025	.558	.574
COLWH	White College Graduates	3,923	.395	.408
Cumulative Years of Experience				
Interaction (Years of Employment Experience and Race/Ethnicity)				
EXP	Years of Experience	354,347	14.0	13.4
EXPBL	Work Experience for Blacks	83,442	14.2	14.6
EXPHI	Work Experience for Hispanic	76,030	11.6	12.8
EXPAS	Work Experience for Asian/Indian	54,524	9.8	10.4
EXPWH	Work Experience for Whites	140,351	14.2	14.6
Cumulative Dollars of Starting Capital				
Interaction (Real Starting Capital and Race/Ethnicity)				
K	Starting Capital	$1,788m	$27,461	$67,450
KBL	Starting Capital used by Blacks	$236m	$13,247	$41,363
K.HI	Starting Capital used by Hispanics	$245m	$14,361	$41,198
KAS	Starting Capital used by Asians	$416m	$41,271	$78,996
KWH	Starting Capital used by Whites	$892m	$27,918	$92,844

Note: N=26,514. All variables are evaluated within their respective race/ethnicity classification to facilitate intergroup cornparisions.
Source: *1987 Characteristics of Business Owners Dataset*. Unpublished Data.

Endogenous variables, on the other hand, are the factors that go into the decision-making process when a business owner enters into business.

There are approximately 29 dummy variables in the Survival Models. The dummy variables serve an important role in describing spatial effects (where the classes, *CR*, refer to different census regions),[11] industrial effects (where the industrial classes, *IND*, refer to industries), gender differences (*SEX*), and race disparities (*BL, HI, AS,* or *WH*). The variable *COL* was hypothesized to influence business survival; hence, the sample observations have been categorized into those business owners who have completed a college degree program. Other dummy variables include the age of firm, *FA*; founder of the business, *FOUN*; franchised business, *FRAN*; home-based business, *HOME*; location within cities or metropolitan areas, *LOC*; and executive/managerial experience, *MGMT*.[12] In this study, interaction terms were calculated by multiplying a dummy variable by the principal factor. The interaction terms in the augmented Survival Models are the interaction between (1) gender and ethnicity; (2) college graduation and ethnicity; (3) years of work experience and ethnicity; and (4) starting capital and ethnicity.

The Basic Survival Model with augmented gender interaction was estimated using data on 26,514 men and women in the sample of individual business proprietors (Table 11). The dichotomous dependent variable, *S*, identifies the owners' 1991 business performance and viability. The values of all independent variables, however, pertained to the owner's characteristics in the survey year of 1987. The results of linear probability estimation (probit) are summarized in Tables 11 through 14. The interpretation of the coefficients will vary with the values of the parameters and with each individual business owner. In interpreting the coefficients the partial derivatives and the probit estimates are based on "weighted" data.

THE BASIC SURVIVAL MODEL AND SPECIFICATIONS

The Survival Models classify the factors that influence business performance and viability by estimating variables that have empirically led to business survival or discontinuance. The basic functional form (the "Basic Model") assumes that the population of all small businesses in the United States have the following common characteristics:

TABLE 11
Basic Survival Model Augmented by Gender: Probit Estimates

Variable		Regression Coefficient	Standard Error	Chi-Square	t-value
	Dependent Variable: S – Business Survival (between 1987 and 1991)				
Intercept	(Constant term)	0.543	0.0038	20,428	142.94
K	(Starting Capital)	0.050	0.0003	32,514	180.09
COL	(Bachelor's degree or greater)	0.247	0.0013	37,066	192.56
IND_1	(Construction)	0.263	0.0027	9,388	96.91
IND_2	(Manufacturing)	0.293	0.0044	4,501	67.09
IND_3	(Transportation, Publ. Utilities)	–0.185	0.0036	2,651	51.50
IND_4	(Wholesale Trade)	–0.169	0.0038	2,007	44.80
IND_5	(Retail Trade)	0.103	0.0026	1,626	40.32
IND_6	(Finance, Ins., Real Estate)	0.091	0.0029	1,015	31.85
IND_7	(Selected Services)	0.023	0.0023	102	10.09
IND_8	(Personal Services)	0.214	0.0029	5,485	74.05
MGMT	(Managerial Experience)	0.144	0.0013	12,419	111.43
EXP	(Years of Work Experience)	0.062	0.0005	15,507	124.55
LOC	(within MSA)	–0.014	0.0014	98	9.91
FA_1	(Firm 1–2 years or older)	–0.736	0.0015	226,385	475.82
FA_2	(Firm 3–9 years or older)	–0.157	0.0016	9,349	96.68
HOME	(Home-Based Business)	–0.060	0.0013	2,150	46.36
FOUN	(Founder of Business)	0.133	0.0016	7,122	84.38
FRAN	(Franchised Business)	–0.279	0.0032	7,622	87.29
SEX	(Women-Owned Businesses)	–0.035	0.0014	642	25.34
SEXBL	(Black Women Businesses)	–0.079	0.0073	116	10.78
SEXHI	(Hispanic Women Businesses)	0.030	0.0076	16	4.01
SEXAS	(Asian Women Businesses)	–0.082	0.0077	113	10.62
BL	(Black)	0.058	0.0044	175	13.25
HI	(Hispanic)	0.046	0.0039	141	11.87
AS	(Asian/Other)	0.054	0.0044	151	12.27
CR_2	(Mid-Atlantic)	0.215	0.0029	5,646	75.15
CR_3	(East North Central)	–0.096	0.0027	1,294	35.97
CR_4	(West North Central)	–0.117	0.0029	1,566	39.57
CR_5	(South Atlantic)	–0.083	0.0027	952	30.86
CR_6	(East South Central)	0.104	0.0035	858	29.29
CR_7	(West South Central)	–0.152	0.0029	2,760	52.55
CR_8	(Mountain)	–0.173	0.0032	2,920	54.04
CR_9	(Pacific)	–0.010	0.0027	15	3.81
–2 Log Likelihood for Normal Distribution		3,142,389			

Note: The Basic Survival Model: Results provides a summary of the relationship between minorities and small businesses owned by non-minoriry business owners. These data also compare businesses in the nine Census Divisions to the New England region; males to females; and younger firms to older firms.
n = 26,514 observations.
All results are in comparison to non-minority business owners.
Source: Characteristics of Businesses Owners Database. Unpublished data.

TABLE 12
Survival Model Augmented by Formal Education: Probit Estimates

Variable		Regression Coefficient	Standard Error	Chi-Square	t-value
	Dependent Variable: S – Business Survival (between 1987 and 1991)				
Intercept	(Constant term)	0.537	0.0038	19,982	141.36
K	(Starting Capital)	0.050	0.0003	32,651	180.51
COL	(Bachelor's degree or greater)	0.258	0.0013	37,338	193.24
COLBL	(Black College Graduate)	–0.085	0,0074	129	11.38
COLHI	(Hispanic College Graduate)	–0,153	0.0078	384	19.59
COLAS	(Asian College Graduate)	–0.153	0.0072	445	21.09
IND_1	(Construction)	0.265	0.0027	9,473	97.33
IND_2	(Manufacturing)	0.294	0.0044	4,525	67.27
IND_3	(Transportation, Publ. Utilities)	–0.185	0.0036	2,652	51.50
IND_4	(Wholesale Trade)	–0.168	0.0038	1,996	44.68
IND_5	(Retail Trade)	0.103	0.0026	1,622	40.27
IND_6	(Finance, Ins., Real Estate)	0.093	0.0029	1,052	32.42
IND_7	(Selected Services)	0.024	0.0023	111	10.52
IND_8	(Personal Services)	0.214	0.0029	5,502	74.18
MGMT	(Managerial Experience)	0.145	0.0013	12,512	111.87
EXP	(Years of Work Experience)	0.062	0.0005	15,497	124.52
LOC	(within MSA)	–0.015	0.0014	110	10.50
FA_1	(Firm 1–2 years or older)	–0.735	0.0015	225,956	475.49
FA_2	(Firm 3–9 years or older)	–0.157	0.0016	9,355	96.72
HOME	(Home-Based Business)	–0.059	0.0013	2,088	46.69
FOUN	(Founder of Business)	0.132	0.0016	7,072	84.09
FRAN	(Franchised Business)	–0.277	0.0032	7,539	86.82
SEX	(Women-Owned Businesses)	–0.035	0.0014	633	25.14
SEXBL	(Black Women Businesses)	–0.074	0.0073	102	10.09
SEXHI	(Hispanic Women Businesses)	0.036	0.0076	22	4.74
SEXAS	(Asian Women Businesses)	–0.078	0.0077	103	10.15
BL	(Black)	0.085	0.0049	292	17.09
HI	(Hispanic)	0.083	0.0043	368	19.19
AS	(Asian/Other)	0.135	0.0059	523	22.86
CR_2	(Mid-Atlantic)	0.217	0.0029	5,731	75.69
CR_3	(East North Central)	–0.095	0.0027	1,265	35.56
CR_4	(West North Central)	–0.115	0.0029	1,533	39.16
CR_5	(South Atlantic)	–0.082	0.0027	930	30.50
CR_6,	(East South Central)	0.104	0.0035	870	29.50
CR_7	(West South Central)	–0.153	0.0029	2,767	52.60
CR_8	(Mountain)	–0.174	0.0032	2,931	54.13
CR_9	(Pacific)	–0.010	0.0027	15	3.86
–2 Log Likelihood for Normal Distribution		3,141,935			

Note: The Basic Survival Model Augmented by Formal Education: Results provides a summary of the relationship between minorities and small businesses owned by non-minority business owners. These data also compare businesses in the nine Census Divisions and the effects of college education on business survival.
n = 26,514 observations.
All results are in comparison to non-minority business owners.
Source: Characteristics of Businesses Owners Database. Unpublished data.

TABLE 13
Survival Model Augmented by Years of Employment Experience: Probit Estimates

Variable		Regression Coefficient	Standard Error	Chi-Square	t-value
	Dependent Variable: S – Business Survival (between 1987 and 1991)				
Intercept	(Constant term)	0.539	0.0038	19.981	141.36
K	log(Starting Capital)	0.050	0.0003	32.448	179.94
COL	(Bachelor's degree or greater)	0.248	0.0013	37.122	192.72
IND_1	(Construction)	0.264	0.0027	9.434	97.13
IND_2	(Manufacturing)	0.294	0.0044	4.515	67.19
IND_3	(Transportation. Publ. Utilities)	–0.185	0.0036	2.647	51.45
IND_4	(Wholesale Trade)	–0.169	0.0038	2.002	44.74
IND_5	(Retail Trade)	0.103	0.0026	1.631	40.38
IND_6	(Finance. Ins.. Real Estate)	0.091	0.0029	1.012	31.80
IND_7	(Selected Services)	0.024	0.0023	104	10.18
IND_8	(Personal Services)	0.215	0.0029	5.533	74.38
MGMT	(Managerial Experience)	0.144	0.0013	12.401	111.37
EXP	(Years of Work Experience)	0.064	0.0005	15.056	122.68
EXPBL	(Black Work Experience)	–0.011	0.0028	14	3.80
EXPHI	(Hispanic Work Experience)	–0.029	0.0026	121	10.99
EXPAS	(Asian/Other Work Experience)	–0.021	0.0029	52	7.19
LOC	(within MSA)	–0.014	0.0014	101	10.04
FA_1	(Firm 1–2 years or older)	–0.736	0.0015	226.537	475.93
FA_2	(Firm 3–9 years or older)	–0.157	0.0016	9.395	96.94
HOME	(Home-Based Business)	–0.060	0.0013	2.144	46.29
FOUN	(Founder of Business)	0.133	0.0016	7.146	84.53
FRAN	(Franchised Business)	–0.278	0.0032	7.589	87.11
SEX	(Women-Owned Businesses)	–0.035	0.0014	630	25.09
SEXBL	(Black Women Businesses)	–0.080	0.0073	120	10.98
SEXHI	(Hispanic Women Businesses)	0.026	0.0076	12	3.41
SEXAS	(Asian Women Businesses)	–0.082	0.0077	112	10.59
BL	(Black)	0.080	0.0072	123	11.09
HI	(Hispanic)	0.099	0.0062	258	16.05
AS	(Asian/Other)	0.098	0.0064	190	13.79
CR_1	(Mid-Atlantic)	0.215	0.0029	5.655	75.21
CR_2	(East North Central)	–0.096	0.0027	1.290	35.91
CR_3	(West North Central)	–0.116	0.0029	1.563	39.54
CR_4	(South Atlantic)	–0.083	0.0027	954	30.89
CR_5	(East South Central)	0.103	0.0035	852	29.19
CR_6	(West South Central)	–0.152	0.0029	2.757	52.52
CR_7	(Mountain)	–0.174	0.0032	2.921	54.06
CR_8	(Pacific)	–0.010	0.0027	14	3.74
–2 Log Likelihood for Normal Distribution		3,142,300			

Note: The Basic Survival Model Augmented by Work Experience: Results provides a summary of the relationship between minorities and small businesses owned by non-minority business owners. These data also compare businesses, in the nine Census Divisions and the effects of work experience on business survival.
n = 26,514 observations.
All results are in comparison to non-minority business owners.
Source: Characteristics of Businesses Owners Database. Unpublished data.

TABLE 14
Survival Model Augmented by Starting Capital: Probit Estimates

Variable		Regression Coefficient	Standard Error	Chi-Square	t-value
Dependent Variable: S – Business Survival (between 1987 and 1991)					
Intercept	(Constant term)	0.542	0.0038	20.332	142.57
K	(Starting Capital)	0.051	0.0003	31.087	176.03
K'BL	(Starting Capital-Black)	–0.006	0.0017	14	3.71
K'HI	(Starting Capital-Hispanic)	–0.007	0.0016	22	6.68
K'AS	(Starting Capital-Asian/Other)	–0.010	0.0016	44	6.66
COL	(Bachelor's degree or greater)	0.248	0.0013	37.085	192.62
IND_1	(Construction)	0.264	0.0027	9.413	97.02
IND_2	(Manufacturing)	0.293	0.0044	4.503	67.11
IND_3	(Transportation. Publ. Utilities)	–0.185	0.0036	2.649	51.47
IND_4	(Wholesale Trade)	–0.169	0.0038	2.001	44.73
IND_5	(Retail Trade)	0.104	0.0026	1.641	40.51
IND_6	(Finance. Ins.. Real Estate)	0.092	0.0029	1.022	31.96
IND_7	(Selected Services)	0.024	0.0023	104	10.19
IND_8	(Personal Services)	0.214	0.0029	5.494	74.12
MGMT	(Managerial Experience)	0.144	0.0013	12.389	111.31
EXP	(Years of Work Experience)	0.062	0.0005	15.484	124.47
LOC	(within MSA)	–0.014	0.0014	96	9.82
FA_1	(Firm 1–2 years or older)	–0.735	0.0015	226.241	475.71
FA_2	(Firm 3–9 years or older)	–0.157	0.0016	9.331	96.60
HOME	(Home-Based Business)	–0.060	0.0013	2.136	46.22
FOUN	(Founder of Business)	0.133	0.0016	7.093	84.21
FRAN	(Franchised Business)	–0.279	0.0032	7.622	87.30
SEX	(Women-Owned Businesses)	–0.035	0.0014	625	25.02
SEXBL	(Black Women Businesses)	–0.081	0.0073	123	11.10
SEXHI	(Hispanic Women Businesses)	0.027	0.0076	12	3.51
SEXAS	(Asian Women Businesses)	–0.088	0.0078	130	11.39
BL	(Black)	0.063	0.0046	190	13.79
HI	(Eispanic)	0.053	0.0041	163	12.71
AS	(Asian/OLher)	0.074	0.0054	191	13.82
CR_1	(Mid-Atlantic)	0.215	0.0029	5.638	75.10
CR_2	(East North Central)	–0.096	0.0027	1.294	35.98
CR_3	(West North Central)	–0.117	0.0029	1.567	39.59
CR_4	(South Atlantic)	–0.083	0.0027	952	30.94
CR_5	(East South Central)	0.103	0.0035	852	29.19
CR_6	(West South Central)	–0.153	0.0029	2.767	52.59
CR_7	(Mountain)	–0.174	0.0032	2.931	54.14
CR_8	(Pacific)	–0.010	0.0027	14	3.76
–2 Log Likelihood for Normal Distribution		3,142,351			

Note: The Basic Survival Model Augmented by Starting Capital: Results provides a summary of the relationship between minorities and small businesses owned by non-minority business owners. These data also compare businesses in the nine Census Divisions and the effects of initial financial capitalization on business survival.
n = 26,514 observations.
All results are in comparison to non-minority business owners.
Source: Characteristics of Businesses Owners Database. Unpublished data.

Let,

$$Basic\ Model = c_0 + c_1AS_i + c_2BL_i + c_3COL_i + c_4CR_i + c_5EXP_i + c_6FA_i + c_7FOUN_i + c_8FRAN_i + c_9HI_i + c_{10}HOME_i + c_{11}IND_i + c_{12}K_i + c_{13}LOC_i + c_{14}MGMT_i + c_{15}SEX_i$$

where i denotes the ith business owner, i = (1,...,n) and c_0 through c_n denote the values of the weighted coefficients.

AS = Asian American-Owned Business
BL = Black-Owned Business
COL = College Graduate
CR = Census Regional Division
EXP = Years of Employment Experience
FA = Age of Firm
FOUN = Original Founder of Business?
FRAN = Franchised Business?
HI = Hispanic-Owned Business
HOME = Home-Based Business
IND = Non-Agricultural Industry of Business Operations
K = Starting Capital in 1987 Dollars
LOC = Location of Business within an MSA?
MGMT = Prior Managerial Experience?
SEX = Gender of Owner

Four versions of the Survival Model were specified: (1) the Basic Model augmented by gender; (2) the Basic Model augmented by interaction terms computing the number in each minority classification that have completed a baccalaureate (college) education; (3) the Basic Model augmented by interaction terms showing the relationship between prior work experience and ethnicity; and (4) the Basic Model augmented by the interaction between starting capital and ethnicity. These four versions were estimated by expanding the basic functional form to include the ethnicity variables of African American (Black), Hispanic/Latino American (Hispanic), and Asian or Native Americans (Asian/Other), with respect to the Nonminority (White) population of small business owners. The augmented Survival Models are as follows:

(i) Basic Model augmented by gender:

$$S_i = Basic\ Model + c_{16}(SEX_i \cdot WH_i) + c_{17}(SEX_i \cdot BL_i) + c_{18}(SEX_i \cdot HI_i) + c_{19}(SEX_i \cdot AS_i) + e_i$$

(ii) Basic Model augmented by formal education:

$$S_i = Basic\ Model + c_{16}(COL_i{\cdot}WH_i) + c_{17}(COL_i{\cdot}BL_i) + c_{18}(COL_i{\cdot}HI_i) + c_{19}(COL_i{\cdot}AS_i) + e_i$$

(iii) Basic Model augmented by years of employment experience:

$$S_i = Basic\ Model + c_{16}(EXP_i{\cdot}WH_i) + c_{17}(EXP_i{\cdot}BL_i) + c_{18}(EXP_i{\cdot}HI_i) + c_{19}(EXP_i{\cdot}AS_i) + e_i$$

(iv) Basic Model augmented by starting capital:

$$S_i = Basic\ Model + c_{16}(K_i{\cdot}BL_i) + c_{17}(K_i{\cdot}HI_i) + c_{18}(K_i{\cdot}AS_i) + c_{19}(K_i{\cdot}WH_i) + e_i$$

Variable Definitions for Basic Survival Model

COL = { 1 if owner completed a college degree or greater; 0 otherwise.

CR is a series of dummy variables denoting the nine Census Regional Divisions:

CR_1 = { 1 if firm is located in New England; 0 otherwise.

CR_2 = { 1 if firm is located in the Mid-Atlantic; 0 otherwise.

CR_3 = { 1 if firm is located in the East North Central; 0 otherwise.

CR_4 = { 1 if firm is located in the West North Central; 0 otherwise.

CR_5 = { 1 if firm is located in the South Atlantic; 0 otherwise.

CR_6 = { 1 if firm is located in the East South Central; 0 otherwise.

CR_7 = { 1 if firm is located in the West South Central; 0 otherwise.

CR_8 = { 1 if firm is located in the Mountain Region; 0 otherwise.

CR_9 = { 1 if firm is located in the Pacific Region; 0 otherwise.

ETHNICITY is a series of dummy variables denoting the race or ethnicity of owner:

$AS = \begin{cases} 1 \text{ if the firm is owned by an Asian or Native American;} \\ 0 \text{ otherwise.} \end{cases}$

$BL = \begin{cases} 1 \text{ if the firm is owned by an African American (Black);} \\ 0 \text{ otherwise.} \end{cases}$

$HI = \begin{cases} 1 \text{ if the firm is owned by a Hispanic/Latino;} \\ 0 \text{ otherwise.} \end{cases}$

$WH = \begin{cases} 1 \text{ if the firm is owned by a White (Non-minority);} \\ 0 \text{ otherwise.} \end{cases}$

EXP = ln(owners' work experience in years).

FA is a series of dummy variables denoting the age of the firm in years:

$FA_1 = \begin{cases} 1 \text{ if firm is 1 to 2 years old;} \\ 0 \text{ otherwise.} \end{cases}$

$FA_2 = \begin{cases} 1 \text{ if firm is 3 to 9 years old;} \\ 0 \text{ otherwise.} \end{cases}$

$FA_3 = \begin{cases} 1 \text{ if firm is more than 10 + years old;} \\ 0 \text{ otherwise.} \end{cases}$

$FOUN = \begin{cases} 1 \text{ if owner of firm was original founder;} \\ 0 \text{ otherwise.} \end{cases}$

$FRAN = \begin{cases} 1 \text{ if owner of firm is a franchisee;} \\ 0 \text{ otherwise.} \end{cases}$

$HOME = \begin{cases} 1 \text{ if business is home-based;} \\ 0 \text{ otherwise.} \end{cases}$

IND is a series of dummy variables denoting nonagricultural industries:

$IND_1 = \begin{cases} 1 \text{ if firm is in the Construction Industry;} \\ 0 \text{ otherwise.} \end{cases}$

$IND_2 = \begin{cases} 1 \text{ if firm is in the Manufacturing Industry;} \\ 0 \text{ otherwise.} \end{cases}$

$IND_3 = \begin{cases} 1 \text{ if firm is in Transportation and Public Utilities Industry;} \\ 0 \text{ otherwise.} \end{cases}$

$IND_4 = \begin{cases} 1 \text{ if firm is in the Wholesale Trade Industry;} \\ 0 \text{ otherwise.} \end{cases}$

$IND_5 = \begin{cases} 1 \text{ if firm is in the Retail Trade Industry;} \\ 0 \text{ otherwise.} \end{cases}$

$IND_6 =$ { 1 if firm is in Finance, Insurance, & Real Estate Industry; 0 otherwise.

$IND_7 =$ { 1 if firm is in the Services Industry (excl. Personal Services); 0 otherwise.

$IND_8 =$ { 1 if firm is in the Personal Services Industry; 0 otherwise.

K =ln(real starting capital used in business formation in 1987 dollars).

$LOC =$ { 1 if firm is located within an MSA; 0 otherwise.

$MGMT =$ { 1 if owner was previously a manager, executive, or supervisor; 0 otherwise.

$S =$ { 1 if business survived under same owner between 1987 & 1991; 0 otherwise.

$SEX =$ { 1 if firm is woman owned; 0 otherwise (i.e., male-owned).

Estimated Models

(i) Definition of augmented variables in gender model:

SEX = { 1 if the firm is owned by a woman; 0 otherwise.

$SEX{\cdot}BL =$ { 1 if owner is an African American (Black) woman; 0 otherwise.

$SEX{\cdot}HI =$ { 1 if owner is a Hispanic/Latino woman; 0 otherwise.

$SEX{\cdot}AS =$ { 1 if owner is an Asian or Native American woman; 0 otherwise.

$SEX{\cdot}WH =$ { 1 if owner is a White (Non-minority) woman; 0 otherwise.

(ii) Definition of augmented variables in formal education model:

$COL =$ { 1 if owner completed a college degree or greater; 0 otherwise.

$COL{\cdot}BL =$ { 1 if the owner is an African American (Black) college graduate; 0 otherwise.

$COL{\cdot}HI =$ { 1 if the owner is a Hispanic/Latino college graduate; 0 otherwise.

$COL{\cdot}AS =$ { 1 if the owner is an Asian or Native American college graduate; 0 otherwise.

$COL{\cdot}WH =$ { 1 if the owner is a White (Non-minority) college graduate; 0 otherwise.

(iii) Definition of augmented variables in employment experience model:
EXP = ln(owner's prior work experience in years).

$EXP{\cdot}BL =$ { ln(owner's years of work experience if an African American); 0 otherwise.

$EXP{\cdot}HI =$ { ln(owner's years of work experience if a Hispanic/Latino); 0 otherwise.

$EXP{\cdot}AS =$ { ln(owner's years of work experience if an Asian/Native American); 0 otherwise.

$EXP{\cdot}WH =$ { ln(owner's years of work experience if a White (Non-minority)); 0 otherwise.

(iv) Definition of augmented variables in starting capital model:
K = ln(starting capital used in business formation in 1987 dollars).

$K{\cdot}BL =$ { ln(starting capital used in business formation if African American); 0 otherwise.

$K{\cdot}HP =$ { ln(starting capital used in business formation if Hispanic/Latino); 0 otherwise.

$K{\cdot}AS =$ { ln(starting capital used in business formation if Asian/Native American); 0 otherwise.

$K{\cdot}WH =$ { ln(starting capital used in business formation if White (Non-minority)); 0 otherwise.

RESULTS

The data sources used in this study are the 1987 and 1992 *Characteristics of Business Owners* database and summary reports. An extract file was created of 26,514 survey responses of sole proprietors and individual owners of subchapter S corporations (IRS Form 1065 or 1120S). Summary statistics (i.e., means and standard errors) for the Survival Models are provided in Tables 9 and 10. The unweighted means provide data on the average of all 26,514 observations, whereas the weighted values can be interpreted as providing information on the population of 14 million small businesses surveyed in the 1987 Economic Census. All dummy variables can be interpreted as the proportion of the sample exhibiting that characteristic. The continuous variables are interpreted in their specified units of measurement.

Human Capital Input as a Catalyst to Business Survival

The relative differences between the economic survival of African American, Hispanic, Asian/Other, and Non-minority businesses were initially introduced as a linear probability model with gender and college education interacting with ethnicity. The effects of these factors on the survival of women-owned businesses is negative—that is, the expected survival rate is lower for women than for men Table 11. When viewing the interaction between ethnicity and gender, only Hispanic women-owned businesses appear to survive longer with increases in formal education as compared to Nonminority women-owned businesses. This is despite the fact that the effects of formal education on business survival are positive and significant.

To test the research question: are the returns to a college education greater for minority business owners than for non-minority business owners?, the Basic Survival Model augmented by formal education interaction was estimated. The specification and results of a linear probability (probit) model of business survival with formal education interaction terms are illustrated in Table 12.

In Table 12, a majority of the signs of the parameter estimates are as hypothesized, based upon prior literature of minority business ownership. By viewing the chi-square statistics in Table 19, it appears that formal education has less impact on the business performance and viability of minority-owned businesses than on non-minority small businesses. Years of work experience, however, enhanced the survivability of single-owner businesses. Furthermore, starting capital is important for all small businesses, regardless of ownership, because it can serve as a way to enhance cash flows during the introduction and growth phases of the business's life cycle. From Table 12, it can be deduced that the most important determinant of business survival is the age of the firm (*FA*). The Firm Age variable indicated that younger firms have a lower probability of survival.

Owners' Prior Experience as an Indicator of Future Business Survival

We have previously hypothesized that business survival may, in addition to formal education, be related positively to the number of years of work experience. The relative survival rates of African American, Hispanic, Asian/Other, and Non-minority businesses were tested using a linear probability model with gender and work experience interacting with ethnicity. Table 13 indicates that the effects of years of employment experience on business survival are positive and significant.

The average years of work experience of the 26,514 business owners surveyed are: 14.2 years for African American business owners; 11.6 years for Latino/Hispanic proprietors; 9.8 years for Asian/Other business owners; and 14.2 years for White entrepreneurs. Overall, the positive effects of years of work experience are slightly lower for minority business owners compared to their non-minority counterparts. This may reflect a secondary labor market in minority communities. This phenomenon could imply that prior work experience may have little relationship to the self-employment line of business.

Table 13 uses the dichotomous dependent variable, S, which identifies the owners' 1991 business performance and viability. The values of all independent variables, however, pertain to the individual owner's characteristics in the survey year of 1987. The empirical results are shown in Table 13, indicating a positive coefficient on years of work experience and business survival. Note that founders of businesses, when controlling for years of work experience, tend to survive longer than those who were not the original owners of their businesses. Note also that previous managerial, executive, or supervisory experience is positively related to firm survival.

Financial Capitalization as an Indicator of Future Business Survival

Many individuals seeking self-employment often do not fully understand the necessity of a financial cushion to protect their fledgling businesses. Prior research has suggested that it is the low initial capitalization that inhibits future growth of minority-owned businesses. For those individuals seeking business ownership, starting capital may reduce the need to return to wage-and-salary employment, which in turn may reduce the overall business dissolution rate of minority-owned businesses.

It was previously hypothesized that business survival is high in industries where starting capital requirements are low; and when capital requirements are low, there are no barriers to entry into certain lines of business. The relative differences between the economic survival of African American, Hispanic, Asian/Other, and Non-minority businesses are introduced in Table 14 as a linear probability (probit) model with gender and starting capital interacting with race and ethnicity. The conjectured influence of this argument upon the survival of women-owned businesses is negative, due to their reduced number of years in the labor force prior to business ownership and to their reduced ability to obtain commercial credit for business ventures. In Table 14, the impact of the utilization of starting capital is indeterminate for the various minority groups of *BL, HI, and AS*; however, most theoretical literature posited a positive and strong relationship between starting capital and business survival regardless of ethnicity.

The *K* variable is derived from business owners' starting capital. The weighted and unweighted means vary significantly by ethnicity and gender. The average financial capital of the business owners surveyed in the CBO extract file revealed weighted starting capital values of $13,247 for African American business owners; $14,361 for Hispanic proprietors; $41,271 for Asian business owners; and $27,918 for White (Non-minority) entrepreneurs (Table 10). Note that the unweighted means for starting capital differ significantly, suggesting some sample selection bias.

The empirical results exhibit a negative coefficient on the interaction between starting capital and each minority group, indicating that minorities have less access to credit and, thus, business survival is lower than for Whites. Note that home-based businesses which are usually started with little or no capital are likely to lead to voluntary business dissolution.

PROBABILITY ESTIMATES

Probability estimates were calculated from the coefficients on the weighted Survival Models (Tables 11–14) to analyze the probability of business survival based on varying amounts of initial financial capital. By using the tools of the cumulative normal density function, the standard normal distribution, and Z-tables, an analysis was conducted based on industry averages and the regional distribution of the four major groups under study: Black (African American), Hispanic (Latino), Asian/Other (Native American or Asian American), and White (Non-minority).

As shown in Table 15, the average probability of survival for firms in this study was approximately 70 percent. The estimated probability of survival differed, however, for each racial and ethnic group, and by industry and region. When controlling for exogenous factors and the amount and sources of starting capital, business survival of minority-owned businesses tended to be lower than for non-minority-owned businesses. The probability of survival increased rapidly up to the mean value of starting capital for each group, and then continued to increase at a decreasing rate.

TABLE 15
Probability of Business Survival by Race and Ethnicity: Evaluation of Probit Estimates for the Normal Distribution (Percent)

Starting Capital	African American	Hispanic American	Asian/ Other	Non-Minority
(Basic Survival Model Augmented by Gender)				
Model Probabilities	70.2	69.2	72.9	71.9
K = 0	65.5	66.6	66.3	59.1
K = $1,000	77.3	77.9	77.9	71.9
K = $5,000	79.7	80.2	80.2	74.5
K = $25,000	81.9	83.4	83.2	77.0
K = $50,000	82.6	83.4	83.2	78.2
(Basic Survival Model Augmented by Formal Education)				
Model Probabilities	69.2	68.8	69.9	71.9
K = 0	64.4	65.2	56.8	59.1
K = $1,000	76.1	76.7	69.9	71.9
K = $5,000	78.5	79.1	72.6	74.5
K = $25,000	80.8	81.3	75.2	77.0
K = $50,000	81.9	82.4	76.1	78.2
(Basic Survival Model Augmented by Years of Employment Experience)				
Model Probabilities	69.2	66.3	70.9	71.9
K = 0	64.4	63.7	64.4	59.1
K = $1,000	76.4	75.8	76.1	71.9
K = $5,000	78.8	78.5	78.5	74.5
K = $25,000	81.1	80.5	80.8	77.0
K = $50,000	81.9	81.3	81.9	78.2
(Basic Survival Model Augmented by Starting Capital)				
Model Probabilities	69.9	68.1	71.6	71.9
K = 0	64.4	65.5	76.7	59.1
K = $1,000	76.1	77.3	76.7	71.9
K = $5,000	79.1	79.7	79.4	74.5
K = $25,000	81.3	81.9	81.6	77.0
K = $50,000	82.1	82.9	82.4	78.2

Note: Probability of Business Survival by Race and Ethnicity provides a summary measure of the business survival rates based on varying degrees of initial capitalization at business formation.
All probabilities in percentages. Mean starting capital and years of work experience were used to evaluate the probabilities for non-minorities. Years of work experience were kept constant allowing only capital to vary.
Source: Characteristics of Businesses Owners Database. Unpublished data.

SUMMARY

This research study investigated empirical evidence on business survival and the choices that business proprietors face when determining continuity or dissolution. The Survival Models used a dichotomous dependent variable, *S*, which is a decision to remain in business or to terminate business operations. In this non-experimental setting, we used the relative frequency approach to estimate the underlying probabilities. Dummy variables and interaction terms were also included in the Survival Models.

The characteristics of business owners were described by the explanatory variables. Probit analysis was selected for the microdata specification because the micromodels used a discrete dependent variable, *S*. The underlying probability function assumed that the estimators were normal rather than logistic. The results of the analysis indicated the most significant contributors to business survival to be the age of the firm, formal education, starting capital, and random exogenous factors.

The racial or ethnic characteristics of the business owners were used as control variables in the Survival Models. The estimated models omitted non-minority-owned businesses to guard against the "dummy variable trap," i.e., singularity.[13] The resulting probabilities that were estimated from models illustrated in Tables 11 through 14 revealed an approximate 70 percent survival rate among the firms in this study; however, individual rates of probability varied between about 55 percent and 85 percent.

CONCLUDING REMARKS

The 1987 CBO survey instrument permitted an investigation of factors influencing small and minority-owned business ownership and viability. The estimated linear probability models of business survival revealed a 70 percent survival rate for minorities among the single-owner firms in this research study and 81 percent for non-minorities; however, the overall probability of survival of a minority-owned business if compared with all small businesses in the United States is only approximately 2 percent.

The findings revealed that the probability of minority business survival is increased with the number of years of formal education to some threshold. After that point, there are many unexplained factors that influence individual success and business performance. In sum, there is much volatility in the minority business community that cannot be explained by the characteristics of the business owner exclusively.

The probability of minority business survival was increased with the greater work experience of the owner. Many have cited obstacles to obtaining the work experience necessary to enter into business. Yet most self-employed business owners were able to compete within their own ethnic markets and business communities by having comparable within-group characteristics.

In an evaluation of the probability of survival based on the Survival Models, the results revealed that capital-intensive industries such as manufacturing and wholesale trade have lower probabilities of survival, while labor-intensive firms in the services and personal services industries require little or no starting capital and have a moderate probability of survival (between 70 and 82 percent for all groups). Minority business survival was increased with the utilization of commercial bank financing to enter into business. A related finding was that there is a slightly higher rate of survival for individuals who use a mix of debt and equity capital in business formation.

One of the greatest determinants of business survival, however, has been the length of business ownership. In essence, the longer an entrepreneur owns a business, the stronger and more viable it will become based on "life cycle" principles.

Hence, the results revealed that minority business owners have lower accessibility to commercial bank credit than their non-minority counterparts. An analysis of the utilization of commercial bank loans within minority groupings revealed that 46.6 percent of African American business owners, 38.7 percent of Hispanic proprietors, 33.4 percent of Asian American business owners, and 55.4 percent of White (Non-minority) business proprietors used commercial bank loans as sources of capital to form new businesses.

Although this research study addressed specifically what sources of equity capital were used in the formation of business enterprises, it can be concluded that higher-income households have greater access to debt capital (with women, African Americans, and Hispanics being the exceptions).

This research effort has concluded that business survival increased as debt to equity increased to some threshold level (which in this study was 65 percent of total capitalization), and that access to commercial sources of capital increased the likelihood of business survival. The type of debt capital was also significant. The relationship between choosing a commercial bank loan, or refinancing a home, to enter into business operations, moreover, had differential effects on business performance and viability.

NOTES

1. Limited educational opportunities, per se, do not hinder an individual from seeking self-employment. In fact, many business owners are self-employed because they were unable to be trained for a higher-paying wage-and-salary occupation or trade. Vocational and educational opportunities, however, have restricted the size and number of minority-owned businesses, which have traditionally been concentrated in the personal services industry and in retail trade.
2. Stevens, Richard L. 1984. "Measuring Minority Business Formation and Failure." *Review of Black Political Economy* 12(4): 71–84.
3. Bracker, Jeffrey S., Barbara W. Keats, and John N. Pearson. 1988. "Planning and Financial Performance Among Small Firms in a Growth Industry." *Strategic Management Journal* 9(4): 591–603.
4. Data for these measures were taken from the 1987 CBO database provided by the U.S. Bureau of the Census.
5. Brigham, Eugene F. and Louis C. Gapenski. 1983. *Fundamentals of Financial Management.* 3rd ed. (New York: The Dryden Press): Business failure has been defined in the following manner: Business failure is the termination of the business because of insolvency and the loss to creditors. Economic failure is when sales and receipts do not cover the true costs of doing business. Technical failure is when the business cannot meet its obligations to creditors when they become due. And legal failure is when courts of law require the business to liquidate, merge, or reorganize.
6. Because of the existence of confidential identifiers the CBO database is not directly accessible for public use and is not available on CD-ROM except in a summary format. In this report, the U.S. Census Bureau incorporated data from the CBO survey and combined them with administrative (institutional) records from the SMOBE and IRS tax information. An attempt was made to minimize the likelihood of an indirect disclosure of a particular business enterprise by restricting the minimum cell sizes for all variables to no less than 35 observations per cell. This rule established by the U.S. Bureau of the Census formally requires that there must be no combination (cross-tabulation) of survey variables yielding a frequency of fewer than 35 observations.
7. Data from the 1987 CBO survey became available for the first time in computer readable form in the summer of 1992. Data from the 1992 CBO survey were available for the first time in late 1997.
8. Owner characteristics including age, race, gender, marital status, business address, and years of ownership were analyzed. The characteristics of multiple-owner firms, however, were excluded from this analysis because of the difficulty in assigning an ethnicity indicator to multi-racial firms.
9. The models presented here were also run with Federal Reserve Districts as the geographic unit of analysis. The results were almost identical to the models using Census Regions and Divisions. Hence, the research results are approximately robust regardless of the selection of geographic sub-divisions.
10. For a stylized example, almost all Metropolitan Statistical Areas (MSAs) with more than 100 black-owned businesses have a significant majority of non-minorities in their population as well. A change in the demographic makeup of

the minority population in a city has little effect on the probability of success of a minority-owned business. However, very large cities that have large minority populations generally possess larger and more diverse ownership of minority-owned businesses.

11. Nucci, Al. 1992. "The Characteristics of Business Owners Database." Washington, D.C.: U.S. Bureau of the Census. Center for Economic Studies. CES 92–7. (August). The weighted responses, also known as universe estimates, were calculated from response-adjusted firm weights. Population estimates of owner characteristics were calculated from the responding cases with weights adjusted to account for non-response. Nucci (1992) stated that the response rate for minorities in the 1987 CBO data was "relatively low compared to rates of household surveys such as the Current Population Survey." In fact, the response rate in the 1987 economic census was 13.2 to 16.3 percent lower for black respondents; 17.1 to 20. 1 percent lower for Hispanic respondents; 5.2 to 8.6 percent lower for Asian/Other respondents; and 22.8 to 25.2 percent higher for non-minority respondents.

12. Starting capital (K) and work experience (Exp) are continuous variables.

13. A matrix in which an inverse does not exist is "singular." The rule of thumb is if a qualitative variable has in categories, then only m-1 dummy variables should be introduced into the regression. The group, or category, that is assigned the value of zero is often called the omitted category. Thus, in this analysis, males are the base or omitted category. The choice of the base category has been determined by a priori considerations. The coefficient attached to the dummy variable is also called the differential intercept coefficient because it shows how much the value of the intercept term of the category that receives the value of 1 differs from the intercept coefficient of the base category.

8

WHAT DETERMINES EXPORTS OF BLACK-OWNED ENTERPRISES?*

N. Frank Ekanem
Charlie E. Mahone, Jr.

INTRODUCTION

It is estimated that about 85 percent of U.S. exports are made by 250 large multinational corporations while only 10 percent of total U.S. exports are made by small businesses.[1] Many black leaders in this country, especially those who have worked so hard to bring about minority empowerment in all aspects of life, have asked why minorities in business, and blacks in particular, have accomplished so little in international trade. This study is therefore an effort to address one of those questions. The study attempts to inquire into how much black-owned enterprises export and what determines how much they export.

In 1987, the U.S. Department of Commerce reported that 424,165 black-owned enterprises were in operation. Thirty-five percent of these firms reported average gross annual receipt of less than $5,000, while 92 percent reported average gross annual receipts of $5,000–$99,999; 7,790, or 6.1 percent, reported average receipts of between $100,000–499,999; and 0.9 percent reported average sales of $500,000 and over. Thirty-one thousand four hundred fourteen, or 7.4 percent of those firms reported no employees, 353,350, or 83 percent, reported no paid employees; while only 70,815, or 16.7 percent, reported paid employees. The statistics also shows that 7,253, or 10 percent, of these firms reported that between 1 and 9 percent of their sales receipt came from exports, while 6,528, or 1.9 percent, reported export sales of between 10 and 100 percent. As few

* The author wishes to acknowledge the assistance of the following individuals; Dr. Alfred Nucci, Bureau of the Census, Dr. Richard Stevens, Minority Business Development Agency, MBDA, U.S. Department of Commerce for providing the data and other facilities required for this study and Ms. Alma Nugent for her painstaking assistance in data analysis.

as 4.6 percent of those firms that exported between 1 and 9 percent of gross sales also reported average gross receipts of over $1,000,000. Only 3.0 percent of the firms that exported between 1 and 9 percent reported average export sales of between $200,000 and $249,999, and 0.6 percent of those that exported 75 to 100 percent of sales reported average gross receipts of over $1,000,000. The distribution of export activity by industry shows that most export activity took place in the wholesale trade, with 4.7 percent of the firms exporting; 82.9 percent of the firms did not export.[2]

According to White's definition firms with less than $5,000 in sales receipts should be classified as small firms.[3] This means that 1,332 or 0.3 percent of black-owned enterprises which were in operation in 1987 were medium-sized enterprises. So much has already been written in the literature on the export activity of small and medium-sized firms generally, but nothing on black-owned enterprises. This is the subject of this study. The 1987 Economic Censuses of business owners provided some characteristics of black-owned business enterprises, which merit some investigation. These characteristics include information on exports, employment, gross sales, payroll, age of owners, education, prior work and managerial experience, and the length of time the enterprises have been in business operation. These characteristics are used to explain the export activities of black-owned enterprises in 1987. In particular, we are interested in the level of export involvement, in terms of the percent of gross sales exported, and the industry distribution of such exports. The statistics report the number of firms that export a given percentage of gross sales. The percentage of sales exported varies between 1 percent and 100 percent. That is why it is important to investigate which enterprises export how much, and what determines the export effort of those enterprises. Also, since exporting firms seem to concentrate in wholesale trade, it is necessary to investigate the distribution of export sales by industry and determine the reasons for this distribution.

LITERATURE REVIEW OF THE THEORIES AND METHODOLOGIES

Much is already known from earlier studies about the determinants of exporting. Some of the issues discussed in the literature in connection with exporting are firm size, and management experience. Many of the studies conclude that small-to-medium sized firms do little exporting because of potential barriers. One such barrier is the cost of exporting.

Bilkey, Edmund, and Sarkis, Hook and Czinkota, and Burton and Schlegelmilch[4] assert that enterprises with relatively young managers engage in exporting because those managers serve as the force behind their companies' export drive. In a recent study, Ekanem and Mahone[5] found that for black-owned enterprises, the threshold age of those managers is between 35 and 54 years. That study found that education and prior working experience also play an important role in exporting. They observe that exports are significantly greater among enterprises run by managers who have a college education and ten or more years of prior working experience than they are among enterprises whose managers do not have these attributes.

Birch[6] discusses the effect of firm size measured in the number of employees. He asserts that since more than one half of the firms he studied had fewer than 100 employees, firms need not be too large before exporting can take place. This is possible where the enterprise is capital intensive and/or efficiently managed. Capital intensity enables the enterprise to operate with fewer employees, while efficient management helps firms to reduce unit costs. These attributes allow an enterprise to become competitive relative to its foreign counterparts. O'Rourke[7] believes that small firms have less export experience and can only rely on the initiatives of the foreign buyers of their exports. The lack of knowledge of foreign markets, inability to assess market conditions, and inability to target export sales are among the problems confronting small and medium-sized firms in export participation.[8] Ali and Swiercz[9] claim that mid-sized firms offer the greatest potential response to efforts designed to increase export performance, especially when sales volume exceeds $5 million.

The lack of unanimous conclusions on the effect of firm size on exports means that a lot of work still needs to be done on this subject. According to Birch, firms with less than 100 employees are able to support export activities, and firms need more than $5 million in sales volume to be able to export.[10] If this is the case, then how much will firms that meet neither the size nor the sales conditions be able to export? Conversely, if firms meet both the sales and size conditions but are lacking in other essential attributes, such as adequate operating capital, will they be able to face the competition involved in international marketing? The effects of export-related, firm-specific attributes and management characteristics are examined in this study.

METHODOLOGY AND HYPOTHESES

Three semi-logarithmic models are for export levels, E_1, E_2, and E_3 corresponding, respectively to export levels 1–24%, 24–74% and 75–100%. The models are:

$$E_1/E_2/E_3 = \alpha_0 + \alpha_1 Log(EM) + \alpha_2 Log(AP) + \alpha_3 Log(SA) + \Sigma\alpha_{4j}SC + \Sigma\alpha_{5j}BC + \Sigma\alpha_{6j}DG + \Sigma\alpha_{7j}AG + \Sigma\alpha_{8j}PE + \alpha_9 ED + \alpha_{10}ME + \alpha_{11}AS + \mu$$

Where EM represents employment, AP represents annual payroll, SA represents annual gross sales, SC represents start-up capital (j=2), BC represents percent of borrowed capital (j=2), DG represents industry group (j=5), AG represents owners' age (j=2), TN represents business tenure or years in business operation (j=2), AS represents business assets, PE represents prior work experience, ME represents management experience, and ED represents education of owners. As seen in Appendix 1.1, the distribution of the exporting firms is such that more firms fall in the 1–24% class range as compared to firms exporting higher percent of their gross sales. Therefore, estimation procedure, which fits this type of firm's distribution, was considered necessary. For this reason the maximum likelihood method was considered appropriate because it allows us to maximize between, and minimize within-class variances.

In our investigation of the effect of firm size on exporting, three size variables are considered namely employment, annual payroll and volume of sales. Three levels of export participation are considered namely 1–24% of sales, 25–74% of sales, and 75–100% of sales. Although these size variables can be jointly or individually related to exporting, joint relationship is assumed in this study. In order to isolate the determinants of exports at various levels, three samples were drawn, one for each export level. The separate sample treatment allows us to effectively handle the estimation problems arising from the concentration of firms exporting low percent of gross sales in a way that allows us to reduce the variance in each of the three groups of exporting enterprises. The continuous variables are employment, annual payroll, and annual gross sales. The categorical variables and their coding procedures are given in Appendix 1.

The literature shows that export involvement varies by firm size. Although the theoretical explanation of this phenomenon has not been offered, this notion can be linked to the standard economic theory of the economies of scale. Economic theory links economies of scale to lower unit costs, because when costs are spread over many units of output, costs per unit fall. Since comparative cost advantage is an important aspect of international trade, the link between firm size, export involvement and average cost of the product exported becomes an important factor, which needs to be explored. This is not the focus of this study.

We investigate the effect of the learning hypothesis, which was popularized by Burton and Schlegelmich.[11] Five variables are used for this purpose, namely the age of managers, prior working experience, education, managerial experience, and the number of years the firm has been in operation. Three age groups are considered. These are less than 35 years, 35–54 years, and 55 years and older. Two categories of education, prior working experience, and management experience are considered. These are respectively, high school and college education; less than 10 years, and 10 or more years of prior working experience; managerial /executive and other managerial experience. The number of years the enterprise has been in operation is broken into the following categories: less than 15 years, 15–24 years, and 25 years or more. We assume that the longer the enterprise has been in operation the more capable it is of handling the responsibilities involved in exporting. The ability to engage in export activity also depends on the nature of the industry and the type of product or service exported. In manufacturing, it is necessary to experiment with various product qualities until an acceptable product quality is found. To discover the acceptable product quality. investment in research and development will be an important consideration. This is a process that will evolve over time.

On the other hand, in the retail or wholesale trade, exporting requires no learning exposure. Export in these industries involves a simple decision on what quality of product is desired by foreign customers. Once this is known, the product is immediately procured for export. Although age is believed to enhance the learning process, the literature claims that enterprises that are managed by younger persons are more likely to be involved in exporting at any given export level. This contradicts the learning process hypothesis. The justification for this is probably to be found in the "managerial attitude" hypothesis, which is not investigated in this study. Young managers are believed to be more enterprising and more ready to take risk than older managers are. Other variables, assumed to be related to export involvement are: industry classification, start-up, and the percent of borrowed capital.

EMPIRICAL RESULTS

The results of the probit analysis are given in the Appendix. The probit results for the black-owned enterprises are shown against those for all minority-owned enterprises. All the three size variables are statistically significant in the all-minority model, but only one size variable, annual payroll, is statistically significant in the black-owned enterprise model. This variable is statistically significant at the 1–24% export level, but not at 25–74% or 75–100% export levels. The negative sign taken by this variable is worthy of note. This means that significantly fewer black-owned enterprises with large payroll export at the 1–24%, compared to other enterprises with less payroll costs. When annual payroll is used as an index of firm size, we can conclude that black-owned firms with large payroll cost do not export significantly more than their counterparts with less payroll cost. This observation applies to each of the five industry groups, namely construction, wholesale, retail trade, FIRE, and services used in the probit model.

Neither employment nor sales receipt are statistically significant at any export level in the black-owned enterprises probit. Employment is, however, directly related to exporting at all export levels, while sales receipt is directly related to exporting only at the 1–24% level. This means that neither employment nor sales receipt supports the hypothesis that firm size has an effect on black-owned enterprises export activity. Annual payroll supports the hypothesis that firm size has an effect on black-owned firms' exports, but according to the results of this study, significantly fewer firms having higher payroll costs export more than firms with lower payroll costs export.

All the "learning process" variables are statistically significant in black-owned enterprises' models at the 1–24% level. Black-owned enterprises whose owners are aged 35–54 years export just as much as those whose owners are younger. But enterprises whose owners are 55 years and older export significantly more at the 1–24% level than those whose owners are younger. Owners' college education variable is directly related to export at the 25–74% and 75–100% levels, implying that more enterprises whose owners have at least a college education export significantly more at these levels than those whose owners have less education. College education is therefore seen as a factor that gives black-owned enterprises the necessary learning exposure to cope with competitive international marketing. The lack of statistical significance among other learning variables implies that black-owned enterprises whose owners have these traits are not better equipped with export ability than those without these qualities. Prior working and managerial experience are two other learning variables that affect minority exporting in different ways. Black-owned enterprises whose owners have ten or more years of prior working or managerial/executive experience export significantly less than other black-owned enterprises at the 1–24% and 75–100% export levels with the same learning exposure except that they have less than ten years of prior working or managerial experience. The export involvement of firms whose owners have ten or more years of prior working or managerial experience at the 25–74% level is not significantly different from that of the enterprises whose owners do not have prior working or managerial experience.

To test the hypothesis that industry characteristics affect the amount of exporting of an enterprise, five industrial groups were considered. For this purpose industry dummy variables were created by scoring 1 if the enterprise belongs to a given industry group and zero otherwise. The industries excluded from the models are agriculture, transportation, and manufacturing, because there were few enterprises in those industries. The excluded industries serve as the reference industry for the purpose of comparing exporting in the industries included. The results show that industry characteristics affect export performance of black-owned enterprises in different ways. For example, black-owned enterprises in each of the four industries included in the model except finance, insurance, and real estate (FIRE), export significantly less at the 1–24% level, but significantly more at the 25–74% level in the construction and retail trades than the enterprises in the reference industries. Also, compared to the reference industries, black-owned enterprises in the five industries export significantly more at the 25–74% or 75–100% levels, than industries in finance, insurance and real estate (FIRE), and the services industries, respectively. None of the variables considered by itself plays any unique role in determining export activity of black-owned enterprises in any industry at any export level.

We also examined the effect of start-up capital and percent of borrowed capital on black-owned enterprises' export activity. Start-up and percent of borrowed capital are considered here as indices of firm size. The results show that significantly fewer black-owned enterprises with start-up capital of $5,000 or more, exported at the 1–24% and 25–74% levels, compared to black-owned enterprises with less start-up capital. Also fewer black-owned enterprises which borrowed 11 percent or more capital exported at 1–24% and 75–100% levels than black-owned enterprises with less borrowed capital. Neither start-up capital nor other financial commitments in borrowed capital offers any additional export advantages. By themselves, they have no direct relationship with the firms' ability to finance current export activities. When start-up capital is allowed to increase to reflect the number of years the firm has been in business operation and inflation, and current sales, one can understand management's desire and pressure to increase sales through export drive.

SUMMARY AND CONCLUSIONS

What determines how much black-owned enterprises export? To be able to answer this question, we have compared exports in black-owned enterprises at three export levels to that of other-minority-owned enterprises in selected industries. The selected industries are services, construction, finance, insurance and real estate (FIRE), wholesale, and retail trades. We have also compared black-owned enterprise exports in these industries to some reference industry group, namely agriculture, manufacturing, and transportation. These industries were excluded from the probit model, because the number of black-owned firms in these industries was too few to warrant a separate treatment. The three export levels studied are 1–24%, 25–74%, and 75–100% of gross sales. We observe that, except in the services and finance, insurance and real estate (FIRE) and construction industries, few black-owned enterprises in these industries export, compared to enterprises owned by other minorities. Significantly more black-owned enterprises, however, export at the 25–74% level in services, finance, retail and construction industries (FIRE) compared to other-minority-owned enterprises. On the other hand more black-owned enterprises export at the 75–100% level in the services, finance and wholesales than in enterprises owned by other-minorities.

Below is a list of variables that yield statistically significant coefficients at the prescribed export levels. The variables which are statistically significant at the 1–24% export level are: annual payroll, start-up capital in excess of $5,000, borrowed capital 11 percent and over, owner's age 55 years and older, ten or more years of prior working experience. Others are education of owner (college or graduate school), executive management experience, and the number of years during which the firm has been in operation. Start-up capital $5,000 or more is not statistically significant at the 75–100% export level. The inverse relationship between export at the 1–24% and 24–74% levels implies that borrowed capital in the amount of $5,000 or more significantly determines black-owned enterprises' export at these levels, but such export is less than the export of enterprises with less borrowed capital. What this means is that black-owned enterprises need not have large amounts of borrowed capital to be involved in international marketing. This contradicts popular belief in the literature that small sized enterprises have considerable export handicaps. Our data suggest that black-owned enterprises with little start-up capital can still be engaged in international marketing if their owners have a college education. College education is one of the means of gaining the necessary experience and knowledge of international marketing. The percent of borrowed capital 11 percent or more, owner's age 55 years and older, and prior work experience ten years or more are also not statistically significant at 25–74% export level. Our data further show that black entrepreneurs who have substantial financial interests in their businesses tend to engage in exporting, probably because they see exporting as a means of making more money to increase their profit. Enterprises that belong to this category export anything between 1–24% and 75% or more of their products.

We have no specific knowledge of what determines the variations in export levels in the industries in which such variations are observed. We can only say that different marketing and management strategies, differences in the type of technology in use, product quality, etc., are among several factors which may make the products of one industry cheaper, or otherwise more appealing to foreign customers than the products of other industries.

Size variables do not seem to have any effect on black-owned enterprises export. Only a few black-owned enterprises with large annual payroll export at the 1–24% level compared to the enterprises owned by other minorities. A few other firms with large annual payroll export more at the 75–100% level, but their number is not significantly more than "other minority-owned" enterprises that export at this export level. Other minority-owned enterprises, as defined by the Bureau of the Census, include enterprises owned by ethnic minorities and women. Since size variables, except payroll, are not statistically significant, we can conclude that the export by black-owned enterprises does not increase as such enterprises become larger. The only size variable that is statistically significant in the export equation is annual payroll variable. The inverse relationship between this variable and the export by black-owned firms means that export by these enterprises at the 1–24% level falls as the firms' payroll obligations increase.

By using owner's age, prior work, and managerial experience as learning indices, we can make conclusions about the effect of "learning exposure" on export activity, especially at the 1–24% export level. Generally speaking, black-owned enterprises export as much as other minority-owned enterprises, given the same learning exposure. However, significantly more black-owned enterprises whose owners are 55 years or older, export at the 1–24% level than enterprises owned by other minorities. This means that age gives black business owners some export advantage over other minorities, provided the volume of export is less than 25% of gross sales. Also, black-owned businesses, which have been in business 15–24 years, export 1–24% of their gross sales, but their number is significantly less than the number of enterprises owned by other minorities. This leads us to the conclusion that newly established business enterprises are aggressively involved in international marketing compared to enterprises that have been in operation for many years, especially when the managers/owners of such businesses are 55 years or older, or have college education.

We acknowledge that the results of this study have raised more questions than we have been able to answer. Among the questions yet to be answered is the effect of firm size on exporting. Although we have found no evidence of the effect of firm size on black-owned enterprise's export, we do not deny that firm size plays an important role in exporting. We suspect that the size effect could be linked to the economies of scale concept, which may or may not be observed in black-owned enterprises.

These findings raise a number of policy issues. Among these is the role of education and work-related experience. This study shows that college education is very crucial in preparing black entrepreneurs for participation in international trade. For those who do not have college education, executive training or seminars that emphasize such topics as cultural shocks, language problems, etc., will go a long way in preparing them to overcome some of the export barriers. Some of these services are provided by the Small Business Development Centers around the country. Black entrepreneurs are therefore encouraged to use these services, wherever they may be provided, if they wish to overcome some of the barriers posed by learning exposure in international marketing.

NOTES

1. Mahone, Charlie E., Jr. (1991). "Factors that restrict exports of small and medium firms: the role of expert financing," *Journal of Small Business Strategy*. November.

2. [Footnote these data]
3. White, Lawrence J. (1982). "The determinants of the relative importance of small business," *The Review of Economics and Statistics*, Volume 64 (1): 42–49.
4. Bilkey, W. J. (1978). "An attempted integration of the literature on the export behavior of firms," *Journal of International Business*, 9, (1) Spring/Summer; Edmund, S. and K. Sarkis (1986). "Export: a necessary ingredient in the growth of small business firms," *Journal of Small Business Management,* 24(4):54–65; Hook, Ralph C. and Michael R. Czinkota (1989). "Export activities and prospects of Hawaiian firms," *European Journal of Marketing*, 23, (11); Burton, F. N. and B. B. Schlegelmilch (1987). "Profile analyses of non-exporter versus exporters grouped by export involvement," *Management Information Review*, 27/1.
5. Ekanem, N. Frank and Charlie E. Mahone, Jr. (1997). "Minority-owned business enterprises' participation in international trade" (Multinational Business Review, Vol. VI, No. 2, Fall 1998).
6. Birch (1988).
7. O'Rouke, A. Desmond 91985). "Differences in exporting practices, attitudes and problems by size of firm," *American Journal of Small Business,* Volume 9, #3, Winter.
8. Ditcht, Erwin, M. Leibold, Hans-George Koeglmayr and Stefan Mueller (1984). "Export decision of small- and medium-sized firms: a review," *Management International Review.* See also Edmonds and Sarkis, op. cit.
9. Ali, Abbas and Swierz, Pal (1991). "Firms size and export behavior: lessons from the Midwest," *Journal of Small Business Management,* April, pages 71–78.
10. Birch (1988).
11. Burton and Schlegelmilch, op. cit.

APPENDIX 1
List of data used

1.	Acemp	employment
2.	acap	1987 annual payroll
3.	acsr1	1987 sales/receipt
	i1	owner's age
4.	Less than 35 years = 1	
5.	35–54 years = 1	
6.	55 years or older = 1	
	i5	highest level of education of owner
7.	Elementary & high school equivalent = 1	
8.	College or graduate school = 1	
	i9a	prior employment experience
9.	Less than 10 years = 1	
10.	10 years or more = 1	
	i9b	management experience
11.	Managerial/executive = 1	
12.	Other types of experience = 1	
	i16	years of business ownership
13.	Less than 14 years = 1	
14.	14–24 years = 1	
15.	25 years or more = 1	
	i17a	percent of start-up debt
16.	No borrowed capital = 1	
17.	1–10% borrowed capital = 1	
18.	11% or more borrowed capital = 1	
	i19a	firms' asset
19.	Less than $25,000 = 1	
20.	$25,000 or more = 1	
	ind	industry group
21	Construction = 1	
22.	Wholesale = 1	
23.	Retail trade = 1	
24.	Finance, etc. = 1	
25.	Services = 1	

APPENDIX 1.1
Export of Minority-Owned Enterprises: Probit Result

	All Minority-Owned Enterprises Export Levels			Black-Owned Enterprises Export Levels		
Independent Variables	1–24%	25–74%	75–100%	1–24%	25–74%	75–100%
Sample Size	841	372	286	201	44	49
Intercept	2.3674	2.4162	2.3725	2.6687	2.5939	2.5232
	(1609.89)*	(1098.40)*	(896.89)*	(495.96)*	(222.37)*	(221.23)
Employment	0.0074	0.0103	0.0356	0.006	0.0016	0.0409
	(3.55)*	(1.69)	(5.79)*	(0.87)	(0.01)	(1.06)
Annual Payroll	–4.27E-07	7.89E-08	5.83E-08	–5.27E-07	–1.03E-07	1.87E-07
	(4.12)*	(0.02)	(0.01)	(2.43)*	(0.01)	(0.01)
Sales Receipt	–3.007E-08	–4.27E-08	–8.95E-08	7.46E-09	–1.67E-07	–7.30E-08
	(1.71)**	(1.05)	(5.44)*	(0.04)	(0.05)	(0.45)
Start-up Capital						
< $5,000	–0.1815	–0.057	–0.0264	0.0059	–0.1414	0.2468
	(15.33)*	(0.72)	(0.15)	(0.01)	(0.88)	(2.81)*
$5,000 or More	–0.1765	–0.5121	–0.1787	–0.1654	–0.4511	–0.1349
	(11.06)*	(59.55)*	(5.52)*	(3.21)*	(7.51)*	(0.77)
Borrowed Capital (%)						
1–10%	0.0741	–0.0393	0.4842	–0.0377	–0.2146	4.792
	(0.68)	(0.14)	(5.18)*	(0.05)	(0.88)	(1.00E-07)
11% or More	–0.228	0.1806	0.0015	–0.1886	–0.0596	–0.2267
	(36.64)*	(12.40)*	(0.0006)	(5.55)*	(0.20)	(2.81)*

APPENDIX 1.1 (Continued)
Export of Minority-Owned Enterprises: Probit Result

	All Minority-Owned Enterprises Export Levels			Black-Owned Enterprises Export Levels		
Independent Variables	1–24%	25–74%	75–100%	1–24%	25–74%	75–100%
Industry Group						
Construction	0.1499	0.4648	1.1545	–0.3026	0.2857	5.0193
	(4.18)*	(23.14)*	(15.05)*	(5.15)*	(2.12)*	(2.80E-07)
Wholesale	–0.4483	0.0303	–0.8734	–0.9214	–0.0925	–0.1783
	(29.70)*	(0.07)	(125.06)*	(28.43)*	(0.08)	(4.81)*
Retail Trade	–0.3288	0.2721	0.1028	–0.5784	0.2795	1.1286
	(50.07)*	(21.55)*	(2.37)*	(29.90)*	(3.25)*	(0.81)
Finance	0.3821	1.166	0.6739	–0.1264	1.3034	–0.1327
	(15.66)*	(28.41)*	(20.78)*	(0.67)	(1.74)**	(3.09)*
Services	0.0947	0.4127	0.492	–0.2125	0.3817	0.3865
	(4.21)*	(60.05)*	(55.84)*	(4.41)*	(9.05)*	(9.17)*
Owner's Age						
35–54 Years	–0.0986	–0.0348	0.1017	–0.008	0.0951	0.1161
	(6.15)*	(0.37)	(2.74)*	(0.01)	(0.43)	(0.59)
55 Years or Older	0.0046	–0.0814	–0.0932	0.2009	0.0541	–0.0091
	(0.007)	(1.32)	(1.48)	(3.73)*	(0.10)	(0.00)
Owner's Education						
College or Grad School	–0.047	–0.0247	–0.1637	–0.1402	0.1874	0.2419
	(1.99)*	(0.28)	(10.32)*	(4.93)*	(1.76)**	(3.22)*

APPENDIX 1.1 (Continued)
Export of Minority-Owned Enterprises: Probit Result

	All Minority-Owned Enterprises Export Levels			Black-Owned Enterprises Export Levels		
Independent Variables	1–24%	25–74%	75–100%	1–24%	25–74%	75–100%
Prior Work Experience						
10 Years or More	0.0607	–0.1035	0.0253	–0.0979	–0.0121	–0.1868
	(3.45)*	(5.45)*	(0.23)	(2.54)*	(0.01)	(2.69)*
Managerial Experience						
Managerial/Exec	–0.1089	–0.2269	–0.4101	–0.2037	0.1085	–0.5139
	(6.51)*	(17.57)*	(51.36)*	(6.88)*	(0.34)	(17.33)*
Years In Business						
25 Years or More	0.1335	0.3197	–0.0118	–0.1303	–0.1281	0.0354
	(1.87)**	(4.74)*	(0.01)	(0.88)	(0.34)	(0.02)
15–24 Years	–0.0288	–0.0457	0.1391	–0.1609	–0.065	0.0811
	(0.25)	(0.40)	(1.74)**	(3.04)*	(0.15)	(0.20)
Business Assets						
$25,000 or More	–0.1901	–0.236	–0.0255	—	—	—
	(26.18)*	(23.79)*	(0.17)	—	—	—
Log Likelihood						
Normal	–3,727.31	–1,888.08	–1,405.80	–984.79	–278.22	–283.94

* Statistically significant at 1% Level
** Statistically Significant at 5% Level

9

IS THE U.S. SMALL BUSINESS ADMINISTRATION A RACIST INSTITUTION?*

Timothy Bates

THEORY: RACISM AS ELUSIVE

Racism and its manifestations are embedded in dynamic social/political/economic processes. It follows necessarily that its meaning changes as these processes evolve and interact, and this periodically gives rise to a need "to reencounter the concept and disrupt its former meanings in order to understand it anew."[1] Such a reencountering is presently taking place in U.S. society, and the struggle to redefine racism is a highly politicized fight, not an impartial analysis of evolving social conditions. John Powell observes that we, as a nation, may no longer know what the term means as we try "unsuccessfully to assign racial issues to a distant past, fooling ourselves into thinking that racism can only faintly make claims on who we are today."[2]

Social context always conditions the construction of meaning. Language is rooted in a system of implicit understandings about social reality. When those understandings diverge along racial lines, as they do today, dialogue deteriorates rapidly. "Whites and blacks see racial issues through different lenses and use different scales to weigh and assess injustice."[3] Thus, whites and blacks are often talking past each other; there is no single, dominant frame of reference for talking about race in America.

A stream of assertions forthcoming from the media, academia, and elected officials indicates that racism has been overcome. A variant of this view is that the racists of today are the people who are always bringing up race, often minorities themselves who want to "inject it into

*The research reported in this study was funded, in part, by the U.S. Small Business Administration under grant SBIC-94-001-01. Findings are those of the author and do not reflect the views of the Small Business Administration. The extensive assistance of Diane Thomas is gratefully acknowledged.

everything."[4] Whites often equate racism with racial consciousness, so that one's affirmation of racial identity gives rise to offense, and color blindness is seen as an absence of racism. Confronted with such reactions, minorities increasingly seem to feel that whites have flipped: "it seems to them misinformed, even ignorant. They in turn sense a kind of racism in the whites' assumption that minorities must assimilate to mainstream values and styles."[5]

In the contested terrain of racial dialogue, one highly developed and refined interpretation of racism appears to be emerging as dominant. Today's neoconservatives condemn racism, which they see largely as past practices: Jim Crow institutional arrangements, Ku Klux Klan chapters, and blatant discrimination in job access and college admissions are opposed as racist. To the extent that such practices linger, the neoconservative is against such racism. Neoconservatives are commonly very impressed by the progress that society has made in the past 50 years: the Supreme Court's *Brown vs. Board of Education* decision in 1954, the 1965 Voting Rights Act, and the like are approved of wholeheartedly. To many, opposition to such blatant discrimination demonstrates that they are opposed to racism. Yet white neoconservatives get decidedly uncomfortable when discussions of racism are cast in terms of underlying structures of power that bias economic opportunities against minorities. At this point, their policy discussions turn to individualistic color-blind advocacy of free market outcomes. On balance, racism is seen as a rather minor force in modern American life and meritocracy is the primary determinant of inequality of outcomes. Stephen and Abigail Thernstrom, in their most recent book, inform us that few whites are now racist: such people have become a tiny remnant with no influence in any important sphere of American life.[6]

Racism today, for the Thernstroms, is more often manifested in the efforts of government that target minorities for preferential treatment. Such affirmative action policies, we are told, produce no gains for blacks, but they generate great resentment among whites. White-owned small businesses, claimed former presidential candidate Patrick Buchanan, lose sales revenues because of race-based government procurement policies known as minority "set-asides." If elected, Buchanan vowed to purge the federal government "agency by agency, and root out the whole rotten infrastructure of reverse discrimination, branch by branch."[7] Modern racial antagonism among whites toward minorities, according to the Thernstroms, has been one of the regrettable results of public policies that stress racial identity.[8]

Have the neoconservatives won the battle over the meaning of racism? In Blauner's view, "by the late 1970s the main usage of racism in the mind of the white public had become undoubtedly that of 'reverse racism.'"[9] The political struggle to define the meaning of racism, however, is ongoing.

PRACTICE: THE U.S. SMALL BUSINESS ADMINISTRATION

As racism continues to be downplayed, one consequence is the current working out of the ramifications of the belief that the nation has won the war against bigotry. Why then does government promote affirmative action? The assumption that white Americans are no longer racist is "central to the argument against race-based affirmative action."[10] If the playing field is level, then affirmative action ceases to be a remedy and becomes reverse discrimination, simple racial entitlement. Newt Gingrich tells us that the history of discrimination against black Americans is no different than that faced by white ethnics: "Virtually every American" has been subjected to discrimination.[11]

Thus far, this article—by design—is written in an armchair academic style: various articles and books are selectively paraphrased and quoted. The resultant synthesis is a subjective interpretation that reflects one point of view. Let's call this a "theory" of racism today. As a test of this theory, the balance of this article is devoted to studying how the U.S. Small Business Administration (SBA) has administered a racially targeted program, the Minority Enterprise Small Business Investment Company (MESBIC) program, from its inception to its recent defunding by Congress. I know a great deal about the SBA and the MESBIC program; my doctoral dissertation, written in 1971 and 1972, was based entirely upon SBA data. Since then, I have worked on numerous studies that focused upon SBA programs, yet I was hugely assisted in my study of the MESBIC program by an industry insider, Diane Thomas, who for fourteen years represented the interests of MESBIC investment companies (chartered by the SBA) day-by-day in their dealings with their regulator and funder, the SBA. In 1994, I was awarded a contract by the SBA to conduct an in-depth study of the MESBIC program. In the process, I had free access to all relevant internal SBA records, and I interviewed all top SBA officials connected with the MESBIC program. Written results of this inquiry to date include my final report to the SBA[12] and various articles in professional journals.[13]

Diane Thomas's overview assessment is that the investment companies chartered under the MESBIC program have long suffered due to actions of racist SBA employees seeking to undermine them. In true academic fashion, I have struggled to define what "racist" means when it is used to label a major federal government agency, indeed one charged with running major programs that have racially targeted beneficiaries.

Robert Stillman, who was directly in charge of the MESBIC program from 1993 to 1995, responded to the racism label as follows: "SBA is a regulatory agency, and as such inevitably has disputes with those whom it regulates. One of the most corrosive aspects of the SSBIC [the legal name of MESBIC became "SSBIC" in the 1990s] program has been the tendency of vocal leaders of the program to attribute these differences to presumed racial prejudice."[14] Stillman adds that "the actions and decisions of the SBA Investment Division cannot in any fair evaluation be termed racist."[15] Why, then, the charge of racism? According to several top SBA officials, treatment of minorities and whites in the context of running their programs was equal and essentially color blind. Nonetheless, vocal minorities often tried to interject racial considerations into their disputes with SBA, and they hollered "racism" whenever they didn't get their way.

Why, indeed the charge of racism? SBA is a large, diverse bureaucracy, and its high-level officials are certainly not like-minded. Many SBA officials are African American, and the black officials, individually and as a group, stand above the agency norm, contributing disproportionately to the gains that were accomplished by the MESBIC program over the years. These leading black officials, furthermore, enjoyed *much* better working relationships with the investment companies chartered under the MESBIC program than their white counterparts. Nor are white officials charged with running the MESBIC program a homogeneous group: some work with a missionary zeal to assist their perceived clients, the nation's downtrodden minorities. Others see the MESBIC program, through a neoconservative lens, as blatant reverse discrimination. The most successful black-owned MESBIC investment companies are typically the ones held in greatest contempt. TSG Ventures, licensed under the MESBIC program, has grown to be one of the nation's most innovative and successful minority-owned investment companies, and its success derives from making venture-capital investments in black-owned businesses. Asked (by Bates) to name a MESBIC licensee that the SBA disliked, a top SBA official responded, without hesitation, "TSG Ventures."[16] Duane Hill, the head of TSG Ventures and one of the pioneers responsible for creating today's multi-billion dollar minority venture capital industry, explains the antagonism. The SBA, according to Hill, prefers to have MESBICs financing unsophisticated minority business owners: "college graduates with corporate expertise are not socially or economically disadvantaged."[17] Yet these are precisely the kinds of owners TSG seeks to finance. Furthermore, TSG is making money; its top managers are highly paid. The SBA bureaucracy does not like this. Describing the capabilities of SBA bureaucrats, Hill adds that it's a case of the "inmates running the asylum."

Thus, we have evidence of disagreement and of differing program conceptions, but none of this merits the racist label. If the SBA is to be called racist and the charge is to be taken seriously, then it is necessary to document actions by the SBA bureaucracy that distinctly handicap minorities relative to whites. Having a control group would be nice. Fortuitously, we have one. The SBA investment division, since 1969, has run two parallel programs—one for minorities, one for whites—whereby MESBIC-licensed investment companies finance minority business enterprises (MBEs) and Small Business Investment Company (SBIC) licensed investment companies finance nonminority-owned business enterprises. Rare instances of cross-over in clientele notwithstanding, MESBICs and SBICs are ideally matched for comparing SBA's treatment of minorities and whites. We now turn to the task of tracking SBA's treatment of MESBICs and SBICs.

MESBIC Program Conception

The MESBIC program was originally created in 1969 as a public sector/private sector partnership to increase the flow of financial capital to MBEs. The federal government approached corporate America: if corporations would commit their capital to investing in MBEs, the federal government would commit to provide matching funds at low cost through creation of the MESBIC program. For each dollar of corporate capital, up to three government dollars would be provided, and the SBA was to fund and regulate the whole scheme. At least 100 major corporations were expected to come forward initially, establishing the SBA-chartered small business investment companies known popularly as MESBICs. Major corporations establishing MESBICs—Sears, Ford, General Motors, Equitable Life, Amoco, International Paper, and others—accounted for at least 15 of the 141 MESBICs chartered over the next ten years. Corporate paternalism, in the form of establishing 100 MESBICs, thus fell short of expectations, and most of these corporate MESBICs were subsequently sold or shut down. MESBICs were largely minority-owned small business investment companies with several million dollars in assets available for making loans or venture-capital investments in MBEs.

MESBICs were designed to fill some of the roles envisioned for the Community Development Financial Institutions created by the Clinton Administration. Conservative Republican Texas Senator John Tower, later nominated by President Reagan to serve as secretary of defense, cosponsored the MESBIC Act. Tower envisioned MESBICs as a means "to facilitate capital formation in the minority community generally." MESBICs were a "self-help approach to curing poverty and unemployment in the minority community."[18]

SBA Tries to Undermine the New MESBIC Program

According to Joe Newell, director from 1988 to 1994, the MESBIC program has always been on "a rocky road with SBA."[19] Many of the SBA investment division staff, according to Newell, did not want the program. They were already administering SBICs—the sister program for providing government funds to SBIC-licensee private investment companies—and the new MESBIC program initially meant more work without additional staffing. The issue of how the SBA investment division staffed the new MESBIC program is vitally important: it is "exhibit A." Existing personnel of the investment division were ranked in order to identify the least productive staff members. The poorest performers thusly identified, those least able to carry their share of the workload, were assigned to run the MESBIC program. Commenting on the slackers assigned to MESBIC, Newell notes that "the staff was bad."[20] I attempted to verify this horror story about choosing the MESBIC program staff by relating the above episode to other long-term senior SBA bureaucrats. The story was confirmed by multiple sources. I learned in the process that the practice of assigning the least capable staff to minority business assistance programs was not confined to the investment division; it was practiced throughout the SBA. Young staffers, assigned to minority assistance programs, often fell into depression, feeling that their chances of advancement in government were ruined by virtue of their working in such stigmatized, dead end areas.

Meanwhile, MESBIC charters were granted, and the program was launched. Most MESBICs were capitalized at less than $1 million, far too small to permit prudent portfolio diversification of risky MBE investments or to achieve scale economies in the operational aspects of running a business investment company.[21] Demonstrating that one had the expertise to run a small business investment company—evaluating credit risk, prudently making venture-capital investments in young MBEs, and the like—was not even a prerequisite for getting a charter. Did the SBA staff know a competent manager when they saw one? Did they care? Of the 141 MESBICs licensed by 1980, 65 had been declared insolvent by 1994 and forced into liquidation by the SBA, 44 had walked away from their charters, and 32 continued to operate.

Some MESBIC managers were highly competent, creative, successful financiers of MBEs; others were competent, creative, successful scam artists. For some of the MESBICs, Newell notes, "circumstances provided a more attractive use of their funds albeit contrary to the purpose and intent for which SBA provided the funds."[22] In English, that means that MESBIC licensees often invested their low-cost funds from the SBA into bank CDs, making a nice profit off the spread between CD yields and the taxpayer-subsidized funds intended to finance MBEs. While MBEs were starved for capital, MESBIC assets often sat in money-market investments, see Dominguez,[23] Bradford,[24] and Bates.[25]

SBA Reneges on Its Commitment to Provide Matching Funds

By the late 1970s, the MESBIC industry had grown to over 100 investment companies licensed by the SBA to make long-term loans and venture capital investments in MBEs. The attraction of entering the MESBIC industry was the government's commitment to provide low-cost matching funds—up to three dollars in SBA funds for each dollar of private capital put up by the MESBIC licensees. The SBA now began to renege upon its matching commitments, providing insufficient funding for the program, at times attempting to reallocate MESBIC funding to other SBA programs, or attempting to eliminate the program altogether. Inadequate congressional funding of the program was sometimes a problem, but the stark fact is that the SBA rarely *requested* from Congress sufficient funds to meet its matching fund commitments to the MESBIC investment companies. Although the Reagan Administration's neglect of the MESBIC industry seemed at times to be part of a larger disdain for the SBICs and MESBICs alike, or even the entire SBA, by the mid-1980s it was clear that the minority side of the industry was a lower priority of its administrators at the SBA.

Having survived the program's early start-up years, industry insiders were deeply concerned with the message government was sending to its private-sector "partner" in its continuing refusal, from 1979 to 1983, to provide adequate matching funds. In retrospect, this funding situation was good news compared to what was forthcoming.[26]

From 1985 through 1987, the Reagan Administration attempted to eliminate the MESBIC program as part of its move to abolish the SBA. Congress did not comply, providing $44.5 million in 1985, $39 million in 1986, and $39 million in 1987; MESBIC demands for these funds exceeded the supply throughout this period. Unable to abolish the SBA legislatively, the administration appointed Charles Heatherly as its chief, and Heatherly's mandate was to dismantle the agency from within.

In addition to raising the effective cost of funds provided to MESBICs, the Agency, in fiscal year 1988, proposed to let MESBICs sell bonds to the general public, with the SBA providing default guarantees. Since this fund-raising procedure was not legally authorized, the net effect was to place potential MESBIC funding into a state of legal limbo. In contrast, the SBICs were legally authorized to raise funds by selling SBA-guaranteed debt to private investors.[27] It was not until March of 1990 that this funding avenue was opened to MESBICs.

Another episode demonstrating the SBA's irresponsible pattern of pledging matching funds and not delivering involved its approval in the 1970s of a regulation permitting the SBA to match funds invested in the MESBIC industry by other federal government agencies. As a result of this incentive, a unique advantage for the MESBIC industry, federal agencies, including the Economic Development Administration, the Department of Housing and Urban Development, and the Department of Transportation made investments in seventeen MESBIC-licensed investment companies. Attracting over $17 million in funds from other agencies by 1980 as a result of the public funds leverage regulation, the SBA then changed its position, seeking to renege on its matching funds commitment. The SBA requested a ruling from the Comptroller General on the legality of its new-found opposition to its own matching public funds regulation. On July 29, 1980, the Comptroller General ruled that the SBA lacked the legal basis to leverage the government funds invested in MESBICs. Completely reversing itself, the SBA now applied its policy of not leveraging public funds *retroactively,* leaving seventeen MESBICs hanging; ten of the seventeen subsequently failed and entered liquidation. Through such acts did the SBA build its reputation as an unreliable partner for the MESBIC-licensed minority business investment companies.

Congress Attempts to Revitalize the MESBIC Industry

Faced with the uncertain and unstable funding situation created by the SBA, the MESBIC industry shifted its focus to attracting more private capital, as did the SBICs. Differential treatment of the MESBIC and SBIC sides of the small business investment company industry by the SBA revealed the minority side would be relegated to the back of the bus as far as expanded private capital access was concerned.

One of the great attractions luring small business investment companies to form and seek charters under the MESBIC program in the 1970s was the promise of cheap matching funds from the SBA. For the MESBIC licensees, the preferred way to raise funds was to sell preferred stock to the SBA. This preferred stock was legally a balance sheet liability for the MESBICs that sold it, but it was highly attractive because it required annual payment of only a three percent dividend to the SBA, *and* this three percent dividend payment could be legally deferred. The effective cost of this source of funds was effectively zero during early years of MESBIC operations. The SBA's willingness to buy three percent preferred stock from MESBICs declined dramatically throughout the 1980s, and this funding source was basically dead by 1989.

The preferred stock repurchase program was passed by Congress and became law in 1989, and this program enabled the MESBIC licensees to repurchase their outstanding preferred stock (all of which was owned by the SBA) at a steep discount. Why would a MESBIC want to repurchase its preferred stock? It carried a dividend obligation, after all, of only three percent annually. In fact, MESBICs did so in cases where they wanted to clean up their balance sheets in order to make themselves attractive to private investors. Once the repurchase program was made operational by the SBA, MESBICs bought back their stock for 35 cents on the dollar. Thus, a MESBIC could buy back five million dollars in preferred stock it had sold to the SBA for only $1.75 million. In the process, the liabilities on the balance sheet of the MESBIC licensees shrunk dramatically, since the five million in preferred was wiped out as a liability by the repurchase transaction. Thus, Congress had passed a preferred stock repurchasing program that would potentially open up vast new possibilities for MESBICs to attract funding from other sources, including pension funds. An exciting transformation of the industry loomed.

Given the opportunity by a sympathetic Congress to restructure itself, the potential for many MESBICs was utterly destroyed by the SBA bureaucrats who administered the preferred stock repurchase program. The most serious damage resulted from the fact that it took the SBA investment division nearly five years to implement the new program. The repurchase program (Public Law 101-162) was passed in November 1989, but it was June 1994 before the first MESBIC licensee was actually permitted to repurchase its preferred stock. MESBICs poised to restructure were left in limbo for five years; many languished and were ultimately driven to failure by this denial of their promised opportunity to restructure.[28] Many MESBICs hoped to sell a new class of 15 year, four percent preferred stock to the SBA, using proceeds to retire their old three percent preferred. During the five year delay, SBA funds available for buying the new 15 year preferred stock from MESBICs sat unused, and were thusly viewed as a potential area of savings by members of Congress seeking to cut budgets. Thus, between the passage of the repurchase program in 1989 and its implementation in 1994, Congressional funding for SBA purchase of preferred stock from MESBICs dwindled from $31 million to $5.8 million. Even this dwindling amount was put in further jeopardy as SBA administrators strove to reallocate it to other programs.

During the five year delay, the SBA kept the MESBIC industry in constant uncertainty over terms of the preferred stock repurchase program. The pricing formula—determining what each MESBIC would pay to repurchase its preferred stock—bounced around. Repurchase prices under three different formulas ranged from less than 35 percent of preferred stock face value to over 60 percent. Further, the SBA changed its position regarding permissible methods of payment for the repurchase transaction, keeping the MESBICs in a state of perpetual turmoil.[29]

In addition to the ongoing changes in the terms and conditions surrounding the repurchase transaction, the agency continued to change the parties responsible for its oversight and implementation. Oversight for the program changed at least six times from passage of the law to its implementation, and the specified group of SBA analysts actually handling the application packages has changed a number of times as well. Primary oversight for the repurchase program changed from former SBA Associate Administrator for Investment Robert Lineberry to his successor Berky Kulik in 1990, to Wayne Foren in 1991, and Robert Stillman in 1994. During this period, responsibility for the program was delegated to SBA office of investment director Joseph Newell for a time in early 1994 and to special assistant to the office of investment Ed Cleveland during 1994 and 1995. Given the specialized nature of the transaction, its vacillating terms and conditions, and the differing signals given by the changing management of the process, SSBICs attempting to participate in the program were not only left confused but were often suspicious of their SBA "partners."

Changing repurchase transaction conditions and terms, in conjunction with a new wave of related regulations, created a period of time during which the MESBICs in the repurchase program found it almost impossible to infuse any type of financial capital into their funds, whether it be new private capital or funding from the SBA.

In summary, the SBA's conduct of the preferred stock repurchase program provides a blueprint for limiting a program's success: delay implementation as long as possible; constantly change the program rules; continually change those responsible for program oversight and implementation and, where possible, use participation in the program as a means of forcing company compliance to SBA positions on unrelated issues. When the repurchase program finally became a reality, it was burdened with technical regulations (restrictions on dividend payments, SBA's liquidating interest in MESBICs; see Bates, 1996),[30] that largely nullified its intent, since these restrictive regulations minimized the MESBIC industry's ability to attract new capital from private investors.

This sorry record stands in stark contrast to the SBA's implementation of the SBIC industry's revitalization effort, the Small Business Equity Enhancement Act (SBEEA). SBEEA was implemented by the SBA in less than two years after its passage by Congress and received the full support of the agency. This became particularly frustrating for MESBIC representatives working on the implementation of the preferred stock repurchase program, who were told by SBA sources that all work on their repurchase program had been put aside to complete work on SBEEA, *an act passed three years after the MESBIC repurchase program.* The SBA's failure to provide adequate and appropriate funding to the MESBIC industry, its actions in diminishing industry revitalization attempts, and its discrimination in favor of regular SBICs paved the way for congressional defunding of the MESBIC program in 1995.

MINORITY BUSINESS ASSISTANCE AND SBA PARALYSIS

Commenting on the SBA's management, head of Dallas MESBICs, Donald Lawhorne, observed, "Political winds may change; fresh input may seek to reshape the MESBIC program; the SBA's long-term career bureaucrats undermine all of this."[31] Several of the more serious problems typifying the SBA's administration have been reviewed in this study, but generalizations about *why* the MESBIC program has suffered need to be drawn out. We might conclude that the SBA's investment division is staffed by a bunch of racists and leave it at that. That is too simple. Rather, the fact that the investment division is staffed and directed by persons holding highly diverse views about minority business assistance is, by itself, an important cause of the agency's ineffectiveness. A serious problem afflicting the MESBIC program is the lack of a unified vision on the part of the SBA regarding what the program is all about. What is the MESBIC program supposed to be accomplishing? Stripping away the generalities, the SBA had no underlying shared set of goals that was unifying the SBA's administrators and investment division employees as they went about the task of administering the MESBIC program.

Having no shared concept of what a sound, successful MESBIC program would look like, the SBA's administration was often micro in nature, focusing upon day-by-day problems. They were fighting the alligators rather than monitoring the health of the swamp. Would they agree on how to delineate a healthy swamp from one that is dying? Not likely. Often, SBA's administrators were fighting each other over the direction of the MESBIC program. The 1989 preferred stock repurchase program, the attempt by Congress to clean up the balance sheet of the MESBIC industry and make the stronger MESBICs attractive to private investors, was particularly divisive.

This program was, indeed, designed to be a boondoggle for MESBICs: the enormous potential benefits that financially sound MESBICs could realize from the 1989 stock repurchase program passed by Congress were unavailable to SBICs (the mainstream investment companies that were not minority business oriented). This was, by design, a preferential program for minorities. In practice, it was nothing of the kind. SBA's bureaucrats took care of that. The torturous five year period from 1989 to 1994, when the SBA was working to implement the stock repurchase program for MESBICs, can only be understood by realizing that some of the SBA's investment division employees really did want to revitalize the MESBIC industry. Others resented the fact that minorities were being singled out for preferential treatment, and their peculiar notion of fairness motivated them to try to weaken the MESBIC program. Part of the reason for the five year delay in implementing the MESBIC stock repurchase program was the infighting between the opposing factions of SBA bureaucrats. That struggle shifted in 1993 when Clinton's appointees began to assert leadership in the SBA bureaucracy: the forces promoting

MESBIC industry reform then managed to overwhelm the forces trying to undermine MESBIC industry reform.

The whole notion that MESBICs were being bailed out by Congress while SBICs were not was moot by 1994. The SBIC bailout package was passed by Congress in 1992, meaning that both the minority and nonminority sides of the industry had the opportunity to restructure their balance sheets on highly preferential terms made possible by subsidies funded by government. By 1994, the SBA had implemented the restructuring programs for both MESBICs and SBICs. But the five year limbo for MESBICs (versus the smoother two year implementation of SBIC restructuring) had poisoned relations between MESBICs and the SBA. Once again, the SBICs had been treated well while the MESBICs had suffered.[32] The stronger minority business investment companies began to exit from the MESBIC program, transforming themselves into purely private small business investment companies. The weaker MESBICs often failed outright or walked away from their charters, their dreams of restructuring destroyed by SBA's five years of dawdling. MESBIC, in practice, had turned out to be a Jim Crow program: consistent with the history of Jim Crow, the treatment of MESBICs by the SBA was separate and unequal.

The temptation to make generalizations transcending details of administering this one SBA program is fraught with risk but, of course, irresistible. One hypothesis about race relations in America is that in the 1970s white Americans, were more favorably inclined toward programs targeting minorities for preferential treatment, while today the tide has shifted toward a micro concern with feathering one's own nest. The history of the SBA's treatment of the MESBIC program provides no support whatsoever for the hypothesis that white America's attitudes toward racially-targeted assistance programs are subject to such cyclical swings. The entire record of the MESBIC program is entirely wrong: the 1990s version of the SBA investment division does not stand out as being noticeably worse that its 1970s predecessor. An alternative hypothesis is that white Americans in the 1970s were less likely to openly express attitudes that could be called racist, while today a new language has evolved that encourages whites to more freely express attitudes that they previously tended to keep to themselves.

White Americans have traditionally been constrained from making blatantly racist statements by the widely shared perception that blatant racists are a rather stupid lot. Being thought of as an ignorant redneck is a deterrent to many, if not all, white Americans, and the applicability of this sort of inhibition does shift through time. Historically, racist attitudes have flourished in this country when they were supported by the appearance of a pseudoscience holding that white European races were superior to others. Racist attitudes grew in intensity and depth from the 1880s into the 1920s, coinciding with growing overseas imperialism of both the United States and Europe.[33] In the United States, this led to passage of Jim Crow laws, lynchings in the South, violence against blacks in the North, increasing attempts to drive black workers (in the South) out of the skilled trades, and so forth. Scholars like William Z. Ripley and the early physical anthropologists and a host of others, Homer Lea, H.S. Chamberlain, Golineau, and so forth, helped create an intellectual environment which encouraged racial discrimination to go largely unquestioned.

My hypothesis is that underlying racial attitudes change slowly but that the willingness to express those attitudes can change relatively quickly; the role of intellectuals, finally, can be important in lessening inhibitions constraining language that recently would have been viewed as racist. Widespread misrepresentation of racial attitudes sometimes is so obvious that it leaps out of social science data and stands in stark contrast to reality. White Americans have routinely expressed their general approval of racially integrated neighborhoods in recent decades. Juxtapose such stated opinions with the reality of racially segregated housing throughout most of the United States and it is obvious to all but the densest of observers that many millions of white Americans are simply lying. Why do they bother to lie?

Racial attitudes are multidimensional and contradictory. If the founding fathers of our nation could endorse concepts like "all men are created equal" while embedding slavery into the U.S. constitution, it should surprise no one to learn that racial dialogue in the U.S. is less than honest. Many whites would prefer to have a language available which would enable them to state sincerely that they opposed discrimination, endorsed equality, and passionately believed in racially homogeneous neighborhoods. This is a challenging, but not impossible task.

A first step entails making whites believe that they—not minorities—are the victims of discrimination in contemporary America. A widely accepted racial stereotype today goes something like this: 1) a black person who is working in a highly paid managerial or professional job typically owes that success to preferential treatment, affirmative action; 2) a white person who is successful most commonly has gotten there because of individual merit. The bottom line is resentment: a minority employee receives an important promotion, and twenty white co-workers feel that they, each of them, would have gotten that promotion if the decision had been based on merit evaluation rather than affirmative action. A black applicant is admitted to the University of Texas law school; this is obviously due to affirmative action, which appears to have magical powers in the case of college admissions. How else can we explain the presence of hundreds of white applicants who *know* that they personally have been denied admission because of the slot in the entering class occupied by the black applicant? When neoconservatives sanction this mass self-delusion by endorsing color-blind policies seeking to root out such "reverse racism," they attract an enthusiastic following. Facts have gotten lost in the process and this is a dangerous development: the masses attracted to the rhetoric of this color-blind society are not color blind; rather, they are just blind.

NOTES

1. Winant, Howard, "The New International Dynamics of Race," in Chester Hartman, ed., *Double Exposure: Poverty and Race In America* (Armonk, NY: M.E. Sharpe, 1996), p. 17.
2. Powell, John, "Introduction," in Chester Hartman, ed., *Double Exposure: Poverty and Race in America* (Armonk, NY: M.E. Sharpe, 1996), p. 3.
3. Blauner, Bob, "Talking Past Each Other: Black and White Languages of Race," *The American Prospect* (Vol. 15), 1992) p. 56.
4. Winant, op. cit., p. 57.
5. Blauner, op. cit., p. 57.
6. Thernstrom, Stephen and Abigail, *America in Black and White* (New York: Simon and Schulster, 1997).
7. Marable, Manning, *Black Liberation in Conservative America* (Boston: South End Press, 1997), p. 122.
8. Thernstrom, op. cit.
9. Blauner, op. cit., p. 60.
10. Lawrence, Charles and Matsuda, Mari, *We Won't Go Back: Making the Case for Affirmative Action* (Boston: Houghton Mifflin, 1997), p. 69.
11. Quoted in Lawrence and Matsuda, op. cit., p. 70.
12. Bates, Timothy, Final Report. *An Analysis of the SSBIC Program: Problems and Prospects*, report to the U. S. Small Business Administration under grant SBIC-94-001-01, 1996.
13. Bates, Timothy, "Institutionalizing a Nonviable Minority Business Assistance Infrastructure: The Specialized Small Business Investment Companies", *Urban Affairs Review* (Vol. 32), May, 1997.

Bates, Timothy, "Michael Porter's Conservative Urban Agenda Will Not Revitalize America's Inner Cities: What Will?," *Economic Development Quarterly* (Vol. 11), February 1997.

14. Bates, 1996, op. cit., p. 220.
15. Bates, p. 220.
16. Bates, p. 188.

17. Bates, p. 86.
18. Bates, p. 29.
19. Bates, p. 188.
20. Bates, p. 189.
21. Bates, 1997, op. cit.
22. Bates, 1996, op. cit., p. 184.
23. Dominguez, John, *Capital Flows in Minority Communities* (Lexington, MA: D. C. Health, 1977).
24. Bradford, William, "The Effectiveness of the MESBIC Program: A Theoretical and Empirical Analysis," (unpublished manuscript, 1980).
25. Bates, 1997, op. cit.
26. Bates, 1996, op. cit.
27. Ibid.
28. Ibid.
29. Ibid.
30. Bates, pp. 198–217.
31. Bates, p. 183.
32. Bates, p. 183.
33. Fusfeld, Daniel, and Timothy Bates, *Political Economy of the Urban Ghetto* (Carbondale: Southern Illinois University Press, 1984).

Income Inequality

10

RACE, COGNITIVE SKILLS, PSYCHOLOGICAL CAPITAL AND WAGES*

Arthur H. Goldsmith, William Darity, Jr., and Jonathan R. Veum

INTRODUCTION

The observation that blacks earn less than otherwise comparable whites has long been an established "stylized fact" for workers in the U.S. The Thernstroms have most visibly challenged the validity of this "stylized fact" and, in turn, the view that black workers are subject to wage discrimination.[1] They argue that poor scholarship—research that neglects the influence of cognitive ability on wages—is responsible for this finding. In general, failure to control for relevant variables leads to inaccurate estimates of the relationship between variables, including the impact of a person's race on their wages.

In the Thernstroms' view, research that adopts an appropriate specification for the wage equation demonstrates that black workers are paid as much as comparable white employees. For instance, in studies that ostensibly account for cognitive ability, a productivity related characteristic, black and white employees earn wages that are essentially identical.[2] Therefore, the Thernstroms assert that black workers in the U.S. do not systematically confront race based wage discrimination.[3]

Findings we report below cast doubt on the validity of the Thernstroms' (1997) claim. Drawing on literature in psychology, we (Goldsmith, Veum, and Darity) have argued that psychological capital is an important determinant of personal productivity, and hence, wages.[4] However, with the exception of recent work by Goldsmith, Veum, and Darity[5] and by Dunifon and Duncan,[6] the influence of psychological capital on wages has been neglected in empirical models of wage determination. Second, using both

* The authors are indebted to Stuart Low who offered valuable insights and suggestions on the ideas addressed in this paper. The views expressed in this paper are those of the authors and do not reflect the policies or views of the U.S. Bureau of Labor Statistics.

the same data and means of measuring cognitive ability as O'Neill[7] and Neal and Johnson,[8] we find that when psychological capital also is included in a model of wage determination, blacks earn significantly less than otherwise comparable white workers. Thus, we present evidence consistent with an important adverse discriminatory affect on black worker wages.

WAGE DETERMINATION: THEORY AND EVIDENCE

Neoclassical theory predicts that a profit-maximizing firm will pay the *ith* worker a real wage, w_i, equal to their marginal product, MP_i. Most economists believe a person's marginal product depends primarily on two factors: (i) a person's skills, typically referred to as human capital, HC_i, and (ii) the physical capital, *Kj*, made available to them by the *jth* firm that employs them. In practice, human capital generally is treated as skills acquired on-the-job, both in training programs and while working, or through formal education.

Psychologists believe that a person's capacity to initiate and complete tasks is influenced by their cognitive ability, CA_i, as well as human and physical capital. Demographic factors such as age, marital status, and dependent children may alter an individual's productivity, as well as institutional phenomena like union membership. Suppose all of these factors are represented by X_i. Thus, the *ith* worker's marginal product, and hence, wage function can be written as

$$(1) \quad w_i = MP_i\,(KJ_i, X_i, HC_i, CA_i)$$

Following the convention initiated by Mincer[9] a person's wage function, equation (2), can be depicted by a linear representation of their marginal productivity function, equation (1):

$$(2) \quad w_i = \alpha_1\,(K_i) + \alpha_2\,(X_i) + \alpha_3\,(HC_i) + \alpha_4\,(CA_i) + \varepsilon_i$$

Measures of cognitive ability are rarely contained in the data sets used by economists to estimate wage equations. Thus, CA_i is typically treated as an omitted variable, which ends up in the error or disturbance term. Therefore, the wage equation usually estimated is of the form:

$$(3) \quad w_i = \alpha_1\,(K_i) + \alpha_2\,(X_i) + \alpha_3\,(HC_i) + \{\varepsilon_i + \alpha_4\,(CA_i)\}$$

Investigators often extend equation (3) to include an indicator for race, R_i. When a person is black, $R_i = R_B$, and when a person is white, $R_i = R_w$.

The race indicator usually is specified as a dummy variable, so that for black workers $R_B = 1$ and $R_w = 0$. Thus, the empirical wage equation is

$$(4) \quad w_i = \alpha_1(K_i) + \alpha_2(X_2) + \alpha_3(HC_i) + \alpha_5(R_i) + \{\varepsilon_i + \alpha_4(CA_i)\}$$

The estimated coefficient on the race indicator variable, ($\hat{\alpha}_5$), reveals any systematic average effect of being black relative to being white on wages. Suppose the set of explanatory variables includes all of the factors that influence a person's productivity. A negative and significant value for ($\hat{\alpha}_5$) indicates that a typical black worker would earn less than an equally productive white worker. Estimation of equation (3) reveals that, *ceteris paribus,* blacks receive approximately 10–13 percent lower annual earnings.[10] However, the status of cognitive ability as an omitted variable potentially mars the validity of this finding.

If the disturbance, $\{\varepsilon_i + \alpha_4 (CA_i)\}$, is correlated with HC_i—those with greater cognitive ability accumulate more human capital—then estimation of equation (4) yields biased or inconsistent estimates of the parameters ($\hat{\alpha}_1$, $\hat{\alpha}_2$, $\hat{\alpha}_3$, $\hat{\alpha}_5$). Since, the size of the estimated coefficients are suspect, the assertion that black workers face wage discrimination, based on ($\hat{\alpha}_5$) being both statistically significant and negative, may be erroneous.

On the other hand, Hernstein and Murray's[11] claim that blacks possess poorer levels of cognitive ability than whites predicts that estimation of equation (4) will yield ($\hat{\alpha}_5 < 0$). However, they would not interpret this as evidence of wage discrimination. In order to understand why this is the case consider the following situation. Suppose there are two types of people in the work force, persons with "high" cognitive ability (CA_i^H), and individuals with "low" cognitive ability (CA_i^L). Suppose that all of the high ability persons are white, while every black person possesses low cognitive ability.

Suppose an investigator wants to estimate equation (2), but does not have a measure of CA_i. They could use R_i as a proxy for CA_i. In this case the econometrician is essentially estimating equation (4')—CA_i *is* no longer in the error term of the estimating equation if it is measured by R_i.

$$(4') \quad w_i = \alpha_1 (K_i) + \alpha_2 (X_i) + \alpha_3 (HC_i) + \alpha_5 (R_i) + \{\varepsilon_i\}$$

However, if equation (4') is estimated, care must be taken in interpreting ($\hat{\alpha}_5$). This coefficient reveals the expected impact of a one unit increase, from 0 to 1, in R_i which is equivalent to a decline in cognitive ability from CA_i^H to CA_i^L. If people with poorer cognitive ability are less productive, and hence earn lower wages, then ($\hat{\alpha}_5$) would be negative. Thus, the finding ($\hat{\alpha}_5 < 0$) can be interpreted as evidence that employers reward cognitive ability, and if blacks possess less of this desired attribute, they are paid less. It need not be interpreted as evidence that employers engage in racial wage discrimination.

Controversy over both the accuracy of the estimated coefficient on a dummy variable representing race in wage equations such as equation (4), and interpretation of the coefficient on the race indicator variable in equation (4′), led O'Neill and Neal and Johnson to conclude that existing evidence shed little light on the question of whether black workers face wage discrimination.[12] They argued that both race and cognitive ability must be included in empirical wage equations in order to assess the wage discrimination hypothesis. Therefore, they estimated a wage equation of the form:

$$(5) \quad w_i = \alpha_1 (K_i) + \alpha_2 (X_i) + \alpha_3 (HC_i) + \alpha_4 (CA_i) + \alpha_5 (R_i) + \varepsilon_i$$

In order to estimate equation (5) the critical step is measurement of the psychological construct "*cognitive ability*." A number of different variables have been used to serve as a proxy for CA_i in literature.[13] For instance, Murnance, Willett, and Levy[14] used a person's score on a test designed to assess mastery of elementary mathematical concepts to measure their cognitive ability.[14] They estimated equation (5) using this measure as well as others drawn from the National Longitudinal Study of the High School Class of 1972 (NLS72) and from the High School and Beyond survey (HS&B). The trio of researchers report that a person's cognitive ability in 1972 was directly related to their wage six years later in 1978 for individuals in the NLS72. Similarly, 1980 math scores for persons in the HS&B sample were positively related to their wages in 1986.

However, they also found that the estimated coefficient on R_i, $\hat{\alpha}_5$, is inversely related to wages for members of both the LHS82 and HS&B samples. Since these researchers had controlled for cognitive ability their finding can be interpreted as evidence consistent with wage discrimination. Moreover, they also discovered that the absolute value of the negative and statistically significant race coefficient in their earnings regressions was larger for the 1980 graduates than the 1972 graduates! Being black had an even stronger negative effect on wages for blacks in 1986 than in 1978, even after measured cognitive ability was taken under consideration.

Mason estimated equation (5) using data drawn from the Panel Study of Income Dynamics (PSID), another longitudinal nationally representative data set.[15] The PSID contains a person's score on a 10–item sentence completion test. Mason used a person's test score to gauge their cognitive ability. He also found that the coefficient on race, $\hat{\alpha}_5$, is negative and significant.

A person's score on the Armed Forces Qualification Tests (AFQT) now is the most commonly used measure of cognitive ability in wage equations. The Armed Forces Qualification Test (AFQT) has been utilized by the armed services for many years to test individuals for fitness for military service. In 1980 this test was administered to 94 percent of the young men and women in the National Longitudinal Survey of Youths (NLSY) sample—a nationally representative data set rich in demographic and economic information.

June O'Neill was the first of several economists to demonstrate that the estimated coefficient on the dummy variable for race is *insignificant* when equation (5) is estimated with data drawn from the NLSY and AFQT scores are used to represent cognitive ability.[16] She also found that persons with greater cognitive ability earned significantly more than otherwise comparable individuals. Her findings have been replicated by Ferguson and by Neal and Johnson.[17] These findings reveal that employers pay the same wage to black and white workers of equivalent cognitive ability. However, the average black person in the NLSY sample scores lower on the AFQT than the typical white individual in the sample. Therefore, Neal and Johnson conclude that the racial wage differential is largely due to a racial skill differential—not discrimination.

Blacks did score lower than whites on average in the NLSY sample of AFQT takers. Whether this indicates that blacks have lower average cognitive ability than whites is contingent upon the credibility one assigns to the AFQT as a measure of cognition. However, important policy implications hinge on what factors govern a person's AFQT score (i.e., why do blacks score lower than whites?). According to Hernstein and Murray, AFQT is ". . . highly g-loaded," and ". . . AFQT is an excellent test, with psychometric reliability and validity that compare well with those of the other major tests of intelligence."[18] Thus, in their view, the AFQT gauges innate intelligence, biologically determined.

In contrast, June O'Neill describes the AFQT as "an achievement test of verbal and mathematical skills that reflects the quality of schooling received as well as the effects of parental background."[19] Performance on an achievement test depends upon both nature (genetic inheritance or intelligence) and nurture (parental inculcation and educational resources). A poor AFQT test score may reflect a relatively high intelligence coupled with few educational resources.[20]

Given the potential importance of cognitive ability's influence on wages, the dispute over what AFQT measures is important from a policy perspective. If AFQT reflects genetic intelligence, AFQT is time invariant and independent of policy. However, if AFQT reflects achievement, the policy can alter community and educational resources, and possibly parental behavior. Therefore, policy action can influence a person's cognitive ability level and hence their wage.[21]

Card and Krueger find a link between school resources and subsequent earnings.[22] They conclude that educational disparities play some role in explaining racial economic disparities. According to Darity this judgment is unsurprising since there is strong evidence that the black-white educational gap was engineered by deliberate social policy.[23]

The dispute over what AFQT really measures (see Rodgers and Spriggs)[24] as well as the accuracy of the claim that blacks score lower on the AFQT, remains. An unfortunate byproduct of this debate is that it has diverted attention from the more fundamental issue of whether equation (5) is a model specification capable of producing reliable estimates of the relation between race and wages.

The Thernstroms argument that all of the black-white gap in wages can be accounted for by racial differences in cognitive skills may be unwarranted.[25] Their conclusion depends on equation (5) being the "correct" model of wage determination. If an important determinant of personal productivity, and hence wages, is unaccounted for in equation (5)—as was the case with equation (4)—then the coefficients estimated suffer from omitted variable bias. If this is the case, reaching a conclusion about the presence of wage discrimination by evaluating the sign and significance of the estimated coefficient on race from equation (5) is inappropriate. In the next section we discuss why equation (5) is likely to be a misspecified model of wage determination.

SPECIFICATION OF THE WAGE MODEL REVISITED: PSYCHOLOGICAL CAPITAL AND PRODUCTIVITY

Most economists believe that a person's human capital—education, experience, and cognitive ability—are the primary determinant of their personal productivity. Of course, the quantity and quality of a person's work also depends on their psychological capital, PC_i—those aspects of personality that influence productivity. Erikson, founder of *Life Span Development Theory,* argued that individuals who were psychologically healthy would be the most productive.[26] Economists acknowledge that the influence of personality on productivity is detectable and is rewarded by employers. Therefore, the appropriate model of wage determination is

$$(6)\quad w_i = \alpha_1 (K_i) + \alpha_2 (X_i) + \alpha_3 (HC_i) + \alpha_4 (CA_i) + \alpha_5 (R_i) + \alpha_6 (PC_i) + \varepsilon_i$$

Most economists have taken the position that personality is either unobservable or unmeasurable. Therefore, empirical studies of wage determination that control for cognitive ability result in the estimation of equation (7):

$$(7)\quad w_i = \alpha_1 (K_i) + \alpha_2 (X_i) + \alpha_3 (HC_i) + \alpha_4 (CA_i) + \alpha_5 (R_i) + \{ \varepsilon_i + \alpha_6 (PC_i)\}$$

Treating psychological capital as an omitted variable, and thereby transferring it to the error term of equation (7), leads to biased coefficient estimates and inaccurate hypothesis tests if PC_i is correlated with any of the other explanatory variables. Because psychological capital is likely to influence the accumulation of human capital, it is necessary to include measures of psychological capital in wage equation (6) to attain an accurate estimate of the relation between race and wages.

Psychological capital encompasses a host of personal attributes expected to influence productivity. Many features of a person's psychological capital are reflected in a person's self-view or sense of self-esteem. Following Rosenberg, psychologists treat self-esteem as a multidimensional construct, comprising notions of worth, goodness, health, appearance, and social competence.[27] The broad scope of factors contributing to self-esteem allows it to capture many aspects of a person's psychological capital. Therefore, self-esteem is an ideal way to measure psychological capital.

Rosenberg[28] and other psychologists have developed and validated measures of self-esteem based upon self-reported responses to an inventory of survey questions.[29] Rosenberg's scale contains 10 questions used to construct six subscales, each yielding a single measure represented on a two point (0,1) scale. Therefore, the Rosenberg measure of self-esteem ranges in value from 0–6, with a higher value representing a greater level of self-esteem.

Brockner[30] found a positive correlation between self-esteem and job performance—evidence consistent with Erikson's[31] assertion that persons with better psychological health are more productive.[32] In spite of Brockner's findings, the notion that self-esteem contributes to personal productivity, and hence wages, was unrecognized by economists—leading them to continue to estimate equation (7)—until the recent work by Goldsmith, Veum, and Darity.[33]

Goldsmith, Veum, and Darity estimate equation (6) using data drawn from the NLSY. The NLSY is a sample of 12,686 males and females who were between the ages of 14 and 21 in 1978 and who have been interviewed each year since 1979. It includes data on wages and numerous aspects of human capital. In also contains a person's responses to Rosenberg's inventory of questions for his Self-Esteem Scale (SES).

In our empirical work, psychological capital (PC_i) is measured by a person's score on the Rosenberg Self-Esteem Scale, and cognitive ability by an individual's score on the AFQT. Thus, apart from our *inclusion* of a measure of psychological capital, we used the same data as O'Neill and Neal and Johnson.[34] Unlike them, we are able to estimate equation (6) rather than equation (5), which on theoretical grounds appears to be misspecified and which in practice becomes equation (7)—an equation estimated subject to omitted variable bias.

We are able to examine the influence of cognitive ability, psychological capital, and race on a person's real wage at two different points in time for NLSY participants, 1980 and 1987. In both of these years respondents were asked the entire set of questions which comprise Rosenberg's Self-Esteem Scale.[35] We limit the 1980 data to persons who were old enough to have a work permit in 1979 and had finished their formal schooling; this gives us 2,225 young people of whom 1,411 were employed in 1980. Our 1987 data set consists of 8,132 observations of persons not enrolled in school in 1987—6,911 of these persons were working in 1987.[36]

Table 1 presents our findings on the influence on a person's wage of human capital (HC_i), cognitive ability (CA_i), psychological capital (PC_i), and race (R_i). The summary table does not include our findings on the contribution to a person's wage of: age, marital status, dependents, wealth, adolescent environment, residence. local labor market conditions, occupation, and industry of employment.[37]

TABLE 1
OLS Log Wage Estimates Equation (6)ψ
(t-statistics in parentheses)

VARIABLE NAME	VARIABLE MEASURE	1980 DATA	1987 DATA
HC_I	EDUCATION	.12e-01 (1.67)**	.27e-01 (6.75)***
HC_I	EXPERIENCE	.76e-02 (5.29)***	.51e-03 (3.92)***
HC_I	TENURE	.69e-03 (3.11)***	.54e-03 (12.07)***
CA_i	AFQT	.19e-02 (2.34)***	.12e-02 (1.58)*
PC_i	SELF-ESTEEM	.13 (2.97)***	.25 (3.73)***
R_i	BLACK	-.53e-01 (1.98)**	-.30e-01 (1.73)**
NUMBER OF OBSERVATIONS		1411	6911
F		18.90*** (34,1376)	115.84*** (34,6876)
R^2		.32	.36

* Statistically significant different from zero at the .1 confidence level.
** Statistically significant different from zero at the .05 confidence level.
*** Statistically significant different from zero at the .0P1 confidence level.
ψ EDUCATION is measured in years of schooling completed, tenure is represented by weeks of employment with current employer, EXPERIENCE is measured by all weeks of employment prior to current job, SELF-ESTEEM is measured using Rosenberg's scale (0–6), and cognitive skills are captured by AFQT scores which range from 0–60.

RESULTS AND CONCLUSIONS

The coefficient estimates on each of three different types of human capital (EDUCATION, EXPERIENCE, TENURE) are positive and significant in both the data set primarily composed of people at a very early stage of their working life-cycle and the data set containing more mature individuals. In addition, self-esteem, a broad measure of psychological capital, is positively and significantly related to the real wage in both the 1980 and 1987 data. For the average person in the entire data set, a 10 percent increase in self-esteem improves the real wage by 4.8 percent using 1980 data and 13.3 percent using 1987 data.[39] Persons with greater cognitive ability, measured by their score on the AFQT, earned significantly more than otherwise comparable individuals for both the 1980 and 1987 data sets.[40]

The striking result, in the context of the debate over the existence of wage discrimination, is that the race coefficient ($\hat{\alpha}_5$) is negative and statistically significant at the .05 confidence level in both 1980 and 1987 despite the presence of a measure of cognitive ability (AFQT score) in the wage equation regression. When the contribution to wages of both cognitive ability and psychological capital are explicitly taken into account we find that black workers, with comparable skill characteristics, still earn significantly less than white employees. For very young workers, persons 16–22 years old, blacks earn 5 percent less *per hour*. When these individuals are still young, 22–29 years of age, black employees earn 3 percent less *per hour*.

Our findings suggest that among working persons there is a positive correlation between being black and self-esteem.[41] Thus, when psychological capital is excluded from the wage equation, the dummy variable identifying black employees captures both the negative effect of being black on wages as well as the positive correlation between greater self-esteem—which black employees possess—and wages. If the positive effect on wages of being black, operating through self-esteem, is offset by the negative impact of being black on wages then being black would be unrelated to wages—the finding reported by O'Neill and Neal and Johnson.[41] When psychological capital is included in the wage equation, the contribution of race to wages is isolated and being black has a negative effect on a person's wage.

What can we conclude? Empirical wage equation specification matters. The Thernstrom's claim that differences in "pre-market factors"—particularly cognitive ability—explain the black-white earnings gap. However, their conjecture is based upon an empirical model of wage determination that neglects the role of psychological capital. Race is an important determinant of wages when the influence of *both* cognitive skills and psychological capital is taken into account in a wage equation.

The average black person in the sample possesses a lower level of psychological capital and a lower AFQT score. However, black workers with identical cognitive talent and equivalent levels of both human and psychological capital still receive lower wages than white workers. The latter finding is inconsistent with the Thernstrom's assertion that labor market discrimination against blacks is negligible or nonexistent. It is consistent with the presence of wage discrimination in the labor market.

NOTES

1. Thernstrom, A., and S. Thernstrom, "The Real Story on Black Progress," *The Wall Street Journal,* September 3, 1997.
2. O'Neill, June, "The Role of Human Capital in Earning Differences Between Black and White Men," *The Journal of Economic Perspectives,* Winter 1990, 25–45; Neal, Derek A. and William R. Johnson, "The Role of Premarket Factors in Black-White Wage Differences," *The Journal of Political Economy,* October 1996, 869–95.
3. Thernstrom and Thernstrom, 1997.
4. Goldsmith, Arthur H., Jonathan R. Veum, and William Darity, Jr., "The Impact of Psychological and Human Capital on Wages," *Economic Inquiry,* October 1997, 815–29.
5. Goldsmith, Veum, and Darity, 1997.
6. Dunifon, Rachel, and Greg J. Duncan, "Long-Run Effects of Motivation on Labor-Market Success," *Social Psychology Quarterly,* 1998, 61:1, 33–48.
7. O'Neill, 1990.
8. Neal and Johnson, 1996.
9. Mincer, Jacob, "On-the-Job-Training: Costs, Returns, and Some Implications," *Journal of Political Economy,* October 1962, S50–S79; Mincer, Jacob, *Schooling, Experience, and Earnings.* New York: Columbia University Press for the National Bureau of Economic Research, 1974.
10. Gottschalk, Peter, "Inequality, Income Growth, and Mobility: The Basic Facts," *Journal of Economic Perspectives,* Spring 1997, 11:2, 21–40.
11. Herrnstein, Richard, and Charles Murray, *The Bell Curve: Intelligence and Class Structure in American Life.* New York: Basic Books, 1994.
12. O'Neill, 1990; Neal and Johnson, 1996.
13. Altonji and Spletzer (1991) use either high school class rank or a person's score on the Scholastic Aptitude Test to measure cognitive ability. Card and Krueger (1990) use secondary school quality to gauge ability. Hanushek, (1986) provides an excellent review of the literature on measurement of personal ability and its subsequent impact on wages.
14. Murname, Richard J., John B. Willett, and Frank Levy, "The Growing Importance of Cognitive Skills in Wage Determination," *The Review of Economics and Statistics,* May 1995, 77:2. 251–66.

15. Mason, Patrick L., "Race, Culture, and Skill: Interracial Wage Differences among African Americans, Latinos, and Whites," *The Review of Black Political Economy,* forthcoming.

16. O'Neill, 1990.

17. Ferguson, Ronald F., "Shifting Challenges: Fifty Years of Economic Change toward Black-White Earnings Equality," *Deadalus,* Winter 1995, 124, 37–76; Neal and Johnson, 1996.

18. Herrnstein and Murray, 1994.

19. O'Neill, 1990, p. 32.

20. Given O'Neill's perspective on what the AFQT reflects, discrimination in the provision of school resources and perceived disparate social and economic treatment could influence AFQT scores.

21. Goldberger and Manski (1995), in their review of the *Bell Curve,* argue convincingly that AFQT scores are influenced by factors including educational attainment and social resources—AFQT is not fixed at birth—and therefore AFQT is a poor measure of cognitive ability. Their view, which is now shared by most economists including O'Neill and Neal and Johnson, is that AFQT reveals mastery level of basic academic skills. In a wage regression that controls for both a person's educational attainment and the resources they received during childhood and adolescence an individual's AFQT score performs better as a measure of cognitive ability, but remains less than ideal.

22. Card, David, and Alan Krueger, "School Quality and Black-White Relative Earnings: A Direct Assessment," *Quarterly Journal of Economics,* February 1992, 107:1, 151–200.

23. Darity, William, Jr., "Programmed Retardation and the Theory of Noncompeting Groups," unpublished manuscript, University of North Carolina at Chapel Hill, May 1997.

24. Rodgers, William M., and William E. Spriggs, "What Does AFQT Really Measure: Race, Wages, Schooling, and the AFQT Score," *The Review of Black Political Economy,* Winter 1996. 24:4, 13–46.

25. Thernstrom and Thernstrom, 1997.

26. Erikson, Erik H., "Identity and the Life Cycle," *Psychological Issues,* January 1959, 50–100.

27. Rosenberg, Morris, *Society and the Adolescent Self-Image.* Princeton, NJ: Princeton University Press, 1965.

28. Ibid.

29. Robinson and Wrightsman (1991) offer an excellent description and psychometric evaluation of all the commonly used measures of self-esteem. See also Wylie (1989) for an extensive discussion of Rosenberg's SES.

30. Brockner, Joe, *Self-Esteem at Work.* Lexington, MA: Lexington Books, 1988.

31. Erikson, 1959.

32. He found self-esteem was directly linked to productivity in two ways. First, managers perceived that high self-esteem workers tend to use their time more effectively. The latter needed less direction from supervisors, leading to shorter periods of "down time." Second, workers high in self-esteem exercised a more efficient use of group time by exhibiting a willingness to consider a wider range of solutions to problems; and they were more confident decision makers. These characteristics led to groups with high levels of cooperation and, groups less inclined to seek guidance from managers.

33. Goldsmith, Veum, and Darity, 1997.

34. O'Neill, 1990; Neal and Johnson, 1996.

35. Rosenberg, 1995.

36. Wage data are only available on working individuals. Unobserved personal characteristics may exists that influence both the decision to work and compensation if employed. We adopt a technique developed by Heckman (1979) to account for these differences.

37. A detailed discussion of our results for equation (6) and the empirical procedures used appears in Goldsmith, Veum, and Darity, 1997.

38. Some caution is called for when comparing the 1980 and 1987 results, since the latter year has a much larger sample size.

39. For complete results as well as a detailed description of how all the variables in equation (7) are measured and the procedure used to estimate equation (7) see Goldsmith, Veum, and Darity, 1997.

40. This finding is consistent with Mason's (1998) speculation that there may be unobservable variables in wage equations that favor black productivity. See Darity and Mason (1998, footnote 13) for a thorough discussion of this argument.

41. O'Niell, 1990; Neal and Johnson, 1996.

11

DETERMINANTS OF REGIONAL INCOME DISTRIBUTION IN THE U.S. SOUTH, 1980–1990: ROLES OF NET MIGRATION AND HUMAN CAPITAL ACCUMULATION

Octavian Ngarambé and Stephan J. Goetz

INTRODUCTION

A number of recent studies of regional income distribution have suggested growing income inequality in the U.S. during the 1980s.[1] This growing inequality has been attributed to the effects of industrial structure, demographic, economic, educational, labor force, and other socio-economic characteristics. Previous studies have also examined the effect of international migration on income distribution using cross-country data.[2] Heretofore, however, the effect of internal migration has generally been given lower importance in the search for explanations of regional income inequality. As a result, our current knowledge is very limited regarding how internal migration measurements and modeling results might influence the distribution of incomes.

The primary purpose of this article is to extend the previous literature a step further by determining the effect of net migration, defined as movement across county or state boundary or abroad,[3] on family income inequality in a county. A second major purpose of this article is to examine simultaneously the effect of increased human capital formation in a county on family income distribution. Furthermore, this study examines the effects of these two factors on the cross-sectional dispersion of black, white, and overall family incomes within counties. Hence, decomposing the components of income inequality by race in the present analysis is another means of extending our understanding of how the central variables for this analysis influence income inequality *within* the three dimensions inequality.

A large literature examines the impacts of population migration and human capital investments on income distribution. However, higher income inequality in a locality may lead to reduced migration flows and educational growth. A third focus of this article is to take into account the simultaneity between these three sets of variables. We choose the U.S. South[4] because it is a region with relatively high income inequality and low schooling, and because numerous U.S. residents and immigrants from abroad moved into the South as a result of the strong economic performance in that region over the decade of the 1980s. Also, during the 1980s, black and white populations redistributed themselves from the rural South where employment opportunities have traditionally been very limited to metropolitan areas associated with relatively rapidly growing labor demand.

The article is organized as follows. Section 2 discusses the method for estimating a Gini coefficient of concentration using grouped family income data. Section 3 describes the variables and the structural equation for family income inequality. A three-stage least squares model of income inequality is then constructed that considers inequality, net migration, and human capital as jointly determined. Section 4 discusses empirical results, and a summary and conclusion are presented in Section 5 with suggestions for future research.

MEASURING FAMILY INCOME INEQUALITY

There are, in general, several ways to measure income distribution. In this study, we use the Gini coefficient following the methodology described in Kakwani and Podder.[5] The coefficient is bounded by zero for perfect equality and one for perfect inequality: the higher the score, the greater the income inequality.

Suppose income Y of a family unit is a random variable with probability density function $f(y)$, defined as:

$$F(y) = \int_0^y f(y)dY \qquad (1)$$

where $F(y)$ represents the percentage of family units receiving income less than or equal to Y. Assume that the mean μ of the distribution exists. Then, the first moment of the distribution is

$$F_1(y) = \frac{1}{\mu}\int_0^y Y\, f(y)dY \qquad (2)$$

which is the share of all income with income less than or equal to Y. The Lorenz curve can be plotted by generating values of $F(y)$ and $F_1(y)$ using equations (1) and (2), and by considering arbitrary values of Y.

Let A denote the ordinate of the Lorenz curve through the origin along the line of perfect equality and B the length of the ordinate from any point on the Lorenz curve to the line of perfect equality. Then,

$$A = \frac{1}{\sqrt{2}}[(F(y) + F_1(y)] \text{ and } B = \frac{1}{\sqrt{2}}[(F(y) - F_1(y)] \tag{3}$$

By integrating both ordinates of the Lorenz curve,

$$\frac{dA}{dB} = \frac{(\mu - y)}{(\mu + y)} \tag{4}$$

The equation for the Lorenz curve is

$$B = cA^{\gamma}\,(\sqrt{2} - A)^{\sigma} \tag{5}$$

where $0<B<\sqrt{2}$; c, γ, and σ are > 0.

The county-level family income data are grouped by income class. Assume there are N families grouped into $Q + 1$ income classes for each time series t, ($t = 1, \ldots, T$). If n_t is the number of families receiving income between Y_{q-1}, and Y_q, $f_{t,q} = n_t/N$ is a consistent estimator of the probability that a family belongs to the qth income earner group. Therefore, $F(y)$ and $F_1(y)$ can be estimated from:

$$f_{t,q} = \sum_{\gamma-1}^{q} \quad \text{for each } t = 1, \ldots, T \text{ and } q = 1, \ldots, Q$$

$$f_{1t,q} = \frac{1}{M}\sum_{\gamma-1}^{q} m_{\gamma} f_{\gamma} \quad \text{for each } t = 1, \ldots, T \text{ and } q = 1, \ldots, Q \tag{6}$$

where m_y is the mean income of Y for group q; and M is the overall mean income for all families grouped into Q+1 and in year t. Expressing $f_{t,q}$ and $f_{1t,q}$ using equation (6), the consistent estimators of A and B are:

$$n_{t,q} = \frac{(f_{t,q} + f_{1t,q})}{\sqrt{2}} \text{ and } p_{t,q} = \frac{(f_{t,q} - f_{1t,q})}{\sqrt{2}} \tag{7}$$

Given (7), the formula for the Lorenz curve is[6]

$$\log p_{t,q} = \log c + \alpha \log n_{t,q} + \beta \log(\sqrt{2} - n_{t,q}) + e_1 \qquad (8)$$

where e_1 is an error term.

By substituting equation (4) into the Lorenz curve equation (5),

$$\frac{M - y_{t,q}}{M + y_{t,q}} \frac{(\sqrt{2} - n_{t,q})n_{t,q}}{P_{t,q}} = \gamma(\sqrt{2} - n_{t,q}) - \sigma n_{t,q} \qquad (9)$$

The Lorenz curve is estimated using equation (8) and the restriction in equation (9). In estimating the Lorenz curve, we use a generalized least squares (GLS) approach. The resulting coefficient estimates, c, γ, and σ are asymptotically more efficient than ordinary least squares estimates.[7] Then the overall Gini coefficient of concentration is

$$GINI = 2c(\sqrt{2})^{1+\gamma+\sigma} B(1+\gamma, 1+\sigma) \qquad (10)$$

where $B(1 + \gamma, 1 + \sigma)$ is the Beta function, $1 + \gamma$, and $1 + \sigma$ are degrees of freedom.

A MODEL OF INCOME INEQUALITY AND THE DATA

Three measures of family income inequality are used, based on the Gini coefficient. First, *black-to-black inequality* measures income inequality *within* the black population in a county. Second, *white-to-white inequality* measures income inequality *within* the white population in a county. Third, *overall inequality* measures family income distribution for the whole population in a county.

We include the initial level of the Gini coefficient at the beginning of the decade to control for inequality convergence across counties. To test for the hypothesized simultaneity between migration and inequality, we include the net in-migration rate measured as the number of in-migrants per county population.[8]

Migration affects income distribution because it changes factor supplies, factor productivity, and factor prices. Since potential in-migrants are more educated on average,[9] an influx of domestic migrants may reduce earnings of higher-skilled original residents, which compresses income distribution. However, greater in-migration may imply that a large share of population has less labor market information, which may act to increase inequality. So, the net effect of a county's population mobility on income inequality is uncertain.

Previous studies have also demonstrated that human capital accumulation is a major determinant of differentials in earnings between social groups in the United States.[10] These authors have found that income inequality and average educational attainment were negatively related. However, recent empirical evidence has demonstrated that technological change that increases demand for skills favors high-income individuals who can afford education at the expense of low-income individuals, leading to higher income disparities.[11] Thus, the model also includes the educational attainment variable measured as change in the percentage of the population 16 years-old and over with one year or more of college education.[12]

We expect that higher county-level family income growth rates are associated with lower income inequality. However, recent literature found a positive relationship between economic growth and income inequality in the U.S.[13] Likewise, others found that economic growth had minimal effects on national income inequality.[14]

A number of cross-sectional studies of income inequality have convincingly demonstrated that inequality is a function of industrial composition of workforce. The industrial composition vector we include contains seven non-agricultural employment shares, where the share in government is omitted to avoid perfect collinearity. Hence, the industry share coefficients are measured *relative* to public sector employment. In general, sectors such as manufacturing and construction pay relatively high wages to less-skilled workers. Thus, greater shares of these industries in a county could reduce income inequality. Similarly, the government sector acts to promote equal employment opportunities, thereby reducing disparities in state, local, and federal payrolls. In contrast, service employment is relatively heterogeneous, ranging from highly paid professionals to lowly paid workers, and thus service sector firms tend to be associated with higher income inequality.

We hypothesize that a county's average wages are positively associated with higher inequality because of the increased wage differentials between skilled and unskilled workers. Because female-headed households are disproportionately low-earning households, counties with higher shares of female-headed households may be associated with higher income inequality. Since there were major changes in tax law resulting in a less progressive income tax during the Reagan Administration in the 1980s, local taxes are expected to be positively related to income in-

TABLE 1
Summary Statistics and Data Sources for Variables Used in Income Inequality Model

$DGINI_{c,t}^{a}$	Change in Gini coefficient for cth county between 1980 and 1990	1.4190	-0.0816	0.0481
$DCLGE_{c,t}^{a}$	Change in percent of persons 16-years-old and over completing one year or more of college (1980-1990)	0.7092	0.4471	0.3952
$MOV85_{c,t}^{a}$	In-migration rate of county population, 1985	0.4410	0.4413	0.4446
$MOV75_{c,t}^{a}$	In-migration rate of county population, 1975	0.4431	0.4922	0.4710
$GINI_{c,t}^{a}$	Gini coefficient for cth county in 1980	0.3942	0.2406	0.2062
$D\ln Y_{c,t}^{b}$	Family income growth rate between 1980 and 1990	0.1198	0.1195	0.1015
$MIN_{c,t}^{c}$	Mining employment (%)	0.0213	0.0214	0.0324
$MFT_{c,t}^{c}$	Manufacturing employment (%)	0.2309	0.2373	0.2219
$CST_{c,t}^{c}$	Construction employment (%)	0.0708	0.0707	0.0729
$TSP_{c,t}^{c}$	Transport and public utilities employment (%)	0.0601	0.0598	0.0609
$SALE_{c,t}^{c}$	Wholesale and retail trade employment (%)	0.1709	0.1684	0.1645
$FIN_{c,t}^{c}$	Financial services employment (%)	0.0357	0.0349	0.0329
$SCE_{c,t}^{c}$	Services employment (%)	0.2293	0.2271	0.2207
$WAGE_{c,t}^{d}$	Mean wage income ($100,000)	0.1339	0.1327	0.1314
$EXP_{c,t}^{c}$	Real local gvnt. gen. expenditures ($1,000/capita)	0.5094	0.5065	0.5060
$TAX_{c,t}^{c}$	Real local gvnt. gen. tax revenues ($1,000/capita)	0.1454	0.1426	0.1568
$FEMHH_{c,t}^{a}$	Households headed by single females (% of total)	0.3550	0.1117	0.1263
$METRO_{c,t}^{e}$	Coded 1 for Metropolitan county and 0 otherwise	0.3136	0.2903	0.2212
Number of Observations		735	874	1,256

Data Sources: a. U.S. Bureau of Census, General Social and Economic Characteristics 1980, 1990. b. U.S. Bureau of Census, Current Population Reports, Series P20, 1980, 1990. c. U.S. Bureau of Census, Statistical Abstracts, CD-ROM 1996. d. U.S. Bureau of Economic Analysis, Regional Economic Information System, CD-ROM 1995. e. U.S. Department of Agriculture (Beale Codes).

equality. On the other hand, public-sector expenditures are either progressive or regressive depending on the distribution of incomes, although they are on balance expected to be progressive. Earlier work has also found that incomes in rural areas are distributed more unequally than in their urban counterparts.[15]

The estimated income inequality model takes the form:

$$DGINI = \alpha_o + \gamma_1 GINI + \gamma_2 MOV85 + \gamma_3 DCLGE + \gamma_4 D\ln Y + \sum_{i=1}^{8} \beta_i JOBPC_i + \delta_1 WAGE + \delta_2 FEMHH + \delta_3 TAX + \delta_4 EXP + \delta_5 METRO + e \quad (11)$$

where *DGINI*=change in the Gini coefficient between 1980 and 1990, *GINI*=the Gini coefficient in 1980, *MOV85*=in-migration rate of county population in 1985, *DCLGE*=change in percent of persons 16 years-old and over completing one year or more of college (1980–1990), *D*ln*Y*=family income growth, *JOBPC*=percent employment in mining; construction; manufacturing; transportation and public utilities; whole/retail sale; finance, insurance, and real estate; and services (government is the omitted category), *WAGE*=mean wage income, *FEMHH*=percent female-headed households, *TAX*=local tax revenues per capita, *EXP*=local government expenditures per capita, *METRO*=metropolitan county, ε=error term. We use 1980 data to measure our explanatory variables in order to avoid simultaneity bias. Table 1 presents brief descriptions of variables used in the model, along with sources, and summary statistics.

ESTIMATION RESULTS AND DISCUSSION

Results for the three-stage least squares estimation of income inequality are reported separately for blacks, whites, and the entire population in the South in Table 2. The coefficient estimate for initial personal income inequality is significant and of the expected negative sign, indicating convergence of inequality. Net migration had mixed effects on income inequality. Counties with higher rates of net migration flows are associated with lower *overall* income inequality. However, net migration has a statistically significant and positive effect on black income inequality. Educational growth is similarly found to have a strong negative effect on *overall* income inequality, but had little impact on income inequality *within* the two broad racial groups in the South.

TABLE 2
Three-Stage Estimates for Income Inequality

	Black	White	All Races
Constant	4.147	0.002	0.620
	(1.60)[a]	(0.01)	(12.08)
$GINI_{c,t}$	-15.626***	-0.556**	-0.730***
	(10.04)	(2.99)	(21.31)
$MOV85_{c,t}$	6.172*	0.444	-0.772***
	(1.65)	(1.54)	(10.62)
$DCLGE_{c,t}$	0.066	0.208	-0.239***
	(0.40)	(0.73)	(7.06)
$DlnY_{c,t}$	1.434	0.285***	0.184***
	(1.36)	(3.08)	(9.53)
$MIN_{c,t}$	9.389**	0.430*	0.076**
	(2.45)	(1.93)	(2.12)
$MFT_{c,t}$	-0.477	0.149	-0.214***
	(0.25)	(0.81)	(8.59)
$CST_{c,t}$	-1.173	-0.585*	0.111*
	(0.17)	(1.64)	(1.88)
$TSP_{c,t}$	11.820*	0.330	0.010
	(1.65)	(0.63)	(0.14)
$SALE_{c,t}$	-8.667	-1.051**	0.354***
	(1.14)	(2.07)	(6.61)
$FIN_{c,t}$	-3.998	0.169	0.056
	(0.19)	(0.15)	(0.38)
$SCE_{c,t}$	-0.535	0.246*	0.062*
	(0.58)	(1.87)	(1.64)
$WAGE_{c,t}$	-11.644**	-0.636	-0.080
	(1.95)	(1.07)	(1.20)
$FEMHH_{c,t}$	-1.083	-0.155	0.272***
	(0.45)	(0.86)	(5.57)
$TAX_{c,t}$	11.060**	0.027	0.560**
	(2.84)	(0.24)	(2.67)
$EXP_{c,t}$	-0.870	0.064	-0.014
	(0.71)	(1.07)	(1.36)
$METRO_{c,t}$	-0.548	0.021	0.011**
	(1.44)	(0.90)	(2.67)

[a]Numbers in parentheses are *t*-statistics, with levels of significance: *= 10%, **=5%, and ***=1% or lower.

Counties with faster income growth were more likely to experience higher income inequality for whites and all *Southerners.* There is a great deal of variation in terms of how industrial composition of workforce affects income inequality of all three types. Relative to the control variable—employment in government—counties with more employment in mining exhibited higher income inequality. The result for mining likely reflects the economic slump for energy counties in the 1980s. Employment in the manufacturing sector had a significant negative effect on the *overall* level of income inequality. Counties with more employment in construction had higher *overall* level of income inequality, but below average level of white income inequality. Counties with more employment in transport and public utilities had statistically higher black income inequality. Counties with more employment in whole/retail sale had higher *overall* income inequality, but lower white income inequality. Also, counties with more employment in services sectors had higher white and *overall* income inequality.

Counties with higher wage-levels had relatively lower level of black income inequality, *ceteris paribus.* The results indicate that the *overall* level of income inequality is higher in those counties that have a relatively large percentage of families headed by a female (with no husband present), suggesting that incomes of female households are predominately concentrated in the lower rings of *overall* income distribution. It is worth noting that family structure played little role in influencing inequality *within* both sub-group populations. Counties with higher local taxes exhibited subsequently higher black and *overall* income inequality, and the impact of taxes is much stronger for blacks. One possible reason for this result is that government taxes collected a large share of low income families, and thus largely contributed to the widening of black family income differentials. The redistributive effect of government expenditures is weak probably because of government decisions to cut programs providing assistance to low and middle family income people in the 1980s. Contrary to expectations, total incomes in urban counties are more unequal than in their rural counterparts. Urban counties may be more likely to have a bimodal income distribution of high and low-wage jobs leading to greater *overall* income inequality.

In order to understand the spatial distribution of incomes *within* the three dimensions inequality, Table 3 provides the estimated regression models of income inequality by county-type. We report only the net migration, educational attainment, and family income growth variables

TABLE 3
Three-Stage Estimates for Income Inequality by County-type

	METRO	NONMETRO ALL	LARGE[a]	SMALL[b]	FRONTIER[c]
Dependent Variable $DGINI_{c,t}$	Black Income Inequality				
Constant	4.224	2.740	-3.355	1.394	23.163
	(2.83)[d]	(0.94)	(1.00)	(0.41)	(2.08)
$MOV85_{c,t}$	0.492	9.224	14.629**	5.00	-26.624
	(0.19)	(1.49)	(2.55)	(0.60)	(0.95)
$DCLGE_{c,t}$	0.313*	0.026	0.388	0.071	-2.274*
	(1.66)	(0.12)	(1.07)	(0.22)	(1.90)
$DlnY_{c,t}$	-0.634	2.391*	1.924	3.561	12.214**
	(0.79)	(1.64)	(1.19)	(1.46)	(2.11)
Dependent Variable $DGINI_{c,t}$	White Income Inequality				
Constant	0.476	0.460	-0.306	1.731	-0.497
	(6.23)	(1.14)	(2.77)	(1.63)	(1.06)
$MOV85_{c,t}$	0.857***	-0.098	0.630**	-1.467	1.893**
	(6.62)	(0.18)	(4.22)	(1.11)	(2.35)
$DCLGE_{c,t}$	0.017**	0.012	0.022*	0.014	-0.118
	(2.29)	(0.62)	(1.73)	(0.38)	(1.52)
$DlnY_{c,t}$	0.190**	0.436*	0.313***	0.755**	0.197*
	(3.96)	(2.91)	(6.95)	(2.08)	(1.64)
Dependent Variable $DGINI_{c,t}$	Overall Income Inequality				
Constant	0.555	0.422	0.273	0.441	0.108
	(10.10)	(8.44)	(4.53)	(6.61)	(1.09)
$MOV85_{c,t}$	-0.557***	-0.405***	-0.321**	-0.445***	0.088
	(8.44)	(5.69)	(3.19)	(4.67)	(0.62)
$DCLGE_{c,t}$	-0.350***	-0.240***	-0.208**	-0.246***	-0.105*
	(8.25)	(7.18)	(3.68)	(5.22)	(2.18)
$DlnY_{c,t}$	0.074***	0.187***	0.180***	0.184***	0.230***
	(3.73)	(8.29)	(5.72)	(5.91)	(4.65)

[a]Large trade center nonmetropolitan counties which contain a town of at least 25,000 persons.

[b]Small trade center nonmetropolitan counties where the largest town has between 10,000 and 25,000 persons.

[c]Rural (frontier) counties in which no town is greater than 10,000 persons.

[d]Numbers in parentheses are *t*-statistics with levels of significance: *=10%, **=5%, and ***1% or lower.

for purposes of discussion. Results indicate significant differences between metro and several types of nonmetro counties. Net migration had a positive impact on black income inequality in large trade center counties. Greater educational attainment tends to reduce inequality among blacks in rural (frontier) counties and increase income inequality in metropolitan counties. These results on educational attainment are sizable, indicating that although education was generally found to be insignificant in explaining income inequality *within* both racial-groups, it was probably due to great variations of the variable across county-types. Family income growth had a positive effect on black income inequality in all nonmetropolitan and frontier counties.

Net migration increased income inequality among whites in urban, large, and frontier counties. Greater educational attainment also tends to increase inequality among whites in urban and large trade center counties. Family income growth generally had a positive effect on white income inequality in all county-types. Results for *overall* levels of income inequality across all county-types are generally similar; net migration and educational growth were found to generally be significant and negatively related to *overall* income inequality, while family income growth increased inequality.

SUMMARY AND CONCLUSION

Previous work on regional income distribution has been quite successful in advancing our understanding of the determinants of income inequality. However, results in this study suggest other dimensions—the effects of broadly defined net migration and human capital investment on inequality vary *within* black-to-black, white-to-white, and *overall* income inequality in southern United States, and more importantly, there is a significant dissimilarity in the impact these characteristics have on the spatial distribution of incomes.

Results indicate that net migration reduced *overall* income inequality but had a positive effect on black income inequality. That is, in-migrants may tend to make counties more heterogenous with regard to the level of black family income. Educational growth is also found to have an equalizing effect on income inequality for the total population in the South. However, the proportion of a county's population that has a college degree does not significantly affect its level of income inequality *within* both racial groups.

Results for income inequality by county-type indicate significant differences between metro and several nonmetro counties. The increase in net migration contributed to the increase in black income inequality in large towns (of at least 25,000). Educational growth also had a positive impact on black income inequality in metropolitan counties, but reduced inequality for blacks in small towns (of less than 10,000). Family income growth had a positive effect on black income inequality in all nonmetropolitan counties. This result can be attributed to changes in regional industrial composition during the 1980s. Much of the economic growth in the rural South has been driven by expanding services and technology industries with a bimodal wage distribution.

Greater net migration rates increased white income inequality in urban, large, and small towns. Educational growth also had a positive impact in urban and large towns. Family income growth generally had a positive effect on white income inequality in all county-types. Concerning the *overall* level of income inequality, results indicate that net migration and educational growth tend to reduce *overall* family income inequality, while family income growth had a positive impact on *overall* income inequality in all county-types.

Through this overview, we highlight the importance of conducting complementary analyses using national-level data to determine whether the relationships noted herein are unique to the South or are generalizable to other U.S. regions as well. The 1980s was a decade of severe economic recessions, and our results may not necessarily hold during economic expansions. We also suggest that one could, for instance, systematically extend these analyses for the 1990s as more data become available for some time.

NOTES

1. Nissan, E., and G. Carter, "Income Inequality Across Regions Over Time," *Growth and Change,* 24 (1993): 303–319; Levernier, W., D.S. Rickman, and M.D. Partridge, "Variation in U.S. State Income Inequality: 1960–1990," *International Regional Science Review,* 3 (1995): 355–378.

2. Chiswick, B., "Illegal Immigration and Immigration Control," *Journal of Economic Perspectives,* 2 (1988): 101–16; Stark, 0., T.J. Edward, and Y. Shlomo, "Migration, Remittances and Inequality: A Sensitivity Analysis Using the Extended Gini Index," *Journal of Development Economics,* 28 (1988): 309–322; Davies, J.B., and W. Ian, "Income Inequality and International Migration," *Economic Journal,* 102 (1992): 789–802.

3. According to the Census Bureau, migration can be defined as longer distance residential relocation, i.e., migration streams can be intracounty (mainly rural-urban migration), intercounty, intrastate, interstate, and migration from abroad.

4. States included are Alabama, Arkansas, Florida, Georgia, Kentucky, Louisi-

ana, Mississippi, North Carolina, Oklahoma, South Carolina, Tennessee, Texas, and West Virginia.

5. Kakwani, N.C., and N. Podder, "Efficient Estimation of the Lorenz Curve and Associated Inequality Measures from Grouped Observations," *Econometrica* 44 (1976): 137–148.

6. For a full derivation of the properties of the Lorenz curve, see Kakwani and Podder.

7. Kakwani and Podder explain in detail this method of estimation and demonstrate that the parameter estimates obtained from the generalized least squares method are more efficient than those obtained from the ordinary least squares method.

8. Accordingly, the first stage of our estimation procedure is to instrument net in-migration rate in the county in 1985 (measured five years before the Census) using fitted values from the reduced form of the county population net migration equation. Independent variables used in the model include: the initial level of migration at the beginning of the decade (1975), change in the distribution of income, educational attainment, family income growth rate, employment growth rate of civilian labor force, manufacturing employment, mean wage income, local government taxes and expenditures, population density and density square (to detect for possible curvilinear effect of the variable on net migration), population growth, and environmental conditions index.

9. Spiers, J., "Where Americans Are Moving," *Fortune,* 132 (1995): 38–39.

10. Bénabou, R., "Theories of Persistent Inequalities: Human Capital, Inequality, and Growth: A Local Perspective," European Economic Review, 38 (1994): 817–826; Davis, T.J., Jr., "Income Inequities between Black and White Populations in Southern Nonmetropolitan Counties," *Review of Black Political Economy,* 22 (1994): 145–158.

11. Slottje, D.J., and K.J. Hayes, "Labor Force Participation, Race and Human Capital: Influence on Earnings Distributions Across States," *Review of Income and Health,* 38 (1992): 27–37.

12. With the assumption that the education variable is endogenous and is correlated with the error term, we also constructed a human capital model to estimate predicted values of educational growth. Independent variables used in the model include, the stock of initial human capital, the distribution of income, family income, unemployment rate, poverty rate, mean wage income, local government taxes and expenditures, fertility rate, the percentage of the population that is "young," crime rate, employment in the professionals, and regional dummy variables.

13. Ram, R. "Kuznets inverted-U Hypothesis: Evidence from a Highly Developed Country," *Southern Economic Journal,* 57 (1991):1112–23.

14. Karoly, L.A., "The Trend in Inequality among Families, Individuals, and Workers in the United States: A Twenty-Five Year Perspective," in *Uneven Tides, Rising Inequality in American* (ed. S. Danziger and P. Gottschalk), New York: Russell Sage Foundation, 1993.

15. McGillivray, M., and M. Peter, "Regional Income Inequality in a Developed Nation: A Cross-Sectional Study of Australian Sub-State Regions," *Review of Regional Studies,* 21 (1991): 137–151; Kassab, C., "*Income and Inequality: The Role of the Service Sector in the Changing Distribution* of *Income,*" New York: Greenwood Press, 1992.

12

ASSESSING THE EFFECT OF THE OCCUPATIONAL CROWDING OF IMMIGRANTS ON THE REAL WAGES OF AFRICAN AMERICAN WORKERS

Lonnie K. Stevans

INTRODUCTION

Do immigrant workers cause the reduction of wages and the displacement of domestic workers? One response to this question holds that immigrants are in competition and are able to displace indigenous workers by working for lower wages—particularly in low-wage, less-skilled, labor markets. The opposing view, as noted by Simcox,[1] posits the argument that non-U.S. citizen workers take employment that domestic workers would not accept and thus serve to preserve jobs and increase consumption levels.[2] The recurring importance of the immigration issue has spurred renewed research interests to determine what impact, if any, immigration has on domestic labor markets—particularly the labor markets of unskilled workers.

IMMIGRATION AND THE DOMESTIC LABOR MARKET

While many previous studies have examined whether immigration displaces indigenous workers, we will focus on research that has analyzed the wage effects of immigration at a point in time. This is most relevant, given the cross-sectional nature of the data we will utilize.

There have been a number of studies that have analyzed immigration and indigenous wages. Espenshade provides evidence on the impact of immigration on native wages in different geographical locations and industries around the United States.[3] In two specific wage studies, Grossman[4] finds that recent flows of immigrants have had small but non-negligible negative effects on the long-run wage level of native workers, and DeFreitas and Marshall[5] observe negative relationship between the percentage of manual workers who are immigrants and the rate of growth of manufacturing wages. In an article by Butcher and Card the evidence is that the labor market consequences of immigration are relatively small.[6] Large differences across cities in the growth rates of wages for low and high paid workers bear no relation to the size of immigrant inflows. Boras and Tienda have illustrated that the stock of foreign workers already in the U.S. is strongly and negatively affected by new immigrants.[7] An increase of 10 percent in the number of new immigrants reduces the average wage of resident foreign workers by two to nine percent.[8]

While there are many further studies that have found slight and negative impacts on wages for indigenous workers and immigrants already in the labor market,[9] few have examined the consequences that immigration has on unskilled native workers, e.g., less-educated whites and African Americans. Altonji and Card[10] have found that earnings of black males and females decline by 20 percent and 14 percent, respectively, for each 10 percent increase in immigrants in a SMSA. Since the percentage of immigrants has been rising in many SMSAs by more than 10 percent per decade in cities such as Los Angeles, Miami, Long Beach, Atlanta, Albuquerque, New York City, and Jersey City, the issue is of great importance.

We will further examine the effects of immigration on the real wages of black workers by utilizing an untapped data source: the 1990 National Longitudinal Survey of Youth.[11] My methodology will use the concept of occupational crowding as the focal point of the inquiry. With one exception, no research to date has used the NLSY or occupational crowding in the stated methodology to investigate the economic consequences of immigration.[12]

OCCUPATIONAL CROWDING

"Crowding" is defined as the exclusion of certain workers from certain occupations which "crowds" them into other occupations, decreasing the wages of those workers and the wages in the latter occupation. This theory finds illustration with blacks and other minorities and with women.[13]

Stewart and Hyclak[14] incorporate a measure of SMSA crowding of immigrants in the U.S. by employing a regression in which black to white earnings by SMSA is the dependent variable and the number of immigrants by country of origin is a subset of the explanatory variables. In their model, they find that differences in relative black earnings across large metropolitan areas are indeed sensitive to the degree of labor force penetration of recent immigrants. Occupational crowding is addressed in a 1978 paper by Mayhew and Rosewell,[15] in an attempt to descriptively determine the extent and nature of the occupational crowding of immigrants in Great Britain. They discover that immigrants are more crowded than the population as a whole, but the extent and type of crowding varies greatly from one group to another.

Many immigrants to this country are likely to be distributed unevenly across occupations. Greenwood and McDowell[16] have noted a difference in occupational distributions for recent entrants. Immigrants from Africa, Asia, and the Middle East will tend to be more frequent in the higher skilled occupations, while those from South/Central America, Mexico, and the Caribbean are more numerous among the less-skilled occupations. This could result because of an association between workers of low productivity and occupations with low productivity. Non-U.S. citizen workers may have low productivity because of language difficulties, lack of education, or the lack of skills suitable to the domestic labor market. Crowding may also be the result of discrimination against non-U.S. citizen workers. Discrimination in the labor market can take the form of either wage or job discrimination—with the latter leading to occupational crowding. The internal or dual labor market is most likely to predict job discrimination, leading to crowding which can give rise to wage discrimination.[17]

Data Collection

As mentioned previously, we use the 1990 National Longitudinal Survey of Youth to examine the effect that the relative number of non-U.S. citizens by world region of origin within an occupation has on the average real wage of skilled/unskilled, black indigenous/foreign-born workers already in the U.S. The 1990 NLSY was chosen because this was the year that a series of immigration questions were asked of all respondents born outside the U.S., its territories, or Puerto Rico. Dates of most recent entrance into the U.S. were recorded as well as the immigration status of the respondent, e.g., whether he/she was the principal entrant or the spouse, child, or other relative of the principal entrant. The total number of non-U.S. citizens in the sample is 653. The most frequent non-U.S. citizens classified by world region of origin in the sample are from Europe (1.9 percent) and South/Central America, Mexico, and the Caribbean (7.1 percent). Moreover, many of the non-U.S. citizens in the NLSY entered the U.S. between 1960 and 1980 (97 percent).

Method

The primary effort is to investigate the effect that the occupational crowding of immigrants has on the real wages of blacks in the domestic labor market. We have chosen four categories based upon two dichotomous variables: non-U.S. citizen or indigenous worker and skilled or unskilled occupation. The four categories are:

(1) indigenous, skilled, black central city resident,
(2) indigenous, unskilled, black central city resident,
(3) non-U.S. citizen, skilled, black central city resident, and
(4) non-U.S. citizen, unskilled, black central city resident.

The focus on central city resident jointly with the black category is relevant, since inner cities are typically associated with low-wage labor markets and housing segregation confines many blacks to declining intraurban areas. This is a major constraint on the labor market options of minorities.

The earnings/wage function may be specified as:

$$W_{1i}, = \beta_0 + D'\beta_1 + C_I'\beta_1 + I_i'\beta_3 + X_i'\beta_4 + \varepsilon_{1i}$$

$$W_{2i}, = \alpha_0 + D'\alpha_1 + C_I'\alpha_2 + I_i'\alpha_3 + X_i'\alpha_4 + \varepsilon_{2i},$$

$$W_i = W_{1i} \text{ when } W_{1i} > W_{2i}$$

$$W_i = 0 \text{ otherwise.}$$

W_i = observed wage, W_{1i} = market wage, W_{2i} = reservation wage, and "i" is the number of individuals in the sample (i = 1, 2, ... 2695). When the market wage is less than the reservation wage, the individual is not working and the observed or measured wage is zero. The specified model is a censored regression with a stochastic and unobserved threshold.[18] In the above model, *D* is a vector comprised of two dichotomous variables, skilled/unskilled and indigenous/non-U.S. citizen, and the two-way interaction effect between the two dummy variables. The vector *C* contains the factors that measure occupational crowding: the ratios of the number of non-U.S. citizens by region of origin to the number of indigenous workers in the individual's occupation, and the *I* vector includes the interactions between the two dichotomous and occupational crowding variables. Including these interaction terms will allow us to determine if the effect on real wages of having a large relative number of immigrants in the occupations of black workers will differ depending upon skill level (skilled/unskilled occupation) and/or resident status (indigenous/non-U.S. citizen).

The explanatory variables that have been selected for inclusion in the vector X_i', D', and C', may be found in Table 1. They encompass different categories used in the specification of earnings functions: human capital (GRADE, TRAINING, PEXP, and WKSILF5), discrimination (GENDER and PHYSCHAL), personal (MARRIED, HEALTH, and AGE), and institutional (COLLBARG, WKSUNOLF, DIFJOBS). The variable STATE was included to capture the overall supply effect of living in a labor market with many immigrants, as put forth in Greenwood and McDowell.[19] The STATE dummy variable takes the value one if the individual lived in one of the following states in the U.S. in 1990: California, Florida, Illinois, Massachusetts, Michigan, New Jersey, New York, Ohio, Pennsylvania, and Texas. We would expect that individuals residing in these states with a larger population of recent immigrants would realize relatively lower real wages on average, *ceteris paribus*. It is important to note that in this analysis, the variables in the vector X are included only as a control. Our primary focus will be on the parameter estimates associated with the vectors D, C, and I.[20]

Empirical Results

The censored regression, equation (1), was estimated by the method of maximum likelihood.[21] Some of the final results may be found in Table 2. Among the continuous control variables, education (GRADE) is found to have the largest effect on real wages. A one standard deviation increase in education is associated with a .06 standard deviation increase in real wages. Real wages are observed to be significantly lower for those workers in unskilled occupations (–.12 in log wage units). Another interesting result is the sign and significance of the STATE variable. Real wages appear to be lower in those states that have a large population of immigrants (–.03 in log wage units). There is a wage premium in being male (.17) and a disadvantage in being a non-U.S. citizen (–.05). The occupational crowding variables, which measure the relative number of immigrant workers by occupation, are analyzed by each of the four worker categories mentioned above in Table 3. The first hypothesis that was tested was that of no interaction between the variables UNSKILL and FORBORN and with each of the crowding variables. A failure to reject this hypothesis would imply that the effect that the occupational crowd-

TABLE 1
Variable Explanations—1990 NLSY

Dependent Variable:	**Natural Log of Real Wage**
Explanatory Variables:	
X Vector:	
GRADE—Highest grade attended since last interview	COLLBARG—Wages set by collective bargaining.
TRAINING (qualitative)	Yes = 1
Vocational Training = 1	No = 0
No Vocational Training = 0	WKSUNOLF—Weeks out-of-labor force
PEXP—Prior job experience (qualitative)	DIFJOBS—Number of different jobs
Experience prior to current job = 1	STATE (qualitative)
No prior job experience = 0	Live in state with large population of immigrants = 1
WKSILF5—Weeks in labor force in last five (5) years	Otherwise = 0
MARRIED (qualitative)	AGE—Age in years
Married = 1	
Single = 0	
GENDER (qualitative)	HEALTH (qualitative)
Male = 1	Health limitation = 1
Female = 0	No limitation = 0
PHYSCHAL (qualitative)	
Physical or mental handicap = 1	
No handicap = 0	
D Vector (No interactions included):	
UNSKILL—Unskilled occupation (qualitative)	FORBORN—U.S. resident status (qualitative)
Service, forestry, farming and fishing, operators = 1	Non-U.S. citizen = 1
All other occupations = 0	Born in U.S. or naturalized citizen = 0
C Vector:	
RATIOSI—Ratio of South/Central American, Mexican, and Caribbean immigrants to indigenous in occupation	
RATIOAFI—Ratio of African immigrants to indigenous in occupation	
RATIOASI—Ratio of Asian immigrants to indigenous in occupation	
RATIOMEI—Ratio of Middle Eastern immigrants to indigenous in occupation	
RATIOEI—Ratio of European immigrants to indigenous in occupation	

TABLE 2
Maximum Likelihood Estimates

Adjusted R-Squared: 62%
Root Mean Squared Error: .5435
N = 2,695

Explanatory Variables	Standardized Estimates[a]
GRADE	.0603**
TRAINING	.1032
PEXP	.0412*
WKSILF5	.0312*
MARRIED	.0231*
AGE	.0123
HEALTH	–.0621*
GENDER	.1721**
PHYSCHAL	–.1165*
COLLBARG	.0245*
WKSUNOLF	–.0465*
DIFJOBS	–.0541*
STATE	–.0319**
UNSKILL	–.1154**
FORBORN	–.0465**

Note: [a]Standardized coefficients are only reported for continuous variables. **Statistically significant at .05 level; *statistically significant at 10 level.

ing of immigrants has on wages would not be dependent upon whether workers were skilled/indigenous, skilled/non-U.S. citizen, unskilled/indigenous, or unskilled/non-U.S. citizen. This premise is rejected, according to the results presented in Table 3. Our remaining focus will be on the examining the effects of the immigration crowding variables, RATIOSI, RATIOAFI, RATIOASI, RATIOMEI, AND RATIOEI, on black real wages for each of the four worker categories.

The relative number of non-U.S. citizens in the occupations of skilled black workers, indigenous or non-U.S. citizen, is found to have no effect on wages—there is no statistical significance. However, a relatively large number of Asians in the occupations of black, unskilled, and indigenous workers, has tended to depress wages for this group (–.08). This interesting finding is evidence that the racial tension existing between the Asian (Korean) and African American communities in many U.S. urban areas is economic in nature—they compete with each other in the same sec-

TABLE 3
Interaction Results

Category	Statistical Significance and Standardized Weight
All interactions	Yes**
Indigenous, skilled, black	No
Non-U.S. citizen, skilled, black	No
Indigenous, unskilled, black	Yes**
Asian	–.0823**
Non-U.S. citizen, unskilled, black	Yes**
South/Central American, Mexican and Caribbean	–.0669**
European	–.0154**

** Statistically significant at the .05 level.

ondary labor market. Among black, non-U.S. citizens who are already in the U.S. labor market, there are negative effects on wages for unskilled workers. A relatively large number of South/Central Americans, Mexican, Caribbean, and European workers in the occupations of black and unskilled workers who are already in the U.S. is associated with lower wages for these workers (–.07 and –.02, respectively). Since the coefficients in Table 3 are standardized, it may be noted that the largest negative parameter estimate is for the effect that the proportion of Asians in the occupations has on the real wages of indigenous and unskilled black workers (–.08).

CONCLUSION

It is indicated by the results of this research that not only are black indigenous workers affected by immigration, but non-U.S. citizen black workers who are already in the U.S. as well. In much of the literature on the wage effects of immigration, the general consensus based on many studies seems to be that the economic impact of immigration is illusory or unimportant.[22] We have shown in this analysis that the wage effects of immigration are very real indeed—in the sense of a strong degree of statistical significance. In fact, not only are there significant negative impacts upon the wages of African/Afro Americans due to the occupational "crowding-out" of immigrants by world region of origin, but there is also an overall adverse effect on wages as a result of residing in a state with a large population of non-U.S. citizens. Moreover, while it is shown that immigration has a statistically significant effect on the real wages of black workers in the U.S., it is also true that the estimated parameters from Table 3 are numerically large. The two largest standardized weights in absolute value (Table 3) are .0823 and .0669. These numbers are larger than any of the reported standardized coefficients for the continuous variables in Table 2.

The U.S. labor market is clearly not segmented or insulated from any immigration effects, given the details of this study. Alternatively, if one were to define segmentation as between skilled and unskilled occupations for black workers, then our results indicate the existence of a primary labor market for skilled workers that is insulated from the wage consequences associated with the occupational crowding of immigrants.

NOTES

1. Simcox, D.E. (1988), *Immigration and the Labor Market: The Repeal of Supply and Demand,* U.S. Immigration in the 1980s: Reappraisal and Reform, Boulder, Co, pp. 31–36, and London: Westview Press and Center for Immigration Studies.
2. Piore, M. (1979), Birds of Passage: Migrant Labor and Industrial Societies, New York: Cambridge University Press.
3. Espenshade, T. J., ed. (1994), A Stone's Throw from Ellis Island: Economic Implications of Immigration, London: University Press of America.
4. Grossman, J.B. (1982), *The Substitutability of Natives and Immigrants in Production*, Review of Economics and Statistics 64:596–603.
5. DeFreitas, G. and Marshall, A. (1984), *Immigration and Wage Growth in U.S. Manufacturing in the 1970s*, Proceedings of the Thirty-sixth Annual Meeting, Industrial Relations Research Association, pp. 148–156.
6. Butcher, K. F. and Card, D. (1991), *Immigration and Wages: Evidence from the 1980s, AEA Papers and Proceedings* 81, 2:292–296.
7. Borjas, G. J. and Tienda, M. (1987), "The Economic Consequences of Immigration," *Science*, February 6.
8. Ibid.
9. Borjas, G. J. 919900, Friends or Strangers: The Impact of Immigrants on the U.S. Economy, New York: Basic Books, Inc. Bean, F. D., Lowell, B. L., and Taylor, L. J. (1988), *Undocumented Mexican Immigrants and the Earnings of Other Workers in the United States*, Demography 25, 1:35-52.
10. Altonji, J. G. and Card, D. (1996), "The Effects of Immigration on the Labor Market Outcomes of Less-Skilled Natives," in Aboud, J.M. and Freeman, R.B., eds.
11. We have used this dataset in a previous publication utilizing an exhaustive set of demographic groups.
12. As mentioned previously, the one exception is a previous publication by this author in the journal *Labour* that utilized an exhaustive set of demographic groups. The reason the NLSY has not been utilized may in fact be due to the small number

of non-U.S. citizens in the 1990 database. However, we did not find this to be a significant problem since from the entire sample that was used in our previous article, (6,258), approximately ten percent were non-U.S. citizens.

13. Bergsman, J. (1982), "Apartheid, Wages, and Production Costs in South Africa: An Application of the Crowding Hypothesis," *The Journal of Human Resources* 17, 4:633–645. Sorensen, E. (1990), "The Crowding Hypothesis and Comparable Worth," *The Journal of Human Resources* 25, 1:55–89.

14. Stewart, J. B. and Hyclak, T. J. (1986), "The Effects of Immigrants, Women, and Teenagers on the Relative Earning of Black Males," *The Review of Black Political Economy*, 15, 11:93–101.

15. Mayhew, K. and Rosewell, B. (1978), "Immigrants and Occupational Crowding in Great Britain," *Oxford Bulletin of Economics and Statistics* 3:223–248. Council of Economic Advisers (1986), *Economic Report of the President*, Washington, D.C.: U.S. Government Printing Office.

16. Greenwood, M.J. and McDowell, J.M. (1986), "The Factor Market Consequences of U.S. Immigration," *Journal of Economic Literature* 24, 4: 1738–1772.

17. See P. Doeringer and M.J. Piore, *Internal Labor Markets and Manpower Analysis*, Lexington, 1971.

18. See G.S. Maddala, *Limited Dependent and Qualitative Variables in Econometrics*, Cambridge University Press, 1983, pp. 174–276

19. Greenwood and McDowell, 1986.

20. The vector I includes the interactions terms between the crowding variables and the variables UNSKILL and FORBORN.

21. The software package used was Eviews 3.0.

22. See Borjas and Tienda (1987), Council of Economic Advisors (1986), Greenwood and McDowell (1986), Papademetriou et al. (1989).

13

ON THE PERMANENCE OR IMPERMANENCE OF BLACK-WHITE ECONOMIC INEQUALITY

Jeremiah Cotton

A great many people in the United States believe that racial prejudice and discrimination, in a word, racism, will eventually be eliminated from American society. These expectations are held by both white people and black people, although perhaps by many more of the former than the latter. They point to the social and economic progress black people have made in recent years as irrefutable evidence of the ongoing, inexorable movement toward a racially equal society. They generally view racism as a hangover from the slave past, an unfortunate relic of the rationales that were used at the time to justify slavery. They therefore essentially agree with Gunnar Myrdal's assessment of racism as "a terrible and inexplicable anomaly stuck in the middle of our liberal democratic ethos."[1]

Racism in this view is out of keeping with and ultimately undermined by the essential American ideals of justice and equity. Indeed America is seen for the most part as a fair, open, meritocratic democracy in which ambition, hard work, initiative, and self-sacrifice should be and are the major determinants of the success and well-being of individuals and groups. A decline in the significance of race is therefore heralded as conventional wisdom.

This belief in the decline and fall of racism is not shared by all concerned. There are a number of social analysts who were and are deeply pessimistic about the prospects of racism ever ending here in the United States. One of the first to give up on America was W. E. B. DuBois. Early on he declared that racism gave the lie to any pretense that this country was or ever would be a democracy, and after seventy years of struggle, he despaired that America would come to grips with the problem; in 1961 he renounced his United States citizenship and emigrated to Ghana.

Most recently the matter has been put in stark terms by Derrick Bell, the former Harvard Law School professor who left his post there in protest over the school's failure up to that time to hire and tenure a black female. The title of his book, *Faces at the Bottom of the Well: The Permanence of Racism*, tells it all. In it he maintains that "racism is an integral, permanent, and indestructible component of American society" and concludes that "black people will never gain full equality in this country" (p. ix). He goes on to cite another scholar, Jennifer Hochschild, who sharply disagreed with Myrdal's claim that racism was an "anomaly." She argued that "liberal democracy and racism in the United States are historically, even inherently, reinforcing" and that America "thrives only because racial discrimination continues. The apparent anomaly is an actual symbiosis" (p. 10).

In a book unambiguously titled *White Racism,* Joel Kovel maintains that America is "saturated" with racism and that it cannot be legislated away "since what is put into law always serves to legitimate the system which generates racism and is defined by it."[2] He thus implies that racism survives now and will survive in the future by changing its form and adapting its expression to changes in its environment. He identifies three historical, overlapping phases of racism. The first is the Southern-style, physically oppressive racism of slavery that he calls "dominative"; the second, "aversive," is the racism of segregation and exclusion that mainly characterized the post-slavery urban North; and the third is "metaracism," the institutionalized racism perpetuated through "economic and technocratic means" that prevails today.

The question of the permanence or impermanence of racism is also a critical theoretical and empirical issue in orthodox and heterodox economics where it is framed in terms of black-white inequality in wages, earnings, employment, occupation, capital ownership, and wealth. Economic orthodoxy acting *au fond* in defense of free-market capitalism predicts the demise of racism in the long-run as a cause of racial economic inequality. It offers two not necessarily competing explanations for the existence of black-white wage or earnings inequality in the short-run. One, generally considered to be legitimate, is the greater white than black endowments of education and training and therefore productivity skills; this is the human capital investment argument. The other is the presence of a so-called white "distaste," of pre-market origin, for economic association with blacks; this is the discrimination or racism hypothesis. It contends that, equal skills notwithstanding, blacks are paid a lower wage than whites in order to compensate the latter for the racially-induced "disutility" they suffer.

Taken together or singly these two explanations are assumed to account for the short-run black-white economic gap. In the long-run, however, only the human capital explanation is plausible because economic discrimination cannot survive in the face of the competitive forces assumed to be inherent in capitalist markets. Equally efficient blacks who are being paid less than their white counterparts will soon attract the attention of entrepreneurs who care more for profits than race. They will hire away the underpaid blacks at a greater wage than they currently receive but slightly less than that received by whites, produce and sell at lower costs and prices, and ultimately drive the discriminators out of the market.

Hence orthodox theory predicts that the proportion of the black-white economic gap that is caused by racism will disappear in the long-run and any economic differences remaining thereafter will be solely due to differences in black-white human capital endowments. It is further predicted that as blacks accumulate more and more human capital and become more and more productive the nondiscriminatory racial economic gap will also close.

Among the most well-received pieces of evidence generated in apparent support of this conclusion was the report by Finis Welch and James P. Smith in their 1986 study, *Closing the Gap: 40 Years of Black Economic Progress.* They found that in 1940 "the typical black male worker earned only 43 percent as much as his white counterpart; by 1980, the average black man in the labor force earned 73 percent as much as the typical white man."[3] And although this earnings advance was most pronounced among younger black males with less than ten years of work experience, it was also enjoyed by all other work experience classes. The finding of this inverse relationship between age cohorts and the size of the black-white wage gap also supported Welch's well-known "vintage" hypothesis. He argued that younger black males entering the labor market were better educated than their older brethren and as the latter were gradually replaced by the former there would be a steady decrease in the black-white skill and wage gaps.

I am among those heterodox analysts who have taken issue strongly with both the upbeat conclusions of the Welch-Smith/human capital project and the vanishing discrimination argument. I am also very much more persuaded by the pessimism of those who do not foresee an end to racism in this society than I am by the racial optimists, but more on that later.

I have argued that the Welch-Smith claim of black economic progress was narrowly based on movements in the earnings of employed black males to the exclusion of other equally, if not more important, indicators of economic progress such as unemployment, family income, wealth, and poverty rates.[4] Broadly, black adult unemployment rates have been twice as high as white rates for nearly fifty years, and the gap has been slowly increasing since the early 1970s. In 1954, the black teenage unemployment rate was about 15 percent and the white rate was 12 percent. Forty-four years later, by early 1998, the black teenage rate had more than doubled to around 31 percent, while the white rate was still just 12 percent.

The amount of income available to the average black family has been at or just under 60 percent of that available to white families for the last 30 years, and lower on average in the 1990s than it was in the late 1960s and early 1970s. And while there are no data on long-term trends in black-white comparative wealth or net worth, what exists paints a less than rosy picture. In 1993, the net worth of the average black family was less than 10 percent of white family net worth; and in 1984 the net worth of a white female-headed family was greater than that of a black married couple family.

Finally, there has been an almost constant three-to-one ratio of black to white poverty rates, whether among children, adults, or the elderly, for nearly forty years.

These are the findings that pose a serious challenge to the Welch-Smith claim of a steadily closing black-white economic gap. But even the black male relative earnings situation on which their claim was initially predicated turned sour in the late 1980s after their report had been issued. Contrary to their expectations very few of the young, presumably better-educated black male cohorts who entered the labor market in the late 1960s and mid-1970s had narrowed the earnings gap between themselves and their white counterparts ten years later in the late 1970s and mid-1980s. In fact, in most cases the gaps had widened.

The presence of a long-lasting unemployment rate gap between blacks and whites shatters the education-economic payoff link promoted by human capital investment theory. Indeed, in 1985, the unemployment rate for young black *college* graduates was almost twice as high as that of white *high school* graduates. In 1979, even white high school dropouts had lower unemployment rates than black college graduates. All of this goes against the grain of the human capital model and leaves its predictive power in doubt. The question that stymies it is this: if the increasing acquisition of human capital by blacks is responsible for the narrowing of the racial earnings and wage gaps, why does it not have the same salutary effect on black unemployment?

I attempted to put the human capital and discrimination models to the test in a number of empirical studies that focused on the black-white wage and earnings gaps. The central strategy was to regress black and white wages or earnings on as many of the proxies for human capital as could be mustered in order to decompose the resulting wage or earnings gap into a component that could be attributed entirely to, or "explained" by, the proxies and a residual, or "unexplained," component that could be considered at the very least an upper bound estimate of discrimination. In most of these studies the human capital model could account for less than 50 percent of the gap, leaving a large unexplained residual.

Under the defining assumption that discrimination confers benefits on whites by overpaying them and imposes costs on blacks by underpaying them, I further partitioned the residuals or discrimination components into estimates of these benefits and costs.[5]

The results of this research confirmed that labor market discrimination was alive and well and that reports of its demise by orthodox economic theory were greatly exaggerated. Human capital theory also came in for some knocks. In one study I compared the earnings gap between better educated blacks and whites in the white collar occupations and the gap between less well educated blacks and whites in the blue collar occupations. The gap at the top turned out to be not only larger than that at the bottom, but a greater proportion was unexplained—presumably due to discrimination.[6]

Of course not everyone is prepared to accept the interpretation of the residuals generated in studies such as mine as indicators and measures of racial discrimination. The interpretation favored by economists such as Thomas Sowell is that the residual along with differential acquisition of human capital is due to cultural differences. Their claim is that black culture does not place a very high premium on the middle-class values espoused by white culture such as hard work, self-reliance, and the postponement of present in favor of future consumption and gratification. Hence even though a black might have the same amount of education and training as a white, their respective cultural nurturing will generate differences in drive, ambition, self-confidence, and the amount of effort they put out, and consequently differences in economic performance and remuneration.

This culturalogical interpretation of differences in black-white economic performance has been vigorously challenged, successfully in my view, by Professor William Darity, Jr. and others.[7] My contribution to the counterattack was a comparative wage study of black Hispanic and non-Hispanic males (controlling thereby for color) and of black and white Hispanic males (controlling for culture). I found that color was a much more potent explanatory factor than culture in these comparisons. In fact, white Hispanic males had less average education and greater average earnings than either black Hispanic males or black non-Hispanic males.[8]

I have found nothing in my research with which to counter the pessimism of Professor Derrick Bell et al. Indeed, if my assumption that racism confers undeserved benefits on whites is correct, then discrimination is more than just an extra-market, psychological predisposition, or "taste," as supposed by the orthodox yea-sayers, but rather it is a market-embedded enterprise that yields profits and privileges for whites. The level of their skills aside, whites on average are given preferments for the best jobs and occupational slots in the economy. In the choice between a white and black of equal productivity, the white more often than not wins the job simply because the white is white. In fact, in the choice between a capable white and a more capable black, the white still usually wins. Therefore it is folly to suppose that advantages such as these will ever be given up voluntarily.

Racism and racial economic inequality also well serves the interests of capitalism. White capitalist employers vouchsafe white workers control over the ports of entry to most jobs and occupations along with their internal promotion ladders. In exchange the capitalists are assured of a relatively docile, system-defending white workforce more conscious and wary of race than of class.

I am convinced that the popular faith in the inevitable demise of racism is based on a belief in the intertwining myths of America as a democratic society and the beneficence of its capitalist economic arrangements. Any general acknowledgement that racism is profitable and therefore here to stay would be damaging to capitalist ideology and painful for most Americans, particularly most white Americans. They have a warm, fuzzy image of themselves and this country as benevolent, just, decent, honest, God-fearing, and God-favored—in short, good people living in a great democracy. Shielded from view are the past and present enormities committed in the course of the establishment and maintenance of this "democracy," notable among which early on was the conquest and decimation of the Native American population and the importation and exploitation of African slave labor, and currently the wretched conditions on the reservations and in the inner cities in which many of the descendants of these two populations find it necessary to live.

Capitalism in its turn is taken to be synonymous with democracy and touted as a system in which individual rewards are distributed solely according to individual contributions to the production process. This is a crucial, all-important tenet of the capitalist faith. For if equally productive individuals are systematically compensated differently solely on the basis of some extraneous characteristic such as their so-called race then the claim that capitalist markets are the most efficient orchestrators of the economic activities of entirely self-interested individuals would have to be abandoned. The capitalist cover would be blown because the prices and wages in product and labor markets would no longer reflect the true values or optimal amounts of the resources employed and goods produced.

Since racism and discrimination embarrass attempts to portray America as a democratic society and capitalism as benign, they must be either denied outright or declared to be rapidly declining in significance.

If the racial optimists are wrong, however, and if Bell et al. are correct in supposing that racism and racial economic inequality are permanent features of the American social and economic landscape, then it means that the struggle against racism if it is to continue must be carried out without hope of ultimate victory. All that can be done therefore can only be ameliorative, not curative. The goals of the struggle must be more modest and yet at the same time their pursuit must be more intense. Past gains or progress against racism have never been safe but are always in danger of being eroded as racist practices adapt to and challenge the changing rules and environment—the current backsliding on affirmative action is a sad case in point.

Because racism is profitable its beneficiaries will concede nothing without a struggle. The last major concession, or ameliorative opening, came as a result of the mass demonstrations, civil disobedience, and riots of the 1960s Civil Rights movement. Racism for a brief spell became unprofitable for America, and the government stepped in with jobs and social welfare programs to placate, or, as some have said, "cool out" the protests. From 1948 to 1965, black family median income averaged only 50 percent of white family income. In 1966, however, the percentage leaped to 57 percent, peaked at 62 percent in 1974, and then started to decline, falling as low as 55 percent in the early 1990s. The 1966–74 plateau, I contend, was the "Civil Rights 'cool out' effect," and it began to wear off as soon as the fires of the movement subsided.

To attempt again to narrow the black-white economic gap, or at least to keep it from widening any further, the ameliorative struggle against racism must be renewed and perhaps reconfigured: not as a civil rights movement this time but as an *economic* rights movement. The demands of such a movement should not only be for black community economic development and equal earnings and employment opportunities but full-employment for the entire economy as well. These are mutually reinforcing projects.

The communities in which most black people live share a common set of dystopian characteristics: a decaying residential and commercial infrastructure pockmarked with dilapidated and abandoned housing; boarded-up storefronts; broken, littered sidewalks; and trash-filled vacant lots. Since the residents of these communities have very little political influence they receive inadequate municipal services and concern. A capital transfer or redistribution to these communities on the order of that used recently to bail out the savings and loan industry ($150 to $200 billion, or less than half of what blacks spend annually on consumption goods) will be needed to begin the repairs and physical improvements of these locales.

Rather than dismantling the state and federal affirmative action programs and other measures designed to insure blacks equal labor and capital market treatment, these programs should be greatly strengthened and compliance with them rigorously monitored and enforced.

Full-employment might very well be the centerpiece of the movement's ameliorative goals. For it would not only greatly benefit blacks but working class whites as well and might help mitigate some of their racist bigotry since much of it is fueled by their perception of blacks as competitors for the scarce jobs they consider to be their's by right. That bigotry is more apt to be on display, and even acted on, in economically tight times than in more prosperous times.

The increasingly high unemployment and underemployment rates experienced by both blacks and whites are completely unnecessary. There is probably more work that needs to be done in this country now than workers to do it. Millions of good-paying jobs could and should be created to rebuild the rapidly deteriorating national infrastructure of roads, highways, waterways and bridges, and to construct new schools and clean up the pollution that is poisoning the nation's land and water arteries.

The models for this endeavor are the public works programs and projects that grew out of the political response to the widespread unemployment of the Great Depression. These efforts not only laid the foundation for the ultimate recovery from that catastrophe but also yielded economic benefits to the country throughout the ensuing half century. The nation is now in desperate need of another such buildup of its physical capital. The amount of public expenditure required for this renaissance, although huge, would be nothing compared to the short- and long-term returns it would yield. The value of the undertaking and the spillover benefits flowing from it would be well-nigh immeasurable. As previously implied, everyone would stand to gain—blacks, whites, the rich, the middle-class, and the poor. Big business would reap substantial benefits because its profitability is strongly affected by the quantity and quality of the public capital stock.[9]

The revitalizing effects on the black community of a full-employment economy coupled with the aforementioned economic development efforts would no doubt be transforming: crimes born out of hopelessness, neglect, and despair might well be greatly reduced; the physical deterioration of the present housing and building stock would be reversed; there would be a burgeoning of businesses offering goods and services not currently available inside many black communities; and many of the now disaffected young people could be reclaimed by the plentiful prospects of jobs that pay decent wages.

An economic rights movement based on the goal of full-employment through public infrastructure investment might draw people from across racial lines—the unemployed, underemployed, poor, and near-poor of all races and ethnic groups should have a strong interest in a full-employment economy—and from across the class lines that separate the imperiled middle class from the imperiled poor classes.

Though the movement would be ultimately beneficial, its demands would put enormous pressure on the social and economic fabric of this country. To meet these demands would require a substantial transfer of market power from capital to labor, and a dismantling of the monopoly of the white working class over the best jobs and job ladders.

Resistance to the demands of an economic rights movement could be expected to be even more fierce than the resistance to the demands for civil and legal rights in the 1960s. To mount and sustain the movement would no doubt require a return to many of the tactics of mass demonstrations, civil disobedience and disruptions, economic boycotts, and perhaps even some broken glass. The system will never cede these rights peacefully they must always be demanded on pain of open social conflict.

Whether these or some other ameliorative actions will ever be undertaken the need for them is as pressing now as we enter the new century and millennium as it has been at any point in the current century. Racism is a deep-seated pathology from which American will not soon, and may very well never recover. The struggle, however, must continue.

NOTES

1. Quoted in Derrick Bell, *Faces at the Botton of the Well* (New York: Basic Books, 1992), p. 9.
2. Joel Kovel, *White Racism: A Psychohistory* (London: Free Association Books, 1988), p. lxiv.
3. James P. Smith and Finis Welch, *Closing the Gap: 40 Years of Black Economic Progress* (Santa Monica, Calif.: Rand Corporation, 1986), p. 23.
4. Jeremiah Cotton, "Opening the Gap: The Decline in Black Economic Indicators in the 1980s," *Social Science Quarterly* Vol. 70, No. 4 (1989), pp. 803–819.
5. See, e.g., Jeremiah Cotton, "On the Decomposition of Wage Differentials," *The Review of Economics and Statistics*, 40: 2 (1988), pp. 236–243.
6. Jeremiah Cotton, "The Gap at the Top: Relative Occupational Earnings Disadvantages of the Black Middle Class," *The Review of Black Political Economy*, 18: 3 (Winter 1990), pp. 21–38.
7. See William Darity, Jr., "What's Left of the Economic Theory of Discrimination?" in Steven Shulman and William Darity, Jr., eds. *The Question of Discrimination* (Middlebury, Conn.: Wesleyan University Press, 1989), pp. 335–374.
8. Jeremiah Cotton, "Color or Culture: Wage Differences Among Non-Hispanic Black Males, Hispanic Black Males and Hispanic White Males," *The Review of Black Political Economy,* 21: 4 (Spring 1993), pp. 53–67.
9. David A. Aschauer, "Is The Public Capital Stock Too Low?" *Chicago Fed Letter.* Federal Bank of Chicago (October 1987), pp. 23–40.

14

THE SHADOW OF THE FUTURE AND THE COMPLEXITY OF COOPERATION

John W. Handy

INTRODUCTION

The early part of the twenty-first century must inevitability confront the issue of social choice among opposing groups competing over public resources and private-sector opportunities. The underlying dynamic of this overarching issue and the choices that will be made will impact such seemingly diverse areas as the concentration of urban poverty; identity politics and the formation of coalitions; affirmative action and minority business firm formation; youth crime; and the allocation of tax revenue between central cities and outlying suburbs.

Many of the profound issues of racial justice and relations reflect a societal-scale prisoner's dilemma: by groups focusing on short-term gains as a reflection of narrow self-interests, social outcomes are often suboptimal.[1] The importance of the repeated prisoner's dilemma centers on the fact that many social phenomena have this dilemma at their core. The conflict between narrow self-interests and socially optimal outcomes is a very common, result of mutual defections from policies and actions where everyone would be better off with mutual cooperation.[2] Conflicts in American society concerning racial justice, the allocation of resources between central cities and suburbs, and affirmative action often reflect a suboptimal zero-sum mentality that there must always be winners at the expense of losers in a never-ending struggle for primary access to resources and opportunities. What cooperative solutions to the repeated prisoner's dilemma can demonstrate is that there are long-term solutions that are more enlightened and which also increase the payoffs to all parties.

It is important to note that cooperative solutions to the repeated prisoners dilemma involve no explicit appeal to altruism, brotherhood, fear, or guilt. While some of these are enviable traits, they are not sufficiently predictable or reliable motivations in a *political environment* over the long-term. It is for this reason that cooperative games can be more accurately described as games of negotiation. The need for cooperation, under games of negotiation, comes from a deeper understanding of what constitutes self-interests in a political environment such that the long-run gains to opposing players are maximized.

This article will explore examples of suboptimal social outcomes as a reflection of the repeated prisoner's dilemma. The first section offers a concise theoretical approach to analyzing these type of outcomes by utilizing Robert Axelrod's important work on the evolution of cooperation among competing players. Necessary conditions for groups to effectively interact over the long-term are explored in subsequent sections of the article by applying the model to important social issues that will continue to have future repercussions.

THE THEORY

The path-breaking work of Robert Axelrod demonstrates that the evolution of cooperation among egoists is enhanced when separate groups have a high probability of continually interfacing with the concomitant condition that each of them have a stake in their mutual future interactions.[3] Therefore, a necessary condition for stable mutual cooperation is that the future relationship among opposing groups must be sufficiently important relative to the present. When this is the case, opposing groups take seriously both the threat of retaliation against their defection, as well as attempts by other parties to signal cooperation. When the future casts a large shadow on the present as reflected by high discount parameters, where the future is highly valued, it pays to cooperate with other players who also seek to cooperate and issue threats of retaliation to those who seek to threaten you. On the other hand, when the discount parameter is low, and future possibilities mean little compared to the present, cooperative arrangements are unlikely and may even be undesirable to a group who would be leaving themselves open to exploitation. For ease of exposition, the discount parameter can be thought of as the rate of association, R_A. This rate of association can be thought of as the probability of significant group interaction or as a measure of the weight of importance attached to the future group interaction. Thus, high rates of association (R_A) denote long-term relationships possessing two characteristics: (i) significant dialogue and interaction, and (ii) meaningful reciprocity.[4]

Low rates of association (R_A) occur when interaction among groups is expected either to be infrequent or there is little strategic significance to any future interaction that might occur. Thus, there are two ways to expand the shadow of the future: by making interactions among competing groups more durable and more frequent; and by each group developing sufficient group importance so that retaliation and the threat of defection or noncooperation is meaningful. Long-term relationships characterized by these features increase the likelihood of cooperative mutually shared gains within a *real politik* environment. A generalized game theory demonstration of these issues is outlined in the endnotes.[5]

A CASE OF EXPECTED LOW FUTURE INTERACTION: THE CLOSING OF FIRE HOUSES

As we have summarized, the evolution of cooperation requires that groups have a sufficiently high chance to meet repeatedly so that they mutually have a high stake in their future interaction. When the chance of group interaction is low or their mutual association is viewed as unimportant by at least one of the players, there is not sufficient incentive to share power or resources. In the 1970s, low-income black and Hispanic neighborhoods in New York City lacked political organization, had a history of weak voter participation and, hence, lacked retaliatory voting or political power to oppose outside threats. In essence these communities were politically marginalized and viewed by other groups as outside the loop of significant political dialogue and on-going political relationships.

Based on Roderick Wallace's study on the impact of budget cuts on poor areas of New York City in the 1970s, Massey and Denton[6] describe the full impact of social disinvestment. Faced with a shortage of funds during the city's financial crisis, the New York City Fire Department eliminated thirty-five companies between 1969–1976, twenty-seven of which were in poor minority areas located in the Bronx, Manhattan, and Brooklyn, areas where the risk of fire was recognized to be quite high. Budget cutting considerations led white politicians to confine their reductions to segregated ghetto and barrio wards whose long-term political association with controlling government decision-makers were low or nonexistent and where, consequently, the political damage could be contained. As Massey and Denton describe it:

> After the closings were implemented, the number of residential fires increased dramatically resulting in an epidemic of building fires within black and Puerto Rican neighborhoods. As housing was systematically destroyed, social networks were fractured and institutions collapsed; churches, block associations, youth programs, and political clubs vanished. The destruction of housing, networks, and social institutions, in turn, caused a massive flight of destitute families out of core minority areas. Some affected areas lost 80% of their residents between 1970 and 1980, putting severe strain on adjacent neighborhoods, which had been stable until then. . . . Black ghettos and Puerto Rican barrios were hollowed out from their cores. . . . Within affected neighborhoods, infant mortality rates rose as did the incidence of cirrhosis, gonorrhea, tuberculosis., and drug use. The destruction of the social fabric of black and Puerto Rican neighborhoods led to an increase in the number of unsupervised males, which contributed to a sharp increase in crime, followed by an increase in the rate of violent deaths of young men.[7]

Throughout the 1970s the rate of association (R_A) with low-income black and Hispanic communities was judged not to be significant enough by New York City white politicians to make the future loom large in their calculation of benefits. Negotiated mutually advantageous outcomes was not triggered by considerations of *real politik* since the removal of public resources in poor areas was expected to result in minimal political fallout. However, the long-term consequences to both the image of New York City and the quality of life of residents of low-income neighborhoods proved to be disastrous.

IDENTITY POLITICS AND THE PIVOTAL VOTE

Coalition formation addresses another aspect of cooperative games. Over the last few years there has been a shift in the formation of urban coalitions around the country. One such coalition has been the political coalition formed among Jewish and Hispanic voters around the country. In Chicago, for instance, this partnership occurred while there was a collateral distancing of the black voting block following the death of Harold Washington. Similarly, Jewish and Hispanic voters have consolidated their political clout and interests in Queens and Manhattan, New York, as well as in such areas as Houston, Texas, California and New Jersey. One political writer has observed:

> Latinos and Jews are in political alliance. In city after city, state after state, the two groups vote the same way. What they do not do . . . is vote like African Americans. . . . The political space that Jews and Latinos are creating in places like New York, Chicago, New Jersey, and California is likely to grow. Jews, although declining in numbers, are a powerful source of campaign money, and the Latino population is increasing fast. Latinos already outnumber African Americans in three of America's four largest cities and will outnumber them in the fourth, Chicago, by early in the next decade.[8]

In each case, these coalitions were formed among groups that assessed their mutual R_A to be high. Moreover, with the increased emphasis on identity politics several black political leaders emphasized the adversarial nature of their relationship with other voting blocks (low R_A).

In a coalitional game, each voting block must decide whether cooperating with others in a potential coalition promises them higher payoffs than they can get by going alone. For instance, if the value of the coalition of B voters and H voters [V(BH)] is such that B voters are perceived as adding and receiving more value to the coalition [V(BH)–V(H)] than they can achieve alone [V(B)], then it makes sense for black voters to formulate the (BH) coalition of B and H voters. In this case, we would have $V(BH)-V(H) > V(B)$.

On the other hand, if as a result of race-conscious identity politics, black voters (B) decide to go it alone, then it must be that black voters feel they can get a higher payoff on their own compared to payoffs from forming coalitions with either ethnic whites (W), Hispanics (H), or Jews (J). Consequently, the perception among black voters would be

$$V(BH) - V(H) < V(B)$$
$$V(BW) - V(W) < V(B)$$
$$V(BJ) - V(J) < V(B)$$

Clearly, the Hispanic voting block in Chicago and New York must have believed that $V(HJ)-V(J) > V(HB)-V(B)$. This means that the payoff value to Hispanics in forming coalitions with Jewish voters in New York and Chicago was considered to be greater than the payoff value of trying to form a coalition with black voters.[9]

Thus, from the point of view of Hispanic and Jewish voters in New York City and Chicago, mutually beneficial, long-term relationships with black voters were deemed to be low. This may have been reinforced by the fact that several influential black political leaders were signaling that they were more concerned with racial conscious politics than with coalition-building. This latter decision would also preclude the possibility of blacks acting in concert with others to be a swing vote for leveraging their influence to exert power and obtain concessions.

Carol Swain in her study of African American representation in Congress concludes that African Americans have made the most of their opportunities to elect black politicians from majority black districts. In calculating the loss of population in black drawn districts particularly in Illinois, Michigan, New York, Ohio, and Pennsylvania, Swain concludes,

> Not only is the strategy of carving out predominately black districts from urban areas with dense concentrations of blacks unlikely to encourage adequate black representation in the South, it is also likely to become ineffective in the future in the Northeast and Midwest, which are presently the largest producers of black members of Congress.[10]

The creation of black districts has certainly had some past benefits, but it also may have had unintended consequences. While consolidating black votes, race-conscious districting also has furthered consolidated conservative, Republican power while moving several Democrats further to the right in an effort to preserve their seats. As a result, black political clout may have peaked. Several of these Democrats who previously favored black initiatives have moved away from supporting affirmative action programs since they no longer have to appeal to black voters who have been drawn out of their districts. In 1990, Newt Gingrich barely won reelection against Ben Jones, by just over 900 votes. What is not widely known is the fact that had black voters turned out in the 1990 election in significant numbers, Newt Gingrich would not have been reelected to Congress. Later, as a result of racial redistricting, the percent of black voters in his new district fell from 15 percent to 6 percent. "And so it was that Newt Gingrich became Speaker of the House," notes Swain.[11]

It is possible that over reliance on identity politics has diverted attention from the strong likelihood that black voters can become a much more potent political force by becoming the preeminent swing vote in elections. If one looks at the *Shapley value* of alternative nonracial voting arrangements which emphasize more coalitional strategies, what emerges is the clear possibility that black voters can become the critical swing vote in many crucial elections.[12] Swing voting blocks wield substantial, disproportionate power in elections since other large voting blocks must then offer substantial concessions to get the black vote. Clearly, Hispanic, Jewish and other ethnic voting blocks have recognized this strategy for increased public policy impact, as the new urban coalitions among Hispanic, Jews, and other ethnics have shown.

AFFIRMATIVE ACTION

Among the most important and convincing empirical research on the impact of affirmative action is the work of Jonathan Leonard in a series of studies from 1984 to 1990.[13] Leonard compared the progress of minority workers at firms with federal contracts with establishments that did not have affirmative action programs. He found that the share of both black male and black female employment in total employment rose significantly faster among federal contracts in comparison to noncontractors between 1974 and 1980. The difference remained statistically significant even after controlling for other factors such as establishment size, region of the country, industry, occupational structure, and corporate structure among noncontractors. Similar effects were also reported by Ashenfelter and Heckman, and Heckman and Wolpin.[14] Smith and Ward found that affirmative action programs had a large affect on the employment of black females.[15]

Leonard determined that compliance reviews of timetables and audits of hiring records played a significant role in black employment growth over and above that required by an affirmative action plan. Leonard found that employment growth for black males in firms undergoing compliance review was twice that of federal contractors generally.

Leonard also concluded that from 1974 to 1980, the growth in skilled black employment was significantly greater among federal contractors: However, after 1980, the Reagan administration's federal enforcement of affirmative action came to a virtual halt. After that time, the federal contract compliance program stopped requiring employers to report separately on their employment and promotion of African Americans. Consistent with this result, Leonard, confirmed that employment growth among blacks was slower from 1980 to 1984 among federal contractors than among noncontractors, especially for black females.

Intergenerational Wealth Transfers

One of the frequently cited criticisms of affirmative action is that the present generation of high wealth and income earners has not significantly benefited from the imposition of past discrimination and unfair advantage of their forebears. To the contrary, there is ample evidence to indicate that past advantages are effectively handed down through future generations. Intergenerational transfers via gifts and bequests account for a large amount of personal wealth in the United States. Studies show that half of all large fortunes appear to be inherited. Research examining the intergenerational effects of wealth, using the coefficient of immobility, where zero indicates no intergenerational correlation of wealth and where a value of one indicates perfect correlation of parental and children wealth, confirms that the correlation between an individual wealth and parental wealth is on the order of 70 percent.[16]

Framing Effects and Chicago Firefighters

The perception of the efficacy and fairness of affirmative action programs is very sensitive to the way in which the issue is framed. When asked whether there should be efforts to promote affirmative action programs to improve economic opportunities for African Americans, the clear majority of Americans favor such policies. When surveyed as to whether they support affirmative action programs based on "racial quotas," the majority of Americans indicate they are against such programs. The game theory framework of this essay offers a clear reason for these framing effects. Framing the question in terms of programs to increase African American success and participation in the economic system reflects a high R_A, whereby such programs are viewed as part of a long-term interaction with the interests of the general society and exposure to mutually beneficial economic growth and advancement. On the other hand, the same programs characterized as racial preferences are perceived to be attempts to permanently deny resources to all non-African Americans. This latter conceptualization is seen as defecting from an implied social contract reflecting noncooperative reciprocity.

Many large corporations have maintained their affirmative action programs in the face of political retrenchment. One of the most powerful incentives for firms maintaining affirmative action programs and promoting cultural diversity is the importance of the changing consumer market, which is for business the quintessential long-term, shared relationship. Blacks, Hispanics, and Asians are now approaching 25 percent of the population, and their combined spending power will reach upwards of $650 billion by the year 2000. A poll of CEOs, primarily from companies with over 10,000 employees, indicated they would continue their affirmative action programs irrespective of federal government requirements.[17]

Resentment over affirmative action is reflected in the continued opposition of white firemen in Chicago to the affirmative action program to increase the number of African American firemen in that city. Pre-affirmative action, the Chicago fire department was nearly 90 percent white. It was well known and accepted practice in Chicago for many decades that the fire department was the virtual exclusive domain of the Irish-controlled patronage system. With the hiring of more black firemen, Chicago totally segregated their fire houses, with the department still remaining over 80 percent white. When interviewed about the affirmative action program, the head of the Irish fire fighters group asserted that the hiring of black firemen should be declared illegal on the grounds that it promoted preferential treatment!

Evidence for the claim of reverse discrimination is very weak. Reverse discrimination against white males is insignificant in terms of actual contract dollars. White men averaged only 1.7 percent of discrimination charges filed with the EEOC between 1987 and 1994 while they filed 82 percent of the age discrimination cases in the 1990s. Eleanor Holmes Norton in reviewing these statistics commented, "Apparently white males are highly conscious of the form of discrimination they are most likely to encounter."[18]

A 1994 study and 1996 follow-up study covering over eighty SMSAs found that African American firms received less than 2 percent of state contracts throughout the U.S., and barely 1 percent in most states. Moreover, state government set-asides for minority businesses resulted in the majority of contracts going to white women-owned firms.[19] Even the more aggressive federal set-aside goal of 5 percent for minority and women-owned businesses has never been met. Thus, white males still receive over 95 percent of the federal contracts. Minority business owners collectively received about 3.5 percent of total federal contract dollars in 1993. In that same year, McDonnell-Douglas alone received 91 percent more in federal contracts than all minority business owners combined.[20]

THE REALITY OF ETHNIC NICHES

The rate of association (R_A) reflects the value placed on future payoffs compared to the present. The more important are future payoffs from the perspective of the present, the higher the rate of future discount or association. High rates of association, therefore, reflect the high value placed on future interaction with other groups, thereby increasing the likelihood of cooperative relations in the future among associated groups. This measure can also be applied to describe a high degree of association within one's own reference group reflecting a high degree of intragroup interaction and shared interest. An individual can therefore have high interaction and shared interests with one's primary reference group, as well as with other groups. Alternatively, an individual can have significant shared interest with one's own primary group and little association or interest in working with outside groups. A third possibility is that of an alienated individual who would have low rates of association with all groups.

The idea that an individual has a high R_A for their own primary (ethnic, racial, social, or professional) group reflects the establishment and operation of *norms*. Norms impose standards of behavior and conformance to group values and actions that no individual member can establish or determine on their own. In fact, *groups* can be defined as a collection of individuals who display a great degree of coordinated behavior largely established by norms which serve to regulate potential group conflict. Thus, within-group cooperation can also serve to promote the interests of group members while imposing a cost on outsiders.

Suzanne Model's work on the history of ethnic employment niches as the basis for group and individual advancement utilizes this framework.[21] Her thesis can be summarized as follows: The ethnic niche is an especially effective agent of social control because reaping its economic benefits requires conforming to the behavioral standards of coworkers who are also friends and neighbors. American ethnic history, therefore, is not a story about *individuals* who struggle to pull themselves up by their own bootstraps in an essentially hostile world. It is a story about how *groups* established themselves in particular occupations and industries and used their collective resources either to control those industries or to upgrade the rewards associated with their occupations. This is the primary route that white ethnics followed in the United States throughout the twentieth century.

In 1910, the Irish were 17 percent of all construction workers and 31 percent of all railroad employees. By 1940, the Irish were dominating public service employment in several cities particularly in the fire and police departments largely as a result of controlling the political patronage system. One in five Irish workers nationally and one in four in New York City were employed in the public sector in the 1940s and 1950s. From 1899–1931, 31 percent of Jews (largely Russian Jewish immigrants) worked in the garment trades, concentrated in New York City. By 1950, the construction industry employed 12 percent of the Italian American workforce which constituted 25 percent of all construction workers in the United States. Similar stories hold for Poles in the steel industry in Buffalo, Koreans in grocery, Greeks in the restaurant business, and Chinese in the laundry business. These ethnic niches offered the advantages of simplified job search for low-skilled workers and the opportunity for individual upward mobility as group members moved over generations from laborers to managers to owners.

African Americans have a different profile. In the early to mid-twentieth century, outside of teaching and church work, black workers in the private sector were dispersed over wide geographic areas in various occupations centering around servant occupations, including janitorial service, heavy labor, and elevator operation. There was one important exception. African Americans developed a niche in railroads while working primarily for the Pullman's Sleeping Car Porters in the 1930s and 1940s, which was at that time the largest single employer of black workers in the country.[22] Of course, after World War II, black workers began to gain a foothold in the Midwest auto industry. In none of these areas, however, were there any significant routes for upward mobility to management and ownership. Thus, unlike unskilled and low-skilled white ethnics, the lack of niche opportunities and mobility for black workers segmented them at poverty and near-poverty levels. Higher skilled African Americans, in turn, were segregated from career tracks leading to upward mobility. Low-skilled white immigrants facing much less discrimination, eventually found working-class security in their niches. This security, in turn, facilitated the education necessary for the next generation to enter the middle class.[23]

A similar concept is utilized by Handy in his general theory on the evolution of black business development.[24] In this article, black entrepreneurs were historically segmented and constrained by the larger society's purposeful withholding of effective demand for black firms' goods and services. As a result, black businesses were confined to a low level development equilibrium trap. Throughout most of the twentieth century, this outcome insured permanent, intertemporal disadvantages in acquiring technology, capital resources, business human capital, and in employing workers. Further, when opportunity costs and measures of risk were explicitly considered, the result was a severe dampening of opportunities for the most prepared black talent to pursue entrepreneurship as a career. Thus, black firm formation rates have consistently lagged behind that of other groups.[25] The impact of this on the economic development of the black community through the capacity to hire black workers has also been noted by Bates and Boston.[26]

YOUTH VIOLENCE

Activities that dramatically increase the likelihood of social and economic isolation also increase the probability of profound prisoner's dilemma with low rates of association. The contemporary phenomenon of politically and economically cordoning-off and isolating high poverty census tracts in the inner-city has changed the conduct of criminal activity and its impact on susceptible neighborhoods. Unlike past organized criminal activity involving bootlegging, prostitution, loan sharking, union racketeering, and illegal gambling which provided adult employment niches and upward mobility to Jewish, Irish, and Italian criminals in the United States, the modern drug-trade at the neighborhood level relies almost exclusively on personal acts of violence to successfully conduct business and establish and maintain reputations among loosely affiliated youth. Drug distribution combined with political and economic isolation has broken down the social fabric of poor neighborhoods, resulting in a substitution of a youth-based control of street-level crime in place of the more traditional adult control of crime.

Alfred Blumstein, on examining a wide range of data on changing crime patterns in recent years, concludes that the predominant change in homicide is attributable to the dramatic growth in youth homicide beginning in the mid-1980s with the emergence of crack cocaine. The growth in the homicide rate, therefore, is linked largely to the recruitment of young people in poor neighborhoods into illicit drug markets.[27] Because these markets employ a disproportionate number of teens and pre-teens to assume the risk of street-level distribution, young individuals are required to arm themselves daily for self-protection and to conduct business. The immaturity of this group resulted in an "arms race" that often led to the frequent use of guns, and a major escalation of violence which often characterizes encounters among violent teenage males. Data shows that the dramatic rise in the juvenile murder rate and the juvenile drug arrest rate from 1984 to 1990 followed each other very closely, after which time the gap between the juvenile murder rate and drug arrest rate widened. Blumstein explained the continuing rise in the murder rate as the drug arrest rate fell after 1990 as follows: "Once the guns are diffused into the community, they are much more difficult to purge."[28]

CONCLUSION

A major contention of this article is that an important challenge for the early part of the twenty-first century is to better understand the complex connection between social choice, resources, and social outcomes among competing groups. This article has tried to outline how various issues of social choice in the form of a prisoner's dilemma game have increased social and economic isolation while simultaneously decreasing political leverage and resources to address racial inequality and problems of the inner-city. Irrespective of class, the political retrenchment in affirmative action employment and contracting programs, along with declining educational opportunities at major state university systems, has also served to reinforce the fact that blacks and whites face vastly different environments in which to live, work, and maintain families. Each of these manifestations has taken the form of decreased political con-tact, deteriorating political dialogue, and lack of meaningful association with other salient groups in the allocation of opportunities and resources. Increased social stratification of African Americans reflects a succession of these kind of sub-optimal outcomes. Social choices which have delivered short-run advantages at the expense of more long-run benefits have fostered social and economic isolation and set the stage for the slow deterioration of social capital which has deprived low-income inner-city residents of resources and mainstream social networks to facilitate social and economic advancement.

By outlining the importance of group niches under which individuals prosper, the game theory perspective of this article also serves to temper over reliance on individualistic explanations of social change. Individual success is a byproduct of individuals taking advantage of shared resources and opportunities developed through group advancement. Conversely, individual success is more difficult to achieve when groups cannot readily advance resources, opportunities, and social capital for its members. The fundamental labor queue and issues of group stratification are not fundamentally altered by individual success.

With the emergence of black political control of the central city, there has been a retreat in surrounding metropolitan area and state-level structural support for interracial cooperation. White politicians in the suburbs have little direct political interest in the welfare of the central city since the city is viewed as competing over limited local and state tax revenues which, in turn, impact property taxes and incomes to the suburbs.[29] Budget cuts made by public officials to lower or balance city budgets are invariably undertaken in poorer black populated areas where the political damage has been calculated as minimal. The widespread phenomena of limiting resources to black-controlled central cities and to black neighborhoods within cities, which represent a minority of state and metro-wide voters, has been well-documented. In addition, lack of leadership and organization in high poverty tract inner-city districts, and even among black middle class voters, has resulted in an inability to leverage black voting power through coalition development and attention to pivotal voting strategies. The political isolation of a significant number of African Americans in high poverty census tracts interacts with declining public resources to create a powerful dynamic for disinvestment in poor communities. This link between social, spatial, and political cooperation is the key to social change in twenty-first century America.

NOTES

1. John Handy, "Community Economic Development: Some Critical Issues," *The Review of Black Political Economy* 24 (4), (Winter, 1993).
2. In game theory terminology, "not cooperating" in the prisoner's dilemma game constitutes the *dominant strategy* for both B and W since, at any point in time, it is the best purely self-interest strategy either side can play regardless of what the other side plays (shown below as noncooperative payoff [30, 30]). From the point of view of group W, in the matrix below, W would not cooperate when B wishes to cooperate since W will receive a higher payoff by being greedy and imposing the sucker's payoff on group B (payoff 60 for W versus 10 for B). Likewise, W would also receive higher payoffs by being distrustful and not cooperating if B decides not to cooperate (30 for W), thereby avoiding the sucker payoff to themselves (10 for W). These strategies are identical for B. As a result, the strategy of not cooperating constitutes a *strong Nash equilibrium* because neither side can see its way clear at any point in time to unilaterally improve its position by cooperating. The result is that the social optimum is never chosen (50 for W and 50 for B) even though it is clearly superior to the pure self-interest dominant strategy and strong Nash equilibrium outcome (30W, 30B).

		W's Strategy	
		Cooperate	Don't Cooperate
B's Strategy	Cooperate	B gets 50 W gets 50	B gets 10 W gets 60
	Don't Cooperate	B gets 60 W gets 10	B gets 30 W gets 30

3. Robert Axelrod, *The Evolution of Cooperation* (New York: Basic Books, Harper Collins, 1984).

4. A long-term relationship means that the importance of future encounters between two or more groups must be significant enough to make defection or noncooperation an unprofitable strategy. Reciprocity is the ability to reciprocate both cooperation and defection effectively. In the case of Axelrod's Tit-for-Tat strategy, this means returning or reciprocating whatever the other player did on the previous move. If the other side cooperates, you cooperate; if the other side plays hard ball, you play hard ball. Other solutions to the reiterated prisoner's dilemma in the cooperative game theory literature like win-stay, lose-leave also have the same preconditions.

5. It can be shown that it is in the vital interest of competing groups to cooperate in a repeated prisoner's dilemma when the rate of association (R_A), showing the importance of future group interaction, exceeds a critical threshold.

Given the general game matrix below for either cooperation (C) or noncooperative defection (D) between two players,

	C	D
C	(R,R)	(S,T)
D	(T,S)	(U,U)

where,
R = reward or payoff for cooperation
S = sucker payoff to player being exploited
T = temptation payoff for exploiting other player
U = payoff to players' non-cooperation

the prisoner's dilemma occurs when $T > R > U > S$ (as shown above in note 2).

When the rate of association $(R_A) > (T-R) / (T-U)$, as well as when $(R_A) > (T-R) / (R-S)$, it is vital to the self-interest of each player to maximize long-term rewards through cooperation. The upshot of these equations is that the desirability for cooperation (R_A) becomes increasingly critical the larger the benefit of cooperation (R_A) and the smaller the payoff for defecting and not cooperating (U). Moreover, (R_A) is increasingly important as the gap between the payoff for being cooperative without being exploited and played for a sucker widens. This reinforces the importance of forming coalitions where each membership group has enough political weight for effective reciprocity, whereby they can effectively reward other competing groups' cooperation and punish their defection.

For proofs and discussions see Philip Straffin, *Game Theory, and Strategy* (New York: The Mathematical Association of America), p. 75; John Casti, *Five Golden Rules: Great Theories of 20th Century Mathematics* (New York: John Wiley & Sons, 1996), pp. 38–39; and Robert Axelrod (1984), pp. 216–218.

6. Douglas Massey and Nancy Denton, *American Apartheid: Segregation and the Making of the Underclass* (Cambridge: Harvard University Press, 1993). The original studies in this area are from Roderick Wallace, "Urban Desertification, Public Health, and Public Order: 'Planned Shrinkage,' Violent Death, Substance Abuse, and AIDS in the Bronx," *Social Science and Medicine* 32 (1991):801–813; Roderick Wallace, "'Planned Shrinkage,' The Contagious Urban Decay, and Violent Death in the Bronx: The Implications of Synergism," Epidemiology of Mental Disorders Re-

search Department, New York State Psychiatric Institute, 1990.

7. Massey and Denton, op. cit., pp. 158–159

8. Peter Beinart, "New Bedfellows," *The New Republic* (August 11 & 18, 1997), pp. 23 and 26.

9. This process of coalition formation between Hispanics (H) and Jews (J) while excluding blacks (B) could more accurately be described by the more technical concept of the "kernal." The kernal expresses the idea that surplus payoff that Hispanics can get against blacks (S_{HB}) over all possible coalitions S and imputations x represents the highest excess payoff that Hispanics can hope to gain without the cooperation of blacks. That is, $S_{HB} = \max e(S,x)$, for $H \in S$; $J \in S$; $B \notin S$. See Guillermo Owen, *Game Theory* (San Diego: Academic Press, 1995), pp. 319–322; and Martin Shubik, *Game Theory and the Social Sciences* (Cambridge: MIT Press, 1984), pp. 342–347.

10. Carol Swain, *Black Faces, Black Interests: The Representation of African Americans in Congress* (Cambridge: Harvard University Press, 1995), p. 201.

11. Ibid., p.232.

12. The Shapley value measures the ability or power of a player (ethnic group) to turn a coalition that is not a winning one into a winning one. The ability of a coalitional player to act as a swing vote across all the possible ways coalitions can form measures the real power of the group. In this sense the Shapley for is considered a power index for the player group compared to other groups. Its formula is,

$$S = \sum \frac{(t-1)!\,(n-t)!}{n!}\,[V(T) - V(t-i)]$$

where [V(T)–V(T–i)] is the marginal contribution of group i to the coalition T, and the other term measures the probability or percent of times winning coalitions can form for a given group's swing vote.

13. See Edward Wolfe, *Economics of Poverty, Inequality, and Discrimination* (Cincinnati: South-Western, 1997), pp.503–507, for a listing of Leonard's research in this area.

14. Ibid., p.500.

15. James Smith and Michael Ward, *Women's Wages and Work in the Twentieth Century* (Santa Monica: Rand Corporation, 1984).

16. Paul Menchik, "Inter-generational Transmission of Inequality: An Empirical Study of Wealth Mobility," *Econometica* 46 (1979); Edward Wolfe, "Trends in Household Wealth in the United States," *Review of Income and Wealth* 40 (2), 1994.

17. "Progressing Beyond Affirmative Action: A Course for the Future," National Planning Association and Joint Center for Political and Economic Studies Affirmative Action Task Force, May, 1996, p. 20, cited in Stephan and Abigail Thernstrom, *American in Black and White: One Nation, Indivisible* (New York: Simon & Schuster, 1997), p.452.

18. Eleanor Holmes Norton, "Affirmative Action in the Workplace," in *The Affirmative Action Debate,* George Curry, ed. (Reading, MA: Addison-Wesley, 1996), p. 44–45.

19. "Local Supply and Demand Analyses of the Minority-Owned Business Sector.: Final Report." D..J. Miller & Associates (Washington, D.C.: U.S. Department of Commerce, Minority Business Development Agency, December, 1994).

20. Kweisi Mfume, "Why America Needs Set-Aside Programs," in Curry, pp. 122–124.

21. Susan Model, "The Ethnic Niche and the Structure of Opportunity: Immigrants and Minorities in New York City," in *The Underclass Debate: Views from History,* Michael B. Katz, ed. (Princeton: Princeton University Press, 1993).

22. Brailsford Brazeal, *The Brotherhood of Sleeping Car Porters* (New York: Harper and Brothers, 1946).
23. Model, 1993, p. 193.
24. John Handy, "A Theory on the Evolution of Black Business Development," in *A Different Vision: Race and Public Policy,* Thomas D. Boston, ed. (London and New York: Routledge. 1997), pp. 380–400.
25. John Handy, *An Analysis of Black Business Enterprises* (New York and London: Garland Publishing, 1989), pp. 12–13.
26. Timothy Bates, *Banking on Black Business* (Washington, D.C.: The Joint Center for Political and Economic Studies, 1993); and Thomas D. Boston, *Some Dynamics of African American Business Growth; Implications for CDFI,* mimeo, 1996.
27. Alfred Blumstein, "Youth Violence, Guns and the Illicit-Drug Industry," *The Journal of Criminal Law and Criminology,* Northwestern University School of Law 86 (1), (Fall, 1995).
28. Ibid., pp. 32–33.
29. Douglas Massey and Nancy Denton (1993), pp. 155–158; William Wilson, *When Work Disappears: The World of the New Urban Poor* (New York: Alfred Knopf, 1996) pp. 218–220; Thomas Edsall and Nancy Edsall, *Chain Reaction: The Impact of Race, Rights, and Taxes on American Politics* (New York: Norton, 1991); David Rusk, *Cities Without Suburbs* (Washington, D.C.: Woodrow Wilson Center Press, 1993).

Economic History and Public Policy

15

W.E.B. DUBOIS AS ECONOMIC ANALYST: REFLECTIONS ON THE 100TH ANNIVERSARY OF THE *PHILADELPHIA NEGRO*

Lynn C. Burbridge

INTRODUCTION

In 1899, *The Philadelphia Negro* was published by a brash, young W.E.B DuBois. This was not his first major work. As shall be discussed shortly, he had already written not one, but two, Ph.D. dissertations. But it was the beginning of a long and contentious debate on African American life in urban America. As we approach the 100th anniversary of the publication of this seminal work, some reflections on its contributions, and the contributions of its author are in order.

This article argues that much of the academic work of W.E.B. DuBois is of great importance to our understanding of economic phenomena currently affecting African American communities, as well as remaining relevant to debates in economic history. Including DuBois in the history of American economic thought may appear to be a stretch, given that he is generally considered a sociologist and a historian. Yet there has been considerable interest in his work by African American economists (e.g. Boston)[1] as well as there being a general revival of interest in DuBois in the social sciences overall.

There are two reasons why DuBois deserves consideration as an economic analyst. First, he was trained in Europe as an economist and only missed obtaining a doctorate in economics because of the shortsightedness of the American philanthropic community at the time. Second, his early work represents some of the very first genuinely scholarly attempts to examine the lives of African Americans at the turn of the century, so that anyone interested in African American economic history—regardless of his or her field—will benefit greatly from DuBois's analyses. In addition, DuBois's methodology, particularly in the *Philadelphia Negro*

(1899/1992),[2] brings insight into issues affecting African American communities that is often lacking in many current economic analyses.

DUBOIS AS ECONOMIST

DuBois has been depicted as a pioneer in empirical sociology (Blackwell and Janowitz,[3] Rampersand,[4]) and his work is also heavily cited by historians of the black experience in the United States (e.g. Wesley,[5] Meier and Rudwick,[6] Foner,[7]). In addition, DuBois stretched his interests beyond the United States to the African continent and is considered an important influence in the study of African history (Hansberry,[8]). His role as a pivotal figure in the gestation of the civil rights movement—as co-founder of the National Association for the Advancement of Colored People (NAACP) and as the fiery editor of *Crisis*, the NAACP's news magazine—and his role as a co-founder of the Pan-African movement, makes him a figure of great interest to political scientists, as well (Smith).[9]

This should be enough accomplishment for one life, but DuBois's reach was greater than this. Harrison[10] discusses his profound influence on the field of anthropology, including St. Clair Drake and Horace Cayton's work, *Black Metropolis*,[11] which was modeled on *The Philadelphia Negro*.[12] Stretching even further, Gaines and Reed[13] propose in a recent article that DuBois's insights should carry into the field of psychology; notably the "double consciousness" experienced by many African Americans, as eloquently described by DuBois in *The Souls of Black Folk*,[14] needs to receive further attention from psychologists and social psychologists. Even philosophers have claimed him as one of their own.[15] The addition of the interest in DuBois by African American economists makes him a scholar of influence in virtually all of the social sciences and in many of the humanities. (DuBois was also a novelist.)

One can only conclude that DuBois's influence in a wide variety of fields is truly extraordinary for one man, even one who was well past ninety when he died. One possible reason for his influence is the simple fact that he was there first. When very few other people were bringing a sharp, analytical lens to American race relations, DuBois was poised and ready to do so with tremendous dedication and vigor. The field was wide open for him. Nevertheless, one cannot ignore the fact that DuBois was an extraordinary man with a brilliant mind, a restless imagination, and a deeply powerful personality that disdained any limitations that others might try to place on him (Rampersand,[16] Lewis[17]).

DuBois was born February 23, 1868 in Great Barrington, Massachusetts. Although his father deserted his mother when he was still very young, he had a relatively happy childhood as something of a prodigy in this Western Massachusetts community.[18] While he certainly experienced racial prejudice and the sense of "otherness" he was to write about later, he was shocked and appalled by the intense racism he encountered in the Nashville area when he went to Fisk University in 1885. After graduating from Fisk, DuBois went to Harvard in 1888 where he was required to repeat his junior and senior years, as was often required of students from "undistinguished" undergraduate colleges.[19] He earned his baccalaureate degree (cum laude) from Harvard in 1890 and went on to pursue graduate studies at Harvard until 1892 when he obtained a fellowship to study abroad from the Slater Fund.

While at Harvard, DuBois was influenced by the eminent psychologist William James and the historian Albert Hart. It was while in Europe that he was exposed to the ideas of economist Gustave Schmoller at the University of Berlin. Schmoller was a leader of young radical economists advocating for a kind of democratic socialism that would ameliorate and mitigate the negative consequences of capitalism.[20] Schmoller was also a proponent of inductive methodology in social science "stressing the primacy of observed phenomena over theory or ideal constructs,"[21] who gave DuBois a deep appreciation for empirical social science.

In his first three semesters at the University of Berlin, DuBois wrote a doctoral thesis, in German, on "The Large and Small-scale System of Agriculture in the Southern United States, 1840–1890" ("Der Gross und Klein Betrieb des Ackerbaus, in den Sudstaaten der Vereinigten Staaten, 1840–90"). Despite the support of Schmoller and other faculty to obtain his doctorate after only three semesters, other professors at the University of Berlin objected to his finishing in so short a time. (There was a four semester minimum and most students took considerably longer than this.) DuBois was required to spend another semester at the university before he could obtain his Ph.D. in economics.[22]

Unfortunately, DuBois did not have the funding to stay an additional summer in Berlin. The Slater Fund, which provided him his fellowship, refused to extend his grant. Lewis, in his detailed analysis of DuBois' funding situation, writes that the Slater Fund had been reluctant to provide DuBois a fellowship in the first place and only did so after vigorous prodding from the aggressive, young scholar.[23]

The philanthropic community in the United States was becoming increasingly influenced by the ideas of Booker T. Washington and others that their primary goal should be to fund the industrial education of the Negro. Helping a brilliant, black scholar obtain a European education did not fit into the ideology of the time. Thus, DuBois was forced to sail for home, having completed all his degree requirements for a doctorate in economics, but unable to finish because of the short-sighted policies of the Slater Fund. Not only was DuBois denied funding, but it was also decided that the Slater Fund would no longer assist any other African American who wanted to study in Europe. Lewis suggests that DuBois's success in Europe might have been more than they could handle.[24]

After returning to the United States, DuBois completed a dissertation in history at Harvard on "The Suppression of the African Slave Trade."[25] A detailed study, drawing on many public documents, it demonstrated the failure of the United States to enforce the ban on slave trading in the pre-Civil War nineteenth century. It was so well received, it was published in 1896 as the first volume of the Harvard Historical Studies. Some sixty years later when the study was re-published, DuBois wrote an "Apologia" expressing his regrets that he did not know more about the works of Freud and Marx when he was a young doctoral student. A knowledge of Freud would have made his admonitions that politicians should have done the right thing with regard to the slave trade "seem less pat and simple."[26] A knowledge of Marx would have enhanced his knowledge of the "economic motives on the action of mankind."[27] Nevertheless, Lewis notes that "if much of *Suppression* reduces social and political conduct to a matter of character . . . its numerous economic pronouncements have a distinctly modern, we might say proto-Marxist, ring."[28] In spite of his later dissatisfaction with this work, it clearly shows DuBois as a conscientious, economic thinker.

Before going on to discuss some of DuBois later work, it should also be noted that while he did not obtain a degree in economics, he did in fact teach economics. Following the completion of *The Philadelphia Negro*, which is discussed shortly, DuBois obtained a position at Atlanta University (AU) where he taught economics, history, and sociology.[29] And while the studies that came out of his tenure at AU were described as "sociological," they were also described as coming out of the Department of Economics and History at Atlanta University.[30] Thus, DuBois had a clear history as a student and teacher of economics.

DUBOIS'S SEMINAL WORK

The Philadelphia Negro

Following an unhappy tenure at Wilberforce University where DuBois taught while finishing his dissertation, he moved to Philadelphia in the fall of 1896 to conduct a study of the living conditions of African Americans residing in the 7th ward of that city. Writing in his autobiography, he described the impetus for the study as follows:

> It all happened this way: Philadelphia, then and still is one of the worst governed of America's badly governed cities, was having one of its periodic spasms of reform. A thorough study of causes was called for. Not but what the underlying cause was evident to most white Philadelphians: the corrupt, semi-criminal vote of the Negro Seventh Ward. Everyone agreed that here lay the cancer; but would it not be well to give scientific sanction to the known causes by an investigation, with imprimatur of the University [of Pennsylvania].[31]

In actual fact the study was jointly sponsored by the University of Pennsylvania and the Philadelphia chapter of the College Settlement Association (CSA), an organization dominated by educated and well-to-do white women involved in charitable and reform work in various cities. While many of the women involved in the CSA were certainly well intentioned, their activities in charitable work often reflected their exclusion from other areas of public life because of the sexism of the time.[32] They certainly were not free of commonly-held race and class biases and, according to Lewis, regarded the poverty and crime of the Seventh Ward as a "virus to be quarantined,"[33] with little understanding of the economic and social causes of the problems existing there. They were further chagrined when blacks in this district did not support their reform-minded candidates against the city political machine.

DuBois was invited to conduct the study as an "assistant instructor" at the university. In spite of his Harvard degree and his training abroad he was given "no academic standing, no office at the University, no official recognition of any kind."[34] He proceeded to undertake, by himself, the monumental task of surveying the 7th ward. According to Aptheker in the introduction to a recent edition of *The Philadelphia Negro,* he visited approximately 2,500 households, a job that was estimated to have consumed 835 hours.[35] He also compiled historical documents and other data (e.g., census data) to supplement his own survey. Most of the work was conducted in 1896 and 1897, with the final published version released by the University of Pennsylvania in 1899.

DuBois was not unaware that his sponsors at the University of Pennsylvania and the CSA were hoping that his study would confirm their own notions about the immorality and criminal behavior of those in the 7th Ward. Nor did he shy away from making a serious critique of the lives of the African Americans living there. Lewis describes *The Philadelphia Negro* as "two books in one—one that would not be immediately denounced or ridiculed by the arbiters of mainstream knowledge . . . and a second one that would, over time, deeply penetrate the social sciences and gradually improve race relations policy through its not-immediately apparent interpretive radicalism."[36] Nevertheless, DuBois' own New England Calvinism may have also contributed to the harshness of his criticism,[37] just as much as any hidden agenda on his part.

Nevertheless, while *The Philadelphia Negro* often supported the claims of others that immorality and crime were serious issues for the 7th Ward, DuBois was quite clear about the reasons: he rejected the popular social Darwinist explanations of the time and pointed his finger at racism as the pre-eminent, underlying cause. *The Philadelphia Negro* is an important study if for no other reason than being one of the first empirical analyses of black urban life in America and one of the first of such studies to link crime, out-of-wedlock births, and poverty to blocked economic opportunities resulting from racism:

> . . . men have a right to object to a race so poor and ignorant and inefficient as the mass of Negroes; but if their policy in the past is parent of much of this condition, and if to-day by shutting black boys and girls out of most avenues of decent employment they are increasing pauperism and vice, then they must hold themselves largely responsible for the deplorable results.[38]

But there are other reasons to pay attention to *The Philadelphia Negro.* Many of the issues facing urban blacks, documented by DuBois, are still very much with us today. One sees in this work intimations of things to come and many of DuBois keen observations seem almost prophetic.

Very early in his discussion, DuBois writes that "scanning the population [statistics] . . . carefully, the first thing that strikes one is the unusual excess of females."[39] DuBois attributes the low male-to-female ratio to the greater ease black women had finding jobs in the city (largely in domestic service) and to the high mortality rates of black males. DuBois describes the shortage of men and their poor economic prospects as contributing to the high percentage of female-headed households in the Seventh Ward (although rates of female headship were low by today's standards). This argument is very similar to that of Darity and Meyers[40] or William Julius Wilson,[41] in their analyses of low marriage rates among African Americans today.

In addition, we find from this work the first indications of the declining fertility rate for blacks that would come with urbanization. "The size of families in cities is nearly always smaller than elsewhere," he wrote, "and the Negro family follows this rule; late marriages among them undoubtedly act as a check to population; moreover, the economic stress is so great that only the small family can survive."[42] It turned out to be the beginning of a trend that has resulted in the convergence of black and white fertility rates by the later part of the twentieth century (e.g., Farley and Allen, 1989).[43]

DuBois also documents high youth unemployment that encouraged crime among young males, but that also left the Seventh Ward without the child labor problems found elsewhere. "[T]he absence of child labor . . . is not voluntary on the part of Negroes, but due to restricted opportunity; there is really very little that Negro children may do."[44] The relation between youth unemployment and crime is an issue currently under debate, just as it was at the turn of the century (e.g., Sullivan).[45] And recent concerns about American youth working too much have not been very relevant to black youth who experience extraordinarily high unemployment rates in urban America (see Greenberger and Steinberg).[46]

The Philadelphia Negro is also extremely important in being the first scientific study to seriously examine class differences within the African American community. DuBois defined four classes. First, he described a middle class as families in which the husband is not engaged in menial work, where the wife is at home, and the children attend school; this represented about 12 percent of the population. Next he estimated a respectable working class with steady work and with children in school as representing 53 percent of the population. Third he identifies a group of "honest poor" (about 30%) not earning enough to live without want but that had "no touch of gross immorality or crime."[47] Finally, there was the "lowest class of criminals, prostitutes, and loafers," a group very similar to what we now refer to as the "underclass" (6% of the population).

DuBois's description of black social classes is interesting for several reasons. It was an early attempt to assert the heterogeneity of the black population to an audience that was disinclined to see African Americans as a highly differentiated group of people. This is an issue that is still with us today as many middle-class blacks complain bitterly that some whites continue treat all blacks, regardless of their education or comportment, as members of the underclass.[48] It is also interesting to note that much of the current work that has been done on black social classes seems to be largely undertaken by African American scholars (e.g., Boston,[49] and Darity and Meyers[50]).

DuBois's description is also interesting since the percentages he attributes to the poor and to the "underclass" are very similar to the percentages now given to describe these groups. DuBois also sounds very much like William Julius Wilson[51] in criticizing the black middle class for distancing themselves from the black poor and underclass and in being ineffectual in helping to rehabilitate those at the bottom of the class structure.

Of course, one can take these analogies too far. In fact much has happened since 1896. What was a trickle of black migration to Philadelphia from the South, became a flood, as African Americans poured into the cities in the 1920s, 1950s, and 1960s. Blacks have made tremendous gains in education, absolutely and relatively to whites. The Civil Rights Movement put an end to some of the more egregious forms of discrimination, if not an end to all of it. The black middle class grew as a result of their access to jobs in the expanding service sector and, for a while, the black working class gained access to industrial employment that strengthened their position as well.

On the negative side, black success in obtaining industrial jobs was short lived, with devastating consequences for non-college educated black males. Whatever hopes of racial peace that arose from the Civil Rights Movement have dissipated with the resurgence of racial violence and various pseudo-scientific theories of racial inferiority. Further, blacks are now more segregated than they were during the time DuBois was writing. In fact, Darity and Myers attribute to segregation the inability of the black elite to obtain the social distance DuBois described them as wanting in 1896.[52]

Massey and Denton[53] provide some support for this: they report segregation indices in Philadelphia of about 46 between 1860 and 1910, compared to an index of 88.8 in 1940, declining to 77–79 percent in the 1980s. (The segregation index measures the percentage of blacks that would have to move to have blacks distributed in neighborhoods throughout the city in the same proportion that they are in the total population of the city. An index of 0 is equivalent to no segregation. An index of 100 is equivalent to total segregation.) Thus, blacks have become increasingly segregated with relatively little change since the 1940s. Unfortunately, these data do not tell us whether blacks have become more segregated by class—even when segregated from whites—as has been suggested by Wilson and Darity and Myers. Massey and Denton argue that the problems of the underclass would have developed regardless of movements by the black middle class, however, because of the increasing concentration of poverty resulting primarily from economic changes.[54]

Perhaps the greatest and most important analogy between the time DuBois wrote *The Philadelphia Negro* and now is that both are times of rapid economic restructuring and change. In 1896 Philadelphia was turning into an industrial city, with large inflows of immigrants from Europe, as well as the more limited immigration from the black South. Now cities are being changed by de-industrialization. In 1896 blacks were losing jobs in their traditional lines of work—such as catering and other service fields—as they faced increasing competition from white immigrants. Now blacks are losing hard-won industrial jobs in the face of increasing competition from abroad. In 1896 the racial climate seemed to be worsening as the nation turned away from the commitments made during the abortive post-Civil War Reconstruction period and embraced social Darwinist theories of racial inferiority, just as now there is a similar retrenchment on civil rights.

The Philadelphia Negro is the story of rapid economic and social change in the context of a seriously compromised racial climate. For those interested in the political economy of race relations, in how discriminated-against minorities fare in times of upheaval and change, it is an important and valuable study.

Studies at Atlanta University

As indicated earlier, DuBois went on to teach in the Department of Economics and History at Atlanta University at the end of 1897. Atlanta University was embarking on a series of studies on the conditions of

African Americans as well. Two annual research conferences had already produced publications before DuBois's arrival—one on "Mortality Among Negroes in Cities" and one on "Social and Physical Condition of Negroes in Cities."[55] DuBois took over leadership for subsequent conferences and studies engendered by them, hoping to bring "higher standards of statistical and empirical work"[56] than was found in these earlier works.

DuBois's ambitions were stymied by the lack of adequate funding available to undertake the quality of research required. This lack of funding was obviously a source of frustration to DuBois. In the introduction to the 1901 publication on "The Negro Common School" DuBois said in comments most probably directed to the philanthropic community:

> . . . the further prosecution of these important studies is greatly hampered by the lack of funds. With meager appropriations for expenses, lack of clerical help and necessary apparatus, the Conference cannot cope properly with the vast field of work before it.
>
> Studies of this kind do not naturally appeal to the general public but rather to the interested few and to students. Nevertheless there ought to be growing in this land a general conviction that a careful study of the condition and needs of the Negro population—a study conducted with scientific calm and accuracy, and removed so far as possible from prejudice or partisan bias—that such a study is necessary and worthy of liberal support.[57]

In spite of lack of funds and the compromises in quality that DuBois invariably had to make, these first studies are still important historical documents for students of African American history. In his autobiography DuBois was able to boast, not without justice, that "these studies with all their imperfections were widely distributed in the libraries of the world and used by scholars . . . [B]etween 1896 and 1920 there was no study made of the race problem in America which did not depend in some degree upon the investigations made at Atlanta University."[58]

The studies produced in the twelve years DuBois was first at Atlanta University include something for everyone. Two of the studies—"The Negro in Business"[59] and "Economic Cooperation Among Negro Americans"[60]—along with DuBois's analysis of black businesses in *The Philadelphia Negro*, have been used by students of black business development from Abram Harris[61] to John Sibley Butler.[62] The two studies on "the Negro Artisan" in 1902 and 1912[63] are important for those interested in the labor history of African Americans (e.g., Foner[64]). "The Negro American Family,"[65] along with DuBois's observations in *The Philadelphia Negro* have set the tone for subsequent discussions on the black family from E. Franklin Frazier[66] to the present (e.g., Stewart).[67]

For those interested in the education of African Americans and the issues facing black schools at the turn of the century, one can find useful information in studies of "The College-Bred Negro"[68] and "The Negro Common School"[69] (e.g., Bond[70]); although DuBois's fight with Booker T. Washington over education policy for black youth clearly stole the limelight. For those interested in social and self-help institutions operating in the black community at the turn of the century (e.g., Wilmor[71]), there are studies on "The Negro Church"[72] and "Efforts for Social Betterment Among Negro Americans".[73]

In spite of these accomplishments, DuBois found it increasingly difficult to obtain funding for his studies, particularly after his fight with Booker T. Washington spilled out into the open. Washington was not without influence in the philanthropic community and there were fears that the annual conferences would soon be coming to an end. In addition he and his wife were devastated by the loss of a son who might have lived had there been access to better medical care in Atlanta. There was also the increasing realization that the intransigence of racism was to persist in spite of DuBois's best efforts to educate through research.[74] So in 1910 DuBois cut his loses and agreed to accept the position of Director of Publicity and Research at the NAACP. DuBois appeared to be turning away from his life as scholar to work as a political activist and propagandist. However good his reasons, it must have been a bittersweet choice for one whose "professional achievements placed him in the vanguard of social science scholarship in America"[75].

In spite of the popularity of NAACP's *Crisis* news magazine, DuBois' frequent fights with the leadership of the NAACP, often centering around his independence from their direction, resulted in DuBois leaving the NAACP and returning to Atlanta University in 1933. He was 65; an age of retirement for many. But DuBois was only entering a new stage in his active life.

Black Reconstruction. In his second tenure at Atlanta University he wrote his seminal work on the reconstruction era, *Black Reconstruction in America: 1860–1880.* Just as *The Philadelphia Negro* was written with a view to undermining stereotypes of African Americans living in urban

America at the turn of the century, with *Black Reconstruction* he was determined to overturn the established historical accounts of the Reconstruction period following the Civil War. Up until *Black Reconstruction,* the post-Civil War period was characterized as a dark time in which Southern politics was overrun with greedy carpetbaggers and incompetent Negroes, as immortalized in the D.W. Griffith film, *Birth of a Nation,* which justified the criminal activity of the Ku Klux Klan as necessary to saving the South from these corrupt forces. DuBois wrote:

> The whole history of Reconstruction has with few exceptions been written by passionate believers in the inferiority of the Negro. The whole body of facts concerning what the Negro actually said and did, how he worked, what he wanted, for whom he voted, is masked in such a cloud of charges, exaggeration and biased testimony, that most students have given up all attempt at new material or new evaluation of the old, and simply repeated perfunctorily all the current legends of black buffoons in legislature, golden spittoons for fieldhands, bribery and extravagance on an unheard-of scale, and the collapse of civilization until an outraged nation rose in wrath and ended the ridiculous travesty.[76]

Black Reconstruction in America: 1860–1880 was published in 1935 and runs over 700 pages, indicating the tremendous vigor of its author. In the introduction to the latest edition, Lewis notes the difficulties involved in doing the research. Many library archives were unavailable to DuBois either because blacks were not allowed or because the proud scholar was unwilling to endure the condescending and hostile behavior exhibited to blacks desiring access to them.[77] Lewis argues that some of the factual errors, for which the work has been criticized, are understandable given the circumstances under which it was written. What is important about this work, Lewis argues, is that it ultimately initiated a revisionist history of Reconstruction, influencing white and black historians alike to write more accurate accounts of this period.

Unlike the case with *The Suppression of the African Slave Trade,* DuBois did not have to later regret not having read Marx. The influence of Marxist analysis is clear in this book. Not that it was well received by Marxist scholars of its time. DuBois rejected the primacy of class issues in explicating what happened in the post-Civil War period. He acknowledges and describes in detail the different class interests at work, but ultimately concluded that the virulence of racism precluded the possibility of a united proletarian in the South, and that the inability of working class whites and blacks to find common ground in the South contributed to the demise of Reconstruction. The white left found DuBois's argument unacceptable. Lewis writes that a reviewer in *The Nation* condescendingly referred to DuBois as "'an old man' who had 'turned to reading Marx.'"[77]

Many may now see this as an old argument between black scholars and the white left, but it is important to remember that DuBois shot one of the first arrows against a simple class-based interpretation of Southern history. He wrote:

> The proletariat is usually envisaged as united, but their real interests were represented in America by four sets of people: the freed Negro, the Southern poor white, and the Northern skilled and common laborer. These groups never came to see their common interests, and the financiers and capitalists easily kept the upper hand.[78]

And again:

> It was not until after the period which this book treats that white labor in the South began to realize that they had lost a great opportunity, that when they united to disfranchise the black laborer they had cut the voting power of the laboring class in two.[79]

For DuBois, the Reconstruction was a brief period of unparalleled democracy, that not only enfranchised the freedman, but that gave political power to poor whites as well. The demise of Reconstruction and the resurgence of the old landed class, according to DuBois, hurt poor whites as well as poor blacks. An opportunity for greater democracy for blacks and whites in the South was lost because of the ease with which the white working class was manipulated by appeals to racial solidarity. Again, this may now seem an old argument, but it was explosive in its time.

Finally, DuBois argues that one important legacy of the enfranchising of blacks did remain after Reconstruction—universal public education. Black legislators throughout the South pushed for the availability of public schools, a policy that remained in effect after the end of Reconstruction. Poor whites may have been the greater beneficiaries, since blacks were eventually confined to lesser schools that served them for fewer hours a year, but the long-term impact on the South that this investment in human capital produced can only be large.

DuBois and Myrdal's Study. It was also during this period at Atlanta University that DuBois developed an idea to write an "Encyclopedia of the Negro." While the encyclopedia never received the backing of the philanthropic community, Lewis[80] suggests that the idea for funding *An American Dilemma* (1944)[81] grew out of discussions between the foundation community and DuBois about the encyclopedia. Rather than funding DuBois's idea, however, it was decided instead to fund the Swedish economist Gunnar Myrdal to conduct an analysis of American race relations. In writing *An American Dilemma,* Myrdal cites DuBois and his work no less than seventy-five times, but one wonders if DuBois appreciated the compliment.

What is interesting about Myrdal's opus is that, in spite of his being an economist, the work gives greater attention to the psychological and political aspects of American race relations. His discussion of class differences in the African American community is particularly short and perfunctory, something that would not have occurred with DuBois at the helm. To Myrdal's credit, he admits as much in the appendix, suggesting the need for community studies to examine the social dynamics within the black community. He concludes this discussion with the following statement:

> We cannot close this description of what a study of a Negro community should be without calling attention to the study which best meets our requirements, a study which is now all but forgotten. We refer to W.E.B. DuBois, *The Philadelphia Negro,* published in 1899.[82]

METHODOLOGICAL ISSUES

Of course, it can easily be argued that DuBois's methodology, particularly in *The Philadelphia Negro*, is more relevant to sociology than to economics. The case study approach is rarely used in economics, although economic historians often relish sorting through old archival data, as did DuBois. The best argument against DuBois as an economic thinker is that his work looks much more like modern sociology than modern economics. Nevertheless, for its time, it was highly empirical and showed the influence of his study of economics in Berlin.

Further, this approach permits an analysis of complex and elusive issues. As mentioned earlier, Myrdal noted the importance of community studies to examine class issues, particularly in the African American community, where class lines are weak and fragile.

In another article, I have raised similar issues with respect to analyses done of black women.[83] One set of studies, noting the occupational gains by black women in recent decades, suggests that black women have been making remarkable economic gains, especially with respect to black men. Another set of studies, focusing on families, finds an increasing "feminization of poverty," with a disproportionate impact on black women. Another set of studies, focusing on time use has found that single mothers are increasingly "time poor," in ways not captured in data on income. A complete understanding of the status of black women requires a more "holistic" approach that can balance and synthesize these findings.[84]

Further, we have to ask the question: does it really make sense to consider the occupational gains of black women as somehow part of a separate process than the industrial losses of black men? In fact the economic restructuring that has been detrimental to black men is the *same process* that has benefited black women: the shift from manufacturing to services has benefited female-intensive fields relative to male-intensive ones. Because of their position in the labor queue black men have born the brunt of the loss of traditionally-male jobs. Black women are also at the bottom of a queue, but theirs—at least until recently—has been moving a lot faster.

In examining a work like *The Philadelphia Negro* one comes away with a more complete understanding of what was happening to black men and black women, and the interaction of these factors, than one often finds in reading more current economic articles. There are more risks to DuBois's approach, and that of many of his contemporaries, however. The research takes longer and probably lays one open for more criticism, because of the breadth of the work being attempted.

For this reason alone, it seems unlikely that the economics profession will change dramatically. The focus will still be on narrowly-defined questions, analyzed using secondary data sources. That does not obviate the need for economists to pay attention to studies like DuBois', however. They often provide important insights into subjects that are of interest to us.

CONCLUSION

DuBois was retired from Atlanta University in 1944 after conflicts with its president, and returned to the NAACP. Now 76, his radicalism continued to be a problem for that organization, and he was forced to leave again in 1948. Nevertheless, he persisted in his activism until his death at the age of 95, one day before the historic March on Washington, in April of 1963.[85]

While DuBois's political activism made an unmeasurable contribution to the evolution of the Civil Rights Movement that led to that march, it is extraordinary to consider that a scientist of his caliber found it so difficult to ply his trade as a scholar, requiring him to sway from this job to that with little economic security for himself and his family. Some may want to argue that his political beliefs created a barrier for him. But DuBois' was 93 when he joined the Communist Party, shortly before leaving for Ghana, where he spent his last years. Further, in a recent interview his stepson—David DuBois—argues that he joined the Communist Party primarily as an act of defiance after years of harassment by the U.S. authorities because of his international social activism.[86] David DuBois noted that his stepfather never abandoned his fundamental critique "that when it came to black people, socialists and communists didn't know what they were talking about"[87].

Rather, it is more likely that it was DuBois' inability to compromise his principles that caused him so much grief. But it was the strength of his personality that ultimately produced seminal works like *The Suppression of the African Slave Trade, The Philadelphia Negro*, *Black Reconstruction*, and the many AU studies. On the anniversary of *The Philadelphia Negro*, it may be useful to reflect on the tremendous challenges posed to a young, African American scholar to write seriously and analytically about black life, with little support or precedents.

REFERENCES

1. Boston, T. D. (ed.) (1997) *A Different Vision: African American Economic Thought,* London: Routledge; and Boston, T. D. (ed.) (1997) *A Different Vision: Race and Public Policy,* London: Routledge.

2. DuBois, W.E.B. (1899/1992) The Philadelphia Negro, Millwood, NY: Kraus-Thomson.

3. Blackwell, J. E. and M. Janowitz (1972) *Black Sociologists: Historical and Contemporary Perspectives,* Chicago: University of Chicago Press.

4. Rampersand, A. (1976) *The Art and Imagination of W.E.B. DuBois,* Cambridge: Harvard University Press.

5. Wesley, C.H. (1970) "W.E.B. DuBois: The Historian," in J.H. Clarke, E. Jackson, E. Kaiser, and J. H. O'Dell (ed.), Black Titan: W.E.B. DuBois, Boston: Beacon Press.
6. Meier, A. and E. Rudwick (1976) *From Plantation to Ghetto,* New York: Hill and Wang.
7. Foner, P. S. (1974) *Organized Labor and the Black Worker,* New York: International Publishers.
8. Hansberry, L. (1970) "W.E.B. Dubois' Influence on African History," in J.H. Clarke, E. Jackson, E. Kaiser, and J.H. O'Dell (eds.), Black Titan: W.E.B. DuBois, Boston: Beacon Press.
9. Smith, R. C. (1992) " 'Politics' is Not Enough: the Institutionalization of the African American Freedom Movement," in R.C. Gomes and L.F. Williams (eds.) From Exclusion to Inclusion: *The Long Struggle for African American Political Power,* New York: Greenwood Press.
10. Harrison, F. V. "The DuBoisian Legacy in Anthropology," *Critique of Anthropology,* 12 (3):239–260.
11. Drake S. and Cayton, H. (1945) *Black Metropolis: A Study of Negro Life in a Northern City,* New York: Harcourt, Brace and Company.
12. DuBois, 1899/1992.
13. Gaines, S. O. and E. S. Reed (1995) "Prejudice: From Allport to DuBois," American Psychologist, 50, No. 2.
14. DuBois, W.E.B. (1903/1965) "The Souls of Black Folk," in Three Negro Classics, New York: Avon Books.
15. Holmes, E. C. (1970), "W.E.B. DuBois: Philosopher," in J. H. Clarke, E. Jackson, E. Kaiser, and J. H. O'Dell (eds.), Black Titan: W.E.B. DuBois, Boston: Beacon Press.
16. Rampersand, 1976.
17. Lewis, D.L. (1993) *W.E.B. DuBois: Biography of a Race, New* York: Henry Holt and Co.
18. Lewis, 1993.
19. Lewis, 1993.
20. Rampersand, 1976.
21. Lewis, 1993. p. 142
22. Lewis, 1993.
23. Lewis, 1993.
24. Lewis, 1993.
25. DuBois, W.E.B. (1896/1969) *The Suppression of the African Slave Trade,* New York: Shocken Books.
26. DuBois, 1896/1969 p. xxxii.
27. DuBois, 1896/1969 p. xxxii.
28. Lewis, 1993, p. 159.
29. Lewis, 1993.
30. DuBois, W.E.B. (1902/1969) "The Negro Artisan," in W.L. Katz (ed.), The American Negro, His History and Literature: The Atlanta University Publications, New York: Arno Press and the New York Times.
31. DuBois, W.E.B. (1968) *The Autobiography of W.E.B. DuBois: A Soliloquy on Viewing My Life from the Last Decade of Its First Century,* New York: International Publishers. p. 194.
32. Burbridge, L.C. (1997) "Black Women in the History of African American Economic Thought: A Critical Essay" in T. Boston (ed.) *A Different Vision: African American Economic Thought,* London: Routledge.
33. Lewis, 1993. p. 188.

34. DuBois, 1968. p. 194.
35. DuBois, 1899/1992.
36. Lewis, 1993. p. 189.
37. Rampersand, 1976.
38. DuBois, 1899/1992. p. 394.
39. DuBois, 1899/1992. p. 53.
40. Darity, W. A. and Myers, S. L., Jr. (1984) "Changes in Black Family Structure: Implications for Welfare Dependency," *Journal of Marriage and the Family*, 46: 756–779.
41. Wilson, W. J. (1987) *The Truly Disadvantaged: the Inner City, the Underclass, and Public Policy*, Chicago: University of Chicago Press.
42. DuBois, 1899/1992. p. 165.
43. Farley, R. and Allen, W. A. (1989) *The Color Line and the Quality of Life in America*, New York: Oxford University Press.
44. DuBois, 1899/1992. p. 111.
45. Sullivan, M. (1989) *Getting Paid: Youth Crime and Work in the Inner City*, Ithaca: Cornell University Press.
46. Greenberger, E. and L. Steinberg (198) *When Teenagers Work: The Psychological and Social Costs of Adolescent Employment*, New York: Basic Books.
47. DuBois, 1899/1992. p. 311.
48. Cose, E. (1993) *The Rage of a Privileged Class*, New York: Harper Collins Publishers.
49. Boston, T. D. (1988) *Race, Class and Conservatism*, Boston: Unwin Hyman.
50. Darity, W. A. and Myers, S. L., Jr. (1994) *The Black Underclass: Critical Essays on Race and Unwantedness*, New York: Garland Publishing, Inc.
51. Wilson, 1987.
52. Darity and Myers. 1994.
53. Massey, D. S. and N. A. Denton (1993) *American Apartheid: Segregation and Making of the Underclass*, Cambridge: Harvard University Press.
54. Massey and Denton, 1993.
55. Lewis, 1993.
56. Rampersand, 1976. p. 55.
57. DuBois, W.E.B. (1901/1969) "The Negro Common School," in W. L. Katz (ed.), *The American Negro, His History and Literature: The Atlanta University Publications*, New York: Arno Press and The New York Times.
58. DuBois, 1968. p. 218.
59. DuBois, W.E.B. (1899/1968) "The Negro in Business," in W.L. Katz (ed.), *The American Negro, His History and Literature, The Atlanta University Publications*, New York: Arno Press and the New York Times.
60. DuBois, W.E.B. (1907/1969) "Economic Cooperation Among Negro Americans," in W. L. Katz (ed.), *The American Negro, His History and Literature: The Atlanta University Publications*, New York: Arno Press and The New York Times.
61. Harris, A. (1936) *The Negro as Capitalist*, Philadelphia: American Academy of Political and Social Science.
62. Butler, J.S. (1991) Entrepreneurship and Self-Help Among Black Americans: A Reconsideration of Race and Economics, Albany: State University of New York Press.
63. DuBois, 1902/1969; and DuBois, W.E.B. (1912/1968) "The Negro American Artisan," in W.L. Katz (ed.), *The American Negro, His History and Literature: The Atlanta University Publications*, New York: Arno Press and The New York Times.
64. Foner, 1974.

65. DuBois, W.E.B. (1908/1968) "The Negro American Family," in W. L. Katz (ed.), *The American Negro, His History and Literature: The Atlanta University Publications,* New York: Arno Press and The New York Times.
66. Frazier, E. F. (1940) *The Negro Family in the United States,* Chicago: University of Chicago Press.
67. Stewart, J.B. (1991) "Back to Basics: The Significance of DuBois's and Frazier's Contributions for Contemporary Research on Black Families," in H.E. Cheatham and J. B. Steward (eds) *Black Families: Interdisciplinary Perspectives,* (eds.), New Brunswick: Transaction Publishers.
68. DuBois, W.E.B. (1900/1969) "The College-Bred Negro," in W.L. Katz (ed.), *The American Negro, His History and Literature: The Atlanta University Publications,* New York: Arno Press and The New York Times; and DuBois, W.E.B. and A. G. Dill (1910/1968) "The College-Bred Negro American," in W. L. Katz (ed.), *The American Negro, His History and Literature: The Atlanta University Publications,* New York: Arno Press and The New York Times.
69. DuBois, 1901/1969; and DuBois, W.E.B. and A. G. Dill (1911/1968) "The Common School and the Negro American," in W.L. Katz (ed.), *The American Negro, His History and Literature: The Atlanta University Publications,* New York: Arno Press and The New York Times.
70. Bond, H.M. (1966) *The Education of the Negro in the American Social Order,* New York: Octagon Books.
71. Wilmore, G.S. (1972) *Black Religion and Black Radicalism,* Garden City, N.Y.: Doubleday and Company.
72. DuBois, W.E.B. (1903/1968) "The Negro Church," in W.L. Katz (ed.), *The American Negro, His History and Literature: The Atlanta University Publications,* New York: Arno Press and The New York Times.
73. DuBois, W.E.B. (1909/1968) "Efforts for Social Betterment Among Negro Americans" in W.L. Katz (ed.), *The American Negro, His History and Literature: The Atlanta University Publications,* New York: Arno Press and The New York Times.
74. Lewis, 1993; and Rampersand, 1976.
75. Lewis 1993. p. 225.
76. DuBois, W.E.B. (1935/1992) *Black Reconstruction in America: 1860–1880,* New York: Touchstone Books, pp. 381–382.
77. Lewis, D. L. (1992) "Introduction," in DuBois, W.E.B. (1935/1992), p. xiv.
78. DuBois, 1935/1992. p. 216.
79. DuBois, 1935/1992. p. 353.
80. Lewis, D. L. (ed.) (1995) W.E.B. Dubois: A Reader, New York: Henry Holt and Co.
81. Myrdal, G. (1944) *An American Dilemma: The Negro Problem and Modern Democracy,* New York: Harper and Brothers Publishers. a.) p. 1132.
82. Myrdal, 1944. p. 1132.
83. Burbridge, 1997.
84. Wallace, P. (1980) *The Black Woman in the Labor Force,* Cambridge: *"Inner City."* Ithaca: Cornell University Press. The MIT Press.
85. Lewis, 1995.
86. Wright, P. (1996) "A Patriot to His Toenails," *Massachusetts,* Volume 7, Number 3. a.) p. 27.
87. Wright, 1996. p. 27.

16

NO MORE SERVANTS IN THE HOUSE

Beth T. Bates

A recent influential strand of social science research entails interviewing employers, asking about their impressions of different worker subgroups, particularly blacks and Hispanics. Joleen Kirschenman and Katherine Neckerman, interviewing Chicago-area employers, found that they were remarkably blunt in their generalizations about racially-defined employee groups.[1] Young black males seeking low-paying jobs clearly stirred up their negative sentiments: they had an attitude; they were unreliable. Some employers lumped immigrants from Latin countries into the same unflattering categories, while others expressed a general preference for Latino workers. Race, in the minds of most employers, interacted with various situational variables: blacks graduating from suburban high schools, for example, were preferable to inner-city graduates; public housing residents were seen as unpromising potential employees.

Roger Waldinger in *Still the Promised City?: African-Americans and New Immigrants in Postindustrial New York* records similar employer sentiments: if you hire black males from Bedford Stuyvesant (a low-income Brooklyn neighborhood), "they don't show up on Monday . . . ." Another observer noted that black Americans lacked the "discipline of the family."[2] General employer sentiment toward immigrant minorities, in contrast, was much more favorable: they were "more pliable," "more flexible," as well as servile and vulnerable.[3] Immigrants represent a desirable labor supply because they are cheap, reliable, safe.[4] Two immigrant traits repeatedly mentioned favorably by employers are reliability and servility.

Pursuing the "what's wrong with blacks" line of inquiry, a common employer perception is that young blacks aspired to something better than the jobs held by their parents and grandparents. The hotel "industry's legacy as a repository of the traditional jobs to which blacks had long been confined deterred younger African-Americans from taking hotel jobs." As a manager of a New York business hotel said, "American-born blacks see hotel work as servitude. They don't want to be a bellperson or a waiter." Moreover, "they're willing to take a lower paying job if it gives them a higher level of self-esteem."[5] Unlike many of the immigrants, notes Waldinger, "African Americans aspire to the rewards and positions enjoyed by whites."[6]

Yet, in the early part of the twentieth century, the Pullman Company actively recruited black Americans over other workers for the position of porter on the Pullman Sleeping Cars. They did so because company officials thought black southerners exemplified the servile characteristics they sought for the position of Pullman porter. This was a perception held by many other employers who hired black workers to be hotel waiters, baggage handlers, and smiling chauffeurs. But the Pullman Company is significant because by the early 1920s, the company was the largest single private employer of black workers in the United States.[7] What made the racial stereotype corporate America held of black workers change so dramatically?

This article explores the legacy of the master-servant narrative in the Pullman Company and argues that not only is the employability of black workers heavily influenced by stereotypes held by employers, but that racial stereotypes are historically contingent. A traditional black service job—Pullman porter—is examined, first through the lens of the employer, George Pullman, and the customer riding in the Pullman car, and then through the lens of A. Philip Randolph and other organizers of the Brotherhood of Sleeping Car Porters [BSCP], the labor union that successfully challenged the politics of servility rewarded by Pullman employers. Examining employer and customer attitudes, a Pullman porter ideal is identified.

At the end of the Civil War, when George Mortimer Pullman manufactured an impressive sleeping car for railroads, he revolutionized the industry. He gained monopoly status for his Pullman Palace Sleeping Car Company by constructing a sleeping car designed to envelop passengers in a luxurious world. Pullman called his sleeping cars hotels on wheels with elaborate interiors of brocaded fabrics, hand-worked wooden door frames, plush carpets, and gilt-edged mirrors reflecting the light of silver-trimmed coal-oil lamps.[8] But what distinguished Pullman as an entrepreneur was his understanding the role that service could play in creating a palatial atmosphere for the passengers. To serve his princes and princesses, Pullman created the position of "porter," to be personal servants of the passengers while riding in the sleeping car, available night and day to prepare berths, clean cars, and render whatever small services patrons desired to make them comfortable. Pullman carefully divided the work of his employees between conductors who sold and collected tickets and porters who were at the beck and call of the clients.[9] That Pullman hired only white men to be conductors and only black men to be porters may have seemed only fitting to him in 1867. Indeed, he once claimed, as historian William Harris notes, that black Americans were chosen out of concern for their welfare in the aftermath of the Civil War, a time when precious few non-agricultural jobs were open for black workers. Nevertheless, black Americans could not be conductors on his sleeping cars, and very few black workers found employment in maintenance shops in Pullman yards until World War I.[10]

George Pullman's official biographer noted that black Americans were his choice for personal servants on the rails because they had been "trained as a race by years of personal service in various capacities." Moreover, Pullman thought they were accustomed, "by nature . . . to perform their duties under circumstances which necessitate unfailing good nature, solicitude and faithfulness."[11] Pullman took advantage of societal caste distinctions between black and white people when he chose black men rather than white men to cater to the needs of his customers sleeping in a bedroom on wheels. Those distinctions had created a "social distance" which made black porters seem less intrusive—indeed, even invisible because they were regarded as inferior—than white workers in the limited and intimate space of a sleeping car. White clients were therefore more comfortable with black Pullman porters performing the job of servant. As was Pullman's intention, a smiling, polite porter increased the comforts of his sleeping cars in the eyes of his clients. Finally, to insure the continued efficiency of the porter as servant to the traveling public, the Pullman Company linked a porter's take-home pay to tips received for services rendered.[12] Tipping reinforced the stereotype of the black worker as servant and served to create a mystique about Pullman porters as happy workers in the eyes of many patrons.[13]

To the public who patronized Pullman Sleeping Cars, porters often were not fully-formed, three dimensional characters; they were just "George"—usually the only way they were summoned—a servant whose identity was shaped by serving the white public. George, the universal call for a Pullman porter, identified porters with George Pullman, classifying them as the property of Pullman and casting them into a category of inferiority and childlike dependency.[14] While slavery images were not necessarily on the minds of their white clients when they called for "George," the person who responded to that call was, as Murray Kempton observed, "at once omnipresent and nonexistent."

> The Pullman porter rode his car, silent . . . [and] always most agreeable when he was of the old school, accepting the generic designation of "George" as though it were a balm instead of an affront, a domestic apparently unaltered by the passage of time or the Emancipation Proclamation. . . . Any white man who spoke to him spoke consciously to a Negro, which is a terrible barrier even for the best of men. . . . [L]ife was a process of enforcing recognition of his personality from a world which treated him as possessed of color without feature. It was always mixing him up with the porter in the car ahead and asking him in simple bewilderment if he was its porter, because he was, after all, only a piece of furniture set out for the convenience of persons who saw no need to be connoisseurs of this sort of furniture.[15]

While on the job, Pullman porters masked their feelings, which contributed to the mystery surrounding porters. It was a protective mechanism that shielded them from the charge of stepping out of place—the place assigned by the white world—or "being uppity," but it was also a weapon which, if used deftly, could give porters a measure of control under servile social relations. The porters learned to utilize their "invisibility" in order to attract tips. Although pretending not to understand or be privy to conversations, for example, porters took mental notes of the likes and dislikes, interests, and habits of clients as a way of anticipating the patrons' needs. One ex-porter in Chicago told his interviewer, "Pullman made hustlers out of us. They had us constantly on our knees." Two other ex-porters, writing for *Coronet* magazine in 1948, revealed that the "porter caters first to your *mental* comfort. He massages your ego, flatters your vanity, helps you enjoy your trip. . . . Most porters would be out of work if they didn't add applied psychology to their job of running errands." Malcolm X, who once worked briefly for the New Haven railroad as a dishwasher and sandwich man, noted that black service employee on railroads were both "servants and psychologists" for white people "so obsessed with their own importance that they will pay liberally . . . for the impression of being catered to and entertained."[16]

In order to validate the stereotype of "George" as the smiling, polite servant, passengers sometimes demanded that porters sing and dance for them. It was the tipping system that promoted such behavior to survive base monthly wages that were $27.50 in 1915 and $60.00 per month in 1919.[17] Thus, certain expectations were built into the relationship between porters and Pullman Sleeping Car clients from the moment the Pullman porter was created. "George" was supposed to be deferential, helpful, and unobtrusive, playing a role one historian noted was assigned to porters by "race as well as by occupation."[18] To protect the possibility of making a good tip, the porter had to recreate, on each trip, the role assigned to him by Pullman as a servant for the traveling public. Thus, as noted by many ex-porters, passengers were not only always right, but could take liberties with porters, which further reinforced the porters' subordinate status.[19]

George Pullman reinforced these social relations through his paternalism. Pullman, his daughter Florence, and Pullman's successors poured money into black institutions on Chicago's South Side and financially backed prominent black citizens, linking the name of Pullman with assistance and philanthropy. Without the financial backing of Florence Pullman, it is doubtful that Provident Hospital, the first large-scale civic project of the black community, begun in 1891, would have succeeded.[20]

The hospital, unlike any other in the country at the time, received black citizens on an equal basis and provided opportunities for black doctors and nurses who were discriminated against at most "white" hospitals. Black and white citizens and medical professionals served as members of the Advisory Board and on the medical staff.[21] Thus when Provident Hospital was established it marked an important departure in the black community, giving black neighbors an unprecedented sense of control over health care. The hospital also became a symbol of the advancement of black professionals.[22]

Opening the Provident, however, was only the first hurdle. During the depression that began in 1893, Florence Pullman's liberal contributions helped save the hospital from foreclosure. Another difficulty, finding properly trained nurses to serve on the staff of Provident, was solved when George Pullman and Marshall Field financed the construction and staffing of a nursing school, which, by World War I, was training an average of twenty-five nurses a year.[23] The close relationship between the financial health of Provident Hospital and the Pullman Company continued well into the 1920s. When the BSCP began organizing in 1925 in Chicago, the president of Pullman Company reminded porters about the company's most recent and substantial contribution to Provident Hospital, and praised the work of the hospital and its training school for nurses.[24]

The Pullman Company also gave large sums to the Wabash Avenue YMCA and the Chicago Urban League.[25] All major employers of black workers sponsored Efficiency Clubs through the Wabash YMCA. Pullman's efficiency club was designed for employees of the Pullman Car Shops and porters. At club meetings, black men were taught that the thing they have to do is to keep out of organized labor.[26] The Chicago Urban League received substantial contributions from Pullman, both during its first financial campaign and in the years that followed its founding in 1915, and close ties between the Chicago Urban League and Pullman Company existed well into the 1930s.[27]

But perhaps most important, in terms of cultivating deep roots in the black community, was the company's long-lasting relationship with the congregation and minister of the city's largest African Methodist Episcopal [AME] Church, Quinn Chapel. The Rev. Archibald James Carey took over Quinn Chapel in 1898 and captured the attention of Pullman executives as a wise administrator, gaining their financial support. Subsequently, the Rev. Carey rose to prominence, made his mark on both ecclesiastical and political affairs, and became a major leader of Chicago's black community.[28] Pullman contributed to the support of the church nursery and kindergarten to care for children of working mothers helping the Rev. Carey expand the role of his church to meet secular needs of his congregation. Civic and community affairs occupied a major place in the weekly activities at the Rev. Carey's church with speakers addressing issues such as human welfare, housing, and racial affairs. The church filled a void and provided a vital center for organizing urban life in black communities.[29]

But when the Rev. Carey established an employment service in his church, he created a strong connection between the Pullman Company and his congregation. During the summer the Pullman Company routinely hired an additional five to six hundred porters. One of the most likely places to hear about these jobs was from the Rev. Carey during a church service. In addition, many black workers got the few coveted jobs in Pullman repair shops and yards through Rev. Carey. While the position often was only as a car cleaner, it held out the promise of advancement to a skilled job in the Calumet shops where, by 1925, there were over 300 black workers.[30] When Rev. Carey announced these positions from his pulpit, Pullman was seen as a friend of black workers.[31] It must be remembered, however, that when Rev. Carey put down roots in Chicago, the city's trade unions did not extend a helping hand to black workers.[32]

Rev. Carey felt so strongly that economic opportunity for black workers would come from cooperation with industrial magnates rather than solidarity between black and white workers that during the 1920s he "forbade the congregations in his bishopric in Chicago to allow A. Philip Randolph to speak before them."[33] His reasoning grew out of his positive experiences with wealthy benefactors who recognized black Americans and opened up jobs for black workers—often the very jobs that labor unions excluded black workers from with their color clauses. In 1924 Carey said he believed "the interest of my people lies with the wealth of the nation and with the class of white people who control it. Labor and capital cannot adjust themselves by rival organizations; they must work together."[34] As a result of Carey's comprehensive approach to ministering, Pullman, as benefactor, had access to networks that reached far beyond the realm of the sacred. Carey's approval of the Pullman Company boosted the company's anti-union approach to labor relations, while cultivating its image as friend of the black community.[35]

Another way the company promoted the idea that it gave black workers unparalleled opportunities was by offering music lessons and organizing porters into bands, orchestras, and choruses. Pullman's President Edward F. Carry hired Major N. Clark Smith, director of music at Tuskegee, to give the porters a "thorough training in fundamentals of music" along with lessons on instruments such as the trombone and saxophone. At least one porter was trained to direct a 60 piece band as a pupil of Major Smith.[36] Hundreds of Pullman porters took advantage of this opportunity to develop their musical talents. Carry did not, however, extend the opportunity to Pullman conductors, perhaps because white conductors were not blessed with African Americans' "racial gift of music," as one promoter suggested. Nor were Pullman maids able to avail themselves of this opportunity.[37]

While the musical program was designed to provide recreation and education for porters, President Carry also hoped the quartets and choruses would "be in a position to sing a song or two for the edification of the patrons."[38] The bands and choruses also performed at Pullman Porters' picnics[39] and special quartets sang throughout the country. One was known as the Hungerford Quartette, named after one of the managers of Pullman Company. Another, and one of the most celebrated, was the

Pullman Porters Quartet of Chicago, whose four harmonizers, personally selected by President Carry, were known as the "president's own." This group traveled extensively, appearing in concerts before "leading men in every branch of commerce, industry and the professions."[40]

Other activities, such as baseball games, field days, and picnics, at which officials of the company were always present, encouraged what President Carry called an "*esprit de corps*."[41] Perhaps the feeling of being part of one big family found its deepest expression in the Pullman Porters Benefit Association of America [PPBAA], a voluntary organization for all black male workers at Pullman Company. Approximately eight thousand of the twelve thousand Pullman Company porters belonged to the Pullman Porters' Benefit Association of America in the late 1920s, attracted by insurance benefits and lavish yearly conventions sponsored by the company. Porters also valued the PPBAA because it provided access to a financial network, one of the few safety nets available to them.[42] Jesse Binga, head of the Binga State Bank, a black-owned institution with large deposits from the Pullman Company, pledged at the 1927 convention to help members get mortgages and loans from Binga State bank, highlighting one of the many benefits to membership in the Pullman family. He also praised George Pullman for showing that "it pays to hire a black man."[43]

When the Brotherhood of Sleeping Car Porters (BSCP) set out to organize Pullman porters, they had to answer the question raised by Binga and the Rev. Carey: why was it in the interests of Pullman porters to challenge the notion that the Pullman Company was a good employer for black workers? Why should black workers bite the hand that feed them?

Several years before the Brotherhood of Sleeping Car Porters [BSCP] began to organize, W.E.B. DuBois provided a partial answer when he described Pullman porters as part of the "million menial workers," which included "upper servants," positions like "hotel waiters . . . janitors, and cooks, who, had they been white, could have called on the great labor movement to lift their work out of slavery, to standardize their hours, to define their duties and to substitute a living, regular wage for personal largess in the shape of tips, old clothes, and cold leavings of food." The major reason menial service lingered was directly related to what DuBois called the "'manure' theory of social organization," a belief that "at the bottom of organized human life there are necessary duties and services which no real human being ought to be compelled to do. We push below this mudsill the derelicts and half-men, whom we hate and despise, and seek to build above it—Democracy!" Because the majority "consciously and unconsciously" still subscribe to this theory, DuBois advocated getting the servants out of the house, and restoring black workers to their full manhood, that is full humanity, by destroying the myth that "Negroes are servants; servants are Negroes."[44]

Organizers for the Brotherhood of Sleeping Car Porters also wanted to destroy the myth connecting black people with the status of servants, for they, too, believed that the historical circumstances that created "George" continued to define social relations restricting freedom for black workers and citizens in 1920s. During the first anniversary celebration of the union, Randolph declared the "Brotherhood was born" to pursue the "quest for the holy grail of economic freedom." But in order to reach that goal, "we must destroy the engines of industrial slavery ere we breathe the air of free men."[45] Industrial slavery and the paternalistic relations embedded in company unions embodied most of the servile relations that the Brotherhood thought held citizens and workers alike in second-class status, as second-place Americans. It was for this reason that the union movement largely concentrated its educational efforts around restoring manhood rights to the porters and maids as a first step in the struggle for economic freedom. Manhood rights and economic freedom, in the minds of BSCP organizers, were inextricably intertwined. Asserting one's "manhood rights" was, therefore, part of the process of regaining one's self-esteem and claiming a place as an equal American citizen.[46]

By employing the rhetoric of manhood and manhood rights, the Brotherhood drew from the legacy of earlier struggles in African American history. Independence from white control, a marker in the black freedom struggle, a stage on the way to gaining full "manhood rights," was resurrected by the BSCP and connected to the legacy of Douglass and the writings of DuBois.[47] Despite the failure of Reconstruction to secure the rights of black Americans as citizens and free laborers, the quest for manhood rights was kept alive through story, song, and history.[48] Frederick Douglass pointed the way with his relentless agitation around the unfinished agenda of Reconstruction. On the twenty-fourth anniversary of Emancipation, Douglass reminded his fellow citizens that the work of the Republican party in enfranchising and emancipating black Americans was "sadly incomplete. We are yet, as a people, only half free. The promise of liberty remains unfulfilled."[49] DuBois raised the issue of manhood and manhood rights in his critique of Booker T. Washington in *The*

Souls of Black Folk.[50] Manhood rights appeared on the agenda of the Second Meeting of the Niagara Movement, formed to secure manhood suffrage and freedom of speech and absorbed by the National Association for the Advancement of Colored People in 1909, where DuBois declared that black Americans would not be satisfied with "one jot or title less than our manhood rights."[51]

Within the larger community, BSCP flyers, handbills, and literature revived the usage, articulated by Frederick Douglass and W.E.B. DuBois, equating manhood with full humanity, first-class citizenship. A popular handbill that was taken from the "Bulletin," published by the Brotherhood, harked back to nineteenth century manhood rhetoric with a sketch of Frederick Douglass and a caption that said: "Douglass fought for the abolition of chattel slavery, and today we fight for economic freedom. The time has passed when a grown-up black man should beg a grown-up white man for anything," a reference to the tipping system that porters and maids had to rely upon to made a "living" wage.[52] Despite the passage of the 13th Amendment, which *The Messenger* called a "dead letter," slavery was not entirely abolished. The Brotherhood proclaimed its task was to abolish the sequel of chattel slavery, "chattel peonage," which held Pullman porters and maids bound to the Company without respect for their rights as free laborers, especially the right to write their own contract and organize to protect their position at work.[53] The Brotherhood's fight for economic freedom was a continuation of what they called the "unfinished task of emancipation."[54]

Within the union movement, to be a "man" meant to become self-reliant, stand tall, and move out from under the control of paternalism. In a widely-circulated poster under the banner, "Reasons why Pullman porters and maids should join the Brotherhood of Sleeping Car Porters now," organizer Ashley Totten wrote: "We appeal to that spark of manhood; that willingness to take the position of a man and not a coward."[55] Independence from white control was the core belief that shaped the Brotherhood's use of self-reliance and manhood rights. To illustrate its view, the Brotherhood evoked slavery to depict the difference between its movement and that of the Pullman Company Union. In BSCP's publication, *The Messenger,* the Brotherhood explained that porters and maids needed their own union to fight off the handicap of "too many Uncle Toms in the service" of the company. These "me-too-boss, hat-in-hand porters" spied, according to BSCP, on "independent manly men." The time was ripe for "porters to stand up like men," and stop having a "wishbone where a backbone ought to be."[56] The struggle for manhood was finally to claim what one organizer called "the humanhood of the Negro race," starting with a company that demanded of its porters the "submersion of their manhood by making public beggars of them."[57]

The BSCP was ultimately successful in organizing the sleeping car porters, despite the resolve of Pullman Company executives never to sit down around the same table with "a bunch of black porters" to write an employment contract.[58] In the process, African Americans voted, under federal supervision, for their economic rights and negotiated the first contract signed between a major American corporation and a black workers' union. The struggle, which took twelve long years, succeeded not just because New Deal labor laws favored unionization, or because Randolph was a charismatic personality as some have suggested, but because of the Brotherhood's actions. Despite the enormous support the BSCP had won from the middle class in Chicago by the mid-1930s, Pullman did not grant the BSCP full recognition until after the Brotherhood's local efforts intersected with protest networks of black Americans at the national level.[59]

Randolph and other organizers of the BSCP clearly had an attitude problem, from the perspective of Pullman employers. Not only were they not grateful for all the company had done for them, they actually "bit the hand that fed them." History reminds us that the definition of a "good employee" is race and class based, not static, and subject to ongoing struggle in the workplace. It is often useful to juxtapose the good employee issue to an inseparable question: what is a good employer? For Pullman Company, the good porter, like the stereotypic immigrant analyzed by Waldinger, was certainly pliable, safe, and servile. Yet when the BSCP began to organize Pullman porters, organizers saw this same porter as degraded, abused, and exploited.

How important are employer attitudes for shaping access to low-paying jobs in modern urban America? The conventional wisdom focuses less upon those attitudes than upon skills mismatches and the exit of manufacturing jobs. Advances in technology, according to John Kasarda, undercut the "traditional goods-producing industries that once constituted the economic backbone of cities, and provided entry-level employment for lesser-skilled African-Americans." Instead, job opportunities in cities are dominated today by "knowledge-intensive white-collar service industries that typically require education beyond high school and therefore precluded most poorly employed inner city minorities from obtaining employment."[60] Thus failures of the education system, not employer attitudes, become the focus of policy concerns about improving the prospects of low-wage and underemployed urban workers.

Yet for many large cities, the emerging reality is that of a polarized economy simultaneously generating high-income professional and managerial jobs, along with low-income, labor-intensive service jobs.[61] Skills mismatch theories tell us nothing about why poorly educated immigrants are flocking to the largest post-industrial cities. Immigrants taking jobs in low-skill sectors have been the biggest gainers of jobs in New York City in recent decades. The vast, continuing exit of low-skill white workers from the New York City economy has been so enormous that minority opportunities have even expanded in both relative and absolute terms in such declining sectors as manufacturing.[62]

As low-wage employment proliferates, particularly in the urban service industries, employer attitudes indeed determine who gets these jobs. Given the employer attitudes described at the beginning of this essay, it is not surprising that rising minority immigrant participation and declining African American participation are the norm in New York, Chicago, Los Angeles, and other post-industrial cities. African Americans aspire to positions enjoyed by whites notes Waldinger. They do so because they have a keen sense of their civic and economic rights.

What is to be done? More schooling? American-born blacks are already much better educated than immigrant Hispanics. Should young urban blacks not attending college become the smiling, servile George of the post-World War I era? Judging from their responses, low-wage urban employers would be thrilled to have indigenous minority youth emanating George, the singing porter. Yet the porters offer another, more powerful lesson to those stuck in the low-wage sectors where servitude and vulnerability are traits that employers seek to foster. The porters organized and fought back against their employer. In the favorable conditions of the New Deal with significant backing from the black community at the local and national level, the porters won the right to shape the terms of their employment, which they declared a fundamental right of American citizenship.

Low-wage workers today need job upgrading; they need better employers. But the experience of Pullman porters suggests that the future shape of labor relations will be determined as much by organization of black workers as by the wish-list of employers. Good employers are the product of the negotiation process between workers and management.

When that process is weighted heavily in favor of management because workers do not recognize the fighting weight of collective organization, then employers will usually take the path of least resistance and hire those who are the weakest and most pliable. Before the BSCP came along, the Pullman Company was benevolent if the porters played by the rules set up by company officials and negotiated with Pullman Company management on an individual basis as part of the Pullman Company "family." The problem, according to the BSCP, was that the parties were not equal under those rules. Unequal fighting weights between employer and employee may worsen in the next century. The tactics used by the BSCP's labor organizing process—expressing demands through mass-based, collective action with the support of the larger community—may represent for many low-wage workers a new language. The language of protest through organized action may be one of the few means available to employees for expressing workplace grievances in the twenty-first century. DuBois articulated the problem of stereotyping a certain group of workers as servants; the BSCP challenged servile social relations and won a measure of economic citizenship. Improved job conditions and better employers, history tells us, are won through struggle, not servility.

NOTES

1. Joleen Kirshenman and Katherine Neckerman, "'We'd Love to Hire Them, But. . . .': the Meaning of Race to Employers," in Christopher Jencks and Paul Peterson, eds., *The Urban Underclass* (Washington, D. C.: Brookings, 1991).

2. Roger Waldinger, *Still the Promised City? African-Americans and New Immigrants in Postindustrial New York* (Cambridge: Harvard University Press, 1996), 288.

3. Waldinger, *Still the Promised City?*, 15.

4. Saskia Sassen-Koob, "Exporting Capital and Importing Labor: The Role of Caribbean Migration to New York City," Occasional Paper, Center for Latin American and Caribbean Studies, New York University, 1981.

5. Waldinger, *Still the Promised City?*, 166.

6. Waldinger, *Still the Promised City?*, 7.

7. For Pullman Company officials perceptions of black workers, see findings of the 1915 Commission on Industrial Relations, which was submitted to the U.S. Congress, see Brailsford Reese Brazeal, *The Brotherhood of Sleeping Car Porters: Its Origins and Development* (New York: Harper & Brothers, 1946), 6, note 1.

8. Stanley Buder, *Pullman: An Experiment in Industrial Order and Community Planning, 1880–1930* (New York: Oxford University Press, 1967), 10.

9. For a history of the early years of George Pullman and the Pioneer, see Buder, *Pullman*, 3–16; Almont Lindsey, *The Pullman Strike: The Story of a Unique Experiment and of a Great Labor Upheaval* (Chicago: University of Chicago Press, 1942), 19–37; and Jervis Anderson, *A. Philip Randolph: A Biological Portrait* (New York: Harcourt Brace Jovanovich, 1973; reprinted, Berkeley, California, 1986), 155–158.

10. William H. Harris, *Keeping the Faith: A. Philip Randolph, Milton P. Webster, and the Brotherhood of Sleeping Car Porters, 1925–1937* (Urbana: University of Illinois Press, 1977), 3.

11. Joseph Husband, *Story of Pullman Car* (Chicago: A. C. Mc Clurg, 1917), 155. This reference was found in Anderson, *A Philip Randolph*, 159, 366–367.

12. For Pullman Company officials testifying before the Commission, see information from Commission on Industrial Relations, *Final Report and Testimony* (Washington, D.C.: Government Printing Office, 1915), Volume X, 9553, which is quoted in Brailsford Reese Brazeal, *The Brotherhood of Sleeping Car Porters: Its Origins and Development* (New York: Harper and Brothers, 1946), 6, see also, pp. 1–2.

13. H. N. Hall, The Art of the Pullman Porter," *The American Mercury* 23:91 (July 1931): 333.

14. Jack Santino interviewed twenty plus retired Pullman Porters between 1978 and 1984. He said the term "George" was associated with the days of slavery. See, Santino, *Miles of Smiles, Years of Struggle: Stories of Black Pullman Porters* (Urbana: University of Illinois Press, 1989), 125.

15. Murray Kempton, *Part of Our Time: Some Ruins and Monuments of the Thirties* (New York: Simon Schuster, 1955), 259, 240–242.

16. Quotes from, Bernard Mergen, "The Pullman Porter: From 'George' to Brotherhood," *The South Atlantic Quarterly* 73:2 (Spring 1974): 224 and Anderson, *A. Philip Randolph*, 162. For Malcolm X quote, see David D./ Perata, *Those Pullman Blues: An Oral History of the African American Railroad Attendant* (New York: Twayne Publishers, 1996), xxviii.

17. Anderson, *A. Philip Randolph*, 162.

18. For an interesting and instructive study of "George," see Bernard Mergen, "The Pullman Porter: From 'George' to Brotherhood," *The South Atlantic Quarterly* 73:2 (Spring 1974): quote from, 224.

19. The nature of the relationship between porters and passengers is commented on by, Jack Jack Santino, *Miles of Smiles*, 107.

20. Beth Tompkins Bates, "The Unfinished Task of Emancipation: Protest Policies Come of Age in Black Chicago." Ph.D. dissertation, Columbia University, 1997, pp. 74–75.

21. Helen Buckler, *Doctor Dan* (Boston: Little, Brown & Company, 1954), 66–84; Junius B. Wood, *The Negro in Chicago* (Chicago: *Chicago Daily News* 1916), 17–18; Allan Spear, *Black Chicago: The Making of a Negro Ghetto, 1890–1920* (Chicago: University of Chicago Press, 1967), 97–98; St. Clair Drake, "Churches and Voluntary Associations in the Chicago Negro Community," Report 465-54-3-386 (Chicago: WPA Publication, 1940), 102.

22. Buckler, *Doctor Dan*, 70–71.

23. Buckler, *Doctor Dan*, 83–84.

24. "Pullman Porters in Session at Y.M.C.A.," *Chicago Defender*, November 21, 1925, p. 9.

25. James R. Grossman, *Land of Hope: Chicago: Chicago, Black Southerners, and the Great Migration* (Chicago: University of Chicago Press, 1991), 200; George R. Arthur, *Life on the Negro Frontier* (New York: Association Press, 1934), 186; George Arthur, "The Young Men's Christian Association Movement Among Negroes," *Opportunity* 1:3 (March 1923), 17; *Chicago Defender*, October 14, 1922; Arvarh E. Strickland, *History of the Chicago Urban League* (Urbana: University of Illinois Press, 1966), 34–36; Sterling Spero and Abram L. Harris, *Black Worker: The Negro and the Labor Movement* (New York: Columbia University Press, 1931), 142.

26. Quote from Tuttle, *Race Riot: Chicago in the Red Summer of 1919* (New York: Atheneum, 1970), 151; see also, James R. Barrett, *Work and Community in the Jungle: Chicago's Packinghouse Workers, 1894–1922* (Urbana: University of Illinois Press, 1987), 213.

27. Grossman, *Land of Hope*, 200; Arthur, "The YWCA Movement Among Negroes," 17; *Chicago Defender*, October 14, 1922; Strickland, *History of the Chicago Urban League*, 34–36; Spero and Harris, *Black Worker*, 142.

28. Joseph A. Logsdon, "The Rev. Archibald J. Carey and the Negro in Chicago Politics," M.A. Thesis, University of Chicago, 1961, 7–11, 17–18, 43, 79–80; Grossman, *Land of Hope*, 230.

29. Logsdon, "The Rev. Archibald J. Carey," 15–16; *Chicago Defender*, April 5, 1913, p.5, and January 17, 1914, p.2; Interview with Rev. S. A. Bryant, Feb. 2, 1934, Folder 5, Box 89, Burgess Papers, Manuscripts Division, Joseph Regenstein Library, University of Chicago; Charles R. Branham, "The Transformation of Black Political Leadership in Chicago, 1864–1942," Ph.D. (University of Chicago, 1981), 36, 66–67.

30. Logsdon, "The Rev. Archibald Carey," 16–18; St. Clair Drake, "Churches and Voluntary Associations in the Chicago Negro Community," Report of Project 465-54-3-386 (Chicago: WPA publication, 1940), 6–12; Branham, "The Transformation of Black Political Leadership in Chicago," 37; Spero and Harris, *The Black Worker*, 308–309; *Heebie Jeebies* 2:41 (Sept. 4, 1926):18.

31. Charles R. Branham, "The Transformation of Black Political Leadership in Chicago," 36, 66–67; Interview with Anabelle Carey, August 26, 1960, by Logsdon in "The Rev. Archibald J. Carey," 18.

32. Eric Arnesen, "Following the Color Line of Labor: Black Workers and the Labor Movement before 1930," *Radical History*, 55 (Winter 1993): 53–87; William M. Tuttle, "Labor Conflict and Racial Violence: the Black Worker in Chicago, 1894–1919," *Labor History*, 10 (Summer 1969): 408–432; Arna Bontemps and Jack Conroy, *Anyplace But Here* (New York: Hill and Wang, 1966), 140; William H. Harris, *The Harder We Run: Black Workers Since the Civil War* (New York: Oxford University Press, 1982), 41–42.

33. Personal interview with Ida Mae Smith by Logsdon, July 10, 1960, in Logsdon, "The Rev. Archibald Carey," 79–80.

34. Chicago *Whip*, March 29, 1924. Quoted in Spero and Harris, *The Black Worker*, 135.

35. Logsdon, "The Rev. Archibald Carey," 15–18; St. Clair Drake, "Churches and Voluntary Associations in Chicago," 6–12; Branham, "The Transformation of Black Political Leadership in Chicago," 36–37; Chicago *Defender*, January 17, 1914, p. 2, April 5, 1913, p. 5.

36. *Heebie Jeebies* 2:41 (Sept. 4, 1926): 18.

37. Report of President Carry of the Pullman Company, 1922, Pullman Company Papers, Newberry Library.

38. Information on these educational programs was contained in two press releases by Associated Negro Press, 1926, see all four pages, Folder 5, Box 278, Barnett Papers, Chicago Historical Society (CHS); see also, Report of president Carry of the Pullman Company, 1922.

39. Milton Webster to A. Philip Randolph, August 10, 1928, BSCP Papers, Chicago Division, CHS.

40. *Chicago Defender*, June 5, 1926, part 2, p. 1; *The Messenger* 8:1 (January 1926): 28.

41. Report of President Carry of the Pullman Company, 1922; *Heebie Jeebies,* 2:41 (September 4, 1926):18; Spero and Harris, *Black Worker,* 440; *The Pullman News* (November 1925): 221.

42. Spero and Harris, *The Black Worker,* 441; Brazeal, *The Brotherhood of Sleeping Car Porters,* 12–13; Harris, *Keeping the Faith,* 17–18; Fred Powell to O.P. Powell, February 4, 1926, O.P. Powell to Fred Powell, February 5, 1926, Perry Parker to J. S. Seese, District Superintendent, February 15, 1926, F.L. Simmons to Fred Powell, June 29, 1926, BSCP Papers, Chicago Division, CHS; "The Pullman Porters Benefit Association of America," Box 4, 06/01/01, Pullman Company Papers, Newberry Library.

43. *Chicago Defender* November 26, 1927, p.3.

44. W.E.B. DuBois, *Darkwater: Voices from Within the Veil* (1920; reprint, New York: Schocken Books, 1969), 113–120 (page numbers refer to reprint edition).

45. A. Philip Randolph, "The Brotherhood's Anniversary," *The Messenger,* 8:9 (September 1926): 263.

46. See Beth Tompkins Bates, "The Unfinished Task of Emancipation: Protest Politics Come of Age in Black Chicago, 1925–1943," Ph.D., diss., Columbia University 1997, 176–188.

47. Behind specific yearnings for freedom, as Eric Foner points out, lay the larger desire for independence from white control. See Eric Foner, *Reconstruction: America's Unfinished Revolution, 1863–1877* (New York: Harper & Row, 1988), 60–123 and Foner, "The Meaning of Freedom in the Age of Emancipation," *Journal of American History* (September 1994): 457–458.

48. Thanks to the oral histories gathered by the Works Progress Administration of former slaves during the 1930s, we know how vivid the recollections were of a time when black Americans held office in the South. See, George P. Rawick, ed., *The American Slave: A Composite Autobiography* (Westport, CN.: Greenwood Press, 1972–1979), 9, pt. 3:30, 81, pt. 4:42, pt. 5:220, 14:145, 361, Supplement 1, 5:1650, 6:134, 7:567, Supplement 2, 1650,4015; Paul D. Escott, *Slavery Remembered* (Chapel Hill: University of North Carolina Press, 1979), 153; Eric Foner, *Reconstruction,* 610–611; Mark D. Naison, "Black Agrarian Radicalism in the Great Depression: The Threads of a Lost Tradition," *Journal of Ethnic Studies,* 1 (Fall 1973): 52–55.

49. Philip S. Foner, ed., *The Life and Writings of Frederick Douglass: Reconstruction and After,* vol. 4 (New York: International Publishers, 1955), 430.

50. W.E.B. Du Bois, *The Souls of Black Folk* (1903; reprint, New York: Signet Classic, 1969), 95 [Declaration of Independence reference], 88 (page references are to reprint edition).

51. David Levering Lewis, *W.E.B. DuBoise Biography of a Race, 1868–1919* (New York: Henry Holt and Co., 1993), 230, 329–330. See also, DuBois, *the Autobiography of W. E. B. DuBois: A Soliloquy of Viewing My Life from he Last Decade of Its First Century* (New York: International Publishers, 1968), 250–251.

52. "Posters, handbills, propaganda of the BSCP," Pullman Company Papers, Newberry Library, from Reel 9 of BSCP Papers, University Microfilm Project.

53. *The Messenger,* 9:6 (June 1927): 207.

54. A. Philip Randolph, "The Indictment," *The Messenger* 8 (April 1926): 114.

55. BSCP poster, Propaganda folder, Box 633–A, Pullman Company Papers, Newberry Library.

56. *The Messenger* 7:7 (July 1925): 290.

57. Frank W. Crosswaith, "Toward the Home Stretch," *The Messenger* 8:7 (July 1926): 196.

58. Anderson, *A. Philip Randolph*, 220–221.
59. For fuller discussion, see Bates, "The Unfinished Task of Emancipation."
60. John Kasarda, "Cities as Places where People Live and Work: Urban Change and Neighborhood Distress," in Henry Cisneros, ed., *Interwoven Destinies: Cities and the Nation* (New York: Norton, 1993), 82.
61. Bennett Harrison and Barry Bluestone, *The Great U-Turn: Corporate Restructuring and the Polarizing of America* (New York: Basic Books, 1988), 70.
62. Waldinger, *Still the Promised City?*

17

THE ECONOMICS OF RACISM

Marcus Alexis

Racism, the collection of negative perceptions and behaviors directed at members of groups with different identifiable physical characteristics, was once thought to be outside the domain of economics as a discipline. In his treatise on the subject of discrimination (a mild form of racism), Becker[1] emphasizes the economic *consequences* of discrimination. In his introduction, Becker observes:

> In view of the importance of discrimination, it may seem surprising that economists have neglected its study. One can only speculate about the reasons for this neglect. Other social scientists, notably sociologists and anthropologists, by their early entrance into this field may have established it as their property; the economist, here as elsewhere, has respected the property right of others.[2]

Also,

> I have attempted . . . developing a theory of discrimination in the marketplace that supplements the psychologists' and sociologists'; analysis of causes with an analysis of causes with an analysis of economic consequences.[3]

The concentration on market discrimination and avoidance of the role that discrimination (racism) plays in the larger social context is an unnecessary limitation on the role that economic analysis can play in understanding racism (discrimination). If racism is not an end in itself but a way of achieving a larger end, emphasis on the consequences needlessly limits the economist's role as a commentor on social phenomenon and a designer of public policies to correct undesirable consequences. I will argue that economics has much to say about the market and nonmarket dimensions of racism.

It is useful at this point to make a distinction between discrimination (in the Becker sense) and racism. Discrimination is defined in the economic literature in terms of willingness to incur some cost. Specifically,

> If an individual has a "taste for discrimination" he must act as if he were willing to pay something, either directly or in the form of reduced income to be associated with some persons instead of others. When actual discrimination occurs he must in fact, either pay or forfeit income for this privilege [sic]. This simple way of looking at the matter gets at the essence of prejudice and discrimination.[4]

This definition is counter to popular thought or conventional wisdom; it asserts that the discriminator "pays" for his discrimination. He does not benefit by increases in either income or profit. Thus there is no "exploitation" in the popular sense. As we shall see, this conclusion is reached on the basis of a very special and limiting set of assumptions.

Segregation, which is often thought to be the same as discrimination is defined thus:

> In general, if various members of different factors (such as laborers and foremen) are combined into one group by a criterion such as color or religion, one can say that market segregation of this group exists if its members are employed with each other to a significantly greater extent than would result from a random distribution of members of such a factor.[5]

The definition of segregation given above can be tested by statistical methods. Thus the definition is operational as it stands.

What has been discussed so far may be called the "traditional" theory of economic discrimination. This is a neoclassical (marginalist) theory in which there is

1. Perfect competition in input and output markets.
2. Full employment of all resources, i.e., no employment of labor or excess capacity of plant.
3. Prices are determined at the margin, including wage rates.
4. Wages of workers are determined by their marginal product.
5. All factors (labor and capital) are completely mobile.
5. Whites are the only owners of capital, blacks supply labor only.

6. Employers are maximizers of something, not necessarily profits; in this case something called "utility" (satisfaction) is the quantity being maximized.
7. Black workers are viewed as undesirable and add to the "cost" of production.
8. Market clearing wages of black workers are lower than corresponding wages for identical (equally productive) white workers.

This is, obviously, a very special world. It is abstracted from the "real world" about which it seeks to make inferences. All theory abstracts in one way or another. The empirical utility of such theory is, however, dependent on the extent to which the theory captures essential elements of the environment of interest. The "traditional" theory has been faulted for its departure from the sense of the real world counterpart and because some inferences which follow from it are not supported by the facts. Few economists believe that the output markets of most industrialized societies are perfectly competitive; market power is widespread. Even nonindustrialized, raw material producing nations now play the market power game; OPEC is the most obvious example. Unemployment of labor is also a fact of life in all industrialized nations.

We also know that, for many reasons factors of production are often not mobile. Workers have attachments to places and do not leave simply because there are better economic opportunities elsewhere. Family considerations, health, immigration barriers, and aversion to change are among the reasons for this immobility. Capital does not move because of concerns about political stability of governments: Folklore and custom may not make efficient operations possible; preferential treatment of nationals, and inhospitable living conditions for managers all act as deterrents.

The quantity called "utility" which is being maximized may be dependent on some variables not included in the theory. In the "traditional" theory, employers are assumed to be concerned only with the number of black workers, the number of white workers and profits. There may also be psychic costs or benefits associated with discrimination. Peer group pressures might cause an employer who is genuinely indifferent about hiring blacks to refrain from doing so. Fear or reprisals from white employees (contrary to the traditional theory) might also cause a color-blind employer to act as a discriminator.[6]

How does racism differ from discrimination? In the traditional theory of Discrimination it is assumed that aversion to certain (black) workers is a private, noncollective decision. Each employer has a utility (satisfaction) determining relation (utility function) which assigns weights to the several variables to be manipulated. These variables in the traditional theory are profits, number of workers (black) to whom the employer is averse and the number of (white) workers to whom the employer is either indifferent of or for whom he has a preference. As in most neoclassical analysis, employers (entrepreneurs, capitalists) prefer more profits to less. Give a choice between two outcomes, employers will chose the one with higher profits, *ceteris paribus*. Employers prefer to have fewer workers from the group to which they are averse. Other things being equal, they will employ fewer of them. If an employer is indifferent to the number of workers from a group (white) he will not pay any attention to the number of them employed, other things being equal. If he has a preference for workers of some group, other things being equal, he will obtain a higher level of utility by having more rather than fewer of them and may pay them a higher wage.

Unfortunately, the world does not present options in this idealized fashion. Employers are often faced with choices that involve more of something and less of something else. Production is related to the number of workers (productive capital being fixed), and profits are related to the difference between the additional cost of production (marginal cost) and the additional revenue from sales (marginal revenue). At some point marginal cost begins to exceed marginal revenue. This acts as a brake on the optimal level of output, the level at which profits are maximized. Thus even for preferred workers, employers must eventually make a choice between additional profits and additional workers. The trade-off between profits and the number of additional preferred workers that an employer is willing to make is a measure of his preference for these workers. Similarly, the reduction in profits (in Becker's model) that an employer is willing to accept to avoid workers to whom he is averse is a measure of his discrimination against them. Each employer acts independently in terms of his own preferences. The losses (reduction in profits) are the private costs they bear.[7]

The traditional approach assumes no malevolence on the part of employers. They merely do not wish to associate with certain workers and can be induced to do so only by a transfer from these workers to them in the form of lower wage rates. The tradeoff between profits and these workers must be large relative to the employer's aversion if they are to be hired. Said another way, the losses incurred by not hiring them are greater than the "price" employers are willing to pay to avoid them. In this formulation there is no comparison between the welfare of the discriminated against workers and the employers. The welfare of each is dependent on the other.

Racism is different. Employers explicitly consider the effect of their action on the welfare of the workers to whom they are averse. This consideration is in firms of black workers as a group versus white workers as a group. There is a sense in which they are mutually opposing groups and the gains that go to one are losses to the other. This is analogous to the zero-sum property of two-persons games.[8]

In the racism analysis, discrimination is against blacks as a group, not as individuals. The discriminator (employer, employee, government, or consumer) explicitly concerns himself with the effects of his actions on blacks as a group. Furthermore, his welfare (satisfaction) is dependent on the welfare of blacks. I have given this approach the name "malice-envy."[9] Specifically, a increase in the relative well-being of blacks is interpreted by a white discriminator as a decrease in his own welfare. In this approach he is no longer interested in maximizing his own welfare *independent* of the welfare of the discriminated blacks. Blacks are viewed as opponents. To appreciate this difference one should make an analogy with the situation in which American policymakers act as if an increase in the supply of Russian nuclear warheads is equivalent to a reduction in their own arsenal. Recent Cold War strategic policies are an outgrowth of this approach.[10] An increase in the nuclear capability of a neutral power would not necessarily be viewed in the same way. An increase in the nuclear arsenal of, say, Switzerland would be an example.

To operationalize the concept of malice-envy it is necessary to have a measuring rod by which to assess the welfare of both parties and a relation which translates the welfare of one into the welfare of the other. Interestingly, under this approach, one party might be willing to reduce its own welfare if by so doing it could reduce the welfare of its competitor by more. The net result would be, through the comparison mechanism an increase in the welfare of the first party. In traditional economics, the utility (satisfaction) schedules (functions) of economic agents are assumed to be *independent.* My approach makes them explicitly interdependent.

The conditions which much be satisfied to have interdependence of the utility functions of opposing individuals or groups are:

1. Each individual must have a measuring rod (an ordered metric) against which to measure his welfare.
2. Members of a group must be able to manifest (demonstrate, reveal) their levels of satisfaction to members of the opposing group. Further, as the level of satisfaction increases the manifestation of it must be in accordance with their increased satisfaction.
3. Members of the opposing group must be able to accurately perceive the manifestation of the other group members, and that perception changes as manifestation changes.[11]

In the case where there is a group conflict the measuring rod could be some overall measure of performance of the opposing group, such as mean income or unemployment rate. This performance statistic is then translated by individuals in the other group into a level of satisfaction for the opposing group. This in turn is converted into a satisfaction level for the members of the former group. If each member of a group has the same correspondence between satisfaction levels of the other group and his own satisfaction level, the group's satisfaction level is easily determined; it is the same as that of any individual in the group. When there are differences in the impact on individual members of a group related to the satisfaction levels of members of another group, a method is needed to aggregate these effects. Fortunately, we do not have to worry about this because behavior in the market is most individualistic in nature. A particular agent may be concerned with the effect on his group, but his actions are typically made on a noncollective basis. Thus employers who are averse to black workers make employment decisions on their own. Similarly, employers who are concerned that black workers will "take over" an occupation at the "expense of whites" will give preference to white workers. Such behavior is consistent with an extensive theory of social relations.[12]

The interdependence of the utility (satisfaction) functions of members of the two groups is expressed through a "vicariousness" relation, V. Using U_1 to represent the utility of the first group and U_2 the utility of the second group and V_1 (I = 1, 2) as the vicariousness function we can connect the utility of the two groups.

$$(1) \quad U_1 = V_1 (U_2)$$

$$U_2 = V_2$$

The three conditions above having been satisfied, the utility of one group directly effects the utility of the other. To the extent that each member of a group respond (positively or negatively) to a given level of utility in another group the direction (though not necessarily the magnitude) of their response is predictable. Thus while we retain the assumption of noncollective action, there being no conspiracy or organized activity to induce a given behavior, members of a group will each behave in a predetermined way. Through group socialization members of a group come to share common perceptions and responses to events. This socialization reinforces group identity and solidarity and rationalizes behavior common to member of a group. This behavior is seen in subgroups also and is often referred to as a lifestyle.[10] Once socialization is effective and the need for organized behavior is absent, the mores of the group assures that the behaviors that promote group interest will dominate. In economic terms, the cost of enforcement are consequently reduced. Loss of status, ostracism or expulsion, act as powerful deterrents to normal violating behavior.

Returning to the independence of the utilities of the two groups—now Blacks and Whites—we graphically demonstrate the working of the model. In figures one through five below, we sketch the functional relationships between utilities, an event and its utility, utility and manifestation, manifestation and perception, and perception and utility in the envy-malice case. For the subscripts 1 and 2 above we now substitute the more general subscripts I and J because these relations hold for any two groups independent of the number of groups that might exist. Also, the model is more general in its application than to Blacks and Whites alone; it applies equally as well to English and French speaking Canadians, Protestants and Catholics in Northern Ireland (Ulster), French and Flemish speaking Belgians, and to any situation in which distinctions can be made between groups of individuals. In the cases cited, these distinctions are easy to detect and make division into opposing groups possible at low or zero cost. When these distinctions are not so easily determined more subtle devices are used to discover them including, but not limited to, credentials, testing "manners", and income or wealth (as in the case of dowries).

FIGURE 1
Correspondence of U_I and U_j.

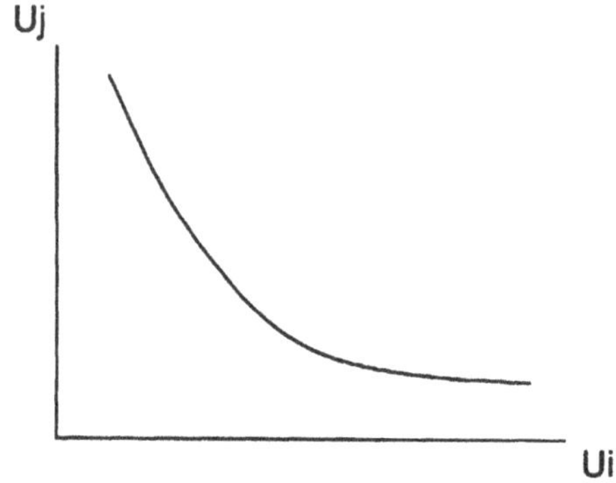

FIGURE 2
Relationship between an event (E) and the utility of the event U(E) to the jth person.

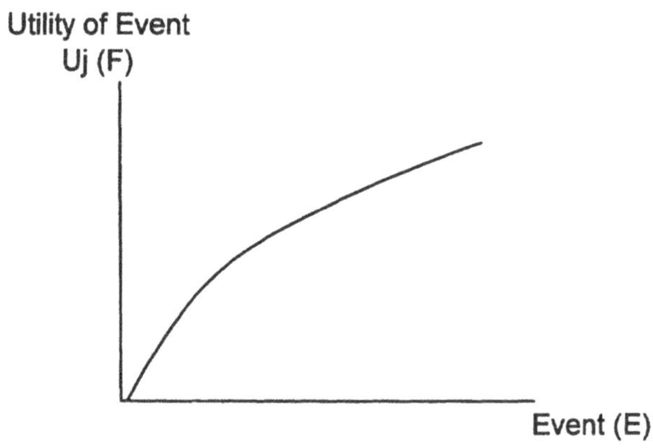

FIGURE 3
Relationship between utility (U_j) and manifestation $M_{ij}(U_j)$.

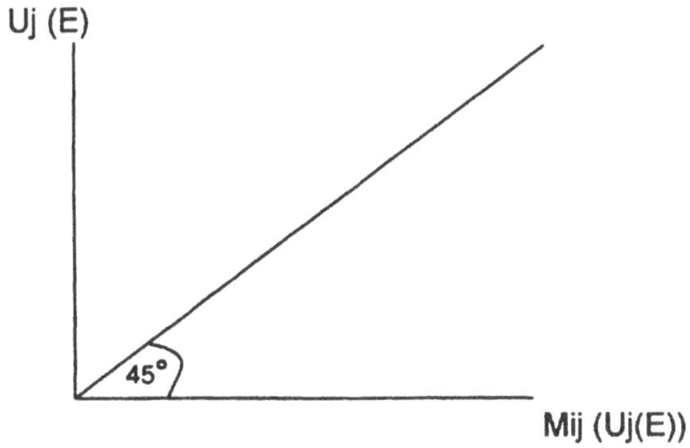

FIGURE 4
Relationship between manifestation (M_{ij}) and perception (P_{ij}).

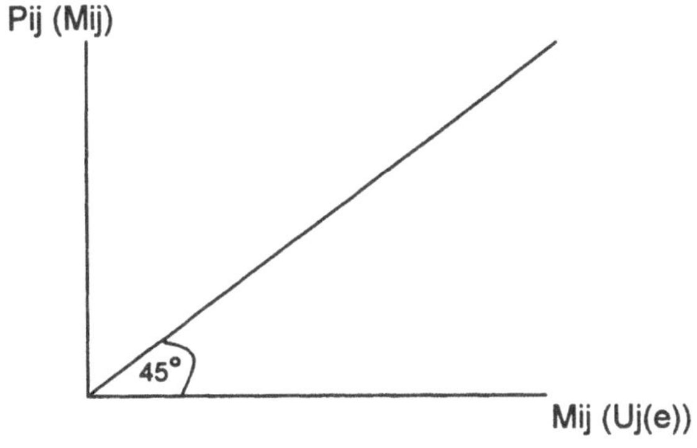

FIGURE 5
Relationship between P_{ij} (M_{ij}) and U_I envy-malice case.

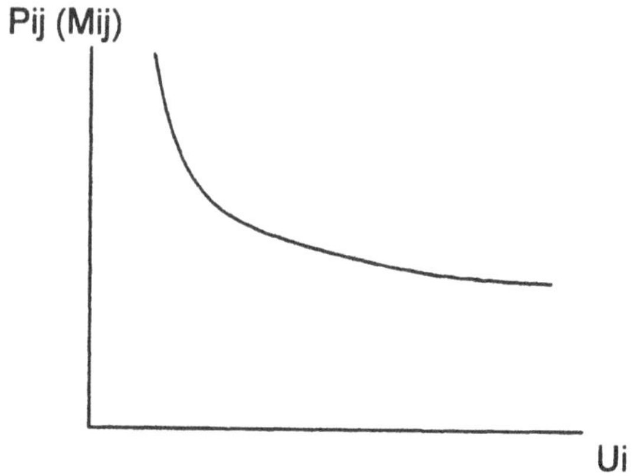

Having discussed the analytical foundations of discrimination and racism, we now turn our attention to the uses of economic methods to achieve the ends of the discriminator (racist). What will concern us is what insights economics can give us into the behavior of the discriminator or racist.

Efficiency occupies a central place in economic analysis. An outcome is efficient if it is accomplished at minimum cost. Alternately, an outcome is efficient if it is accomplished by using the minimum resources required to produce it. Another way to think of the efficiency is in terms of accomplishing the outcome by using a given quantity of resources and obtaining the maximum benefits (desired results) from the use of those resources. Thus the discriminator (racist) seeks to achieve a given amount of discrimination against members of some group at the minimum cost (in terms of profits or other valuable resources) to him. Or, for a given allocation of valuable resources to the discriminatory (racist) activities, he would seek to achieve as much discrimination (racism) as possible. Succinctly stated, the discriminator (racist) does not want to overpay for the results achieved.

We have already learned from Becker that discrimination costs. But it should not be exorbitant. Even discriminators (racists) are rational economic agents. They do not wish to pay any more than is required for a given result. What they must pay is determined by the state of the arts, so to speak. One can think in terms of technical relationship that associates with each level of discriminatory (racist) output minimum dollar cost or use of resources. The best that can be hoped for is to be at the efficient point of that relationship, that is points at which the use of resources or dollar cost are not associated with higher possible levels of desired discrimination (racism).

The technical relation is the production function. When physical output is the end result one can think of the production function as an engineering relation between output and the required inputs (factors of production) such as labor, physical capital, land, and natural resources. In recent years the concept has been extended to include non-physical output. For example, in education there is a production function the output or outcome of which may be achievement scores on standardized tests. The inputs are such things as teachers, physical plant, curriculum, family background, outlay per student, and attributes of the student. In terms of discriminatory behavior, the output is a measure of discrimination (racism), and the inputs may be forgone profits and lost outputs. In functional form such production functions are specified as follows.

Where

K = A constant

O = Output

I_1 = First input

I_2 = Second input

•

•

•

I_n = Nth input.[11]

These inputs are substitutes in production, meaning that as more of one is used less of the others need be used. Consequently, one obtains a family of output curves which are negatively sloped and which curve in such a way that as one uses one unit less of a given input more of the other must be used. Furthermore, as the quantity of the first input continues to decrease progressively more of other inputs must be used. This is illustrated in to dimensions in Figure 6.

All inputs have prices which do not vary with the quantity used by any particular user. Multiplying the quantities of all inputs by their prices one gets the cost. Thus

FIGURE 6
Output as a function of input levels corresponding to every production function is a cost function.

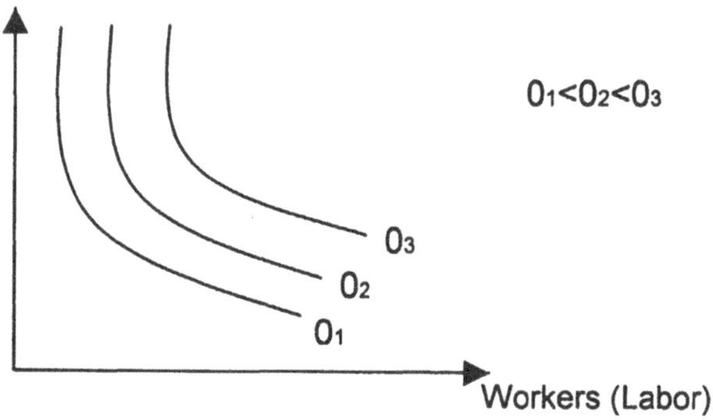

(3) $C = P_1I_1 + P_2I_2 + \ldots + P_NI_N = (I_1, I_2 \ldots I_N)$

where

C = Total cost
P_1 = Price of the first input
P_2 = Price of the second input
•
•
•
P_N = Price of the Nth input
I_1 = Quantity of the first input
I_2 = Quantity of the second input
•
•
•
I_N = Quantity of the Nth input.

Obviously, the less of any input that is used the lower will be the cost. The change from our production example above, which is the standard textbook representation, let us introduce inputs more appropriate to discrimination (racism).

FIGURE 7
Racism and a function of identification and enforcement inputs

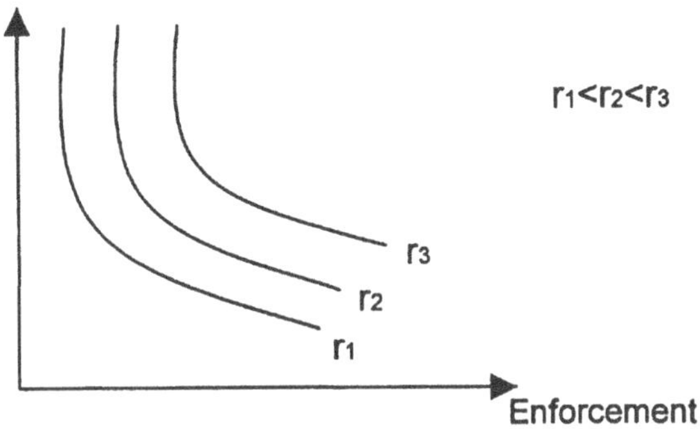

Imagine that one is a totally racist society, South Africa will do. In such a society, the discriminator (racist) wants to make sure all non-whites are known and that they observe all the restrictions imposed by the state. In that case there is a cost of identification and enforcement, among others; resources must be allocated to each activity. Now, we identify outputs as levels of racial separation R.

There are also costs associated with producing the given levels of R. They include inspectors, court systems, punishment centers, and identification systems—infamous South African passbooks.

The optimizing (rational economic agent) faces two choices. First, given the costs of inputs, a choice must be made between the levels of identification and enforcement. Second, the level of racism (R) must be chosen. The first is chosen on the basis of the relative prices. That is, for each curve there exists a unique (single point) which is the maximum quantity of R that can be obtained with a given expenditure,

(4) $C_R = p_I \neq p_E E = C_R (I, E)$

Where

C_R = Cost of production

P_I = Weighted sum of prices of resources used in identification activities

I = Level of identification activities

P_E = Weighted sum of prices of resources used in enforcement activities

E = Level of enforcement activities

The solution to the second problem depends on the total expenditures to be made on racism. This is the budget constraints—B.

(5) $B = P_I I^* + P_E E^* = B(I^*, E^*)$

Where the * indicates the optimal levels consistent with the prices and total budget. Thus for a budget B, I*, and E* are the optimal levels of identification and enforcement respectively.

Over time the levels of racially antagonistic activity that can be achieved with a given level of resource use or budgetary expenditure changes. Technological innovation makes possible the use of fewer resources and hence lowers the real cost of such activity. If the prices of inputs used in such activities do not increase the dollar cost also falls. Thus technological innovation makes the cost (to the practitioner) of racism less. Advances in identification, classification, information storage and retrieval, communications, pharmacology (mood altering substances), psychology (conditioning), and transportation (moving large numbers of people at low cost from places of work to places of residence), to name a few, all have the potential for making the practice of racism efficient.

Political and legal developments may have the opposite impact on the costs. Overt racism is less sustainable in most Western societies. Distinctions which have racial impact are more likely to be indirect. Larger fractions of some groups are disadvantaged under these circumstances because of some designated deficiency—educational attainment, behavioral defect, or inadequate socialization than others, but race per se is usually not the disqualifying factor. If the changed political and legal environment makes overt racism more difficult it may increase the costs of such activity and hence reduce the amounts (levels) observed. A determined racist is not without opportunities to indulge his tastes (preferences) albeit it must be done at a higher cost. Those racist not willing to pay the increased cost will no longer be able to satisfy their desire to practice racial discrimination. The aggregate level of racism then falls.

Technological innovation and political-legal changes go on simultaneously. What determines the resultant changes in costs of each. If technology reduces cost more than political-legal changes increase them, then even in a society with changing racial mores, more "racialism" will result. It may be less overt, less visible, less detectable, but equally corrosive. It is one of the paradoxes of a democratic society that a majority may abhor racist behavior but that it may persist nonetheless, a complete analysis of this is beyond the scope of this paper, but an example will be given of a not unlikely situation in which the majority is for a "color-blind" society but in which racism persists.

Consider a society in which political power is diffuse but economic power is not and in which those with economic power cannot easily translate their economic power into political power. Many examples immediately come to mind. Economic power in the United States is more concentrated than is political power. Wealthy persons seeking direct political power have to appeal to a large electorate for support. Examples of such individuals are the Rockefellers (Nelson in New York, Winthropp in Arkansas, and Jay in West Virginia), Heinz in Pennsylvania, Danfort in Missouri, and DuPont in Delaware. Other examples are the Roosevelts and Harriman in New York, and Saltonstall and Lodge in Massachusetts. One might argue that they sought public office because they are particularly enlightened members of their class or that they used their positions to limit the encroachment of the masses on the privileges and rights of property. Whatever the reason, they could not have been elected without convincing the electorate that their interests converged, or at least were not in direct conflict.

The powers that such wealth exerts in the marketplace is quite another thing. It is less exposed to public view. Those with market power intent on preserving racial distinctions have the opportunity to do so as employers, and as customers. By clever designs they could and did determine the racial, religious and ethnic composition of their workforces and boardrooms. In some cases this was accomplished by the uses of codes on application blanks. It is alleged by some industrial relations (personnel) people that some firms inferred Jewish ancestry if an applicant gave his parents' occupation as New York City garment worker, or retailer. Another way of accomplishing the same thing by hiring from certain schools known to have students with the desired backgrounds. Not until after World War II did Princeton, Johns Hopkins, Vanderbilt, and Washington University (St. Louis) admit black students. Other well known distinguished universities had quotas on many groups. Other ways of excluding nonwhites from the workforce include background checks, personal interviews, and matching addresses to areas known to be inhabited by some groups. A Harlem address unambiguously identifies one as black.

More subtle devices include the design of tests which maximize the differences between the scores of preferred and nonpreferred groups, and the use of weighted application forms with the same property. Whether by design or not, many screening instruments used in employment have the effect of disqualifying proportionately more blacks than whites who otherwise have very similar profiles—education, grades, recommendations, and interests. The legal status of such outcomes is still the subject of intense litigation.

The literature on discrimination emphasizes the wage differential aspects of labor market discrimination. Most observers, including economists, realize that wage discrimination is only part of the story. Discrimination can exist even when people with the same job classification or doing the same job receive unequal wages. This can come about because discriminated against workers are "overqualified." Indeed, it is part of the folklore of discriminated against groups that they have to "be better" in order to obtain certain positions. Jewish professors have to be brighter; blacks holding civil service positions (teachers, postal workers) have to be better educated. Thus equality of wages is either a necessary or sufficient condition for the absence of discrimination. What has to be demonstrated is that workers are, except for some identifying characteristics such as race, identical as productive agents.

One often hears that blacks are not discriminated against in professional sports (baseball, football, and basketball). It is instructive to point out that prior to World War II, blacks were absent from both professional baseball and basketball. Indeed, even though some now contend that basketball is overwhelmingly black, it was not until 1956 that the first black professional basketball player (George "Sweetwater" Clifton) was hired by the New York Knickerbockers, and that Jackie Robinson did not break the "color bar" in baseball until 1947. Interestingly, it was once contended that black athletes in these sports could not compete successfully because of inadequate training or preparation. It is amazing how quickly black athletes acquired the preparation to not only compete successfully, but in the case of basketball, dominate the sport. If one pays attention to occupational discrimination within these sports, one observes the near absence of black coaches in both, even though superstars abound. In an insightful study of professional baseball, Pascal and Rapping demonstrate that wage differentials do not reveal the basis for discrimination in professional baseball. They show that black and white athletes with the same productivity receive equal wages. What they do find is that black athletes have to be better to be playing baseball at all.[12]

Much work remains to be done on occupational discrimination. It is possible for a discriminating employer to employ a black master plumber as a plumber's helper, have him do master plumbers' work and pay him the helper's wage and not be detected for discriminating because all "helpers" receive the same wage. In many occupations the tasks are so varied and complex that it is difficult, if not impossible, to determine the existence of discriminatory differentials. What is commonly done in research is to use some statistical procedure that gives weights to different attribute of workers and to sum the payments associated with each attribute and then compare the payments to blacks and whites to see if there is evidence of wage disparity. This procedure has its shortcomings because the determination of what attributes workers will bring to the market is in part determined by the opportunities they see available to the members of their group. Thus blacks who have reasons to believe that they will have difficulty in entering certain occupations do not prepare themselves for those occupations. The statistical analysis will conclude that blacks are underrepresented because they lack the skills for these jobs. The direction of causation in these cases is not clear. What is needed is a model of social dynamics which explains the underrepresentation.

It should be clear that all the current status of blacks is in large measure attributable to imitations placed on them in the past. In this sense, no study that makes use of variables whose present values are dependent on past discrimination can isolate the effect of these variable and the process that gave rise to them. That is to say, current data on the distribution of income, occupations, and education reflect discrimination over time. Therefore, the effect of such variables on observed outcomes is misleading. The measures do not mean the same thing for blacks as they do for whites. Discrimination affects both the distribution of the income, occupation, and education variables and their effect on observed outcomes.

The likelihood that a black person will complete a given number of years of schooling is less than it is for a white person. In addition, the quality of the schooling is likely to be poorer for the black person. If education is a key variable in determining occupation and income, then the black individual will also have a lower-status occupation and less income. Discrimination affects the observed outcomes in yet another way. Blacks with the same education, as measured by school years and achievement, do not receive as high returns on their investment in education as whites.[13] It has been argued that difference in employment security of blacks and whites is partially due to differences in their distribution of job skills and partially to discrimination.[14] However, since the distribution of job skills is itself a function of discrimination, this argument understates the effect of discrimination on the economic status of blacks.

The point of all this is that static analysis, such as we find in most published papers, cannot deal adequately with the interdependence of discrimination and its effects on variables affecting income and wealth. It can only tell us that given the distribution of the certain variables, differences in such variables as income and wealth are the result of current discrimination. This is a serious problem and must not be lost sight of, a possibility that is all too likely when attention is focused on the measures in an economic model ad not on the more general questions. "How did the variables come to be distributed the way they are and why do the measures attached to them have their particular signs and values?"

One model that has been used to study differences in black-white wealth/income ratios is Milton Friedman's "Permanent Income Hypothesis."[15] In his formulation Friedman argues that household income consists of two components, a permanent income based on such factors as age and labor-market skills (human capital) and a random (transitory) component. In the absence of discrimination, blacks and whites with the same characteristics would have the same permanent income. But this, as we know, is not the case. How then do we explain differences in black and white incomes and wealth?

> The integration in the North means that Negroes tend to be specialized, their lower average incomes reflect very largely the fact that they engage in lower paid occupations; they depend on the white community, as it were, for the services of the most highly paid occupations. In the South, being less fully integrated in this sense in the society, Negroes may tend to depend more on their own community for these more highly paid occupations; their lower average income reflects not only their concentration in lower paid occupations but also, to a much greater extent than in the North, a lower return for each activity separately. The effects would presumably tend to be much more marked in large communities than in small

> cities or villages. A minor bit of evidence supporting this interpretation is that although the average income of nonrelief Negro families is more than 20 percent lower in Atlanta than in Columbus (Ohio), a slightly higher percentage of all Negro families, 10.3 compared with 9.8 are classified as business or professional families, independent or salaried.[16]

What this quote illustrates is that the lower average income of blacks is not an accident. In the North, blacks are more concentrated in lower paying jobs and in the South, where the concentration of highly skilled professional blacks is greater, the compensation for their skill is less. One can argue that the effects of present discrimination are greater in the South and past discrimination affects are greater in the North. This is why it is important to make clear the point that discrimination—past and present—is an integral part of any analysis of the economic status of blacks.

Becker argues that discrimination results in higher returns for black capital. This is certainly not the case if one considers human capital as documented by the quote from Friedman.

The unhappy message of all this is that blacks are still a long way from achieving anything approaching economic parity. The culprit is continued, if with superior education and skills do not reap the full fruits of their labor or endowments. The effect is to discourage younger blacks from acquiring the requisite education or skills in the numbers required to lift the entire income distribution of blacks—and not merely that of what was formerly called "The Talented Tenth."

The remedy to the economic plight of blacks is not to be found in economic activity alone. Until and unless blacks achieve some degree of effective political power (i.e., command over institutions—public and private—that establish the rules of the game and determine the payoffs) they will continue to suffer from second-class economic citizenship.

The measures commonly employed to assess the relative positions of blacks and whites—income, wealth, wages, prices, unemployment rates, for example—often fail to yield unambiguous conclusions. The "correct" interpretation is in the eye of the beholder.

Wattenburg and Scammon,[17] in an article that received considerable public attention, concluded that real progress had been made by blacks and that more progress was likely. This view is challenged by Brice[18] and Gregory.[19] In this case the debate is more about the representativeness of the data and less about whether the right things are being measured.

Even when there is agreement about the accuracy and representativeness of the statistics used to measure the status of blacks and of whites, however, differences of opinion regarding interpretation might still arise. Consider, for example, the controversy over whether the relevant measure of black versus white income is the ratio of the two incomes or the differences between them. During the 1960s the ratio of black to white increased but so did the dollar gap between median black and median white income.

Which is a better measure of relative position is a question which cannot be dismissed lightly. Using more complete income distributions, such as income quarterlies, as is done by Wohlstetter and Coleman[20] does not resolve the problem.

The reasons we are supposedly interested in data on economic conditions is because we believe there is a relation between economic conditions and "well being." Economic resources places at our disposal command over a wide range of goods and services. And these goods and services in turn serve the useful purpose of satisfying some appetite (desire) we have. In the standard textbook treatment the goods and services that are consumes are marker goods, But economic resources can be used to purchase nonmarket goods. For example, peace of mind or goods for which there are informal markets—influence, prestige, name recognition, and the like.

When blacks and whites are compared in terms of income, the implicit welfare measure is a bundle of goods and services purchasable with an income of a given size. If for example, blacks are found to have an income 3/5 white income then blacks can consume only .6 times the goods and services available to whites. But at some point this ratio of available consumption approach looses its attractiveness. Suppose the income ratio of blacks (B) to whites (W), B/W = 1/1,000, with median black incomes equal to $1,000 and median white incomes equal to $1,000,000. Does anyone really believe that the millionaire consumes 1,000 times the *same* goods and services as the person with a $1,000 income? Hardly. As incomes rise, wealthy persons can consume more of the goods poorer persons consume but can also include in their consumption possibilities goods not available to poor consumers at all. So the wealthy can consume yachts, chateaux, original paintings of the old Masters, political influence, positions of honor (university trustees, titles, etc.), and the like—goods unavailable to those with lower incomes. Goods consumption and social and political opportunities are not continuous linear functions of income. Consumption opportunities available at some incomes include elements unavailable at lower ones.

In an earlier paper I pointed out that power relations are at the heart of discrimination and that while economists focus on the marketplace the importance of income and wealth is in the ways in which they give individuals and groups opportunities to determine the social, economic and political environments.[21]

Traditional theory assumes that individual behavior conforms to economic rationality. That is, in making choices an individual will choose the course that will give him (her) the greatest satisfaction—maximizing behavior. In viewing how collections of individuals act in consort to achieve common objectives I reject the individualistic assumption. This departure from the traditional mode of analysis has been applied in my work,[22] and in the work of Buchanan[23] and Saposnik.[24]

Alexis and Buchanan are concerned with economic externalities effects experienced by parties not involved in the transaction. In the former this externality is an interdependence of utility functions, and in the latter it is an externality in the consumption of a (quasi) public good.

Saposnik is concerned with the way in which particular economic environments are determined. He defines power as the ability of individuals (groups) to influence the choice of environments by society. In each environment there is associated with an individual an index of power. The economic environment is not totally determined by individualistic market behavior, witness the size if the public sector which is one element of the environment. The environment may be viewed as a set of outcomes, each relating to a particular variable subject to control—size of the public sector, unemployment rates, levels of inflation, black/white wage rate, and so forth.

As usual, nothing is said about how these preferences come about. But if, as in Alexis (1973), it is assumed that members of some collection(s) perceive that their interests are related, they will be more likely to coalesce. And if they have a larger aggregate power index their preferences will obtain. One should not assume that the power index is determined by absolute numbers of individuals. A numerical minority can be an economic majority in the sense that it has a larger power index. South Africa presents such a case, where the white minority is an economic majority.

Riker has shown that there are incentives to have the winning coalition as small as possible.[25] The reason for this is that the benefits are then divided over a smaller number of persons. This is of some importance in cases where some privilege is conferred by a particular environment. This preferred treatment may be in the form of taxation of income and/or wealth, wage rates (as in South Africa), occupational or residential choice (as in the United States), or any number of cases in which with particular environments is associated specific preferences.

There are sometimes costs involved in forming coalitions. These costs may be generally described as organization costs. The optimal size of the coalition will then depend on the marginal benefits of membership and the marginal costs of organization. Some desired outcomes require larger power coalitions than others. A simple majority will do to revise the Internal Revenue Code, but larger majorities in the Congress and the state legislatures are required for constitutional amendments abolishing the income tax or limiting the size of the public sector to some specified fraction of GNP.

Suppose one starts with a situation in which one group is at a disadvantage; they are never in the winning coalition and are therefore unable to choose environments favorable (or neutral) to them. The outcomes of the social process exercise leave them with lower wage rates, lower incomes, higher unemployment, unfavorable occupational distribution (more seasonal and cyclically sensitive), and smaller endowments of human capital. These are the characteristics of the black population in the United States.

The relative power index of an individual is not merely his share of total income; it can be greater or less than that. Power flows from economic resources—income and wealth—and from ability to persuade others to behave in a manner so as to increase the chances that one's preferred outcome(s) are realized. The ability to persuade others to act in the desired manner might depend on other attributes of the individual, say his race, religion, kinship. Fraternal ties (Masons, Elks, Knights of Columbus, etc.).

Because of the size of the public sector, attention must be paid to ways in which bureaucrats and elected officials act so as to increase the likelihood that preferred outcomes of some individuals or group(s) are more likely to be realized. The recent successes of the "right-to-life" groups in withholding government funds from elective abortions can be seen as an example of one group producing a more preferred environment (E_I)

through governmental intervention. In this case, a less powerful group (the poor) was forced to accept a change in the environmental which is not binding on more affluent groups. This is an example of a group which would face a different set of market opportunities if their incomes were to increase by a few thousand dollars.

The affluent in our society have very different opportunity sets that the nonaffluent. They, almost exclusively as individuals, are the contributors to political campaigns, charitable and philanthropic causes, and to campaigns designed to influence the opinions of others. It would be surprising if the elected officials to whose campaign they contribute, the churches, colleges, community fund drives, hospital capital drives and lobbying efforts to which they contribute, are not responsive to their preferences. Indeed, some elected officials are said to be known as "friends" of special interest groups—organized labor or big business. The poor and members of minority groups do not appear to have such steady supporters and are dependent on "good will."

CONCLUSION

Improvements in the economic political and social status of blacks are joint effects. Improvement in one is unlikely without concommitant improvements in the others, this is a multi-edge sword. Success in any of the areas is correlated with improvement in the others—synergism. On the other hand, failure to realize the interdependencies makes unlikely success or improvement in either.

The task for black leadership is to organize the resources in black communities into coalitions which have the greatest potential for leveraging gains in one area into gains in other areas. Since these gains feed on themselves, the goal should be to assure positive movement at all times. Thus, political gains can be translated into less cyclical exposure for low-income blacks. Economic gains can be converted into greater political participation in decision making. Social (status) gains can be translated into economic gains. And so the cycle goes.

One can expect an equilibrium where outcomes favorable to the preferences of blacks are proportional to their numbers. This is a stronger condition than merely achieving proportionate power, for as a numerical minority it would be possible to be a minority in every outcome determining decision. Equality, to be meaningful, must mean to be in the winning coalition on a proportionate basis.

NOTES

1. Garry S. Becker, *The Economics of Discrimination*, Chicago, 1957.
2. *Ibid.*, p. 2.
3. *Ibid.*, p. 3.
4. *Ibid.*, p. 6.
5. *Ibid.*, p. 49.
6. These points are discussed in Marcus Alexis, "A Theory of Labor Market Discrimination with Interdependent Utilities," *The American Economic Review*, 63 (May, 1973), 296–303; and Marcus Alexis, "The Political Economy of Labor Market Discrimination; Synthesis and Exploration," George von Furstenburg, Ann R. Horowitz and Bennett Harrison (eds.), *Patterns of Racial Discrimination, Vol. II, Employment and Income*. Lexington, 1974, 63–84.
7. In point of fact, these costs are not all private. The decline in available output is a social loss. There is less real output to be consumed. These losses are permanent; they cannot be made up at a later time.
8. For a nontechnical, lucid discussion, see Lenoid Hurwicz, "The Theory of Economic Behavior," *American Economic Review*, 35 (1945), 909–25, reprinted in George J. Stigler and Kenneth E. Boulding, *A.E.A. Readings in Price Theory*. Vol. 6, Homewood, Richard D. Irwin, 1952, 505–26.

For a more thorough discussion, see R. Duncan Luce and Howard Raiffa, *Games and Decisions*, New York, John Wiley & Sons, 1957, ch. 4.

9. Marcus Alexis, "A Theory of Labor Market Discrimination with Interdependent Utilities," *Loc. Cit.* For a less technical treatment, see Marcus Alexis, "Two Theories of Discrimination," Peggy Reeves Sanday (ed.), *Anthropology and the Public Interest: Fieldwork and Theory*, New York, Academic Press, 1976, 147–65.
10. Thomas A. Schelling, *The Strategy of Conflicts*, Cambridge, Harvard, 1960.
11. Marcus Alexis, "A Theory of Labor Market Discrimination with Interdependent Utilities," *Loc. Cit.* See also, Marcus Alexis, "Two Theories of Discrimination," in Peggy Reeves Sanday (ed.), *Anthropology and the Public Interest: Fieldwork and Theory*, New York, Academic Press, 1976, 147–65.
12. *Ibid.*

10. For some examples of the literature on subgroup behavior, see Elliot Liebow, *Tally's Corner*, Boston, Little Brown, 1967; William Foote Whyte, *Street Corner Society: The Social Structure of an Italian Slum*, Second Edition, Chicago, University of Chicago, 1961. Claude Brown, *Manchild in the Promised Land*, New York, Macmillan, 1965. Oscar Lewis, *Five Families: Mexican Case Studies in the Culture of Poverty*, New York, Basic Books, 1959; also by Oscar Lewis, *La Vida: A House*, 1966. Joyce A. Ladner, *Tomorrow's Tomorrow The Black Woman*, Garden City Doubleday, 1971; Lola M. Irelan (ed.), *Low-Income Life Styles*, Washington, D.C., U.S. Department of Health, Education and Welfare, Welfare Administration, Division of Research, 1966.

11. In more general notation, $O = F(I_1, I_2 \ldots I_N)$.

12. Anthony H. Pascal and Leonard A. Rapping "The Economics of Racial Discrimination in Organized Baseball," Anthony H. Pascal (ed.), *Racial Discrimination in Economic Life, loc.cit.*, 119–56.

13. Randall D. Weiss, "The Effect of Education on the Earnings of Blacks and Whites," *The Review of Economics and Statistics*, 52, 2 (May, 1970), 150–59.

14. Harry J. Gilman, "Economic Discrimination and Unemployment," *American Economic Review*, 4 (December, 1965), 1077–1096.

15. Milton Friedman, *A Theory of the Consumption Function*, Princeton, 1957, 20–26.
16. *Ibid.*
17. Ben J. Wattenberg and Richard M. Scammon, "Black Progress and Liberal Rhetoric," *Commentary* (April, 1973), 35–44.
18. Herrington Bryce, "On the Progress of Black—A Comment on Wattenberg and Scammon," Joint Center for Political Studies, 1973.
19. Karl Gregory, "Brief Report on the State of the Black Economy," 1973, *The Review of Black Political Economy*, 4 (1973), 3–15.
20. Albert Wohlstetter and Sinclair Coleman, "Race Differences in Income," Anthony Pascal (ed.), *Racial Discriminations in Economic Life*, 1972, 3–81.
21. "The Economic Status of Blacks and Whites," *The American Economic Review*, 68 (May, 1978), 179–85.
22. *Ibid.*
23. James M. Buchanan, "An Econonmic Theory of Clubs," *Economica*, (February, 1965), 1–14.
24. Rubin Saposnik, "Power, The Economic Environment and Social Choice," Econometrica, 42, no. 3 (May, 1974), 461–70.
25. William Riker, *The Theory of Political Coalitions*, New Haven: Yale University Press, 1962.

18

REPARATIONS AND PUBLIC POLICY

Richard F. America

The concept of reparations is key to understanding the public policy aspects of the race problem and fundamental to resolving them. Increasingly, economists will find it rewarding to address a wide range of policy issues through this lens. It will sharpen their understanding and analyses, and help them develop effective policy.

Until now, most Americans, including most policy analysts, politicians, journalists, legislators, judges, and business leaders, have had little grasp of how slavery or discrimination operated in the overall economic development of the United States. They are largely unaware of slavery's scope. It was significant in manufacturing, mining, and services, as well as in agriculture and in urban as well as in rural areas.

It is often not understood that slavery and discrimination freed up many whites who would otherwise have been allocate to employment in lesser skilled and unskilled occupations, who were able to gain advanced skills and experience in more rewarding job categories. This was a massive and sustained form of "affirmative action" that continues to benefit them to this day relative to blacks, as a class.

They are not aware that slavery created much, if not most, of the infrastructure that was needed to support development and continental expansion in all activities. People do not realize that it produced massive benefits, directly and indirectly, actively and passively, to large numbers of people, North and South, during slavery, who never came into contact with any slaves. A large number of immigrants, who came to the country after slavery, were better able to enter a growing economy, owing to the foundation that slavery built.

Nor do they see how this continues to produce large unjust enrichments to them, currently, as a class.

And the same applies to discrimination after slavery. It, too, produced broad class benefits for generations of whites. These are people who never individually discriminated against anyone in a hiring, training, promotion, educational admissions, contracting, or lending decision, but all those decisions were systematically made by white decisionmakers, against blacks as a class, in favor of other whites as a class, and for the benefit of their posterity, through intergenerational class transfers of income and wealth—especially in wealth in the form of human capital.

To resolve the race issue, Americans need to first come to terms with these continuing economic realities that are based in slavery and discrimination. They need to grasp how those practices, policies, and systemic patterns produced massive benefits to whites as a class at the expense of blacks as a class, and how those benefits were then transferred over the generations and compounded. This accumulated wealth, in many forms, real, financial and human, makes whites better off, relative to blacks than they would otherwise have been, absent all those immoral past transactions.

THE RESTITUTION PRINCIPLE

That brings us to the Restitution Principle. It says that whenever a social group, a nation, or a race decides that past behavior—say, slavery, and discrimination—was wrong, and has made it illegal, then it is wrong to receive and retain the benefits produced by those actions. It is, therefore, necessary to make restitution, giving back the wrongful benefits, by some explicit redistributive action, public, private, or both.

Racial income and wealth disparities have persisted for generations. Now we can do historical auditing to measure the current consequences of past racial injustice. And that knowledge can help us adopt policies of redistributive justice based on the Restitution Principle. Affirmative action, as we know it, may not survive the current attack, but the Restitution Principle will remain until its imperatives are satisfied through affirmative action, in some form, under some label, and in other ways.

The self evident truth is that whites owe blacks money. This should inform and guide public policy thinking in every race related matter in housing, education, transportation, employment, business assistance, health, criminal justice, and in affirmative action in all its forms.

The Sunset Principle

Affirmative action policy—whatever it comes to be called—should have a sunset. That's another key principle: the sunset principle. Compromise solutions to contentious social policies should carry a time limit.

Reparations should be paid in about two generations or 50 years. If we had applied these principles in the 1960s, we probably could have avoided much political conflict these past decades and would be closer to real closure and resolution of the actual problems.

Reparations should emphasize investment in education and training, housing, health, and business development. But merely subsidizing underclass subsistence won't work, and should not count as payment on reparations; that's not an investment in development. That's another key principle, the Development Principle.

The Development Principle

Redistributive investments, based on the restitution principle, should be made in ways that enhance recipients' human capital and ability to compete. They should not simple support and offer indefinite subsistence assistance.

And public policy should also help develop discipline, and what we call "character" and "values," such as the work ethic, respect for law, and other "middle class" ways of looking at life and behaving.

Done right, it will benefit the whole economy. but the policies should be based on the principle that restitution is owed. Then they will help the poor and marginal become independent and fully functioning contributors.

Historical Auditing

These public policy innovations have to be based on measured unjust enrichments. And that process can be called historical auditing.

The historical auditing will become the basis for conflict resolution in many situations. Groups have tried to economically dominate and exploit other groups throughout history. But now we can measure the consequences. That is an innovation.

THE SOCIAL DEBT TO AFRICAN AMERICANS

Whites owe blacks money—several trillion dollars. Actually only some whites owe blacks money; most do not. And most of the debt is owed to poor blacks. But all blacks have been victimized by centuries of economic injustice, in ways that benefit whites in the top wealth percentiles.

The three indigenous or quasi indigenous minorities, Native American

Indians, Native Mexican Americans, and African Americans, are owed reparations. These are all very long term residents, with similar experiences in relations with European Americans. Yale Law School's, Boris Bittker, clearly outlined much of the concept in 1972 in his path breaking, but little noted book, *The Case for Black Reparations.*

Restitution as Redistributive Justice

The Unjust Enrichment is on the order of $5—10 trillion. Most of this wealth is embodied in white human capital. It was created by the systematic diversion of funds that should have been invested in black education and training, to whites, instead. They received disproportionate education and training relative to blacks. And now it is reflected in their ability to generate future income and wealth—expected lifetime earnings beyond what they would have, relative to blacks, but for the wrongful and coercive diversion of human capital investment.

It's over and above what they would have earned—relative to what blacks earned—if slavery had ended much earlier and if there had been no long period of post slavery discrimination. It rightfully belongs to, and would have gone to, blacks had there not been this systemic injustice.

Whites, as a class, whose income, or probable future income, is in the top 30 percent of the income distribution—over $60,000 a year—owe blacks. That includes second and third generation Americans, whose ancestors come through Ellis Island or other ports, as well as those whose ancestors fought in the Revolution, or the Civil War, or arrived in the seventeenth century.

The debt is principally to blacks in the bottom 30 percent, earning income or receiving transfer payments of under $25,000 a year. So, the idea of reparations are about group benefits, "preferences," as it's cynically labeled, losses, right, wrongs, obligations, and entitlements.

The Supreme Court has moved to narrow the focus of affirmative action and of other race related matters. It has tried to create a rule that would apply a strict construction. It has tried to insist on proof of specific individual damages. Justice Scalia has said that there "are no debtor or creditor races." He got it exactly *wrong*. The restitution principle recognizes the reality that systemic, broad based policies and practices are the issue, not isolated incidents.

The restitution principle also provides a way to think and act constructively on the tangled problems of general economic inefficiency, global competitive disadvantage, urban decay, social disintegration, poverty, crime, and self destructive behavior.

Slavery directly enriched those who bought, sold, transported, financed, bred, leased, and managed slaves in agriculture. But it was also important in other sectors, including mining, transportation, manufacturing, and the development of major public works—roads, bridges, dams, canals, levees, railroads, clearing land, and so on.

It indirectly benefited millions who had no first hand role in slavery. It afforded them the benefits of slave produced goods and services. And it released them from low level occupations that allowed them to pursue more rewarding life's work. It freed them to receive education and training of greater value to them and, as it turns out, to their descendants, than they would otherwise have had, absent slavery.

Second, there was discrimination especially in education and in employment. Most Americans now disapprove of discrimination. We say we believe it is not fair. But it produced tangible benefits. These were realized largely indirectly and passively, and that makes the subject difficult to explain and easy for many to deny.

There's a broad and, to use the Supreme Court's language, "amorphous" injustice operating throughout the economy. And the restitution principle helps clarify heretofore unrecognized wrongs, and remedy them. But this principle runs up against our widely shared assumptions: (a) that we have individually arrived at our place in society, fair and square on "merit"; (b) that equal individual opportunity has been secured for all; and (c) that everyone can now go forward, unfettered by membership in any class, group, or race, to make it by adopting working/middle class values, because we should live in a colorblind society.

So, the restitution principle challenges and contradicts long standing assumptions and beliefs. It respects and shares the assumption that individual responsibility is the basis for social progress. At the same time, it asserts that group dynamics still powerfully account for much of our personal well-being or misfortune, as the case may be.

Perhaps many Americans will want to acknowledge the debt and pay reparations as a matter of principle. But many will wonder how all that really affects overall national ability to produce, grow, innovate, and maintain or improve our standard of living and our competitive position in a dynamic world economy. How is it relevant to those practical terms?

The answer is that millions of people are relatively miserable. They're disenchanted, alienated, and underperforming, committing crimes, having babies irresponsible, dropping out, and abusing themselves and others in many ways. Many intuitively sense that they are victims of a massive historic and ongoing injustice. And many also sense a connection between their situation, as a class, and other peoples' affluence and general relative good fortune. Their self defeating and dysfunctional behavior costs them.

And it also costs society, directly and indirectly, because we have had to pay for their dysfunction. So, we should help upgrade their lives and performance, both because it's right and because it makes practical sense. If they come to live according to the Development principal—obey the law, stay healthy, get educated, and perform economically—then social "safety net" costs—health, welfare, remedial education, housing subsidies and police, which are grossly and unnecessarily high—will be greatly reduced.

If behavior improves, the burden on budgets—municipal, county, state, and Federal—will decline. Then those who are poor and marginal will see their output, and enhanced capacity to earn, produce, consume, save and invest, increase. And that improvement will be felt throughout the entire economy at every level.

Regarding education, the restitution principle says that, over centuries, blacks have been wrongfully and systematically deprived by whites of investment in their training and education. This diversion of resources, from a common pot of money that blacks helped produce, primarily benefits whites. And this pattern and practice is cumulative. It produces compounded benefits to whites' descendants, and it creates compounded loss of knowledge, skills, and abilities to blacks' descendants.

The result is, after 375 years of theft of human capital, education, too many blacks, especially those in the underclass, can't function in the modern world. They have been deliberately, deprived of adequate training and education in order that those educational resources could instead go to whites. And, as a result, they are relatively handicapped and cannot carry their share of the load.

Their defects drag down the whole economy. They don't contribute a the level they could, and they require support and subsistence subsidies, wealth that could be better spent if invested to make mistakes. But economic advance requires that we make restitution.

Schools produce too many ill prepared graduates. Factories are, too often, idle, undercapacity, or obsolete. Buses, subways, parks, freeways, and downtown streets are too dangerous. Taxes are wasted in supporting the wretched when they could be invested to help them join the mainstream. But we can do better if policy is informed by the restitution principle.

The middle class refuses, as the political majority and swing vote, to support the needed reforms at the needed scale. They oppose capital redistribution. And they decline to tax and spend adequately for housing, health, education, proper prisons, and the kind of training that would help the poor and marginal stabilize, improve and contribute. But by taking this attitude, the middle class unwittingly prolongs and deepens the difficulty and heightens their risks.

Economic policy formulations will finally have to include explicit direct attention to the restitution principle. Its logic will be undeniable, and it will clarify our choices, and dissolve the policy logjam to everyone's ultimate benefit.

Health, Welfare and Development

19

21ST CENTURY POLLINATION: FEDERAL HOUSING AND HEALTH POLICIES

Wilhelmina A. Leigh

The interactiveness between housing and health has been known since the late 1800s, when it was discovered that infectious diseases easily spread among persons living in crowded tenements.[1] Although this awareness has spawned debate about the influence of housing on health and of health on housing, federal policies and programs in these two areas have been largely shaped separately.

Federal interventions in the markets for housing and health-care services (i.e., the markets for insurance, hospital care, and provider services) have differed in both concept and magnitude. Many federal health programs have been funded as entitlements, with enough money made available so that all who meet the eligibility standards can be served.[2] Federal housing assistance, however, is generally discretionarily funded, meaning that the amounts appropriated are not determined with the objective of meeting the total need.[3] Thus, only a portion of the eligible population receives assistance. For example, of the 15.8 million lower-income renter households eligible for federal housing assistance, only 4.1 million (26%) get it.[4] In addition, among all families with incomes less than the federal poverty level, in 1993, only 18 percent received housing assistance.[5] The housing assistance programs of the U.S. Department of Housing and Urban Development (HUD) constitute only 1.7 percent, but federal health expenditures constitute 20 percent, of the federal budget in fiscal year 1995, further evidence of the different funding principles for housing and health programs.[6]

Because federal health care expenditures are also 33 percent of total national health expenditures (federal, state and local, plus personal), in recent years, steps have been taken to reduce them.[7] Efforts to reduce health care spending have focused on the two largest federal programs—Medicaid, which provides health insurance for the poor and disabled, and Medicare, which insures the elderly.[8] In many localities, efforts to reduce spending in the Medicaid program, for example, have bifurcated the low- and moderate-income populations into those with Medicaid managed care and those without health insurance. At the same time, other market forces have transformed these two groups into those who receive health-care services and those who do not, especially in states that do not fund health care for the uninsured.[9] This trend toward two subpopulations among those eligible for assistance to get health-care services may become entrenched if there are further cuts in federal dollars for health programs. The result may be the official transformation of health-care entitlement programs into discretionarily funded programs.

The purpose of this article is to examine features of existing discretionarily funded federal housing assistance programs and their outcomes to suggest how one federal health program—Medicaid—might be altered if program features from discretionarily funded programs were applied to it in the 21st century. Implications for Black Americans of these changes are a major focus of this article. The first section briefly describes the federal role in the markets for housing and health-care services and the resulting outcomes for Black Americans. The next section discusses selected design features of discretionarily funded federal housing assistance programs (primarily Low-Rent Public Housing (LRPH) and Section 8) and speculates how these features might transform the Medicaid program and the assistance received by African Americans there from. The final section draws conclusions based on the analysis.

FEDERAL ROLE IN MARKETS FOR HEALTH-CARE SERVICES AND HOUSING

Neither health-care services nor housing is sold in a perfectly competitive market—that is, with such large numbers of suppliers and demanders that neither the suppliers nor the demanders can influence the prices of goods. Perfectly competitive markets would also have a free flow of information among suppliers and demanders, which serves as an impediment to attempts to influence prices.[10] Major distortions in price exist in these markets due to both interruptions in the free flow of information (e.g., providers have more information than health-care consumers) and third party payments (by providers of health insurance or housing subsidies) that place a wedge between the demander and the full cost of the goods demanded. In addition, racial segregation—the result of the "separate but equal" concept, which explicitly governed the affairs, policies, and programs of the U. S. government between the 1890s and the 1960s—has distorted access to and prices for both health-care services and housing among African Americans.[11] Federal interventions in these markets have failed to eliminate these distortions and restore competitiveness.[12]

Federal interventions in the markets for health-care services and housing are both indirect and direct. Direct interventions are exemplified by funds appropriated for specific health programs such as Medicaid, or for housing programs such as Section 8 certificates/vouchers and LRPH. The major directly funded federal health programs are entitlements, while most directly funded federal housing programs are discretionarily funded. Indirect interventions or subsidies are provided in the form of taxes not collected and are generally administered as entitlements for both housing and health. Examples include the exclusion from taxation of capital gains on home sales and the deductibility from taxable income of expenditures for health insurance premiums and out-of-pocket expenses that exceed 7.5 percent of adjusted gross income.

Markets for Health-Care Services

The federal government intervenes in the markets for health-care services to fund biomedical research (mainly through the National Institutes of Health), to fund services, to construct facilities, and to train researchers and providers. Health-care services are supported primarily via grants from the federal government and include the maternal and child health block grant to states, the new block grant to states for child health insurance (mandated by the 1997 Balanced Budget Act, P.L. 105–33), special project grants to health profession institutions, and Medicaid grants to states.[13]

Medicaid is the major public financing program that provides for low-income and disabled people with both health insurance coverage and third-party payments for long-term care. Although Medicaid is jointly funded by the federal government and the states (with the federal share based on each state's per capita income and ranging between 50 percent and 80 percent of total Medicaid expenditures), the program is administered by the states, each of which establishes eligibility rules. In 1995, more than 1 in 10 Americans (35.2 million people) were covered by Medicaid, and expenditures of $152.4 billion were made. In 1996, 13.3 million Medicaid beneficiaries were enrolled in managed care plans, and, in 1997, about 40 percent of Medicaid beneficiaries, primarily poor children and their parents, received services through managed care.[14] This coverage and these expenditures, however, reach only half of poor Americans, largely because many states set their eligibility thresholds low as a means to reduce their share of program expenses.[15]

Because they are overrepresented among the low-income population, African Americans are overrepresented among Medicaid beneficiaries. Although only 12.6 percent of the 1996 U.S. population, African Americans were 29.3 percent of all persons below the federal poverty level, and 28.8 percent of all Medicaid beneficiaries (1995).[16] In addition, over a fourth (9.2 million or 27 percent) of all African Americans reported coverage by Medicaid in 1995.

Market for Housing

Federal intervention in the market for housing has included the construction and leasing of housing, subsidizing rents, subsidizing interest rates, insuring mortgages, and supporting and regulating the secondary market for home loans.[17] This article will center around the LRPH and Section 8 certificate/voucher programs, the two largest federal housing assistance programs and the programs targeted to the population most likely to also be Medicaid beneficiaries.

The LRPH program provides reduced-rent publicly owned dwellings for families with incomes less than or equal to 80 percent of the area median income (i.e., lower-income households) and for elderly, handicapped, and displaced individuals. Because of additional program regulations, most of the recipients of federal housing assistance have very low incomes—i.e., less than 50 percent of area median income.[18] The construction of developments in the LRPH program has been funded by both the sale of tax-exempt bonds and direct federal grants, and developments have also been leased for this program.[19] In the Section 8 program, the federal government alters market prices by subsidizing the rents of tenants. Monthly payments are made to private landlords to cover the difference between the tenant's rental payment and the Fair Market Rent (FMR) set by HUD for each unit (based on its size and geographic location). Section 8 beneficiaries get certificates/vouchers, which they give to their landlords to guarantee that these payments will be made.

Although these federal rental assistance programs are discretionarily funded (i.e., all eligibles are not served), African American households are overrepresented relative to their share of eligible very-low-income renter households. Relative to their share of all households (11.6%), African American households are overrepresented among very-low-income renter households (26%) and also are overrepresented among very-low-income renter households who receive federal housing assistance (40%).[20] However, the 40 percent average share for Black households among recipients of federal rental assistance obscures differences in the racial/ethnic mix among the various programs. Blacks are more than half (53%) of the residents of LRPH but less than a third (30%) of the residents of private, project-based, federally subsidized developments.[21] About a third of Section 8 certificate/voucher recipients in 1991 were Black.[22]

21ST CENTURY POLLINATION

By definition, under discretionarily funded federal housing assistance programs some of the eligible population receive assistance and some do not. Although an entitlement program, in recent years Medicaid has also divided the low- and moderate-income population into those covered by Medicaid and those not covered and likely to be uninsured and, therefore, without access to care. Before the rapid spread of managed care within Medicaid, however, uninsured persons defined as ineligible for this program were often able to get health-care services at public health clinics, which were supported in part with Medicaid funding. Medicaid funds kept afloat many health facilities that served not only Medicaid beneficiaries but also provided uncompensated care to the uninsured.[23] The increasing implementation of managed care, however, has altered the access of care for the uninsured poor, because it has enhanced the ability of poor persons enrolled in Medicaid managed care plans to get services at private medical facilities and, thus, has removed the funding cushion for the public facilities that had provided uncompensated care for the uninsured. The removal of this source of funding threatens to convert the service outcomes of the Medicaid program (an entitlement) into the service outcomes of a discretionarily funded program—i.e., some get aid and some do not, without any means by which aid to program beneficiaries can be used to help those who are not beneficiaries.

This section examines selected features of discretionarily funded federal housing assistance and draws inferences about what could happen within the Medicaid program if it becomes operationally more like a discretionarily funded program, and less like an entitlement program.

Block Granting

Whenever separately funded programs are consolidated into a discretionary block grant, one concern is that total funding will be reduced. Another concern is that decisions for allocating funds among competing uses will be determined by a process that is locally idiosyncratic and may violate the spirit of the block grant. If the pattern associated with the implementation of housing-related discretionary block grants shows up in the health sector, what is likely to happen?

The HOME Investment Partnership program (1990 Cranston-Gonzalez National Affordable Housing Act, P.L. 101–625), the latest generation of federal block grants to state and local governments for housing assistance, provides a discretionary block grant that requires each applicant jurisdiction to hold community meetings to determine spending priorities. Thus, funded programs reflect the priorities and interests of those included in the consensus building process leading to preparation of the program application. The top priorities identified in the Comprehensive Housing Affordability Strategies (CHAS) submitted by a sample of jurisdictions for first year funding under the HOME program, included addressing the needs of the low-income, ending homelessness, and improving affordability.[24] Eliminating the causes of racial/ethnic concentrations, developing self-sufficiency programs, and alleviating overcrowding—initiatives that could especially benefit African Americans—were the least frequently mentioned program strategies, included in only 19 percent, 11 percent, and 11 percent of applications, respectively.

The block grant mechanism to distribute funds and determine the nature of housing assistance challenges Black Americans to take steps to insure that their interests are reflected in the application. If health block grants become discretionarily funded and jurisdictions are required to apply for them, this application process may be fraught with peril for underserved populations, whose voices may not be fully reflected in the deliberations that precede the application.

Cashing Out the Subsidy

Although making cash assistance payments to eligible individuals remains an unpopular policy tool in the U.S., the concept has been more thoroughly debated in the context of housing policy than in health policy and programs. The Experimental Housing Allowance Program (EHAP) was a social experiment undertaken between 1974 and 1983 to determine the impacts of cash assistance payments on housing markets.[25] Lessons learned from the EHAP have been incorporated in the Section 8 certificate/voucher program. Although beneficiaries of Section 8 housing assistance do not receive cash payments, in this program the federal government intervenes in the housing market by providing payments toward rent on behalf of tenants to their private-market landlords. Because the Black beneficiaries of the Section 8 program generally reside in neighborhoods that are less poor and racially concentrated than the neighborhoods surrounding LRPH developments, the Section 8 program with its pseudo-cash assistance payments seems to improve both the housing and the neighborhoods of its black beneficiaries.[26]

If health assistance programs become more like housing assistance programs with an unbridged gap between services received by "haves" and "have nots," cash payments for health care for the "haves" are likely to get little popular support. However, in certain types of markets for health-care services—i.e., those with an existing infrastructure of facilities, providers, and good public transportation—if valued properly, vouchers for health care could work well. In markets for health-care services lacking this infrastructure, vouchers would work less well.

The effectiveness of a voucher program is related to the establishment of ceilings or standards for prices for the various services and how these relate to the existing market prices. Housing vouchers illustrate this in markets with sizable vacancy rates, they work well, while in markets with very low vacancy rates, they work less well. As an example, in the Section 8 program in markets with rents above the rent ceilings (i.e., the HUD-established FMRs) before program implementation (i.e., likely markets in which to find low vacancy rates), tenants found it difficult to locate units.[27] In the context of health, similar phenomena would likely appear. If prices for health-care services in a given area were initially below the prices set for health-care vouchers, then local prices would inflate to the levels set by the vouchers. If prices for services were initially above the control levels, voucher holders would have difficulty getting health-care services, as a result of facilities closing due to their persistent financial shortfalls.

Waiting Lists

Because federal housing assistance programs serve just over a fourth of those eligible for aid, the local/public housing authorities (LHAs/PHAs) that administer the LRPH and Section 8 programs maintain waiting lists of unassisted people eligible for and desirous of assistance. Some close their waiting lists if they determine that, based on normal turnover, persons on the lists would have to wait such a long time for assistance that the promise of assistance would no longer be meaningful.[28]

Federal health-care assistance under the Medicaid program can be provided as an entitlement primarily because the states set income eligibility levels such that they can enroll all who qualify and serve them with the total program funds (federal and state government shares). Thus, eligibility is defined to enable Medicaid assistance to be provided as an "entitlement," and there should not be a waiting list.

As states move their Medicaid beneficiaries into managed care and get waivers to alter eligibility criteria and service provision, the program may face constraints more commonly associated with discretionarily funded programs than with entitlements. If a more generous eligibility definition is used, without increased federal or state funding, then a gap in coverage will exist, as it does with discretionarily funded programs. What would a waiting list for discretionarily funded Medicaid imply? Would it correlate with people being untreated for serious, chronic illnesses? Would it translate into the expectation of increased morbidity and mortality in places with the longest waiting lists? Who are likely to be the "first come, first served" among beneficiaries in a world with discretionarily funded Medicaid and its associated waiting lists? Would complicated enrollment procedures for Medicaid managed care discourage enrollment by the least educated and the poorest, among whom racial/ethnic minorities are overrepresented?

An even more important question for African Americans would be whether racially discriminatory practices would be evident when ordering the potential enrollees on the waiting lists and removing them there from.[29] Would the federal government allow localities to establish preferences to move people to the tops of waiting lists, as it does with housing waiting lists? Households that pay more than half of their income for rent, or live in substandard housing, or have been involuntarily displaced receive federally established preferences to move to the tops of waiting lists for housing assistance. However, localities may now override the federal preferences with others that better reflect particular market conditions.[30] How would this translate into waiting lists for Medicaid enrollment? Would people with certain illnesses have priority over others? If so, how would illnesses be ranked? Would conditions such as hypertension, homicide, unintentional injuries, and sickle cell anemia receive a lower preference ranking than conditions not found as often among racial/ethnic minorities? These questions could have many answers, but none will be easy to derive.

Cost Sharing and Income Mixing

Because federal housing assistance is discretionarily funded and most beneficiaries are the "poorest of the poor" (i.e., households with incomes less than 50 percent of the area median income, or very-low-income households), cost sharing with tenants is implemented to increase rent collection and overall revenues. Most tenants contribute toward each month's rent one of the following: 30 percent of adjusted family income, 10 percent of unadjusted family income, the shelter allowance in their welfare check, or a minimum rent ranging in value from $0 to $50.[31] However, since the amount paid toward rent by tenants is usually a percentage of their incomes, and tenant incomes are low, unless adequate supplemental funding is provided from other sources, full operating costs may not be covered. Funds to help meet operating expenses, capital costs, and maintenance come either from federal assistance contract payments (such as Section 8 certificate/voucher payments to landlords), or from operating subsidies for federally owned properties, which are never enough to cover all the costs. Deterioration and loss of the federal housing stock sometimes result from the financial shortfall.

Although historically the Medicaid program has allowed copayments in limited circumstances, the Balanced Budget Act of 1997 expands this authority to allow managed care organizations (MCOs) to charge copayments to their Medicaid beneficiaries, if these entities charge copayments to their fee-for-service Medicaid enrollees.[32] Coupled with recent reductions in provider[33] reimbursements, allowing copayments by beneficiaries of Medicaid MCOs (some of whom will not be able to pay them) may portend a further limiting of the resources available to serve Medicaid beneficiaries. The loss of units from the inventory of federally assisted housing when the various sources of funding do not cover total expenses, would translate in the health-care services sector into the closing of health-care facilities, the lack of access to care, and increased morbidity and mortality.

Income mixing is a strategy being used by LHAs/PHAs to lessen the payment squeeze they face as the result of housing so many clients whose contributions toward their rents are small. Once LHAs/PHAs own the developments and have the flexibility to modify their target tenantry, many try to attract tenants with a broad mix of incomes.[34] Federally assisted housing developments that have been successful at attracting tenants with a mix of incomes have been found to have good location and both excellent design and management. Developments located in high-poverty areas are less successful in attracting tenants with a mix of incomes.[35]

Although the incomes of Medicaid beneficiaries are very low, by the design of the various state programs, the concentration of low-income persons with Medicaid coverage as clients at certain medical facilities (usually termed "safety net") has historically been an asset and has helped these facilities meet their expenses. However, the separation of publicly assisted clients from these safety net providers, due to the inroads of managed care in the Medicaid program, has threatened the financial solvency of many.[36] Attracting clients with a greater mix of incomes to safety net providers is difficult, because these facilities often lack the "location and the excellent design and management" found to be essential in getting tenants with a greater mix of incomes to move into LRPH developments. In addition, safety net providers are often found in high-poverty areas, where many persons seeking health care might not want to go.

Regardless of its potential effectiveness, the use of income mixing as a strategy to enhance solvency within the various state programs may be discouraged by federal rules related to the implementation of Medicaid managed care. Medicaid managed care programs may now contract with Medicaid-only health maintenance organizations (HMOs) to serve enrollees.[37] Because these HMOs would have only Medicaid beneficiaries as their clientele, their reimbursements for services would be constrained by the rate schedule for this program, which pays lower fees than are customarily charged in most localities for health-care services. Since the populations to be served by Medicaid managed care are poor and, thereby, both sicker and more likely than the general population to be African Americans,[38] Medicaid-only HMOs could reasonably expect to incur expenses for remedial health care that other HMOs might not have to bear. The 1987 National Medical Expenditure Survey revealed that African Americans were more than 16 percent of those with the highest health care expenses, even though they were only 12 percent of the U.S. population at that time.[39] The combination of low reimbursement rates with high health care expenditures could spell financial insolvency for Medicaid-only HMOs, a circumstance that could leave enrollees without access to care.

Portability

Portability is a feature of the Section 8 certificate/voucher program enacted to give recipients of the limited number of certificates/vouchers the greatest opportunities to find a way to use them. A certificate/voucher recipient has sixty days in which to locate a unit in standard condition that is available for rent, before the potential beneficiary must return the unused certificate or voucher to the LHA/PHA that issued it.[40] Portability allows the renter to look for qualifying units in jurisdictions other than the one that issued the certificate/voucher. The Gautreaux Assisted Housing Program (Chicago) and the now defunct Moving to Opportunity demonstration program in five cities (Baltimore, Boston, Chicago, Los Angeles, and New York) are small scale initiatives based on the portability concept that have helped racial/ethnic minorities relocate to lower-poverty, often suburban and predominantly white areas.[41]

Portability in discussions of health care usually refers to the ability to retain health insurance coverage when changing jobs. In the context of a discretionarily funded Medicaid managed care program, portability would mean the ability of the limited numbers of beneficiaries to have the greatest possible opportunities to get health care based on their insurance coverage. These opportunities would include getting services in a state other than the one that originally enrolled the beneficiary. Portability within Medicaid managed care would mean that the public clinics and safety net providers in low-income neighborhoods would not necessarily be the places beneficiaries would receive care. Managed care, by its nature, defines for all its enrollees some facilities as valid for use and others as not. Although managed care has given many Medicaid enrollees a "health-care home," other enrollees have not been able to reap the full benefits of this. Some Medicaid beneficiaries find their health-care home to be inaccessible by public transit (their only travel option) and certainly would find travel across state lines to get the best available care inaccessible.[42] Other beneficiaries, for a variety of reasons, simply may refuse to go to their newly assigned health-care homes. Some will try to continue to use the safety net providers who have treated them all along but may not be compensated by a third party for caring for these individuals, now covered by Medicaid managed care. Thus, portability within Medicaid managed care may improve access to health-care services for those willing and able to do what they must to exercise their expanded options for getting health care; it will not help those either unwilling or unable to seek the best available care.

CONCLUSIONS

Although the federal government has traditionally intervened in the markets for health-care services to provide for the poor and underserved by establishing entitlement programs to serve all who are eligible, as the 21st century approaches, market forces may make the outcomes from entitlement programs equivalent to those under discretionarily funded programs. The Medicaid program, one such entitlement program, now is undergoing changes that may force it to operate akin to the LRPH and Section 8 programs, two discretionarily funded federal housing assistance programs. This article examined selected features of these housing programs for implications relevant to a discretionarily funded Medicaid program.

Although attention has focused on the implications for African Americans within the Medicaid program, this article has raised issues that may affect all beneficiaries of federal health-care assistance. For example, priority setting for the use of funds in discretionary block grants has implications for all potential beneficiaries, not just African Americans. The use of a voucher to cover the costs of health-care services is likely to influence prices for these services throughout a metropolitan area, and this, of course, would affect all who use such services. Similarly, the allocation and portability of limited health-care assistance are likely to have notable impacts among African Americans and other disproportionately poor and underserved populations first, but also to have implications among other such populations as well.

Thus, the restructuring that would take place if health-care services were to be funded discretionarily by the federal government, rather than as entitlement programs, would have broad implications and market spillover effects for enrollees and non-enrollees of all racial/ethnic groups and within all such programs. The program features discussed here illustrate only a few of the issues that may arise as a result of this restructuring. To the extent that the early 21st century is an era with greater program consolidation and more discretion given to the states and localities that operate federal programs, the pollination of entitlement programs with discretionary program features will become an increasing concern.

NOTES

1. See "APHA Founders Grapple with Today's Health Issues," *The Nation's Health* 27(4), (April 1997): 1, 12–13.

2. See Alan Weil, "The New Children's Health Insurance Program: Should States Expand Medicaid?" *New Federalism—Issues and Options for States* Series A (13), (October 1997).

3. The only directly funded housing program of the U.S. Department of Housing and Urban Development (HUD) that provides some entitlement money is the Community Development Block Grant (CDBG) program. The CDBG program has an entitlement subprogram, under which all eligible localities get formula-based funding for community development initiatives that often include housing. Discretionary funding for federal housing assistance programs has remained the norm, despite the fact that the March 1988 report of the Rouse/Maxwell National Housing Task Force, entitled *A Decent Place to Live* implicitly envisioned housing assistance as an entitlement by the year 2000. See, for example, Langley C. Keyes and Denise DiPasquale, "Housing Policy for the 1990s," in DiPasquale and Keyes, eds., *Building Foundations: Housing and Federal Policy* (Philadelphia, PA: University of Pennsylvania Press, 1990).

4. "HUD's Housing Programs Serve Diverse Groups," *Recent Research Results* (Newsletter from HUD User) (June 1997): 1–2.

5. Jan Tin, "Who Gets Assistance?" *Current Population Reports* (Dynamics of Economic Well-Being: Program Participation, 1992–1993), pp. 70–58, (July 1996): 4.

6. See Peter Dreier and John Atlas, "U.S. Housing Policy at the Crossroads: A Progressive Agenda to Rebuild the Housing Constituency," *Working Paper,* International and Public Affairs Center, Occidental College, January 1996. See National Center for Health Statistics, *Health, United States, 1996–97 and Injury Chartbook* (Hyattsville, MD: National Center for Health Statistics, 1997).

7. Ibid.; National Center for Health Statistics, 1997.

8. See Wilhelmina A. Leigh, "Implications of Health-Care Reform Proposals for Black Americans," *Journal of Health Care for the Poor and Underserved* 5 (1), (1994): 17–32.

9. Dennis P. Andrulis, "The Public Sector in Health Care: Evolution Or Dissolution?" *Health Affairs* 16(4), (July/August 1997): 131–140.

10. James M. Henderson and Richard E. Quandt, *Microeconomic Theory: A Mathematical Approach* (New York: McGraw-Hill Book Co., 1971).

11. See Wilhelmina A. Leigh, "Civil Rights Legislation and the Housing Status of Black Americans: An Overview," in Leigh and Stewart, eds., *The Housing Status of Black Americans* (New Brunswick, NJ: Transaction Publishers, 1992); See Sara Rosenbaum, Rafael Serrano, Michele Magar, and Gillian Stern, "Civil Rights In A Changing Health Care System," *Health Affairs* 16(l), (January/February 1997): 90–105.

12. See James Heilbrun, *Urban Economics and Public Policy* (New York: St. Martin's Press, 1974; See Wilhelmina A. Leigh, "Will Greater Competition Improve

the Markets for Health Care Services and the Health Outcomes for Black Americans?" in Mason and Williams, eds., *Race, Markets, and Social Outcomes* (Boston, MA: Kluwer Academic Publishers, 1997).

13. See Teresa A. Coughlin and David Liska, "The Medicaid Disproportionate Share Hospital Payment Program: Background and Issues," *New Federalism—Issues and Options for States* Series A (14), (October 1997); Marsha Lillie-Blanton and Ana Alfaro-Correa, *In the Nation's Interest: Equity in Access to Health Care* (Washington, D.C., Joint Center for Political and Economic Studies, 1995); Sara Rosenbaum and Julie Darnell, *A Comparison of the Medicaid Provisions in the Balanced Budget Act of 1997 (P.L. 105–33) with Prior Law* (Washington, D.C.: George Washington University's Center for Health Policy Research for the Kaiser Commission on the Future of Medicaid, 1997); and Louise B. Russell and Carol S. Burke, "The Political Economy of Federal Health Programs in the United States: An Historical Review," *International Journal of Health Services* 8 (1), (1978): 55–77.

14. See The Kaiser Commission on the Future of Medicaid, "The Medicaid Program At A Glance," *Medicaid Facts,* July 1997, and The Kaiser Commission on the Future of Medicaid, "Medicaid and Managed Care," *Medicaid Facts,* November 1997.

15. *Ibid.*; Leigh, 1994, *Op. cit.*; and David Liska, Karen Obermaier Marlo, Anuj Shah, and Alina Salganicoff, *Medicaid Expenditures and Beneficiaries: National and State Profiles and Trends 1984–1994* (2nd edition) (Washington, D.C.: The Kaiser Commission on the Future of Medicaid, 1996).

16. U.S. Bureau of the Census, *Statistical Abstract of the United States: 1997* (117th edition) (Washington, D.C.: 1997): 22, 49, 120.

17. See Wilhelmina A. Leigh, "U.S. Housing Policy in 1996: The Outlook for Black Americans," in Rowe and Jeffries, eds., *The State of Black America 1996* (New York: National Urban League Inc., 1996).

18. For more detail on the targeting of federal housing assistance, see "Glossary of Federal Housing Subsidy Programs," in Leigh and Stewart, eds., *The Housing Status of Black Americans* (New Brunswick, NJ: Transaction Publishers, 1992).

19. *Programs of HUD* (Washington, D.C.: U.S. Department of HUD, 1977).

20. See U.S. Department of Housing and Urban Development, Office of Fair Housing and Equal Opportunity, *1993 Consolidated Annual Report to Congress on Fair Housing Programs,* HUD-1531-FHEO (Washington, D.C.: U.S. Department of HUD, 1995): 55, and U.S. Department of Housing and Urban Development, *Annual Report 1990* HUD-329-PA (19) (Washington, D.C.: U.S. Department of HUD, 1992): 40.

21. U.S. Department of Housing and Urban Development, 1992, *Ibid.*

22. U.S. Department of Housing and Urban Development, 1995, *Op. cit.*, 58.

23. Andrulis, 1997, *Op. cit.*

24. See James Hoben and Todd Richardson, *The Local CHAS: A Preliminary Assessment of First Year Submissions,* U.S. Department of Housing and Urban Development: Washington, DC, April 1992, 6. Note also that the CHAS (Comprehensive Housing Affordability Strategy) has been supplanted by the Consolidated Housing and Community Development Plan, the application to be completed by jurisdictions seeking Community Development Block Grant (CDBG) and homeless funds, as well as HOME monies.

25. See Katharine L. Bradbury and Anthony Downs, eds., *Do Housing Allowances Work?* (Washington, DC: The Brookings Institution, 1981).

26. See John Goering, Ali Kamely, and Todd Richardson, *The Location and Racial Composition of Public Housing in the United States: An Analysis of the Racial Occupancy and Location of Public Housing Developments* HUD-1519-PDR

(Washington, D.C.: U. S. Department of HUD, 1995): 2, and U.S. Department of Housing and Urban Development, 1995, *Op. cit.*, 58.

27. John C. Weicher, "The Voucher/Production Debate," in DiPasquale and Keyes, eds., *Building Foundations: Housing and Federal Policy* (Philadelphia, PA: University of Pennsylvania Press, 1990): 279.

28. For example, in early 1996, the waiting lists for LRPH in Philadelphia and Washington, DC contained 16,620 people and 15,683 people, respectively. Both of these lists would be candidates to be closed. See "5.3 M People Can't Afford Decent Housing," *Housing Affairs Letter* 96–11, (March 15, 1996): 3.

29. Rosenbaum, Serrano, Magar, and Stern, 1997, *Op. cit.*

30. See "Glossary of Federal Housing Subsidy Programs," *Op. cit.*, 261, for a discussion of the federal preferences for admission to federally assisted housing established by Title V, Section 501 of the Cranston-Gonzalez National Affordable Housing Act (P.L. 101–625). The Balanced Budget Downpayment Act, I (P.L. 104–99) suspended federal preferences for fiscal year 1996, and the Departments of Veterans Affairs and Housing and Urban Development, and Independent Agencies Appropriations Act, 1998 (P.L. 105–65) extended the suspension for fiscal years 1997 and 1998. While federal preferences are suspended, the LHAs/PHAs that operate LRPH and Section 8 are allowed to establish preferences for the allocation of housing assistance to tenants.

31. In the LRPH and Section 8 certificate programs, tenants pay a maximum of 30 percent of adjusted family income for rent. In the Section 8 voucher program, however, tenants are allowed to pay more than 30 percent of adjusted family income for rent, if they wish, in order to acquire a standard quality unit in a given neighborhood. For additional information about rent setting for beneficiaries of federally assisted housing, see: Center for Community Change, *The 104th Congress: Less Money, Fewer Rules, More Power to the States* (Washington, DC: Center for Community Change, 1996), and "Glossary of Federal Housing Subsidy Programs," *Op. cit.*, 254, 263. Changes were made in the Balanced Budget Downpayment Act, I (P.L. 104–99), Title IV, Section 402, and in the Departments of Veterans Affairs and Housing and Urban Development, and Independent Agencies Appropriations Act, 1997 (P.L. 104-204).

32. Rosenbaum and Darnell, 1997, *Op. cit.*

33. Providers are defined to include disproportionate share hospitals (DSH), nursing homes, intermediate care facilities, home health agencies, federally qualified health centers, and rural health clinics.

34. LHAs/PHAs operate and manage LRPH developments without owning them, while project indebtedness is being paid off—40 years in many cases. For further information, see Leigh, 1996, *Op. cit.*

35. See Paul C. Brophy and Rhonda N. Smith, "Mixed-Income Housing: Factors for Success," *Cityscape: A Journal of Policy Development and Research* 3 (2), (1997): 3–31, and Jill Khadduri and Marge Martin, "Mixed-Income Housing in the HUD Multifamily Stock," *Cityscape: A Journal of Policy Development and Research* 3 (2), (1997): 33–69.

36. Andrulis, 1997, *Op. cit.*

37. Rosenbaum and Darnell, 1997, *Op. cit.*

38. See Peggy McDonough, Greg J. Duncan, David Williams, and James House, "Income Dynamics and Adult Mortality in the United States, 1972 through 1989," *American Journal of Public Health* 87 (9), (September 1997): 1476–1483. See U.S. Bureau of the Census, 1997, *Op. cit.*, Tables 12, 14, and 739, for data supporting the contention that the poor are more likely to be African Americans or members of

other racial/ethnic minority group than the U.S. population overall. Specifically, in 1995, African Americans were nearly 13 percent of the U.S. population, but 27 percent of the poor U.S. population. Similarly, Hispanics were 10.4 percent of the total population, but 24 percent of the poor U.S. population.

39. U.S. Department of Health and Human Services, "One Percent of Americans Account for 30 Percent of Health Expenditures," *Research Activities* (AHCPR Publication No. 167) (August 1993): 12–13.

40. "Glossary of Federal Housing Subsidy Programs, " *Op. cit.*, 261.

41. See John Goering, Abdollah Haghighi, Helene Stebbins, and Michael Siewert, *Promoting Housing Choice in HUD's Rental Assistance Programs: A Report to Congress* HUD-PDR-1543 (Washington, D.C.: U.S. Department of HUD, 1995): vii; "The Promise of Housing Mobility Programs," *The Urban Institute Policy and Research Report* (Winter 1995–96): 4; and U.S. Department of Housing and Urban Development, "Residential Mobility Programs," *Urban Policy Brief 1* (September 1994).

42. See U.S. General Accounting Office, *Medicaid: Tennessee's Program Broadens Coverage but Faces Uncertain Future* GAO/HEHS-95-186 (Washington, D.C.: U.S. General Accounting Office, 1995).

20

BLACK INFANT HEALTH: WHERE TO IN THE 21ST CENTURY?

Geoffrey Warner

INTRODUCTION

Edward H. Beardsley, a medical historian, opens his book, *A History of Neglect*, with a quote from a passage by G. H. Kimball in his report to the North Carolina Board of Health:

> It is bad enough that a man should be ignorant, for this cuts him off from the commerce of men's minds. It is perhaps worse that a man should be poor, for this condemns him to a life of stint and scheming, and there is no time for dreams and no respite for weariness. But it is surely worse that a man should be unwell, for this prevents his doing anything much about either his poverty or his ignorance.[1]

This passage sheds light on the struggle of Africans and their descendants in the United States from their debarquement at Jamestown Virginia in August of 1619 up to the present.[2] Once denied opportunities for the accumulation of knowledge and wealth, the Black American community has finally forced open some doors of opportunity wide enough for unfettered crossing. But many of its members, too many, are too weak to and too feeble to avail themselves of these hard fought opportunities.

Michael Grossman's health capital model holds that healthy time is an input to the production of human capital.[3] Greater amounts of healthy time permit greater acquisition of skills and knowledge. In this model, health stock, during the investment period of childhood through early adulthood, is an important determinant of productive capacity during middle through late adulthood. Birthweight is one indicator of the amount of health stock during infancy. The lower the weight at birth, the less healthy time can be expected for the acquisition of knowledge and skills. From the group's point of view, it is necessary to produce a sufficient number of adults for it to perpetuate itself. The proportion of newborns surviving past their first birthday, the inverse of the infant mortality rate, is a strong indication of a group's viability. The state of Black infant health reflects the ability of the Black community to perpetuate itself in America.

THE PROBLEM OF INFANT HEALTH

The importance of the health of infants lies in the observation that the manner in which a life starts out significantly shapes how it continues. Infants who are born normal weight and full-term are more likely to survive their first year of life than are infants born low weight or pre-term. In addition, infants born low weight or pre-term and surviving past their first birthday have higher rates of illness and disability in later life than do infants born normal weight and full-term who survive past their first birthday. Currently, Black Americans have approximately double the rates of infant mortality and prematurity as White Americans.

White American newborns weigh on average 3,400 grams or 7 pounds 8 ounces. Black American newborns weigh on average 150 grams less or 7 pounds 3 ounces.[4] Direct comparisons of birthweight are not straightforward because birthweight varies considerably with birth order. Notwithstanding, the racial difference in average birthweights is minuscule and does not explain the large racial differences in rates of adverse birth outcomes.

Low birthweight is defined by the World Health Organization as newborn weight below 2,500 grams or 5 pounds 8 ounces. Very low birthweight is defined as newborn weight below 1,500 grams or 3 pounds 5 ounces. A premature delivery is defined as birth occurring before 37 completed weeks of gestation compared to the normal gestation of 40 weeks. It should be noted that these standards of infant health, adopted in 1950, are arbitrary in that they do not correspond to any biological event related to fetal development.

The infant mortality rate (IMR) is defined as the number of deaths per thousand live births of persons aged 0 through 364 days. It has two components, the neonatal mortality rate, deaths of those aged 0–27 days, and the post-neonatal mortality rate, deaths of those aged 28–364 days.

Early infant death is more often due to problems of the fetus, pregnancy, or delivery, such as congenital birth defects, extreme prematurity, or a difficult delivery that injures the infant. These problems are of a medical nature. Late infant death is more often due to problems associated with hygiene, nutrition, or shelter, such as diahrrea and dehydration, insufficient nutrients essential to infant growth, and pneumonia. These problems relate to environmental factors. The neonatal mortality rate (NMR) reflects inadequacies in the medical and prenatal care both during pregnancy and prior to conception. The post-neonatal mortality rate (PNMR) reflects inadequacies in the social and economic environment in which the mother lives and into which the child is being born. Investigation into the effect of income on infant mortality has found that in both 1937 and 1965 the PNMR was 2.5 times more sensitive to income changes than the NMR.[5]

The correlation between infant mortality and birthweight is strong. There are two pathways by which weight at birth increases the likelihood of infant death. One is by the fetus growing too slowly so that after 40 weeks the fetus, ready for delivery, weighs less than 2,500 grams. The other is by being born too early so that even if growing at an appropriate rate, the fetus does not have sufficient time to reach the 2,500 gram threshold before being born. A danger in being born too small, but on time, is that the newborn's body does not have enough muscle mass to generate on its own heat to reach normal body temperature or enough body fat to keep the body warm. In addition, it can be too weak to suck with sufficient force and sufficiently to feed adequately. The danger with being born too early, even if normal weight, is that the fetus' organs have not had sufficient time to mature to a stage where they can support independent life.

Even when poor birth outcomes do not lead to infant death, they can lead to disability or other impairments. A small newborn who cannot feed sufficiently may not obtain enough critical nutrients at the time of most rapid brain development. This can lead to reduced cognitive ability later in life, and in fact this has been observed.[6] The lungs and liver are among the last organs to mature. In the crucial moments after delivery, an impaired ability to breath will reduce oxygen flow to the brain and possibly lead to some sort of brain damage. Cerebral palsy, epilepsy, and chronic lung disease are associated with prematurity and low birthweight.[7] The history of rates of infant mortality, low birthweight, and prematurity of Blacks in the U.S. will give a sense of where we have come from, where we are now, and where we are going in terms of the health of the newest generation.

BLACK INFANT HEALTH: SLAVERY (1662–1865)

The health of Black infants in the U.S., even today, has been influenced by the event of slavery and the policies of the South. The migration out of the South in the 20th century simply spread ill health to other parts of the country; the roots of Black ill health lie in the South.[7a]

During slavery, large plantations had infirmaries. As documented by Fogel and Engerman slave owners were concerned for the health of their slaves and informed their overseers of it.[8] For example, J. Acklen's instructions to his overseer included "The preservation of the health of the negroes and the care of them when sick, will require your best attention; and to be ignorant of the best mode of discharging your duties in these particulars, is to be unfit for the responsible station you hold."[9] These duties often included insuring that slaves were personally clean, their clothing was clean and intact, and their cabins periodically thoroughly cleaned and painted. Using survey data from 1850 on 545 slaves on fifteen plantations, Fogel and Engerman calculate that the average slave in the sample lost twelve work days per year to illness, which was taken to imply a high level of health.[10] Critics of Fogel and Engerman's work claim they have miscalculated.[11] They further claim that this figure is biased downward because the owner or overseer and not the slave made the determination of how ill the slave was. Therefore, their estimate overstates the true level of slave health.

Fogel and Engerman characterized the care of pregnant slaves as the best of slave health. One owner instructed his overseer, "Pregnant women must be treated with great tenderness, worked near home, and lightly."[12] Work was further reduced or eliminated in the last month of pregnancy. Light work close to quarters was started four weeks after delivery. The slave mothers nursed for a year during which they worked at half effort. The two claim that the maternal mortality rate for slave mothers was less than that for White Southern mothers. Using 1850 Census data they calculate the slave infant mortality rate to be 183 and the Southern White infant mortality rate to be 177.[13] David et al. maintain that Fogel and Engerman present misleading calculations. They claim that the original source for Fogel and Engerman's White IMR gives an estimate of 104.[14] They further charge Fogel and Engerman with ignoring published estimates of slave and free IMR's. David et. al. cite Jack Eblen's IMR estimate on twelve plantations as 176.4, and Richard Steckel's estimate of Slave IMR as 210. Steckel further calculates the White IMR to be 113.[15] Rather than being almost equal, the slave to White IMR ratio may be double.

One weakness of Fogel and Engerman's work is that it relies heavily on the records of large plantations which were much better organized than smaller farms. Such large farms (over 150 slaves) may not be representative of the many small and medium farms (less than 15 slaves).

Few slave owners adopted a laissez-faire attitude to slave reproduction. Generally, slave owners saw potential profit in breeding slaves. Some former slaves remember plantations that "raised" only slaves, converting the food crops grown into cash when the slave children were sold as adolescents.

Fogel and Engerman present data that show the distribution of age at first birth of slave mothers to be about 4 percent for under fifteen years of age, 36 percent for age fifteen to nineteen, and 30 percent for age twenty to twenty-four, with a median age of twenty and eight-tenths years.[16] They interpret this as evidence that slave women were physically mature when becoming mothers, implying abstinence during the early teenage years. David et. al. challenge this conclusion by claiming that Fogel and Engerman use age at first surviving child as age at first birth in their calculations.[17] David et. al., using the records of four plantations in four states each having between twenty-five and fifty slave women and covering the years 1776–1865, and after adjusting for infant mortality, obtain a median age at first birth of less than nineteen, which implies a median age at first coitus of less than eighteen.[18] Their evidence contradicts that of Fogel and Engerman and supports the observations of former slaves. Hilliard Yellerday explains:

> When a girl became a woman, she was required to go to a man and become a mother. There was generally a form of marriage. The master read a paper to them telling them they were man an' wife. Some were married by the master laying down a broom and the two slaves, man and woman, would jump over it. The master would then tell them they were man and wife, and they could go to bed together. Master would sometimes go and get a large, hale, hearty Negro man from some other plantation to go to his Negro woman. He would ask the other master to let this man come over to his place and go to his slave girls. A slave girl was expected to have children as soon as she became a woman. Some of them had children at the age of twelve

and thirteen years old. Negro men six feet tall went to some of these children.[19]

Using census data from 1850 and 1860, David et. al. provide additional evidence of slave breeding. They found that the fertility rate for slave women in states exporting slaves was higher than that for slave women in states importing slaves.[20] Using data on 248 farms in 1860 with at least five slave women, (the Parker-Gallman sample), they found a strong positive correlation between the ratio of slave women to slave men and the ratio of slave children to slave adults.[21] The ratio of children to adults increases with fertility. This indicates that some slave owners invested in farms with predominantly or exclusively slave women and recouped their investment through the sale of the children the slave women bore.

This section and its anecdotes are not meant to sensationalize but to show that the state of pregnancy of Black women and the creation of new Black life had little other than economic significance for White Southern planters. The slave owning class' interest in Black health stemmed directly from the value of slave labor which was derived from cotton production.

BLACK INFANT HEALTH: RECONSTRUCTION THROUGH WWI (1865–1914)

The economic motive for White concern about slave health vanished with the end of the Civil War. The tenuous health status slaves experienced plummeted when they became free persons. Part of the problem was routed in neglect. But most of the problem was embodied in the horrendous urban living conditions Blacks faced as they migrated from farms to cities in the South. The sharecropping and other farm tenancy arrangements of the Reconstruction and Post-Reconstruction eras mired Blacks in debt and poverty. Prior to World War I, most Black migration was intra-South, that is from farms to cities in the South. Southern cities did not adequately absorb this influx of Blacks. As such, overcrowded housing and inadequate sanitation were the rule in the Black neighborhoods. (Living and working conditions for Blacks were not substantially better than during slavery.) Black health deteriorated so precipitously during this period that urban mortality actually exceeded rural mortality. This high mortality rate, especially the infant mortality rate, was noticed by the Southern health establishment. It blamed high urban mortality among Blacks on poor physiological and behavioral traits caused by inherent racial inferiority. Believing Blacks to be uneducable about hygienic issues, southern White doctors used the lower rural mortality rates to claim that plantation life was preferable for Blacks. Using flawed censuses from 1870 through 1890 which had Black mortality exceeding natality, Whites predicted that the Black race would become extinct, the loser in social evolutionary selection.

By the turn of the century, the debate had reached the academic literature couched in the form of "The Negro Question." One side held that Black mortality, particularly infant mortality, was due to Black behavior, reflective of low morals (low marriage rates and high syphilis infection rates) and ignorance (patronization of "hoodoo" medicine).[22] This view is exemplified by Frederick Hoffman, a statistician with the Prudential Insurance Company, who was commissioned by the American Economic Association to investigate the well-being of Blacks. He investigated population growth and migration, statistics on births and deaths, especially age-, sex-, and marital status-specific death rates, disease prevalence including syphilis and mental disorders, anthropometry and its relation to physical stamina, the patronage of religious and educational institutions, the numbers and health of racially mixed children, and economic aspects such as labor supply, productivity, wages, wealth accumulation, and the interaction between White and Black labor. In the conclusion to his monograph Hoffman writes:

> The central fact deducible from the results of this investigation into the traits and tendencies of the colored population of this country, is plainly and emphatically, the powerful influence of *race* in the struggle for life. . . .[23]

The other side held that poor social and living conditions and their influence on behavior were responsible for the high rates of Black mortality. This view was exemplified by the attendees of Atlanta University's annual Conference for the Study of Negro Problems.

> How much is the Negro death rate affected by environment? One has only to compare the wretched quarters of Charleston and New Orleans, with a death rate of over 40 per 1,000, with the far better, although not ideal, conditions in Atlanta and Louisville, with a death rate of 30 per 1,000. . . .
>
> All of the foregoing shows that the death rate in this country does

TABLE 1
Infant Mortality Rates in 1900

Southern Cities	IMR	Northern Cities	IMR
Atlanta GA	259	Boston MA	173
Charleston NC	323	Buffalo NY	137
Jacksonville FL	234	Chicago IL	134
Memphis TN	214	Detroit MI	177
Mobile AL	271	Minneapolis MN	95
Norfolk VA	236	New York NY	171
Richmond VA	250	Philadelphia PA	162
Savannah GA	300	San Francisco CA	136
Washington DC	233	Seattle WA	96

Source: Meckel, 1990. p. 106, based on 1890 census.

> not altogether depend upon climate; that it is a factor which can be easily overcome, and the Negroes of this population are rapidly overcoming it. That there is something more important than climate may be gained from the observation that almost uniformly the Northern White death rate, like the Northern Negro death rate, is lower than that of the South. Indeed, the Northern Negro death rate is lower than that of the Whites in many Southern cities. . . . And the infantile mortality among the Negroes of Pittsburgh, Indianapolis, Cincinnati, Chicago, and Boston, is lower than that of Savannah Ga. among the Whites; Boston's Negro mortality is lower than Atlanta's, Charleston's and Savannah's White infant mortality.
>
> The high infantile mortality of Philadelphia today is not a Negro affair, but an index of a social condition.[24]

No reliable infant death data from which enlightening statistics can be calculated were available before 1915. Infant mortality rates were calculated from the change in age-specific populations from one census to the next. The 1900 Census published infant mortality rates for selected cities (some displayed in Table 1). At this time, Black infant mortality was believed to be almost double that of Whites. Northern Blacks were better off financially than the Southern Blacks and so did not suffer mortality and morbidity to the same extent. The attention of the Northern medical establishment was on the plight of recent immigrants. They lived in squalid conditions in New York, Boston, and Philadelphia and had very high infant mortality rates. Responding to a health department bulletin that reported at least *one hundred* infant deaths on *each day* of the preceding week, a New York Times newspaper editor wrote in July 1876, that the most depressing feature about American cities was their annual slaughter of children[25] (emphasis mine).

EFFORTS TO IMPROVE INFANT HEALTH: RECONSTRUCTION THROUGH WWI (1865–1914)

Concern over the high rate of infant mortality in cities started in the 1850s. Cities had been growing at a tremendous pace during the previous two to three decades as the result of European migration, the development of canals and railroads, and domestic migration from farms. Urban infrastructures (housing, water, and sanitation), became overtaxed. Northeastern cities such as Boston and New York created boards of health to enact tenement housing regulations similar to those in Europe. But landlord opposition and laws favoring property rights removed the teeth from these efforts.

Near the turn of the century digestive tract disorders were shown to be one of the most common causes of infant death. The summers were particularly deadly as scores of infants born to the urban poor would die of diarrhea. The newly created American Pediatric Society (1887) helped focus attention on nutrition as an important aspect of infant health and improper or unclean nutrition as a factor in infant death. Breast feeding was encouraged but only wealthy women had the time and the diets to nurse sufficiently. Poor women, working full-time and eating what they could afford, were unable to nurse and relied on cow's milk. A first wave of milk reform aimed at outlawing "swill" milk occurred in 1830. "Swill" milk is produced by cows fed exclusively waste products of distillates. The second wave occurred in the 1890s and was aimed at purifying milk. The availability of pasture land for dairy farm products diminished as cities grew, increasing the distance to market for fresh milk. Cows were sick and dirty, milk was unrefrigerated and retailers sold milk in bulk and not individualized containers. In addition, when (not if) milk spoiled, wholesalers would add sugar, molasses, or other products to mask the foul taste. Despite resistance from milk dealers, cities began to set standards. In 1905, the U.S. Supreme Court upheld New York City's licensing of milk dealers and barring from trade any dealers who failed to meet the standards. Though milk pasteurization had been practiced in Europe since 1870, it was not until 1920, after several well publicized instances of milk contamination, that the proportion of pasteurized milk sold in large cities exceeded 90 percent.[26]

BLACK INFANT HEALTH: WWI TO WWII (1915–1945)

With regard to infant health, many things happened very quickly during the First World War. In 1915, the Vital Statistics Registration Act was passed creating registration areas and requiring states to record all births and deaths occurring in these areas. Initially, only cities participated and they were almost entirely Northern. As such, this act did not affect the majority of Black births. It was not until 1935 that birth registration covered almost all of the country and not until the 1950s was the data collected sufficiently accurate.

The war effort and especially the recruitment of soldiers in 1916–17 was an eye-opener to all Americans, especially Southerners. The country found itself unprepared for war. In the North, munitions production created a demand for labor which, combined with the mechanization of farms, caused a migration to Northern cities. While pre-WWI intra-South migration had been between farm and city with little migration North, there was now substantial migration from Southern cities to Northern cities. The migration from Southern farm to Southern city continued. There was still apparently little direct Southern farm to Northern city migration. The importance of this migration was that the poor health performance of Black infants was being recorded through birth registration and was beginning to be noticed, for the first time, by the Northern medical establishment. Northern public health workers were appalled and applied the techniques learned with European immigrants in the previous decades to the new Black "immigrants." In the South, medical examinations of recruits occasionally uncovered epidemic levels of syphilis and malaria in the rural areas. In South Carolina in 1917, one third of recruits failed the physical exam and 10 percent were found to be infected with syphilis.[27] To combat these problems, anti-malaria campaigns were started that were aimed at draining swamps and providing screens for doors and windows to the mostly Black residents. Additionally, anti-venereal disease campaigns were initiated to test and treat the populations close to army camps. This had the effect of raising living standards for rural Blacks and improving infant health.

During the 1920s opposition grew to governmental initiative programs to improve health. Organized medicine in particular perceived this as a threat to the private practice of medicine. The dismantling of infant health programs during the 1920s paved the way for devastating consequences during the Depression. The majority of Blacks still lived in the South and this region was hit particularly hard by the Depression. Due to lack of funding, Southern states closed many public health clinics and ended other public initiatives. Blacks were among the poorest groups in America and Southern Blacks were the poorest of the poor. Black infant mortality rates increased in the early 1930s and did not stabilize until Roosevelt's New Deal program replenished Southern states' public health budgets, relieved hunger, and perhaps most importantly, provided jobs for the unemployed.

War again brought an improvement in Black infant health. Soldiers' wives were beneficiaries of the Emergency Maternal and Infant Care (EMIC) program. This program paid for the delivery of children and the related medical care. This was especially beneficial to Southern women, Black and White, because it encouraged hospital deliveries. Many White women and the great majority of Black women were attended at home by midwives. Some, possibly many, midwives were excellent, providing better prenatal care than physicians. Others were dangerous and did more harm than good. The EMIC shielded Black women from the erratic quality of midwifery services and provided a place for delivery that was usually cleaner and better protected from the elements than were their homes.

EFFORTS TO IMPROVE INFANT HEALTH: WWI TO WWII (1915–1945)

In the early twentieth century voluntary professional societies were formed to examine one or another aspect of U.S. health. In 1909 some attendees at one such society meeting decided to form the American Association for the Study of the Prevention of Infant Mortality. The AASPIM was very active politically, it lobbied all levels of government to take a more active role in promoting the nation's health. Two of its founding members, Lillian Wald and Florence Kelley, conceived of and successfully lobbied for the creation of a federal children's agency. The Federal Children's Bureau was created in 1912 with Julia Lathrop as its chief. Lathrop and AASPIM, wanted to bring more rigor to the analysis of infant mortality. As such, they pushed the Census Bureau to create, in 1915, birth registration areas. Initially they covered only 31 percent of the population in ten states and the District of Columbia. The AASPIM also concerned itself with the medical care that mothers received while pregnant. At the time only wealthy women saw doctors during pregnancy and the examination was modest owing to Victorian sensibilities. In 1914 AASPIM President Whitridge Williams believed that reductions in infant mortality could be achieved through better prenatal care and that improving the quality of prenatal care could only come about with the elimination of midwives. Few native White women were midwives, they were mostly Black or foreign born, and the AASPIM generally succeeded in characterizing them as dirty and superstitious. However, their elimination caused most poor women to go without any prenatal care. The economic need for midwives was acknowledged and some, notably Josephine Baker, argued for the regulation of midwifery rather than its abolition, a position eventually adopted by New York City.

Most infant health activists looked to Europe for inspiration and models to emulate. Several European countries had laws prohibiting the employment of women shortly before and after delivery. A handful of American states passed similar laws but supporters noted that without an income supplement during this period such laws may do more harm than good. No state had income supplements for parturient women and the concept of maternity insurance was conceived as a remedy. Between 1915 and 1920 sixteen states voted on and defeated sickness insurance and maternity insurance bills. Responsibility for this outcome was attributed to the private insurance lobby. Despite the resounding defeat of maternity insurance, WWI did bring about the belief that children were an important national asset and something should be done to safeguard that asset. Lathrop, chief of the Children's Bureau, proposed legislation that would provide matching federal funds for states to provide motherhood training for poor women. Representative Jeanette Rankin (R. MT), the first woman member of the House of Representatives, introduced the bill to Congress in 1918, but it was tabled. The bill was reintroduced the next year by Sen. Morris Sheppard (D. TX) and Rep. Horace Towner (R. IA); it died in committee. The two introduced a third version of the bill in January of 1921 and after stiff opposition it passed as the Maternity and Infancy Act in November of that year. A fatal flaw was that its final version was funded for only five years; it had to be evaluated and re-approved in 1927. During the 1920s fiscal conservatism strengthened and Congressional support for social programs like Sheppard-Towner waned. Though it won a two year extension in 1927, the Sheppard-Towner

Act was repealed in 1929 after the 1928 election resulted in an even more conservative political climate.

Despite the hardship of the Depression, it was not until President Roosevelt's 1935 Social Security Act (SSA) that the federal government took steps to improve the nation's health. Even these steps were tentative in that a maternity insurance provision was dropped because of expected opposition from organized medicine. The SSA did have two sections devoted to infant and child health issues. Title IV provided states with funds for helping families with dependent children. Title V provided states with funds for maternal and infant health services, for handicapped children's services, and general child health services. The maternal and infant health part of Title V was the resurrection of the old Maternity and Infancy Act (Sheppard-Towner).

BLACK INFANT HEALTH: POST-WAR ERA (1946–1980)

The 1950s had both positive and negative developments for Black health. The growing Black urban population began to exploit opportunities for better education, higher incomes, and the commensurate better housing, nutrition, and access to higher quality health care. But there was still at least one third, possibly up to one half, of the Black American population, located mostly in the rural South, who were very poor, limited to low paying dead-end jobs, and essentially living outside the modern education and health care infrastructures. Prior to the 1950s, declines in infant mortality were due to advances in medicine (vaccines), better maternal and child care, better medical facilities, and improving socio-economic conditions. For example, the development of anti-microbial drugs helped reduce infant deaths due to illness. Between 1935 and 1950 the IMR declined at an annual rate of 4.3 percent.[28] This reduction was concentrated in the PNMR as its proportion of the IMR declined from 60 percent in 1900 to 30 percent in 1950.[29]

During the 1950s declining marginal returns began to set in, especially for Blacks. Centuries of poverty and deprivation had left female descendants of slaves, especially those still living in poverty in rural areas, smaller statured (shorter with smaller builds), in poorer physical condition, and, because of poor nutrition during childhood and adolescence, with less properly formed pelvises, relative to White urban women. Each of these three factors is sufficient to result in a small at-risk newborn. The combination of all three was beyond the capabilities of the medical infrastructure to alleviate. The annual rate of decline in the IMR for the nation fell to 1.1 percent for the years 1950 through 1965.[30]

The strong economy of the 1950s and the material gains of the Civil Rights movement did not benefit Blacks evenly. Stevans, Register, and Grimes found evidence suggesting that a sex difference existed between Black men and Black women regarding the employment gains from civil rights legislation.[31] Heckman claims that federal civil rights policy was directed at the South and the resulting gains were concentrated in the South.[32] Many of the relief programs of the Depression and the war were dismantled in the 1950s because they were perceived as no longer being needed. Medical care stagnated because the medical compass shifted to a concentration on investigating basic biological functions rather than providing service related programs. In addition, there were no major scientific breakthroughs.[33] The continuing mechanization of the agriculture sector, especially in the South, was causing unemployment and displacement among the rural poor. Despite the strong inverse relationship between socio-economic status (as measured by father's occupation) and mortalities of all types, the large socio-economic gains of the 1950s for most Americans did not translate into a substantial reduction in infant mortality. As can be seen in Table 2, White infant mortality declined from 26.8 per thousand in 1950 to 22.9 per thousand in 1960, while Black infant mortality rose from 43.9 per thousand in 1950 to 44.3 per thousand in 1960. The effects of migration are partly responsible for the lack of progress in Black infant health during the 1950s. Suburbs began to grow as Whites migrated from cities. Rural Blacks continued to migrate to the cities. As in Reconstruction, there was a lag in the response of community facilities to the Black migration. The result was overcrowding and poor sanitation, making Black housing an incubator of disease rather than a barrier against it. Outside the U.S., all other developed countries continued their prewar downward trend in infant mortality causing the U.S. to fall behind most European countries by the mid-1960s.

The 1960s saw the War on Poverty legislation of 1965 with the Medicaid Act providing medical care for the poor and disabled. Evaluations of its effectiveness in reducing infant mortality and morbidity are numerous. Of note with regard to Blacks is that in the South restrictions were set so that many Blacks were unable to participate in the Medicaid program. The 1967 poverty tour by U.S. senators yielded estimates as high as 10 million Americans in hunger. Raymond Wheeler of the University

TABLE 2
Infant Mortality Rates 1950–1995
(Per Thousand)

	50	60	70	80	81	82	83	84	85	86
Total	29.2	26.0	20.0	12.6	11.9	11.5	11.2	10.8	10.6	10.4
White	26.8	22.9	17.8	10.9	10.3	9.9	9.6	9.3	9.2	8.8
Black	43.9	44.3	32.6	22.2	20.8	20.5	20.0	19.0	18.9	18.8

	87	88	89	90	91	92	93	94	95
Total	10.1	10.0	9.8	9.2	8.9	8.5	8.4	8.0	7.6
White	8.5	8.4	8.1	7.6	7.3	6.9	6.8	6.6	6.3
Black	18.5	18.6	18.0	17.6	17.6	16.9	16.5	15.8	15.1

Source: National Center for Health Statistics, 1998.
http://www.cdc.gov/nchswww/

of North Carolina felt that the degree of hunger went beyond simple malnutrition to the point of starvation. Arnold Schaefer, the nutritionist at the Public Health Service responsible for investigating and determining the extent of malnutrition in the country, reported in 1969 that malnutrition in the rural South was so severe that nutrition related diseases and conditions, previously only seen in developing countries, were common.[34]

The 1960s also saw the development of safe and reliable methods of birth control. The greater use of birth control methods and the federal subsidization of family planning services are credited with causing the marked decline in fertility (16.6%) observed in the late 1960s and early 1970s.[35] The decline in fertility meant that fewer high risk births, those of high parity or high maternal age, were occurring. This contributed to the decline in infant mortality observed over the 1970s.

The 1970s were notable for the marked decline in infant mortality for both Blacks and Whites. However, the decline reflects advances in medical technology and not increases in infant health. That decade saw improvements in synthetic surfactants which speed the maturation of a newborn's lungs, improvements in incubators, improvements in assisted breathing devices (ventilators), improvements in the nutrition of premature babies, and the development of micro-intubation. The invasive devices used on adults are far too large to be used on small or premature newborns. The ability to produce quality small needles and tubes for intravenous lines and intra-nasal feeding (directly to the stomach via the nasal passage) was important in lowering the viability threshold to smaller sizes and earlier ages.

These technological developments permitted the growth of a new organizational development, the neonatal intensive care unit (NICU). The NICU's with their specially trained nurses and neonatologists and high technology were not cheap and contributed to rising medical care expenditures. Between 1970 and 1980, the rate of low birthweight declined 1.2 percentage points for both Blacks and Whites. The declines in infant mortality over the same decade are 10.4 percentage points for Blacks and 6.9 percentage points for Whites. The declines in infant mortality over this decade were due exclusively to technology, particularly for Blacks.

The 1970s were also notable for the culmination of several years of liberalized state laws regarding abortion with the national legalization of abortion occuring in 1973. With abortion legal, any unwanted pregnancy could be terminated.

EFFORTS TO IMPROVE INFANT HEALTH: POST-WAR ERA (1946–1980)

The years leading up to the 1939 amendment to the SSA were filled with talk of a national health program. A universal health program for enlisted men's families, the Emergency Maternal and Infant Care program (1943–46) and President Truman's talk of the need for national health care failed to move the U.S. forward on this issue. All such efforts were labeled communistic and were fiercely opposed by conservatives and organized medicine. However, there was support for expanding the private provision of health care. To this end Congress passed the Hospital Survey and Construction Act of 1946 (Hill-Burton Act) which financed the construction of health facilities in areas then deficient. Areas populated by Blacks such as the rural South especially benefitted from this program. The focus shifted from infant health as the Children's Bureau was transferred in 1946 from the Labor Department, a Cabinet department, to the Federal Security Administration (FSA), a non-Cabinet agency. In 1953, even as the FSA was being transformed into the Department of Health, Education, and Welfare and elevated to cabinet status, the Bureau was buried deeper in it. In 1963 it was transferred to the Welfare Department, and in 1969 it was stripped of its authority to administer Maternal and Child Health programs by President Nixon.

The response in the 1960s was part of the general war on poverty. The income supplement program called Aid to Families with Dependent Children (AFDC) was set up in 1962 and Medicaid, health insurance for the poor or disabled, was passed in 1965. The war in Vietnam probably put a hold on many other projects, but Congress still managed to create the National Health Service Corps which financed the educations of medical students who later worked in under-served areas of the country. Partly in response to the hunger tours and the relationship between maternal malnutrition and infant health, the Special Supplemental Food Program for Women, Infants, and Children (WIC), was set up in 1972.

The Medicaid Act was intended to increase access to medical care primarily for recipients of AFDC benefits. The extent to which improved Black birth outcomes is difficult to determine because of the many other social and economic changes occurring at the same time. The increasing availability and effectiveness of contraceptives and the expansion of the eligibility of legal abortions changed the composition of new mothers. At the same time, civil rights progress increased the economic opportunities for Blacks and improved their standard of living. New advances in medical technology were becoming widespread and having an influence on infant health. In addition, states implemented the Medicaid program and differences in the benefits and eligibility thresholds caused wide variations in outcomes.

Eisner et al. describe the rapid decline in IMR, annualized rate of 4.1 percent over the years 1965–73.[36] The decline was predominantly in the post-neonatal component, especially in rural areas where the annualized rate of decline in the PNMR was three times that of the NMR (8.9% versus 2.8%). The period was particularly beneficial for Black infants. The IMR for non-Whites, while still double that for Whites, declined at an annual rate of 1.5 times that for Whites (5.4% versus 3.8%).[37] Eisner et. al. identify Medicaid as only one of several factors responsible for the IMR decline. More recent research evaluating the expansion of Medicaid eligibility in the 1980s comes to stronger conclusions. Piper, Ray, and Griffin evaluated the 1985 Medicaid expansion in Tennessee and concluded that "our findings do not support the premise that expansion of Medicaid coverage per se will increase early use of prenatal care and decrease adverse [birth] outcomes."[38] Braverman et. al. found that in 1990 in California, Medicaid insured women were significantly more likely to obtain no or inadequate prenatal care as compared to privately insured women.[39] Guyer states in an editorial that "Insurance is necessary but not sufficient to insure better prenatal care and birth outcomes."[40]

The liberalization and legalization of abortion during the late 1960s and early 1970s may have influenced the IMR by reducing the number of "unwanted" infants born. Grossman and Jacobowitz (1981) evaluated the effects of both Medicaid and abortion policy on the race-specific county average NMR over 1970–72. They found that the coefficients on the Medicaid policy variables were rarely significant and always of small magnitude for both Blacks and Whites. The coefficients on the abortion reform variables were significantly negative for both Blacks and Whites supporting the hypothesis that the liberalization of abortion laws had a beneficial impact on NMR rates.[41] Further, the magnitude of the coefficients was three times greater for Blacks than for Whites. Their results suggest that greater control over reproductive events may have benefitted birth outcomes more than greater access to medical care.

BLACK INFANT HEALTH: MODERN DAY (1980–2000)

The main issues regarding infant health for the past twenty years have been demographic and behavioral. Newborns no longer die from the diarrheal and respiratory ailments as they did 100 years ago. Today infant death is greatly influenced by the choices made by the mother, and to a lesser extent the father, regarding her reproductive activity. In the 1990s teenage child bearing received a lot of attention. The norm is that child bearing should be delayed until the prospective parents are capable of providing a supportive home for the child. During the 1950s baby boom, the norm was to start families very young. A quarter of all women had their first child as a teenager.[42] In 1996, 11.3 percent of White births were to teenagers, 22.9 percent and 17.4 percent of Black and Hispanic births respectively were to teenagers.[43] During the earlier period, most women were married. In fact, half of all women married in their teens.[44] Provided there has been nutritional adequacy during childhood, a sixteen to nineteen year old has no greater risk of a poor birth outcome than an adult woman, all else constant.[45] Marital status is a different story. Single motherhood has been identified as a risk factor for infant death and low birthweight.[46] In 1996, 25.7 percent of White births were to single mothers, 69.8 percent and 40.9 percent of Black and Hispanic births respectively were to single mothers.[47]

In the 1990s, due to widely available and effective birth control and better income earning opportunities, women, especially middle class women, have been postponing child bearing. The women who have continued to bear children as teenagers are those with poor economic prospects and who have many of the problems that accompany a bleak life outlook. Well-to-do women have fewer children than poorer women and they invest a great deal to assure the good health of those children, whereas poorer women have more children and invest less in the health of each.[48] This results in a higher proportion of infants being born to women at higher risk of poor birth outcomes in two ways. One, through younger women who are at-risk due to adverse behavioral and socio-economic characteristics. Two, through older women with favorable behavioral and socio-economic characteristics but who are at-risk because of advanced age. The Black community, in particular, is affected by this phenomenon because its middle class is smaller, its poverty rates higher, and post-secondary education rates lower than those of White America.

During the 1990s more attention was also paid to substance use by pregnant women. The extent of use of illegal drugs such as heroin and cocaine by pregnant women and their effect on birth outcomes have been and continue to be extensively investigated.[49] The extent of the use of legal drugs such as alcohol and tobacco by pregnant women and their effect on birth outcomes have also been investigated.[50] Mittendorf et. al. estimate that cigarette smoking and alcohol consumption are responsible for 42.3 percent of preventable low birthweight cases while narcotics addiction is responsible for 13.5 percent of preventable low birthweight cases.[51] Chomitz, Cheung, and Lieberman estimate that 16.6 percent of low weight births in 1990 were due to maternal smoking. They also claim that the prevalence of smoking is ten times greater than that for cocaine use, 25 percent of pregnant women in 1990 smoked while 2.6 percent of them used cocaine. They state that "(c)igarette smoking is unequivocally the largest and most important known modifiable risk factor for low birthweight and infant death."[52] There has been a steady decline in the prevalence of maternal smoking, and in 1993, 16. 8 percent of White mothers smoked during pregnancy, 12.7 percent and 5.0 percent of Black and Hispanic mothers, respectively smoked during pregnancy.[53]

EFFORTS TO IMPROVE INFANT HEALTH: MODERN DAY (1980–2000)

The election of President Reagan lead to a severe tightening of AFDC eligibility in 1981. One result of this was that the proportion of poor children receiving AFDC fell to 50 percent in 1982 from a high of 80 percent in 1973.[54] In addition, states were prevented from paying cash assistance to a first-time pregnant mother until her sixth month. Funding for Part I of Title V of the SSA, (the maternal and infant health part), was converted to state controlled block grants. Blacks were disproportionately affected by these actions and, not surprisingly, by the mid 1980s the rate of decline in the Black infant mortality decreased greatly and low birthweight among Blacks actually increased. Faced with this consequence Congress decided, starting in 1985, to reverse some of the 1981 restrictions. This was done primarily by expanding Medicaid coverage to poor women not on AFDC primarily and raising the poverty threshold.

The most recent federal effort to reduce infant mortality was the 1991 Healthy Start program. Fifteen cities or large communities with historically high rates of infant mortality were selected with the goal of reducing mortality by 50 percent over five years. The program intends to reduce infant mortality through four strategies; reducing the proportion of high risk pregnancies, reducing the incidence of low birthweight and prematurity, increasing birthweight specific survival rate, and reducing specific cause mortality rates. The program is ambitious and has its critics. The number of cities affected by this program is small relative to the country as a whole so a significant impact on population statistics is not expected.

INTERNATIONAL COMPARISONS

How U.S. infant mortality rates compare to the rest of the world can give an indication of how effective U.S. efforts to reduce infant mortality have been. The logical comparison is to other developed countries because of similar levels of infrastructural support (sanitation, housing, transportation, energy, etc.). These are proxied by the members of the Organization for Economic Cooperation and Development (OECD), of which there are currently twenty-nine mostly European countries. The overall U.S. rank fell from twentieth in 1985 to twenty-first in 1990 and then to twenty-second in 1995. The U.S. White infant mortality rank fluctuated over this ten year period. U.S. Whites had a rank of sixteen in 1985, rising to thirteen in 1990 (tied with Spain), but falling to eighteen in 1995 (tied with Ireland). The rank of the U.S. Black infant mortality rate has held steady. U.S. Blacks ranked twenty-sixth in both 1985 and 1990, falling to twenty-seventh in 1995. In comparison to the world's top seven economies, the U.S. has ranked dead last throughout the ten year period. Considering only the U.S. White rate, the U.S. ranked fifth among the G-7 ahead of the United Kingdom and Italy, in both 1985 and 1990. However, in 1995 the U.S. White rank slipped to seventh out of seven. It should be noted that the U.S. is the only G-7 country without a national health care or health insurance system.

The OECD countries are not representative of the entire world, only of Europe. How does the U.S. infant mortality rate compare to non-OECD countries including developing countries? Table 6 lists the infant mortality rates of some Caribbean, Latin American, African, and Asian countries in 1994. As expected, most developing countries are doing badly with regard to infant mortality but some are doing surprisingly well. Barbados and Jamaica, predominantly Black countries, have lower infant mortality rates than do Black Americans, as does Costa Rica, whose population is predominantly of European descent. Malaysia's infant mortality rate is better than that of U.S. Blacks and Singapore's is better than that of U.S. Whites. Even economically struggling countries like Panama, Trinidad, and Mauritius are closing in on the U.S. Black infant mortality rate.

THE 21ST CENTURY

Where does the Black community go from here? How does the Black community step into the 21st century from the 20th and bring the health of its young along with it? The Black community needs to decide how important infant health is to it compared to other concerns.

Adverse labor market outcomes result in high rates of poverty for the Black community and poverty is strongly correlated with infant mortality and morbidity. Incarceration and low marriage rates restrict the ability of Black men to contribute to family life. During the 1980s, approximately 67 percent of Black single female-parent households were in poverty compared to 19 percent of Black single male-parent households.[55] An increase in the level of infant health cannot be sustained while these other sociological problems are present to a significant degree. But neither can rates of low birthweight and prematurity be reduced without a direct effort. While this is obvious to some, "(t)he American public health system has failed to address the contribution of other sectors (education, employment, housing, sanitation, and so on) to health outcomes in its preventive health programs."[56]

The trade-off for the Black community is between allocating resources at the direct medical causes of poor infant health outcomes and allocating resources at the indirect sociological factors influencing infant health outcomes. The dilemma is that the former will result in a relatively quick but temporary improvement in the infant health of those with the best access to medical health care, while the latter will result in a long-lived but slow improvement in the infant health of those living under sociologically adverse conditions.

EPILOGUE

I would sum up the things that, in my opinion, the Black community must do to assure healthy future generations in the following manner.

Since healthy infants mostly come from healthy women the Black community needs to reconceptualize infant health as integrated with women's health. This means that infant health should comprise all aspects of women's reproductive health starting from childhood and have the goal of ensuring that Black women are healthy enough to bear two or three normal weight full-term children and healthy enough to live long enough with sufficient daily activity to parent the children to adulthood. Universal reproductive health care for Black women and expansion of nutritional programs would be the logical policy tools. The tools should be administered to manifest a trade-off of higher mortality, i.e., fewer survivors, for lower morbidity among the survivors. For example, the threshold for starting newborn survival protocol could be artificially raised from the current 500 grams to, say, 1800 grams. The cost of caring for a very low weight infant is enormous.[57] The money saved from not putting newborns weighing less than 1800 grams in a neonatal intensive care unit could be used to increase the quantity and quality of pre-pregnancy and prenatal health care in an effort to reduce the rates of low birthweight and prematurity. Joyce, Corman, and Grossman found that NICU's were by far the costliest way of reducing infant death. The pathway of improving infant health should be through the improvement of women's health.[58]

The economics of the Black community cannot be ignored. Health care delivered by the market will not supply enough to the Black community because of its relative poverty. An alternative that is not dominated by organized medicine is needed for the Black community. Its characteristics should include a lower technological level (which should translate into lower cost), greater decentralization, an emphasis on preventing ill health and adverse health events, and a social welfare component. Resources should be allocated entirely to the provision of services and none on technological or biological research. Europe has successfully shown that substantial improvements in infant health are waiting to be realized with already existing technology and knowledge. This alternative health care delivery system could be a national health maintenance organization for the Black community. While suitable models may be hard to come by in the U.S., any health care system in the rest of the developed world will be a more than adequate model. For example, The Netherlands permits the choice of home births for low risk pregnancies, which comprised about one third of total births from the 1980s through early 1990s.[59] Home births are supervised by a midwife working in the area of residence of the mother. The midwife must be able to reach the mother's home within fifteen minutes of being called. An ambulance is on call in case of unexpected difficulties with the delivery that require transportation to a hospital. This practice certainly could not be copied in every detail. But an alternative health care system becomes even more attractive when one realizes that the causes of infant death differ by race. Prematurity and low birthweight are the leading causes of infant death for Blacks; congenital anomalies are the leading cause of infant death for Whites.[60]

The current generation has an obligation to improve the health of Black infants. Failing this obligation will more than condemn future generations in the Black community to ill health. As implied by the words which opened this essay, it will also condemn future generations of Blacks to remain in poverty and ignorance.

NOTES

1. Beardsley, Edward (1987), *A History of Neglect: Health Care for Blacks and Mill Workers in the Twentieth-Century South* Knoxville: The University of Tennessee Press, a.) p. vii, b.) p. 133.
2. Quarles, Benjamin. (1987), *The Negro in the Making of America (3rd ed.)* New York: Macmillan.
3. Grossman, Michael (1972), "On the Concept of Health Capital and the Demand for Health." *Journal of Political Economy* 80:223–225.
4. Paneth, Nigel (1995), *The Problem of Low Birthweight. The Future of Children* 5(1):19–34, p. 24.
5. Fuchs, Victor (1974a), *Some Economic Aspects of Mortality in Developed Countries. In the Economics of Health and Medical Care*, Edited by Mark Perlman, New York: John Wiley and Sons, pp. 174–93.
6. McCormick, Marie, Steven Gortmaker, and Arthur Sobol (1990), "Very Low Birthweight children: Behavior Problems and School Difficulties in a National Sample," *Journal of Pediatrics* 117(5): 687–93.
7. Paneth, 1995.

7a. Theory on the economics of migration predicts and empirical analysis confirms that the most capable and healthiest of a population migrate first and most

(Borjas, Bronars, and Trejo, 1992). This implies that the early Black migrants out of the South were among the healthiest of Southern Blacks. However, the health of the healthiest of Southern Blacks hardly compared favorably with that of the average Northern White as Table 1 suggests. (see Borjas, George, Stephan Bronars, and Stephen Trejo, (1992), "Self-Selection and Internal Migration in the United States," *Journal of Urban Economics* 32(2): 159–85.

8. Fogel, Robert and Stanley Engerman (1974), *Time on the Cross: Economics of American Negro Slavery*, Boston: Little Brown).

9. Fogel and Engerman, 1974. pp. 117–8.

10. Fogel and Engerman, 1974. p. 126.

11. David, Paul, Herbert Gutman, Richard Sutch, Peter Temin, and Gavin Wright (1976), *Reckoning with Slavery: A Critical Study in the Quantitative History of American Negro History*, New York: Oxford University Press, p. 283.

12. Fogel and Engerman, 1974. p. 122.

13. Fogel and Engerman, 1974. pp. 123–24.

14. David, et. al., 1976. p. 284.

15. David, et. al., 1976. p. 285.

16. Fogel and Engerman, 1974. pp. 137–138.

17. David, et. al., 1976. p. 139.

18. David, et. al., 1976. pp. 142–43.

19. Mellon, 1988. p. 147.

20. David, et. al., 1976. p. 155.

21. David, et. al., 1976. p. 157.

22. Meckel, Richard (1997), *Racialism and Infant Death. In Migrants, Minorities, and Health*, edited by Lara Marks and Michael Worboys, London: Routledge, pp. 70–93.

23. Hoffman, Fredrick (1896), "Race Traits and Tendencies of the American Negro," Publications of the American Economic Association 11(1): 1–329. New York: Macmillan.

24. DuBois, Burghardt (1906), *The Health and Physique of the Negro American*, Atlanta University Publications 11: 1–112, Atlanta: Atlanta University Press.

25. Meckel, Richard (1990), *Save the Babies: American Public Health Reform and the Prevention of Infant Mortality, 1850–1929*, Baltimore: The Johns-Hopkins University Press. p. 11.

26. Meckel, 1990. p. 89.

27. Beardsley, 1987. p. 133.

28. Fuchs, Victor (1974b), *Who Shall Live?: Health, Economics, and Social Choice*, New York: Basic Books. p. 32.

29. Fuchs, 1974. pp. 32–33.

30. Fuchs, 1974. p. 33.

31. Stevans, Lonnie, Charles Register, and Paul Grimes (1984), "Civil Rights legislation and Racial Employment Differentials," *Review of Black Political Economy* 13(3): 49–61.

32. Heckman, James (1990), "The Central Role of the South in Accounting for the Economic Progress of Black Americans," *American Economic Review* 80(2):262–26.

33. Shapiro, Sam, Edward Schlesinger, and Robert Nesbitt (1968), *Infant, Perinatal, Maternal and Childhood Mortality in the U.S.*, Cambridge MA: Harvard University press.

34. Beardsley, 1987. p. 293.

35. Eisner, Victor, Margaret Pratt, Alfred Hexter, Marion Chabot, and Naresh

Sayal (1978), "Improvement in Infance and Preinatal Mortality in the United States, 1965–1973: Priorities for Intervention," *American Journal of Public Health* 68(4):359–64.

36. Eisner, et al., 1978. p. 361.
37. Eisner, et al., 1978. p. 360.
38. Piper, Joyce, Wayne Ray, and Marie Griffin, (1990), "Effects of Medicaid Eligibility Expansion on Prebatl Care and Pregnancy Outcome in Tennessee." *Journal of the American Medical Association*. 264(17): 2219–23.
39. Braverman, Paula, Trude Bennett, Charlotte Lewis, Susan Egerter, and Johnathan Showstack (1993), "Access to Prenatal to Care Following Major Medicaid Eligibility Expansions," *Journal of the American Medical Association* 269(10):1285–91.
40. Guyer, Bernard (1990), "Medicaid and Prenatal Care: Necessary but Not Sufficient," *Journal of the American Medical Association* 264(17):2264–65.
41. Grossman, Michael and Steven Jacobowitz (1981), "Variations in Infant Mortality Rate Among Counties of the United States: The Roles of Public Policies and Programs," *Demography* 18(4): 695–713.
42. Creighton-Zollar, Ann (1993), *The Social Correlates of Infant and Reproductive Mortality in the U.S.*, New York: Garland Publishing. p. 17.
43. National Center for Health Statistics (1997), Monthly Vital Statistics Report 46(1). p. 13.
44. Creighton-Zollar, 1993. p. 17.
45. Geronimus, Arlene and Sanders Korenman (1993), "Maternal Youth or Family Background? On the Health Disadvantages of Infant with Teenage Mothers," *American Journal of Epidemiology* 137(2):213–225; and Kleinman, Joel and Samuel Kessel (1987), "Racial Differences in Low Birthweight," *New England Journal of Medicine* 317(12):749–53.
46. Institute of Medicine (1985), Preventing Low Birthweight, Richard Behrman, Chair: Committee to Study the Prevention of Low Birthweight. Washington, D.C.: National Academy Press.
47. National Center for Health Statistics (1996), Health United States, 1995. Hyattsville, MD: Public Health Service. p. 14.
48. Beciser, Gary and Gregg Lewis, (1973), "On the Interaction of Quantity and Quality of Children," *Journal of Political Economics* 81(2) (Part II): 5279–88.
49. Institute of Medicine (1985), Preventing Low Birthweight, Richard Behrman, Chair: Committee to Study the Prevention of Low Birthweight. Washington, D.C.: National Academy Press; and Chasnoff, Ira, Dan Griffith, Scott MacGregor, Kathryn Dirkes, and Kayreen Burns (1989), "Temporal Patterns of Cocaine Use in Pregnancy," *Journal of the American Medical Association* 263(14):1741–44.
50. Institute of Medicine, 1985; and Olsen, Jorn, Altomiro da Costa Pereira, and Sjurdur Olsen (1991), "Does Maternal Smoking Modify the Effect of Alcohol on Fetal Growth?" *American Journal of Public Health* 81 (1): 69–73.
51. Mittendorf, Robert, Marguerite Herschel, Michelle Williams, Judith Hibbard, Atef moawad and Kwang-sun Lee (1994), "Reducing the Frequency of Low Birthweight," *U.S. Obstetrics and Gynecology* 83(6):1056–58.
52. Chomitz, Virginia, Lilian Cheung, and Ellice Lieberman (1995), "The Role of Lifestyle in Preventing Low Birthweight," *The Future of Children* 5(1):121–138.
53. National Center for Health Statistics (1996).
54. Hughes, Dana and Lisa Simpson (1995), "The Role of Social Change in Preventing Low Birthweight," *The Future of Children* 5(1):87–102.
55. O'hare, William (1989), "Black Demographic Trends in the 1980s," In *Health*

Policies and Black Americans edited by David Willis. New Brunswick, NJ: Transaction Publishers, pp. 35–55.

56. Avery, (1992). p. 41.

57. Racine, Andrew, Theordore Joyce, and Michael Grossman (1992), "Effectiveness of Health Care Services for Pregnant Women and Infants," *The Future of Children* 2(2):40–57.

58. Joyce, Corman and Grossman (1988).

59. Treffers, P. and R. Lann (1986). "Regional Prenatal mortality and Regional Hospitalization at Delivery in The Netherlands." *British Journal of Obstetrics and Gynecology* 93(7):690–93. p. 690.

60. Singh, Gopal and Stella Yu (1995), "Infant mortality in the U.S.: Trends, Differentials, and Projections, 1950 through 2010," *American Journal of Public Health* 85(7):957–64.

21

ECONOMIC COMMUNITY OF WEST AFRICAN STATES: FROM AN ECONOMIC UNION TO A PEACEKEEPING MISSION?

E. Ike Udogu

INTRODUCTION

African countries were not part of that great industrial revolution of the eighteenth century that spawned the process of modernization and industrialization in western Europe and North America.[1] Indeed, they were colonies of some of the European powers. As a result, they were sometimes referred to as regimes of delayed industrialization[2] because they only started industrializing following independence. Hitherto, they served fundamentally as the sources for raw materials.

Even after they gained their sovereignty on paper, it was discovered that they still relied heavily on the colonial powers for trade and economic survival. If African countries were to exculpate themselves from what was later termed neocolonialism, by some scholars, it was incumbent upon them to do business with each other. This philosophy was generally attractive and welcomed by some of the political actors who believed that economic sovereignty was a *sine qua non* for political sovereignty. How might these newly independent nations pursue their objective of continental economic autarky? The initial strategy was the creation of regional economic unions.

So, in East Africa, there was the East African Economic Community. In French-speaking African states, there were a host of economic unions of which L'Organization Commune Africaine et Malagache (OCAM), L'Union Douaniere et Economic de L'Afrique Centrale (UDEAC), and L'Union des Etats d'Afrique Centrale (LTEAC) were some examples. And, in West Africa was created the Economic Community of West African States (ECOWAS). This essay examines the *raison d'etre* of the ECOWAS, and its contemporary peacekeeping role, against the backdrop of economic crisis in the area. Additionally, it seeks to briefly examine the role of Nigeria, the area's hegemonic power in the peace building enterprise within the context of the republic's foreign policy and national interest.

ECONOMIC COMMUNITY OF WEST AFRICAN STATES (ECOWAS)

The widespread trend toward some form of regional economic grouping in both developed and developing countries is no doubt due to growing awareness of the importance of economic interdependence for the promotion of the economic well-being of the peoples of these countries, and for solving and facilitating the solution of some of the knotty economic problems which face individual countries. Even developed countries, which in the 1950s shunned regional integration, have since altered their views and style. For example, the European Coal and Steel community was formed in 1952, and the European Common market in 1957.[3] These were some of the precursors to the modern European Economic Community and European Union.

The United Nations has also encouraged regional integration. Indeed, the Resolution on the "International Development strategy for the second UN development decade, urged developing countries to continue their attempts to put into effect plans for sub-regional and regional development."[4] It has also been recognized that self-reliance and growing cooperation among developing nations will further strengthen their role in the new international economic order.

The beginning of the idea of regional economic grouping in West Africa can be traced back to initiatives emanating from the Economic Commission for Africa.[5] Representatives of the various African countries have held several meetings called by that Commission. For example, there was the Lagos Conference on Industrial Coordination in West Africa in November, 1963; the Niamey Conference on Economic Cooperation in October, 1963; and the Accra Conference of April, 1967, where the article of Association for the establishment of an Economic Community for West Africa was signed.[6]

In 1968, heads of state of the West African group met in Monrovia, Liberia and signed the Protocol establishing the West African Regional group. The only achievement of the group was the preparation by Nigeria and Guinea of priority studies of areas of cooperation. The agreed areas of cooperation were trade, transport, communication, education, cultural exchange and information, research, health, energy, and heavy industries.[7]

A number of attempts made at regional cooperation ended up in fiasco, but these failures did not stop the West African leaders from seeking other means of cooperation. It was to this end that Togo and Nigeria worked assiduously for the creation of regional economic cooperation.

THE BIRTH OF ECOWAS

The treaty establishing the ECOWAS was signed on May 28, 1975, by fifteen countries. These countries were Dahomey (now the Republic of Benin), the Republic of Gambia, the Republic of Ghana, the Democratic Republic of Guinea, Guinea Bissau, the Republic of Ivory Coast, the Republic of Liberia, the Republic of Mali, the Islamic Republic of Mauritania, the Republic of Niger, the Federal Republic of Nigeria, the Republic of Senegal, the Republic of Sierra Leone, the Republic of Togo, and the Republic of Upper Volta (now Burkina Faso). Cape Verde joined later, and that brought the total membership to sixteen.

The aims of ECOWAS are stated in Article Two of the treaty of the Community:

1. It shall be the aim of the Community to promote cooperation and development in all fields of economic activity particularly in the fields of industry, transport, monetary and financial questions and in social and cultural matters for the purpose of raising the standard of living of its peoples, of increasing and maintaining economic stability, of fostering closer relations among its members and of contributing to the progress and development of the African continent.
2. The Community shall by stages ensure:
   a. the elimination of custom duties and other similar charges in respect of importation and exportation of goods among Member States;
   b. the abolition of quantitative and administrative restrictions on trade among the Member States;
   c. the establishment of a common custom tariff and a common commercial policy towards third countries;
   d. the abolition as between the Member states of the obstacles to the free movement of persons, services and capital;
   e. the harmonization of agricultural policies and the promotion of common projects in the Member States notably in the field of marketing, research and agro-industrial enterprises;

f. the implementation of schemes for the joint development of transport, communication, energy and other infrastructural facilities as well as the evolution of a common policy in these fields;
g. the harmonization of the economic and industrial policies of the Member States and the elimination of disparities in the levels of development of Member States;
h. the harmonization required for the proper functioning of the Community, of the monetary policies of the Member States;
i. the establishment of a fund for cooperation, compensation and development; and
j. Such other activities calculated to further the aims and objectives of the Community as the Member States may from time to time undertake in common.[8]

There exist a number of factors that made it difficult and sometimes impossible for West African states to implement the aims contained in the treaty. Such difficulties and problems have included inadequate infrastructure; road, railway, telecommunications, and other vital links for free movement of goods and persons. There have also been vested desires for the preservation of the existing state of affairs and the persistence of semi-colonial ties, sometimes referred to as neocolonialism, and lack of grassroots involvement.[9] These are the same as the problems that have prevented the realization of African unity at the continental level.

Other difficulties known to have prevented economic union in West Africa in the past include the small proportion of world trade taking place within the sub-region, the different commercial and financial policies pursued by the countries as a result of their past colonial experience; over dependence of many of the African countries on revenues from Import duties and in some, manipulation of such duties to encourage foreign capital inflow and to protect industries; the existence of different currencies and payment arrangements and competition among them to have visible signs of development even when these are uneconomic.

It is significant to note that the lesson to be learned from these problems and difficulties confronting earlier attempts to bring the West African nations together is that integration is a long term task subject to the uncertainties that characterize many international attempts.

The formation of ECOWAS does not mean an instant solution to the problems confronting the area. It, however, provides the mechanism for combating the problems. One notable issue is that West African countries are mainly primary producers, the agricultural sector employing over 60 percent of the labor force.[10] The member states' products are oriented to the market of developed countries. And until the economies of ECOWAS states undergo structural transformation through which agriculture (as is practiced today) will lose its preponderance to industry, ECOWAS member countries may not significantly be each other's customers. Economic integration under such circumstances is not likely to bring about a sizeable expansion of intra-ECOWAS trade in the immediate future.

Another issue confronting the ECOWAS states is that of common payment, a problem that even the European Union is facing today. West African currencies which are tied to different major international currencies are not all convertible into each other. Article 38 of the ECOWAS treaty provides for creation of a Committee of West African Central Banks which would determine a clearing system of payments for the region.[11] Currency unification would serve as an effective response to the problem of disparate exchange rates within an integrated scheme. It is hoped that under one currency the liberty for capital movement will be improved, and it would also take care of problems of balance of payments in intra-union trade.

Moreover, a major problem that ECOWAS faces is that of determination of location of major industries. Indeed, every country wants industries, since they provide jobs and are believed to enhance modernization.[12]

ECONOMIC AND THEORETICAL RATIONALE FOR ECOWAS

The theoretical rationale of economic integration in West Africa is generally based on possible ways in which economic integration affects the rate of growth of Gross National Product (GNP) of participating countries. Such economic integration should therefore result in some of the following: 1. Enlargement of the size of the market for firms otherwise producing below optimum capacity. A large market catering for about 130–200 million consumers is also considered significant to sustain heavy industries such as engineering and chemical plants. These would be vehicles for modernization. 2. Economic integration will increase the level of economic activity through increased trade, and at the same time allow the exploitation of external economies and inter-industry linkages and also lead to lowering of production cost. 3. The economic integration envisaged by ECOWAS would lead to economic cooperation, and promotion of economic efficiency through specialization. In short, economic integration would bring about more adequate use of resources and harmonization of economic and trade policies among member states.

The significance of developing the infrastructure cannot be over-stressed and remains one of the important objectives of the ECOWAS. And indeed, without an efficient regional transport and communication network, economic integration and later political union would have little meaning.

One of the most important anticipated outcomes of the present economic union of West African States is the eventual continental union which could emerge from such an integration. This dream is reinforced by Article 27 (1 and 2) of ECOWAS Treaty, which states that:

> Citizens of Member States shall be regarded as Community citizens and accordingly Member States undertake to abolish all obstacles to their freedom of movement and residence within the Community.
>
> Member States shall by agreement with each other exempt Community citizens from holding visitors visas and resident permits and allow them to work and undertake commercial and industrial activities within their territories.[13]

Social intercourse is extremely important in any kind of politico-economic relations. Such intercourse in the past has been mitigated by the problems of visas and, generally, free travel among the various countries. It could be argued that as more Africans travel and meet with other Africans outside their own states, this could kindle a spirit of understanding which is helpful for African unity.

Thus, Article 27 (1 and 2) provides not only the groundwork for economic integration in West Africa, but also a model which is very significant for a future continental union. Optimism was even expressed that ECOWAS working together with other regional groupings could further the 1991 African Economic Treaty aimed at establishing a common market in A..D. 2025. Indeed, it is also hoped that like in Europe, this treaty could lead to the inauguration of an elected African Parliament with a supranational characteristic.[14]

In sum, it is one thing to formulate policies and quite another to implement them. The quest to address the problem of underdevelopment in the sub-region is without doubt very urgent. Unfortunately, it is over two decades now since ECOWAS was created, yet the area has not come close to satisfactorily resolving the fundamental issues contained in its treaty.

To be sure, trade flows between member nations of ECOWAS appear to have increased since the organization's inception. But, contended Mamit Deme, "the volume of trade flows between ECOWAS member countries and industrial countries is proportionately much larger than the intraregional trade flows. For ECOWAS members as a whole, the average annual volume of imports from industrialized countries during the 1981–1992 period was US$13.22 billion. For the same period the average annual volume of imports from African countries was merely US$1.59 billion, of which US$1.24 billion is from ECOWAS member countries."[15]

Arguably, the above issue is not based on ECOWAS' lack of efforts; it is based on both internal and external conditionalities. Internally, the area has been faced with numerous civil wars, military coups, and counter coups. Externally, the international lending organizations have made the region completely dependent on the creditors, such that a majority of member states of the ECOWAS lack the major elements of sovereignty.[16] The economic misery suffered by the poor in these states is so poignant that a majority of the citizens have been forced to develop antagonistic attitudes toward the state; indeed, they may have in their vexation toward the state "deligitimized" it.

The Human Development Index (HDI), of the 1997 Human Development Report, of the sixteen member states of the ECOWAS is not reassuring against the backdrop of the aims and objectives of the organization. Sierra Leone ranked (175), Niger (173), Burkina Faso (172), Mali (171), Guinea (167), Gambia (165), Guinea Bissau (163), Senegal (160), Mauritania (150), Togo (147), Benin (146), Cote d'Ivoire (145), Nigeria (141), Ghana (132), and Cape Verde (123); Liberia was omitted in the survey because of the civil war in that country.[17] But there were a total of 175 nations measured for this report. The Human Development Index report combines life expectancy, literacy, and distribution of income or basic purchasing power as generally linked with a nation's overall economic prosperity. In short, the "statistics reflect people's well-being and the opportunities that they actually enjoy."[18]

Given the aims and objectives of ECOWAS as stated in the organization's treaty and its poor economic record so far, why did the group embark upon a risky and unpredictable peacekeeping mission in Liberia? Furthermore, could this mission signal a shift in its emphasis on economic development in the area to that of peacekeeping in a region that is fraught with ethnic and political problems?

PEACEKEEPING MISSION: A CONCEPTUAL AND THEORETICAL ANALYSIS

Arguably, peacekeeping attempts predate the modern nation-state system. This is especially so when defined within the context of maintaining international peace and security. It was, however, during the birth of the modern state system that the quest for peace and stability took on an added dimension. This policy was pursued within the framework of a balance of power system. Historically, two major epochs, among others, might illustrate the move toward peace and security in Europe. The first period was from 1648 (the treaty of Westphalia) to 1789 (the French Revolution), commonly referred to as the first golden age of classical balance of power. The second period was from 1815 to 1914, generally touted the second golden age of classical balance of power.

During the former, religious conflict was reduced, mercantilism was superseded by free trade, and absolute monarchies gradually started to lose their significance to popular sovereignty. Although wars between nation-states persisted, they were of low intensity.[19] The latter saw such powers as England, France, Prussia, Austria-Hungary, and Russia pursue a policy of stable and ideologically similar or uniform international politics.[20] This state of relative peace provided opportunities for free movement of people and trade.

Following WWII and in the aftermath of the decolonization process in Africa and elsewhere, the proliferation of independent sovereign states with their distinct and often conflicting national interests created international tensions. Indeed, the character of the post-colonial state in Africa, and the balkanization of Eastern Europe into independent sovereign states following the collapse of communism in that area created severe ethnic strains (for example, the Republic of Georgia), and in some cases irredentist wars (for instance, Bosnia-Herzogovina and Yugoslavia).

The formation of the League of Nations after WWI and its successor, the United Nations after WWII, were intended to ameliorate activities by nation-states that were likely to threaten international peace and security. It was in attempts to avoid the catastrophic consequences of both wars, that the international community, *inter alia*, encouraged the use of peacekeeping missions when measures such as the use of the good offices of the UN and regional endeavors failed to lead to the pacification of a conflict.

The general strategy of a peacekeeping operation is the interposition of a multinational force between combatants to provide the enabling environment for peaceful resolution of a political dispute. In this regard, the views propounded by the International Peace Academy in the early 1980s is instructive and approximates the overall mechanism of the process, viz: "the prevention, containment, moderation and termination of hostilities between or within states through the medium of third-party intervention organized and directed internationally, using multinational military, police, and civilian personnel to restore and maintain peace."[21]

The activities of the UN in the area of peacekeeping, peace making, and peace enforcement have been daunting. Indeed, it has had its successes and failures in Central America, the Middle East, Asia, and elsewhere. The intensification of the peacekeeping role of the UN appears to have gathered momentum following the end of the Cold War. Indeed, soft states that were pawns in the superpower rivalry and the politics of the zero-sum-game, were now free to exercise their right to national self-determination. The consequences were disastrous for such dependencies as Mozambique, Zaire, Angola, Ethiopia, and others. In fact, of the thirty-eight peacekeeping missions sponsored by the United Nations since its inception in 1945, twenty-five were put into force between 1988 and 1995.[22]

Moreover, with the emergence of the "new international world order," the political calculus within the UN as to its strategy for handling conflicts had to be adjusted in accordance with contemporary realism—i.e, the collapse of communism in the Soviet Union. This demise, in the thinking of many observers, not only signaled the victory of democracy over communism, but also illustrated its superiority. With the Russian Federation, the major remnant following the implosion of the former USSR, now a full fledged member of the democratic club in the UN, and with the wind of change and euphoria of political liberalization blowing across Africa and elsewhere, the UN was "compelled" to assume two non-traditional roles. The first was the enforcement of peace, such as in Yugoslavia and Somalia, and the second was to take on the role of an instrument for democratic transition.[23] The latter was designed to build and promote the conditionalities for the sustenance of democracy and peace. This philosophy was propagated in 1992 by the erstwhile Secretary-General Boutros Boutros-Ghali who termed this genre of UN peacekeeping strategy in his Agenda for Peace, *Postconflict Peace Building*.[24]

In Africa, UN peacekeeping missions have taken on different forms because of the complexities of the political issues in the area. For instance, in Angola and Mozambique, it took on the onerous task of implementing political as well as democratic transitions. In Namibia, it conducted elections to establish an independent state of Namibia, and is presently preparing Western Sahara for a national referendum intended to lead to the area's independence from Morocco.

In sum, with all its good intentions, the UN is generally plagued with a number of contradictions—rooted in its axioms of sovereignty, neutrality, and attaining democratic peace. To compound the organization's problems is the fact that UN agents are often confronted with both international and indigenous obstacles, as for example, Somalia, that sometimes render their missions impossible. The situation in Liberia falls within this framework, and hence the allurement for a regional solution to a common problem in the continent.

THE LIBERIAN CRISIS

The frequency of civil wars in the continent is commonplace due to economic and ethnopolitical crisis. The sometimes overt and covert involvement of African states in the internal affairs of countries experiencing such wars, in contravention of Article 2, paragraph 4 of the UN charter, which forbids member nations of the UN from doing so, is not novel. In West Africa, though, the collective action of member states of the Economic Community of West African States (ECOWAS) in the Liberian political crisis was unique. This was so because provisions were not made in the ECOWAS treaty for a military action to bring about peace to a member state. To be sure, African countries have been involved in peacekeeping efforts, but these were carried out under the auspices of the United Nations which has the infrastructure for such an undertaking. Witness for example, the UN peacekeeping operation in the Suez Canal in 1956 to resolve the British, Israeli, and Egyptian crisis, and the Congo issue of 1960.[25] Moreover, such actions were generally implemented on an *ad hoc* basis to tackle conflicts that were construed to be a threat to international peace and security.

It is true that such regional organizations as the Organization of American States (OAS) has been successful at regional peace operations in the Americas. The OAS operated in the Dominican republic in 1965 and more recently in Haiti to restore democracy. In these operations, the United States remained the hegemonic power and generally acted on the basis of her national interest, and within the context of the Monroe doctrine, which places the area within the sphere of its influence. In Africa, however, no regional organization has ever taken a peacekeeping mission before ECOWAS interloped in Liberia.[26]

The major regional power in the region and ECOWAS itself is Nigeria, which like any other regional hegemon, tends to equate its national interest with that of the group. Nigeria became the major *dramatis personae* in the Liberian political saga, when it created ECOWAS Cease-fire Monitoring Group, whose acronym was ECOMOG. Despite initial opposition within its ranks spearheaded by Cote d'Ivoire and Burkina Faso, ECOMOG pursued with resiliency its twin objectives of making and enforcing peace.[27] The following discussion centers on Nigeria, whose participation was paramount for the successful conclusion of the mission.

NIGERIA AND ECOMOG

There are two possible contending theories, or schools of thought, regarding Nigeria's involvement and leadership in the operation. Scholars of the first school argue that the internal political dynamics in the country accounted for Nigeria's active participation in the peace mission, especially since such matters are generally within the purview of the United Nations. The second school stresses the importance of Nigeria in the region and the centrality of its foreign policy in West Africa in particular, and Africa in general.

According to the first school, President Babangida's transition program to a democratic rule in Nigeria from 1989–1993 appeared to be going nowhere. Primary elections were canceled and rescheduled. Babangida and his administration's ability to dribble the political entrepreneurs and society "maradonically," by the late 80s and early 90s had created profound anxiety and frustration, particularly, among members of the informed public and the media. Indeed, the general opinion in the country regarding the transition program was that it was a farce, if not a ruse. They contended that despite the administration's timetable for handing over power to a democratically elected politicians, Babangida had his own "hidden" agenda. The print medium and others who belonged to this school were relentless in their criticism of the administration on this score. They insisted that Nigeria's profound involvement in ECOMOG was intended to divert the people's attention from the political blunders at home. They argued, that the assumption on the part of the regime was, that Nigerians would rally behind their government at a time of crisis involving a preponderant number of Nigerian soldiers. Within this school, moreover, were those who contended that, Babangida, having survived a military coup, wanted to keep the soldiers busy by sending the possible "trouble" makers in the military away from Lagos and Abuja. In this way, they would be less likely to foment another coup in light of the internal political dislocation and unsteadiness.

The second school of thought which I shall term the national interest school, attempts to explain Nigeria's activities in the ECOWAS and ECOMOG within the context of Nigerian foreign policy. It is on the assumptions of this school that I will focus my succeeding analysis.

ECOMOG AND THE NATIONAL INTEREST SCHOOL

The ethnically induced civil war in Liberia between the Americo-Liberian and the indigenous population which was triggered following sergeant Samuel Doe's coup d'etat of April 1980 had reached its crescendo by the late 1980s. The activities of Charles Taylor and his National Patriotic Front of Liberia (NPFL) and the other forces were causing casualties both in human life and property. The refugee problem was taxing the resources of the neighboring countries.[28] Furthermore, in the carnage, foreign nationals became a pawn in the civil war. For whatever tactical reasons, Nigerian citizens living in Liberia became the major *bete noire* and target for NPLF's retribution.[29] Arguably, Nigeria's prestige as the hegemon in the area and harassment of its citizens living in Liberia, the political instability in Sierra Leone, the refugee problems in the neighboring countries, and the possible domino-effect of the civil war in the region served as the rationales for Nigeria's military *putsch* in Liberia—a mission which General Sani Abacha claimed cost the Nigerian government over US$3 billion.[30]

Theoretically, a hegemon assumes a leadership stance in a community of nations for the purpose of expanding its power, influence, authority, and control in order to obtain greater economic and security advantage.[31] Within this context, it seeks a policy of expansionism through economic, political, and military control. A hegemonic power tends to succeed in its endeavor because of its overbearing and sometimes intimidating presence. Such an imposing stature is furthered by its ability to provide goods and services that are needed by the "lesser" and weaker states. Indeed, Pax Britannica and Pax Americana have been cited as examples of hegemonic states enforcing peace and security on the international scene and system as a strategy to promote the interest of the hegemonic state.[32] Today, in the political conversation in West Africa and Nigeria in particular, there is already talk of Pax Nigeriana[33] in the wake of Nigeria's successful performance in the Liberian crisis. In fact, with a population of 80–100 million, a GDP of $30 billion and a strong military to match, Nigeria is on course to pursue its interest in the region.

In order to pursue its foreign policy objectives within the African and regional context,[34] Nigeria invoked the tenets of Chapter VIII, Article 52 of the charter of the United Nations on Regional Arrangements. In this way, ECOMOG was able to receive support from the international community, because its actions could not be misconstrued as usurping the powers of the Security Council under Article 34 and 35.[35]

Indeed, Article 52 states:

> 1. Nothing in the present Charter precludes the existence of regional arrangements or agencies for dealing with such matters relating to the maintenance of international peace and security as are appropriate for regional action, provided that such arrangements or agencies and their activities are consistent with the Purposes and Principles of the United Nations.
> 2. The Members of the United Nations entering into such arrangements or constituting such agencies shall make every effort to achieve pacific settlement of local disputes through such regional arrangements or by such regional agencies before referring them to the Security Council.
> 3. The Security Council shall encourage the development of pacific settlement of local disputes through such regional agencies either on the initiative of the states concerned or by reference from the Security Council . . . [36]

Having cleared the above hurdle, as it were, Nigeria was now prepared to pursue its foreign policy interest within the framework of ECOMOG. To this end, President Babangida declared:

> We are in Liberia because events in that country have led to massive destruction of property, the massacre by all parties of thousands of innocent civilians including foreign nationals, women, and children, some of whom have sought sanctuary in the churches, mosques, diplomatic missions, hospitals, and under Red Cross protection contrary to all recognized standards of civilized behavior and international ethics and decorum.[37]

Although the above assertion represented the official view of the administration, there may be two other remote causes for Nigeria's reaction to the Liberian upheaval. First, the war was affecting Nigeria's economic interest (both governmental and non-governmental). Second, the Samuel Doe regime was friendly to the Babangida Administration, and Babangida, for his own personal interest, did not want to see a friendly government replaced by a hostile one—i.e., Charles Taylor. After all, Nigeria established the Ibrahim Babangida School of Political Science and Strategic Studies in Monrovia for a cost of US$20 million in appreciation of the cordial relations between both governments.[38] Furthermore, Nigeria was concerned that if Taylor was allowed to succeed, he might foment trouble in Gambia, Guinea, and Sierra Leone, countries that were considered friendly to Nigeria.

Economically, and because of its share size and wealth in the region, Nigeria's export to member nations of ECOWAS is substantial. However, it is difficult to observe the effect of economic growth in intra-ECOWAS trade in the overall well-being of the citizens of member states. In fact, Mamit Deme in his study discovered that "imports from industrialized countries by Nigeria, Cote d'Ivoire, Liberia, Ghana and Senegal on the average grew (or decreased) by –3%, –1%, 24%, 6% and –2%, while those from ECOWAS partner countries grew by 8%, 14%, 22%, 3%, and 5%."[39] These figures are represented in Table 1.

The figures presented below represent business flows at the official level. The volume of trade between private citizens at the informal level that are unaccounted for, is phenomenal. This involves the underground economic intercourse which is rampant in the region.[40] Also, the table shows that the ECOWAS still spend more for goods and services from Western Europe.

Nigeria created the ECOWAS because it was in her interest, realist scholars would argue. Economically, too, political instability in the area could not further its interest of economic integration and mutual cooperation.[41] In fact, the desire for regional stability has always been a major objective of the various Nigerian regimes from Prime Minister Sir Abubakar Tafawa Balewa to General Sani Abacha. For example, General Yakubu Gowon who was a signatory to the ECOWAS treaty in 1975 observed that such a grouping was likely to mitigate the role of France among Francophone West African states. Economic health in the area could promote political security and the protection of Nigerian borders.[42] General Olusegun Obasanjo also noted that Nigerian foreign policy objective included the establishment of the desired political and economic

TABLE 1
1981–1992 Average Annual Volume and Rate of Growth of Import by Each ECOWAS Member Country

	Imports from Partner Countries		Imports from Industrialized Countries	
ECOWAS	Rate of Growth (%)	(Million $)	Rate of Growth (%)	(Million $)
1. Benin	13	30	16	341
2. Burkina Faso	9	118	2	235
3. Cote d'Ivoire	14	323	–1	1,350
4. Cape Verde	*	*	*	*
5. Gambia	–1	6	7	113
6. Ghana	3	215	6	740
7. Guinea	7	8	16	55
8. Guinea Bissau	12	0.5	5	342
9. Liberia	22	22	24	1,209
10. Mali	8	129	2	254
11. Mauritania	16	20	–2	298
12. Niger	–3	58	3	232
13. Nigeria	8	82	–3	6,099
14. Senegal	5	138	–2	746
15. Sierra Leone	45	7	1	118
16. Togo	23	55	–1	360

Source: Mamit Deme, "The Impact of ECOWAS on Intraregional Trade Flows: An Empirical Investigation" *The Review of Black Political Economy*, Vol. 23, No. 3 (Winter 1995), p. 119.
* Cape Verde was not included in the table.

conditions in the area to promote Nigeria's economic development.[43] President Babangida summed up Nigeria's interest thus: "When certain events occur in this sub-region . . . which are bound to affect Nigeria's politico-military and socio-economic environment we should not stand by as helpless and hapless spectators."[44]

Moreover, the fact that the internal economic dynamics of a nation-state tends to influence foreign policy decisions is illustrated in the concern and pressures from multinational corporations who stand to lose a lot of money in unhealthy political climates. For example, Cadbury Nigeria Limited, one of several major corporations doing business within the ECOWAS member states brought pressure to bear on the Nigerian government to create an enabling environment in Liberia for it to do business. Indeed, Margaret Vogt wrote: "The Managing Director of Cadbury Nigeria Limited [a confection company] stated that his company had lost over N$10million in export proceeds since the beginning of the Liberian crisis. If this was true for Cadbury, it was bound to be true for other Nigerian companies doing business with Liberia . . . "[45]

Another area of concern to Nigeria in her foreign policy and ultimate participation in the peacekeeping effort in Liberia relates to its claim that West Africa is within her sphere of influence—a sort of "Nigerian Monroe doctrine." The interference of Libya, United States, France, and other external powers in Liberia was considered to be inimical to the overall interest of Nigeria. The United States and France aside, Libya, Nigeria's political nemesis in Chad, was known to be supplying arms and ammunition to Charles Taylor's NPLF. Such successful "external" encroachment was bound to create the impression that Nigeria was not only weak, but also unable to resolve a political crisis in her "backyard." Nigeria's failure to act in Liberia might further the notion that Nigeria was only a "paper tiger" in the region. Faced with these circumstances, as it were, Nigeria was determined to do whatever it took to bring peace to Liberia even in the light of mounting criticisms at the home front and billions of nairas it had spent on the operation.

END OF THE WAR

The general assumption, noted Eva Bertram, is that peace building attempts tend to share certain fundamental characteristics: 1. they deal with conflicts within rather than between states; 2. the host government is one of the parties to the conflict; 3. their aim is to develop and/ or implement a political transition following or accompanying an end to military hostilities; and 4. a central component is the reform or establishment of basic state institutions.[46] Retrospectively, the development in Liberia followed the above chronological order.

Indeed, the painstaking efforts toward peace came to fruition as a result of a series of complex negotiations in which Nigeria as the leader of ECOMOG played a major role. The formation of an interim legislative body, and the multiparty elections that followed culminating in the victory of Charles Ghankay Taylor were some of the important, yet occasionally problematic, steps undertaken by ECOMOG. On August 2, 1997, at the swearing-in ceremony of Taylor as the twenty-first President of the Republic of Liberia, General Sani Abacha, current chairman of ECOWAS, said:

> Indeed, as we look back on the many attempts at finding peace for Liberia, the victory which we celebrate becomes even more precious and uplifting. The catalogue of all those conferences which resulted in so many peace accords from Banjul in 1990 to Yamousoukro—a series of talks, from Geneva to Cotonou and then Akosombo to Accra should remind us how difficult and fraught with frustration and even [how dangerous] this whole process had been. The Abuja agreement of 1995 and its Revised Schedule of implementation of August, 1996, were a culmination of all these efforts.[47]

It goes without saying that the ECOWAS intervention in Liberia under the auspices of ECOMOG is epochal in spite of the antinomies and intermittent political, diplomatic, and military setbacks. This is even more so because unlike the UN, ECOMOG lacked both the structural and institutional mechanisms for peacekeeping. Yet, when push came to shove, the group, despite members limitations and contradictory national interests, the complexities of the ethnic character of the civil war itself, succeeded in this important mission. It must be noted, though, that the outcome of the operation would have been more difficult were it not for the support of the United Nations. To this end, it could be argued that such a regional attempt at solving regional problems, with the assistance of the international community, might become a model in the "New International World Order."

LOOKING AHEAD

If there was any lesson to be learned from the Liberian crisis, it might be to remind ourselves of one of Sir Winston Churchill's dicta regarding wars when he said: "It is easy to start a war, but difficult to end one." This view was echoed by General Sani Abacha at the inauguration of Charles Taylor when he affirmed: " . . . if the difficulties we have encountered teach any lessons, it is that wars, especially civil wars, are easy to ignite on the raw emotions of ethnic chauvinism, but difficult to stop, even when our instincts of nationalism finally compel us to draw back from the brink."[48] In spite of these words of wisdom, ECOMOG is poised to undertake a somewhat similar mission in Sierra Leone following the military coup of Major Johnny P. Koroma on May 25, 1997, that toppled the regime of President Ahmad Tejan Kabbah.

Whatever might become of the Sierra Leonean operation, ECOWAS must not become oblivious to the fundamental objectives of economic growth and solvency in the region. It is true that civil wars tend to affect the flow of trade, but ethnically motivated crisis and political instability in the sub-region issue from the problems of underdevelopment and scarce resources. Indeed, it is the competition for the meager resources in the area that, *inter alia*, trigger ethnic and racial conflicts in Africa.

ECOWAS was not created as a war machine; it was established as an economic union for the purpose of assailing the intractable condition of poverty existing in this region.[49] While ECOWAS/ECOMOG deservedly celebrates its triumph in Liberia and now attempts to plunge itself into the Sierra Leonean imbroglio, it must also be prepared to pursue its policy of economic revival with equal, if not more, vigor than the peace efforts in Liberia. In this way, ECOWAS would not be placing the cart before the horse. Normatively, too, as the area marches toward the next millennium, it should be noted that economic revitalization is a *sine qua non* for peace and stability. Indeed, it is only when member states of the ECOWAS pursue vigorously the tenets of its treaty within the context of liberalization and democracy that the area might be spared of the crisis that engulfed Liberia and now rages in Sierra Leone.

NOTES

1. E. Ike Udogu, "The Issues of Development and Environment in Africa: An Overview," in Rukhsana A. Siddiqui (ed.) *Sub-Saharan Africa in the 1990s: Challenges to Democracy and Development* (Westport, CT: Praeger, 1997), p. 189.
2. Mary Matossian, "Ideologies of Delayed Industrialization: Some Tensions and Ambiguities," *Economic Development and Cultural Change*, Vol. 6 (1958), pp. 217–218.
3. Emmanuel I. Udogu, *The Problems of African Unity and the Awakening of Regional Cooperation* (Carbondale, IL: MA Thesis, Southern Illinois University, 1977), p. 89.
4. *Economic Community of West African States* (FGP 1936/(75)176/25,000), p. 12.
5. *Ibid.*, p. 4.
6. *Ibid.*
7. Udogu, *The Problems of African Unity and the Awakening of Regional Cooperation*, p. 90.
8. *Treaty of the Economic Community of West African States* (New York: Nigerian Consulate, 1975), pp. 7–8.
9. Mamit Deme, "The Impact of ECOWAS on Intraregional Trade Flows: An Empirical Investigation," *The Review of Black Political Economy*, Vol. 23, No. 3 (Winter 1995), p. 116
10. Uke Ezenwe, "The way ahead for ECOWAS: Two," *West Africa*, (27 September, 1976), p. 1043.
11. *Treaty of the Economic Community of West African States*, p. 29.
12. Udogu, "The Issues of Development and Environment in Africa: An Over-

view," in Siddiqui (ed.), *Sub-Saharan Africa in the 1990s: Challenges to Democracy and Development*, pp. 192–194.

13. *Economic Community of West African States*, p. 8

14. Julius O. Ihonvbere, "Evolving sovereignty in an interdependent world: The challenge of democratization in sub-Saharan Africa," *International Politics (formerly Coexistence)*, Vol. 33, (September 1996), p. 264.

15. Deme, *op. cit.*, pp. 117–118

16. Ihonvbere, *op. cit.*, pp. 245–267.

17. *Human Development Report 1997: United Nations Development Programme* (New York: Oxford University Press, 1997), pp. 142–147.

18. *Ibid.*, p. 143.

19. Theodore A. Columbus and James H. Wolfe, *Introduction to International Relations: Power and Justice* (Englewood Cliffs, NJ: Prentice-Hall, 1990), p. 44.

20. *Ibid.*

21. International Peace Academy, *Peacekeeper's Handbook* (New York, 1984), p. 7.

22. Eva Bertram, "Reinventing Governments: The Promise and Perils of United Nations Peace Building," *Journal of Conflict Resolution*, Vol. 39, No. 3 (September 1995), p. 388.

23. *Ibid.*

24. Cited in *Ibid.*

25. Ademola Adeleke, "The Politics and Diplomacy of Peacekeeping in West Africa: The ECOWAS Operation in Liberia," *The Journal of Modern African Studies*, Vol. 33, No. 4 (1995), pp. 570–571.

26. *Ibid.*, p. 571.

27. *Ibid.*, p. 569.

28. Toyin Falola, "Nigeria in the Global Context of Refugees: Historical and Comparative Perspective," *Journal of Asian and African Studies*, Vol. XXX11, No. 1–2 (June 1997), pp. 5–6.

29. Terry Mays, "Nigerian Foreign Policy and the Liberian Civil War," A paper presented at the annual meeting of the South Carolina Political Science Association, Clemson University, (March 29, 1994), pp. 4–6.

30. "President Sani Abacha's Speech Delivered at the Inaugural Ceremony of President Charles Ghankay Taylor," *The [Liberian] INQUIRER*, (Tuesday, August 5, 1997), p. 6

31. Robert Gilpin, *War and Change in World Politics* (New York: Cambridge University Press, 1981), pp. 29, 145.

32. *Ibid.*

33. "Nigeria's Fourth Republic looms," *West Africa*, No. 4168 (29 September–5 October 1997), p. 1528.

34. Julius O. Ihonvbere, *Nigeria: The Politics of Adjustment & Democracy* (New Brunswick, NJ: Transaction Publishers, 1994), pp. 35–71.

35. Article 34 states that: The Security Council may investigate any dispute, or any situation which might lead to international friction or give rise to dispute, in order to determine whether the continuance of the dispute or situation is likely to endanger the maintenance of international peace and security.

Article 35 affirms that: Any Member of the United Nations may bring any dispute, or any situation of the nature referred to in Article 34, to the attention of the Security Council or of the General Assembly.

36. Robert E. Riggs and Jack C. Plano, *The United Nations: International Organization and World Politics* (Chicago, Ill.: The Dorsey Press, 1988), p. 377.

37. "Taylor Rejects Bamako Initiative," *West Africa*, (November 12–18, 1990), p. 2836.
38. Adeleke, *op. cit.*, p. 578.
39. Deme, *op. cit.*, pp. 118–119.
40. Zaki Ergas, "In Search of Development: Some Directions for Further Investigation," *The Journal of Modern African Studies*, Vol. 24, No. 2 (1986), pp. 305–312.
41. Emenike Okorie, Yakubu Mohammed and Abdulrazaq Magaji, "Celebration of Wishes," *Newswatch*, Vol. 14, No. 3 (July 15, 1991), p. 20.
42. Alajide Aluko, *Essays on Nigerian Foreign Policy* (London: George Allen and Unwin, 1981), p. 13.
43. Alaba Ogunsanwo, *The Nigerian Military and Foreign Policy 1975–1979: Processes, Principles, Performance, and Contradictions*, (Princeton, NJ: Princeton University Press, 1980), p. 16.
44. *Nigeria and the ECOWAS since 1985*, (Enugu: Fourth Dimension Publishing Co., and the Nigerian Institute of International Affairs, 1991), p. 104.
45. Mays, *op.cit.*, p. 13.
46. Bertram, *op.cit.*, p. 388.
47. "President Sani Abacha's Speech Delivered at the Inaugural Ceremony of President Charles Ghankay Taylor," *op.cit.*, p. 6. For a superb discussion of the intricacies of the operation, see Carolyn M. Shaw and Julius O. Ihonvbere, "Hegemonic Participation in Peace-Keeping Operations: The Case of Nigeria and ECOMOG," *International Journal on World Peace*, Vol. XIII, No. 2 (June 1996), pp. 31–60; George Klay Kieh, "Combatants, Patrons, Peacemakers, and the Liberian Civil Conflict," *Studies in Conflict and Terrorism*, (April/June 1992), pp. 131–132.
48. *Ibid.*, pp. 6–7
49. M. N. Ogbonna and Abraham E. Nwankwo, "A Dynamic View of Dependency Within Integration: The Case of Ecowas," *African Studies*, Vol. 10 (January 1986), p. 186.

22

DEVELOPMENT PROSPECTS AND POLICY FOR AFRICA: STRUCTURAL ADJUSTMENT AND BEYOND

Kempe Ronald Hope, Sr.

INTRODUCTION

In most of Africa, post-independence development policy was formulated through a statist ideological framework, which was then implemented by experimentation. That produced disastrous results. Among other things, poverty and socioeconomic inequalities increased, the external debt burden became heavier, the brain drain intensified, capital flight deepened, the balance of payments weakened, the physical infrastructure deteriorated, unemployment and crime escalated, famine and malnutrition became more pronounced, budget deficits soared, agricultural productivity declined, urbanization burgeoned, environmental degradation expanded, political and civil strife worsened, and corruption became much more rampant.[1]

These disastrous development results were, in turn, the catalyst behind the deepening economic crisis in Africa and, consequently, provided the imperative for policy reform in these countries. Incidentally, the impact of that economic crisis was so devastating that the 1980s are now correctly referred to in the literature as "Africa's Lost Decade."[2] One analyst has even gone further by arguing that the "the first three decades of African independence have been an economic, political and social disaster."[3] This economic deterioration at the national level, and the ensuing economic deprivation at the human level, resulted in the emergence of policy reform which was dominated by donor-sponsored structural adjustment programmes (SAPs). Despite the fact that SAPs have had mixed results, they have been successful, for the most part, in restructuring and liberalizing African economies.[4] Consequently, as we approach the 21st century, we are now able to talk of economic recovery as a number of performance indicators have been showing positive upturns in Africa since the early 1990s. In other words, performance is most definitely responding to policy reforms.

This paper reviews the positive economic recovery impact of SAPs in Africa and analyzes development prospects and policy for the continent in the post-SAPs era beyond 2000.

STRUCTURAL ADJUSTMENT AND ITS IMPACT IN AFRICA

The deepening of the economic crisis in Africa, which began in the 1970s and intensified in the 1980s, as mentioned above, presented a difficult challenge to the political leadership, policy advisers, and the development community. It required policy measures to reverse the declining trends and place those economies on a path of sustainable growth and development. There was a need to, among other things, arrest the deepening poverty, reduce the socioeconomic inequalities, lighten the external debt burden, reverse the brain drain, create new employment opportunities, improve the efficiency of the physical infrastructure, narrow down the fiscal deficits, and improve the balance of payments. To avert famine and malnutrition, there was also a critical need to increase productivity.

In the early 1980s, SAPs became the policy response to Africa's economic crisis. SAPs were formulated by and with the support of the International Monetary Fund (IMF) and the World Bank, and they are a combination of two types of policy responses—stabilization policies which are the domain of the IMF, and structural adjustment policies which are the province of the World Bank.[5] Generally, as a precondition for a country to enter into a structural adjustment programme, agreement must first be reached on a set of stabilization measures with the IMF.

To achieve the objectives of SAPs, the primary policy instruments employed are: (1) exchange rate adjustment, primarily devaluation; (2) control of the money supply and credit ceilings; (3) interest rate policy, allowing interest rates to respond freely to market forces; (4) debt rescheduling; (5) fiscal policy, including measures to reduce public expenditure and mobilize resources; (6) deregulation of prices of goods, services, and factor inputs; (7) liberalization of trade and payments arrangements; and (8) the reform of institutions with an emphasis on building capacity for policy analysis, implementing public investments, and privatization of public assets.[6] These instruments are interdependent and, in some cases, they are mutually reinforcing.

In the majority of the African countries that implemented SAPs, there has been a marked improvement in economic performance beginning in the early 1990s.[7] That, in turn, led to a process of economic recovery on the continent, reversing the trend of persistent negative growth in the 1980s. Table 1 depicts the primary macroeconomic indicators and shows that real GDP growth, which continues to broaden, was estimated at 4.8 percent in 1996—the highest in 20 years. However, there are variations in individual country performances as well as by region. Had it not been for the slower growth in South Africa and Nigeria, for example, the real GDP growth rate in Africa would have been much higher at this point in time.

The Eastern, Southern, and West African regions all grew at or above the continent's average, while the Central African region's growth was below average. Ghana maintained its reputation as one of the star pupils of structural adjustment. The country grew at 4.4 percent in 1995 and 5 percent in 1996. Similarly, Uganda continued its high rates of growth at 11.5 percent in 1995 and 9.8 percent in 1996, while, in Tanzania, economic growth was well over 4 percent in both 1995 and 1996. Mozambique has also been recording significant growth and recovery, as it pursues structural reforms. In 1996, the country had real GDP growth of 6.4 percent. Following the CFA franc devaluation in 1994, many CFA franc zone countries began to exhibit signs of strong or restored growth. After years of recession Côte d'Ivoire, for example, had real GDP growth in excess of 6 percent in both 1995 and 1996, while Cameroon seems to be emerging from an extended period of economic stagnation with GDP growth of 3.5 percent in 1995 and 5 percent in 1996.

Under SAPs, there have been serious attempts to reduce the rates of inflation. In 1996, the average inflation rate in Africa was estimated at 27.3 percent compared to 40.4 percent and 32.5 percent in 1994 and 1995, respectively. The median rate of inflation was even lower at 9.3 percent in 1996.[8] This suggests that the average rate of inflation is heavily influenced by the high inflation in a few countries. From a regional perspective, only Eastern Africa had recorded single-digit inflation (8.9 percent) by 1996 while Southern Africa had rates of inflation averaging in excess of 70 percent. In Zambia, for example, the inflation rate exceeded 110 percent.

Large fiscal deficits indicate the extent of government failures to achieve fiscal balance. In Africa, there has been a progressive improvement in the fiscal situation compared to the pre-adjustment period. In the 1990s, fiscal policy continued to emphasize budgetary restraint and the overall budget deficit was consistently reduced from 7.5 percent of GDP in 1993

TABLE 1
Africa: Macroeconomic Indicators, 1992–96

Indicators	1992	1993	1994	1995	1996
Real GDP Growth Rate[a]	0.3	0.8	2.6	2.9	4.8
Inflation[a]	28.3	27.6	40.4	32.5	27.3
Fiscal Balance[b]	–5.9	–7.5	–5.3	–3.3	–2.9
Money Supply Growth[b]	39.5	29.5	40.8	27.1	17.5
Merchandise Export Growth (volume)[a]	2.5	0.9	–0.5	8.3	10.1
Merchandise Import Growth (volume)[a]	–1.4	–0.3	2.7	6.7	7.7
Terms of Trade[a]	–8.8	–4.4	0.0	–2.1	–3.3
Trade Balance[c]	0.2	–2.5	–5.6	–7.2	–9.8
Current Account[c]	–5.8	–9.2	–11.1	–12.9	–16.1
Current Account[b]	–1.3	–2.0	–2.5	–2.4	–2.8
Debt Service[d]	29.9	27.1	21.5	25.5	25.1

Sources: African Development Bank, *African Development Report 1997* (New York: Oxford University Press, 1997); p. 1; Global Coalition for Africa, *African Social and Economic Trends: 1996 Annual Report* (Washington, D.C.: Global Coalition for Africa, 1997), Statistical Annex; and World Bank, *African Development Indicators* (Washington, D.C.: World Bank, Several Years).
Notes: [a]Percent; [b]Percent of GDP; [c]US$ billion; [d]Percent of Exports.

to 2.9 percent in 1996. Several countries, including Lesotho, Gabon, Botswana, and Algeria, either recorded or maintained budget surpluses.

Fiscal policy (changes in government expenditures and revenues) is important for short-term attempts to stabilize the macroeconomy and for longer-run efforts to make key structural changes to the economy. Consequently, the impact of SAPs on fiscal deficits is determined through a set of conditions, including the reduction of government spending. It has also been increasingly recognized that unless the role of government is limited to those activities where market failures predominate, growth of the private sector could be crowded out and stifled. In Africa, the share of government expenditure in GDP has declined from an average of 33 percent in the 1980s to approximately 28 percent in 1996. Uganda has had the most dramatic decline from 109 percent of GDP in 1980 to 42 percent in 1995. Public sector wage bills account for a large proportion of total government expenditures. Typically, in the adjusting African countries, the public sector wage bill accounts for more than 20 percent of total government spending. As a fiscal weight, the central government wage bill in Africa has been declining from 10 percent of GDP in the 1980s to 6.7 percent of GDP in the 1990s.[9]

Apart from reductions in government expenditures, maintaining a healthy fiscal balance also necessitates measures to increase revenues. Unfortunately, in Africa, the performance of total government revenue has been mediocre, increasing slightly from 23.3 percent of GDP in 1980 to 24.7 percent in 1995. In some countries such as Tanzania, Uganda, and Zambia, for example, government revenue declined during the adjustment period, and this, in turn, increased their dependence on external financing. Almost all African countries have weak and narrow tax bases. In addition, in some countries, such as Zambia, for example, the decline in revenues has also been caused by the erosion in the real value of tax revenues associated with very high rates of inflation.[10] While adjustment policies for public expenditure have received a great deal of attention, and have been subject to much criticism due to a generally false perception that they result in draconian cuts in public spending, changes in tax policy have gone relatively unnoticed.[11] The primary fiscal problem in many African countries pertains to the lack of revenue and inadequate allocation of the existing resources, and this was found to be particularly true in those economies, such as Ghana, that suffered serious economic collapse before commencing their adjustment programs.[12]

The African countries have been adjusting under a somewhat difficult international economic environment. That environment has been characterized by deteriorating commodity terms of trade; a heavy burden of servicing debts; and a recession in some industrial countries.[13] Nonetheless, promoting growth and diversifying exports have been central to SAPs. Notwithstanding declines in major commodity prices in 1996, export volume continued to show the strong growth which began in 1995 and stood at 10 percent in 1996. The value of exports has also been growing steadily since 1993 and stood at US$116.4 billion in 1996. Since exports have a major impact on growth, all African countries should strive to remove policies that impede their export competitiveness, particularly with respect to the manufacturing sector which is one of the major sectors that continues to show slow progress, in terms of both growth and structural change, with an average contribution to total GDP in many countries at less than 12 percent.[14] During the past decade, Africa's share of world manufacturing value added remained less than 1 percent.[15]

With respect to imports, the gains made in the volume and value of exports have been offset by increases in the value of imports; leading to a current account deficit which has been increasing over the years and which stood at 2.8 percent of GDP in 1996. There have also been major strides toward the liberalization of imports. In the pre-adjustment period, most African countries had over-valued exchange rates and they rationed their foreign exchange through administrative measures. However, domestic currency depreciations, combined with appropriate macroeconomic policies, have now eliminated foreign exchange rationing and reduced the import-scarcity premiums which tended to be reflected in the prices in the parallel markets. For instance, Tanzania and Zambia experienced severe distortions in their foreign exchange markets. The ratio of the parallel market to that of the official exchange rate decreased from 4.9 in 1986 to 1.4 by 1992 in Tanzania, while in Zambia the ratio increased from 1.3 in 1986 to a peak of 7.8 in 1989 before the black market for foreign exchange was wiped out in 1991.[16] In many other African countries, the black market premium has declined in the 1990s, in some cases to virtually zero, as market-based exchange rate policies were introduced.

Further evidence of import liberalization has been the progressive elimination of nontariff barriers (NTBs). Barriers to imports were pervasive in the pre-adjustment era. To have access to foreign exchange, for example, required a valid import license. In some sense, licensing had become a mechanism for rationing foreign exchange and a conduit for graft and corruption. Import licenses were also used to protect inefficient domestic production from foreign competition. Significant progress has also been made on reducing the number of goods requiring approval for import. In such countries as Ghana, Malawi, Tanzania, Zambia, and Zimbabwe, before the implementation of SAPs, all imports were subjected to NTBs, including quantitative restrictions and special licensing requirements other than for health and safety reasons.

Reforming trade policies has been a central feature of SAPs and, coupled with exchange rate policy, the most controversial. All of the adjusting countries in Africa have embarked on trade liberalization. This has contributed to improved trade performance, measured in terms of export growth and some diversification, as noted earlier. Increases in imports have also been the immediate impact of trade liberalization, as domestic demand (primarily private consumption) has been increasing. With a contribution of 4.3 percentage points, domestic demand was responsible for about 90 percent of the overall growth of GDP in 1996 with private consumption accounting for more than half (2.7 percent) of that growth.[17]

For macroeconomic policy reforms to succeed, they should be implemented with corresponding changes in the social and political institutions. Even if the reforms, purely in economic terms, may initially be sustainable, if economic liberalization is politically unacceptable, policy reversals would be inevitable. Such reversals and reinstatements have occurred in Zambia and Zimbabwe. These oscillations in economic policy reflected the vacillations in the political arena on the efficacy of SAPs. The role of politics as a major determinant of the sustainability of economic policy reforms has also been demonstrated in Malawi.[18] Unless there is political will, implementing public sector reforms will continue to be intractable. And yet, improving public sector management has been deemed essential for the success of policy reforms. For example, an effective civil service is central to ensuring that a sound macroeconomic framework can be implemented. However, under SAPs, considerable progress has been made toward the restructuring of the public sector. For instance, in Zimbabwe, during the first phase of the structural adjustment programme (1991–1995), between 16,000–22,000 public sector employees were retrenched.[19] Several other countries, including Tanzania, Malawi, Ghana, Gambia, and Guinea, have also significantly reduced the size of their civil services.[20]

In addition, reforms have also been directed at improving civil service pay and the restructuring of grade levels. In many of the countries, the erosion of average salaries was the major issue to be addressed by pay reform. This took the form of attempts to decompress the wage structure so as to be able to recruit and retain higher-level staff whose salaries had sunk to very low multiples of the lowest-ranked employees. In Mozambique, for example, the decompression ratio widened from two to one in the early 1980s to nine to one by the early 1990s; in Uganda it moved from six to one to eight to one; and in Ghana it moved from six to one to ten to one during the same period.[21]

Besides the attempts at public sector reform in the African countries, there has also been some progress in the reduction of state ownership of enterprises. These public enterprises are generally inefficient and are in various stages of dilapidation. Moreover, they absorb large amounts of funds that could be better spent on basic social services. In many of the countries, central government subsidies to public enterprises exceeded 50 percent of central government spending on education and more than 100 percent of central government spending on health.[22] The currently available data suggest that privatization is proceeding in Africa, albeit at a mixed pace and with mixed results. Some noteworthy examples of countries with relatively good privatization records are Ghana, Tunisia, and Zambia.

Perhaps the most controversial aspect of the debate on SAPs has been their impact on the poor. In Africa, the majority of the poor live in the rural areas. As producers of agricultural commodities, they have benefited from policy reforms in agricultural marketing and also from foreign exchange and trade liberalization. Prices paid to the rural farmers have increased and the delivery of agricultural commodities has improved. However, to cushion the impact of rising food and other prices, many of the adjusting countries have implemented government-sponsored social safety net programs, as part of their SAPs, which include direct cash transfers, subsidies on basic goods and services, social infrastructure development in deprived areas, employment-generating public works schemes, targeted nutrition programs, employment services and retraining programs, and direct delivery of basic goods and services to the poor. Most of these programs are, or have been, supported by the World Bank. They include, for example, the Social Dimensions of Adjustment (SDA) program in Zimbabwe; the Program for the Alleviation of Poverty and the Social Costs of Adjustment (PAPSCA) in Uganda; the Social Recovery Fund, the Public Welfare Assistance Scheme, and the Program Against Malnutrition (PAM) in Zambia; the Social Dimensions of Adjustment (SDA) project in Cameroon; and the Program of Action to Mitigate the Social Costs of Adjustment (PAMSCAD) in Ghana.

BEYOND STRUCTURAL ADJUSTMENT AND ECONOMIC RECOVERY: DEVELOPMENT PROSPECTS AND POLICY

SAPs have made a positive impact on the economic recovery of the African countries beginning in the early 1990s. SAPs were necessitated by the type of African economy that emerged in the early decades after independence which was influenced by various types of socialist theories; by an emphasis on Keynesian economics; by government administered price controls and increasingly regulated labour, commodity, and financial markets; by increasing the share of the public sector in the economy through, among other things, appropriation and nationalization of private enterprises and financial institutions, as well as the creation of public monopolies for the marketing of agricultural products; by administratively allocating foreign exchange and credit (which primarily benefited the public enterprises and the political elite; and by a restrictive trade policy and an inward-looking import-substitution strategy.[23] All of these anti-market interventionist policies rapidly overextended the African governments and gave birth to the region's economic crisis.[24]

Africa's economic performance is now improving and responding to policy reforms. The prospects for sustainable growth and development are encouraging and are much better now than at any time since the crisis became concentrated in the 1980s. However, the recovery is fragile and there are a number of policy issues that need to be tackled before these economies can remain firm on the path toward market-oriented sustainable development. To be sure, some analysts still regard Africa as a continent in chaos—a lost continent whose citizens are powerless to rid themselves of predatory governments or force existing ones to adopt the right policies in a peaceful way.[25] In most of the continent, growth is not nearly sufficient to make a dent in poverty reduction, and despite recent improvements, Africa's GDP and export growth rates, savings and investment levels, and social indicators, for example, remain below those of other continents. Below, we discuss the primary outstanding policy issues which need to be given greater attention as African countries move beyond SAPs into the 21st century, utilizing a more indigenously based and self-reliant policy framework as opposed to reliance on external assistance and ideas.

Debt Management and Control

The external debt and debt-servicing obligations of the African countries continue to pose a major threat to the sustainable development of the region. Africa's outstanding external debt was estimated at US$320.6 billion in 1996. As a ratio, this was equivalent to 211 percent of exports and 57 percent of GDP. Of the World Bank's list of 41 Highly Indebted Poor Countries (HIPCs), 33 are in Africa. Debt servicing amounts to 25 percent of export earnings.

The capacity of African countries to service their debt has therefore not improved despite major efforts at both scaling down their debt burden and reduction in the volume of arrears within the framework of existing debt reorganization and forgiveness measures. The debt situation of Africa has, therefore, left the majority of those countries in a debt trap with substantial resources being siphoned away from supporting the transitional reform process. The need to control and manage debt is therefore an obvious one. Debt ceilings should be observed and, as argued by Jeffrey Sachs, further debt relief should be deep, phased over time, and conditional on fundamental reforms.[26]

In that regard, the World Bank and IMF have reacted by agreeing to provide debt relief to highly indebted poor countries undertaking serious reforms. The African Development Bank has also now joined this initiative in relationship to African countries. As part of the package, the Paris Club of bilateral creditors will forgive up to 80 percent of the debt owed by eligible countries. In April 1997, Uganda was designated as the first African country to benefit from the initiative with debt relief taking effect in April 1998, subject to the country's satisfactory performance with its reform program. The intent of the HIPCs initiative is to leave beneficiary countries with sustainable debt stocks and debt service obligations, which would reestablish their creditworthiness and improve the prospects for increased private capital flows.

Promoting Savings and Investment

The achievement of sustainable development, particularly so in the context of free markets, requires high levels of domestic savings and private investment as amply demonstrated in the East Asian countries. However, in Africa, as seen in Figure 1, both the savings and investment to GDP ratio continue to be much lower in the 1990s than they were in 1980. In 1996, the savings ratio was 16.2 percent of GDP compared to 27 percent in 1980 while the investment ratio was 17.8 percent of GDP compared to 23.3 percent for the same two periods.

Historically, in Africa, private savings have been low and foreign investment has been concentrated in natural resource industries, such as mining and oil, rather than manufacturing. With low domestic savings, private investment has also been low. However, in the context of the post-SAPs period, African countries must move rapidly in the implementation of strategies to mobilize domestic savings and private investment and particularly foreign direct investment, in the case of the latter. To be sure, part of Africa's economic recovery is the result of the improved foreign direct investment inflows in the 1990s. As seen in Figure 1, the gross domestic investment ratio had caught up with the savings ratio in 1991 and has exceeded it ever since. But, while the recent increase in the volume of foreign direct investment inflows is encouraging, Africa has experienced a downward trend in the share of such investment it attracts. In the 1970s, Africa received an annual average of more than 16 percent of all foreign direct investment flows to developing countries, compared with 10 percent in the 1980s, and approximately 5 percent in the 1990s.[27]

Perhaps, one of the primary factors contributing to weak domestic savings and investment in Africa is the inadequacy of the financial system. Although SAPs have resulted in considerable financial liberalization

FIGURE 1
Gross Domestic Savings and Investment in Sub-Saharan Africa Percent of GDP

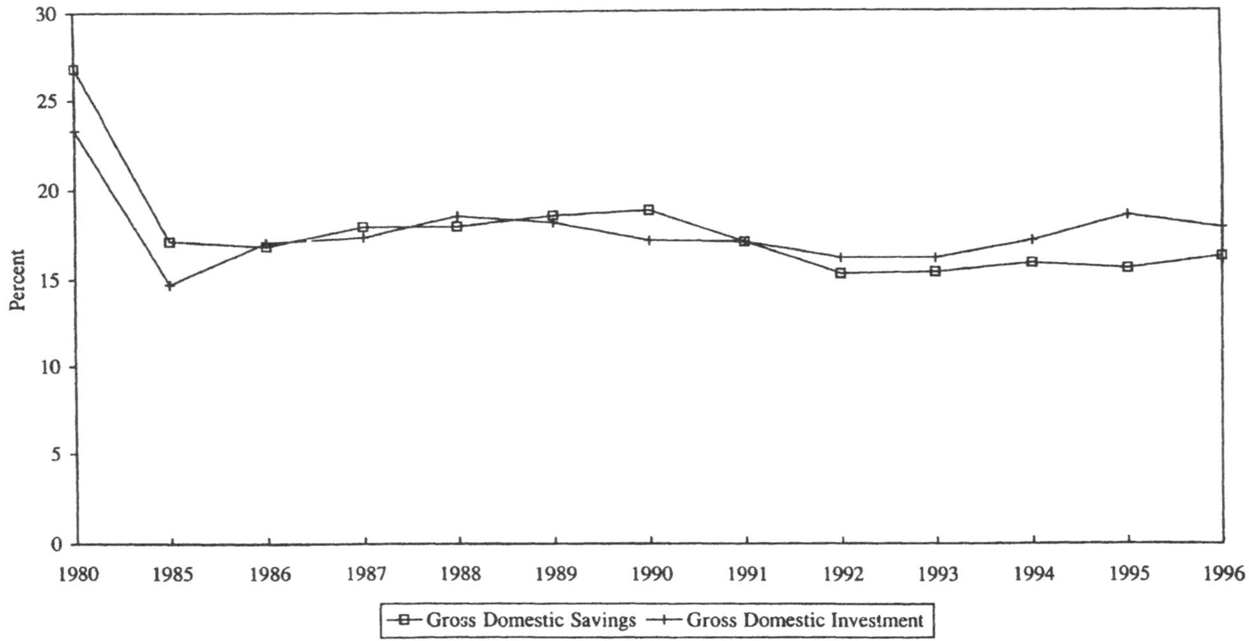

(including the development of stock markets in countries such as Ghana, Malawi, Zambia, and Zimbabwe, for example), the inadequate savings and investment ratios in Africa is clearly associated with a stagnant or declining performance of the formal financial sector as measured by the standard indicators of financial deepening such as the ratio of money and quasi-money to GDP, the ratio of deposit money to the money supply (M2), and the ratio of the banking system's claim on the private sector in relation to national income.[28]

African countries, therefore, need to take steps to further liberalize and develop their financial markets. Developed financial markets and liberalized financial systems enable all individuals, no matter how limited their means, to share in the increased wealth provided by competitive private enterprise. At the same time, savings may increase, at any level of income, if the financial markets afforded greater opportunities for individuals to increase their future income by saving in the present. Moreover, foreign investor confidence is likely to be enhanced and the resilience of the economies and their financial systems, to external and internal shocks, will be increased.

Outward-Looking Economic Diversification

African economies have paid a heavy price as a result of their highly protectionist policies from independence through to the 1980s. Those economies that liberalized trade from the outset, such as Botswana and Mauritius, have considerably outperformed the rest of Africa, and those that have liberalized their trade under SAPs have begun to perform better. One study has determined that trade liberalization alone should raise average growth rates by 0.7 percent per year, in the formerly protected economies.[29]

In the mid-1950s, sub-Saharan Africa accounted for 3.1 percent of global exports. However, by 1990 this share had fallen to 1.2 percent. A major and extensive loss of Africa's international competitiveness played a key role in its decline in world trade. If sub-Saharan Africa, for example, had merely retained its 1962–1964 OECD market shares, its exports now would be 75 percent (US$11 billion) higher.[30] Trade restrictions and domestic policy interventions created a bias against tradeables, especially exports in the region. In the current context of globalization, and looking beyond SAPs, African countries need to fully embrace trade liberalization and economic diversification away from dependence on a few traditional primary exports.

Undoubtedly, this will enhance international competitiveness, permit local exporters to capitalize on opportunities in foreign markets, and encourage capital flows from such initiatives as the 1998 United States African Growth and Opportunity Bill of the administration of President Clinton. The latter seeks to establish a trade-based United States-Africa relationship which would allow more African goods to be exported to the United States while creating a US$650 million equity and infrastructure fund for the African continent. This initiative would only be available to those African countries pursuing market-oriented policies and observance of human rights.

Developing Institutions and Building Capacity

When institutions are weak, then there is limited implementation capacity. In such an environment, economic development cannot be sustained irrespective of the performance of the growth indicators. Sustainable development beyond SAPs requires relatively stable rules of the game for regulating economic and political interactions. The lack of institutional capacity in Africa translates into inability to regulate property rights, enforce contracts, maintain law and order, and control official acts of corruption and abuses of power, among other things.[31]

However, institutional change can be a complicated and lengthy process. Institutions typically change incrementally rather than in discontinuous fashion. Informal cultural constraints embodied in customs and traditions tend to be much more impervious to deliberate policies.[32] Consequently, the relative success of institutional change would be a function of the environmental factors which the political leadership have been instrumental in setting in place. In Africa, there is a degree of disconnect between the formal and informal institutions which largely explains problems in capacity building and institutional performance. As a result, economic and political achievements are generally not fully institutionalized with the required enforcement and incentive mechanisms to make them sustainable, and they are therefore prone to reversal with changes of regime and leadership.[33]

Nonetheless, institutional development and capacity building are central to African development. Capacity is the combination of human resources and institutions that permits countries to achieve their development goals. "It engenders the self-reliance that comes with the ability of people to make choices and take actions to achieve the objectives they set for themselves. This entails the ability to identify and analyze problems, formulate solutions and implement them."[34] Central to capacity are an effective bureaucratic machinery, skilled and committed leaders and officials, and ample financial resources. Four dimensions to capacity have been identified. These are regulatory, administrative, technical, and extractive.[35]

Regulatory capacity involves the ability of the state to establish and enforce the rules that guide, or regulate, behaviour in society so as to eliminate mismanagement, inefficiency, pervasive corruption of the public sector, and political instability. Administrative capacity is the routine ability to manage the personnel and resources of the state and to ensure accountability and efficiency in service delivery. It is a critical capacity because it affects the ability of private economic agents to achieve their goals, the availability of a well-trained and healthy workforce, and the satisfaction of the basic needs of society.[36] Technical capacity includes the expertise and knowledge required to make and implement technical decisions as well as the policy tools and instruments necessary to implement those decisions effectively. Extractive capacity is the ability of the state to raise the revenues it needs to pay for the expenses of implementing its policies and goals.

Capacity is now widely recognized as the missing link in Africa's development thrust beyond the era of SAPs despite the donor driven creation of the African Capacity Building Foundation in 1990.[37] Lacking capacity, neither government nor the private sector can adequately perform the tasks that make an economy function. The need for capacity exists in virtually all sectors and areas of African economies. Consequently, capacity building is important because, among other things, it generates the capability for those countries to develop indigenous and self-reliant development policies.[38]

Moreover, the relevant skills would be developed without which Africa would be unable to transform its agriculture, effectively link its industrialization with its natural resource base, and become scientifically and technologically advanced.[39] In addition, a skills base would emerge for establishing linkages and complementarities among the production sectors, serving as an effective domestic catalyst for growth and socio-economic development, and following strategies that are most appropriate to the region's needs and realities.[40] That is the challenge for the post-SAPs era.

Curbing Corruption

From being widespread to systemic, corruption in Africa has reached cancerous proportions and now has a demonstrable negative impact on the development process in the continent. Corruption is of special concern in Africa because graft and poverty tend to go hand in hand, and particularly so where civil society is weak and good governance is lacking. Whether in the public or private sphere, corruption results in the abuse or misuse of scarce resources that significantly affect an entire economy through multiplier effects. Corruption restricts investment and employment opportunities and also undermines programs designed specifically to assist the poor.

Moreover, corruption in Africa is a pervasive and endemic pattern of behaviour that is incongruent with good governance, economic freedom, and competition—all three of which are significant elements of market-oriented economies. The control of corruption, as is currently emphasized by donor agencies and other aid partners, is a fundamental condition for the long-term sustainability of economic progress in Africa. Corruption should therefore be made a high-risk activity—a high risk that kleptocrats and other perpetrators will be caught and severely punished.[41]

The entrenchment of corruption in Africa points to the fact that something has gone wrong in the governance of the individual nation-states. Institutions, which were designed for the regulation of the relationships between citizens and the state, are used instead for the personal enrichment of public officials (politicians and bureaucrats) and other corrupt private agents (individuals, groups, businesses). However, and as has been argued elsewhere, "opportunistic bureaucrats and politicians who try to maximize their take without regard for such perdition on the 'size of the overall pie' may account for the particularly adverse impact corruption has in some countries of Africa. . . ."[42]

That corruption adversely affects the development process in Africa is no longer in doubt. Static efficiency, investment, and growth, for example, are all affected. A payment of a bribe to get an investment license will reduce the incentive to invest as well as the composition of investment. Moreover, those who pay and receive bribes can expropriate a nation's limited wealth. However, even those African countries well endowed with natural resources may fail to develop under a regime of systemic corruption.[43] Nigeria and the former Zaire (under Mobutu) are classic examples in this latter observation. In both scenarios, governments and/or their leaders are not constrained by countervailing forces or national legitimate institutions. As a matter of fact, upon assuming power, many African governments equate the state with their ruling parties and set about to monopolize national resources and thereby infiltrate all facets of economic life.

By violating the public trust and corroding social capital, corruption has far-reaching externalities including the slow erosion of political legitimacy to the point where even honest officials and members of the public see little point in playing by the rules, with the greatest victims being the poor. The curbing of corruption in Africa must, therefore, be made a priority area in African development policy in the post-SAPs era.

CONCLUSION

Africa's economic recovery in the 1990s, though somewhat fragile, is very encouraging. Policy reforms, primarily in the form of SAPs, have led to improved economic performance. However, as we approach the post-SAPs era of the 21st century, African countries need to intensify efforts in the pursuit of sound policies and further structural reforms. Much higher growth rates, exceeding 7 percent annually, are deemed as necessary to be attained and maintained over a longer period for there to be meaningful reductions in poverty.[44]

This paper has advocated a set of policy areas which need to be given priority in Africa as the 21st century approaches. African countries are in a better position now, than anytime since the crisis of the 1980s, to build a path toward sustainable development. In that regard, maintaining market-oriented policy reforms remains the imperative for the immediate future and beyond.[45] It is now up to Africa's leaders to provide the requisite leadership for a home-grown, rather than donor driven, attempt at sustainable socio-economic development.

NOTES

1. Kempe Ronald Hope, Sr., *African Political Economy: Contemporary Issues in Development* (London: M.E. Sharpe, 1997), pp. 3–4.
2. A thorough exposition of this viewpoint can be found in Philip Ndegwa and Reginald Herbold Green, *Africa to 2000 and Beyond: Imperative Political and Economic Agenda* (Nairobi: East African Educational Publishers, 1994).
3. Pierre Landell-Mills, "Governance, Cultural Change, and Empowerment," *Journal of Modern African Studies* 30(4), 1992, pp. 543–567.
4. See Kempe Ronald Hope, Sr. (ed.), *Structural Adjustment, Reconstruction and Development in Africa* (Aldershot: Ashgate, 1997).

5. A good review of the nature of SAPs can be found in Lionel Demery, "Structural Adjustment: Its Origins, Rationale and Achievements" in G.A. Cornia and G.K. Helleiner (eds.), *From Adjustment to Development in Africa: Conflict, Controversy, Convergence, Consensus* (London: Macmillan, 1994).

6. See Bela Balassa, *A Conceptual Framework for Adjustment Policies* (Washington, D.C.: World Bank, 1989); and Finn Tarp, *Stabilization and Structural Adjustment: Macroeconomic Frameworks for Analyzing the Crisis in Sub-Saharan Africa* (London: Routledge, 1993).

7. Discussions and analyses of the individual country performances since the 1980s can be found in the various studies and annual reports of the World Bank, African Development Bank, Global Coalition for Africa, and the United Nations Development Programme. See also Kempe Ronald Hope, Sr. and Gladson Kayira, "Development Policies in Southern Africa: The Impact of Structural Adjustment Programmes", *South African Journal of Economics* 65(2), 1997, pp. 258–74; and David E. Sahn, Paul A. Dorosh, and Stephen D. Younger, *Structural Adjustment Reconsidered: Economic Policy and Poverty in Africa* (Cambridge: Cambridge University Press, 1997).

8. African Development Bank, *African Development Report 1997* (New York: Oxford University Press, 1997), p. 12.

9. Salvatore Schiavo-Campo, Guilio de Tommaso, and Amitabha Mukherjee, *An International Statistical Survey of Government Employment and Wages* (Washington, D.C.: World Bank, 1997), p. 5–9.

10. Kempe Ronald Hope, Sr. *African Political Economy*, p. 125.

11. David E. Sahn, Paul A. Dorosh, and Stephen D. Younger, *Structural Adjustment Reconsidered*, pp. 95–180.

12. *Ibid*, p. 180.

13. Colin Kirkpatrick and John Weiss, "Trade Policy Reforms and Performance in Africa in the 1980s," *Journal of Modern African Studies* 33(2), 1995, pp. 285–298.

14. African Development Bank, *African Development Report 1997*, pp. 24–25.

15. *Ibid.*

16. See World Bank, *Adjustment in Africa: Reforms, Results, and the Road Ahead* (New York: Oxford University Press, 1994).

17. African Development Bank, *African Development Report 1997*, pp. 6–7.

18. Tony Killick, "Structural Adjustment and Poverty Alleviation: An Interpretative Survey," *Development and Change* 26(2), 1995, pp. 305–331.

19. John M. Makumbe, *The Zimbabwe Civil Service Reform Programme: A Critical Perspective* (Birmingham: Development Administration Group, University of Birmingham, 1997), p. 6.

20. See Kempe Ronald Hope, Sr., *African Political Economy*, p. 129; and David L. Lindauer and Barbara Nunberg (eds.), *Rehabilitating Government: Pay and Employment Reform in Africa* (Washington, DC: World Bank, 1994).

21. Salvatore Schiavo-Campo, Guilio de Tommaso, and Amitabha Mukherjee, *Government Employment and Pay: A Global and Regional Perspective* (Washington, DC: World Bank, 1997), p. 44–45.

22. See World Bank, *Bureaucrats in Business: The Economics and Politics of Government Ownership* (New York: Oxford University Press, 1995).

23. Janine Aron, "The Institutional Foundations of Growth," in Stephen Ellis (ed.), *Africa Now: People, Policies and Institutions* (London: James Currey, 1996), pp. 93–118.

24. Kempe Ronald Hope, Sr. and Gladson Kayira, "The Economic Crisis in Southern Africa: Some Perspectives on its Origins and Nature", *Development Southern Africa* 13(6), 1996, pp. 881–894.

25. George B.N. Ayittey, *Africa in Chaos* (New York: St. Martin's Press, 1998), pp. 1–21.
26. Jeffrey Sachs, "Growth in Africa: It can be Done," *The Economist*, June 29, 1996, pp. 23–25.
27. African Development Bank, *African Development Report 1997*, pp. 11–12.
28. Delphin G. Rwegasira, "A Policy Framework for Resource Mobilization: An African Perspective" in Claire Liuksila (ed.), *External Assistance and Policies for Growth in Africa* (Washington, D.C.: IMF, 1995), pp. 34–40.
29. Jeffry Sachs and Andrew Warner, *Sources of Slow Growth in African Economies*, Development Discussion Paper No. 545 (Cambridge: Harvard Institute of International Development, 1996), p. 6.
30. Francis Ng and Alexander Yeats, *Open Economies Work Better: Did Africa's Protectionist Policies Cause Its Marginalization in World Trade?* (Washington, D.C.: World Bank, 1996), p. 28.
31. Merilee S. Grindle, *Challenging the State: Crisis and Innovation in Latin America and Africa* (Cambridge: Cambridge University Press, 1996), p. 31.
32. See Douglas C. North, *Institutions, Institutional Change and Economic Performance* (Cambridge: Cambridge University Press, 1990).
33. Mamadou Dia, *Africa's Management in the 1990s and Beyond: Reconciling Indigenous and Transplanted Institutions* (Washington, D.C.: World Bank, 1996), pp. 28–29.
34. World Bank, *Partnership for Capacity Building in Africa* (Washington, D.C.: World Bank, 1996), p. 5.
35. Deborah Brautigam, "State Capacity and Effective Governance," Benno Ndulu, Nicholas van de Walle, and Contributors, *Agenda for Africa's Economic Renewal* (Washington, D.C.: Overseas Development Council, 1996), pp. 81–108.
36. Merilee S. Grindle, *Challenging the State*, p. 37.
37. The African Capacity Building Foundation focuses on projects that create technical capacity in African countries to increase their ability to improve their development prospects through their own initiatives and abilities. It is located in Harare, Zimbabwe.
38. Kempe Ronald Hope, Sr. "The Political Economy of Policy Reform and Change in Africa: The Challenge of the Transition from Statism to Liberalization," *Regional Development Dialogue* 18(l), 1997, pp. 126–138.
39. *Ibid.*
40. See Kempe Ronald Hope, Sr., *African Political Economy;* and John Mukum Mbaku, *Institutions and Reform in Africa: The Public Choice Perspective* (Westport, CT: Praeger, 1997).
41. Kempe Ronald Hope, Sr. and Bornwell C. Chikulo (eds.), *Corruption and Development in Africa: Lessons From Country Case Studies* (London: Macmillan, 1999).
42. Daniel Kaufmann, "Corruption: The Facts," *Foreign Policy*, No. 107, p. 120.
43. Susan Rose-Ackerman, "Corruption and Development," Paper Presented at the Annual World Bank Conference on Development Economics, Washington, D.C., April–May, 1997.
44. Global Coalition for Africa, *African Social and Economic Trends: 1996 Annual Report* (Washington, D.C.: Global Coalition for Africa, 1997), p. 12.
45. Kempe Ronald Hope, Sr., "Development Solutions for Africa: The Need for Policy Reform and Good Governance," *Issue: A Journal of Opinion* 25(l), 1997, pp. 35–38.

Discrimination, Affirmative Action and Public Policy

23

HOW DOES IT FEEL TO BE FREE?: REFLECTIONS ON BLACK-WHITE ECONOMIC INEQUALITY IN THE ERA OF "COLOR-BLIND" LAW

Rhonda M. Williams and William E. Spriggs

This article is a product of our shared reflections on late twentieth century legal, economic and policy conversations on Black-White economic inequality. Our entry point is recent developments in human capital theory and color-blind jurisprudence. We take as a given that economists, lawyers and judges shape public policy on racial economic inequality; their research and rulings are constitutive of the "common sense" that shapes popular opinions and political conversations. We choose these traditions for two reasons. First, each articulates the normality and inevitability of a present-day racial economic inequality characterized by white economic domination and Black subordination. Second, we believe that color-blind jurisprudence and human capital theory are deeply complementary narratives of white economic supremacy. This essay explores the ideological terrain shared by economists and jurists who continue to normalize and institutionalize Black-White economic inequalities.

What we see is this: both mainstream economists and today's high courts have reached closure on racial inequality. By 'closure' we mean that each community articulates a hegemonic account of Black-White inequality. Neoclassical economists remain largely unresponsive to colleagues who argue for the persistence of racial discrimination. Although a generation of political economists (some more Marxist than others), institutionalists, and feminists have penned many a robust critique of human capital-based explanations of racial inequality (and crafted numerous alternatives), the leading U.S. departments of economics continue their march to the beat of the human capital drum. They remain largely undaunted by the conceptual, (methodo)logical, historical and empirical challenges to their works, comfortably affirming the wonders of labor markets that, for the most part, reward equals equally.[1]

When confronted by the secular increase in Black-White wage inequality in the 1980s, human capital theorists marshaled their ideological and quantitative resources to assure the professional and policy mainstream that rising discriminations was not the causal culprit. As Rodgers and Spriggs recently noted in the pages of this journal, standardized test scores are the human capital variable of choice for labor econometricans in the 1990s in hot pursuit of a "missing variable" to explain the recent slowdown in interracial wage convergence.[2] Today's residual analysts use AFQT score analysis to reassert the link between racial gaps in "social and cultural skills" and Black-White wage differences.[3] Although scholarly critiques of this line of research abound, the blitzkreig continues, largely unabated, toward the now familiar conclusion: although "pre-market" forms of institutionalized White racism may persist, labor market discrimination plays only a minor role in the determination of African Americans relative employment and wages.[4] Labor markets reward equals equally—it's just that, as was the case in George Orwell's *Animal Farm*, some are less equal than others.

A decade (or more) of Circuit Court and Supreme Court rulings demonstrate that today's judicial leaders are ideological kin to neoclassical economists. Recent rulings indicate the Courts' commitment to the "formal equality" doctrine. Formal equality requires only equality-before-the-law, or procedural equality. Moreover, conservative jurists articulate an understanding of economic inequalities shared by the neoclassical mainstream—i.e., economic outcomes generally reflect the preferences and abilities of market agents. Unless shown the workings of some intentional malfeasance, they accept the distributive outcomes of a "private" economy. When confronted by Black-White disparities in employment or contractor status, the Supreme Court reminds us that the playing field is level. Like many human capital theorists, today's judges lean toward the assumption that discrimination is not a significant social relation. Whatever role racism and discrimination have played historically in allocating the resources social competitors now bring to the game is none of the Courts' business. Like the discrimination-bashing entrepreneurs who erode purely discriminatory wage differentials, the Supreme Court sees only "color," not racialized and gendered social subjects and class relations. Hence their pledge to be "color-blind."

In what remains of this essay, we explore in greater depth the content of and connections between these twin narratives of racial inequality. We note their nineteenth century roots and show how they jointly function to consolidate White economic privilege, to legitimate African American economic deprivation, and to enable those who resist a reckoning with the past and present legacies of White economic power.

NINETEENTH CENTURY FOUNDATIONS: FORMAL VS. SUBSTANTIVE RACIAL EQUALITY

Today's conjuncture of economic and judicial theory has historical precedent. We are specifically interested in turn-of-the century court rulings and economic theories that simultaneously narrate and deny the consolidation of White economic domination. Consider, for example, the Supreme Court's shift in the years between *Dred Scott* and *Plessy v. Ferguson.* In his infamous ruling that denied runaway slave Dred Scott's claim to citizenship (and therefore the right to self-ownership), Chief Justice Taney clearly stated the court's commitment to White supremacy:

> The question is simply this: can a negro, whose ancestors were imported into this country and sold as slaves, become a member of the political community formed and brought into existence by the Constitution of the United States . . . The only matter before the courts, therefore, is whether the descendants of such slaves, when they shall be emancipated, or who are born of free parents . . . are citizens of a state . . . We think they are not, and that they are not included, and were not intended to be included, under the word 'citizens' in the Constitution . . . They had for more than a century before been regarded as being of an inferior order; and altogether unfit to associate with the white race, either in social or political relations; and so far inferior, that they had no rights which the white man was bound to respect. . . . It was regarded as an axiom in morals as well as in politics, which no one though of disputing . . . ; and men in every grade and position in society daily and habitually acted upon it in their private pursuits, as well as in matters of public concern.[5]

Taney's strong language makes clear the state's position on the economic and social relations between Blacks and Whites. The "axiomatic" ideology of White supremacy naturalized racial domination in (so-called) private and public life; by definition, African Americans and Whites were non-competing groups, and Blacks were not members of the community of citizens. Taney's ruling does more than simply restate the bizarre ideological madness of White supremacy; the Court's action sanctifies White racial rule as the law of the land, the right and good end of White agency in matters economic and social, public, and private.

The judiciary provided additional affirmation to Whites dedicated to the economic exclusion of freedmen and freedwomen in the sometimes overlooked Civil Rights Cases of 1883. In ruling that Congress could not enact legislation forbidding discrimination in public accommodations, the Court explained that the Fourteenth Amendment to the Constitution applied only to the "public" sector. White citizens were at liberty to practice whatever forms of "private" racial discrimination they so choose. This ruling exemplifies what critical race theorist Cheryl Harris describes as the role of law in constructing "whiteness" as property.[6] In this case, the law constitutes whiteness as property in that owners of "whiteness" may exclude others from the privileges thereof:

> The right to exclude was the central principle, too, for whiteness as identity, for mainly whiteness has been characterized, not by an inherent unifying characteristic, but by the exclusion of others deemed to be "not white." The possessors of whiteness were granted the legal right to exclude others from the privileges inhering in whiteness; whiteness became an exclusive club whose membership was closely and grudgingly guarded. The courts played an active role in enforcing this right to exclude . . . In that sense, the courts protected whiteness as any other form of property.[7]

Thus, were the possessors of whiteness entitled to create, define, and protect White spaces and places in the social economy. However, lawyers and judges continued to debate the legal distinction between public and private discrimination. In the case of housing market discrimination, the Supreme Court again affirmed the White right to exclude. During the late nineteenth century, private developers began using race restrictive covenants when selling their properties. Lower federal courts and state courts upheld the use and enforcement of the covenant provisions. In May 1911, the city of Baltimore passed a segregation ordinance, mandating separate residential sections of the city by race. Cities in other states followed in passing similar ordinances. State courts upheld such ordinances (*Ashland v. Coleman*, 86 *Southeastern* 140). The U.S. Supreme Court, however, overturned such laws. The Court ruled against public laws to create residential segregation, but let stand private efforts to get the same result. Not until the 1940s, did the U.S. Supreme Court also outlaw the enforcement of race restrictive covenants in private deeds.[8]

Thus, did the turn-of-the century rulings confer constitutional legitimacy upon the practice of racial exclusion in each and every sector of the market economy. Proprietors could and did exclude Black customers, employers could and did exclude Black workers from specific industries and jobs. Notwithstanding several noteworthy cases of interracial class solidarity, White employers and workers crafted a system of racial job segregation that would be longstanding. By the end of the 1800s, native born Whites and "newly white" European immigrants collectively dominated Blacks in the struggle for land and jobs, each a lynchpin in the struggle for wealth and economic security.[9] Whiteness was not simply a color; it was a social construct premised on discrimination-as-exclusion and racial domination of those deemed "non-white."

Yet, it was thirteen years later that the judges begin to define "equality" in terms that bears a striking resemblance to the rhetoric used in today's court rulings against affirmative action. As deployed by the courts in *Plessy v. Ferguson*, formal equality addresses neither the context nor consequences of substantive racial economic inequality.[10] Recall that in *Plessy*, the Supreme Court justifies "separate but equal" railroad cars by invoking a symmetry thesis. Legal theorist Kimberle Crenshaw explains the symmetry thesis as follows:

> The strategy they chose was to formalize equality basically to constitute only symmetrical treatment and then to render the social, material context of segregation as well as its effects . . . private or unknowable. This strategy would be achieved through distinguishing between the civil, which was protected, and the social, which was not.[11]

Because the railway officials had provided separate cars and prohibited each race from entering the other's car, "civil" equality was achieved. If Blacks didn't like the conditions of their car—well, that was a social or "private" matter for Blacks to take up with the railway industry. After all, Whites did not feel degraded by the two-car system.

Crenshaw's additional observation is of equal import: the Court's chosen definition of equality masks substantive racial inequality—in Plessy's case, the discomfort of the Black cars. We also note that the Court retreats from Judge Taney's bold assertions of White supremacy. Rather than asserting White superiority, they justices argued that segregation was not inherently a mark of inferiority; if blacks felt stigmatized by segregation, that was simply an unfortunate by-product of their interpretive schema. Now the jurists imagine segregation as the unfortunate outcome of a marketplace where whites devalued "Blackness." Crenshaw's observations are insightful:

> If social equality were to be achieved, blacks would essentially have to earn the respect of whites within the private social sphere. I call this racial marketplace ideology. In this market the state cannot interfere to redistribute racial value. Such redistribution is an illegitimate end that would upset the natural outcomes of the market. If blacks wanted social equality, they would have to get in there (in the market) and work for it.[12]

We note that the Court's verdict did more than simply enshrine the economist's notion of a market place of free and equal subjects—*Plessy also sanctions white economic valuations of Blackness as true and valid.* Unfortunately for African Americans, White agents of the market were not predisposed to value Blacks highly or what they brought to the marketplace. Loud dirty cars, dangerous jobs, segregated housing and employment in low wage industries simply were the market manifestations of that valuation. Racial economic inequality reflected "private," not "public" assessments of Black worthiness. The presumption of Black inferiority governed market interaction, and it was up to Blacks to change White minds.

Notions of Blacks inferiority also ruled the paradigms of the turn-of-the-century U.S. economics profession. Like most of their educated White male peers, early U.S. economists held their own in the great eugenics campaign to preserve a genetically strong nation. Whereas genetic determinists and environmentalists disagreed as to the precise cause of southern and eastern European inferiority, they agreed that Blacks were inferior by nature. "Progressives" John R. Commons and Walter Willcox argued that Blacks were biologically ill-prepared for freedom; the lack of industry, self-discipline, and sexual morality preordained "the Negro" to the loser's corner when competing with Whites. For the turn of the century profession, African American economic subordination was not a puzzling social phenomena. Thus, notions of Black deficiency were pervasive, governing the minds and actions of those who professionally interpreted the laws of the land and explained the mysteries of the marketplace.[13]

Before leaving the 1800s, we offer a footnote on the legacy of *Plessy v. Ferguson. Plessy* also enshrined whiteness-as-property, only this time it is the "status" of whiteness that receives Court sanction. In a less well-known part of his case, Homer Plessy argued that when state officers forced him out of the white cars and into colored cars, they deprived him of his status and reputation as a White person of good character; in so doing, they did injury to his social standing (recall that with only one Black great-grandparent, Plessy "passed" as white), and Homer Plessey sued for civil damages. In a remarkably candid judicial validation of the "status-value" of whiteness, the majority opinion affirms this claim—with one small caveat. According to the laws of Louisiana, Plessy simply was not White. However, had he been White under Louisiana law, the Court ruled, he would have had a valid claim.[14]

The doctrine of "separate but equal" legitimated substantive racial inequality in the public spheres and white financial control over black human capital development; moreover, southern governments routinely denied African Americans equal protection of property and life, thus enabling white efforts to achieve racial domination in economic and political life. The law declared that Blacks were non-citizens by nature and subject to White whim. Free from the fear of legal reprisal, Whites continued to practice private economic exclusion. Industry and job-based employment discrimination was the norm in union and non-union settings, and neither competition nor Black acquisition of human capital proved sufficient to erode substantive racial inequality. Although twenty-five percent of Black farmers owned their own land by 1900 and small Black owned businesses grew by more than tenfold between 1867 and 1917, African Americans entrepreneurs competed in racially segregated markets. By the turn of the century, Black artisans competed in an economy increasingly dominated by White-only craft unions, Black children attended poorly funded schools, and Blacks collectively faced the rising tide of a homicidal White terrorism. In markets for housing, land, jobs, and education, whites openly and effectively exercised their rights as "Whites" to exclude and reap the benefits thereof.[15]

FIRST CLASS CITIZENS WITH SECOND CLASS JOBS: FROM AN ASSUMED TO AN INFERRED INFERIORITY

One of the *Plessy's* more striking legacies is its juridical validation of White judgement. "Discrimination," as economists understand it, was not an issue. Although the Supreme Court abstained from a Taney-like proclamation of white supremacy, its demarcation of the private social sphere as the fair arbiter of racial value indicates an absence of discrimination.

Whites were not rewarding Blacks less than comparable whites; Blacks simply *were not* comparable to whites. The Court's ruling implicitly accepts white assessments of Black human capital, and puts the burden of proof upon Blacks to prove otherwise.

Like the justices in *Plessy*, neoclassical theorists assume that racialization will not affect white valuations of Black human capital[16] ("racialization" refers to the social processes by which we learn to define human capacities in racial terms—the legacy of white supremacy is negative valuations of Black bodies and abilities). Hence evidence of longstanding racial disparities are prima facie evidence of Black deficiencies. *Alternatively stated, economists and jurists are at liberty to infer black deficiency from the extant racial distribution of economic outcomes.* The object of the human capital research agenda thus becomes the identification of the precise nature and size of those deficiencies.

In much of today's mainstream literature on Black-White wage and employment gaps, researchers infer that African Americans suffer "pre-market" disabilities (ostensibly due to racial differences in family, cultural background, and school quality) that inhibit our acquisition and use of human capital.[17] Yet young Blacks closed much of the racial education gap (measured by years of school completed) during the 1970s and 1980s. Moreover, African American youth steadily increased their SAT scores relative to whites since 1976, and the National Assessment for Educational Progress shows Black scores rising from the late 1970s through 1990, an era of economic crisis in working class African America. Remarkably, this widely available evidence of Black academic achievement does not disrupt the professional mainstream's dedication to the deficit thesis.[18]

And what of discrimination? Past discrimination remains the elusive culprit, appearing in the aforementioned conjectures about familial and cultural deficits. Present-day discrimination, or so the story goes, is just plain unlikely in a competitive environment. Moreover, orthodox economists disregard or endlessly dispute the direct evidence of market discrimination provided by audit studies. The ostrich has his head in the sand, and case studies are no match for theory and ideology rooted in the notion of African American inferiority.[19]

Today's Supreme Court also advances a color-blind vision. As was the case in the *Plessy*, the Fourteenth Amendment and the rights of whites, as whites, to exclude, assume center stage. Consider the 1989 case of *Richmond V. Croson*. Here the Supreme Court ruled against an affirmative action program adopted by the Richmond, Virginia City Council.

Richmond's post-1978 majority Black council viewed with suspicion the data in contracting left behind by their predecessors, a white dominated council. African Americans were 50 percent of Richmond's population, but received only 1 percent of the city contracts. The new council established an affirmative action set-aside program that required minority businesses to receive 30 percent of city contracts. The Supreme Court terminated the program in 1989; one year later, minority contractors again received 1 percent of the city's business.[20]

The Black council members were deeply aware of Richmond's long history of white racial domination. Black plaintiffs and their allies had sued the city before; in cases covering voting, education and housing, the city had appeared as defendant before the Supreme Court. Moreover, the white business elite had a one hundred-year record of systematically thwarting Black artisans' efforts to become contractors; loan refusal was a favorite strategy. A good-ol'-boy alliance between the white commercial establishment and the all-white city council governed the allocation of city contracts:

> While some of this elite circle believed that African Americans ought to be allowed equality in farming and trade pursuits (so long as they were willing to accept Jim Crow laws), there was no place for African-American businessmen outside of the African-American community.[21]

Croson is significant because it was the first time a majority of the Court used a "strict scrutiny" standard to evaluate an affirmative action program under the Equal Protection Clause of the Fourteenth Amendment. "Strict scrutiny" means that the Court is inherently suspicious of state policies that invoke racial classifications—i.e., it is predisposed to view race-based state policies as violations of the Fourteenth Amendment's guarantee of equal rights for each person without regard to her or his race. Critical race theorists Matsuda and Lawrence offer the following explanation of contemporary invocations of formal equality:

> Racial classifications are presumed invidious and are looked on with suspicion, because when we judge a person based on her race we disregard her human individuality and thereby deprive her of dignity and freedom of self-determination and self-actualization . . . The Supreme Court relies on America's strong tradition of liberal individualism when it tells us that we can ensure human dignity and equality by promising each person fair governmental process . . . Under this

view, it matters not whether the purpose of the policy is the perpetuation of racial subordination or its demise.[22]

Here again, we see the re-assertion of the doctrine of formal equality. As was the case in *Plessy*, the Court's invocation of equal treatment *both* "disappears" the different histories and meanings of Blackness and whiteness *and* reduces race to a mere accident of skin color. The application of color-blind formal equality obliterates the link between individual harm and harm done to individuals on a group basis. By using law to assert that white identity is identical to all other group identities, the Court denies that "whiteness" is based on racial exclusion and privilege. It insulates historically accumulated white privilege and further *de facto* codifies the status and property derived from the possession of whiteness.[23] Or, as Crenshaw observes, "Formal equality in conditions of social inequality becomes a tool of domination, reinforcing that system and insulating it from attack."[24]

The Court also turns a blind eye to past and present discrimination. Whereas neoclassical economists look to past societal discrimination to explain present day Black-white gaps in labor market outcomes, the Court offers no account of the past, thus disconnecting it from the present. Again, *Croson is* a powerful case-in-point. In writing the majority's opinion, Justice Sandra Day O'Connor rejected the city of Richmond's claim that set-asides were a remedy for past and continuing discrimination. She labeled the defendant's argument an "amorphous" and "unsupported" assertion of "societal discrimination."[25] But O'Connor did not stop there. In crafting her account of the absence of Black city contractors, she invoked neoclassical economists' old friend, "culturally based preferences." Remarkably, O'Connor went so far as to speculate that African Americans simply were disinterested in contracting work. Once again, Black culture is the culprit, this time predisposing African Americans to reject entrepreneurial life.

Thus, the two traditions are deeply connected ideological kin. The blood tie that binds is the denial of white racial domination. For orthodox economists, white racial identity is a non-starter. In a competitive world, whites are race-less entrepreneurs, heroically dismantling irrational wage and price differentials. Past discrimination—presumably more robust due to its legal foundations—injured Blacks, but apparently *neither* helped whites in any cumulative manner *nor* substantively altered their capacities to critically assess Black ability. Today's white market agents are color-blind by assumption.

In the halls of the highest courts, color-blindness also reigns. By denying both the past intentionality of white supremacist social relations and present-day institutional discrimination, the Supreme Court makes invisible both historic white privilege and the accrued socioeconomic benefits thereof. Yet in the rejection of indemnification programs, the court nonetheless affirms whites' collective right, as whites, to compete for each and every contract. And when, as was the case in Richmond, the post-affirmative action competition yields Black exclusion—well, 'tis simply the natural outcome of private actions in a market assumed well-ordered unless proven otherwise. In their narratives of Black-white economic inequality, the courts and our professional mainstream sing a disturbing, harmonious duet that renders African American economic exclusion both normal and just.

NOTES

1. Because the critical literature is voluminous, our list is only suggestive of sources available to the interested reader. See William A. Darity, Jr.'s "The Human Capital Approach to Black-White Earnings Inequality: Some Unsettled Questions," *Journal of Human Resources* 17 (1982): 72–93; Paula England, "The Failure of Human Capital Theory to Explain Occupational Sex Segregation," *Journal of Human Resources* (Summer, 1982): 358–70; Barbara Bergmann, *The Economic Emergence of Women* (New York: Basic Books: 1986); Rhonda M. Williams, "Beyond Human Capital: Black Women, Work and Wages," Wellesley College Center for Research on Women, Working Paper No. 183, 1988; Patrick Mason, "The Divide-and-Conquer and Employer/Employee Models of Discrimination: Neoclassical Competition as a Familial Defect," *Review of Black Political Economy* 20 (Spring 1992); Jeremiah Cotton, "Labor Markets and Racial Inequality," in William A. Darity, Jr. (ed.), *Labor Economics: Problems in Analyzing Labor Markets* (Boston: Kluwer Academic Press: 1993): 183–208. For an elegant summary of the Marxian and radical tradition's alternatives, see Patrick Mason, "Some Heterodox Models of Inequality in the Market for Labor Power," in Thomas D. Boston (ed.), *A Different Vision.-Race and Public Policy-Volume 2* (New York: Routledge, 1997): 350–379.

2. William M. Rodgers III and William E. Spriggs, "What Does the AFQT Really Measure: Race, Wages, Schooling and the AFQT Score, " *Review of Black Political Economy* 24 (Spring, 1996):13–46.

3. See Rodgers and Spriggs for a more thorough discussion of the recent literature.

4. Mason, 1997 discusses radical economists' analyses of racial inequality in capitalist economies. For other examples of economic analyses that address the class and gender dimesions of racial inequality, see Rhonda M. Williams, "A Reconsideration of Racial Earnings Inequality," *Review of Radical Political Economics* 19:2 (Summer, 1987): 1–15; Rose Brewer "Theorizing Race, Gender and Class," in S.M. James and A.P.A. Busia, ed. *Theorizing Black Feminisms* (New York: Routledge, 1993): 13–30; Julie Matthaei, "Why Marxist, Feminist and Anti-Racist Economists Should be Marxist-Feminist-Anti-Racist Economists, *Feminist Economics* 2 (Spring, 1996): 1–21; and Rhonda M. Williams and Robert E. Kenison, "The Way We

Were?: Discrimination, Competition, and Inter-Industry Wage Differentials in 1970," *Review of Radical Political Economics* 28:2 (June, 1996): 1–32.

5. *Dred Scott v. Sanford,* 60 U.S. 393 19 Howard 393 (1857).

6. Cheryl Harris, "Whiteness ass Property," *Harvard Law Review* 106:8 (June, 1993): 1707–1791.

7. Harris, p. 1736.

8. See William E. Spriggs, *Afro-American Wealth Accumulation, Virginia, 1900–1914* (Ph.D. Dissertation, University of Wisconsin, 1984) for a discussion of private developers use of race restrictive covenants during the late 1800s. See Charles S. Johnson, *Patterns of Negro Segregation* (New York: Harper and Brothers, 1943) for a discussion of the Supreme Court's eventual outlawing of private deed covenants in the 1940s.

9. For discussions of white economic power at the turn of the century, see Sterling.D. Spero and Abram Harris, *The Black Worker: The Negro and the Labor Movement* (New York: Antheourn, 1972-originally published in 1931); Robert D. Higgs, "Black Progress and the Persistence of Racial Economic Inequalities, 1865–1940," in Steven Shulman and William Darity, Jr. (ed.) *The Question of Discrimination: Racial Inequality in the U. S. Labor Market* (Middletown, CT: Wesleyan University Press, 1989):9–31; Herbert Hill, "Black Labor and Affirmative Action: An Historical Perspective, " in Shulman and Darity, *op cit:* 190–267. Oliver and Shapiro's analysis of race, land acquisition and home ownership provides long needed insights into the historical emergence of the much underexamined Black-white wealth gap. See Melvin Oliver and Thomas Shapiro, *Black Wealth, White Wealth: A New Perspective on Racial Inequality* (New York: Routledge, 1995).

10. *Plessy v. Ferguson,* 163 U.S. 537 (1869).

11. Kimberle Crenshaw, "Color Blindness, History and Law," in Wahneema Lubiano (ed.), *The House That Race Built: Black Americans, U.S. Terrain* (New York: Pantheon, 1997): 280–288.

12. Crenshaw (1997), p. 283.

13. See Robert Cherry, "Myrdal's Cumulative Hypothesis: Its Antecedants and Its Contemporary Application,'.' in Boston, (ed.): 17–37 an analysis of turn of the century racial thought in the economics profession.

14. I credit Cheryl Harris (1993), op cit, for introducing me to this part of the *Plessy* decision.

15. See Higgs (1989).

16. By "racialization," we mean the social processes that encourage the reading of specific body types as indicative of "naturally" ocurring and distinct breeding populations, or "races" (each "race" is understood to include patterns of gender differentiation).

17. See Rodgers and Spriggs (1995) for a concise summary of and critique of this literature. Another variation on the human capital theme attempts to explain the decline in African American relative wages in the 1980s as the result of a general widening of the U.S. wage distribution. That is, the shift in labor demand toward better educated and more skilled workers reduced the relative wages of all less-skilled employees and increased the rate of return to skill. However, William Rodgers' rigorous distributional analysis shows that it is better educated African Americans moreso that the less well educated, who have lost ground relative to their white peers because of the general increase in wage inequality. See his chapter "Measuring Wage Discrimination During Periods of Growing Overall Wage Inequality," in Patrick L. Mason and Rhonda M. Williams (ed.), *Race, Markets and Social Outcomes* (Boston: Kluwer Academic Press, 1997): 67–90.

18. Rodgers and Spriggs (1995) address the phenomena of rising test scores in

their conclusion; Jared Bernstein's "Where's the Payoff? The Gap Between Black Academic Progress and Economic Gains," (Washington, D.C.: Economic Policy Institute, 1995) presents the NAEP test score data for the years between 1975 and 1990.

19. Marxian economists continue to articulates a theoretical, historical, and empirical tradition that reconciles competition and discrimination. For examples, Williams (1987), Williams and Kenison (1996), Mason (1992, 1997) and William A. Darity, Jr. "What's Left of the Economic Theory of Discrimination?" in Shulman and Darity (1989): 335–376.

20. Mary Frances Berry, "Affirmative Action: Political Opportunists Exploit Racial Rears." *Emerge* (May, 1995): 29–42.

21. Peter Charles Hoffer, "Blind to History: The Use of Affirmative Action Suits: Another Look at *City of Richmond v. J.A. Croson Co.*," 23 *Rutgers Law Journal* 270 (1992): 289–290. Also, see *City of Richmond v. J.A. Croson*, 488 U.S. 469, 485 (1989).

22. Charles R. Lawrence III and Mari Matsuda, *We Won't Go Back: Making the Case for Affirmative Action.* (New York: Houghton Mifflin, 1997): 80–81.

23. Here I paraphrase Cheryl Harris' conclusions.

24. Crenshaw, 285; Matsuda and Lawrence make a similar critique.

25. Matsuda and Lawrence, 79–80.

24

IS THERE DISCRIMINATION IN MORTGAGE LENDING? WHAT DOES THE RESEARCH TELL US?

Harold A. Black

The research and discussions of discrimination in lending are extensive. Due to the magnitude of the research, this article does not attempt to be exhaustive in its literature review. Rather it is more selective and presents representative studies on each of the areas delineated. In general, researchers fall into two camps. First, are those that believe that discrimination is pervasive and who will criticize any study whose conclusion differs from their view. Second, are those that believe that discrimination exists but not in mortgage lending and who criticize any study whose conclusion differs from their view. I fall into the third camp. I have no agenda and in the twenty or more years that I have contributed to the literature, I report what the data tell me. As a consequence, I have noted the existence of discrimination in some research and its absence in others.

With nationwide rejection rates of blacks and Hispanics almost three-to-one above that of whites (and Asians), many people argue that discrimination must exist. The question is, if discrimination exists, then why are there so few cases that document it? Indeed, very few cases of discrimination have been documented in the research, few cases are uncovered in the regulatory examination process and even fewer complaints are made by applicants of unfair treatment. Where discrimination is alleged, often the investigation is dropped by the regulator or a settlement is reached. Often such settlements are greeted in the popular press as implying the institution is in fact discriminating against applicants. However, in at least one such instance, statistical analysis on the lender's application files showed no discrimination, but the lender accepted the settlement because it was less costly than litigation.

Asians also present an interesting case. Generally, Asians are excluded from the research on discrimination because their rejection rates are equal to or lower than those for whites. But why is this the case? Also, Hispanics are generally considered as one group. However, housing studies have shown that only black Hispanics are subject to discrimination similar to that of black non-Hispanics. White Hispanics appear to suffer less discrimination. As a consequence, should white Hispanics be deleted from a data set that includes black Hispanics?

THE RESEARCH

The research in the area can be divided into the following areas, many of which overlap.

Redlining versus Racial Discrimination

Redlining is lending discrimination against properties rather than individual applicants. A review of the redlining literature can be found in Benston.[1] If lenders were engaging in redlining some observers asserted that this created economic decline in certain geographic areas. It was contended that certain areas are perceived, rightly or wrongly, as being high risk. Therefore, individuals who applied for mortgage loans in those areas were considered by the lender to be purchasing property that is of a higher risk than alternative properties. Thus, redlining is discrimination against *properties* rather than against individuals. As a consequence, the application could be denied due to property location or the loan could be accepted but on less favorable terms. Although acceptance by the loan on less favorable terms could be an appropriate compensation for the additional perceived riskiness of the loan, some view such differential terms as prima facie evidence of discrimination.

The research on redlining has taken two approaches. The first is the survey method and the second is analysis of statistical data. The survey approach relies on reports of personal experiences of the respondents. As such, the surveys may report on the respondents perception of discrimination and the responses are seldom if ever verified.[2]

Statistical studies of redlining have found little evidence that such discrimination exists.[3] Avery and Buynak do find that whereas neighborhood racial composition has little impact on mortgage lending, majority black neighborhoods do have a lower incidence of conventional mortgage financing. Nonetheless, such is not *prima facie* evidence of redlining discrimination despite some claims to the contrary. Generally, these studies are of specific urban areas and mainly show that the lower incidence of lending is correlated with factors such as low income and low home appraisals.[4]

As to studies on loan terms, the results are also mixed. Black and Schweitzer[5] study mortgage lending terms at commercial banks and find that race and gender play significant roles in determining lending terms at the banks that they analyzed. This is consistent with the possibility of discrimination in the loan terms established for accepted loans. However, Black and Schweitzer note that although these applicants made larger downpayments, their mortgages were at lower interest rates and longer years to maturity than comparable white male applicants. Similarly, Crawford and Rosenblatt[6] look at yield premiums over market rate for loans that had been originated. These premiums are compared across three racial groups over a two year period in the late 1980s. In contrast to the results of Black and Schweitzer,[7] they find little evidence of significant differences across racial groups, although small premiums were observed for VA and FHA loans.

RACIAL DISCRIMINATION

The literature on racial discrimination in lending finds mixed results. Galster[8] reviews much of this literature. The major problem that has hampered researchers has been the lack of data. The most readily available data source is the Home Mortgage Disclosure Act (HMDA) data base. Racial disparity drawn from HMDA have widely been cited as evidence of discrimination. But racial disparities are inadequate for such a conclusion. The HMDA data do not contain information on data that are important in the lending decision making process such as the financial characteristics of the applicant: liquid assets and net worth, credit history, employment history, or information regarding the property to be purchased.[9]

Ideally, bank applicant data would be the source to study. For those researchers not privy to the applicant files at lenders, there are two widely cited works that indicate lender discrimination. The first is a Department of Justice study of an individual lender and the second was a study of the Boston MSA by the Federal Reserve Bank of Boston.

The Department of Justice (DOJ) case involved DOJ analyzing loan files and using multivariate statistical analysis.[10] The analysis utilized a statistical model to analyze the variables that included income, credit history, and debt levels. The finding was that race was a significant factor in the lending decision of the lending institution.

However, Rachlis and Yezer[11] show that the statistical technique employed in the DOJ study can be used to demonstrate the absence of discrimination when the coefficient on the race variable is insignificant, but cannot be used to show discrimination. Moreover, the econometric literature indicates that DOJ's statistical technique was employed incorrectly and does not yield a unique solution.[12]

The study by the Federal Reserve Bank of Boston[13] was the first publicly available study that employed econometric methods to find strong statistical evidence of discrimination against minority applicants. Previously, studies had shown either the absence of discrimination or weak statistical evidence of discrimination in lending.[14]

The Boston study finds discrimination in lending in its analysis of the Boston MSA. However, it does not reveal discrimination at the institutional level. As the authors of the Boston study note "a systematic bias in mortgage lending is very difficult to document at the institution level, particularly when the number of minority applications is small, as it is in the vast majority of institutions".

The Boston study has been carefully scrutinized. It has generated studies that support its conclusion[15] and studies that do not support its conclusions.[16] Using the Boston data set that includes FDIC-supervised lenders, Horne first generates similar results. Then he addresses the variable omission problem, re-estimates the model and finds no evidence of lending discrimination.

Analysis of Defaults

It has been suggested that average default rates rather than average rejection rates be used as a test of discrimination. If the average default rate on loans to black borrowers were lower than that for loans to white borrowers, the implication is that black borrowers are being held to a higher credit standard. As Galster[17] and Ferguson and Peters[18] have noted, a credit policy that is uniform across races will result in a higher average default rate for black borrowers if average credit risk for black borrowers is higher than that for whites. Instead of differences in average default rates, the literature stemming from seminal work suggest testing for differences in the marginal probability of default, holding borrower characteristics constant.[19] Berkovec, Canner, Gabriel and Hannan[20] indicate that rather than lower default rates on FHA loans, black borrowers have a *higher* marginal likelihood of default than white borrowers holding other characteristics of the mortgage constant. This result has led to spirited criticism by Galster,[21] Yinger[22] and Ross[23] on the value of such an approach.

SOME FINAL OBSERVATIONS

Despite those who contend that discrimination in lending must exist, it is less probable now than when I first began to study the problem. When I conducted one of the first econometric studies of lending discrimination,[24] I fully expected to find evidence of lending discrimination. There was no CRA and no HMDA. There was little competition in the financial institution arena. Economics tells us that discrimination is more likely to occur when competition is absent.

However today the federal regulatory agencies, HUD, the Justice Department and state regulators are all aggressive in monitoring for lending discrimination making such activity on the part of lenders highly costly and irrational.

Moreover, today's competitive environment is radically different than in the 1970s. Studies have shown that the influx of competitors has reduced the value of a bank charter throughout the 1980s. Where there were few providers there are now many. Benston[25] has noted that the likelihood that discrimination exists is lessened by the presence of so many competitors in the mortgage market. He notes that there are at least 540 mortgage lenders listed in the Atlanta telephone book, many of whom offer mortgages mainly by telephone. Thus, in an environment of aggressive regulators and competition, we should find less discrimination assuming of course that discrimination is a rational act. Of course, if it is an irrational act it would still occur.

Discrimination could be due to something that is subconscious. A banker does not want to make a bad loan. But a banker does not want to turn away good business to the bank's competitors either. However, if the banker knows that a certain group is more likely to default than another, then that group would have higher rejection rates than similar individuals in another group. This would mean that the marginal black applicant is more likely to be rejected than the marginal white applicant.

This action is illegal and is often referred to as the cultural affinity hypothesis.[26] That is why many banks are employing more minorities as loan officers, reevaluating their lending procedures, and instituting awareness seminars for their loan officers and executives.

However, the cultural affinity hypothesis may be independent of the race of the lender. As commonly presented, the applicant is a minority and the lender is a majority. However, the issue is one of information and information costs. If similarly situated blacks have higher default rates than whites, then the color of the lender is irrelevant. Indeed Black, Collins and Cyree[27] have found that under certain conditions black banks show statistical evidence of discrimination against black customers while white lenders do not.

One other point. The banks may not be discriminating but a particular bank representative may be. This is an agency problem. Let us assume that a loan officer is biased while the bank itself is not. It would be difficult to discover such an individual given a random distribution of minority applicants among the loan officers. The bank could then let the loan officers be production agents who do not make the final decision. Some lenders—including FNMA—are relying more heavily on credit scoring. However, it is well known that given income, black applicants have worse credit than white applicants. If scoring were employed, rather than lender discretion, black rejection rates would likely rise.

The major problem facing lenders today is therefore one of uncertainty. If lenders know what rejection rates are likely to elicit a response from the regulators, then they may engage in some type of window dressing to achieve such rejection rates.[28] Although the acceptance of the best of the clearly rejected black applicant pool may result in higher defaults and foreclosures, such actions are not likely to impair the financial viability of lenders but will result in more severely damaging already poor credit histories of applicants.

CONCLUSIONS

The literature is rich with research and commentary on discrimination in mortgage markets. But what does the literature tell us? Does lending discrimination exist? The answer appears to be that if lending discrimination does exist, it is far from pervasive. Despite high rates of racial disparities in accept/reject decisions, when factors such as job stability and credit history are taken into account, most studies show little evidence of discrimination.

There are very few statistical studies that provide an indication of discrimination. The ones that do often have serious flaws and analyses of the same data set by other researchers have yielded conflicting results. However, this does not imply that lending discrimination is absent from all institutions. If it exists, it is either an irrational act in the face of aggressive regulatory monitoring or is a result of cultural affinity. Regardless, there is little doubt that the lending environment is radically different today that when the earliest research was conducted. It is apparent that the presence of regulators and competition lessen the likelihood of lending discrimination occurring. Perhaps this is the message that the literature is telling us.

NOTES

1. Benston, G. J. (1979). "Mortgage Redlining Research: A Review and Critical Analysis," *Journal of Bank Research*, Spring, 8–23.
2. Massey, D. S. and N.A. Denton. *American Apartheid.* Harvard University Press, Cambridge, MA, 1993.
3. See Avery, R. B. and T. M. Buynak, "Mortgage Redlining: Some New Evidence," *Economic Review,* Federal Reserve Bank of Cleveland, Summer 1981. Becker, G. S. (1971). *The Economics of Discrimination*, Chicago: University of Chicago Press; Bentson, G. J. and D. Horsky, (1991) "The Relationship Between the Demand and Supply of Home Financing and Neighborhood Characteristics: An Empircal Study of Mortgage Redlining," *Journal of Financial Services Research* 5, 235–260; Holmes, A. L. and P. Horvitz (1994). "Mortgage Redlining: Race, Risk, and Demand," *Journal of Finance,* 49, 81–99.
4. Benston, G.J. (1979). "Mortgage Redlining Research: A Review and Critical Analysis," *Journal of Bank Research*, Spring, 8–23.
5. Black, H. A. and R. L. Schweitzer, (1985). "A Canonical Analysis of mortgage Lending Terms: Testing for Lending Discrimination at a Commercial Bank," *Urban Studies,* 13–19.
6. Crawford, G. and E. Rosenblatt, (1995). "Discrimination and Racial Differences in Home Mortgage Interest Rates," working paper, Federal National Mortgage Association
7. Black, H. A. and R. L. Schweitzer, (1985). "A Canonical Analysis of mortgage Lending Terms: Testing for Lending Discrimination at a Commercial Bank," *Urban Studies,* 13–19.
8. Galster, G.C. (1992). "Research on Discrimination in Housing and Mortgage Markets: Assessment and Future Directions," in *Housing Policy Debate.*
9. Black, H. A. (1995). "HMDA Data and Regulatory Inquiries Regarding Discrimination," in *Fair Lending Analysis,* Anthony J. Yezer, Ed., American Bankers Association, Washington, D.C.
10. Siskin, B. R. and L. A. Cupingood, "Use of statistical models to provide statistical evidence of discrimination in the treatment of mortgage loan applicants: a study of one lending institution," in *Home Mortgage Lending and Discrimination,* 1993.
11. Rachlis, M. B. and A. M. J. Yezer, "Serious Flaws in Statistical Tests for Discrimination in Mortgage Markets," *Journal of Housing Research,* May 1993.

12. Hosmer, D. W. and S. Lemeshow, (1989), *Applied Regression,* (Wiley-Interscience).

13. Munnell, A. H., L. E. Browne, J. McEnerney and G. M. B. Tootell, (1996). "Mortgage Lending in Boston: Interpreting HMDA Data," *American Economic Review,* 86, 25–53.

14. Black, H. A., R. L. Schweitzer and L. Mandell, (1978). "Discrimination in Mortgage Lending," *American Economic Review,* 68, 234–241; Black, H.A. and R. L. Schweitzer "Discrimination in the Lending Decision of Banks: The Case of Home Improvement Loans," *Journal of Bank Research,* Autumn 1980, v. 11, n. 3 pp. 184–186.

15. Carr, J. H. and I. F. Megbolugbe (1993), "The Federal Reserve Bank of Boston Study on Mortgage Lending Revisited," *Journal of Housing Research,* 4(2), 277–313; Glennon, D. and M. Stengel (1994). "An Evaluation of the Federal Reserve Bank of Boston's Study of Racial Discrimination in Mortgage Lending," Working Paper 94–2, office of the Comptroller of the Currency, Washington, D.C.

16. Horne, D. K. (1997). "Mortgage Lending, Race, and Model Specification," *Journal of Financial Services Research* 11, 43–68. Day, T. and S.J. Liebowitz (1994). "Mortgages, Minorities, and Discrimination," Working Paper, University of Texas at Dallas.

17. Galster, G.C. (1993). "The Facts of Lending Discrimination Cannot Be Argued Away by Examining Defaults Rates," *Housing Policy Debate.*

18. Ferguson, M.F. and S. R. Peters (1995). "What Constitutes Evidence of Lending Discrimination?", *Journal of Finance* (June), 739–748.

19. Becker, 1971. Arrow, Kenneth (1973). "The Theory of Discrimination," in *Discrimination in Labor Markets.* Ashenfelter and Rees (eds.), Princeton, NJ: Princeton University Press.

20. Berkovec, J. A., Canner, G. B., Gabriel. S. A. and T. H. Hannan (1996). "Mortgage Discrimination and FHA Loan Performance," Cityscape 2 (1), 9–24.

21. Galster, G. C. (1996). "Comparing Loan Performance Between Races as a Test for Discrimination," Cityscape 2(l), 33–40.

22. Yinger, J. (1996). "Why Default Rates Cannot Shed Light on Mortgage Discrimination," *Cityscape* 2(l), 25–32.

23. Ross, S. L. (1996). "Flaws in the Use of Loan Defaults to Test for Mortgage Lending Discrimination," *Cityscape* 2(l),41–48.

24. Black, H. A., R. L. Schweitzer and L. Mandell, (1978). "Discrimination in Mortgage Lending," *American Economic Review,* 68, 234–241.

25. Benston, G. J. (1997). "Discrimination in Financial Services: What Do We Not Know?", *Journal of Financial Services Research* 11, 209–214.

26. Calomiris, D. W., Kahn, C. M. and Longhofer, S. D. (1994). "Housing-Finance Intervention and Private Incentives: Helping Minorities and the Poor." *Journal of Money, Credit and Banking* 26 (Part 2), 634–674; Hunter, W.C. and M. B. Walker (1996). "The Cultural Affinity Hypothesis and Mortgage Lending Decisions," *Journal of Real Estate Finance and Economics* 13, 57–70.

27. Black, H. A., Collins, M. C. and K.B. Cyree (1997)."Do Black-Owned Banks Discriminate Against Black Borrowers?," *Journal of Financial services Research* 11, 189–204.

28. Evanoff, D.D. and L.M. Segal (1996). "Strategic Responses to Bank Regulation: Evidence from HMDA Data," *Journal of Financial Services Research* 11, 69–94.

25

ANOTHER LOOK AT MORTGAGE LENDING DISCRIMINATION: A REVIEW OF FINDINGS

Thomas D. Boston
Usha Nair-Reichert
Willie Belton
Haizheng Li

Decades ago the civil rights struggle focused the nation's attention on the unfulfilled constitutional promise of equal treatment. This unfulfilled promise was epitomized in the various practices that denied minorities equal access to social, political and economic institutions and fostered separate and unequal life chances between whites and blacks.

Today, most of the extreme vestiges of inequality have disappeared. But economic parity between minority and non-minority groups in income and wealth remains an enormous challenge. One primary manifestation of this inequality is in homeownership. The 1998 Survey of Consumer Finances indicates that non-financial assets are still the largest component of the value of household assets even though their share has declined from 69.6% in 1989 to 59.4% in 1998. Among all family assets, homeownership is the most important, accounting for 47.1% of the value of non-financial assets of all American families. But, 71.8% of non-Hispanic white families are homeowners while only 46.8% of minorities own their primary residence.

The relative importance of homeownership as a component of family wealth and the enormous wealth gap between minorities and whites make understanding the factors that influence the mortgage lending decision very important. In particular, it is important to know whether the gap in homeownership between minorities and non-minorities is influenced by discriminatory practices. Recently, a number of studies have examined this issue and their findings have been the subject of a great deal of controversy. While some leading researchers in this area have statistically validated the presence of discrimination in the lending process, others criticize these findings, citing flaws in the quality of data and methodology.

OBJECTIVE

This chapter examines the literature on mortgage lending discrimination. Its purpose is to determine whether the findings of that literature suggest that discriminatory practices continue to exist among financial institutions engaged in the mortgage lending and administration process.[1]

We look at the three distinct stages of the lending process: the pre-application stage, the loan approval/rejection stage, and the loan administration stage. Among these three, the greatest amount of empirical data and largest number of studies have been conducted for the loan approval/rejection stage. Yet, researchers still disagree about the conclusiveness of the findings. The same is true for the other stages where much less research has been conducted. Our analysis leads us to conclude that despite methodological and data limitation, the preponderance of the empirical and anecdotal evidence suggests that mortgage lending discrimination occurs at all three stages of the lending process.

Legally, lending discrimination is classified in two ways: (1) "Disparate Treatment," and (2) "Disparate Impact." The first type of discrimination occurs when lending standards are applied differently by race. The difference in application of standards may center on any part of the lending process where criteria that are used to make loans to whites differ from those used to make loans to minorities. As an example, this type of discrimination would exist if a lending institution considered the non-labor income of whites as a compensating factor in determining the debt-to-income ratio while the same consideration is not given to similarly situated minorities.

By contrast, a disparate impact occurs when lending criteria that are facially neutral have an adverse impact on minorities. This might exist, for example, if a bank establishes a minimum mortgage threshold below which it will not make loans. Although the threshold is neutral on the surface, the ultimate impact might be to disqualify a larger percentage of minorities because the average size of their mortgage loan requests is smaller than that of whites.

The legal treatment of these two forms of discrimination has a long established history in employment discrimination litigation which dates back to Title VII of the 1964 Civil Rights Act, as amended in 1972.[2]

These acts prohibit discrimination in employment on the basis of race, color, creed, national origin, religion or sex.

Under Title VII, an employer is liable to a claim of disparate treatment when it treats certain employees less favorably than others based on race, color, religion, sex or national origin. To establish this claim, proof of motive is required. This can be either direct proof or proof inferred from the preponderance of the evidence or the mere difference in the facts of the treatment.

Under Title VII, an employer is also liable for a claim of disparate impact if the employer uses a facially neutral employment practice which falls more harshly on minority groups. In an adverse or disparate impact case, the plaintiff will typically use statistics to show a significant difference in the treatment of the protected group, and/or that a policy or practice has a disparate and adverse effect on the protected class. If an employee makes a prima facie case of discrimination by using statistics that show a disparate impact of an employer's practices, the burden of proof then shifts to the employer to justify the challenged practice. Using this standard, it has been suggested that the empirical evidence of lending discrimination is such that the burden of proof should shift to lending institutions themselves.

PRE-APPLICATION STAGE OF MORTGAGE LENDING

The pre-application stage refers to activities that occur before a potential homeowner actually applies for a mortgage. It includes the buyer's interaction with both the realtor and the lender. The realtor provides information on the location, availability, and pricing of housing units. In addition, they provide information regarding the availability of mortgages. Lenders rely heavily on realtors for referrals and often advertise their loan products through them. The realtor's recommendation to the buyer often influences their choice of a lender, especially in the case of first time homeowners. Similarly, the realtor's referral to the lender causes the latter to be more favorably pre-disposed towards the buyer. As such, the realtor can use this unique relationship as a screening device that may discriminate against minorities. Some researchers have noted that it is during this stage that most of the discriminatory acts take place.[3]

Measurement of discrimination in the pre-application stage is challenging because discrimination can take subtle forms and customers are not fully aware of how other racial groups are treated. It is also difficult to distinguish, especially in a legal sense, between a profit-maximizing decision by the realtor or lender that also adversely affects minorities and one that is discriminatory. In addition, records maintained by banks and realtors regarding the pre-application stage are often incomplete.

Some of the approaches used to identify discrimination at this stage include audits using matched pairs, personal interviews with loan applicants, and an analysis of the history of branch openings and closings. Researchers then statistically control for applicant, property and loan characteristics and determine whether there are statistically significant differences in the treatment of minority and white applicants. Typically, regression analyses or paired differences-of-means tests are used. Audits of realtors have been conducted on a large scale; but for lenders, most of the audits have been pilot studies.

FAIR HOUSING AUDITS

The fair housing audit was developed to determine whether or not complaints of discrimination are valid. Auditing is used for both research and enforcement. Research auditing is designed to identify the existence of discrimination and requires a large number of tests to obtain statistically robust findings. Enforcement audits are conducted by auditors to develop evidence of discrimination in legal proceedings, and requires a much smaller sample to prove discrimination. This method was used on a small scale in the 1950s and 1960s. It became a very visible tool when the U.S. Department of Housing and Urban Development sponsored the Housing Market Practice Survey (HMPS) in 1977 to study housing discrimination against African American households.

In 1989, the Housing Discrimination Study (HDS) sponsored by the U.S. Department of Housing and Urban Development conducted about 3,800 audits in twenty-five metropolitan areas. This study also supported findings of discriminatory practices against minorities in the housing market.

An audit is a survey technique that helps to isolate the impact of a person's minority status on the treatment the person receives when making inquiries about the availability of housing or mortgages. Auditing for discrimination involves identifying matched pairs of auditors. Each member of a matched pair is similar with respect to all relevant characteristics except race. An audit consists of successive visits to the same realty firm or lender by the two audit teammates. The treatment that the minority tester and the majority tester receive and the outcomes of the transactions are closely observed, documented and analyzed for differential treatment on the basis of race. The key aspect of the audit design is to make teammates as comparable as possible, so that the differences in the treatment of the black and white auditors cannot be attributed to factors other than race. In order to build comparability and isolate the impact of race, the HDS carefully used the four tools of audit design, namely, matching, assignment, training and timing. Audit teammates are matched so that they have the same general set of fixed characteristics such as sex, age, and general appearance. They are also assigned similar economic and family characteristics for the purpose of each audit. Training helps minimize differences in the teammates' questions and behavior. Teammates also visit the same realtor or lender within a relatively short time of each other, in order to make the circumstances they encounter at the office as similar as possible. In the case of the HDS audit the sample of realtors visited was based on randomly selected newspaper advertisements.

ADVANTAGES AND LIMITATION OF THE AUDIT METHODOLOGY

Among the chief advantages of auditing are the comparative level of confidence and political persuasiveness of its results, its ability to detect subtle forms of discrimination, and its effectiveness as an enforcement tool. Some analysts have expressed concerns that auditors' feedback regarding subtle discriminatory behaviors by loan officers may be unreliable and highly subjective. It is also very difficult to match auditors on all characteristics that the realtors perceive as relevant. Strategies used to recruit, train and compensate the auditors may also affect the outcome of the audits. Other important issues that influence the results of the audit include sampling strategies such as the selection of realtors and lenders to be audited, the types of housing units to be used in the audit, and the mechanism through which auditors gain access to the agent. Additional small-scale audits may also be necessary to determine the optimal size of the sample needed to discern discriminatory behavior. There is also some concern that the lenders discovering that they are being audited may compromise the integrity of an audit.

Another disputed area is the measurement of unfavorable treatment. It may not always be possible to measure unfavorable treatment unambiguously. For example, minority auditors may be shown more dwellings than their majority teammates, but these may be in minority neighborhoods, or in places with low-quality housing and poor public services. Even though minorities were "favored" with respect to the number of units shown to them, this is clearly a case of steering. However, including the quality of housing in the audit greatly increases the scope for subjectivity and bias in the results.[4] Critics of audits have also pointed to several ethical issues such as breach of the realtors'/lenders' privacy, entrapment of realtors/lenders in the case of enforcement audits, and the institutionalization of deceptive practices. Despite these criticisms, the technique has served to identify discrimination and in this regard it has influenced public policy. Clearly, the methodology must be continually refined. Recent empirical work in this direction includes pairs of same race auditors, "sandwich" audits that involve three auditors, two of one race and a third of the other, and repeat audits of the same agent.[5]

Most of the information regarding lender behavior at the pre-application stage is from pilot audits. However, the methodology has been used extensively to audit realtors. These pilot studies of lender behavior do not meet the standards of research design or reporting required for research purposes; nonetheless, they provide insight into the incidence and types of discriminatory practices of lenders.

DISCRIMINATION IN HOUSING AVAILABILITY

Existing evidence suggests that minority and white auditors are often treated differently by the realtor with regard to the number and type of housing units they are shown. Upon arrival at the realtor's office, an auditor usually inquires about the advertised unit and the availability of similar units. Two measures of discrimination are the net incidence of discrimination and the severity of discrimination. The net incidence of discrimination for any type of realtor behavior (such as denying an auditor access to all available housing) is the share of audits in which the minority auditor was treated less favorably than her teammate less the share of audits in which the white auditor was treated less favorably. The severity of impact in this case is the difference between the average number of units shown to white auditors and those shown to minority auditors.

Realtors have considerable latitude in deciding which units to recommend and show to prospective customers. The net incidence of discrimination against black auditors regarding the total units available (which is the sum of the total units recommended and total units shown) was 19.4 percent. The HDS audits also tried to identify whether minorities were excluded from the market. Exclusion occurred if a minority auditor was told that nothing is available while her teammate was recommended or shown at least one unit. The net incidence of exclusion was 6.34 percent for black-white sales audits.[6]

While these results reveal the incidence of discrimination in housing availability, there is also the need to identify the severity of its impact. Evidence from the HDS indicates that blacks are shown 23.7 percent fewer units than their white counterparts. Exclusion and withholding information about some units denies minorities access to over 2 housing units in sales audits. The study also revealed that discrimination increases in relation to the number of units agents have to sell. The severity of discrimination against blacks increases when the number of units other than the advertised one available to be inspected is larger. With a single unit available, the severity of discrimination is only 0.11 houses, but this increases to 2.26 houses when 15 additional units are available.[7]

A 1995 study using the 1989 HDS data suggests that customer prejudice and racial stereotyping influence agent behavior, particularly towards black customers. Specific estimates indicate that discrimination levels vary across cities.[8] There is also evidence that widespread discrimination occurs because of the realtor's personal prejudice and the prejudice of white clients.[9] The perception of discrimination by brokers may also limit the use of realtors by black home-seekers. Data from Detroit collected in 1992 suggests that blacks were significantly less likely than whites to consult brokers, and relied more on search techniques such as talking to friends, newspaper advertisements and driving through neighborhoods.[10]

RACIAL STEERING

Steering occurs both in the treatment of individual home-seekers and in the marketing practices of realtors. Steering takes place at the individual level when minorities are shown housing units but are steered away from predominately white neighborhoods into already integrated or minority neighborhoods. Steering in the marketing of homes may involve discriminatory practices by realtors such as differential efforts at advertising, holding open houses, listing houses, or the use of multiple listing services (MLS) for homes in largely black or integrated neighborhoods as compared to white neighborhoods. Racial steering imposes significant constraints on minority individuals in their choice of housing and promotes segregation in residential neighborhoods.

Some of the steering at the individual level may be motivated by the perceptions of the realtor. For example, a realtor may perceive customers from different races and ethnic groups as having different neighborhood preferences. Hence, in order to save time and effort, they may not show whites homes in predominantly black neighborhoods and vice-versa. A realtor may also perceive a white seller in a predominately white neighborhood as being less willing to sell to minorities, and hence steer his minority clients away from such listings.[11]

Racial differences in the way that realtors provide information to minority customers about mortgages have a large impact on their ability to obtain a mortgage, since realtors are often the primary source of information regarding mortgages for many potential homeowners. The Housing Discrimination Study found substantial and statistically significant differences in the willingness of brokers to help white and minority customers obtain mortgages.[12] In black-white audits, 24.4 percent of the white auditors were provided assistance in finding mortgages as compared to 13.3 percent for black auditors. In addition there were significant differences in the information provided to white and black auditors about fixed and variable rate mortgages, as well as FHA loans. White auditors were 21.5 percent more likely to be told about fixed loans and 15.1 percent more likely to be told about adjustable rate mortgages than were black auditors. On the other hand, black auditors were 6.7 percent more likely to be told about FHA loans than white auditors.[13] This supports earlier findings that realtors were more likely to inform white prospects about conventional mortgages and creative financing opportunities.[14]

The literature review suggests that the actions of realtors, such as their office location, advertising practices, racial steering, and poor dissemination of information to prospective minority customers severely constrain the ability of many minority households to buy homes, and exacerbate residential segregation by race. A 1996 study, using the Boston Fed data, was able to empirically identify the effects of race and neighborhood separately, and show weak evidence of redlining. Tests indicate that lenders are not directly redlining minority neighborhoods when deciding on a mortgage loan; however, they are indirectly redlining these neighborhoods, as they impose a higher price on stronger applications from minority areas by requiring them to get private mortgage insurance (PMI).[15]

The outcome-based approach provides considerable evidence of redlining. Most outcome-based studies examine whether the number of mortgage loans per individually owned housing units in a neighborhood is negatively associated with the proportion of minorities in a neighborhood's population. Other factors that influence loans are controlled. One study found that after controlling for a large number of neighborhood characteristics, predominantly black neighborhoods received fewer loans per housing units during 1982-87 than white neighborhoods.[16] Some recent evidence regarding redlining in Atlanta follows up on the results in the study "The Color of Money," which documented wide lending disparities between black and white neighborhoods of similar income levels in 1988.[17] This analysis, using data from 1992 to 1996, reveals that Atlanta's depository lenders made 4.2 times as many conventional home purchase loans per owner occupied unit to middle income white neighborhoods as they did to middle income black neighborhoods. The comparable figure for 1988 was 5.2, suggesting that redlining of minority neighborhoods is still a problem in Atlanta, even after the sweeping changes experienced by the mortgage industry in the past decade. However, a study using 1988 to 1991 HDMA data for Houston finds that the racial composition of a neighborhood does not have a significant effect on the number of conventional mortgage loans. One speculation regarding this finding is that a disproportionately large percentage of loans in minority neighborhoods are going to white residents.[18]

A major problem with the outcome-based methodology is that it is not possible to identify the exact cause of the loan deficit. The latter could also be caused by any of the other players in the mortgage market such as realtors, underwriters, appraisers etc., and not just the lenders. Nonetheless, it points to the need to investigate further the striking deficit in the flow of credit to minority neighborhoods, as compared to white neighborhoods. It has also been argued that empirical studies of mortgage redlining cannot identify redlining because multivariate regression analysis suffers from serious problems such as data availability, model specification, and aggregation into census tracts or neighborhoods.[19]

The default rate approach to redlining suggests that systematic lender discrimination may result in applicants from minority neighborhoods being held to a higher standard than other borrowers. This implies that the default rates on loans to marginally qualified minority borrowers should be lower in comparison to loans extended to other borrowers. The default-risk characteristics of FHA-insured single-family residential mortgages were used to test this prediction. The results did not provide evidence of redlining in minority neighborhoods.[20] It is important to point out however that higher default rates for minorities than for whites do not provide conclusive evidence to reject the hypothesis that redlining occurs. If certain determinants of defaults are omitted from the regression equations and these omitted variables are correlated with race, the estimates could be biased upward. A study based on interviewing people involved in the sale or purchase of homes in Cincinnati, Indianapolis and Nashville did not find a difference between houses in redlined areas and those in the control group in terms of their ability to secure mortgages.[21]

Some theoretical models attempt to show how imperfect information can potentially result in redlining.[22] These models assume that there are economies of scale associated with collecting information about the neighborhood characteristics that affect housing values. The larger the number of loan applications processed in a neighborhood, the more lenders learn about the neighborhood. This information may be used in evaluating subsequent loan applications in the same neighborhood. This may create problems for minority neighborhoods where the number of housing sales in a neighborhood are low. This circumstance may cause the perception of risk to be greater. Lenders are less certain about appraised home values or face greater per unit cost of processing loans since they cannot exploit neighborhood-based economics of scale. Some empirical evidence using mortgage application data in 1990 and 1991 suggests that there are considerable economies associated with the scale of operations in a neighborhood, and that the inability to exploit these economies explains a substantial portion of the higher denial rates observed in minority neighborhoods or census tracts.[23] To the extent that neighborhood scale economies are information-related, recent technological advances may reduce their importance as a causal factor in redlining.

PRE-APPLICATION INQUIRIES AT BANKS

Lender discrimination against minorities at the pre-application stage can be evaluated using information given to auditors regarding interest rates, points, debt ratios, credit history, terms of application, documentation requirements, types of credit products offered and recommended, helpful qualifying information, quality of treatment, processing time and procedures, referrals to other lending institutions, probable qualification of the applicant and closing costs and procedures. The Chicago Fair Housing Alliance conducted pilot studies on ten institutions using female auditors. They found evidence of differential treatment in seven out of the ten institutions tested.[24] Black auditors had more difficulty gaining access to loan officers for a preliminary meeting; their debt ratios were not calculated as often; they were not given an assessment of the likelihood of qualifying for a loan as frequently; and were not given as much helpful information or suggestions for creative financing. Loan officers in some cases refused to meet with minority auditors until they had completed the loan application and paid the loan fee.

Pilot tests in Toledo, Ohio have identified policies that have a disparate impact on minorities and minority neighborhoods, discourage loan applications by minorities and lead to reduction in service and branch closures in minority neighborhoods. The tests focused on pre-screening factors such as minimum mortgage amount policies, race and sex of applicant, location of property, and tiering of interest rates. The tests provided evidence that loans of less than $40,000 were steered to FHA or other special programs rather than conventional loans, and that small loan applicants were often discouraged from applying. Tiering of interest rates for loans below $40,000 also have a disparate impact on minorities and those attempting to purchase homes in minority or integrated neighborhoods.[25] A pilot study by the Philadelphia Commission on Human Relations in 1991 found discrimination in the form of racial steering, differential treatment in down payment requirements, and a refusal to entertain low value loan requests.[26]

LOAN APPROVAL/REJECTION ANALYSIS

The majority of the research on mortgage lending discrimination has employed statistical analysis in an attempt to document discrimination in mortgage lending behavior. The underlying model in this literature starts out with the notion that profit maximizing lenders attempt to select investments, i.e. mortgages that will deliver a high rate of return. The probability of rejecting an application for a loan increases as the expected rate of return on the loan falls.

Discrimination exists when loan applications from minorities are more likely to be rejected than loan applications from whites when there is no significant difference in the expected return from the loans. In a similar fashion, redlining exists when loan applications for houses in largely minority-dominated neighborhoods are more likely to be rejected when the expected return on the loans are not significantly different. The underlying model reveals that the probability of rejecting a loan is dependent upon the expected return, the race of the applicant and the neighborhood in which the mortgaged property is located. From a statistical point of view, discrimination exists when the race of an applicant and the location of the property have a positive impact on the probability that a loan is rejected.

One of the major problems with this research is that the expected return on a mortgage is difficult to observe explicitly. Munnell et al (1992, 1996) and Peterson (1981) have found that the expected return on a loan depends on the terms of the loan such as the loan-to-value ratio, the rate of interest, the probability of default, and the impact of default on the return.[27] The probability of default depends on the characteristics of the loan applicant such as credit history, the characteristics of the property, the characteristics of the neighborhood, and the terms of the loan. The cost of default also depends on the characteristics of the neighborhood as well as the term of the loan.

The underlying model suggests that the probability of rejection for a mortgage loan depends on characteristics of the applicant, characteristics of the property, loan characteristic, and the existence of discrimination and/or redlining.

Black, Schweitzer, and Mandell (1978), King (1980), Schafer and Ladd (1981), Maddala and Trost (1982), and Munnell et al (1992, 1996) have all used a variant of the analytical model outlined above. The most widely cited of the studies above, Schafer and Ladd (1981) and Munnell et al (1992, 1996) both find evidence of discrimination in loan rejection data. Although these studies find discrimination, the methodological approach used has been the subject of much debate.[28]

At the core of the debate on mortgage lending discrimination is the issue of whether people with similar creditworthiness characteristics belonging to different ethnic groups experience significantly different outcomes from a mortgage market where racial, gender and other forms of discrimination are illegal. The task of the origination/underwriting process is to determine the creditworthiness of each mortgage applicant, i.e. render a decision as to whether an applicant's past credit history, as well as past, current, and future income generating potential, makes extending credit to the applicant a reasonable risk for the mortgagor to undertake. Since much of current evidence appears to reveal wide disparities in origination/underwriting outcomes between white and minority loan applicants, the examination of the origination/underwriting process is of paramount importance in understanding what appears to be widespread violations of the law.[29]

This line of research has encountered major criticisms because of omitted variable problems and many other methodological flaws. Before the 1996 Boston Federal Reserve study most data sets did not contain information on personal characteristics of loan applicants and were therefore thought to be inadequate in attempting to determine the significance of race in loan rejection models. In effect, the omission of such variables limited the interpretation of the race variable in most studies.

The well known 1992 Boston study finds that minorities in the Boston metropolitan area were approximately fifty percent more likely to be rejected for a mortgage loan than whites, even after controlling for factors that banks use to determine an applicant's creditworthiness.

There are three general areas on which the loan rejection approach to examining discrimination has been challenged. Many argue that key variables that affect the lending decision and are correlated with race have been omitted from loan rejection models and that these omissions tend to bias the coefficient associated with race in these models. More precisely, if variables that are positively correlated with race are left out of regression models, the size of the coefficient associated with race will overstate the impact of race on loan rejection rates. Secondly, Carr and Megbolugbe (1994) and Horne (1994a,b) have both criticized loan rejection models on the basis of data errors. Carr and Megboulgbe (1994) suggests that miscoded data could undermine the credibility of the Boston Fed study, whereas Horne (1994) finds that many of the applications which had the lowest probability of being rejected were indeed rejected.[30] This reveals bias in the data collection process. These studies generally argue that mistakes in data entry or coding may distort results—possibly over-estimating the importance of minority status. Finally, the issues of incorrect specification and the endogeny of explanatory variables used in these models are a third area of debate. Yezer, Phillips and Trost assert that the simultaneous determination of the loan action taken (i.e. to reject or approve the application) and the loan-to-value ratio could bias the coefficient on race. The direction of the bias is dependent upon the correlation between the race of the applicant and the loan-to-value ratio.[31]

LOAN DEFAULT APPROACH

Academic researchers and popular media have proposed that tests for mortgage discrimination should focus on the outcome of the mortgage process, namely defaults.[32]

Becker argues that if mortgage-granting institutions discriminate against minorities, then we should observe minorities defaulting less frequently than whites on average. That is, the rates of defaults on loans approved for blacks and hispanics by discriminatory institutions should be lower, not higher, than those on mortgages for whites. This is because lending institutions would only accept the very best minority candidates.[33] In effect, discriminators who are following their taste will pass up better-qualified minority applicants for less qualified whites ones. Hence, the average creditworthiness of minority applicants who actually receive loans will be higher than that of whites.

Using Becker's argument, several authors develop theoretical models that start by assuming that the world consists of individuals that do not have sufficient funds to purchase a home and must depend on credit markets to obtain a loan.[34] The individuals in this world have two distinguishing characteristics. The first is that the likelihood of loan repayment differs across individuals. The second is that each member belongs to one of two groups: W (white applicants) and group M (minority applicants). The typical assumption is that the average creditworthiness of group W is higher than that of group M and that lending institutions are aware of the differences in creditworthiness across the two groups. Lending institutions set a minimum level of acceptable creditworthiness for loan approval. It is assumed that lenders cannot observe the true creditworthiness of each individual. However, lenders can observe signals such as past credit history, income ratios, and other characteristics that are correlated with creditworthiness. Using signals that are correlated with creditworthiness, as well as the average creditworthiness of the group, the lender derives an estimate of an applicant's expected creditworthiness. This expectation is formed over the lender's posterior beliefs about the applicant's creditworthiness. This posterior belief will depend on the distribution of credit risk in the overall applicant pool, the relative distribution of credit risk across groups W and M, and the specific signal sent by the applicant. Given these conditions, if the applicant's expected creditworthiness exceeds the minimum level required for loan approval, then the loan is approved.

If discrimination exists, then discriminating institutions should accept less creditworthy white applicants while accepting only the highest quality minority applicants. If this is the case, then the marginal white applicant should be less creditworthy than the marginal minority applicant. If defaults are highly correlated with creditworthiness, then the probability of default should be higher for less creditworthy white applicants than the more creditworthy minority applicants. Using this approach, most research has failed to find evidence of discrimination. More specifically, black loan applicants have a higher default rate than white applicants. [35] But the approach leaves many unanswered questions.

The default approach is based on examining loan performance. If lenders are engaged in discrimination, they would set a higher cutoff standard in terms of creditworthiness for minority borrowers than for white borrow-

Table 1
Loan Default Studies and their Findings

Loan Default Studies	Main Findings	Remarks
1. Van Order and Zorn (1995)	Racial difference in default rates in the southeast do provide evidence of discrimination.	Examine average default rates.
2. Berkovec, Canner, Gabriel, and Hannan (1994)	Reject the hypothesis that minorities encounter discrimination.	Regression analysis using a sample of FHA mortgage from 1987 through 1989.
3. Berkovec, Canner, Gabriel, and Hannan (1996)	Find a statistically significant black-white differential in default rate. Reject the hypothesis of mortgage discrimination against black borrowers.	Examine average default rates and regression analysis, using FHA data.
4. Berkovec, Canner, Gabriel, and Hannan (1998)	Find no evidence of (taste-based) discrimination.	Regression analysis using market concentration as a proxy, based on FHA data.

ers. As a result, loans given to minorities would be expected to perform better than those given to whites, i.e. average loan default rates for minorities would be lower than for whites. Table 1 summarizes the findings of default studies. Despite these findings, substantial controversy continues. We discuss this controversy below.

LOAN ADMINISTRATION

After a loan is approved with specific terms and conditions, it enters the stage of mortgage administration. If the borrower makes payment on time and remains current on the loan, then nothing needs to be done. If, however, the borrower has problems in making loan payments on time, the lender has the option to take some action. In particular, the lender can either accept some late payments or arrange a repayment plan with the borrower. Finally, the lender can declare the borrower in default on the loan and initiate foreclosure proceedings. But what if some lenders take a more favored stance toward white borrowers than toward minority customers in accepting late payments or in arranging repayment plans? If such preferential treatment occurs, it may bias downward statistical estimates of discrimination in the loan approval stage.

Existing studies of discrimination using the loan default approach include Berkovec as well as and Van Order and Zorn (1995).[36] Most of these studies do not find evidence of discrimination in the loan approval process. The Berkovec study is based on a large sample of single family mortgage loans that were originated between 1987 and 1989. They found that, for the 1987 cohort of borrowers, the default rate was 9% for blacks and 4.3% for whites. Even with the additional statistical controls for loan and borrower characteristics, the default rate for blacks was still two percentage points higher than that for whites, and the difference was statistically significant. These findings are very controversial from a methodological standpoint. In a 1998 study, Berkovec et al controlled market concentration and still concluded that discrimination could not be proven.

The default approach to studying mortgage discrimination has drawn intensive criticisms. The first criticism centers on the assumptions used in the approach, and the second is related to the empirical methods.

The first controversy on the default approach concerns the assumption about the average quality of approved minority loan applicants. Ross and Yinger argue that the average quality of approved minority loans is substantially lower than that of white applicants.[37] Thus, the natural average default rate for minorities should be higher than that for whites. Discrimination against minorities might cause a higher standard in loan approval for minorities, and therefore lower the average minority default rate. However, it might not lower the average default rate enough to offset the higher average quality of loans given to whites. In short, the extent of discrimination may not be severe enough to make the default rates for minority loan recipients lower than that of whites. Thus, a higher average default rate for minorities cannot be interpreted as evidence that discrimination does not exist. A lower default rate for minorities is sufficient but not necessary to show discrimination (Van Order and Zorn 1995).[38]

The second controversy on the default approach concerns the direct comparison between white and minority loan recipients. Ideally, to investigate discrimination, the observed likelihood of default for minority borrowers needs to be compared to the likelihood of minority default that would have occurred without discrimination, not with the likelihood of default by white borrowers. Unfortunately, the "would-be default" rates for minorities, absent discrimination, are not observable. Clearly, without knowing the minority-white difference in default likelihood caused by unobserved heterogeneity in the absence of discrimination, it is difficult to estimate racial discrimination based on the observed difference in default.

Third, an additional difficulty in the default approach using regression analysis to investigate discrimination is the simultaneity problem between the dependent variable and some explanatory variables (Galster 1996, Ross 1996).[55] If all underwriting variables are observable, some of these variables are likely to be endogenous. More specifically, the likelihood of default is affected by some underwriting variables, such as credit history. At the same time, the values of these underwriting variables are affected by the likelihood of default, which has been taken into account in the underwriting process. If the lenders think that the default likelihood for minority applicants is high, they will set a higher requirement for those underwriting variables for minorities. Thus, the procedure in loan approval becomes correlated with the outcome, that is, default.

If all underwriting variables are observable and included in the regression, discrimination will be controlled by these variables themselves and will not show up in the minority dummy variable. More specifically, lenders can set a higher standard in terms of the value of these variables during the underwriting process. But the estimates for the coefficients of these underwriting variables will be biased because of the endogeny problem. Only if some underwriting variables or individual characteristics are not observable will discrimination be shown on the minority dummy variable. However, these omitted variables are likely to be correlated with the dummy variable for minority status, and thus will bias the estimates of discrimination.

THE DEFAULT APPROACH AND MARKET CONCENTRATION

Faced with so many problems and criticisms of the methodology, it seems difficult for the default approach to generate any convincing results. However, a new default approach using an alternative strategy proposed by Berkovec et al (1998) is designed to overcome these shortcomings.[39] This new method utilizes the extent of market concentration within the industry as a proxy to aid in identifying discrimination.

The basic assumption is that taste-based discrimination, if it exists, should be higher when lenders have more market power. Therefore, market concentration in the mortgage lending industry can be a proxy variable to estimate discrimination.[40] In other words, if lenders have more market power, they set a higher cutoff standard for minority borrowers in approving a loan, which lowers the default rate for minorities. Berkovec et al, using data on FHA loans, finds that the coefficient of the interaction term is statistically insignificant. Hence, they conclude that lenders do not engage in discrimination because the market power of lenders has no influence on the minority default rate.

This new version of the default approach has also been criticized by researchers. First, they note that the assumption that discrimination is stronger in locations where the lending industry is more concentrated has not been tested. Second, a higher market power may lead lenders to be more selective in rationing to any group, including whites. An increase in the cutoff of mortgages may drop a large number of low-quality white mortgages but only a small number of minority mortgages. As a result, the average quality of white loan receipts may increase a great deal, while the average quality of minority loan receipts only increases slightly. Thus the inter-group difference in the loan default rate increases. Finally, it is noted that the interaction term of minority status and market concentration can still be correlated with the error terms, because market concentration may change the standards of some underwriting variables (observed and unobserved). Thus, it is possible for the estimate of this coefficient, which gives the extent of discrimination, to be biased.

Turner and Skidmore conclude, "the default approach produces unreliable estimates of the incidence of discrimination."[41]

NOTES

1. For a recent survey of mortgage discrimination literature see Turner, Margery Austin, and Felicity Skidmore, ed. (1999). "Mortgage Lending Discrimination: A Review of Existing Evidence." (Washington: The Urban Institute), pp. 1-168; Yinger, John. 1996. "Discrimination in Mortgage Lending: A Literature Review." In *Mortgage Lending, Racial Discrimination, and Federal Policy*, edited by John Goering and Ron Wienk (Washington: Urban Institute Press), pp. 29-74; Cloud, Cathy and George Galster, 1993. "What do we know about Racial Discrimination in Mortgage Markets?" *Review of Black Political Economy*, Vol 22, no. 1 (summer) pp. 101-120; Black, Harold A., 1999. "Is there Discrimination in Mortgage Lending? What Does the Research Tell Us?" *Review of Black Political Economy*, Vol 27, no. 1 (summer) pp. 23-30.

2. Two of the amending statutes are the 1972 Equal Employment Opportunity Act and the 1991 Civil Rights Act.

3. For example see, Fix, Michael, George Galster, and Raymond Struyk. 1993. "An Overview of Auditing for Discrimination." In *Clear and Convincing Evidence*, edited by Michael Fix and Raymond Struyk (Washington: Urban Institute Press), pp. 1-68.

4. Ibid.

5. Ibid.

6. Yinger, John. 1996. "Discrimination in Mortgage Lending: A Literature Review." In *Mortgage Lending, Racial Discrimination, and Federal Policy*, edited by John Goering and Ron Wienk (Washington: Urban Institute Press), pp. 29-74.

7. Ibid, pages 34-36.

8. Page, Marianne. 1995. "Racial and Ethnic Discrimination in Urban Housing Markets: Evidence from a Recent Audit Study." *Journal of Urban Economics*. 38. 183-206.

9. Ondrich, Jan, Alex Stricker, and John Yinger. 1998. "Do Real Estate Brokers Choose to Discriminate? Evidence from the 1989 Housing Discrimination Study." *Southern Economic Journal*. 64(4), 880-901.

10. Farley, Reynolds. 1996. "Racial Differences in the Search for Housing: Do Whites and Blacks Use the Same Techniques to Find Housing?" *Housing Policy Debate*. 7(2). 367-85.

11. Yinger, 1996.

12. Yinger, John. 1991. *Housing Discrimination Study: The Incidence and Severity of Unfavorable Treatment*, Washington, DC.: US Department of Housing and Urban Development.

13. Yinger, John. 1993. Access Denied, Access Constrained: Results and Implications of the 1989 Housing Discrimination Study." *Clear and Convincing Evidence: Testing for Discrimination in America*, ed. By M. Fix and R. Struyk, pp. 69-112, Washington, D.C. Urban Institute Press; Op. cit. Yinger, John, 1996, page 81.

14. Feins, Judith D., Rachael G. Bratt, and Robert Hollister. 1981. *Final Report of a Study of Racial Discrimination in the Boston Housing Market*. Cambridge, Mass.: Abt Associates.

15. Tootell, Geoffrey M. B. 1996. "Redlining in Boston: Do Mortgage Lenders Discriminate against Neighborhoods?" *Quarterly Journal of Economics*. 111(4). 1049-79.

16. Bradbury, Katharine L., Karl E. Case, and Constance R. Dunham. 1989. "Geographic Patterns of Mortgage Lending in Boston, 1982-87." *New England Economic Review (September/October)*: 3-30.

17. Wyly, Elvin and Steven R. Holloway. 1999. "'The Color of Money' Revisited: Racial Lending Patterns in Atlanta's Neighborhoods." *Housing Policy Debate*. 10(3). 555-600.

18. Holmes, Andrew and Paul Horvitz. 1994. "Mortgage Redlining: Race, Risk, and Demand." *Journal of Finance*. 49(1). 81-99.

19. Perle, Eugene D., Kathryn Lynch, and Jeffrey Horner. 1993. "Model Specification and Local Mortgage Market Behavior." *Journal of Housing Research*. 4(2). 225-43.

20. Berkovec, J.A., G.B. Canner, S.A. Gabriel, and T.H. Hannan. "Race, Redlining, and Residential Mortgage Loan Performance." *Journal of Real Estate, Finance, and Economics*, vol. 9, no. 3 (November 1994), pp. 263-94.

21. Benston, George and Dan Horsky. 1992. "The Relationship between the Demand and Supply of Home Financing and Neighborhood Characteristics: An Empirical Study of Mortgage Redlining." *Journal of Financial Services Research*. 5(3). 235-60.

22. Lang, William W., and Leonard I. Nakamura. 1993. "A Model of Redlining." *Journal of Urban Economics 33* (March): 223-234; Gruben, William C., Jonathan A. Neuberger, and Ronald H. Schmidt, 1990. "Imperfect Information and the Community Reinvestment Act." *Federal Reserve Bank of San Francisco Economic Review.* 3. 27-46.

23. Avery, Robert B., Patricia E. Beeson, and Mark S. Sniderman. 1999. "Neighborhood Information and Home Mortgage Lending." *Journal of Urban Economics.* 45. 287-310; Ling, David C., and Susan M. Wachter. 1998. "Information Externalities and Home Mortgage Underwriting." *Journal of Urban Economics 44* (November): 317-332.

24. Smith, Shanna L. and Cathy Cloud, 1996. "The Role of Private, Nonprofit Fair Housing Enforcement Organizations in Lending Testing." From *Mortgage Lending, Racial Discrimination, and Federal Policy.* Urban Institute Press. Washington, D.C. 589-610.

25. Ibid.

26. Lawton, Rachael, 1996. "Preapplication Mortgage Testing Program: Lender Testing by a Local Agency." From *Mortgage Lending, Racial Discrimination, and Federal Policy.* Urban Institute Press. Washington, D.C. 611-22.

27. Munnell et al. (1992); Munnell et al (1996); Peterson, Richard L. 1981. "An Investigation of Sex Discrimination in Commercial Banks' Direct Consumer Lending." *Bell Journal of Economic* 12(2) 547-561.

28. Black, Schweitzer, and Mandell (1978); King (1980); Schafer and Ladd (1981); Maddala and Trost (1982); Munnell et al (1992); Munnell et al (1996); Schafer and Ladd (1981); Munnell et al (1992); Munnell et al (1996).

29. Temkin, Kenneth, et al. 1998. A Study of GST's Single Family Underwriting Guidelines. *Report for U.S. Department of Housing and Urban Development* (Washington: Urban Institute) October; Calomiris, Charles W., Charles M. Kahn, and Stanley D. Longhofer. "Housing-Finance Intervention and Private Incentives: Helping Minorities and the Poor," *Journal of Money, Credit, and Banking*, vol. 26, no. 3, pt. 2 (August 1994). pp. 634-74; Calomiris, Charles W., Charles M. Kahn, and Stanley D. Longhofer. "Housing-Finance Intervention and Private Incentives: Helping Minorities and the Poor," *Journal of Money, Credit, and Banking*, vol. 26, no. 3, pt. 2 (August 1994). pp. 634-74; Longhofer, Stanley D., and Stephen R. Peters. "Self-Selection and Discrimination in Credit Markets," Federal Reserve Bank of Cleveland, Working Paper No. 9809, July 1998 (revised February 1999); Longhofer, Stanley D., and Stephen R. Peters. "Self-Selection and Discrimination in Credit Markets," Federal Reserve Bank of Cleveland, Working Paper No. 9809, July 1998 (revised February 1999); King, Thomas A. "Discrimination in Mortgage Lending: A Study of Three Cities." Working Paper No. 91, Office of Policy and Economic Research, Federal Home Loan Bank Board, Washington, D.C. 1980; Schafer, Robert, and Helen F. Ladd. 1981. *Discrimination in Mortgage Lending.* Cambridge: MIT Press; Maddala, George S., and Robert P. Trost. 1982. "On Measuring Discrimination in Loan Markets." *Housing Finance Review 1*: 245-268; Munnell, Alicia H., Lynn E. Browne, James McEneaney, and Geoffrey M.B. Tootell. "Mortgage Lending in Boston: Interpreting HMDA Data," Federal Reserve Bank of Boston, Working Paper No. 92-7, October 1992; Munnell, Alicia H., Lynn E. Browne, James McEneaney, and Geoffrey M.B. Tootell. "Mortgage Lending in Boston: Interpreting HMDA Data." *American Economic Review*, 86(1), March 1996, 25-53.

30. Carr, James H. and Isaac F. Megbolugbe. "The Federal Reserve Bank of Boston Study on Mortgage Lending Revisited." Office of Housing Research, Fannie Mae, November 1993; Munnell et al (1994); Horne, David K. 1994a. "Evaluating

the Role of Race in Mortgage Lending." *FDIC Banking Review*, vol. 7, no. 1 (Spring/Summer 1994), pp. 1-15; Horne, David K. 1994b. "Mortgage Lending, Race, and Model Specification." Preliminary draft. Federal Deposit Insurance Corporation, Division of Research and Statistics.

31. Yezer, Anthony M.J., Robert F. Phillips, and Robert P. Trost. "Bias in Estimates of Discrimination and Default in Mortgage Lending: The Effects of Simultaneity and Self-Selection." *Journal of Real Estate, Finance, and Economics*, vol. 9, no. 3 (November 1994), pp. 197-215.

32. Becker (1993). Brimelow, Peter. 1993. "Racism at Work?" *National Review*, April 12, p. 42; Brimelow, Peter, and Leslie Spencer. "The Hidden Clue." *Forbes*. January 4, 1993, p. 48. Peterson (1981); Berkovec et al (1994).

33. Becker, Gary (1993).

34. Calomis, Kahn, and Longhofer (1994); Longhofer and Peters (1998); Longhofer (1999).

35. Berkovec et al (1994); Calomis et al (1994); Ferguson, Michael F., and Stephen R. Peters. "Cultural Affinity and Lending Discrimination: The Impact of Underwriting Errors and Credit Risk Distribution on Applicant Denial Rates." *Journal of Financial Services Research*, vol. 11, nos. 1-2 (April 1997), pp. 153-67; Ferguson, Michael F., and Stephen R. Peters. "Is Lending Discrimination Always Costly?" University of Illinois, unpublished manuscript, September 1998; Quercia, Roberto G., and Michael A. Stegman. 1992. "Residential Mortgage Default: A Review of the Literature." *Journal of Housing Research 3*: 341-380.

36. Berkovec et al. (1994, 1996a, b, 1998); Van Order, Robert, and Peter Zorn. 1995. "Testing for Discrimination: Combining Default and Rejection Data." *Fair Lending Analysis: A Compendium of Essays on the Use of Statistics*, edited by Anthony M. Yezer (Washington: American Bankers Association), pp.105-112.

37. Ross and Yinger (1999).

38. Van Order and Zorn (1995).

39. Berkovec et al. (1998).

40. More specifically, because of unobserved underwriting variables and individual characteristics, the dummy variable of minority status will be correlated with the error terms and thus will bias the estimate of the coefficient of minority status. Thus, the resulting estimate regarding discrimination will be biased. The market concentration, however, will not correlate with these individual unobserved variables. As a result, the coefficient on the interaction of race and market concentration could provide information on whether lenders engage in taste-based discrimination. Because market concentration is exogenous, the estimate for the coefficient of the interaction term will be unbiased. If this coefficient is negative and significant, then a higher market concentration will lower default likelihood of minority applicants.

41. Turner and Skidmore (1999, page 12).

26

BLACK MALE EMPLOYMENT AND TIGHT LABOR MARKETS

Robert Cherry

Despite what is widely considered to be the most favorable labor market conditions in thirty years, black male unemployment rates remain double white rates. In the past, liberal economists would have recommend even tighter labor markets to break racial employment barriers. For example, James Tobin[1] wrote,

> We know how to operate the economy so that there is a tight labor market. . . . The government could choose to control it so that unemployment *averaged* 3.5 or 3 percent instead of remaining over 4.5 percent except at occasional business cycle peaks. . . . Running the economy with a tight labor market would mean a somewhat faster upward creep in the price level. The disadvantages of this are, in my view exaggerated and are scarcely commensurable with the real economic and social gains of higher output and employment. . . . The vast comfortable white middle class who are never touched by unemployment prefer to safeguard the purchasing power of their life insurance and pension rights than to expand opportunities for the disadvantaged and unemployed.

In the 1980s, Richard Freeman echoed similar thoughts. He found that young black male high school graduates disproportionately benefitted from the 1980s expansion. Freeman[2] concluded: "Although a strong job market may not be a panacea for all the problems of the disadvantaged, it does improve their employment and earnings."

Unfortunately, this in no longer the perspective of most liberal economists. Tobin now believes that demand-side stimuli do not appear to be as effective as in the past in aiding the disadvantaged. Tobin[3] shows that poverty rates declined dramatically between 1959 and 1969 in response to per capita income growth. Since then, however, increasing per capita income has had no significant impact on poverty rates. Blank and Card[4] also find that a rising tide no longer lifts all boats. For them, the problem has been that economic growth, whether measured by per capita income, employment growth, or declining unemployment rates, is now quite skewed so that it is no longer associated with rising real wages for the bottom half of the income distribution. They find that without real wage increases for these workers, economic growth no longer lowers poverty rates.

Most liberals now perceive that black employment problems primarily stem from cultural inadequacies, which are often compounded by employer attitudes. William Julius Wilson claims that cultural inadequacies stem from the social isolation of poor blacks in dysfunctional neighborhoods. As a result, he finds that both black and white Chicago employers are unwilling to hire any black workers who live in these neighborhoods. Echoing James Tobin's recent thoughts, Wilson[5] asserts: "Today, it appears that inner-city residents who are not in the labor force tend to be beyond the reach of monetary or fiscal policy." Similarly, Robert Reich[6] suggests, "Only in metropolitan areas where the official level of unemployment is under 3 percent are we beginning to see employers recruit from central city and train employees in basic skills."

Darity and Myers[7] also question the likelihood that low national unemployment rates will aid black workers, though they have a different explanation for the dysfunctional behavior of black inner-city workers. They focus on the difficult employment situation black men have faced since the early 1970s. In particular, Darity and Myers reject any notion that black workers need a black middle class to instill the proper behavior traits. Instead, they emphasize that perceived black dysfunctional behavior grows out of the marginality imposed on them by a managerial class that has grown indifferent to their plight. Darity and Myers note that with a generation of low employment and consistent discrimination—whether the statistical discrimination Wilson documents or pure discrimination—it is quite rational for black youth to reject schooling and other societal norms. Darity and Myers[8] contend:

> [T]he increase in marginality feeds back upon the behaviors that contribute to or at least justify the expansion of institutionalization. Marginality also contributes to self-destruction, explaining the rise in homicides, which we find in our empirical work directly contributes to the decline in marriageable mates. . . . [We] see members of the middle class as supporting means for further control and institu-

TABLE 1
Black and White Male Employment Rates at the Peak and Trough of Recent Business Cycles

	Black Men			White Men		
	Emp	Δ(Emp)	Δ(Emp)	Emp	Δ(Emp)	Δ(Emp)
Year	16 years and older		20–64	16 years and older		20–64
1973	67.5			76.5		
1975	60.6	–7.1	–7.8	73.0	–3.5	–3.8
1979	63.4	2.8	3.0	75.1	2.1	2.3
1982/83	56.2	–7.2	–8.2	70.5	–4.6	–4.7
1989	62.8	6.6	5.8	73.7	3.2	3.9
1992	69.1	3.1	–4.1	71.1	–2.6	–2.6
1997	61.4	2.3	2.7	72.7	1.6	1.9

tionalization of unwanted, superfluous inner-city residents, creating further marginalization of many young black males, thereby males, thereby increasing observed pathologies like crime and violence.

Historically, black employment rates have been more sensitive to the business cycle, rising disproportionately during expansions and falling disproportionately during contractions. Table 1 illustrates this by looking at male employment rate changes between the peaks and troughs of the business cycle. Notice that the volatility is even greater for the adult prime working-age population, 20 to 64 years old, for the entire working-age population, 16 years and older.

Though the disproportionateness continued in the current expansion, this disguised an important occurrence. While the white male employment rate increase has been continuous throughout the current expansion, the black rate was greater in 1995 than in 1997. In particular, for the entire working-age population, the black male rate fell from 6.17 to 61.1 percent. These developments support the Wilson, Reich, Tobin, and Darity-Myers thesis that strong impediments to male black employment growth may exist even when labor demand is quite strong.

Official unemployment statistics paint a somewhat different picture. Table 2 presents unemployment statistics for comparable years in each of the last three economic expansions. It includes the official black and white unemployment rates for all men, 16 years and older, and for the adult working-age population, 20 to 64 years old. For both populations,

TABLE 2
Male Unemployment Rate Measures
Official Unemployment Rate

	White Men		Black Men	
Year	16 Yr older	20–64 Yr Old	16 Yr Older	20–64 Yr Old
1979	4.5	3.5	11.8	9.5
1988	4.7	4.2	11.7	10.3
1997	4.2	3.6	10.2	8.5
Δ(79–97)	–0.3	0.1	–1.6	–1.0

black rates are more than double white rates. However, when comparing 1979 and 1997, the changes are relatively better for black men than for white men. Moreover, during the recent expansion, the official unemployment rate for black men, aged 20 to 64 years old, fell from 13.8 percent in 1992 to 8.5 percent in 1997.

Official unemployment rates can decline because employment rates rise, or because labor force participation rates decline. During this 18 year period, Table 3 indicates that there was a disproportionate drop in the participation rates of black men, which increased the gap between the black and white male labor force participation rates, especially during the last decade. In particular, between 1988 and 1997, the white participation rate fell by 0.6 percentage points while the black rate fell by 3.3 percentage points.

TABLE 3
Labor Statistics for Black and White Men,
Aged 20 to 64 Years Old

	Labor Force Participation Rate		Employment Rate	
Year	White	Black	White	Black
1979	90.2	84.1	87.0	76.1
1988	89.4	82.7	85.5	74.1
1997	88.8	79.4	85.5	72.7
Δ(79–88)	–0.8	–1.4	–1.2	–2.0
Δ(88–97)	–0.6	–3.3	0.3	–1.4

FIGURE 1
Unemployment Rates, 1972–1997
Black Men, 20 to 64 Years Old

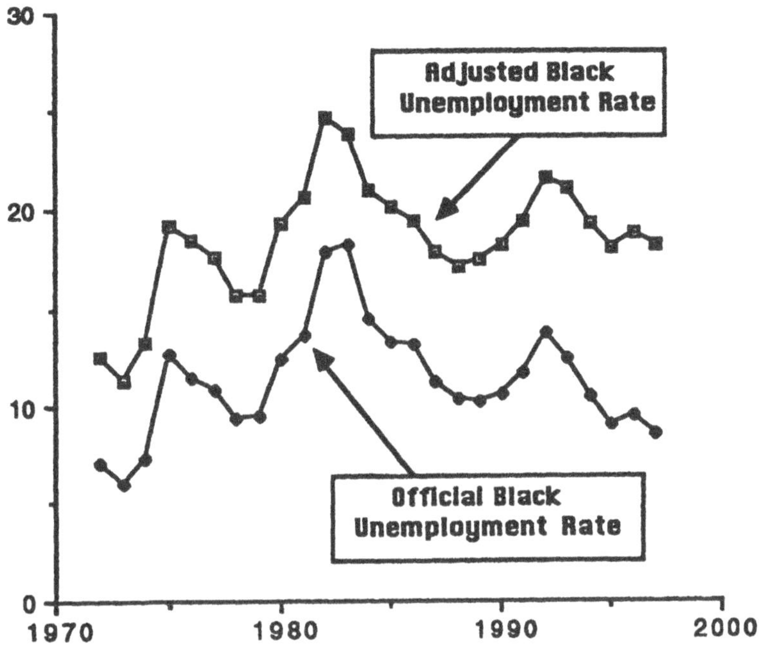

Juhn[9] has documented that racial differences in labor force participation rates among men is substantially the result of a lack of employment opportunities, particularly for black men seeking employment in low-wage labor markets. Holzer[10] documents that in these markets, the most important method used by firms to attract job applicants is informal networks. The presence of such networks tends to increase the proportion of discouraged workers among blacks.

In order to assess the impact that labor force withdrawals have on black employment, I constructed an alternative unemployment measure for adult prime-age black men. The alternative measure uses the actual black employment rate but assumes that the "true" black labor force participation rate equals the white rate.[11] Figure 1 depicts the relationship between the official and adjusted black unemployment rate.

Both rates move together over the business cycle. However, since the mid-1980s, the gap between the two rates has increased continuously.

FIGURE 2
Labor Force Participation and Unemployment Rate Gaps
Men, 20 to 64 Years Old

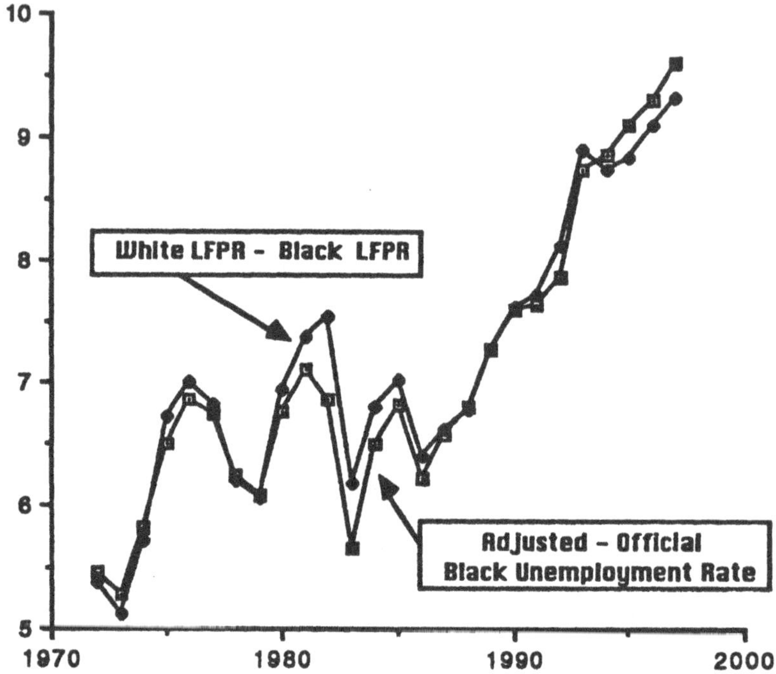

Figure 2 illustrates that the growing gap between the two black unemployment rates is directly related to the growing gap between black and white LFPRs.[12] As a result, the decline in the adjusted rate during the most recent expansion is much more modest than the official rate; so modest that the adjusted black unemployment rate increased between 1988 and 1997 from 17.1 to 18.1 percent while, as Table 3 indicates, the official rate declined from 10.3 to 8.5 percent. Most importantly, the adjusted unemployment rate of adult working-age black men remains at depression levels despite robust economic growth.

The issues raised are quite important. With the weakening of affirmative action and the labor market impact of welfare changes, it is quite important to assess the prospects for black men in an economy with high labor demand. Can a rising tide lift all boats, as Tobin once believed, or are structural and/or behavioral impediments too significant to be overcome simply by providing a strong demand for labor? This paper will begin by assessing variations in black employment growth rates among states.

DATA

This study looks at variations in state black employment rates for the most recent four years for which census data is available, 1992 through 1996. This period covers the first four years of the current economic expansion. I decided to only include the seventeen states which had the largest employment numbers for black men in 1992. These states have over 85 percent of total black employment. There were another ten states for which census data was available; however, these states had too little employment for the government year-to-year estimated changes to be reliable and they comprised only 9 percent of total black employment.[13]

Table 4 provides employment estimates for black men for each of these states. It also includes both black and white male employment rates. The states are listed in descending order, based on the black male employment rate for 1996. It is important to remember that these employment rates are the ratio of employment of a noninstitutionalized population. Given the disproportionate black incarceration rates, the racial gap would be larger if employment was calculated as a percentage of the entire male population. Also note that the second group of nine states has substantially lower black employment rates. This group includes the rustbelt states (IL, OH, MI, PA, and NY) and three deep South states (MS, AL, and LA). For white men, only two of these states (NY and PA) have employment rates which deviate substantially from the first group of eight states. These state racial employment rate differences are consistent with regional differences in the 1980s reported by Cotton.[14]

Finally, I present data for 1995 and 1996 to highlight the relative weakening of the black employment situation in 1996. Notice that for a number of states, the absolute number of black men working declined. In particular, this occurred in Texas and California, the two states in which black employment would have been most likely to be adversely affected by the North Atlantic Free Trade Agreement (NAFTA).

TEST RESULTS

This study's dependent variables are the absolute growth rate of black male employment (AGR) and the black male employment growth relative to white male employment growth (RGR). They were calculated

TABLE 4
Employment Changes of Black and White Men, 1992–1996

	Employment (000) Black			Employment Rate (percentage) Black			White		
States	92	95	96	92	95	96	92	95	96
Maryland	321	312	309	66.6	71.3	69.7	74.6	74.8	74.8
Texas	432	490	473	64.1	67.9	67.0	74.6	75.8	75.8
Florida	415	474	461	61.9	68.3	65.7	64.3	66.3	66.5
Virginia	302	308	308	69.3	66.7	65.3	75.5	76.5	72.6
Georgia	410	464	460	62.2	63.3	65.3	73.2	76.0	76.5
North Carolina	335	323	299	63.8	64.6	64.6	73.9	73.8	74.7
New Jersey	198	201	210	57.7	60.2	63.4	71.2	71.3	71.6
South Carolina	218	225	222	62.8	62.6	62.3	73.3	72.8	71.3
Ohio	195	217	254	55.0	54.7	58.8	71.1	72.7	72.2
Alabama	190	200	230	57.6	56.0	58.7	70.0	71.2	71.8
Mississippi	160	170	178	56.3	55.4	58.2	70.9	73.0	71.7
Michigan	213	223	209	53.4	55.8	57.2	70.3	72.5	72.4
New York	500	491	503	54.6	54.1	56.8	66.7	66.7	67.8
Illinois	302	297	315	53.6	54.9	56.6	74.0	75.2	75.8
California	370	440	421	58.8	60.4	56.4	70.5	69.8	71.1
Pennsylvania	178	199	203	52.5	52.8	55.6	68.6	68.6	69.2
Louisiana	196	216	211	53.6	51.9	53.0	70.4	70.0	70.9

annually, generating a potential sixty-eight observations, four for each of the seventeen states.

There were three explanatory variables tested for each of the dependent variables. First, I included the state's unemployment rate (UN). This was the starting unemployment rate for each of the annual changes. Second, I desired a measure of each state's total production in order to test whether there was a positive relationship between total production and black employment growth rates. Unfortunately, I did not have a direct measure of each state's annual production. Instead, I used each state's annual growth rate of total employment (GRTE). GRTE was also included in the relative growth equation. This enables us to test the possibility that in states with faster growing total production, black male employment growth would be even more robust relative to white male employment growth.

Since black male employment is part of total employment, this creates an upward bias in the likelihood that GRTE and AGR will be positively correlated. However, this bias may be modest, since in no state was the black male proportion of total unemployment at least 15 percent, and in 9 states it was less than 7 percent. I could have eliminated this bias by including instead a net total employment variable by subtracting black male employment from total employment. This net total employment variable, however, is not a proxy for total production. For this reason, I decided to use the unadjusted total employment growth variable despite its bias.

Finally, black employment may be influenced by a composite sectoral relative growth variable (CSRG). In particular, I tested the influence of various sectors (construction, manufacturing, government, etc.) to determine whether individually or in combination they could explain variations in either absolute or relative black male employment growth rates among states. Thus, the two regressions tested were:

$$AGR = a_1 + a_2\,(GRTE) + a_3(UN) + a_4(CSRG)$$

$$RGR = b_1 + b_2\,(GRTE) + b_3(UN) + b_4(CSRG)$$

The *strong* rising tide thesis maintains that a state's unemployment rate should have no impact on either its absolute or relative growth rates (i.e., $a_3 = b_3 = 0$). In contrast, the new view articulated by Tobin, Wilson, Reich, and Darity-Myers, would suggest that as unemployment rates decline and the pool of unemployment black male workers becomes dominated by those with perceived or actual dysfunctional traits, employers are increasingly reluctant to seek their employment. As a result, there should be a positive relationship between both the absolute and the relative black male employment growth and unemployment rates (i.e., $a_3 > 0$ and $b_3 > 0$).

The weak rising tide hypothesis is the following: Even if the tightening of labor markets reduces the rate at which black employment grows during expansions, rising total production increases black male employment. In this case, there should be a positive relationship between the absolute black employment and total production growth rates, (i.e., $a_2 > 0$).

Table 5 presents the test results. I first ran simple unweighted regressions for 1992–1995 data (51 observations) with all the potential explanatory variables. Whether black male employment growth is measured absolutely or relative to white male employment growth, each state's unemployment rate is statistically significant. The unemployment rate was positively correlated with the absolute and relative growth rate in opposition to the *strong* rising tide hypothesis. Holding state employment growth constant, the absolute black male employment growth rate is predicted to decline by at least 1.4 percent for each one percentage point the unemployment rate is lowered. This is substantial given that, for the entire four-year period, the growth of black employment averaged 1.6 percent annually across these seventeen states.

Consistent with the *weak* rising tide hypothesis, the absolute black male growth rate was positively correlated with total employment growth rates.[15] Finally, neither absolute nor relative black employment growth rates were significantly related to particular sectors. Each dependent variable was mildly positively correlated with relative growth in manufacturing and government employment but mildly inversely correlated with relative growth of construction employment. I constructed a simple relative sectoral growth rate variable (RSGR), reflecting these tendencies and it was somewhat more robust than any of the individual sectoral relative growth measures. However, it still was not quite significant at the 90 percent confidence level for any of the dependent variables, so I have included the statistical results with and without this variable.[16]

Next, I added the 1996 observations which increased to sixty-eight the number of observations. I also ran regressions excluding the 1996 observations for Texas and California since, as mentioned earlier, their perverse changes in black employment may be related to NAFTA. Since no composite variable of relative sectoral growth was even remotely significant, the regressions which included them are not presented. For both

TABLE 5

Variation in the Absolute and Relative Growth Rates of Black Male Employment, 1992–1996

(t-scores in parentheses)

	Relative Growth Rates				Absolute Growth Rates			
Independent Variables	92–95	92–95	92–96	92–96*	92–95	92–95	92–96	92–96*
Constant	–0.125	0.885	0.916	0.909	–1.120	0.313	0.254	0.231
	(0.17)	(17.2)	(20.3)	(20.1)	(1.61)	(0.68)	(0.60)	(0.54)
UN	0.019	0.018	0.014	0.015	0.016	0.016	0.014	0.015
	(2.51)	(2.44)	(2.02)	(2.22)	(2.33)	(2.25)	(1.83)	(2.01)
GRTE	0.532	—	—	—	1.556	1.205	0.679	0.696
	(1.01)	—	—	—	(3.13)	(2.69)	(1.62)	(1.67)
CSRG**	0.161				0.155	—	—	—
	(1.51)				(1.54)			
F-Ratio	3.23	5.94	4.09	4.91	4.80	5.85	3.04	3.47
R-Square	0.16	0.14	0.06	0.07	0.23	0.20	0.09	0.10
N	51	51	68	66	51	51	68	66

* — Deleted Texas and California for 1996.

** — Composite = 4(Relative Mfg. Growth Rate) + 1(Relative Govt. Growth Rate) – 2(Relative Construction Growth Rate).

sets of observations, the unemployment rate continues to have a statistically significant adverse impact on either relative or absolute black employment growth. Of interest is the reduced positive relationship between each state's total employment growth and its growth rate of black employment. It is now barely significant at the 90 percent confidence level. Given the upward bias due to the proxy variable used, this indicates that even the *weak* rising tide hypothesis is problematic when labor markets tighten.[17]

Finally, I ran the same set of regressions for the six year expansion, 1983–1989. In no specification was an unemployment variable even remotely statistically significant. Once again, there was mild support for the weak rising tide hypothesis since there was a statistically significant relationship between the unadjusted total employment and absolute black employment growth rates (t=2.12, F=4.51).

DISCUSSION

This paper suggests that as labor markets tighten, it may be unlikely that the disproportional benefits black male workers experience during economic expansions continue. Whether it is due to the negative stereotypes employers exhibit toward inner-city low-skilled black men, or a dysfunctional set of behavior traits, or black adaptation to persistent adverse employment experiences, there seems to be a significant core of black workers who will not gain paid legal employment despite robust economic growth in periods of high employment.

When data from 1996 are included, there is a substantial reduction in the statistical significance of the positive relationship between each state's employment growth and its growth of black employment. This suggests that as an expansion matures and begins to stall, black men begin to experience employment difficulties before white men. There were some hints of this in the last expansion. Between 1988 and 1989 while the white employment rate for adult working-age male workers grew from 85.7 to 86.2 percent, the black rate fell from 74.1 to 74.0 percent. This strongly suggests that even the weak rising tide hypothesis no longer holds for employment as expansions mature, just as it no longer holds for poverty rates.

In addition, the descriptive statistics in Table 3 and the recent work by Holzer[18] seem to indicate that black men in the rustbelt states may have particular difficulties. In Pennsylvania, Michigan, Ohio, and Illinois, black male employment rates were 14 to 19 percentage points lower than white rates in 1996. Unusually large racial male employment gaps also exist in the three deep South states of Louisiana, Alabama, and Mississippi. California is the only other state with such a large racial employment rate gap which should not be surprising since it had the lowest total employment growth (4.8 percent) among the seventeen states over the four-year period. While the racial employment rate gap was more modest in New York, this was little consolation to black men since it reflected a very low white male employment rate, not a significantly higher black rate. Moreover, as noted in the introductory section, the adjusted black unemployment for adult working-age black men was still 18.1 percent even after five years of economic expansion. This supports the Darity-Myers' thesis that black workers have been quite rational to adapt in ways which may be perceived as dysfunctional.

If my results are correct and there will be a significant core of black men who will not be reached simply by the general tightening of labor markets, we should demand specific programs which will aid in this transition. We should demand them not simply because it makes sense from a benefit-cost standpoint. We should demand them because, as many researchers[19] have documented, government slow-growth policies are primarily responsible for the weak employment prospects that victimized black men during much of the 1970s and 1980s.

Since 1996, labor markets have tightened considerably, causing substantial wage and employment gains for those on the margins of the economy. In cities experiencing low unemployment, the black employment rate among young workers with limited education jumped from 52 to 64 percent between 1992 and 1998.[20] In early 1999, despite these gains 19 percent of black men 16 to 24 years old were neither in school nor at work, slightly higher than at the peak of the 1980s expansion.[21] As Wilson[22] contends: "It would take sustained tight labor markets over many years to draw back those discouraged inner-city workers who have dropped out of the labor market altogether, some for very long periods of time."

Unfortunately, Federal Reserve Chairman Allan Greenspan may only temporarily be willing to allow such tight labor markets to persist. Thus, we should demand continued robust growth to protect the employment of those who are gaining a foothold in the economy for the first time.

NOTES

1. Tobin, James (1965). "On Improving the Economic Status of the Negro." In *The Negro American*, edited by Talcott Parson and Kenneth Clark, pp. 457–458. Boston: Houghton Mifflin.

2. Freeman, Richard (1991). "Employment and Earnings of Disadvantaged Young Men in a Labor Shortage Economy." In *The Urban Underclass*, edited by Christopher Jencks and Paul Peterson, pg. 119. Washington, D.C.: Brookings Institute.

3. Tobin, James (1994). "Poverty in Relation to Macroeconomics Trends, Cycles, and Policies." In *Poverty and Policies*, edited by Sheldon Danziger and Daniel Weinberg, pp. 147–167. Cambridge, MA: Harvard University Press.

4. Blank, Rebecca and David Card (1993). "Poverty, Income Distribution, and Growth: Are They Still Linked?" *Brookings Papers*, 2:285–339.

5. Wilson, William J. (1996). *When Work Disappears*, pg. 146. New York: Vintage.

6. Reich, Robert (1997). *Locked in the Cabinet*, pg. 333. New York: Knopf.

7. Darity, William and Samuel Myers (1994). *The Underclass*, p. 57. New York: Garland Publishing.

8. There is a simple reason why the benefits of the current expansion seem less for the adult working-age population then for the entire population. We can divide the total population into three groups: the teenage population, which has a high unemployment rate, has become a smaller share of the total population while the retirement age population, which has a low unemployment rate, has become an increasing share of the total population, Thus, the shifting age distribution would lower the unemployment rate for the entire population even if there were no changes in the rate for each of the three subpopulations.

9. Juhn, Chinhui (1992). "Decline of Male Labor Market Participation." *Quarterly Journal of Economics*, 107 (Feb.):79–121.

10. Holzer, Harry (1996). *What Do Employers Want?* New York: Russell Sage.

11. Juhn (1992) finds that about one-half of the racial labor force participation rate gap among men is a result of racial wage differences. That is, she finds that if white men had as low wages as black men they would also have somewhat lower labor force participation rates, since they too would become discouraged and use informal networking activities.

12. The difference between the adjusted and the official black unemployment rate, $\Delta UN_b = (LFPR_w - LFPR_b)(X)$ where X = (Black Employment Rate)/ $[(LFPR_w)(LFPR_b)]$. X has been very close to 1.0 for the entire period.

13. Tennessee was the 18th state but it revised its sampling procedure, which led to a 65 percent rise in reported black male employment during this period. The ten states in order of black male employment (000) in 1992 were as follows: TN 138; MO 84; IN 74; CT 71; AR 60; KY 57; MA 49; OK 36; KS 36; and DE 30.

14. Cotton, Jeremiah (1993). "A Regional Analysis of Black Male-White Male Wage Differences." *Review of Black Political Economy* 22 (Summer).

15. Due to the bias of using total employment as the independent variable, I ran a regression using instead total employment minus black male employment. This adjusted variable was not statistically significantly related to black employment. However, the unemployment variable was still statistically significant (t=1.99, F=3.96).

16. I also included a dummy variable for the rustbelt states (IL, MI, OH, PA, and NY) to test if growth rates were highest in these states which also had high employment rates. In none of the specifications did this dummy variable even remotely approach statistical significance (t-scores were always less than 0.50). Finally, the

unemployment rate was not significantly related to the absolute or relative employment growth rates for black females, white female, or white male employment.

17. When I ran AGR regression with the net total employment growth variable, it was not significantly correlated with black employment growth. However, the unemployment variable was still mildly statistically significant (t=l.84, F=3.79).

18. Holzer, Harry (1996). *What Do Employers Want?* New York: Russell Sage.

19. Blank, Rebecca and Robert Blinder (1996). "Macroeconomics, Income Distribution, and Poverty." *In Fighting Poverty: What Works and What Doesn't*, edited by Sheldon Danziger and Daniel Weinberg, pp. 180–208. Cambridge, MA: Harvard University Press.

20. Freeman, Richard and William Rodgers, III (forthcoming). "Area Economic Conditions and the Labor Market Outcomes of Young Men in the 1990s Expansion. In *Prosperity for All? The Economic Boom and African Americans*, edited by Robert Cherry and William Rodgers III. New York: Russell Sage.

21. Nasar, Sylvia and Kirsten Mitchell (1999). "Booming Job Market Draws Young Black Men into the Fold." *New York Times* (May 23): A1.

22. Wilson, William J. (1996). *When Work Disappears*, p. 146. New York: Vintage.

27

COOPERATIVE ECONOMICS—A COMMUNITY REVITALIZATION STRATEGY

Curtis Haynes, Jr., and Jessica Gordon Nembhard

The debate in the Fall 1995–Winter 1996 Special Issue of *The Review of Black Political Economy*[1] (*RBPE*) reveals a growing interest among academic and community service providers in the economic component of community revitalization strategies for inner-city development. Many of the discussants challenge Porter's conventional notions of economic growth and development through individual self interest and the profit motive. Many imply that if revitalization is to target both human needs and human potential, then cooperation and collaboration are key components of a comprehensive and holistic strategy. Our own research corroborates this trend.[2]

The debate, however, centers on policy alternatives with little discussion of economic theory and the potential for alternative models. In light of this deficiency in areas with immense potential for both research and practice, we add the following three propositions to the debate:

(1) Political economy and the corresponding strategy of cooperative economics are underutilized theoretical and applied tools which link broad holistic strategies of community revitalization to current socio-economic urban conditions;

(2) The cooperative firm is a viable and competitive method of enterprise organization—including but not limited to small businesses, cooperative corporations, or industrial districts—capable of sustainable growth under conditions dictated by modern industrial organization; and

(3) The collaboratives stemming from and associated with cooperative industry can facilitate the increasing importance of involving local community business and service providers in the community-building ventures currently pursued among the public, private, financial, and academic sectors.

Our exploration into the potential of cooperative entrepreneurship is not an aberration. Throughout the U.S. and the world, thousands of cooperative firms produce goods and services for the market and provide social conditions and work opportunities capable of responding to human needs and developing human potential. As with traditional business formations, these cooperative structures range in sizes similar to sole proprietorships and partnerships, to that of medium and large corporations. In the U.S. more than 100 million people are members of 47,000 producer-owned, consumer-owned, and worker-owned cooperatives spanning almost every sector of the economy, in both rural and urban areas.[3] In 1995, continuing an upward trend, the revenues of the top 100 cooperatives in the U.S. increased to $110.4 billion. Every industry group registered increased revenues, with Agriculture, Finance, and Supermarkets accounting for the majority of the gains. Internationally the largest six cooperatives have larger total combined revenues than Citicorp, Merrill Lynch, Apple Computer, Texas Instruments, ITT and Bell Atlantic combined.[4]

The most renown example of a cooperative enterprise is the Mondragon Cooperative Corporation (MCC). This corporation evolved from a small cooperative firm built in the economically depressed Basque lands of northern Spain, in the 1950s, into a modern-day multinational corporation with over $8 billion in assets and $3.5 billion in sales in 1993. The MCC is currently operated by almost 30,000 worker-owners organized into financial, industrial, and distributional groupings. The MCC has become a powerful force in shaping regional development strategies and is a model of economic collaboration which is highly respected throughout the world. Moreover, the MCC is not the only successful example of cooperative entrepreneurship.[5] Models in Asia, Africa, Latin America, Europe, Canada, and the U.S. proliferate.

The cooperative enterprise can be the cornerstone of a progressive urban revitalization strategy, but to date this model has been left out of the debate. Why? A major reason is that neo-classical economic theory, at the root of Porter's and other urban development analyses, has been effective in its prominence[6]—keeping at "bay" significant challenges to its construct and core assumptions. This may explain why the Special Issue critiques of Porter's work tend to be policy debates and not theoretical challenges. Although many of the reviewers implicitly recognize weaknesses in Porter's neo-classical economic policy, none challenge the theory behind it. Since current economic development strategies are typically rooted in neo-classical theory, acknowledgment of this theoretical hegemony would contribute to the debate. Any challenge to the mainstream strategies would be helpful since their core assumptions and policy prescriptions may no longer be appropriate, as we search for solutions to urban redevelopment in the 21st century.

In the following pages we explore the need for alternative paradigms, sketch an alternative framework for analyzing inner-city development, and propose cooperative enterprise development as a viable economic strategy for inner-city redevelopment. We will present political economy as an appropriate tool in understanding current socio-economic conditions in U.S. cities, and explain its effectiveness in describing the relationship between corporate forms of business and the cooperative enterprises advocated for in the industrial policy of cooperative economics. We will review the ways in which current conditions in industry can be enhanced with democratic ownership and governance. It is through the lens of political economy and cooperative economics that we analyze the cooperative enterprise as an important component of policy designed to respond to the total condition of depressed communities.

THE NEED FOR AN ALTERNATIVE PARADIGM

> *Revitalizing inner cities is one of the nation's most challenging problems. The failure to meet this challenge has led to an enormous waste in human and economic resources.*[7]

Each of the contributors to the *RBPE* Special Issue confirm that the current conditions of U.S. inner cities must be addressed. The twenty-two reviews of his essay, "The Competitive Advantage of the Inner City," affirm Michael Porter's assertion that the economic distress of U.S. inner cities is one of the most pressing issues facing the nation. All agree that the task facing inner cities is formidable, and that the consequences of continued inadequacies in urban development policies will only add to the travesty of urban economic and social conditions—much of which is not completely measurable through traditional means. Porter's call for a "radically different approach" resounds through the halls of urban planning departments, some business schools, and down inner-city streets. It is prophetic and challenging:

> The time has come to recognize that revitalizing our nation's inner cities requires a radically different approach. We must stop trying to cure the problems of these distressed urban areas by perpetually expanding social programs and hoping that economic activity will

> follow. Our nation's urban policies and programs have fallen into the trap of only redistributing wealth.[8]

In his own defense, Porter reasserts his position that his strategy should be one component of a larger strategy, albeit the leading one. Alluding to assumptions upon which neo-classical economic theory is founded, Porter expresses disappointment in current government programs and reveals his theoretical bias, as he outlines the premise of his work:

> . . . a sustainable economic base can be created in the inner city only as it has been elsewhere: through private, for-profit initiatives and investments based on economic self-interest and genuine competitive advantage instead of artificial inducements, government mandates, or charity.[8]

In challenging "social programming" Porter assumes that the economics of inner cities is, "as elsewhere," based on self interest and can only manifest itself in private, for profit indicatives. Many of Porter's reviewers, however, suggest that a sustainable inner-city economy will be built not on the profit motive as a manifestation of individual self interest, but rather through collaborations and partnerships based on the shared and mutual interests of the participating parties.[9] They take exception to his narrow solutions and harsh attack on social service programming. They expose weaknesses in Porter's policy and practice in a variety of ways, and in so doing implicitly attack the main tenets of neo-classical economic theory. These critics counter that community revitalization is not just about the development of small private firms or providing low-paying, dead-end service sector jobs.[10] In today's climate of unprecedented market activity and wealth accumulation, inner-city communities still end up having to beg just for a few crumbs. Our central cities need jobs that are family-supporting and wealth-creating, and economic activities and opportunities that are accessible and sustainable.

The narrow framework of mainstream economic theory upon which Porter's ideas are based does not respond to the broad dimensions of community needs, nor does it capture the value of the activity (labor) expended in the service of bettering community, with the profit motive tangential. The sterile mathematical models of the modern economic theoretician are not synchronized with or reflective of the policies and activities of the practitioners who are attempting to respond to the needs and assets of inner city communities. If anything, those models are used to justify the status quo. Indeed, traditional economic theory rules out many vital relationships and activities (such as learning by doing, networking, team work, concern for community, and the sharing of capital) as not being resources for community economic development. The option of cooperative enterprise development is ignored; hence, its potential for bettering community and the accumulation of wealth is missed.

Traditional economic thinking does not capture the dynamics of our changing economy, nor does it adequately respond to the unique needs of urban areas. Blakely and Small's recognition, for example, that "doing well is moving out," captures a major component of the resource drains endemic to inner-city communities:

> The real reason for the continuing distance from the labor market among a large segment of the ghetto population is that there is little connection between work and better outcomes for ghetto dwellers or for their communities. The signals are very clear. To move up economically requires moving out. As a result, the link between job and social betterment is lost collectively as achievers move out of the ghetto rather than pass on social and networking skills to the community or act as the magnets for community human resource recovery. Porter does not suggest ways to capture this social capital in the community as it is developed.[11]

If inner cities are merely places that people move out of and do not want to live in, then no wonder there is not good policy about how to sustain and revitalize them. They are just "throw-away" places. They are supposed to become obsolete, or at best are just places in constant transition, not real communities that need much attention or concern. However, there is a problem because people inhabit them and continuously live there—everyone does not transition out; and as abundant empirical research shows, those who stay are often the ones with the least prospects and the fewest resources and skills. These enclaves of defeat and underdevelopment persist and cannot be ignored; neither can they be solved in the usual way.

Shipp[12] contends that purely entrepreneurial, single proprietor strategies narrow the focus from the community to individuals, and thus are only able to help a small group, with limited impact on the entire community. This in turn limits the entrepreneur's ability to expand the service area and be self-sustaining enough to reinvest in the community. Thus, both the single proprietor and the community lose. Shipp concludes that "this capitalistic approach has proven incapable of solving the multidimensional problems within the black community"[13]; thus, the need for alternative paradigms.[14]

Porter's strategy, however, is not new and is not "radical." His model is based on the tenets of dominant economic theory. Policy prescriptions similar to Porter's have led to sterile actions that have combined in the past to create economic policy which has allowed the private sector to run from its responsibility to rebuild the cities from which it operated. The government, taking up the slack, throws new money after old into a black hole of expanding despair. Sawicki and Moody remind us of the limitations of these solutions.[15] We see that Porter's model is unable to tackle the complexities of economic change, and clashes in values, activities, and people in an increasingly shrinking and interactive world, in a way that effectively addresses the conditions of the most depressed in urban communities. It is particularly unable to respond to the conditions of African Americans, the majority of whom are urban dwellers in an urbanized society.

Further, Porter's call for private enterprise development is actually industrial policy under the mistaken assumption that the building of industry is community economic development. Even among his critics, many of the solutions manifest themselves in economic policy built around one component of the economy—Industry. We acknowledge that building effective industry is a critical component of community revitalization, but argue that the current methods of organizing private enterprise through sole-propriety, partnerships and corporations are too limited to fulfill community needs for empowerment. The current view of industry blinds us to the strong links between the structure of industry and the living conditions in communities, and the need to respond to both simultaneously. Not surprisingly, economic activity stemming from current forms of industrial organization is becoming increasingly ineffective in turning inner-city economies around.[16] A new direction is needed.

If the comprehensive needs of urban communities are not satisfied solely through private enterprise development, accessing traditional market processes, then what other economic strategies might work? The critics of Porter's thesis have not provided a collective vision for how to proceed. Indeed, among all sides there appears to be strong disagreement and even mistrust of the variety of strategies proposed or reported on by others. None of the reviewers in the *RBPE* Special Issue expand their analysis to fully investigate the strengths and weaknesses of our economic system—particularly its inability to deliver comprehensive economic and community development to our inner cities—or offer new paradigms to adequately address the needs. This helps to explain why Porter is able to respond to his critics by continuing to call for "economic" strategies and admonishing them for continuing to worry more about "social" programs. The striking omission, in almost all the reviews and in Porter's work, of any serious attention to the work being done in cooperative enterprise development, self management, worker-ownership and regional cooperative development through networking is especially disturbing and counter-productive. By not discussing alternatives in discourse, and by excluding these forms of enterprise development, a variety of theoretical, empirical, and applied research and policy is left unmined; and viable solutions are left unimagined.

POLITICAL ECONOMY AND COOPERATIVE ECONOMICS

The distress of the inner city is not fundamentally about dilapidated buildings and worn out infrastructures. It is about conditions that deprive individuals of the capacity to fulfill their human potential. Dilapidated buildings are important mainly because they house the broken spirits of those who have lost all hope of attaining a better life."[17]

These powerful words challenge us to rethink the meaning of economic development—particularly in an urban setting. They also operate as a mandate for practitioners and theoreticians to redirect their community revitalization tactics. The very pragmatic policies designed to respond to dilapidated housing and all that it represents through the "necessity and the real opportunity [of] creat[ing] income and wealth. . . ."[18] must equally contribute to the pursuit of human perfectibility and spiritual growth. To make sense of cooperative economics as a response to human needs we must challenge the very foundation of social thought, including what we understand today as economics, and redefine the structure and function of economic activity. It is to this challenge that political economy and cooperative economics speaks.

In this new theoretical space, cooperative economics becomes the outcome of an analytic tool—political economy—and becomes a practical response to the concerns of inner city communities. We shift the analysis from the study of the production and distribution of goods and services through the pursuit of profit and individualistic self interest, to focus on social reproduction. Hogan[19] defines a political economy as "a human population undergoing the act of social reproduction, over a protracted period of time, under a set of rules promulgated and enforced by a political state, within a bounded geographical domain." Through this analytical model, people are understood as the "*dramatis personae*" of a social activity of which they are the subject, object and results. Political economy describes the relationship between the survival of community members and the human potential of each individual. As a tool this framework allows us to examine cyclical and long term trends in addition to race, class, and ethnic dynamics in communities; investigate how communities grow from the past, are lived in the present, and set the foundation for the future; and explore the interactions between community members, labor markets, work-sites, goods and services, and wealth accumulation.

Political Economy

Hogan builds a political-economic analysis from the traditions of Adam Smith, Karl Marx and W.E.B. DuBois. Hogan's research responds to the theoretical and methodological rationalizations in the discipline which "justify the existing conditions in which wage workers find themselves." Particularly concerned with the shortcomings of dominant economic thought's analysis of African Americans, he develops an analytical tool designed to explain the mechanisms by which this black population in the United States reproduces itself as a particular grouping of human beings. In this essay we adopt the mode and structure of Hogan's general political economy to focus on urban populations as a whole.[20]

A political-economic analysis of urban social reproduction understands "the complex set of interrelations, that link the individual members of the human population, one to another, in stable and regularly recurring bonds of cooperative existence." Together six minimal parameters define the analysis:

(a) the geographical space within which the political economy functions,
(b) the human population whose social reproduction is the underlying motivating force of the political economy,
(c) the institutional mechanisms which are the instrumentalities of social reproduction,
(d) the historical period during which the people are being reproduced,

(e) the political state which oversees the political economy, and
(f) the geographical domains outside of the political economy in question.[21]

People are the key factor, and their labor which is generated and expended on themselves and the material means of their survival is the driving force of the political-economic system. For continued social reproduction, members of the population must be created and others must be maintained as living beings. A set of institutions which provide for this, subject to the constrains of the local area and region, are what Hogan calls the "institutional mechanisms of social reproduction." These mechanisms operate as the organizing principle of his thesis which recognizes human labor as "two continuous, synchronized, and complementary alternating phases of the most fundamental activity that drives the political economy." These phases of human labor are referred to as "external labor" and "internal labor" respectively. The first uses up human beings and their energy, through the process of creating the material means of survival for the human population. The second uses this material to create human energy, and consequently the human population itself.[22] The social reproduction of the population involves the unified and continuous performance of both phases of labor. The analysis is completed by specifying the nature of two distributive mechanisms, which are preconditions for the alternating phases of human labor. Through these mechanisms human energy is distributed, first, from the internal labor process (ILP) where it is created to the external labor process (ELP) where it is used. Second, material goods are distributed from the external labor process where they are created to the internal labor process where they are used.

Accumulated wealth, in a form characteristic of the particular historical epoch in which the human labor is being generated, is the natural "terminus" completing the cycle of labor. It is the social switching mechanism which allows the cycle to be restarted within the same social arrangements as before, ensuring the continuation of the political economy.

By blending the insights of three significant social scientists, Hogan reveals a way to deconstruct current models of social thinking. Political economy facilitates an interdisciplinary response to the broad needs and assets of a typical urban society. Through concepts such as energy expenditure in both the transformation of the material means of existence (the external labor process), and the reproduction of a human population (the internal labor process), Hogan lays the groundwork for a discussion of why a particular grouping of the human species is reproduced as a "people." Such a focus also brings to the forefront of political-economic analysis the struggle over the control of this human energy. When applied to inner cities, the model allows us to (1) understand the past development (and underdevelopment) of inner cities and the ethnic and racial groups who reside in them, and (2) create new political-economic realities in inner cities that address the needs of the current populations, and rebuild more responsive, productive and just economic activities, relationships, and institutions.

Political economy as pioneered by Lloyd Hogan can be used to understand the current socioeconomic conditions of today's inner cities and provide a framework which facilitates the building of comprehensive and holistic strategies of economic development which can be implemented with other social policies designed to better life in America's inner cities. One of these policies is cooperative economics.

Cooperative Economics as a Social Safety Net

Indeed, the policy outcome of political-economic analysis when focused on the urban and black condition in the current capitalist political economy is cooperative economics. Political economy and cooperative economics combined, enables us to focus our economic analysis on people—as a few of the reviews[22] suggest is needed. It is the economic development of a people, not of a place, or even a nation, that should concern us. "The first line of basic capital formation is the people themselves."[23] In addition, Williams (1993) reminds us, "cooperation was one of nature's more important schemes for survival."[24]

Williams advocates for cooperative economics as the natural solution to the social condition of underdeveloped peoples.

> Poor and underdeveloped peoples, it seems to us, have no other alternative to self-help cooperative organization if they wish to develop as a whole and, at the same time, remain free to develop individually. The socio-economic society we envision is one so truly democratic in fact that the people, having always the freedom of choice, will not be frightened by the bugbear of "regimentation" when organization and united action are urgently necessary for their own economic and social salvation and progress.[25]

Hogan finds it to be a political-economic imperative that African Americans build a safety net in their communities to ensure the material means of their survival, and capture "black labor in the total interest of black people." This net must be built to assert their "complete control" over both the internal and external labor processes.[26] Hogan suggests further that the safety net be built "grounded in the principle of the creation of a black laboring population which is molded in the true spirit of human perfectibility."[27] The depressed conditions in inner cities, of which so many are now aware, are forcing urban communities to build social safety nets in the interest of their own survival. The plethora of social betterment policy presented in the *RBPE* Special Issue attests to this. The policies and activities that will develop an economic safety net and ensure economic empowerment are slower to be advocated, and take longer to build. We can see, however, that cooperative economic ventures are a logical strategy for achieving such social and economic control.

Hogan points us to the external labor process as the site which requires the most decisive change. Williams suggests that democratic control of regimentation is necessary. The cooperative form of industrial organization with its governance structure built on decentralized control and centralized administration responds to these concerns. Cooperative economic policy responds to the call from political economy theoreticians and the needs of the people. It opens the door for comprehensive, community-wide strategies and structures for social and individual betterment linked closely to changes in the external labor process.

Economic cooperation happens everywhere from the home environment, to motivating the actions of racial and ethnic groups, nation-states, corporations, and countless other social organizations. At the root of this focus is the awareness that the conditions for cooperative economic action exist in urban areas, particularly when understood as an extension of the rich history of self help in both immigrant populations and African American communities. Many immigrant groups, for example, find ways to defend themselves against the harshness of urban life. More often than not, this self defense has been organized through ethnic institutions of self help.[28] Combined with the numerous attempts by African Americans to implement self-determination through collective actions, deliberate and coordinated cooperative economic activity becomes a rational (dare we say, even promising) strategy for economic revitalization in inner-cities. Moreover, economic development can be built on a collective and cooperative movement which has always been a part of the "American tradition," whether organized through religious, worker, ethnic, or racial groupings.[29]

The cooperative complex can be seen as an appropriate response to today's conditions, and one aspect of a continual battle to free the energy and labor of working people. African Americans can be involved in the restructuring of production through democratic firms in a cooperative inter-firm relationship. Community controlled economic development is a possible means of development which can incorporate flexible methods of production and organization using a democratic governance structure. Cooperation can be stimulated as a resource for economic development, giving African Americans a critical role in economic and industrial development in the United States. With this focus, community interests and collective action are modeled as rational behaviors in response not only to an awareness of community needs and assets, but also to competitive conditions in capitalist industry.

Current Conditions in Industry

Even though we live in one of the world's greatest political representative democracies, many in the U.S. face a dilemma which signifies that political representation does not ensure economic security. Too many Americans face poverty, unemployment, underemployment, and social stress, even in times of relative prosperity. The inability of many of the working poor to negotiate the labor market effectively, has closed the door to some of the most desired employment in the external labor process. The traditional market relationships where labor negotiates with capitalists, either as individuals or as a group, have led to a loss of jobs and lost prosperity in inner-city communities. Many of the urban poor are left to experiment with various worthy and courageous methods of coping, while all too many engage in economic activities that are detrimental to themselves and their own communities.

The changes that took place in the external labor process during the 1970s and 1980s have isolated the urban poor from, and left too many ill prepared to participate in, the new forms of competition that have come with deindustrialization and globalization. Big business grew in the United States using competitive methods designed to enhance profit making through the control of wage labor (and labor expenditure within the firm and the legitimizing of the market relationship outside). These relationships developed into rigid price- and market-orientated structures. Government industrial policy basically bailed out, and favored ailing and increasingly obsolete firms. Today's conditions, however, provide a unique opportunity to extend the democratic process into economic production processes as a method of inducing economic security. Mainstream economic thought does not acknowledge the importance of this.

New competitive methods used throughout the world are built on entrepreneurial strategies of firms gaining market advantage by pursuing well-defined methods of competition and cooperation. Today's successful industries, for example, use different methods of production and organization both among firms and within firms, with the government playing a more coordinating role. To be effective within this "new competition," principles within the firm are transformed; buyer and vender relationships are distinguished; inter-firm associations are developed; and concerted efforts are made to establish effective industrial policies. The strategy is production-based, focused on entrepreneurial firms organized to pursue continuous improvement in methods, products, and processes. Entrepreneurial activity is moved from a traditional individualist approach, to one which is more collective in concept. Firm relations range externally from giant coordinated organizational structures, to a variety of inter-firm complexes of small firms linked by cooperative associations. Within the firm, worker-management relations range from direct labor consultation to direct labor control. The differences between these methods are in the organizational shells, not the basic principles. A key to their success is their flexibility and varying degrees of worker participation.

Modern strategy is one of permanent innovation, an accommodation to ceaseless change reflected in flexible multi-use equipment, skilled workers, and governance structures which restrict forms of competition in favor of innovation. U.S. industry has slowly experimented with new methods of participation ranging from suggestion boxes to personal supervision through "quality circles." Economic incentives are instituted through employee stock ownership plans.

Neither the hierarchical firms, nor horizontally integrated industrial complexes define success within the current epoch. The general nature of the external labor process is not necessarily the structure or the shell of the competing organizations, but rather the use of relevant productive and organizational principles. The cooperative complex is effective in the use of these key principles in their organizational and productive strategy. More importantly, perhaps, is that the cooperative complex contributes to the positive economic and social development of the human being (killing several "birds" with "one stone").

The task is to integrate a theoretical analysis of the expenditure of human energy to that of economic policy, to show that worker self-management and ownership is effective and can contribute to a continuing process toward self-sufficiency and human liberation. Democracy, particularly through the democratic firm, can stimulate economic development in urban economies. The principle of one-person, one-vote elicits community control of capital, governance, and organization. This can be the foundation for the new competitive firm. Decentralized control through participatory governance and organization, in conjunction with centralized and strategic management, lessens worker alienation and allows for a quickened response to technological and market changes through increased flexibility in the production and assembly processes.

The networking of democratic firms into industrial groups evokes cooperative relationships through the sharing of information and long-term commitments. It is assumed that regions dominated by small firms are functional in today's international economy. The flexibility of the cooperative system in both production and organization is a particular strategy for competitive success open to groups of small firms. Regions dominated by small firms through a network of dynamic industrial districts and the market-share-dominating corporations, can be understood as different faces of flexible specialization.

The challenge today is to establish means of cooperation that generate common benefits for the cooperators within the firms and for the community, without stifling effects of individual responsibility. Enforcing individual responsibility to the common interest is to establish institutions of inter-firm cooperation. This precludes privately rational acts which can undermine collective rationality. Cooperation ensures that commitments are made to long-term infrastructural development. This is to be tempered with a method to ensure that business enterprises remain innovative and responsive to new challenges and opportunities.

Resource-limited economic activities can take advantage of the organizational process of cooperation, using it as an "invisible glue" to bind people together in a voluntary attempt to better their condition collectively. This cooperation can be harnessed to produce a sort of social energy which can be a resource in cooperative economic development. The democratic use of labor entails an organizational advantage when competing in a market system.

The cooperative way can be a feasible undertaking if the strategic action of putting into practice critical production and organizational principles, appropriate to the times, is carried out. The "Mondragon Experiment" is proving itself as a practical method of economic development, maintaining democratic principles of governance and contributing to a high standard of worker satisfaction and participation, and is effective within international economics. Japanese industry integrates the thinking and doing of its workers through "quality circles" and team concepts, while still maintaining the capitalist business structure.

The U.S. needs an industrial policy that encourages the combining of constitutional and economic rights—not simply for a utopian vision, but rather in the name of good business. The expansion of democracy into the economic sphere can expedite the response of U.S. industry to the "new competition" and bring a new wave of economic security. The spillover of democracy from the political to the economic arena can help bring both material and spiritual security.

COOPERATIVE ENTERPRISE STRATEGY FOSTERS COMMUNITY DEVELOPMENT/REVITALIZATION

> *. . . the original organizers of the Mondragon cooperatives acted as catalysts bringing forth collective actions and talents which previously lay outside of the realm of economic activism. This catalytic action facilitated by a "learning by doing" process of organization exhibited tangible success as Mondragon proved its ability for economic and employment growth and long term survival.*[30]

Through political economy and cooperative economics, cooperative enterprises become a critical component of a comprehensive plan of community revitalization which can respond to the current conditions in industry. Through this alternative vision, industry can be conceptualized in its broader relationship to the process of social reproduction within a particular political economy. This has begun to be theorized and documented through applied and participatory research. While much more research needs to be done in this area, we are beginning to know and understand what makes successful cooperative enterprises, and the implications of this knowledge for economic policy.

Cooperative development, clustering and collaboration, and human capital development are all economic activities. Economics does not mean only private, for profit businesses. Those are just specific types of economic activity. The social transformation of goods and services, whether in primary, intermediate or final industry, can be accomplished using the cooperative as the organizing formation. Cooperatives operate effectively when gauged by traditional criteria. Also, when seen in another light, cooperative entrepreneurship and enterprise development bring to the debate a comprehensive tool for community building, combining many of the elements and addressing many of the needs to which all the contributors to the *RBPE* Special Issue[31] call to our attention.

Collective power and collective use of community resources help to solve many of the challenges facing inner cities, problems the Special Issue contributors, including Porter, find daunting and disconcerting: the anti-business attitude of residents and excessive reliance on the profit motive[32]; the need to incorporate the unique social dynamics of the inner city and promote social and distributive justice[33]; the political-economic milieu of laissez-faire practices and government deregulation[34]; the need for "employment anchors"[35]; the lack of understanding the talent, skills and resources in the inner city[36]; fool proof ways to hire inner-city residents themselves[37]; and the need for a coherent "economic strategy," "the necessity and the real opportunity" to "create income and wealth."[38]

How better to "raise the expectations of the people, forge bonds of community and trust, improve social justice and equity, and establish a sense of accountability and ownership within the community,"[39] than to promote and teach collective entrepreneurship and community enterprises? This is also a way to "involve local residents and institutions in solving the problems their communities face[40]; to capitalize on feelings of nationalism and remedy the racial monopoly of business[41]; and to develop new social organizations.[42]

Cooperatives help to build and nurture talent, skills, and confidence in an atmosphere of cooperation and support. Cooperatives help to minimize risk, use collective resources to solve many credit and capitalization limitations, and use social energy alongside labor power and collective labor, specific skills, technology and information to produce goods and services and enhance productivity. Cooperative enterprises combine the social energy and productive activity of their members with their shared resources to produce competitive businesses, which are able to reproduce themselves over time. They have the potential to engage the energies and little tapped resources of poor and other economically unsuccessful economic agents (i.e., community members) into successful economic activities.[43] Cooperative enterprise development enables us to uncover hidden assets and nurture and utilize skills, energies and resources that were being wasted or used in illegal or unproductive activities. In addition, cooperative enterprise development can create a favorable climate for business (of any kind), because business development is a part of any community's development and can be viewed as cooperative, skill building, resource-enhancing ventures which benefit everyone. Cooperation can improve efficiency and productivity.

Hard work is not only motivated through the profit motive and individual self interest. Many people in this society are also highly motivated in attempting to better social conditions. The effect can be much different because the community receives the fruits of their labor.[44] Economic cooperativism can effect the social reproduction of people using competitive institutions able to survive the market economy. We each fulfill the personal interests of living in a thriving and vibrant community conducive to human personal and spiritual development through methods of economic and social cooperation as a motivation for survival.

Morris[45] summarizes many of these elements:

> This is a moment in history that screams out for an organizational form that can bridge the ethics of the 1930s and the 1990s, that can bridge the market and the community, competition and cooperative, stability and innovation. . . . Cooperatives marry means and ends. Their "one person, one vote" principle and their local orientation build community and democracy while their business orientation allows them to offer high-quality and low-cost services and products. They allow us to become part of something bigger than ourselves but no so big that we lose a sense of ownership and participation.

There are many highly successful cooperative businesses ranging from the thousands of small enterprises throughout the country and the world, to the multimillion- and billion-dollar revenue-generating collaboratives such as the Mondragon Cooperative Corporation of the Basque lands in Spain, the Sekatsu Consumer Cooperative of Japan, the Industrial District of the Third Italy, and the Cooperative Commonwealth of Ottawa Canada.[46]

The main successes and potentials of cooperative enterprise development are summarized as the following:[47]

a. Cooperative economic development provides employment and educational opportunities. Throughout the world, consumers and workers are experimenting in cooperative forms of enterprise development. They are competitive, democratic and committed to community education. In many comparative cases they do better than traditional forms of work organization.
b. Many cooperative structures have generated revenues and capital for sustainable economic growth. That the work-sites provided by

cooperative firms are not easily susceptible to capital flight has been shown to be critically important. Personal rights, manifested in voting rights in the form of one person, one vote, rather than property rights through stock ownership, allow membership a greater impact in determining the course of action, and tend to keep capital at home (or at least make it harder to flee). Moreover, moving from rights based on property (and stock ownership) to rights based on patronage (labor or consumer) or personal rights will make a key difference in how wealth remains in or returns to the community.

c. Cooperatives are competitive. The key difference between the cooperative and traditional form of enterprise is the governance structure and wealth distribution based on patronage. The performance structures can be designed to respond to current competitive conditions, and have successfully done so.
d. Cooperative economic organization contributes to the development of community members, through provision of employment, quality goods and services, and a commitment to community building. Cooperative enterprise mobilization is built around community concern. It creates dedicated workers and responsible citizenship through the mobilization of community members and resourccs, in a way that can not be understood with traditional theory, and in alternative forms of industrial and economic development.
e. Accumulated wealth (fruits of labor) is returned to the community and cooperative members in the form of lower prices, dividends, and safety (material and non-material forms).

CONCLUSION

. . . it should be clear that all that we have been saying about economic development through organized cooperative programs has the single purpose of a fuller, happier life. These are things of the spirit. Our various enterprises would be pushed to increase the wealth of the community in order to increase the happiness and well-being of all its members.[48]

Although Williams was speaking to Africans about *The Rebirth of African Civilization* on that continent, his analysis and advice are appropriate worldwide, especially for those of us concerned with the political-economic conditions facing U.S. inner cities. Many who worry about the survival of our cities recognize that collaboration and cooperation are and will continue to be critical elements in any strategy of community revitalization. The public sector, granting agencies, and community organizations are all considering partnerships around these principles, with increased discussion of economic development (through collaborations and cooperation) as a key component of social development. Firms in the private sector, in pursuit of profits, recognize an increased role in worker participation through team work and employee ownership, making these the norm rather than the exception. School reformers celebrate the successes of their incorporation of "new competition" principles into schools and classrooms that reduce class sizes, enhance teaching and learning, empower teachers and students, and facilitate school and community partnerships without increasing costs. Organized labor is accelerating its efforts to build meaningful and long-term community links. Community service organizations are overwhelmingly emphasizing the need for "one stop shops" which combine. social services with work force development, job creation, and other economic development activities. The motivation behind these institutions and the people who are their members, is not purely the profit motive—it is more complex than that. What is clear is that many involved see a need for collaboration, teamwork and "workplace" democracy, whatever the activity, and understand that bettering their own condition is in some way connected to bettering that of others. More and more people realize that many of the current trends in urban environments are not only detrimental to the communities themselves, but to U.S. society as a whole.

In this essay we suggest that much of the problem of finding and recognizing solutions lies in economic theory and its corresponding policy implications. The proposed strategy of income and wealth accumulation through private enterprise development is not broad enough to respond to community concerns associated with housing, economic development, neighborhood revitalization, infrastructure development, health care, job training, education, crime prevention, and planning and community organizing, in a post-industrial, globalized economy. The reality is that the needs in these areas call for a comprehensive, holistic, and well coordinated community-wide set of strategies which incorporate the building of creative, productive, and sustainable mechanisms of survival and prosperity which better the quality of life. Inner-city revitalization and community economic development must mean good jobs, economic empowerment, and community cultural, political, and social development—simultaneously. Materialist and individualistic solutions are no longer enough.

As we enter the 21st century, the world still faces the problem of a color line. However this line is part of a larger quilt of contradictions woven into the social fabric. Political economic theory responds to this complexity. We can understand the historical struggle for control of the labor of the African American as a critical feature of those "broader [and] deeper matters of social condition" which "lie behind the concept of race."[49] In the United States, capitalism has rendered a certain amount of urban labor significantly useless. A possible method of bringing productivity to this group may be through economic restructuring (which will require theoretical restructuring). Economic restructuring may be done according to organizational principles of a new period of international competition, and conceptual restructuring may be done connecting social reproduction with industrial organization.

The omission of such a discussion in previous critiques of Porter's and similar "solutions" to inner-city underdevelopment, is an example of how conceptual debates play a role in promoting, sustaining, and undermining economic institutions.[50] Working together to better a collective condition is a concept that traditional economics at best ignores and usually condemns. Hence, little of it has been studied and the potential to direct collective efforts toward cooperative enterprise development is untapped. We hope that this article has set a conceptual base for understanding that real world situations in inner cities are conducive to the creation of cooperative complexes in the United States. Methods of participatory economics bolstered by the non-material resource of social energy open the door for increased, and more universal, economic prosperity. They make possible more varied forms of expression of the human potential.

We conclude, therefore, that an equally valid response to Porter's challenge to develop the competitive advantage of cities is to:

1. Recognize cooperative enterprise development as an economic (actually a political-economic) activity,
2. Understand how collaboration and cooperative enterprise development address the unique experiences and many of the socio-economic needs of African Americans and all inner-city populations,
3. Document the ways in which such cooperative ventures are viable and competitive,
4. Research cooperative enterprise development as a community development strategy, and

5. Design ways to use cooperative enterprises and cooperative entrepreneurship to redevelop and revitalize inner cities.

Much work needs to be accomplished in this area. As we all struggle to revitalize our cities, we challenge Porter, his critics, and the readers to broaden their research and consider new paradigms to include investigation of cooperative economic activity—its energies, resources, various methods of organization, and achievements—and its ability to engage and empower heretofore underdeveloped, impoverished, and exploited communities.

NOTES

1. Fall 1995/Winter 1996. *The Review of Black Political Economy*. Vol: 24:2/3.

2. Curtis Haynes, Jr. is a co-founder of the HUD-funded Resurgent City for Cooperative Community Development (RCC) at Buffalo State College. The RCC operates on the premises laid out in this paper. Jessica Gordon Nembhard, senior economist at The Institute for Urban Research, Morgan State University, also uses applied and theoretical research in the areas of political economy and cooperative economics.

We would like to thank our colleagues who gave comments and took the time to read various versions of this article, particularly Lloyd Hogan for his encouragement and advice. Of course the controversial analysis and any general short comings are our own doing.

3. Approximately thirty percent of farmers' products are marketed through cooperatives in the U.S. More than 50 million Americans use insurance companies that are owned by or closely affiliated with cooperatives. More than 20 co-ops have over $1 billion in annual sales. And over 67 million people are members of credit unions with assets greater than $100 billion. See National Cooperative Business Association. (No date.) "Cooperatives Are . . . Cooperative Business in the United States." Pamphlet, circa 1997. Washington, DC: NCBA.

4. National Cooperative Bank. (No Date.) "The NCB Co-op 100." Brochure, circa 1996. Washington DC: NCB.

5. According to the National Cooperative Bank, ibid., the Mondragon is the seventh largest cooperative internationally, after France's Credit Agricole, Japan's Morinchukin Bank, and the Swiss Migros—to name the top three.

6. Neo-classical economics is one of the many competing paradigms of economic thought. Its current prominence is the result of historical, political, cultural, economic and natural processes associated with the development of the current political economic system. Also see our note #14.

7. Boston, Thomas D. and Catherine L. Ross, Fall 1995/Winter 1996. "Location Preferences of Successful African American-owned Business in Atlanta," *The Review of Black Political Economy*. Vol: 24:2/3, 337.

8. Porter, Michael E., Fall 1995/Winter 1996. "An Economic Strategy for America's Inner Cities: Addressing the Controversy," *The Review of Black Political Economy*. Vol: 24:2/3, 303 and 304.

9. Reichert, Usha Nair, Fall 1995/Winter 1996. "Revitalizing the Inner City: A Holistic Approach," *The Review of Black Political Economy*. Vol: 24:2/3, 185; Ameri-

can, Richard F., Fall 1995/Winter 1996. "Reparations and the Competitive Advantage of Inner Cities," *The Review of Black Political Economy*. Vol: 24: 2/3, 193; and Johnson, James H., Jr., Walter C. Farrell, Jr., and Geraldine R. Henderson. Fall 1995/Winter 1996. "Mr. Porter's 'Competitive Advantage' for Inner-City Revitalization: Exploitation or Empowerment?" *The Review of Black Political Economy*. Vol: 24: 2/3, 259.

Johnson, Farrell, and Henderson, for example, suggest the mobilization of a broad range of the nation's assets. "What is needed are institutions capable of designing and implementing cooperative, collaborative, and coordinated strategies that draw upon and fully utilize the complete range of community assets to deal with heretofore intractable problems of inner cities." "An emerging school of thought posits that providing greater access to individual and community-based social resources is the key to resolving . . . [crime] and related problems of distressed urban neighborhoods." They conclude with an imperative to empower inner-city workers and entrepreneurs rather than exploit inner-city resources with outside majority-owned businesses.

In addition, Graf, Special Issue . . . , 1995/1996, recognizes the need to solve the problem of who benefits from the fruits of the development when addressing issues of capital formation in inner cities.

10. Bates, Timothy. Fall 1995/Winter 1996. "Political Economy of Urban Poverty in the 21st Century: How Progress and Public Policy Generate Rising Poverty," *The Review of Black Political Economy*. Vol: 24: 2/3, 111. For example, notes that by "adopting the laissez-faire practices of the informal economy, narrowing the gap between the off-the-books sweatshops and the inner city, the above ground small business sector may increase employment in poor urban areas, but poverty will not decline."

In addition, Sawicki, David S., and Mitch Moody. Fall 1995/Winter 1996. "Deja-vu All Over Again: Porter's Model of Inner-City Redevelopment," *The Review of Black Political Economy*. Vol: 24: 2/3, 75. Remind us that " . . . the country needs a more radical look at the changing nature of work, private—and public-sector hiring policies, and an attitude that should hold our society to blame for creating too few jobs, rather than blaming those that lose in the competition for those jobs. In our opinion, Porter contributes to another misformulation of the problem, and therefore a sure loser of a solution" (p. 92).

11. Blakely, Edward J., and Leslie Small. Fall 1995/Winter 1996. "Michael Porter: New Gilder of Ghettos," *The Review of Black Political Economy*. Vol: 24: 2/3, 166.

12. Shipp, Sigmund C. 1996. "The Road Not Taken: Alternative Strategies for Black Economic Development in the United States," *Journal of Economic Issues*. Vol: 30

13. Also see Shipp, ibid., p. 92, about the need for strategies that focus on the entire group and the collection of factors contributing to the quality of life of a community.

Ofari, Earl. 1970. "The Myth of Black Capitalism," *Monthly Review Press*, New York, NY, provides lucid illumination of the weaknesses of Black Capitalism.

Handy, John W. 1993. "Community Economic Development: Some Critical Issues," *Review of Black Political Economy*. Vol: 21 (Winter): 41–46.

14. The debate about inner-city revitalization should include challenges to the theory behind Porter's assertions about economic and community development, and his research and development policy. Yet these challenges are scarce. Decades ago, W.E.B. Du Bois extolled the importance of cooperative enterprise in the social development of African Americans and for the U.S. as a whole. He challenged the structure and function of contemporary economic and social thought, but too few followed his lead.

Haynes, Curtis, Jr. 1993. "An Essay in the Art of Economic Cooperation: Cooperative Enterprise and Economic Development in Black America," Unpublished Ph.D. dissertation. University of Massachusetts, Amherst, attributes this to "A partially completed strategy exasperated by the bigotries of American society and the engulfing power of an evolving capitalist political economic system" (p. 6).

There does exist a rigorous body of economic literature challenging the neo-classical paradigm in general. We will not reproduce those works here or summarize the debate because we want to use our space to delineate an alternative paradigm and support our initial propositions.

See Fishlow, Albert. 1991. "Review of *Handbook of Development Economics*," *The Journal of Economic Literature*. Vol: 7, 1728–1737, for a review of several different schools of thought on economic development;

And for a general critique, see Keynes, John Maynard. 1964. *The General Theory of Employment, Interest and Money*, New York: Harcourt, Brace & World (first edition 1936).

15. Sawicki and Moody point out, for example, that social programs designed by the government are and were under the strong influence of the private sector and were never designed to succeed. Rather, they were designed to "ameliorate some of the damage caused by the failure of free-market economic development of the inner city and, most importantly, the disappearance of living-wage jobs for the unskilled in these areas" (p. 81). They continue, "Private sector failure, infrequently discussed today, is even more likely now, given the well-documented diminishing number of jobs that demand lower-skilled workers" (p. 83). op. cit. (note #10).

16. Bates, op. cit. (note #10), for example, reminds us that "The social contract is being substantially rewritten. The rise of the informal economy is a reflection of fundamentally changing political-economic processes at the core of society" (P. 115).

17. Boston and Ross, op. cit. (note #7), p. 337.

18. Here we agree with Porter, op. cit. (note #8), p. 303, and a number of authors in the volume.

19. Hogan, Lloyd. 1984. *Principles of Black Political Economy*, Boston, MA: Routledge & Kegan Paul, p. 12. Hogan is a former editor of the *Review of Black Political Economy*.

20. Buffalo State College's RESURGE (Resurgent City Research Group) has gathered data, using participatory and applied research, which shows that the political-economic characteristics of many urban communities—particularly in Buffalo, NY—reflect those of the African American population. Effectively responding to the conditions of U.S. cities, therefore, is inseparable from bettering the condition of the African Americans, and vice versa.

21. Hogan, op. cit., p. 12 (the six parameters). Hogan is the source throughout this section.

22. The study of embodied human energy is pursed actively in the field of biochemistry. The concept has long been the mainstay of many forms of Eastern philosophy. Yang, Jwing-Ming. 1989. *The Root of Chinese Chi Kung*. Jamaica Plain, MA: YMAA Publicaton. Center. Fall 1995/Winter 1996. *The Review of Black Political Economy*. Vol: 24: 2/3

23. Williams, Chancellor. 1993. *The Rebirth of African Civilization*. Chicago, IL: Third World Press (reprint from 196 1), p. 15 1. He asks us to remember that what is faced in African nations is not so much the development of a nation for which capitalism and communism have done wonders, but that we are faced with the economic development of a people.

24. Ibid.

25. Ibid., p. 151.

26. Hogan, op. cit. (note #19), speaking of the role of black Americans in the "social reconstruction" of the future states:

In short, unemployment among the members of the black population signals the growing liberation of black people from direct capitalist exploitative mechanisms. [I]t therefore becomes extremely urgent that a black "safety net" be installed by blacks themselves to capture these unemployed black workers to be used to exert black labor in the total interest of black people (p. 160).

Hogan describes the nature of the net:

The net must preserve black personal freedom. The net must give to the freed black households complete control over their Internal Labor. The net must give to the freed black households complete control over their External Labor. [T]his latter characteristic of the net is the most decisive change of status which the social revolution requires. In practical terms this condition requires that the freed black households devise their own system for the creation of their material means of survival.

27. Hogan, op. cit. (note #19). Also see DuBois, W.E.B. 1909. *Efforts for Social Betterment Among Negro Americans*. Atlanta, GA: Atlanta University Press; and DuBois, W.E.B. 1907. *Economic Co-operation Among Negro Americans*. Atlanta, GA: Atlanta University Press.

28. For more details on the various traditions of self help, see Cummings, Scott. 1980. *Self-Help in Urban America*. Kennikat Press, National University Publications.

29. Also see National Cooperative Business Association, op. cit. (note #3).

30. Haynes, Curtis, Jr. 1994. "A Democratic Cooperative Enterprise System: A Response to Urban Economic Decay," *Ceteris Paribus*. Vol: 4:2 (October), 22.

31. *The Review of Black Political Economy*. Fall 1995/Winter 1996. Vol: 24: 2/3.

32. Henry, C. Michael. Fall 1995/Winter 1996. "The Porter Model Competitive Advantage for Inner-City Development: An Appraisal," *The Review of Black Political Economy*. Vol: 24: 2/3, 131.

33. Reichert, op. cit. (note #9), p. 185.

34. Bates, op. cit (note # 10), p. 111.

35. Johnson, op. cit. (note #9), p. 259.

36. Smith, Jane. Fall 1995/Winter 1996." A Dialogue on The Atlanta Project with Jane Smith, Executive Director," *The Review of Black Political Economy*. Vol: 24: 2/3, 291.

37. Peoples, James. Fall 1995/Winter 1996. "Reparations and the Competitive Advantage of Inner Cities," *The Review of Black Political Economy*. Vol: 24: 2/3, 193.

38. Porter, op. cit. (note #8), p. 303–4.

39. Reichert, op. cit. (note #9), p. 185.

40. Boston and Ross, op. cit. (note #7), p. 337.

41. American, Richard F. Fall 1995/Winter 1996. "Reparations and the Competitive Advantage of Inner Cities," *The Review of Black Political Economy*. Vol: 24: 2/3, 193.

42. Graf, Arnold. Fall 1995/Winter 1996. "Economic Development or Social Development? A Strategy for Rebuilding Inner Cities," *The Review of Black Political Economy*. Vol: 24: 2/3, 251.

43. Haynes (1993), op. cit. (note #14); Shipp (1996), op. cit. (note #12); and Shipp, Sigmund C. 1997. "Social Capital, Cultural Capital, and Collective Economic Enterprises in Inner City Neighborhoods." Unpublished. Department of Urban Affairs and Planning, Hunter College, NY.

44. Compare this to "buy Black" campaigns, which benefit primarily black capi-

talists, which makes a point, but does not go far enough with what is needed. Perhaps this explains the difficulty of "buy Black" campaigns.

45. Morris, David. 1997. "A New Cooperative Commonwealth," *The Proceedings of the 1997 Cooperative Development, Building Blocks for Development*, St. Paul, Minnesota, June 13–15; edited by National Cooperative Business Association, Washington, D.C., p. 48.

46. Haynes, Curtis, Jr. 1997. "Mondragon and the African American Community: An Interview with Curtis Haynes, Jr." GEO #10 (January-February): 8–9; Shipp, op. cit. (note #43); Whyte, William F. and Kathleen K. Whyte. 1991. *Making Mondragon*. Ithaca, NY: ILR Press, 2nd edition; Wiener, Hans and Robert Oakeshott. 1987. *Workers-Owners: Mondragon Revisited*. London: Anglo-German Foundation for the Study of Industrial Society; Thomas, Henk and Chris Logan. 1982. *Mondragon*. Boston, MA: George Allen & Unwin Ltd.; Curl, John. 1980. *History of Work Cooperation in America*. Berkeley, CA: Homeward Press; and National Cooperative Bank, op. cit. (note #4).

47. See Thomas and Logan, ibid.

48. Williams, op. cit. (note #23), p. 173.

49. Hogan, op. cit. (note # 19).

50. Here we paraphrase Best, Michael H. 1990. *The New Competition*. Boston, MA: Harvard University Press.

28

MINORITY PROCUREMENT: BEYOND AFFIRMATIVE ACTION TO ECONOMIC EMPOWERMENT

Sherri Leronda Wallace

INTRODUCTION

In these times of post-deindustrialization, deunionization, deregulation and downsizing, the efficacy of the affirmative action strategies has come into question. Since capital and technology are more mobile, many believe that economic development can occur independent of its surrounding community. Debates over whether or not social and public policies are able to address historical inequalities among the American citizenry are being discussed from various theoretical perspectives. In the midst of these discussions, little attention has been focused on existing programs, such as minority procurement contracts, that are plausible solutions to and avenues for community revitalization and economic empowerment for targeted minority communities. Given this conceptual context, the object of this article is to examine to what extent minority procurement activities can be effective strategies in facilitating minority community economic development in the absence of federally mandated goals. Utilizing one case study that focuses on structural barriers to access information for women and minority-owned firms (MWBEs), this article makes the claim that continued minority procurement activity is necessary for overall community economic development.

In largely minority communities, the effectiveness of government procurement policies on long term community economic development will be enhanced if women and minority-owned firms (MWBEs) are incorporated into government vendor pools.[1] *Community economic development* is taken to mean the promotion of economic activity within area neighborhoods, especially in those with large numbers of poor and unemployed residents.[2] Inherent in community economic development goals is the notion of democratic influence over the local political economy and the equitable allocation of costs and benefits commonly disbursed through business investments and job creation. This community-centered approach requires building capacity for appreciable economic development with an infrastructure of local institutions, including small businesses, local labor unions, not-for-profit community organizations, religious groups, and collaborative networks linking such institutions together. It also applies normative principles of democracy and pluralism to the economic sphere as well as embodying strategic ideas for local "empowerment."[3] This notion is underscored by McDougall[3a] who argues that the wealth of more and more U.S. citizens has come to depend not on their ownership of private property, but rather on their relationship to government and their receipt of 'government largess,' such as social security, public insurance and compensation, licenses, franchises, benefits, subsidies, use of public resources, and government contracts."[4] What McDougall describes here is the view that sustainable community development depends not only on the level of economic development initiatives, but also on the level of political power a community wields through access to information via cross-collaboration and networking structures. This broad theoretical framework bodes well with understanding the internal dynamics of community economic development.

In this vein, community economic development fosters the social goals of a community and not just economic growth. Thus, a community-centered approach to economic development directly supports labor and community interest, and does not assume that the mere presence of increased business profits alone will necessarily benefit the social goals of the locale. Concisely stated, community economic development attempts to "change the way a local economy relates to external markets and political forces by mobilizing local resources and reinforcing local control to better capture broader opportunities, rather than passively relying on beneficence of government or private enterprise."[5] Critical to the community economic development perspective is the notion of linkage. Cross collaboration with, and/or among local groups and governmental bodies provides economies of scale in doing business, whether locally and/or regionally as well as needed political clout.[6] Situated within this theoretical framework, the goal of this article is not to make definitive statements about the level of minority procurement activity, but to heighten our awareness of the nature and role that this policy can play in facilitating minority community economic development.

Increased minority procurement activity does not have to be viewed as "set-asides," it can be viewed as one of many possible effective economic development strategies. In this vein recent Supreme Court rulings on the use of race as a criterion in awarding procurement contracts should have no impact on the implementation of this program. By approaching economic empowerment through access to information via collaboration and networking structures, this study centers on the assumption that the lack of information regarding possible contracts constitutes the primary problem for many MWBEs. Without access to information on procurement contracts, MWBEs are at an economic disadvantage compared to nonminority-owned businesses.

An historical overview on minority procurement demonstrates that the transition from small- and/or marginal-businesses to economically viable businesses for many MWBEs is a complex process that occurs overtime and requires carefully constructed systems for on-going support between governmental and community coalitions at various levels. A reexamination of past minority economic development programs shows their relation to the economic, political and social wealth of communities. Basically, these programs provided the avenue through which minority procurement activity, as well as African American upward mobility, became reality.

The degree to which women and minority-owned firms participate in the Erie county minority procurement program is gauged through an analysis of the response rates from MWBEs in the bidding process in Erie county. Although this study is part of an on-going community-based project of information collected via mail and telephone surveys on minority and women-owned businesses (MWBEs) in Erie County over a two year period, this inferential case study is based on their response rates to the bidding process which includes information collected via mail surveys during the Spring of 1996 and Fall of 1997. I argue that most women and minority-owned businesses are at a disadvantage with regards to information about procurement contracts compared to non-minority firms, especially when bidding on formal contracts which yield greater economic wealth. It is not the intent in this work to present conclusive data that will increase procurement contracts to MWBEs, but only to merely suggest through gleaning pieces of evidence from this preliminary case study with minority/women-owned entrepreneurs, that access to information is crucial to their participation in the program. To my knowledge, it is the first case study in upstate New York of the economic activities of women and minority-owned firms in government purchasing activity. The results should be of interest to local governmental officials in evaluating the effectiveness of their current policies and practices in increasing minority procurement activity in Erie County.

Policy analysts who seek new ways to define, characterize, and implement more comprehensive public policies will find the results of use to them as well.

MINORITY PROCUREMENT: A BRIEF DISCUSSION

Historically, minority business firms were uninvolved in the contracting and procurement activities of government agencies and authorities.[7] As a response to this non-involvement, the Minority Small Business and Capital Ownership Program (also referred to as the SBA 8(a) program), emanating from the Nixon Administration, was designed to assist minority entrepreneurs to obtain federal procurement contracts.[8] This assistance to minority-owned small businesses consisted of contract "set-asides"[9] and procurement goals,[10] management and technical assistance,[11] grants for education and training,[12] and surety bonding assistance and loans.[13] It is important to note that although "set-aside" programs were adopted by the federal government to support the development of underutilized businesses owned by women and minorities at a goal of only 10 percent, they are viewed as preferential treatment for minorities. Before its elimination under the Reagan Administration, SBA 8(a) program was designed as a business development program that required certified firms to develop comprehensive business plans with specified goals, targets and objectives. Program participation was limited to nine years. As small and minority-owned companies moved through the program, they were required to obtain a larger share of their revenues from non-8(a) companies in order to enhance their economic viability and long-term survival.[14]

Controversy over government set-aside programs was heightened in one of the most recent cases, *Adarand Constructors, Inc. v. Pena* 115 S. Ct. 2097 (1995), where the Supreme Court held that government set-aside programs must meet the "strict scrutiny standard" that narrowly tailors the federal presumption of "socially and economically disadvantaged," based on past discrimination which, in this particular case, is the awarding of subcontracts without competitive bidding. The *Adarand* decision has been characterized by some as a direct challenge to the federal government's practice of giving general contractors on government projects a financial incentive to hire subcontractors categorized as "socially and economically disadvantaged individuals."[15] In addition, it questioned government's use of race-based presumptions in identifying all MWBEs as victims of discrimination in the awarding of governmental procurement contracts. Although the Clinton Administration announced on July 19, 1995, that its position was "to mend, not end" affirmative action programs, the *Adarand* decision underscores the question of whether or not minority procurement programs can continue to distribute wealth to minority communities without federally mandated goals.

Interestingly, the Business Opportunity Program (BOP) in Erie County is not viewed as an affirmative action program. In its role of identifying MWBEs for procurement contracts, it is not restrained by the use of quotas or goals in increasing the level of procurement contracts awarded to MWBEs. Understandably, the phrase affirmative action conjures up a myriad of opinions; however, in this analysis it is viewed as minorities simply having greater access to public policy programmatic decision-making bodies and to agency or municipal jobs[16] and economic wealth. Thus, affirmative action goals remain vital to the success of minority procurement programs nationwide.

MINORITY BUSINESS DEVELOPMENT: A BRIEF DISCUSSION

Before there was a formal procurement policy to develop and expand viable minority-owned businesses, minority entrepreneurs were left to their own ingenuity to create and operate in the free market economy. Throughout American entrepreneurial history, government has always been a prominent player in economic development and success. Through various federal, state and local legislative initiatives (procurement programs), grants of monopoly, land grants, permits, licenses, loans and favorable supreme court opinions; government aided the growth of multinational and national scale industries. Prior to, during and after segregation, many minority-owned businesses were able to penetrate markets outside their communities; however, they were met by larger, better financed, more diverse, and racially restrictive non-minority-owned companies which enjoyed favorable tax, regulatory and competitive positions not accessible to minority-owned business.[17]

The federal government attempted to level the playing field by enacting a series of economic development and restructuring programs targeted at racial minorities mostly through housing and small-business loan programs. This developmental approach dominated federal urban initiatives soon after President Johnson's declaration on the War on Poverty in 1965, when forces of entrepreneurship were recruited into the revitalization process.[18] The literature reveals that beginning with theoretical concepts as "Black capitalism," economic development has emerged in such forms as public programs to develop minority-owned businesses through managerial training and subsidized financing, business incubators, procurement "set-asides" for firms owned by minorities or located in areas of high unemployment, corporate placement of branch plants in inner cities, public private partnerships between commercial firms and local governments, enterprise zones, commercial real estate development and business ownership by community development corporations, self-employment for recipients of public income support, to name a few.[19]

By way of review, most research has concluded that urban economic redevelopment projects cleared slums to make room for upper- to middle-income housing for whites, while worsening the housing and social problems of the poor minority communities. At best, it merely shifted slums from one place to another, which reduced the supply of low-cost housing and destroyed neighborhoods that attempted to improve on their own. Also, urban redevelopment perpetuated and intensified existing patterns of racial segregation which displaced small and/or marginal (such as minority-owned) businesses. Subsequently, the lack of sufficient participation on the part of neighborhood groups in the planning process resulted in insufficient coordination and communication among the various federal programs and agencies involved. As a result, the entire matter of urban redevelopment was left to the whims of private enterprise, as the federal program achieved negligible results at high cost while endangering the right of private property to its local citizen.[20]

On the other hand, some sympathetic scholars maintained that hundreds of communities have shown that urban renewal was a necessary and desirable means of eliminating blight, aiding those neighborhoods afflicted by blight, and rebuilding the physical, economic and social vitality of urban areas. These scholars also believe that redevelopment helped to rationalize land use patterns, encourage aesthetic considerations, aid educational expansion, induce industry to remain and relocate in the city, salvage deteriorating central business districts, and provide both high and low rent housing, and that the program has increased tax benefits to the city while at the same time providing decent housing for displaced persons.[21] But as Thomas[22] and others argue, in reality, "Model cities" and other economic development programs suffered from inadequate resources, local political battles, uneven performances, and poor federal leadership.

In spite of all the political and social debates surrounding the validity of these programs as a coherent and long-term economic development policy for city governments to pursue, interestingly, no scholar questioned the futility of developing neighborhoods without incorporating long-term comprehensive economic development for its minority entrepreneurs who, most likely, live and work in their communities. Thus, it was never understood whether the very structure of the programs offered equity in terms of economic benefits for sustainable community economic development to begin.

We know that the economic development programs from 1960–1970 provided tremendous upward mobility to a significant number of aggressive and talented racial minorities. Thomas[23] informs us that the programs were designed to appeal to its urban constituency by encouraging residents to participate in defining and supervising neighborhood improvement and by funding multifaceted rejuvenation. Each program had to have CEOs, managers, and a professional staff to implement them. Thus, a new source of minority managerial talent was tapped. Before this, the most talented minorities still had not been incorporated into private industry, and could only be found in traditional government agencies, or their own businesses. Thus, for many minority entrepreneurs, the "poverty" programs were the point of entry for a number of managers and entrepreneurs who otherwise would never have had the opportunity to gain the administrative experience of managing firms and/or agencies. This was the case for many African Americans. In effect, these social programs replaced the Postal Service as the "bulwark of the Black middle class."[24] This new "Black middle class," having access to prestigious university educations, and disposable capital, constitutes the rise in emerging capital-intensive as well as labor-intensive lines of minority-owned enterprises such as: business services, wholesale, transportation and communication, finance, insurance and real estate.[25]

However, overtime, while larger white business have historically accumulated sufficient land, work force, capital and political influence, smaller white businesses have basically thrived on ethnic markets and selective networks that overlap but transcend many minority communities. As a result, while government has anchored the position of majority-owned multinational and large-scale businesses, minority-owned business—especially African American businesses—have steadily lost traditional and selective markets to their larger white-owned counterparts.[26] It is within this historical context of minority business development that we seek to develop a new understanding of the role of minority procurement in facilitating economic empowerment for MWBEs.

THE STATE OF WOMEN AND MINORITY-OWNED BUSINESSES IN ERIE COUNTY

Nationally, our cities face their greatest social and economic challenges to date—including increasing unemployment, concentrated poverty, and racial and ethnic conflict. At the same time, downsizing, privatizing, and outsourcing are combining with the dispersal of both white- and blue-collar jobs to places outside the United States.[27] In upstate New York, cities are in danger of becoming environmental dinosaurs whose fossils are an eyesore as they decay. The suburbs are expanding at the expense of the inner cities, which means that the lifeblood of these cities rest on political and economic choices made outside the scope of their domain.

Cities such as Cleveland, Philadelphia, and Chicago, have found ways to link community churches,[28] civic organizations,[29] and the local government[30] in community-based projects that will foster economic development and neighborhood stability through housing and home improvement programs. David Rusk[31] argues that only cities with direct political and economic links to their surrounding suburban towns can expect to survive; however, I argue that if the right coalitions are formed within the city, whereby local residents and businesses have a stake in the outcome, long-term community economic development can be successful. As embedded residents and small businesses operating in the city of Buffalo, MWBEs can serve as a vital link to full scale comprehensive economic development through the increase of minority procurement contracts. Unlike global and regionally-based businesses, urban minority-owned businesses cannot escape from the poverty, crime, and physical deterioration in their communities. Minority entrepreneurs have a direct stake in their community's long-term stability.

MINORITY PROCUREMENT AS A COMMUNITY ECONOMIC DEVELOPMENT: A THEORETICAL FRAMEWORK

As stated previously, McDougall argues that the wealth of more and more U.S. citizens has come to depend not on their ownership of private property, but rather on their relationship to government and their receipt of government largess through such venues as government contracts. What McDougall describes here is the view that the key to sustainable community development depends on not only the level of economic development initiatives, but also the level of political power a community wields.

McDougall[32] broadly applies this argument as he examines the impact of participatory democracy and community empowerment on defining the "public interest" through self-help efforts of Black and Latino "based communities"[33] in Baltimore, Maryland. His approach is noteworthy in that he finds that community economic development is achieved through the interdependence of human processes of interrelation such as conversation, collaboration, cooperation, and networking; as a means of making connections informally to more formal and impersonal government agencies. This broad theoretical framework bodes will with understanding the internal dynamics of community economic development. Also, it is applicable to understanding the activities and survival rates of women and minority-business owners in Erie County as well. For more often than not, survival for MWBEs rest on informal avenues of communication and networks about business opportunities. It underscores the commonly held notion that community is understood from a geographical as well as political psycho-cultural context—that is, that politics is local. Thus, community in a political sense, always entails the notion of place.[34] That is to say that once ideas and policies become a material force through political coalitions or group interests, they have impacts on place because of the direct links to local government whereby these group interests intermingle and vie for geographical and vertical mobility and/or power.

The context of community economic development and the realization of participatory democratic principles are important to understanding minority procurement activity as a possible economic development strategy instead of as preferential treatment for MWBEs. In order for communities to be rejuvenated, there must be an integral plan that will allow for community participation in decision-making capacities for long-term economic development. If we understand economic development to mean the process whereby individuals and organizations engage in the production, distribution, and consumption of goods and services,[35] it implies the social interactions of people within the community space as well as the values of traditions that define the culture. Understanding and incorporating the views and needs of minority entrepreneurs' input into the formal decision-making process underscores long-term stability for the community and economic development.

As an illustration of this argument, we turn our discussion to research conducted through the Center of Urban Studies as an example of a possible strategy for increasing minority economic development through an Erie County program in minority procurement. This research serves as a potential tool for governmental officials and also as a field of research for faculty involved.

MINORITY PROCUREMENT PROGRAM: A CASE STUDY

The Office of Urban Initiatives (OUI)

OUI is a product of interdisciplinary type of thinking. Beginning in the early 1990s as a nonprofit community development corporation, OUI emanated through the formation of the Commission on Urban Initiatives which was a political organization of leaders from Buffalo and Erie County. As a university-community based project, its goal is to develop community economic development models for Buffalo's minority community that are centered on business development and community education. The university assists mainly as a place for OUI to house its day-to-day operations. As a public service initiative, OUI programs are vehicles through which researchers can bring to bear their own theoretical precepts about social and economic issues as well as basic and applied research projects to carry out analyses on community-oriented problems.

In developing its minority economic development program, the Commission was concerned with addressing the downward spiral of Buffalo's economy, loss of job, and the rise in unemployment of its minority community. Like in most large urban cities many African Americans have lost their jobs to deindustrialization and downsizing. The Commission's strategy for minority economic development was to find ways to create jobs, train minority entrepreneurs, and build the city's minority neighborhood's capacity for long-term development, linking neighborhood revitalization to business development through entrepreneurial and job training opportunities.

OUI, which originally began as a home improvement company, has initiated an economic development program with the primary objectives of increasing access to public and private sector procurement markets for MWBEs; informing and educating minority and women entrepreneurs, community leaders and local residents of business opportunities through its publications on social, economic and political issues; increasing access to financial capital for minority and women entrepreneurs/businesses; and encouraging the development of public/private collaborative efforts with other minority and non-minority organizations, institutions and individuals on business and community development initiatives. These objectives are achieved through a number of programs; however, this paper shall focus on the Business Opportunity Program (BOP) which facilitates the minority procurement program, the subject of this case study.

Business Opportunity Program (BOP)

The BOP seeks to increase business opportunities for MWBEs through participation in Erie County's procurement program. In recognition of the disparity in the awarding of procurement contracts to MWBEs, one legislator urged OUI—in partnership with research scholars in the university's Center for Urban Studies and Erie County's Division of Purchase—to develop a public sector procurement program. The purpose of the procurement program is twofold.

One goal is to increase the number of MWBEs selling goods and services to the county. This is done by utilizing OUI as a "clearinghouse" in helping these companies to submit bids. Another goal is to increase the market share of procurement contracts awarded to MWBEs in metropolitan Buffalo. This is facilitated through the dissemination of literature and/or advertisements that alert MWBEs of more lucrative procurement contracts available.

METHODS[36]

Our analysis of women and minority-owned procurement activity in Erie County begins with a look at the evolution of the Business Opportunity Program as a university-community initiative response to the lack of minority business opportunities in metropolitan Buffalo. The framework is based on an inferential case study approach to explore the potential of minority procurement as an effective tool for minority economic development. Our examination of MWBEs responses to the bidding process as one aspect of procurement activity suggests that minority procurement has some benefits, particularly for MWBEs in Erie County, and that the problems and benefits can provide guidance to local government officials for strengthening the existing program.

There are some caveats, however. This study is part of an on-going project on minority procurement activity in Erie County, thus the full evaluation is not complete. This will limit our ability to make definitive statements about the Erie County program's overall effectiveness, although there is enough data to provide a rudimentary pattern that resembles previous studies on minority procurement activity. In addition, we do not make comparisons between jurisdictions with an equivalent minority procurement program to test continuity, nor do we test the impact of the program on non-minority contractors. Thus, the conceptual flaws come from our own interpretation of program success as defined by the theoretical framework. Our theoretical framework is situated in the belief that community economic development is achieved through the interdependence of human processes of interrelation—conversation, collaboration, cooperation, and networking—as a means of making connections informally to more formal and impersonal government agencies. Thus, it centers around a residential perspective of empowerment as opposed to that of governmental policymakers standards.[37] It also encompasses a diverse and multicultural approach to policy analysis in that policy problems are defined according to various points of view.

The subject of study in which investigation of implementation processes took place was the Business Opportunity Program over a period of roughly one-year. The research design occurred in two steps. The first was through 315 bid response mail surveys to MWBEs in Erie County to gauge their level of procurement activity. The purpose of these mail surveys was to gain insight into the structure and culture of MWBEs to get a sense of why they placed certain bids on certain products. In the mail surveys, we asked companies to report to OUI whether or not they would place a procurement bid as well. With each mail survey we sent a cover letter introducing the Business Opportunity Program. The purpose of the cover letter with the mail survey was to establish an informal network with these companies and the commission facilitating the program. There were some problems with using this method, however.

One problem was that of the minimal interaction between OUI and BOP companies. As our graduate assistant reported, the interpretation of the cover letter that was included was confusing. It asked MWBE companies to respond to OUI "if they participate in the bidding process," which implied if they did not, we did not care to hear from them. Thus, the format of the letter was revised to include a check box "Bid" or "No Bid" response to return to OUI.

The main problem overall has been with the process of tracking the MWBE companies. Currently, the Center for Urban Studies is in the process of evaluating the county bidding process to answer these questions. At the time that this paper is being written, the data obtained from 1,248 bids were randomly mailed to various companies along with a letter from OUI requesting confirmation of their intent to bid on specific products. This volunteer submission of information to OUI was the method for tracking individual MWBEs. The 1,248 bids represent 344 different commodities sent to 1 to 10 companies for each of the bids. Of the 1,248 bids mailed, we have received 315 responses, where 163 are reportedly "bid" (representing 92 different bids[38]) and 152 "no bid." This gives us a

TABLE 1
Minority and Women-owned Businesses (MWBEs)
Formal and Informal "Bid" and "No Bid" Responses/Results

Category	Number of Different Bids	Number of Bids Submitted*	Total % of Bids Submitted	Number of Bids Awarded	Percentage** of Bids Awarded	Total % of Bids Awarded	Monetary Value of Bid	% of Total Monetary Value
Automotive	1	1	.60	0	0.0	0.0	N/A	0.00
Bldg. Services	2	2	1.20	1	50.0	3.6	$5,750.00	12.73
Chemicals	4	8	4.82	2	25,0	7.1	$3,143.25	6.96
Clothing	2	6	3.61	2	33.3	7.1	$5,933.00	13.14
Computers/Supplies	2	4	2.41	0	0.0	0.0	N/A	0.00
Construction Supplies	2	3	1.81	0	0.0	0.0	N/A	0.0
Craft Supplies	1	1	.60	0	0.0	0.0	N/A	0.0
Equipment	8	9	5.42	0	0.0	0.0	N/A	0.0
Electrical/HVAC	6	8	4.82	1	12.5	3.6	$2,688.12	5.95
Hardware/Safety	27	43	25.90	5	11.6	17.9	$3,296.49	7.30
Furniture/Home Needs	2	2	1.20	0	0.0	0.0	N/A	0.0
Janitorial	14	45	27.11	13	28.9	46.4	$17,739.33	39.29
Medical	4	5	3.01	1	20.0	3.6	$2,691.30	5.96
Miscellaneous	4	5	3.01	1	20.0	3.6	$715.96	1.59
Office Supplies	6	12	7.23	1	8.3	3.6	$736.80	1.63
Printing	5	10	6.02	1	10	3.6	$2,461.00	5.45
Sports Related	2	2	1.20	0	0.0	0.0	N/A	0.0
TOTALS:	92	166	100	28		100	$45,155.25	100

* These numbers reflect that multiple MWBEs may submit a quote for the same bid.
** The estimate is derived from Number of Bids awarded divided by the Total Bids submitted. It reflects the level of competition for the same bid.
Sources: Erie County, New York, Division of Purchase and Office of Urban Initiatives, Inc. mail survey responses from MWBEs.

total response rate of 25.24 percent overall, a "bid" response rate of 13.06 percent and a "no bid" response rate of 12.18 percent. Of the 163 "bid" responses, 28 bids were awarded to MWBEs mostly for janitorial supplies and hardware items, a 17.18 percent success rate representing a monetary value of $45,155.25 (see Table).

Aside from these initial problems, there were some additional concerns that came from the response surveys with MWBEs in Erie County. These issues centered on the current state of minority procurement activity in Erie County. These issues were categorized into four commonly felt problems by minority entrepreneurs that contributed to MWBE competitive disadvantages in acquiescing procurement contracts: (1) the lack of direct access to products, (2) the lack of disposable capital, (3) the lack of human capital, and (4) the lack of administrative and technical support.

Competitive Disadvantages: Explanations for the Small Percentage of MWBE Procurement Contracts

Based on our preliminary findings, we know that minorities still do not get the 10 percent level of contracts stipulated in the federal provisions. Perhaps, the main reason for the lack of minority participation in the Erie County BOP minority procurement program is related to competitive disadvantages from which many of the businesses suffer. For instance, in addition to bidding on low-cost products or contracts, MWBEs responses showed that they were more likely to submit higher bids than other non-minority owned firms for most commodities due to basically four reasons.

The first problem is the lack of direct access to products. The data revealed that MWBEs are simply not able to supply the commodities requested. A large volume of the requested commodities remain beyond the purview of many of these small firms which may have to go through a number of channels and/or networks to obtain their products. This, in turn, raises their overhead costs, which results in a higher bid to the County's Division of Purchase.

Secondly, the lack of disposable capital prevents MWBEs from being competitive bidders with more economically viable firms. Since most MWBEs lack access to capital and credit, many run their day-to-day operations by sweat and brow, which means that they depend on fast turn-around of their investments. This being the case, many MWBEs are not able to wait the thirty to forty-five days that it takes for the county to pay for the products requested. Most companies have to pay their suppliers within thirty days, which is ten to fifteen days before they can expect payment from the county. This is a luxury that larger and more established companies enjoy, while it can lead to "out of business" for small businesses.

Thirdly, the lack of human capital prevents MWBEs from having adequate manpower to facilitate contracts. This problem is more salient for small MWBEs, but is also relevant to some of the larger MWBEs that have just enough employers to carry out one or two contracts at a time. It relates back to the lack of access to capital because this reduces the opportunity to hire additional workers quickly and/or part-time basis to fulfill contracts. Larger companies are in better positions to do this. These businesses employ mostly family members (sometimes at low wages) which means there is insufficient staff to handle day to day operations, let alone the additional hours of labor on paperwork that formal bids may require.

Last and most crucial is the lack of administrative and technical support on all the paperwork involved in submitting formal bids. Small MWBEs do not have the time to complete the cumbersome paperwork required to obtain MWBE certification as well as to submit formal county bids. Often times, when these companies do obtain their MWBE status as well as submit their bids, they are then subjected to the long waiting periods required for payment of service. Thus, many MWBEs find that this first step is more costly than the optimal benefits received. Perhaps the rethinking of this step in the process can go a long way in increasing the amount of MWBEs in the county procurement vendor pools. It can also aid in the long-term expansion of the economic development of these businesses and the communities in which they operate. Although our study reveals an embryonic pattern of MWBE activity, the assessment of the bidding process is best understood in the context of previous minority procurement program studies.

AN ASSESSMENT OF THE ERIE COUNTY BIDDING PROCESS

Recent studies on minority procurement programs have been concerned with the effectiveness of government procurement policies that will both increase competition and raise the level of MWBE firms in government vendor pools. From the perspective of most minority-owned (African American, Hispanic, Asian, American Indian) firms, the government is viewed as a somewhat inadequate business partner in the current bid process structure because of its inability to address "special difficulties in the lack of [perceived] business skills and experience [for newly created firms], restrictions to markets with lower purchasing power, limited access to capital, and discrimination"[39] experienced by these firms. On the other hand, some studies question whether or not most MWBEs are viable as potential partners with government to begin.[40] This is a salient point in the case of Erie County and deserves more discussion here.

Minority Procurement Activity in Erie County

County and city procurement contracts represent a largely untapped market for most MWBEs operating in upstate New York. With its $70 million dollar expenditures[41] on commodities and contractual services for Erie County, there exists tremendous opportunities for small-scale, as well as mid- to large-scale MWBEs to partake in this economic largesse. Unfortunately, MWBEs competed for only $310,000 in Erie County procurement contracts, which resulted in roughly 3 percent of the total contracts awarded. This percentage seems consistent with the nation as a whole, where it has been reported that minority vendors account for only 3.5 percent of total federal contract dollars awarded (according to the SBA 1993 annual report).[42] This has lead scholars to offer various explanations as to why municipal contracts have not achieved their goal of 5 percent for MWBEs. The significant point to be made here is that businesses owned by non-minority men continue to receive more than 95 percent of government contracts.[43] History reveals that non-minority-owned companies have always had the competitive advantage in access to municipal contracts as well as the economic marketplace.

The core purpose of the BOP program is to identify MWBEs in the city of Buffalo participating in the County procurement program in order to increase their competitive advantage as bidders. This is done through a series of informal workshops and the dissemination of literature and publications, but mostly through the oversight of the county's bidding process through the county's Division of Purchase.

The Division of Purchase is a commodity driven and demand oriented department. Local government agencies as well as school districts submit requests for supplies here. It is the responsibility of the Division of Purchase to provide these commodities at the lowest available price to its buyers. There are two basic types of bids: informal and formal bids. Informal bids can range in price from $1,000 to $9,999 in costs. Suppliers, determined by the lowest bid submitted, are selected at the discretion of the buyer.

Formal bids begin at $10,000 and higher. These bids are required by county law, administrative code 306, to be publicized in newspapers and/or publications with at least 50,000 subscribers one to three week(s) prior to the bid date to ensure open competition. Companies are given at least three weeks to put together a formal bid. Formal bids, unlike informal bids, are generally more involved in terms of commodities requested and require more paperwork. For MWBEs seeking procurement contracts that involve set-asides, it requires additional minority participation certification and/or proof of insurance which, as stated above, directly affects the participation rates of MWBEs pursuing these types of contracts. This is yet another possible barrier that impacts an MWBE firms ability to make competitive bids on products.

Interestingly, when one looks at the amount of formal bid contracts awarded to MWBEs, it is relatively small compared to that of white-owned businesses. In the BOP minority procurement program, in 1994 only $84,000 of the $70 million contracts went to African American-owned businesses, while approximately $1.7 million contracts were awarded to women-owned businesses. The 1994 county procurement data indicated that a total of 460 MWBEs were currently active in the county's procurement program. The active MWBEs were comprised of 14 percent African American-owned businesses, 8 percent Asian-owned businesses, 5 percent Hispanic-owned businesses, 3 percent Native American-owned businesses, and 70 percent women-owned businesses.[44]

The percentage of procurement contract expenditures flowing to MWBEs also indicated that a greater percentage of the contracts were awarded to MWBEs located outside of Erie County (A total of 275 MWBEs were located in the city of Buffalo). Approximately 57 percent of the procurement contracts awarded to African American-owned businesses were to those located outside of the county, as well as to Hispanics (61%), Native American businesses (52%) and Asian businesses (67%). This net flow leads us to consider whether local MWBEs are being hindered in expanding their business opportunities within their own communities.[45]

Formal Procurement Contracts in Erie County

When placing formal bids of $10,000 or more, generally MWBE bidders are required to complete large amounts of paperwork. This is a competitive disadvantage for most MWBEs which are mostly small microenterprises in Erie County. In order to increase the market-share of MWBEs seeking procurement contracts in the county, there must be a recognition of the barriers within the bidding process that reduce the opportunities for MWBEs to be suppliers to the county in this market.

The case study revealed that the major barriers are the paperwork and the deadlines for submitting formal and informal bids. Formal bids are usually for contractual services for periods of one to three years. For instance, certain maintenance contracts for clinics, prescription drug contracts, and equipment (such as office, computing and building) contracts are rendered on an "annual" basis with the possibility of yearly extensions, depending on the nature of the product or capital demand. Thus, bids are placed one year prior to the awarding of the contracts. However, informal bids (which tend to be more economically feasible for MWBEs) are placed daily to yearly, depending on the nature of the bid. The commodities are usually for demand driven office products and supplies such as paper, toner, writing instruments, and janitorial supplies (e.g., cleaners, soap, and towels), as well as electrical, plumbing, and printing services. As a result, the inform **Cherry** ket is saturated with MWBEs competing with non-minority owned businesses. However, the formal bid market, which entails more expensive products (i.e., customized computer software, general binding, embossing, construction services, etc.), and yields the more lucrative profits, goes virtually untapped by MWBEs. Consequently, this market is monopolized by nonminority firms.[46]

Although some of these larger products by their nature require various levels of certification, many are simply local monopolies that have been able to establish a partnership with the county via political patronage over a number of years. As a result, many MWBEs in Erie County are not able to adequately participate in this sector, which leads to their inability to obtain federal and municipal set-asides. This finding is consistent with one study on construction that found that politics and strong internal networks played a large part in obtaining construction contracts. Waldinger[47] has shown in his study that this is definitely the case for construction contracts awarded by municipal governments.

In his study, Waldinger[48] makes the case that construction contracts are the hardest area for racial minorities to permeate because construction skills are socially generated and neophytes learn the proficiencies they need on the job through interaction with experience workers. This implies a close-knit social and economic network. Developers and suppliers tend to hold newcomers on a tight rein, while allowing ample leeway for customers "with a 25-year record of paying their bills."[49] This makes it difficult for newcomers to compete with the more established or viable companies.[50]

In the case of African American contractors, they are viewed as outsiders. African American constructors have to acquire skills and knowledge without the social capital that their white counterparts enjoy. These traditionally discriminatory practices have had the greatest effect on those African American tradesmen who moved up through the trade union as well as those possessing more education, coming from technical or managerial jobs:

> Market factors make it particularly hard for Black builders to develop the relevant occupational identity. While the demand for contractors' services comes from property owners, disproportionately few Blacks own property of any kind, let alone engage in the development activities that comprise the bread and butter of most contractors' work. Consequently, Black construction entrepreneurs must go outside their communities to find a customer base; practically speaking, this entails confronting a white clientele that many be distrustful or untrustworthy, when not actively hostile. Whites enjoy the golf course advantage.[51]

Construction, like other local and/or small business markets, represents the quintessential ethnic niche: the ties among co-ethnic workers and owners provide the mechanisms whereby information is circulated, skills are obtained, and contracts acquired. This concentrated niche provides a selective identity that is not willing to be permeated by newcomers or perceived outsiders. It is also indicative of the theory behind base community construction. In order for community and economic revitalization to occur, one has to be able to create incentives that will permeate those strong vernacular networks to distribute more egalitarian strategies to benefit the whole community, not just "niches."

Viewing minority procurement activity from a different perspective, Bates and Williams[52] found that, unfortunately, the most common element operating in unsupervised state procurement programs is that "no legitimate MBE is performing a commercially useful function in fulfilling the procurement contract" due to misinformation and over-extension that may result in fraud, fronts with viable non-minority owned firms for quick profits, and business failure which does not create jobs in the minority community. Thus, more supervised programs with clear policy guidelines would lead to more viable small minority-owned businesses that can utilize procurement contracts to create jobs in the minority communities. In the case of Erie County, the problem of "fronts" does not seem as salient to minority-owned businesses which are mostly small to mid-size firms. However, the supervisory role can be strengthen in determining the extent to which these firms participate in the procurement program.

RESULTS

So far, the results from this preliminary on-going case study tell us that the bid rate among MWBEs is problematic and is one of the aspects that needs to be addressed in future research. For instance, the fact that only 13 percent of the 1,248 bids mailed were returned with a bid/no-bid response, suggests that there are embedded barriers to MWBEs optimizing their opportunities to participate fully in procurement programs. Some of the reasons reported are directly related to the four main competitive disadvantages gathered from the mailed-in response surveys in which MWBEs have to contend. Overall, the responses pointed to the lack of direct access to products, lack of disposable financial capital, lack of human capital, and the lack of administrative and technical support to aid in the application process.

For example, bids mailed to these companies and returned as "no bids" or "no response bids" were not for products that they supplied. This relates to a lack of direct access to the commodities. Another assumption could be related to problems with the design of the mail survey, as our graduate intern implied. In the initial stages, these companies were not responding. The problem could have been as simple as revising the cover letter, or it could have meant that these companies did not fully understand the commodity codes/specifications and/or were mailed inappropriate information by our office. Interestingly, MWBEs did submit formal bids for procurement contracts. Of the nine formal bids (8 for electrical services and 1 for printing submitted), none were awarded to MWBEs. However, MWBEs failed to bid upon 291 procurement contracts in 24 different categories. These categories, or classifications, were for products/commodities involving automotive, communications, construction/public works, electrical, heavy-duty equipment, hardware/safety, laboratory/research, medical, and building and equipment services as defined by the United States SIC codes. As mentioned above, these items require formal bids because of the costs and technical/specialized expertise involved in the operations. The commodities awarded were supplied by mostly capital-intensive firms, as opposed to labor-intensive firms that are service-oriented. A significant proportion of MWBEs in Erie County tend to concentrate on the labor-intensive sector[53] (see earlier Table).

In relation to the lack of capital and/or credit, the "no bid" or "no response bid" rates could refer to MWBEs feeling that they are unable to be competitive with other more established companies in the supply the commodities requested. This relates to the lack of human capital that does not allow these companies to function at their full capacity. Last and more importantly, the paperwork seemed to be a direct barrier, in that few MWBEs were able to complete the application process according to specifications. This resulted in many desiring not to participate in the bidding process at all. The argument by Bates and Williams[54] in finding ways to increase the supervisory role of agencies in reviewing the procurement application activity of these companies seem warranted here.

The emerging pattern of the data allows us to make the assumption that government procurement programs have potential in assisting in the development and expansion of minority-owned businesses. Unlike the complaints waged against the federal and state empowerment zone programs that emphasize attracting large immigrant firms into distressed areas, this program seeks to utilize local existing businesses, large or small, in creating community wealth. Governmental officials misunderstood that the main reason for selecting blighted neighborhoods was that these areas contained untapped resources—both human and capital—that needed to be unleashed, although many state empowerment programs were not designed with this in mind.[55] Thus, very little success was realized because of this lack of attention to internal and long-term community development which depends on the economic viability of existing neighborhood businesses more than anything else. Targeted procurement opportunities for minority-owned businesses also represent a largely untapped market for minority and women-owned businesses.

CONCLUSION

The findings from this embryonic analysis, which identifies possible barriers to increased minority procurement activity, supports MacManus[56] argument that the effectiveness of government procurement policies would be greatly enhanced if access to the vendor pools was distributed on a more equitable basis. It also supports Bates and Williams's[57] argument that procurement programs most commonly benefit the larger than average more viable MWBEs. Few of the small mom and pop retail stores of personal service operations are capable of serving government clients. Government procurement accrues naturally in MWBEs that function in the broader non-ghetto economy, particularly in wholesale, construction, business service, and other skill-intensive service industries. Also, the above average firm size and higher survival rates observed among MWBEs that sell to state/local government clients may suggest real benefits to participating businesses. Although larger firm size is strongly associated with viability, it is possible for economically viable and small scale enterprises to compete for procurement contracts. The question of whether or not this can be accomplished in the absence of federally mandated goals still remains to be answered.

We know that it is the viable firms, after all, that permit further business expansion and job creation. Profitable MWBE operations build additional capital and reinvestment, resulting in further creation of income and jobs. Thus, successful small businesses create jobs. Successful minority owned businesses create jobs for minorities. Wealth creation and job creation in the small business sector go hand in hand. Acceptance of this fundamental fact would permit government to "remove the fetters that too often cripple the economic development potential of the minority business community.[58] Ideally, OUI's Business Opportunity Program seeks to ensure that Buffalo minority owned businesses continue to receive a significant portion of the county contracts so that more jobs can be created for minority workers. This case study makes the case that access to information can go a long way to leveling the playing field for minority procurement activity, albeit a partial attempt.

Finally, this analysis of minority procurement activity in Erie County raises some interesting questions about the future progress of minority community economic development initiatives. In this world of more global change and less life certainty, the status of our communities are much more important to our existence as a whole. If the urban community ceases to exist as a safe place to live and work, it matters little whether one has accrued sufficient capital for a comfortable lifestyle. The evidence gathered from this initial study shows that there are still fundamental and institutional barriers to fair competition for MWBEs. Unfortunately, this study cannot provide a definitive statement explaining how to eliminate these barriers, however, it does offer some insights as to how the future of minority procurement programs may be affected in the absence of federally mandated goals. The goal is to find ways to continue the necessary policies that will have a direct impact on continued community revitalization in minority neighborhoods. It is our duty as scholars and political actors in our communities to find ways to help facilitate that end.

NOTES

1. MacManus, S. 1993. "Minority Contractors' Views of Government Purchasing and Procurement Practices." *Economic Development Quarterly*, Vol. 7 No. 1, February: 30–49.

2. Teitz, M. B. 1989. "Neighborhood Economics: Local Communities and Regional Markets." *Economic Development Quarterly*. Vol. 3 No. 2, May: 111–122.

3. Teitz, M. B. 1989. "Neighborhood Economics: Local Communities and Regional Markets." *Economic Development Quarterly*. Vol. 3 No. 2, May: 111–122.

3. Imbroscio, D. L. 1997. *Reconstructing City Politics: Alternative Economic Development and Urban Regimes*. Newbury Park: Sage.

3. Pitegoff, P. 1993. "Child Care Enterprise, Community Development and Work." *The Georgetown Law Journal*. Vol. 81 No. 5, June: 1897–1943.

3a. McDougall, H. A. 1993. *Black Baltimore: A New Theory of Community*. Philadelphia, PA: Temple University Press.

4. See "Beyond the New Property: An Ecological View of Due Process" by Charles Reich *Brooklyn Law Review* 56 (1990): 731.

5. Pitegoff 1997, 1916

6. Pitegoff 1997, 1916

7. Bates, T. and D. Williams. 1995. "Manipulating Minority Procurement Programs: Preferential Procurement Programs and Minority-owned Businesses." *Journal of Urban Affairs*. Vol. 17 No. 1: 1–17.

8. Curry, G.E, editor. 1996. *The Affirmative Action Debate*. United States: Addison-Wesley. See particularly "Why America Needs Set-Aside Programs" by Kweisi Mfume, pg. 121–129.

9. Set-aside programs refer to the practice of allocating a certain proportion of government contracts to minority (including white-women) owned and operated businesses. Many of set-aside programs established levels that approximated the targeted minority's proportion in the general population. However, Government "goals" programs differ from set-asides (although some refer to them as set-asides) in that private companies that do business with government agencies must meet certain minority representation criteria in the selection of their contractors. Source: P. Smith and R. Feagin, *The Bubbling Cauldron*. Minneapolis: University of Minnesota, 1995:99–120.

10. Bates, T. 1985. "Minority Business Set-Asides: Theory and Practice." In *Affirmative Action in Employment and Minority Business Set-Asides*. U.S. Commission on Civil Rights. Washington, D.C. Government Printing Office.

Bates, T. 1992. *Banking on Black Enterprise: The Potential of Emerging Firms for Revitalizing Urban Economies*. Joint Center for Political and Economic Studies, University Press of America.

11. Bowman, A. 1987. *Tools and Targets: The Mechanics of City Economic Development*. Washington, D.C.: National League of Cities.

12. Pitegoff, P. 1993. "Child Care Enterprise, Community Development and Work." *The Georgetown Law Journal*. Vol. 81 No. 5, June: 1897–1943.

13. Bendick, Jr., Marc and Mary Lou Egan. 1993. "Linking Business Develop-

ment and Community Development in Inner Cities." *Journal of Planning Literature.* Vol. 8 No. 1 (August): 3–19.

14. Curry, G.E, editor. 1996. *The Affirmative Action Debate.* United States: Addison-Wesley. See particularly "Why America Needs Set-Aside Programs" by Kweisi Mfume, pg. 121–129.

15. Jackson, J.J. 1995. "Race-based Affirmative Action: Mend it or End it?" *The Black Scholar,* Vol. 25 No. 3, Summer: 30–42.

16. Thomas, J.M. and M. Ritzdorf, editors. 1997. *Urban Planning and the African American Community: In the Shadows.* California: Sage.

17. Henderson, L. J., Jr. 1984. "Black Business Enterprise and Public Policy." *Contemporary Public Policy Perspectives and Black Americans: Issues in an Era of Retrenchment Politics,* Mitchell F. Rice and Woodrow Jones, Jr. eds. Connecticut: Greenwood Press.

18. Bendick, Jr., Marc and Mary Lou Egan. 1993. "Linking Business Development and Community Development in Inner Cities." *Journal of Planning Literature.* Vol. 8 No. 1 (August): 3–19.

19. Bendick, Jr., Marc and Mary Lou Egan. 1993. "Linking Business Development and Community Development in Inner Cities." *Journal of Planning Literature.* Vol. 8 No. 1 (August): 3–19.

20. Ginsberg, B. 1971. "Berman v. Parker: Congress, The Court, and The Public Purpose." *Polity.* vol. IV, no 1: 49–75.

21. Ginsberg, B. 1971. "Berman v. Parker: Congress, The Court, and The Public Purpose." *Polity.* vol. IV, no 1: 49–75.

22. Thomas, J.M. and M. Ritzdorf, editors. 1997. *Urban Planning and the African American Community: In the Shadows.* California: Sage.

23. Thomas, J.M. and M. Ritzdorf, editors. 1997. *Urban Planning and the African American Community: In the Shadows.* California: Sage.

24. McGuire, C. 1976. "The Urban Development Act of 1974: Community-Development Funds and Black Economic Programs." Emerging Issues in Black Economic Development. United States: D.C. Heath and Company.

25. Bates, T. and D. Williams. 1995. "Manipulating Minority Procurement Programs: Preferential Procurement Programs and Minority-owned Businesses." *Journal of Urban Affairs.* Vol 17 No. 1:1–17.

26. Butler J. S. 1991. *Entrepreneurship and Self-help Among Black Americans.* New York: State University of New York Press.

27. Taylor, H. L., Jr. 1997. "No More Ivory Towers: Connecting the Research University to the Community." *Journal of Planning Literature,* Vol. 11 No. 3, February: 327–32.

28. Ramsay, M. 1998. "Redeeming the City: Exploring the Relationship Between Church and Metropolis." *Urban Affairs Review,* vol. 33, no. 5, (May): 595–626.

29. Delgado, G. 1993. *Beyond the Politics of Place: New Directions in Community Organizing in the 1990s.* Oakland, CA: Applied Research Center.

30. Imbroscio, D. L. 1997. *Reconstructing City Politics: Alternative Economic Development and Urban Regimes.* Newbury Park: Sage.

31. Rusk, D. 1993. *Cities Without Suburbs.* Baltimore: Johns Hopkins University Press.

32. McDougall, H. A. 1993. *Black Baltimore: A New Theory of Community.* Philadelphia, PA: Temple University Press.

33. McDougall defines base communities as "a small, intimate social action unit that serves to supplement rather than replace the mediating institutions of community or the political mechanisms of government in their respective imperfect roles" page 22.

34. Taylor, H. L., Jr. 1997. "No More Ivory Towers: Connecting the Research

University to the Community." *Journal of Planning Literature*, Vol. 11 No. 3, February: 327–32.

35. Beauregard, R.A. 1993. "Constituting Economic Development: A Theoretical Perspective." *Theories of Local Economic Development: Perspectives across the Disciplines.* Richard D. Bingham and Robert Mier, eds. Newbury Park: Sage Publications, 267–283.

36. Michelle Kubant's, our graduate assistant and intern for OUI, project data on the bidding process contributes significantly to this discussion.

37. Thomas, J.M. and M. Ritzdorf, editors. 1997. *Urban Planning and the African American Community: In the Shadows.* California: Sage.

38. Most MWBEs were competing against each other as well as other non-minority owned firms for the same products and/or contracts.

39. MacManus, S. 1993. "Minority Contractors' Views of Government Purchasing and Procurement Practices." *Economic Development Quarterly*, Vol. 7 No. 1, February: 30–49.

40. Bates, T. and D. Williams. 1995. "Manipulating Minority Procurement Programs: Preferential Procurement Programs and Minority-owned Businesses." *Journal of Urban Affairs.* Vol. 17 No. 1: 1–17.

41. These expenditures were taken from 1994 Erie County procurement data.

42. Curry, G.E, editor. 1996. *The Affirmative Action Debate.* United States: Addison-Wesley. See particularly "Why America Needs Set-Aside Programs" by Kweisi Mfume, pg. 121–129.

43. Curry, G.E, editor. 1996. *The Affirmative Action Debate.* United States: Addison-Wesley. See particularly "Why America Needs Set-Aside Programs" by Kweisi Mfume, pg. 121–129.

44. Office of Urban Initiatives, Inc. 1996. *Business Opportunity Program Report: April 1–December 31*, unpublished project and publication.

45. Office of Urban Initiatives, Inc. 1996. *Business Opportunity Program Report: April 1–December 31*, unpublished project and publication.

46. Office of Urban Initiatives, Inc. 1996. *Business Opportunity Program Report: April 1–December 31*, unpublished project and publication.

47. Waldinger, R. 1995. "The 'other side' of embeddedness: a case-study of the interplay of economy and ethnicity." *Ethnic and Racial Studies*, Vol 18 No. 3, July: 555–80.

48. Waldinger, R. 1995. "The 'other side' of embeddedness: a case-study of the interplay of economy and ethnicity." *Ethnic and Racial Studies*, Vol 18 No. 3, July: 555–80.

49. Waldinger, R. 1995. "The 'other side' of embeddedness: a case-study of the interplay of economy and ethnicity." *Ethnic and Racial Studies*, Vol 18 No. 3, July: 555–80.

50. Bates, T. and D. Williams. 1995. "Manipulating Minority Procurement Programs: Preferential Procurement Programs and Minority-owned Businesses." *Journal of Urban Affairs.* Vol. 17 No. 1: 1–17.

50. MacManus, S. 1993. "Minority Contractors' Views of Government Purchasing and Procurement Practices." *Economic Development Quarterly*, Vol. 7 No. 1, February: 30–49.

51. Waldinger, R. 1995. "The 'other side' of embeddedness: a case-study of the interplay of economy and ethnicity." *Ethnic and Racial Studies*, Vol 18 No. 3, July: 555–80.

52. Bates, T. and D. Williams. 1995. "Manipulating Minority Procurement Programs: Preferential Procurement Programs and Minority-owned Businesses." *Journal of Urban Affairs.* Vol. 17 No. 1: 1–17.

53. Office of Urban Initiatives, Inc. 1996. *Business Opportunity Program Report: April 1–December 31*, unpublished project and publication.
54. Bates, T. and D. Williams. 1995. "Manipulating Minority Procurement Programs: Preferential Procurement Programs and Minority-owned Businesses." *Journal of Urban Affairs.* Vol. 17 No. 1: 1–17.
55. Vidal, A. C. 1995. "Reintegrating Disadvantaged Communities into the Fabric of Urban Life: The Role of Community Development." *Housing and Policy Debate*. Vol. 6 No. 1:169–230.
56. MacManus, S. 1993. "Minority Contractors' Views of Government Purchasing and Procurement Practices." *Economic Development Quarterly*, Vol. 7 No. 1, February: 30–49.
57. Bates, T. and D. Williams. 1995. "Manipulating Minority Procurement Programs: Preferential Procurement Programs and Minority-owned Businesses." *Journal of Urban Affairs.* Vol. 17 No. 1: 1–17.
58. Bates, T. and D. Williams. 1995. "Manipulating Minority Procurement Programs: Preferential Procurement Programs and Minority-owned Businesses." *Journal of Urban Affairs.* Vol. 17 No. 1: 1–17.

PROFILE OF THE CONTRIBUTORS

1. Introduction and Overview

Andrew F. Brimmer

Andrew F. Brimmer is the president of Brimmer & Company, Inc., an economic and financial consulting firm. He is also the Wilmer D. Barrett Professor of Economics, University of Massachusetts at Amherst, Amherst, Massachusetts.

2. The Declining Social and Economic Fortunes of African American Males: A Critical Assessment of Four Perspectives

James H. Johnson, Jr., Walter C. Farrell, Jr., and Jennifer A. Stoloff

James H. Johnson, Jr. is the E. Maynard Adams Distinguished Professor of Business, Geography, and Sociology and the Director of the Urban Investment Strategies Center in the Frank Hawkins Kenan Institute of Private Enterprise at the University of North Carolina at Chapel Hill.

Walter C. Farrell, Jr., is professor and chair of the Department of Educational Policy and Community Studies and a member of the graduate faculty in urban studies at the University of Wisconsin-Milwaukee. He is also a National Research Scientist in the Urban Investment Strategies Center in The Frank Hawkins Kenan Institute of Private Enterprise at the University of North Carolina at Chapel Hill and in the Center for the Study of Urban Poverty at the University of California, Los Angeles.

Jennifer A. Stoloff is a doctoral student in the Department of Sociology and a research associate in the Urban Investment Strategies Center of the Frank Hawkins Kenan Institute of Private Enterprise at the University of North Carolina at Chapel Hill.

3. Economics Research at Historically Black Colleges and Universities: Rankings and Effects on the Supply of Black Economists

Jacqueline Agesa, Maury Granger, and Gregory N. Price

Jacqueline Agesa is an assistant professor in the Department of Economics at North Caroline A&T State University, Greensboro, NC 27411.

Maury Granger is an assistant professor in the Department of Economics at North Caroline A&T State University, Greensboro, NC 27411.

Gregory N. Price is an associate professor in the Department of Economics at North Caroline A&T State University, Greensboro, NC 27411.

4. Worker Re-training and Labor Market Outcomes: A New Focus for Labor Research Published in *The Review of Black Political Economy*

James B. Stewart

James B. Stewart is professor of labor studies and industrial relations at Pennsylvania State University, State College, Pennsylvania.

5. Employment and Training Solutions for the Economically Disadvantaged: An Essay

Bernard E. Anderson

Bernard E. Anderson is assistant secretary of labor, U.S. Department of Labor, Washington, D.C.

6. Long-Term Trends and Prospects for Black-Owned Businesses

Andrew F. Brimmer

Andrew F. Brimmer is the president of Brimmer & Company, Inc., an economic and financial consulting firm. He is also the Wilmer D. Barrett Professor of Economics, University of Massachusetts at Amherst, Amherst, Massachusetts.

7. Minority Business Formation and Survival: Evidence on Business Performance and Viability

Jan E. Christopher

Jan E. Christopher is an associate professor of Economics at Delaware State University, Dover, Delaware.

8. What Determines Exports of Black-Owned Enterprises?

N. Frank Ekanem and Charlie E. Mahone, Jr.

N. Frank Ekanem is a professor in the School of Business at Howard University, Washington, D.C.

Charlie E. Mahone, Jr. is a professor in the School of Business at Howard University, Washington, D.C.

9. Is the U.S. Small Business Administration a Racist Institution?

Timothy Bates

Timothy Bates is professor of labor and urban affairs at Wayne State University. He also works as a consultant for the U. S. Department of Justice Civil Rights Division, the U.S. General Accounting Office, and the Small Business Administration.

10. Race, Cognitive Skills, Psychological Capital and Wages

Arthur H. Goldsmith, William Darity, Jr., and Jonathan R. Veum

Arthur H. Goldsmith is a professor in the department of economics at Washington and Lee University, Lexington, Virginia.

William Darity, Jr. is the Cary C. Boshamer Professor of Economics in the department of economics at the University of North Carolina, Chapel Hill, North Carolina.

Jonathan R. Veum is employed with the U.S. Bureau of Labor Statistics, Washington, D.C.

11. Determinants of Regional Income Distribution in the U.S. South, 1980-1990: Roles of Net Migration and Human Capital Accumulation

Octavian Ngarambé and Stephan J. Goetz

Octavian Ngarambé is a postdoctoral scholar in the department of agricultural economics, University of Kentucky, Lexington, Kentucky.

Stephan J. Goetz is an associate professor in the department of agricultural economics, University of Kentucky, Lexington, Kentucky.

12. Assessing the Effects of the Occupational Crowding of Immigrants on the Real Wages of African American workers

Lonnie K. Stevans

Lonnie K. Stevens, Ph.D., is an associate professor in the Zarb School of Business, Department of BCIS/QM, Hofstra, University, Hempstead, New York.

13. On the Permanence or Impermanence of Black-White Economic Inequality

Jeremiah Cotton

Jeremiah Cotton is a professor of economics at the University of Massachusetts-Boston.

14. The Shadow of the Future and the Complexity of Cooperation

John W. Handy

John W. Handy is a professor of economics in the department of economics and business administration at Morehouse College, Atlanta, Georgia.

15. W.E.B. DuBois As Economic Analyst: Reflections on he 100th Anniversary of the *Philadelphia Negro*

Lynn C. Burbridge

Lynn C. Burbridge is an assistant in the department of public administration, Rutgers (The State University of New Jersey) Newark, New Jersey.

16. No More Servants in the House

Beth T. Bates

Beth Tompkins Bates teaches African history in the department of Africana Studies at Wayne State University.

17. The Economics of Racism

Marcus Alexis

Marcus Alexis is a professor of economics and professor of management and strategy at Northwestern University. He is also member of the board of trustees of Northwestern University, Evanston, Illinois.

18. Reparations and Public Policy

Richard F. America

Richard F. America is an adjunct lecturer at the School of Business Administration at Georgetown University, Washington, D.C.

19. 21st Century Pollination: Federal Housing and Health Policies

Wilhelmina A. Leigh

Wilhelmina A. Leigh is a senior research associate for the Joint Center for Political and Economic Studies, Washington, D.C.

20. Black Infant Health: Where to in the 21st Century?

Geoffrey Warner

Geoffrey Warner, Ph.D. is a professor in the department of maternal and child health at Harvard School of Public Health.

21. Economic Community of West African States: From an Economic Union to a Peacekeeping Mission?

E. Ike Udogu

E. Ike Udogu is professor of African and international politics at Francis Marion University, Florence, South Carolina.

22. Development Prospects and Policy for Africa: Structural Adjustment and Beyond

Kempe Ronald Hope, Sr.

Kempe Ronald Hope, Sr., is a professor of development studies, University of Botswana. His two most recent books are *African Political Economy: Contemporary Issues in Development* (M.E. Sharpe, 1997) and *Structural Adjustment, Reconstruction and Development in Africa* (Ashgate, 1997).

23. How Does It Feel to be Free?: Reflections on Black-White Economic Inequality in the Era of "Color-Blind" Law

Rhonda M. Williams and William E. Spriggs

The late Rhonda M. Williams was a political economist and associate professor of Afro-American Studies at the University of Maryland, College Park, Maryland. She wrote extensively on the race and gender dimensions of economic inequality, affirmative action, and economic discrimination.

William E. Spriggs is a former senior economist at the Joint Economic Committee, U.S. Congress. He is currently the director of research for the National Urban League.

24. Is There Discrimination in Mortgage Lending? What Does the Research Tell Us?

Harold A. Black

Harold A. Black is James F. Smith Professor of Financial Institutions at the University of Tennessee, Knoxville, Tennessee.

25. Another Look at Mortgage Lending Discrimination: A Review of Findings

Thomas D. Boston, Usha Nair-Reichert, Willie Belton, and Haizheng Li

Thomas D. Boston is a professor of economics in the School of Economics at Georgia Institute of Technology. He also edits *The Review of Black Political Economy.*

Usha Nair-Reichert is an associate professor of economics in the School of Economics at Georgia Institute of Technology.

Willie Belton is an associate professor of economics in the School of Economics at Georgia Institute of Technology.

Haizheng Li is an assistant professor of economics in the School of Economics at Georgia Institute of Technology.

26. Black Male Employment and Tight Labor Markets

Robert Cherry

Dr. Robert Cherry is a professor of economics at Brooklyn College. His recent work includes articles on the origins of the culture-of-poverty thesis in economics, a rational choice model of marriage, and the economic implications of the integration of baseball before civil rights legislation.

27. Cooperative Economics—A Community Revitalization Strategy

Curtis Haynes, Jr. and Jessica Gordon Nembhard

Curtis Haynes, Jr. is a co-founder of the HUD-funded Resurgent City Center For Cooperative Community Development (RCC) at Buffalo State College.

Jessica Gordon Nembhard is a senior economist at The Institute for Urban Research, Morgan State University.

28. Minority Procurement: Beyond Affirmative Action to Economic Empowerment

Sherri Leronda Wallace

Sherri Leronda Wallace is an assistant professor in the department of planning and Center for Urban Studies at the State University of New York at Buffalo, Buffalo, New York.